What Business Students Need to Know about MIS.

Previews of cutting-edge innovations liven up each chapter.

One **Team Work** exercise and three **Web Search** exercises per chapter get students "doing" as well as "learning".

Global Perspective

Each chapter explores how IS impacts the world's businesses— to illustrate the big picture.

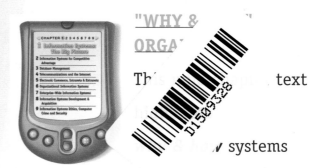

"WHY & ORGA...

Th... text ... systems are used: **why** the... ...e relevant, and **how** they are built, as well as, **how** they are integrated, and **how** they are safeguarded.

Each chapter begins with the **"big picture"** for relevance, and then moves through the specifics of the material.

Every chapter ends with comprehensive end-of-chapter material that ties to the text Web site, [**www.prenhall.com/jessup**], for reinforcement of key concepts.

INFORMATION
SYSTEMS
TODAY

INFORMATION SYSTEMS TODAY

Leonard M. Jessup
Joseph S. Valacich

Prentice Hall

PRENTICE HALL
Upper Saddle River, New Jersey 07458

Executive Editor:	David Alexander
Executive Editor:	Bob Horan
Publisher:	Natalie E. Anderson
Editorial Project Manager:	Lori Cerreto
Editorial Assistant:	Maat Van Uitert
Media Project Manager:	Joan Waxman
Senior Marketing Manager:	Sharon K. Turkovich
Marketing Assistant:	Scott Patterson
Managing Editor (Production):	Gail Steier de Acevedo
Production Editor:	Vanessa Nuttry
Permissions Supervisor:	Suzanne Grappi
Associate Director, Manufacturing:	Vincelt Scelta
Manufacturing Buyer:	Natacha St. Hill Moore
Design Manager:	Maria Lange
Art Director:	Patricia Smythe
Interior Design:	Jill Little
Cover Design:	John Romer
Cover Photo:	Christian Liewig/ Getty Images
	Stone Allstock
Infographics:	Kenneth Batelman
Line Art Studio:	Matrix Publishing Services
Manager, Print Production:	Christy Mahon
Composition/Full Service Project Management:	Pre-Press Company, Inc.
Printer/Binder:	Quebecor World Color-Versailles

Credits and acknowledgments borrowed from other sources and reproduced, with permission, in this textbook appear on appropriate page within text.

Microsoft Excel, Solver, and Windows are registered trademarks of Microsoft Corporation in the U.S.A. and other countries. Screen shots and icons reprinted with permission from the Microsoft Corporation. This book is not sponsored or endorsed by or affiliated with Microsoft Corporation.

Library of Congress Cataloging-in-Publication Data

Jessup, Leonard M., 1961-
    Information systems today / Leonard M. Jessup, Joseph S. Valacich
        p. cm.
    Includes bibliographical references and index.
    ISBN 0-13-009414-5
    1. Information technology. 2. Information storage and retrieval systems—Business. I. Valacich, Joseph S., 1959- II. Title.

    T58.5 .J47 2002
    658'.05—dc21

                                                    2002030779

Pearson Education LTD.
Pearson Education Australia PTY, Limited
Pearson Education Singapore, Pte. Ltd
Pearson Education North Asia Ltd
Pearson Education, Canada, Ltd
Pearson Educación de Mexico, S.A. de C.V.
Pearson Education–Japan
Pearson Education Malaysia, Pte. Ltd

10 9 8 7 6 5 4 3 2 1
ISBN 0-13-009414-5

 **Leonard M. Jessup** is the Dean of the College of Business and Economics, and the Philip L. Kays Distinguished Professor of MIS, at Washington State University. Professor Jessup received his B.A. in Information and Communication Studies in 1983 and his M.B.A. in 1985 from California State University, Chico, where he was voted Outstanding MBA Student. He received his Ph.D. in Organizational Behavior and Management Information Systems from the University of Arizona in 1989. He is a member of the Association for Information Systems and Alpha Iota Delta, associate editor for the *Management Information Systems Quarterly*, a member of the Editorial Board for Small Group Research, was program cochair for the Association for Information Systems Americas Conference, and is conference cochair for the International Conference on Information Systems, to be hosted by WSU and held in Seattle in December of 2003.

In addition, he has held administrative, and/or reviewer responsibilities for a number of other research journals, research conferences, and book publishers. He teaches in various areas of Management and Management Information Systems and has published, presented, and consulted on electronic commerce, computer-supported collaborative work, technology-supported teaching and learning, and on related topics. With Joseph S. Valacich, he coedited the book *Group Support Systems: New Perspectives* for Macmillan Publishing Company. With his wife, Joy L. Egbert, he won Zenith Data Systems' annual Masters of Innovation award.

 **Joseph S. Valacich**, the Marian E. Smith Presidential Endowed Chair and the George and Carolyn Hubman Distinguished Professor in MIS, joined the faculty at Washington State University in 1996. He received his Ph.D. from the University of Arizona in 1989, and his M.B.A. and B.S. from the University of Montana. His teaching interests include Systems Analysis and Design, Collaborative Computing, and Management Information Systems. Professor Valacich served on the national task forces to design "IS '97: The Model Curriculum and Guidelines for Undergraduate Degree Programs in Information Systems" and "MSIS 2000, the Master of Science in Information Systems" curriculum. He served on the executive committee, funded by the National Science Foundation, working to define IS program accreditation standards and is on the board of directors for the Computing Sciences Accreditation Board (CSAB), representing the Association for Information Systems (AIS). He is the general conference cochair for the 2003 International Conference on Information Systems that will be held in Seattle.

He has conducted numerous corporate training and executive development programs for organizations, including: AT&T, Dow Chemical, EDS, Exxon, FedEx, General Motors, and Xerox. His research interests include Technology Mediated Collaboration and Distance Education. His past research has appeared in publications such as *MIS Quarterly*, *Information Systems Research*, *Management Science*, *Academy of Management Journal*, *Communications of the ACM*, *Decision Science*, *Organizational Behavior and Human Decision Processes*, *Journal of Applied Psychology*, and *Journal of Management Information Systems*. He is a coauthor of the best-selling *Modern Systems Analysis and Design* (3rd edition); *and Essentials of Systems Analysis and Design* (2nd edition); both published by Prentice Hall.

Chapters:

Brief Table of Contents

Chapter

Organizational Systems   168

Chapter

Enterprise-Wide Information Systems   204

To Joy, Jamie, and David, for your love and support.
—Len

To Jackie, Jordan, and James for your sacrifices, encouragement, and support.
—Joe

Dedication

APPROACH

One of the greatest challenges that we face in teaching information systems courses is how to keep pace in the class with what is happening out in the real world. Hardware, software, telecommunications, and networking equipment—all of it continues to become faster, cheaper, and better, and business organizations continue to adopt and adapt these new technologies rapidly. In fact, whereas a decade ago large businesses would spend two or three percent of their revenues on information technology, today, spending on information technology for many large businesses can range from seven to 10 percent of their revenue. Most important, organizations are now relying on that technology as a fundamental part of their business strategy and their competitiveness.

As a result of this pervasiveness and the fast pace of technology change and use in organizations, teaching people about information systems has never been more valuable or challenging.

Given the dynamic nature of information systems, and given that it is difficult to find introductory information systems textbooks that are both up-to-date and student-friendly, we wrote *Information Systems Today* with three primary goals in mind. First, we wanted readers not only to learn about information systems, but also to feel as excited as we do about the field and about the amazing opportunities available in this area. Second, we did not simply want to spoon-feed students with the technical terms and the history of information systems. Instead, we want students to understand exactly what innovative organizations are doing with contemporary information systems and, more important, where things are headed. Third, we wanted to empower students with the essential knowledge they need to be successful in the use and understanding of information technology in their careers.

To this end, we wrote *Information Systems Today* so that it is contemporary, fun to read, and useful, and includes the essential body of knowledge regarding information systems.

AUDIENCE

Information Systems Today is primarily for the undergraduate introductory information systems course required of all business students. This course is typically offered in the junior year of four-year undergraduate programs and in the second year at two-year institutions. The introductory information systems course typically has a diverse audience of students majoring in many different areas, such as accounting, economics, finance, marketing, general management, human resource management, production and operations, international business, entrepreneurship, and information systems. Given the range of students taking this type of course, we have written this book so that it is a valuable guide to all business students and provides them with the essential information they need to know. Students majoring in areas outside of business may also attend the introductory information systems course. Therefore, this book has been written to appeal to a diverse audience.

Information Systems Today can also be used for the introductory course offered at the graduate level—for example, in the first year of an MBA program.

KEY FEATURES

As authors, teachers, developers, and managers of information systems, we understand that in order for students to best learn about information systems with this book, they must be motivated to learn. To this end we have included a number of unique features to help students quickly and easily assess the true value of information systems and their impact on everyday life. We show how today's professionals are using information systems to help modern organizations become more efficient and competitive. Our focus is on the application of technology to real-world, contemporary situations. Below we describe each of the features that contribute to that focus.

Cases: A Multitiered Approach

Opening Scenario: Each chapter begins with an opening scenario describing a real-world company, technology, and/or issue to spark students' interest in the chapter topic. We have chosen engaging scenarios that relate to students' interests and concerns. A photo or illustration is included with each scenario.

BRIEF CASE: Each chapter also includes several brief cases that are taken directly from the news and discuss contemporary companies and technologies. These are embedded right in the text of the chapter and highlight concepts from the surrounding chapter material.

End of Chapter Case:

To test and reinforce chapter content, we present two real-world cases at the end of each chapter. Sources for these cases include *Information Week, Business Week, CIO Magazine*, and various Web sites. Like the Brief Cases within the chapter, these are taken from the news and are contemporary. However, these are longer and more substantive than the Brief Cases and are followed by discussion questions that help the student apply and master the chapter.

In order to show students how the material from each chapter applies to their individual career tracks, we have created a "Career Implications" feature. This feature maps the material to the fields of accounting and finance, marketing, information systems, human resource management, and operations management in each chapter. That means there are five "Career Implications" in every chapter. For example, an aspiring accountant will find an explanation within every chapter of how that chapter's material applies to the field of accounting. Similarly, every chapter has such a feature for a marketing major, for an operations management major, and so on.

We worked hard to ensure that this book is contemporary. We cover literally hundreds of different emerging technologies throughout the book. In order to drive the point home, we also included a "Coming Attractions" in each chapter, which describes some specific new technology and how it is or will be used.

It is rare to find an information systems textbook that describes what not to do, but this can be very helpful to students. In each chapter we provide a feature called "When Things Go Wrong," which enables students to learn about a real-world situation in which information systems did not work or were not built or used well.

In addition to end of chapter material, within each chapter we provide several opportunities for students to work alone or in teams to research topics on the Web that relate to chapter material.

Within each chapter we also provide an opportunity for students to work in teams to solve a problem and/ or address an issue related to the chapter material. These and the Web Search exercises are great for livening up a class or study session.

Global Perspective

In addition to scores of international issues and examples throughout every chapter, we also provide a feature called "Global Perspective" in each chapter. With this feature, we show specifically how some aspect of the chapter applies to people, organizations, and technologies from around the world.

End-of-Chapter Material

Our end-of-chapter material is designed to accommodate various teaching and learning styles. It promotes learning beyond the book and the classroom. Elements include the following:

Key Terms

Highlight key concepts within the chapter

Review Questions

Test students' understanding of basic content

Self-Study Questions

Enable students to assess whether they are ready for a test

Matching Questions

Check quickly to see if students understand basic terms

Problems and Exercises

Push students deeper into the material and encourage them to synthesize and apply it

PEDAGOGY

In addition to our use of cases, chapter openers, and the other unique features described, we provide a list of learning objectives to lay the foundation for each chapter. At the end of the chapter, the Key Points Review repeats these learning objectives and describes how each objective was achieved. A list of references is located at the end of the text, organized by chapter.

ORGANIZATION

The content and organization of this book are based on our own teaching, as well as on feedback from reviewers and colleagues throughout the field. Each chapter builds on the others to reinforce key concepts and allow for a seamless learning experience. Essentially, the book has been structured to answer three fundamental questions:

1. What are contemporary information systems, and how are they being used in innovative ways?
2. Why are information systems so important and interesting?
3. How best can we build, acquire, manage, and safeguard information systems?

To answer these questions, we wrote and ordered the chapters in a special way. To continually show

you where you are in the book, we begin each chapter by describing the "Big Picture" and literally provide students with an image of the "Big Picture" that shows you where the current chapter lies within the framework of the book.

The chapters are organized as follows:

■ **Chapter 1: "Information Systems: The Big Picture"**—This chapter helps you understand what information systems are and how they have become a vital part of modern organizations. We walk the student through the technology, people, and organizational components of an information system, and we lay out types of jobs and career opportunities in information systems and in related fields. We use a number of cases and examples, such as that of Ticketmaster, to show the student the types of systems being used and to point out common "best practices" in systems use and management.

■ **Chapter 2: "Information Systems for Competitive Advantage"**—In this chapter we talk about Microsoft's use of information systems to support the Xbox product, along with other business examples, to show how to use information systems to support organizational strategy and enable competitive advantage. We also show the student how to formulate and present the business case for a system, and we explain why and how companies are continually looking for new ways to use technology for competitive advantage.

■ **Chapter 3: "Database Management"**—Databases have become the engine running underneath all information systems and business processes. In this chapter, we use the examples of the Hard Rock Cafe and other businesses to describe what databases and database management systems are and to show why they have become very important for successful, modern organizations.

■ **Chapter 4: "Telecommunications and the Internet"**—Just as databases are the underlying engines, telecommunications and networks are the veins through which vital information flows in organizations. Here we use examples from Pepsi and other companies to show you how people use telecommunications and networking equipment effectively. We also focus on how the Internet and the World Wide Web function and are used heavily by business organizations today.

■ **Chapter 5: "Electronic Commerce, Intranets, and Extranets"**—Perhaps nothing has changed the landscape of business more than the use of the Internet for electronic commerce. In this chapter, we describe how a number of firms, such as Amazon, are using the Internet and Web to do business with customers, building intranets to support internal processes, and building extranets to interact with other firms.

■ **Chapter 6: "Organizational Information Systems"**—Given how many different types of information systems organizations use, in this chapter we use examples from

J.Crew and other firms to describe the various types of systems. We provide ways to categorize the systems so that you can better make sense of them all.

■ **Chapter 7: "Enterprise-Wide Information Systems"**—In this chapter we focus on enterprise systems, which are a popular type of information system used to integrate information and span organizations' boundaries to better connect a firm with customers, suppliers, and other partners. We show you how John I. Haas, a global producer of fine hops for beer making, and other firms use Enterprise Resource Planning, Customer Relationship Management, and other popular types of software packages to compete.

■ **Chapter 8: "Information Systems Development and Acquisition"**—How are all these systems built? In this chapter we show you how Tower Records and other firms build and acquire new information systems. We walk you through the traditional systems development approach, as well as more contemporary approaches such as prototyping, rapid application development, and object-oriented analysis and design.

■ **Chapter 9: "Information Systems Ethics, Computer Crime, and Security"**—In this chapter we describe the ethical dilemmas associated with information systems, as well as common forms of computer crime and various methods for providing computer security. We show you how Microsoft and other firms deal with hackers and ensure the safety and integrity of their critical systems.

In addition to these nine chapters, we include three appendixes focusing on basic hardware, software, and networking concepts. Although our market research found that many students have a solid understanding of these technological building blocks, this material is provided as a reference or to be used as a central part of the course. By delivering this material as appendixes, we provide instructors the greatest flexibility in how and when they can apply it.

SUPPLEMENTARY SUPPORT

Instructor's Resource CD-ROM

The convenient Instructor's CD-ROM includes all of the supplements: Instructor's Manual, Test Item File, Windows PH Test Manager, PowerPoint Lecture Notes, and Image Library (text art). The Instructor's Manual includes answers to all review and discussion questions, exercises, and case questions. The Test Item File (Test Bank), written by Jack Van Deventer of Washington State University, includes multiple-choice, true-false, and essay questions for each chapter. The Test Bank is delivered in MS Word, as well as in the form of the Windows PH Test Manager. The PowerPoint Lecture Notes, also by Jack Van Deventer, highlight text learning objectives and key topics. They are also available on the text's Web site at **http://www.prenhall.com/jessup**. Finally, the **Image Library** is a collection of the figures and tables from the text, supplied on the Instructor's

Resource CD-ROM for instructor use in PowerPoint slides and class lectures.

Companion Web site: www.prenhall.com/jessup

This text is supported by a companion Web site that features:

a. A password-protected faculty area where adopters can download the Instructor's Manual.

b. PowerPoint lecture notes (as described above).

c. Interactive Study Guide includes multiple-choice, true-false, and essay questions for each chapter. Each question includes a hint and coaching tip for students' reference. Students receive automatic feedback upon submitting each quiz.

d. Web Search exercises. All of the Web Search exercises from the text margins appear on the Web site for convenient student use.

e. Chapter updates, posted periodically to help both students and instructors stay up-to-date with what is happening in information systems and how it relates to chapter material.

Online Courses

 WebCT **www.prenhall.com/webct** Gold Level Customer Support, available exclusively to adopters of Prentice Hall courses, is provided free of charge upon adoption and provides you with priority assistance, training discounts, and dedicated technical support.

Bb Blackboard BlackBoard **www.prenhall.com/blackboard** Prentice Hall's abundant online content, combined with BlackBoard's popular tools and interface, result in robust Web-based courses that are easy to implement, manage, and use—taking your courses to new heights in student interaction and learning.

CourseCompass CourseCompass **www.prenhall.com/coursecompass** CourseCompass is a dynamic, interactive online course management tool powered exclusively for Pearson Education by BlackBoard. This exciting product allows you to teach market-leading Pearson Education content in an easy-to-use customizable format.

REVIEWERS

We wish to thank the following faculty who participated in reviews of this text:

Audrey Bollinger, Penn State University, DuBois

Quidong Cao, Winthrop University

Lei-da Chen, Creighton University

James Frost, Idaho State University

Albert Hayashi, Loyola Marymount University

George Kelley, Moorhead State University

Deborah LaBelle, Penn State University, Delaware County

William Leigh, University of Central Florida

David Lewis, University of Massachusetts, Lowell

Chang-Yang Lin, Eastern Kentucky University

Murli Nagasundaram, Boise State University

Robbie Nakatsu, Loyola Marymount University

Denise Nitterhouse, DePaul University

Fawzi Noman, Sam Houston University

Margaret O'Hara, East Carolina University

Richard Platt, University of West Florida

Mark Schmidt, St. Cloud State University

William Stewart, University of Maryland University College

Edward Williams, University of Michigan, Dearborn

Bill Wresch, University of Washington, Oshkosh

ACKNOWLEDGMENTS

Although only our two names will be listed as the authors for this book (in alphabetical order), this was truly a team effort that went well beyond the two of us. Prentice Hall has been an outstanding publishing company to work with. They are innovative, have high standards, and are as competitive as we are.

Among the many amazingly helpful people at Prentice Hall, there are a handful of people we wish to thank specifically. David Alexander, executive editor, MIS, helped us to strategize well for this book throughout the project. Sharon Turkovich, senior marketing manager, helped us to be creative in writing, packaging, and selling this book. Lori Cerreto, our project manager, helped to whip us and this book into shape and get it finished on time. Finally, our executive editor, Bob Horan, guided the book and us from its inception, and he dared us to dream of and to write the best introductory information systems textbook ever.

There are also a number of other people who conducted background research and helped to craft early drafts of materials. They are Darren Nicholson, Jennifer Nicholson, Saonee Sarker, Anna Sidorova, Clay Looney, and Carol Wysocki. Thanks, team! We could not have done it without you.

Most important, we thank our families for their patience and assistance in helping us to complete this book. Len's wife Joy and his daughter Jamie and his son David were a constant inspiration, as were Joe's wife Jackie, his daughter Jordan, and his son James. This one is for you all.

INFORMATION SYSTEMS TODAY

Information Systems:
The Big Picture

OPENING: "Living" Online

Ticketmaster[1], which began in 1978 as a small company that handled tickets to college events for Arizona State University, has quickly grown to be the world's largest online ticketing resource. Headquartered in the mid-Wilshire district of Los Angeles, California, Ticketmaster uses a mix of online services, cutting edge technology, and traditional distribution.

Ticketmaster sells nearly 100 million tickets to more than 350,000 events each year, including concerts and professional sports, arts, family and comedy events. Ticketmaster comprises approximately 3,300 retail Ticket Center outlets, 20 worldwide telephone call centers, and Ticketmaster.com, the online transaction arm for Ticketmaster and the number two e-commerce site on the Web.

Much of Ticketmaster's success is due to its award-winning Citysearch Web sites, which are online city guides for 128 cities worldwide. These have been recognized as the leading online city guides because of their depth of information, their expert recommendations, and because they enable users to conduct transactions online.

At a Citysearch Web site, such as that shown in Figure 1.1 for Los Angeles, California, you can find and purchase event tickets, find romance through Match.com, book golf tee times, book hotel rooms, make restaurant reservations, decide which movie or dance club to go to, figure out where to shop, plan a camping trip (including booking reservations for state and federal parks across the United States), or create, send, and manage online invitations to your business event and/or party with your friends.

One important reason that Ticketmaster is able to provide these services for you is that it is constantly on the lookout for ways to integrate cutting-edge information technologies and systems into its business. For example, it is currently integrating wireless technologies, developing applications for handheld computers, and making it even easier and faster for you to get tickets. For some venues, you now just go online, make your purchase, and print your own ticket on your local printer.

Ticketmaster is a great example of a company that is using computer-based information systems in innovative ways to make your life easier and better. You may be thinking to yourself, "I just want good tickets at low prices, and I want to get them quickly and easily. . . . I didn't know any of this computer stuff was going on in the background." Indeed, that is exactly what Ticketmaster wants you to think.

[1]For more information, see
www.ticketmaster.com

[**Figure 1.1** ➡ The Citysearch Web site makes it easy to plan your evening out.]

Organizations from Wal-Mart to Walt Disney use computer-based information systems to conduct business in much the same manner as that described in the preceding scenario. These organizations use leading-edge information systems to provide high-quality goods and services and gain or sustain competitive advantage over rivals.

Our objective for Chapter 1 is to help you understand what information systems are and how they have evolved to become a vital part of modern organizations. After reading this chapter, you will be able to do the following:

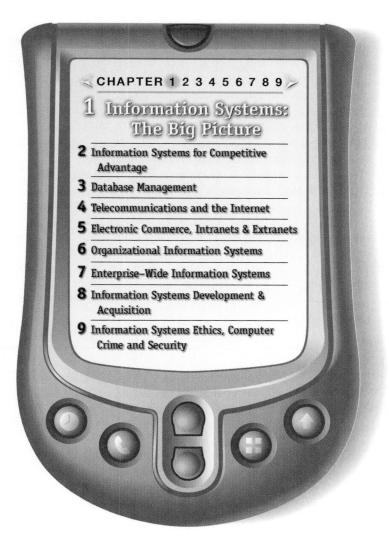

CHAPTER 1 2 3 4 5 6 7 8 9

1 Information Systems: The Big Picture

2 Information Systems for Competitive Advantage

3 Database Management

4 Telecommunications and the Internet

5 Electronic Commerce, Intranets & Extranets

6 Organizational Information Systems

7 Enterprise-Wide Information Systems

8 Information Systems Development & Acquisition

9 Information Systems Ethics, Computer Crime and Security

_1._ Define and understand the term information systems (IS).

_2._ Explain the technology, people, and organizational components of an information system.

_3._ Describe types of jobs and career opportunities in information systems and in related fields.

_4._ Describe the various types of information systems.

_5._ Describe the dual nature of information systems in the success and failure of modern organizations.

_6._ Understand and plan for the future of managing IS.

[Figure 1.2 ➡ The Big Picture guiding this book is a handheld computer with a "to do" list that represents everything you need to know about using and managing computer-based information systems in organizations.]

THE BIG PICTURE

Figure 1.2 provides The Big Picture, which is the guiding framework for this book. The Big Picture is in the shape of a puzzle illustrating how the different parts of this book fit together.

In this first chapter we introduce you to the field of information systems and help to prepare you for what you will learn throughout the rest of this book. In Chapter 2 we talk about why information systems are critical to creating a successful organization and how to use information systems to support organizational strategy and enable competitive advantage.

We then describe the essential elements of information systems. In Chapter 3 we describe databases and their management. Next, in Chapter 4, we discuss the growing importance of telecommunications and the Internet. For those who want and need to learn more about these essential information technology building blocks, we provide more detailed briefings on hardware, software, and networking in appendixes at the end of this book.

We then describe information systems in practice in modern-day organizations. Building on what you learned in Chapter 4 about telecommunications and the Internet, in Chapter 5 we focus on electronic commerce and the use of Intranets and Extranets. In Chapter 6 we describe each of the various kinds of information systems that firms use. Then, in Chapter 7, we focus on enterprise-wide information systems, including Enterprise Resource Planning, Customer Relationship Management, and Supply Chain Management systems, all relatively new, special types of information systems that help integrate the entire organization and help connect the firm to customers, suppliers, and partners.

Next, in Chapter 8, we describe how information systems are developed and/or acquired. Then, in Chapter 9, we discuss key issues in managing computer crime, security, and ethics. We will refer back to The Big Picture at the beginning of every chapter. That way you will know exactly what we will be talking about in each chapter and how it fits within The Big Picture.

INFORMATION SYSTEMS DEFINED

Information systems, such as the online ticket service in the opening scenario, are combinations of *hardware*, *software*, and *telecommunications networks* that people build and use to collect, create, and distribute useful *data*, typically in organizational settings. In Figure 1.3, we show the relationships among these IS components.

People in organizations use information systems to process sales transactions, manage loan applications, and help financial analysts decide where, when, and how to invest. Product managers also use them to help decide where, when, and how to market their products and related services, and production managers use them to help decide when and how to manufacture products. Information systems

---

Brief Case: **Information Systems at Washington State University**

At Washington State University, information systems have changed drastically over the past 20 years. Gone are the long lines to wait to register for classes. Today, students can register for a course over the Internet with a username and password. Information is available about how many seats there are in the classroom, how many students have registered, and whether the course is closed or overloaded. Using a personal computer connected to the Internet, students can quickly and easily add and drop courses without having to get instructor, department chair, and dean signatures. As a result, students can change their course schedules many times until they are just right. Upon completion of the course, students can view grades on-screen as soon as they are entered by the professor. Similarly, professors can find all the information they need online about students, courses, and enrollments. With a few keystrokes, professors can input grades over the Web, saving paper and time.

Information systems have also improved communication between professors and students. Students and professors utilize e-mail for both distance and classroom-based courses. The ease of sending and receiving e-mail along with attachments is very convenient. Professors' Web sites may provide syllabi, assignments, and other pertinent information. Gone are the days of trudging up to the professor's office to replace a lost copy of a syllabus or handout. Today's students are very fortunate with the way technology enhances the communication and learning process.

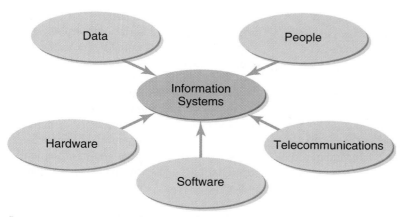

[Figure 1.3 ➡ An information system is a combination of five key elements: people, hardware, software, data, and telecommunications networks.]

also enable us to get cash from ATMs, communicate by live video with people in other parts of the world, and buy concert tickets.

The term *information systems* is also used to describe the field comprising people who develop, use, manage, and study information systems in organizations. In Figure 1.4, we show the essential ingredients of the definition of IS.

Several terms are used to describe the field of information systems: management information systems, data processing management, systems management, business computer systems, computer information systems, and just systems. People most commonly use the term *information systems*; therefore, we will stick with this term and its acronym, *IS*. In the next section, we describe how the information systems field has evolved into a dominant force in modern organizations and in the economy.

The Information Technology Revolution

Computers are the core component of information systems. Over the past decade, the advent of powerful, relatively inexpensive, easy-to-use computers has had a major impact on business. To see this impact, look around your school or place of work. At your school, you may register for classes online, use e-mail to communicate with fellow students and your instructors, and complete assignments on networked personal computers. At work, you may use a personal computer and e-mail. Your paychecks are probably generated by computer and automatically deposited in your checking account via high-speed networks. Chances are you see more technology now than you did just a few short years ago, and this technology is a more fundamental and important part of your learning and work than ever before.

One characteristic of the computer industry is how fast computers change. More than 90 percent of the billions of dollars in revenue earned by computer chip manufacturing giant Intel comes from products that did not even exist just a few short years ago. Now that is change. Even with the cyclic nature of the economy, Microsoft, Oracle, Cisco Systems, and many other companies in the computer industry often experience annual sales growth that is relatively high (as high as 30 percent) when compared to the median growth rate for all other industries (typically more like five to 10 percent). Just 20 or so years ago, the computer industry was a relatively minor player in the world's economy; today, it has become the 800-pound gorilla!

The information technology revolution has been chronicled in the popular business press.

Information systems are combinations of hardware, software, and telecommunications networks
which
people build and use
to
collect, create, and distribute useful data,
typically in
organizational settings.

[Figure 1.4 ➡ The essential ingredients of the definition of IS.]

[Figure 1.5 ➥ Two business magazine covers with stories related to technology.]

Fortune Magazine, *Forbes* Magazine

For example, the cover stories in many issues of *BusinessWeek, Fortune,* and other business magazines have focused on technology or a technology company or industry. Figure 1.5 shows recent business magazines with technology related covers. In fact, *BusinessWeek* recently started adding an *e.biz* supplement to its magazine to focus more on technology and related issues. These articles in the popular business press mirror what is happening in the real world. Information technology is pervasive in everything we do and is the engine driving business productivity and economic success. While stocks for technology companies are not as high as they were at their peak a couple of years ago, technology is still hot.

The Rise of the Knowledge Worker

In 1959, Peter Drucker predicted this rise in the importance of information and of information technology, and at that point over four decades ago he coined the term ***knowledge worker***. Knowledge workers are typically professionals who are relatively well educated and who create, modify, and/or synthesize knowledge as a fundamental part of their jobs.

Drucker's predictions about knowledge workers were very accurate. As he predicted, they are generally paid better than their prior agricultural and industrial counterparts; they rely on and are empowered by formal education, yet they often also possess valuable real-world skills; they are continually learning how to do their jobs better; they have much better career opportunities and far more bargaining power than workers ever had before; they make up about a quarter of the workforce in the United States and in other developed nations; and their numbers are rising quickly.

Drucker also predicted that, with the growth in the number of knowledge workers and with their rise in importance and leadership, a ***knowledge society*** would emerge. He reasoned that, given the importance of education and learning to knowledge workers and the firms that need them, education would become the cornerstone of the knowledge society. Possessing knowledge, he argued, would be as important as possessing property once was (if not more so). Indeed, research shows that people with a college education earn far more on average than people without a college education, and that gap is increasing (see, for example, Farrell, et al., 1998).

People generally agree that Drucker was accurate about knowledge workers and the evolution of society. While people have settled

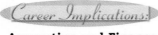

Career Implications:

Accounting and Finance

Information technology affects each and every aspect of our lives. Even law enforcement personnel are realizing that technology can be of enormous value in their day-to-day jobs. A detective in Florida had the responsibility of regularly checking the financial transaction data in pawnshops for stolen merchandise. Given that this required the detective to pore over mounds of paper, this was a time-consuming job. In order to make his life a little better, the detective bought a laptop with database software and started entering the transaction data from all the pawnshops (even those outside his jurisdiction) into the computer. It took quite a while to get all that financial data entered into the system, but once the job was finished it became clear how efficient and useful the system was. The project became a hit, and soon other detectives started asking whether the original detective would search the database of financial transactions to help them find their suspects. Unable to handle the load, the detective sought the help of the Broward County Sheriff's Office's IT department. The IT department

felt that this was a good idea, and developed a new application system called Pawn Trac that automated the collection, storage, and querying of pawnshop transaction data throughout the entire county. The detective's original database was transferred to a better client-server system. The IT department used a Microsoft SQL Server 7.0 database, which now contains about 4.5GB of data and information about 2.1 million pawned items. The county also provided pawnshops with laptops loaded with the software Pawn Power, which enables pawnshops to store all the transaction data easily. The pawnshops now download the data onto a floppy disk and send it to their local police stations, who send the data via modem to the sheriff's office. The IT department is now working on enhancements to the system that will enable pawnshops to send the data directly to the sheriff's office. The system has made it much easier for detectives to track pawnshop transaction data and, thus, recover stolen property. Who would have thought that police and private detectives would have to become savvy computer users too?

[Adapted from J. C. Perez, "Sheriff's Office Uses Technology to Catch the Crooks," *InfoWorld* 22, no. 50 (2000): 47.]

on Drucker's term, *knowledge worker*[2], there are many alternatives to the term *knowledge society*. For example, Manuel Castell has written that we now live in a network society. *Wired* magazine has published that we now live in a **new economy** and described it as follows:

> "So what is the new economy? When we talk about the new economy, we're talking about a world in which people work with their brains instead of their hands. A world in which communications technology creates global competition—not just for running shoes and laptop computers, but also for bank loans and other services that can't be packed into a crate and shipped. A world in which innovation is more important than mass production. A world in which investment buys new concepts or the means to create them, rather than new machines. A world in which rapid change is a constant. A world at least as different from what came before it as the industrial age was from its agricultural predecessor. A world so different its emergence can only be described as a revolution."

(Excerpt from *Wired* magazine's "Encyclopedia of the New Economy," 1998, a series published in the March, April, and May issues.)

Others have referred to this phenomenon as the digital society, the network era, the Internet era, and by other names. All of these ideas have in common the premise that information and information technology have become very important to us and knowledge workers are vital.

Some have argued, however, that there is a downside to being a knowledge worker and to living in this new economy. For example, Sims-Taylor has argued that knowledge workers will be the first to be replaced by automation with information technology. Rifkin has argued that our overreliance on information technology has caused us to think and act hastily and to lose our perspective. Others have argued that in the new economy there is a **digital divide**, where those with access to information technology have great advantages over those without access to information technology.

To be sure, there is a downside to overreliance on knowledge workers and information technology, but one thing is for certain ... knowledge workers and information technologies are now critical to the success of modern organizations, economies, and societies.

Data: The Root and Purpose of Information Systems

Let us break down and discuss the definition of IS. Earlier we defined IS as combinations of

hardware, software, and telecommunications networks that people build and use to collect, create, and distribute useful data, typically in organizational settings. We will begin by talking about data, the most basic element of any information system.

Before you can understand how information systems work, it is important to distinguish between **data**, and **information**, terms that are often erroneously used interchangeably. Data is raw material—recorded, unformatted information, such as words and numbers. Data has no meaning in and of itself. For example, if I asked you what 465889724 meant or stood for, you could not tell me. However, if I presented the same data as 465-88-9724 and told you it was located in a certain database, in John Doe's file, in a field labeled "SSN," you might rightly surmise that the number was actually the social security number of someone named John Doe.

Data formatted with dashes or labels is more useful than unformatted data. It is transformed into information, which can be defined as a representation of reality. In the previous example, 465-88-9724 was used to represent and identify an individual person, John Doe. Contextual cues, such as a label, are needed to turn data into information that is familiar to the reader. Think about your experience with ATMs. A list of all the transactions at a bank's ATMs over the course of a month would be fairly useless data. However, a table that divided ATM users into two categories— bank customers and non–bank customers— and compared the two groups' use of the machine—their purpose for using the ATM machines and the times and days on which they use them—would be incredibly useful information. A bank manager could use this information to create marketing mailings to attract new customers. Without information systems, it would be difficult to make data useful by turning it into information.

In addition to data and information, **knowledge** and **wisdom** are also important. Knowledge is needed to understand relationships between different pieces of information. For example, you must have knowledge to be aware that only one social security number can uniquely identify each individual. Knowledge is a body of governing procedures, such as guidelines or rules, which are used to organize or manipulate data to make it suitable for a given task.

Finally, wisdom is accumulated knowledge. Wisdom goes beyond knowledge in that

---

[2]There are exceptions, however. For example, former U.S. Secretary of Labor Robert B. Reich has used the more precise term *symbolic analyst*.

it represents broader, more generalized rules and schemas for understanding a specific domain or domains. Wisdom allows you to understand how to apply concepts from one domain to new situations or problems. Understanding that a unique individual identifier, such as a social security number, can be applied in certain programming situations to single out an individual record in a database is the result of accumulated knowledge. Wisdom can be gained through a combination of academic study and personal experience.

Understanding the distinctions between data, information, knowledge, and wisdom is important because all are used in the study, development, and use of information systems.

The Technology Side of Information Systems

When we use the term information system, we are talking about **computer-based information systems**. Computer-based information systems are a type of technology. **Technology** is any mechanical and/or electrical means to supplement, extend, or replace human, manual operations or devices. Sample machine technologies include the heating and cooling system for a building, the braking system for

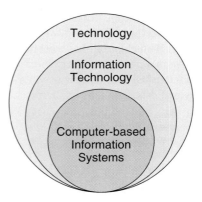

[**Figure 1.6** ➡ Computer-based information systems are a subset of information technologies and of technologies in general.]

an automobile, and a laser used for surgery. In Figure 1.6, we show the relationship between technologies and computer-based information systems.

The term **information technology** refers to machine technology that is controlled by or uses information. One type of information technology is a programmable robot on the shop floor of a manufacturing firm that receives component specifications and operational instructions from a computer-based database.

Operations Management

As we head further into the 21st century, the nature of organizations and how information technology can be used to support such operations are changing dramatically. A recent survey of CIOs conducted by Market Data Group LLC for *Computerworld* suggested that in the coming years, the roles of technology and of information systems will be in supporting the operations of virtual corporations. A virtual corporation may have team members working together remotely, organizations partnering with each other electronically, and literally little or no physical workplace. The CIOs further feel that although the battle between Linux and Windows seems to be a major source of IT-related news in recent times, they are not the technologies that will have the largest impact on organizations. Instead, the CIOs believe that network infrastructure will be the key organizational IT-related issue. Organizational IS departments will now have to focus on making significant improvements in terms of quality of service and connection reliability to the existing virtual private networks in order to serve virtual,

nimble corporations effectively. Intelligent, or policy-enabled, networks will become the new technological trend. These intelligent networks will help to "identify and prioritize data streams," and will require new switching and routing technologies and policy management capabilities. The network capacities will also increase by 25 to 50 percent, and the servers will have to be larger. In order to support the virtual corporations, most employees will have to be mobile and will need to access company servers remotely. As a result, IS departments' primary focus will be on technologies that will enable faster connections, including enhancements to copper-based Digital Subscriber Lines, cable modem technologies, and satellite connections. In short, some of the technological trends in the new century will include the network infrastructure for supporting the operations of virtual corporations, middleware and collaboration tools for enhancing electronic commerce, and object-oriented tools for component reuse. If you are thinking of managing a firm, you had better think carefully about how wired you and your firm are going to be.

[Adapted from Kevin Burden, "The Technology," **www.computerworld.com** (April 12, 1999) and Kevin Burden, "Tomorrow's IT," **www.computerworld.com** (April 12, 1999).]

We could argue that any technology makes use of information in some fundamental way, as does each of the three examples of basic technology listed earlier (heating system, braking system, and a laser). However, information technologies, such as programmable manufacturing robots, use more information and in a more sophisticated way. It may appear that we are splitting hairs by distinguishing among technologies and information technologies. While the distinction is subtle, it is important. Information technologies use machine technologies as building blocks and then combine them with computing and networking technologies. A technology such as a mechanical drill press is useful, but it is more useful when combined with a computer database that instructs that drill press when and how to act.

Information technologies and information systems are also similar. Remember that we defined an information system as a combination of hardware, software, and telecommunications networks that people build and use to collect, create, and distribute data. The goal of an information system is to provide useful data to users. An example of an information system is the use of specialized software on a computer-controlled, mechanical machine used to produce compact discs (CDs), combined with other shop floor equipment that allows a person to monitor and control the production of each CD from a separate, possibly remote, computer.

Other examples of information systems include a series of integrated electronic spreadsheets used for a budget, an order-fulfillment system for managing customers' purchases, or a set of linked pages on the World Wide Web. You may be asking, "Does my PC at work or school count as part of the company's or university's overall information system?" Our answer is, yes. IS includes personal, group, organizational, interorganizational, and even global computing systems.

The People Side of Information Systems

The information systems field includes a vast collection of people who develop, maintain, manage, and study information systems. The career opportunities for a person with IS training have never been better, and they are expected to continue to improve over the next 10 years. *Money Magazine* recently reported that being a systems analyst—a common IS job—is one of the best jobs in the world today.

The U.S. Department of Commerce is predicting huge labor shortages over the next decade for people with skills in using, designing, developing, and managing information systems. Nearly every industry, not just computer hardware and software companies, relies heavily on IS professionals; therefore, the shortage in skilled technology workers may have a big impact on the economy if these jobs go unfilled. The U.S. Bureau of Labor Statistics has reported that high demand for technology-related workers and escalating salaries could lead to inflation and lower corporate profits as companies scramble to offer competitive salaries to these people and, subsequently, have to drive up the prices of their goods and services.

Careers in IS

The field of IS includes those people in organizations who design and build systems, those who use these systems, and those responsible for managing these systems. In Table 1.1, we list careers in IS and the salaries you might earn in those positions. The people who help develop and manage systems in organizations include systems analysts, systems programmers, systems operators, network administrators, database administrators, systems designers, systems managers, and chief information officers.

Another significant part of the IS field is the group of people who work in IS consulting firms such as IBM, Electronic Data Systems (EDS), and Accenture (formerly Andersen Consulting). These consultants advise organizations on how to build and manage their systems and sometimes actually build and run those systems. Companies such as IBM, which have traditionally been hardware/software companies, are now doing a lot of systems consulting and related work. Similarly, companies such as Accenture, which specializes in systems consulting, are very successful—hiring more people, opening new offices, taking on new business, generating lots of revenue, and so on.

University professors are another group of people in IS. These professors conduct research on the development, use, and management of information systems. Nonacademic researchers who conduct research for agencies such as the Department of Defense or for large corporations such as IBM, Xerox, Hewlett-Packard, and AT&T face almost unlimited opportunities. These professionals generally conduct more applied research and development than academic researchers. For example,

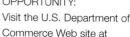

Web Search

WEB SEARCH OPPORTUNITY: Visit the U.S. Department of Commerce Web site at **home.doc.gov/** to find information and publications about the effect of IT on the economy and growth in jobs in this area.

[Table 1.1] *Careers and salaries in the information systems field.*

IS Activities	Typical Careers	Salary Ranges
Develop	Systems analyst	$40,000–$80,000+
	Systems programmer	$50,000–$80,000+
	Systems consultant	$50,000–$100,000+
Maintain	Database administrator	$75,000–$100,000+
	Webmaster	$40,000–$75,000+
Manage	IS director	$80,000–$120,000+
	Chief information officer	$125,000–$250,000+
Study	University professor	$60,000–$200,000+
	Government scientist	$60,000–$200,000+

a researcher for a major computer manufacturer might be developing a new computer product or examining ways to extend the life of a current product by integrating leading-edge components with the older architecture.

The Advent of the Chief Information Officer

A number of important indications show that organizations are trying hard to manage information systems better. But perhaps nothing better demonstrates the growing importance of information systems in organizations than the advent of the ***chief information officer*** (CIO) and related positions in contemporary organizations.

Evolution of the CIO
In the early 1980s, the CIO position became popular as the new title given to executive-level individuals who were responsible for the information systems component within their organizations. The CIO was charged with integrating new technologies into the organization's business strategy. Traditionally, the responsibility for integrating technology and strategy had not officially rested with any one manager. Responsibility for managing the day-to-day information systems function had previously rested with a midlevel operations manager or, in some cases, with a vice president of information systems. Ultimate responsibility for these activities would now rest with a high-level executive, the CIO. People began to realize that the information systems department was not simply a cost center—a necessary evil that simply consumed resources. They realized that information systems could be of tremendous

strategic value to the organization. As a result, this new IS executive would work much like other executives, sitting at the strategy table, working right alongside the chief executive officer, chief financial officer, chief operating officer, and other chief executives and key people in the organization. When strategic decisions were to be made, technology would play a major role, and the CIO needed to participate in the strategic decision-making process.

Not surprisingly, many organizations have jumped on the CIO bandwagon and either hired or named a CIO. As a result, many people thought that the CIO boom was a fad that would soon end, as do many other popular management trends. In fact, in early 1990, *BusinessWeek* printed a story entitled, "CIO Is Starting to Stand for 'Career Is Over': Once Deemed Indispensable, the Chief Information Officer Has Become an Endangered Species" (Rothfeder and Driscoll, 1990). In this story, and in the cartoon in Figure 1.7, the authors reported statistics showing that in 1989, the CIO dismissal rate had doubled to 13 percent, which was noticeably higher than the nine percent for all top executives. They explained that the primary reasons for CIO dismissals included tightening budgets for technology and management's overblown expectations of CIO functions. Apparently, many organizations had been caught up in the rush to have a CIO without thinking enough about why they needed to have a CIO in the first place. The authors countered, however, that given the growing trend toward using information systems to achieve competitive advantage, the CIO could become relevant and important again. How right they were.

[**Figure 1.7** ➡ *BusinessWeek* cartoon showing the dangers of being a CIO.]
© Dave Cutler.

Brief Case: Information Systems Top Job: Brewing Success at Starbucks Coffee

In the field of information systems, the ultimate success in terms of career advancement is the position of CIO. However, being a successful CIO is no easy task, and many obstacles block the way. Deborah J. Gillotti, senior vice president and CIO of Starbucks Coffee Company in Seattle, faces several immediate challenges to her success: the creation of a strategic plan for IT investment, the maximization of the utilization of new technologies, and the development of new relationships between IS and business groups (Field, 1997). In addition, while individual members of the IS staff are highly praised, the other business units have had very low opinions of the IS department. Gillotti must convince the planning committees and her bosses that a greater IT investment and utilization of new technologies are crucial for the company. Gillotti must also forge ahead by building relationships with the other business managers who need her department's services and expertise. After these business managers get what they want and what Gillotti believes they need, she will be judged successful by her peers at the executive level. So far, she has made great strides toward the challenges that face her, but only time will tell. ⬤

The CIO Today

Today, most large organizations have a CIO or an equivalent position[3]. It is also now common for midsized and smaller organizations to have a CIO-like position within their organizations, although they may give this person a title such as Director of Information Systems. Even the United States Internal Revenue Service named its first-ever CIO in 1990. The current IRS CIO, John Reece, is leading a $15 billion modernization program with the goal of delivering e-services to every taxpayer by the end of the decade. On the industry side, eight CIOs were named as "Chiefs of the Year" in December of 2001 by *InformationWeek* (see Figure 1.8), a magazine for business and technology managers. These CIOs were selected not only for their success in managing technology within their firms but also for the roles they played in leading their companies and staffs through the cataclysmic events of September 11, 2001. These and other CIOs are as critical to their organizations as the technologies that they manage.

---

[3]Not to be confused with the chief technology officer, a post usually held by a person within a technology company who helps to chart the course for the company's technology products

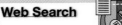

The software industry of late has been highly affected in terms of quality, consistency, and simplicity due to the overarching power of the vendors. The vendors have succeeded in increasing the cost of switching from one software to another, and have thus significantly weakened the power of the customers. Industry experts feel that for the long-term stability of the software industry, it is important to bring about an immediate change. However, the dilemma is who will initiate the change. The software vendors are reluctant to bring any change since the current situation is to their benefit. On the other hand, the customers have too little power to initiate any change. Some people believe that the responsibility of bringing about this change should fall on the CIOs of the organizations. From a human resource management point of view, what type of employee should organizations be looking for in their CIO? Some believe that the new millennium CIO should focus not on technical issues but on relationships, and thus nurture a certain level of collaboration between vendors and customers, which may ultimately lead to a more balanced distribution of power within the industry. In order to foster collaboration between the two parties, CIOs need to think more long-term than short-term. One way to make CIOs think more long-term is to base their rewards on the success of the organization rather than the return on investment of specific IS projects. The new generation CIO's primary goal should hence be on building a customer-oriented workforce in the IS industry, which can help in developing collaborative relationships between customers and vendors, and thus lead to the "continuous improvement of the information assets and the organizations that manage them."

[Adapted from Leon A. Kappelman, 'Rebalancing Acts," **www.cio.com**, *CIO Magazine* (December 15, 1999/January 1, 2000).]

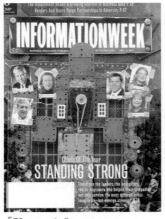

[**Figure 1.8** ➡

InformationWeek cover with Chief Information Officers of the Year.]

IS Managerial Personnel

In large organizations, in addition to the CIO position there typically are many other different management positions within the IS function. In Table 1.2, we describe several such positions. This list is not exhaustive; rather, it is intended to provide a sampling of IS management positions. Furthermore, many firms will use the same job title, but each is likely to define it in a different way. As you can see from Table 1.2, the range of career opportunities for IS managers is very broad.

What Makes IS Personnel So Valuable?

In addition to the growing importance of people in the IS field, there have been changes in the nature of this type of work. No longer are IS departments in organizations filled only with nerdy men with pocket protectors. Many more women are in IS positions now. Also, it is now more common for an IS professional to be a polished, professional systems analyst who can talk fluently about both business and technology. Similarly, today's systems programmers are well-trained, highly skilled, valuable professionals who garner high wages and play a pivotal role in helping firms be successful. For example, good programmers with skills in hot software platforms such as SAP R/3 (Systems, Applications, and Products in Data Processing, Release 3) or Java are so valuable that some organizations are willing to pay $150,000 a year or more to get them.

Many studies have been aimed at helping us understand what knowledge and skills are necessary for a person in the IS area to be successful (see, for example, Todd, McKeen, and Gallupe, 1995). Interestingly, these studies also point out just what it is about IS personnel that makes them so valuable to their organizations. In a nutshell, good IS personnel possess valuable, integrated knowledge and skills in three areas—technical, business, and systems—as outlined in Table 1.3.

Technical Competency

These three areas of knowledge and skills—technical, business, and systems—are the core competencies that make IS professionals valuable to organizations. The technical competency area includes knowledge and skills in hardware, software, and networking. In a sense, this is the "nuts and bolts" of IS. This is not to say that the IS professional must be a high-level technical expert in these areas. On the contrary, the IS professional must know just enough about these areas to understand how they work and how they can and should be applied. Typically, the IS professional manages or directs those who have deeper, more detailed technical knowledge.

The technical area of competency is, perhaps, the most difficult to maintain because

Job Title	Job Description
CIO	Highest-ranking IS manager. Responsible for strategic planning and IS use throughout the firm.
IS director	Responsible for managing all systems throughout the firm and the day-to-day operations of the entire IS unit.
Account executive	Responsible for managing the day-to-day operations of all aspects of IS within one particular division, plant, functional business area, or product unit.
Information center manager	Responsible for managing IS services such as help desks, hot lines, training, consulting, and so on.
Development manager	Responsible for coordinating and managing all new systems projects.
Project manager	Responsible for managing a particular new systems project.
Maintenance manager	Responsible for coordinating and managing all systems maintenance projects.
Systems manager	Responsible for managing a particular existing system.
IS planning manager	Responsible for developing an enterprise-wide hardware, software, and networking architecture and for planning for systems growth and change.
Operations manager	Responsible for supervising the day-to-day operations of the data and/or computer center.
Programming manager	Responsible for coordinating all applications programming efforts.
Systems programming manager	Responsible for coordinating support for maintenance of all systems software (for example, operating systems, utilities, programming languages, and so on).
Manager of emerging technologies	Responsible for forecasting technology trends and for evaluating and experimenting with new technologies.
Telecommunications manager	Responsible for coordinating and managing the entire voice and data network.
Network manager	Responsible for managing one piece of the enterprise-wide network.
Database administrator	Responsible for managing database and database management software use.
Auditing or computer security manager	Responsible for managing ethical and legal use of information systems within the firm.
Quality assurance manager	Responsible for developing and monitoring standards and procedures to ensure that systems within the firm are accurate and of good quality.
Webmaster	Responsible for managing the firm's World Wide Web site.

[Table 1.2] *Some IS management job titles and brief job descriptions.*

Domain	Description
Technical Knowledge and Skills	
Hardware	Hardware platforms, peripherals
Software	Operating systems, application software, drivers
Networking	Networking operating systems, cabling and networking interface cards, LANs, WANs, Internet
Business Knowledge and Skills	
Business	Business processes, functional areas of business and their integration, industry
Management	Planning, organizing, leading, controlling, managing people and projects
Social	Interpersonal, group dynamics, political
Communication	Verbal, written, and technological communication and presentation
Systems Knowledge and Skills	
Systems integration	Connectivity, compatibility, integrating subsystems and systems
Development methodologies	Steps in systems analysis and design, systems development life cycle, alternative development methodologies
Critical thinking	Challenging one's and others' assumptions and ideas
Problem solving	Information gathering and synthesis, problem identification, solution formulation, comparison, and choice

the popularity of individual technologies is so fleeting. In Table 1.4, we list some technical skills areas that are currently popular. Many of these would not have appeared on this list a few years ago, and many will probably not appear on the list in a few years.

Business Competency

The business competency area is one that sets the IS professional apart from others who have only technical knowledge and skills. It is absolutely vital for IS professionals to understand the technical areas and the business and the technology/strategy fit. IS professionals must also be able to understand and manage people. These business skills propel IS professionals into project management and, ultimately, high-paying middle- and upper-level management positions.

Systems Competency

Systems competency is another area that sets the IS professional apart from others with only technical knowledge and skills. Those who understand how to build and integrate systems and how to solve problems will ulti-

mately manage large, complex systems projects, as well as manage those in the firm who have only technical knowledge and skills.

Perhaps now you can see why IS professionals are so valuable to their organizations. These individuals have a solid foundation in, and have integrated, technical, business, and systems knowledge and skills. Perhaps most important, they also have the social skills to understand how to work well with and motivate others. It is these core competencies that make IS professionals a hot commodity.

Given how important technology is, what does this mean for your career? Technology is being used to radically change how business is conducted—from the way products and services are produced, distributed and accounted for, to the ways they are marketed and sold. Whether you are majoring in information systems, finance, accounting, operations management, human resource management, business law, or marketing, knowledge of technology is critical to a successful career in business.

Office/E-Mail	Languages & Data Formats	Applications
Microsoft Office	SmallTalk	Any Enterprise Resource Planning package (e.g., those from SAP or Oracle)
MS Internet Explorer	C, C++, and C#	
Netscape Navigator	Java and JavaScript	Any Customer Relationship Management package (e.g., those from Siebel)
MS Project	HTML/CGI	
Microsoft Exchange	Perl	Any Supply Chain Management package (e.g., those from I2, Ariba, or CommerceOne)
Lotus Notes	ASP/VBScript	
POP mailers	PHP	
IMAP mailers	Python	PeopleSoft
	Visual Basic	SAS Enterprise Miner
	XML and UML	

[Table 1.4] *What technical skills are hot?*

RDBMS Administration	Development Tools	Internetworking
Sybase	Oracle Developer 2000 Uniface	Cisco
Oracle	Lotus Domino/Designer	Lucent
DB2	Microsoft Visual Studio	Juniper
MS SQL Server	Microsoft .net platform	
MySQL	BEA Weblogic	
	IBM WebSphere	
	Sun's J2EE	

Operating Systems	NOS LAN Administration	Networking
Solaris	Windows 2000 Advanced Server	TCP/IP
HP-UX	Novell NetWare	IPX/SPX
AIX	SAMBA	SNMP
OS/2		IEEE 802.11a & b (wireless Ethernet)
Windows XP		Frame Relay
Windows 2000 Professional		ATM
Windows CE		Voice over IP
Linux		VLANs
		VPNs
		Optical networking

Marketing

The explosion in information technologies in the last few years, and the rapid rate at which applications are being introduced, are posing a real challenge for IS professionals, who are finding it hard to cope with the required knowledge and the skills, and also to keep up with their peers and competitors in their respective industries. Many of them focus on reading magazines meant for CIOs or attending conferences to keep up with the new technological trends. IS professionals with retail companies are, however, using another method to keep up-to-date. They are relying on the services of a trade association called National Retail Federation (NRF). The primary responsibility of this association is to talk to retail companies and gather information about how retailers are using different types of technologies, including information about what they are implementing, the tools they are using, and whether it has worked for them. All this information is then compiled in the form of "best practices" documents and peer get-togethers. Twice a year, the association organizes roundtable discussions around the country, which are attended by a number of IS professionals from different retail companies. Vendors are not allowed into these meetings, and retailers are provided with a fairly relaxed environment to discuss each other's experiences regarding new technological trends, implementation of information technology, infrastructure, IS legislation, and so on. Retail IS professionals are arguing that this has significantly increased their ability to cope with the technological explosion. In fact, one meeting lasted for more than eight hours without a break. Members were not even keen on going to the restroom, since they were afraid that they might miss something critical while they made their short exit. If you plan on going into retail, you had better get in on these meetings (or at least send your IS staff).

[Adapted from Cathy Hotka, "Power in Numbers," **www.cio.com**, *CIO Magazine* (December 1, 2000).]

The Organizational Side of Information Systems

We have talked about data versus information, the technology side of IS, and the people side of IS. The last part of our IS definition is the term *organization*. People use information systems to help their organization to be more productive and profitable, to help their firm gain competitive advantage, to help their firm reach more customers, or to improve service to the customers their organization serves. This holds true for all types of organizations—professional, social, religious, educational, and governmental. In fact, not long ago the U.S. Internal Revenue Service launched its own site on the World Wide Web for the reasons just described (see Figure 1.9). The IRS Web site was so popular that approximately 220,000 users visited it during the first 24 hours and more than a million visited it in its first week—even before the Web address for the site was officially announced.

In Chapter 6 we will talk in detail about the types of information systems commonly

[**Figure 1.9** ➡ Web site of the U.S. Department of the Treasury, Internal Revenue Service]
www.irs.ustreas.gov/.

used in organizations. It makes sense, however, for us to describe briefly here the various types of systems used so that you will know exactly what we mean by the term "information system" as we use it throughout the rest of the book. Table 1.5 provides a list of the major types of information systems used in organizations.

Topping the list in the table are some of the more traditional, major categories that are used to describe information systems. These include **transaction processing systems**, **management information systems**, **executive information systems**, **decision support systems**, **expert systems**, and **functional area information systems**. Five to 10 years ago it

Type of System	Designed To	Sample Application
Transaction Processing System	Process day-to-day business event data at the operational level of the organization	Grocery store checkout cash register with connection to network
Management Information System	Produce detailed information to help manage a firm or a part of a firm	Inventory management and planning system
Executive Information System	Provide very high-level, aggregate information to support executive-level decision making	News retrieval and stock update information system
Decision Support System	Provide analysis tools and access to databases in order to support quantitative decision making	Product demand forecasting system
Expert System	Mimic human expert in a particular area and provide answers or advice	Automated system for analyzing bank loan applications
Functional Area Information System	Support the activities within a specific functional area of the firm	System for planning for personnel training and assignments
Office Automation System (a.k.a. Personal Productivity Software)	Support a wide range of predefined, day-to-day work activities of individuals and small groups	Word processor
Collaboration System	Enable people to communicate, collaborate, and coordinate with each other	Electronic mail system with automated, shared calendar
Customer Relationship Management System	Support interaction between the firm and its customers	Siebel's suite of e-business software products, including Siebel Sales
Electronic Commerce System	Enable customers to buy goods and services from a firm's Web site	www.amazon.com
Enterprise Resource Planning System	Support and integrate all facets of the business, including planning, manufacturing, sales, marketing, and so on	SAP R/3 (Systems, Applications, and Products in Data Processing, Release 3)

[Table 1.5] *Types of information systems used in organizations.*

would have been typical to see systems that fell cleanly into one of these categories. Today, with *internetworking* and *systems integration*, it is difficult to say that any given information system fits into only one of these categories (i.e., that a system is a management information system only and nothing else). Modern-day information systems tend to span several of these categories of information systems, helping not only to collect data from throughout the firm and from customers, but also to integrate all that diverse data and present it to busy decision makers, along with tools to manipulate and analyze those data. *Customer Relationship Management systems* and *Enterprise Resource Planning systems* are good examples of these types of systems that encompass many features and types of data and cannot easily be categorized.

Office automation systems and *collaboration systems* are typically bought "off-the-shelf" and enable people to 1) perform their own work, and 2) work with others. There are a handful of software packages that dominate this sector of the software industry and are commonly found on personal computers in people's homes and offices. Microsoft Office is an example of a very popular office automation system that provides word processing, spreadsheet, and other personal productivity tools. Microsoft's Exchange/Outlook and Lotus Notes are good examples of very popular collaboration systems that provide people with e-mail, automated calendaring, and online, threaded discussions.

Systems for *electronic commerce*, such as corporate Web sites, are also very popular and important. These systems are typically Internet-based and enable 1) consumers to find information about, and purchase, goods and services from each other and from business firms, and 2) business firms to electronically exchange products, services, and information. Given the pervasive use of the Internet to support electronic commerce, we devote a great deal of time to this topic in subsequent chapters. In Chapter 4 we talk about the nuts and bolts of how the Internet works. Then, in Chapter 5, we talk about how people are using the Internet to conduct electronic commerce.

While many modern-day information systems span several of these IS categories, it is still useful to understand these categories. Doing so enables you to better understand the myriad approaches, goals, features, and functions of modern information systems.

We have talked about each of the parts of our definition of IS, shown again in Figure 1.10, and we have talked about different types of information systems. In the next section, we focus on how information systems can be applied within organizations.

THE DUAL NATURE OF INFORMATION SYSTEMS

Technology is like a sword—you can use it effectively as a competitive weapon, but as the old saying goes, those who live by the sword sometimes die by the sword. The two following cases illustrate this dual nature of information systems.

Case in Point: An Information System Gone Awry: The Denver International Airport

What happens when an information system is implemented poorly? Perhaps the most notable example of an information system gone wrong in recent years is the automated baggage-handling system for the new, $4.2 billion Denver International Airport (DIA), which is shown in Figure 1.11.

Like the newly constructed DIA, the new underground, automated baggage-handling system for the airport was intended to be amazing. This information system would not only coordinate the automated check-in and routing of all luggage for all customers throughout the airport, but it would also enable airport employees to monitor the flow

Information systems are combinations of
hardware, software, and telecommunications networks
which
people build and use
to
collect, create, and distribute useful data,
typically in
organizational settings.

[**Figure 1.10** ➡ A representation of the definition of IS, as shown in Figure 1.4.]

Disaster Plans Found Lacking

The tragic events in the United States on September 11, 2001, pointed out how important it is for business managers to make contingency plans for the information systems that are used to run their businesses. Surprisingly, while companies have had to rely more and more on their information systems, you would think that business executives would spend more time thinking about disaster recovery. Unfortunately, they have not.

According to an online poll conducted from May 21 to June 3 of 2001 by St. Louis–based trade publication *Disaster Recovery Journal*, 65.5 percent of the 2,223 respondents said their company had not enacted its business contingency/disaster recovery plan in the last 10 years. The poll also found that about 26 percent had enacted their plans between one and three times.

In another survey, also taken during the spring of 2001, 38 percent of 2,151 respondents reported that the biggest challenge in planning disaster recovery efforts was funding. Doran Boroski, a senior consultant with Compass Group, a Chicago-based management consulting firm, is not surprised by that. Boroski says cost is often a barrier to proper disaster recovery and testing.

"Even if they have a plan, they don't test it, mostly for financial reasons," Boroski says. "Testing is the first thing to go out of the IT budget."

Bob Zimmerman, an analyst at Giga Information Group who specializes in storage management, says disaster recovery tests need to be random events, just like the disasters they are supposed to simulate. Too often, he says, companies schedule tests for a specific time, on a specific day, on a specific application, and when specific personnel are available.

"Very few businesses could pass a rigorous disaster recovery test," Zimmerman says. In surveying 150 Compass Group clients over the past 12 to 18 months, Boroski has found that one area where companies are sorely lacking in disaster readiness is their midrange data centers, which are likely to store information related to such things as payroll and HR. Just 25 percent of companies had a disaster recovery plan for their midrange data centers and one-third of the companies with a disaster plan had actually tested it.

After the tragic events of September 11, business leaders are thinking a lot more about how they might recover from a similar disaster. Disaster recovery planning has taken on new meaning and importance since then.

[Adapted from Jon Surmacz, "Disaster Plans Lacking," *CIO Magazine* (September 26, 2001). **www2.cio.com/ metrics/2001/metric269.html**]

>>When Things go Wrong :-(:-| :-0

[**Figure 1.11** ➡ The $4.2 billion Denver International Airport.] ©Getty Images, Inc.

of baggage and literally locate bags anywhere in the airport. The system, which cost $200 million, included the following features:

- 21 miles of steel track
- 4,000 independent "telecars" that would route and deliver luggage among the counters, gates, and claim areas of 20 different airlines
- 100 networked computers
- 5,000 electric eyes
- 400 radio receivers
- 56 bar-code scanners

Due to problems in the software, the system opened, damaged, and misrouted cargo, forcing airport authorities to leave the system sitting idle for nearly a year. Because of this and other delays, the airport did not open and wasted $1.1 million a day in interest and operating costs for quite some time.

The DIA story has a happy ending, or beginning, as it were. They fixed the software and the automated baggage system is now operational. The airport is now making money and winning awards. Indeed, the baggage-handling system is one of many ways that this organization is attempting to be innovative and to outdo the competition. However, the airport is still useful as an example of how a problematic information system can adversely affect the performance of an organization.

Case in Point: An Information System That Works: FedEx

Just as there are examples of information systems gone wrong, there are many examples of information systems gone right. For example, take the innovative use of information systems on the FedEx website (see Figure 1.12).

FedEx Express, the world's largest express transportation company, delivers more than 3 million packages and more than 7 million pounds of freight to over 200 countries each business day. FedEx Express uses extensive, interconnected information systems to coordinate more than 140,000 employees, 644 aircraft, and more than 45,000 ground vehicles worldwide.

To improve its services and sustain a competitive advantage, FedEx now offers services on the World Wide Web. Millions of customers visit the FedEx Web site to track FedEx Express and FedEx Ground shipments anywhere in the world, find out about FedEx's delivery options and costs, or use tools to prepare their own packages, verify them online, and print barcoded shipping documents. These and other information systems assure FedEx a position of dominance in the shipping business for many years to come.

[Figure 1.12 ➡ The Web site for Federal Express.] **www.federalexpress.com**

The growing demand for inexpensive yet competent programming talent is pushing the offshore-outsourcing market beyond its roots in India and encouraging U.S. IT service providers to increase their use of overseas workers.

"The technology skills needed to program in languages such as C++, Cobol, and even Java are available in China, the Philippines, Russia, and other countries, but offshore outsourcing is most mature in India, where the government has been supportive of IT for decades and has continued to improve on the solid educational systems built by the British," says Mukesh Mehta, VP of corporate systems for Metropolitan Life Insurance Company, which has an offshore-outsourcing contract with Cognizant Technology Solutions Corp. For instance, the Indian Parliament granted the Indian Institute of Technology its charter in 1961, and the school has evolved into a center for teaching, research, and industrial consulting.

While India is the biggest resource for offshore programmers and project managers (see Figure 1.13), Forrester Research predicts that demand for

offshore workers will outstrip that country's supply in a few years. India has about 445,000 IT workers, a population that is expected to grow to 625,000 by 2005. But Forrester also predicts that demand for offshore IT workers will reach more than 1 million by 2005, compared with about 360,000 this year.

United States executives are becoming increasingly comfortable with outsourcing projects to companies that do the work in remote locations at lower prices than can be found domestically. "A 25 percent cost savings on an outsourcing contract is a realistic goal when working with an offshore provider," Forrester analyst Christine Overby says. To mitigate risk, many offshore companies have management personnel in the United States who act as liaisons with overseas staff. The continued reliance on offshore talent by well-known service providers, such as Accenture, EDS, and IBM Global Services, also lends credence to the offshore model.

Fifty IT executives interviewed in a recent Forrester study of offshore outsourcing say they spent an average of $8 million on these services in 2000—roughly 12 percent of their IT budgets. The research firm projects that the average outlay will jump to $28 million, or 28 percent of IT budgets, in 2003.

What began more than a decade ago as a cheap way to supplement overworked internal application developers with workers from India has grown into a worldwide search for the right mixture of talent, resources, and cost savings to create and manage today's most complex IT environments.

───────

[Adapted from, Larry Greenemeier, "Offshore Outsourcing Grows To Global Proportions," *InformationWeek* (February 11, 2002).
www.informationweek.com/story/iwek2002 020750011]

Information Systems for Competitive Advantage

The Denver International Airport and FedEx information systems are typical of those used in large, complex organizations. These systems are so large in scale and scope that they are difficult to build. It is important to handle the development of such systems the right way the first time around.

Not only were these systems large and complicated, but they were, and continue to be, critical to the success of the firms that built them. The choices made in developing the new systems at both DIA and Fedex were *strategic* in their intent. These systems were not developed solely because managers in these organizations wanted to do things faster or because they wanted to have the latest, greatest technology. These organizations developed these systems strategically to help gain or sustain some *competitive advantage* (Porter, 1985; Porter and Millar, 1985) over their rivals. Let us not let this notion slip by us—technology should be strategic and can be a powerful enabler of competitive advantage.

Although we described information systems' uses at two relatively large organizations, firms of all types and sizes can use information systems to gain or sustain a competitive advantage over their rivals. Whether it is a small, mom-and-pop boutique or a large government agency, every organization can find a way to use information technology to beat its rivals. In the next chapter we will talk more about this opportunity to use information systems strategically.

THE FUTURE OF THE IS FUNCTION WITHIN THE FIRM

The current emphasis on the use of technology within businesses is not a fad. Indeed, all indicators point to the increased use of technology and organizations' continued awareness of the importance of technology, both as a tool for productivity and as a vehicle for achieving competitive advantage and organizational change. In this section, we briefly discuss some likely future trends.

From Ownership and Control to a Consulting and Service Mentality

Early IS departments typically had huge project backlogs, and IS personnel would often deliver systems that were over budget, were completed much too late, were difficult to use, and did not always work well. In addition, many of these old-school IS personnel believed they owned and controlled the computing resources, that they knew better than users did, and that they should tell users what they could and could not do with the computing resources. Needless to say, this was not a recipe for success and good relationships. Indeed, relations between IS personnel and users within a firm were often sour and were sometimes bitter.

For a long time, users were forced to put up with the poor service and the poor attitude. Then technology started to become significantly better—faster, easier to build and use, and cheaper. As a result, end users began to develop their own computing applications. Disgruntled users simply said, "If the IS staff cannot or will not do this for us, then we will build our own systems." In many cases, they did just that, and they did it well, much to the dismay of some of the IS managers.

Business managers soon became more savvy about technology and the possibilities and opportunities that it offered, and they reasoned that the possibilities and opportunities were too great to let the IS function simply wither away as end-user development took

over. In addition, smart, concerned IS personnel realized that they needed an attitude adjustment. Some people believe that the changes in the nature of technology forced people to cooperate more. For example, the shift from mainframes to a client-server model may have forced people within the IS function to improve their operations and their relationships with people in other units of the firm. The client-server model required a new kind of relationship between IS and other people throughout the firm (Stevens, 1994). As a result of these forces, in modern IS units that do a good job, the atmosphere, attitude, and culture are very different and much more sensitive and responsive than they used to be (see Figure 1.14).

In these more responsive IS units, the personnel have taken on more of a consulting relationship with their users. The IS personnel believe that, fundamentally, they are there to help the users solve problems and be more productive. Indeed, in many cases, the IS personnel do not even refer to the users as "users." They are "clients" or "customers." This new attitude is a major change from the old days, when IS personnel did not want to be bothered by users and thought that the techies knew better than users. It is unfortunate that this old-school mentality still exists in some organizations.

The new IS culture is much like that found in successful service organizations. Think of how customers are treated in service organizations, such as Salomon Smith Barney or Ernst & Young, or in product-based organizations where service is also important, such as McDonald's or Nordstrom. Great service to the customer is absolutely critical, and employees do everything they can to please customers. They often live by the credo that "the customer is always right."

[Figure 1.14 ➡ IS personnel are professional and helpful, and they add value to the organization.]
©Getty Images, Inc.

The same holds for IS units that have taken on this new *service mentality*. The IS personnel do everything they can to ensure that they are satisfying their systems customers within the firm. They reach out to customers and proactively seek their input and needs, rather than waiting for customers to come in with systems complaints. They modify the systems at a moment's notice just to meet customer needs quickly and effectively. They celebrate the customer's new systems ideas rather than putting up roadblocks and giving reasons that the new ideas cannot or will not work. They fundamentally believe that the customers own the technology and the information and that the technology and information are there for the customers, not for the systems personnel. They create help desks, hot lines, information centers, and training centers to support customers. These service-oriented IS units structure the IS function so that it can better serve the customer.

The implications of this new service mentality for the IS function are staggering. It is simply amazing how unproductive it can be when the IS personnel and other people within the firm are at odds with one another. On the other hand, it is even more amazing how productive and fun work can be when people in the IS function work hand in hand with people throughout the organization. Technology is, potentially, the great lever, but it works best when people work together, not against each other, to use it.

The Spread of Technology in Organizations

Another phenomenon that shows how integral and vital information systems and their proper management have become to organizations is the extent to which the technology is firmly integrated and entrenched within the various business units (accounting, sales, marketing).

In many organizations today, you will find that the builders and managers of a particular information system or subsystem spend most of their time out in the business unit, along with the users of that particular system. Many times, these systems personnel are permanently placed—with an office, desk, phone, and personal computer—in the business unit along with the users.

In addition, it is not uncommon for systems personnel to have formal education, training, and work experience in information systems as well as in the functional area that the system supports, such as finance. It is becoming increasingly difficult to separate the technology from the business or the systems staff from the other people in the organization. For this reason, how information systems are managed is important to you, no matter what career option you pursue.

As information systems are used more broadly throughout organizations, IS personnel often have dual-reporting relationships—reporting to both the central IS group and the business function they serve. Therefore, at least some need for centralized IS planning,

Team Work

How to Find Out What is Current in IS

Working with other members of your class, visit the Web sites of *InformationWeek*, *Computerworld*, and *CIO Magazine*, and scan the current headlines. What are the hot technologies and related issues? Which seem to be most important to business managers? You can find these online resources at **www.informationweek.com**, **www.computerworld.com**, and **www.cio.com**.

Brief Case: Developing a Consulting Mentality at Texas Instruments

The notion of a consulting mentality could not have been more appropriate than at Texas Instruments, the Dallas-based electronics manufacturer (Koch, 1998). When Pallab Chatterjee became CIO at Texas Instruments, the IT department had a very tight grip on decision making. Chatterjee soon realized that the control was so tight that the business units were literally scared to ask the IT department for anything, and they relied on "underground" IT projects without the help of the IT department. To combat this problem, Chatterjee has reorganized Texas Instruments' worldwide IT department and services into two subunits. The first, referred to as the worldwide utility, is responsible for the physical networks, the data center, the numerous local LANs, and the global WAN. This group is mainly responsible for efficiency, control, and reliability. The second subunit, the consultants, is composed of all IT staff members who are not part of the utility group. These consultants work both at the central, corporate level as well as at the business-unit level. At the business-unit level, these consultants are able to work closely with the managers to develop and manage systems that do not require centralized control. The systems that do require more control are handled by the consultants at the corporate level. This model has proven to be very successful for Chatterjee and Texas Instruments because business units are no longer afraid to ask for corporate support and know that if they need corporate support, it will be there.

deployment, and management continues—particularly with respect to achieving economies of scale in systems acquisition and development and in optimizing systems integration, enterprise networking, and the like. Even in organizations that are decentralizing technology and related decisions, a need for technology and related decisions to be coordinated well across the firm still persists. This coordination is likely to continue to happen through some form of a centralized (or, at least, centrally coordinated) IS staff. Organizations are likely to continue to want to reap the benefits of IS decentralization (flexibility, adaptability, and systems responsiveness), but it is equally likely that they will not want to, and will not be able to, forego the benefits of IS centralization (coordination, economies of scale, compatibility, and connectivity).

Changing Skill Set and Human Resource Planning

Given the trend toward pushing people from the IS staff out into the various business units of the firm, and given the need for people within each of the functional areas of the business to have technology skills, there is clearly a need for people who know the technology side and the business side of the business well. We suspect that the need for people to play these boundary-spanning roles will continue. Many of these people will be hired into and located within the IS departments of firms, but they are likely to spend a lot of their time working out in the business unit with their clients (see Figure 1.15). Indeed, their work space is likely to be physically located out in the business unit. Staffing the

[Figure 1.15 ➡ IS personnel are likely to be put out in the business unit, working directly with the people who will use the system being implemented.]
©Getty Images, Inc.

IS group with these kinds of boundary spanners is and will continue to be critical to the success of the IS group and to the success of the organization.

Downsizing of Organizations and IS Departments

Many organizations that are **downsizing**, or rightsizing, as some call it, are looking toward the IS function and technology as the lever for simultaneously shrinking the organization and

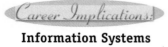

Information Systems

There are a number of different forces causing restructuring within the IS units of business firms. First, IS departments are increasingly finding it difficult to get skilled personnel for their most important and valuable projects. Even with the recent slowdown in the economy, finding qualified IS personnel is still difficult. Second, while many firms have been focused on growing the IS staff as quickly as possible, these firms are now under more pressure to show the value of their information systems expenditures. There is increased pressure to show exactly how new systems will contribute to the bottom line. Finally, the increase in the use of IS to support globalization is leading to problems related to differences in culture, infrastructure, and so on. All of these factors are initiating the need for a rethinking, and in some cases a restructuring, of IS departments within organizations. Industry analysts suggest that the types of changes we are seeing are increased power of CIOs, better use of shared resources within the organization, and growing use of outsourcing, but with the use of internal groups of people and internal project managers to oversee these outsourcing projects, and an increase in regionalization, where regional IS shops will be formed to deal better with differences in culture, geography, and technology.

[Adapted from Marc Cecere, "Adjusting Your IT Organization Design," **www.cio.com**.]

making it more productive. In short, they are using technology to streamline business functions and, in some cases, to slash costs and replace people. Although this approach may not be fair for the people who lose their jobs, many firms are forced to do this to remain competitive and, in some cases, to continue to exist. Such uses of information systems have interesting implications for the size and structure of organizations and for the size and structure of the IS function.

Career Prospects and Opportunities

Although technology at some levels continues to become easier to use, there is still and is likely to continue to be an acute need for people within the organization to have the responsibility of planning for, designing, developing, maintaining, and managing tech-

nologies. Much of this will happen within the business units and will be performed by those with primarily business duties and tasks, as opposed to systems duties and tasks. However, we are a long way from the day when technology is so easy to deploy that a need no longer exists for people with deep information systems knowledge and skills. In fact, many people believe that this day may never come. Although increasing numbers of people will incorporate systems responsibilities within their nonsystems jobs, there will continue to be a need for people with primarily systems responsibilities. In short, IS staffs and departments will likely continue to exist and play an important role in the foreseeable future.

While many organizations are downsizing, and while some are shrinking their IS staffs, overall hiring within IS is growing. With hiring

IS IT A PHONE OR IS IT A COMPUTER?

Microsoft Corp. and its manufacturing partners introduced gadgets based on Microsoft's new Wireless Pocket PC platform at the 2002 3GSM World Congress in Cannes. Attendees were given a hands-on preview of the Pocket PC 2002 Phone Edition (see Figure 1.16) and the Windows-powered Smartphone 2002 device (previously known by its code name, Stinger), which recently went on sale in Europe and the United States.

"The Smartphone devices are primarily mobile phones with some personal digital assistant (PDA) functions, and the new Pocket PCs are PDAs that also function as mobile phones," said Magnus Ahlberg, Microsoft's mobile marketing manager EMEA (Europe, the Middle East, and Africa).

"A big part of the wireless device market is going to be about how many services you can offer users, and Microsoft already has a variety of attractive services," said Paolo Pescatore, a senior wireless mobile communication analyst at Framingham, Mass.-based IDC. According to Ahlberg, there are more than 10,000 registered MS Mobility applications developed for the Wireless Pocket PC platform that will enable people to communicate, collaborate, and coordinate with each other in a number of ways. In addition, the Pocket PC phones include such applications as Pocket Word and Pocket Excel.

Now, imagine that you manage a business. Think about how your employees and customers could use such a device. The possibilities are endless.

[Adapted from, Laura Rohde, "Microsoft, Partners Unveil Smartphone, Wireless Pocket PC," *Computerworld* (February 19, 2002). **www.computerworld.com/ mobiletopics/mobile/story/0,10801,68460, 00.html**]

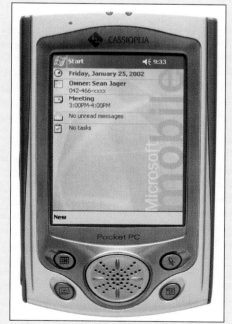

[**Figure 1.16** ➡ The new Pocket PC with phone capabilites from Microsoft and its partners.]

©Casio, Inc.

of systems personnel in a variety of positions at a fever pitch, and with the management of technology a critical business issue, it is not likely that IS departments will go away or even shrink significantly. Indeed, all projections are for growth of IS both in scale and scope.

The future opportunities in the IS field are likely to be found in a variety of areas, which is good news for everyone. The diversity in the technology area can embrace us all. It really does not matter much which area of IS you choose to pursue—there will likely be a promising future there for you. Even if your career interests are outside IS, being an informed and strong user of information technologies will greatly enhance your career prospects.

As we discuss throughout this book, by all accounts, the future of the IS field looks very promising. All current growth indicators and forecasts for the future show that the use of information systems in organizations, the development of new technologies and systems, and, perhaps most important, the demand for IS personnel will continue to grow. If you had to choose a field to go into based on its growth potential and opportunities, you would most likely choose IS.

KEY POINTS REVIEW

1. **Define and understand the term information systems (IS).** Information systems are combinations of hardware, software, and telecommunications networks, which people build and use to collect, create, and distribute useful data typically in organizational settings. When data are organized in a way that is useful to people, these data are defined as information. The term *information systems* is also used to represent the field in which people develop, use, manage, and study computer-based information systems in organizations. The field of IS is huge, diverse, and growing, and encompasses many different people, purposes, systems, and technologies.

2. **Explain the technology, people, and organizational components of an information system.** The technology part of information systems is the hardware, software, and telecommunications networks. The people who build, manage, use, and study information systems make up the people component. They include systems analysts, systems programmers, information systems professors, and many others. Finally, information systems typically reside and are used within organizations, so they are said to have an organizational component. Together, these three aspects form an information system.

3. **Describe the types of jobs and career opportunities in information systems and in related fields.** The people who help develop and manage systems in organizations include systems analysts, systems programmers, systems operators, network administrators, database administrators, systems designers, systems managers, and chief information officers. All of these types of people are in heavy demand and, as a result, salaries are high and continue to rise. The field of IS has changed such that IS personnel are now thought of as valuable business professionals rather than as "nerds" or "techies." The need for technology-related knowledge and skills has spread to other careers as well in fields such as finance, accounting, operations management, human resource management, business law, and marketing.

4. **Describe the various types of information systems.** Types of information systems include transaction processing systems, management information systems, executive information systems, decision support systems, expert systems, functional area information systems, Customer Relationship Management systems, Enterprise Resource Planning systems, office automation systems, collaboration systems, and systems for electronic commerce. While many modern-day information systems span several of these categories, it is still useful to understand these categories. Doing so enables you to better understand the myriad approaches, goals, features, and functions of modern information systems.

5. **Describe the dual nature of information systems in the success and failure of modern organizations.** If information systems are conceived, designed, used, and managed effectively and strategically, they can enable organizations to be more effective, to be more productive, to expand their reach, and to gain or sustain competitive advantage over rivals. If information systems are not conceived, designed, used, or managed well, they can have negative effects on organizations, such as loss of money, loss of time, loss of customers' good will, and, ultimately, loss of customers. Modern organizations that embrace and manage information systems effectively and strategically tend to be the organizations that are successful and competitive.

6. **Explain how you can plan for the future of the IS function.** The future is difficult to predict. Nonetheless, we can expect that there will be broad and continued growth for IS applications, spread of technology and IS personnel throughout organizations, a new service mentality toward technology and IS personnel, and continued downsizing supported by IS. The career opportunities for IS professionals will increase at a rapid pace, making the management of the IS function and the IS human resources an important part of managing all modern organizations.

KEY TERMS

chief information officer 10

collaboration system 18

competitive advantage 21

computer-based information system 8

Customer Relationship Management
  system 18

data 4, 7

decision support system 17

digital divide 7

downsizing 24

electronic commerce 18

Enterprise Resource Planning system 18

executive information system 17

expert system 17

functional area information system 17

hardware 4

information 7

information systems 4

information technology 8

internetworking 18

knowledge 7

knowledge society 6

knowledge worker 6

management information system 17

new economy 7

office automation system 18

service mentality 23

software 4

strategic 21

systems integration 18

technology 8

telecommunications network 4

transaction processing system 17

wisdom 7

REVIEW QUESTIONS

1. Define and understand the term information systems (IS).
2. Explain the technology, people, and organizational components of an information system.
3. Define and list four business knowledge and/or skills core competencies.
4. Describe the three or four types of jobs and career opportunities in information systems and in related fields.
5. What are some reasons that the position of CIO has grown in importance?

6. Define the term knowledge worker. Who coined the term?
7. How does the textbook define technology? Give some basic examples.
8. List and define four of the systems knowledge and skills core competencies.
9. List and define five types of information systems used in organizations.
10. Describe key factors in the future of the IS function within the firm.

SELF-STUDY QUESTIONS

Answers are at the end of the Problems and Exercises.

1. Information systems today are _____ .
   A. slower than in the past
   B. continuing to evolve with improvements to the hardware and software
   C. utilized by only a few select individuals
   D. stable and should not change

2. Information systems are used in which of the following organizations?
   A. professional
   B. educational
   C. governmental
   D. all of the above

3. Whereas data are raw unformatted pieces or lists of words or numbers, information is _____ .
   A. data that has been organized in a form that is useful
   B. accumulated knowledge
   C. what you put in your computer
   D. what your computer prints out for you

4. Computer-based information systems were described in this chapter as _____ .

   A. any complicated technology that requires expert use
   B. a combination of hardware, software, and telecommunications networks that people build and use to collect, create, and distribute data
   C. any technology (mechanical or electronic) used to supplement, extend, or replace human, manual labor
   D. any technology used to leverage human capital

5. In the 1980s, which of the following became a popular new title given to executives who were responsible for the information systems function?
   A. CFO
   B. CIO
   C. CEO
   D. CMA

6. Which of the following positions is typically the highest ranking in an IS department of a modern company?
   A. systems analyst
   B. systems programmers
   C. IS director
   D. networking professional

7. Which of the following IS job titles is used for a person whose primary responsibility is directly doing maintenance on an information system?

   A. IS director
   B. Webmaster
   C. systems analyst
   D. chief information officer

8. Which of the following is **not** classified as business knowledge and skills?

   A. management
   B. communication
   C. systems integration
   D. social

9. Which of the following was not discussed as a common type, or category, of information system used in organizations?

   A. transaction processing
   B. decision support
   C. Enterprise Resource Planning
   D. Web graphics

10. Which of the following is **not** an example of an information system?

    A. an accounting system in a business
    B. a concession stand
    C. a combination of different software packages in a company
    D. a database of customers

PROBLEMS AND EXERCISES

1. Match the following terms with the appropriate definitions

   _____ Transaction processing system

   _____ Systems competency

   _____ Information

   _____ Knowledge society

   _____ Electronic commerce

   _____ Customer Relationship Management

   _____ Systems analyst

   _____ Chief information officer

   _____ Information systems

   _____ Service mentality

   a. A society with a high proportion of knowledge workers who play an important, leadership role
   b. An executive-level individual who has overall responsibilities for the information systems component within the organization and is primarily concerned with the effective integration of technology and business strategy
   c. The use of typically Internet-based systems to enable consumers to find information about, and purchase, goods and services from business firms
   d. A system that processes day-to-day business event data at the operational level of the organization
   e. Data that have been formatted in a way that is useful
   f. Systems that enable employees to manage interaction with customers better
   g. A job title for a person who helps to develop information systems
   h. Ability to solve complex business problems and to build and integrate business systems
   i. The mindset that your goal is to enable others to be successful and that the "customer is always right"
   j. Combinations of hardware, software, and telecommunications networks that people build and use to collect, create, and distribute useful data, typically in organizational settings

2. How has Federal Express updated its information systems with current technology? Is the investment in technology a good one? How has this investment affected Federal Express' competitors? Visit their Web site and look at how to track a package.

3. Peter Drucker has defined the knowledge worker and knowledge society. What are his definitions? Do you agree with them? What examples can you give to support or disprove these concepts?

4. List three major IS professional core competencies or general areas from the textbook. Do you agree or disagree that all three are needed to become a professional? Why? What competencies do you currently possess, and what do you need to improve on or acquire? What is your strategy to acquire new skills? Where and when will you acquire them?

5. Of the 10 information systems listed in the chapter, how many do you have experience with? What systems would you like to work with? What types of systems do you encounter at the university you are attending? Read the Brief Cases in this chapter for application of information systems. The World Wide Web is also a good source for additional information.

6. Consider an organization that you are familiar with, perhaps one that you have worked for or have done business with in the past. Describe the type of information systems that organization uses and whether or not they are useful or up-to-date. List specific examples for updating or installing information systems that improve productivity or efficiency.

7. Identify someone who works within the field of information systems, as an information systems instructor, professor, or practitioner (for example, as a systems analyst or systems manager). Find out why this individual got into this field and what this person likes and dislikes about working within the field of IS. What advice can this person offer to someone entering the field?

8. The case of the Denver International Airport provides insight into the resources used to build large information systems. Is this problem unique to airlines, or do you think other companies have experienced similar problems? What are the tangible or observable costs and the hidden costs when a system takes time to get working as planned?

9. What type of information system do you use at the university you attend to register and add or drop courses? Are course Web sites and e-mail available? How does your university setting compare with Washington State University in the Brief Case? Are improvements to your current system planned?

10. Electronic commerce has changed purchasing over the Web. Have you bought anything over the Web yet? If you have not made any purchases, what is holding you back? Are you comfortable with the payment system of sending credit card information over the Internet?

11. What collaboration system are you using? Do you find e-mail a good communication method? What are the pros and cons of having one or more e-mail accounts? How often do you check your e-mail? Do you consider e-mail time effective? How comfortable are you with e-mail?

12. Based on your previous work and/or professional experiences, describe your relationships with the personnel in the IS department. Was the IS department easy to work with? Why or why not? Were projects and requests completed on time and correctly? What was the organizational structure of this IS department? How do your answers compare with those of other classmates?

13. As a small group, conduct a search on the World Wide Web for job placement services. Pick at least four of these services and find as many IS job titles as you can. You may want to try The Monster Board at **www.monsterboard.com/**. How many did you find? Were any of them different from those presented in this chapter? Could you determine the responsibilities of these positions based on the information given to you?

14. What type of IT investment should Starbucks Coffee have and how would it be used in the corporate office and the individual stores? What would it need to track for inventory and sales? Search the Web or visit a Starbucks Coffee store in your city to determine whether you can see what technology is available in your local store.

15. The IS support group within the School of Business at Indiana University changed its name from "Business Computing Facility" to "Technology Services." Along with the change in name came an appropriate change in services and offerings to their clientele. Ford IT units are another example of an organization that changed its name and focus. Find an example of an organization that changed the external name of its IT or IS unit but did not change the internal structure or attitude. Why were these not changed as well? Was the name change merely to make it sound better to the outsider? Has anything been done to correct this problem?

ANSWERS TO THE SELF-STUDY QUESTIONS

1. B   2. D   3. A   4. B   5. B   6. C   7. B   8. C   9. D   10. B

CASE 1:   *Clinical Information System Adoption At PeaceHealth*

Over the last few years, health-care officials have increasingly realized that information technology can be used in innovative ways to increase efficiency and provide safe, high-quality care to patients. One of the primary categories of health-care providers is that of nurses, who regularly deal with a high volume of data and information in addition to dealing first-hand with patients. It is said that nurses spend at least 20 percent of their time in processing written information and another 30 percent of their time in verbal communication with patients and coworkers (Hovenga, 2001). Nursing data can come in four types: patient/client demographics, activity data, resource data, and health service provider data. Manual processing of all this information often takes huge amounts of time and increases the chances of errors both in information processing and in the care

given to patients. Advanced information systems provide the opportunity to automate many of these processes, increasing staff efficiency and patient care, and at the same time protecting patients and the caregivers (Opperman, Clark, and Harris, 2001). However, until recently, few health-care providers realized the advantages of using a clinical information system. PeaceHealth illustrates this idea nicely.

PeaceHealth is an integrated health-care provider with establishments in various parts of the northwestern United States, including Washington, Oregon, and Alaska. The organization has been plagued for a long time by the shortage of nurses. According to a report by the American Nurses Association, there is an increasing shortage of nurses in the country. Most of the nurses argue that this shortage is a result of their increasing dissat-

isfaction arising out of the labor and paper-intensive documentation that they have to complete every day. As a result of a shortage of nurses, there is an increasing demand on the time of the existing nurses, resulting in poor-quality care provided to patients. While many different clinical information systems have been produced and sold, most organizations shy away from them, given their high costs and complexity. PeaceHealth, however, is different. Suffering from the dissatisfaction of nurses, the company has invested heavily in information technology to make the day-to-day work of nurses easier and thus improve the quality of the health-care service.

As a first step, the company invested in acquiring the clinical information system called LastWord® Enterprise Clinical System from IDX Systems Corporation. The tool supports not only nurses but also therapists and other health-care professionals in providing superior care to patients. The tool helps in performing a varied range of tasks from assessments to charting. To start with, the tool makes patient record information available to all caregivers irrespective of their location. They no longer have to spend time looking for charts or for any kind of missing information. The views of the nurses or other caregivers can be customized to their needs, and the system provides a variety of views from spreadsheets to graphs. This helps in more efficient analysis of the data. The patient information is entered into the system during their first visit. For every return visit, nurses do not need to ask for the same information again and can simply download it from the system. This helps them to assess patients much more efficiently. One of the primary responsibilities of nurses is to chart the activities required for each patient during the course of their shift. Initially, such activities were done manually, resulting in the nurses spending the bulk of their time only on charting. Now the system automates that process and automatically signs, dates, and time-stamps those activities. Further, online charting enables caregivers to get details of a patient's medication (be it inpatient or outpatient), their doses, allergies, and so on, and helps them to administer medication more efficiently and without as many errors.

Nurses are also required to provide a shift report at the end of each of their shifts. Previously, the nurses would tape record these reports, or convey them face-to-face. Now, these reports are inserted into the system, which provides a summary of all activities that took place during a shift, along with short notes from each of the nurses or caregivers. This helps the oncoming shift to look at a general summary without having to go through each report. Nurses have also expressed increased satisfaction with this new system of reporting as opposed to the earlier face-to-face or tape-recorded reporting system. Given that patient history and information are now all stored in the system, disease management has also become much more efficient, especially for those with chronic conditions. When a patient suffering from a chronic condition walks into the care provider facility, the nurse is immediately aware of the tests, checks, and examinations that will need to be performed, by just pulling up the patient information on the screen. In short, the new information technology has made the work of nurses significantly easier.

While many of the nurses' tasks have been automated by the system, PeaceHealth is continuing to work to further enhance the system in order to provide additional benefits to the nurses and other caregivers. Currently, they are focused on ensuring that the system is capable of providing long-term data that will help in conducting outcome improvements. They are in the process of removing redundant data from their system, cutting down on unnecessary documentation, and eliminating duplicative processes that add little value to patients, in order to streamline the jobs of nurses further.

The organization acknowledges that the adoption of this new technology has been a tremendous success. Their nurses are more satisfied now, and health care is being provided more efficiently to patients. They argue that they have learned two major lessons during this adoption. First, they have learned that simplification is best. While their system contains a lot of data, their main screens are fairly simple and extremely user-friendly. Second, they have learned that, when adopting the system to support certain activities, it is best to involve the people who will be actual users of that system. PeaceHealth worked very closely with the nurses (the users of the system) and, in the process, was able to tailor the system to match their needs exactly, thus increasing their satisfaction.

[Adapted from D. Rewick and E. Gaffey, "Nursing System Makes a Difference," *Health Management Technology* 22, no. 8 (2001): 24–26.]

Discussion Questions

1. In what ways has the automation of the day-to-day activities reduced the workload of the nurses? In what ways has it increased their workload? Overall, how has automation been an improvement?
2. What else should the organization do to ensure that the implementation of the new information technology will prove to be successful in the long run?
3. Apart from the nurses and the caregivers, who else do you think will be positively affected by the new clinical information system implemented at PeaceHealth, and in what ways?
4. What additional lessons did you learn form this case narrative?

References

Hovenga, E. J. S. 2001. "Nursing Information and the Use of Electronic Health Records," *Australian Nursing Journal* 8(11): 39–40.

Opperman, J., K. Clark, and J. Harris. 2001. "Automating the Medication System: Yesterday's Impossibilities Are Today's Realities," *Nursing Management* 32(7): 48–49.

CASE 2:   *High Tech, High Touch at Edward Jones*

Edward Jones is not your typical brokerage firm. Its average customer lives in a small town and is more likely to read *USA Today* than *The Financial Times*. In an industry that has gorged itself on virtually every technology fad and fashion, the St. Louis–based Jones stands out for its low-tech, no frills, relationship-focused approach to investing. Unlike nearly all of its competitors, Jones has yet to offer online trading to its clients. Instead, trades require a phone conversation or face-to-face meeting with a broker. In fact, customers cannot even contact brokers directly by e-mail; the Jones way dictates that customers wishing to e-mail must fill out a form on the company's Web site. Those e-mail messages are then routed through the main office in St. Louis, sorted, and then dispatched to brokers via the corporate intranet, a two-day process.

Jones's refusal to trade online, its lack of direct e-mail, and its small-town focus have led many to label the company a technology dinosaur, trying to get by on show-string IT budget and midwestern charm. Others would argue, however, that just the opposite is, in fact, the case. Jones invests a great deal of effort and money in technology (11 percent of its annual revenue is spent on IT, compared with an industry average of nine percent). It recently made huge investments in two new data centers (an $85 million one in Tempe, Arizona, and a $30 million one in April, 2002, in St. Louis). The company has begun overhauling its satellite-based network and plans to implement digital document technologies that will cut down on the amount of paper traveling between almost 8,000 field offices and St. Louis headquarters. It also has not neglected the Internet: Customers can check their account balances, pay bills, apply for mortgages, and view their statements on the company's Web site.

Where the company draws the line is investing in a technology that might get between its customers and brokers. Jones believes that a relationship should be inviolate and that technology should support it but never replace it. As for Jones's behind-the-times image, Managing Partner John Bachmann shrugs it off, adding "We've never been hurt by being underestimated."

Jones caters to individual investors, many of whom are retirees and small-business owners in rural communities and suburban towns. "Their market is the mom-and-pop business with $10,000 to invest," says Heber Farnsworth, an assistant professor of finance at Washington University, based in St. Louis. "And the Jones model has been to try and take the level of service and atten-

tion that millionaires get and give it to those mom-and-pop investors."

The company provides that personal touch through its field offices in Canada, the United States, and the United Kingdom. Each new location is built from the ground up with investment reps going door-to-door to grow their clientele.

Keeping all of Jones's remote offices connected to the markets and to corporate headquarters is one of the company's biggest technical challenges. "We have only one profit center: [the branches]," says CIO Rich Malone, "so the network is critical. It's how we get information back and forth, and it connects us to the exchanges. If the network doesn't work, we've got problems." Currently all the offices are connected by a satellite network, but during the past few years it has become clear to Malone and the rest of the management team that the current network will soon be insufficient for their growing technology needs. Bandwidth needs are rapidly outstripping what the satellite network can provide, and that problem is likely to get worse as the company begins digitally storing and sending the reams of paper it processes each day. Jones is also using an increasing number of Web applications, which tend to perform better on terrestrial networks (fiber-optic land-based cable).

Some analysts are doubtful that Jones can continue its present rate of growth without eventually offering online trading. "It puts them in the position of weakening the

relationship, and when you add to that a little bit of poor performance or some other niggling problem, that's when you lose the relationship," says Jaime Punishill, a senior analyst at Cambridge, Massachusetts–based Forrester Research.

Jones has been incredibly successful in the last decade, and even in these times of economic stringency, the company has managed to avoid the layoffs that have plagued so many of its competitors. In fact, though the company has instituted a hiring freeze at its St. Louis headquarters, the company is still hiring at a brisk clip of 200 new employees per month in the field offices.

Some analysts are still wondering, however, if the company will be able to keep up the brisk growth without bending a little on its no-online-trading policy—especially as its client base gets older and the need to lure younger, more tech-savvy customers increases. But Bachmann sees hope that the Edward Jones brand of conservative, relationship-focused investing will have some appeal for a younger audience. "Our fastest growing segment is young people," he claims. "They know that Social Security will not be there for them, and they don't want to take the chance of putting their money into something that will blow up."

[Adapted from, Daintry Duffy, "At Edward Jones, The Handshake Still Rules," *CIO Magazine* (February 1, 2002) **www.darwinmag.com/read/ 020102/rules.html**]

Discussion Questions

1. Of the various categories of information systems described in this chapter, which types are talked about in this case?
2. What do you think of Edward Jones's use of information systems? Is the company on the right track?
3. Should the company move into online trading? Why or why not?
4. What advice would you give Edward Jones for better utilizing information systems?

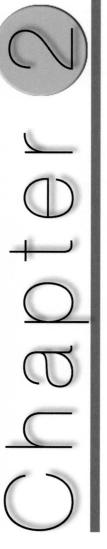

Chapter 2

Information Systems for Competitive Advantage

OPENING: Living on the Edge with Xbox

Microsoft hopes that the Xbox™ video game system (see Figure 2.1) will provide the company with a competitive edge over rival firms such as Nintendo, which sells the competing GameCube system. Microsoft, Nintendo, and others in the video game industry are constantly packing the latest, greatest technology into their systems to make them better than the competition. Better and faster processors, more memory, more high-tech designs and colors for the product, ways to connect multiple TVs and players, ways to play DVDs, more cool games—these firms are constantly improving on their technology so that their products will be more competitive.

Similarly, these firms are also busy using information systems to better support these products and the customers who use them. For example, Microsoft provides a useful Web site to support Xbox users, provides an online Retail Locator for the product, offers downloads for Xbox, hosts an online community for Xbox fans, and does much more with information systems to help Xbox be successful.

It must be working. Microsoft Corp. sold 1.5 million Xbox units in North America with the initial launch, making the Xbox™ video game system one of the most successful launches in video game history. In addition, gamers bought more than three games with every Xbox system, the highest-ever game attach rate for a video game console launch. Finally, the Microsoft action game "Halo: Combat Evolved" is a recipient of multiple industry awards for excellence and is the fastest million-unit seller ever for any next-generation game console. Now that is competitive advantage!

[Figure 2.1 ➡ Microsoft uses information systems to achieve competitive advantage with the Xbox.]
©Microsoft Corporation

The purpose of this chapter is to show you how information systems should be used strategically and how they can enable firms to gain or sustain *competitive advantage* over their rivals. As described in Chapter 1, a firm has competitive advantage over rival firms when it can do something better, faster, more cheaply, or uniquely when compared with its competitors. In addition, we will show why it is vital, but sometimes difficult, for people to determine the value of a new system. The same difficulties face those evaluating an existing system that is being considered for modification, continued support, scaling back, or elimination. Presenting the "case" for an information system is necessary for making good investment decisions.

After reading this chapter, you will be able to do the following:

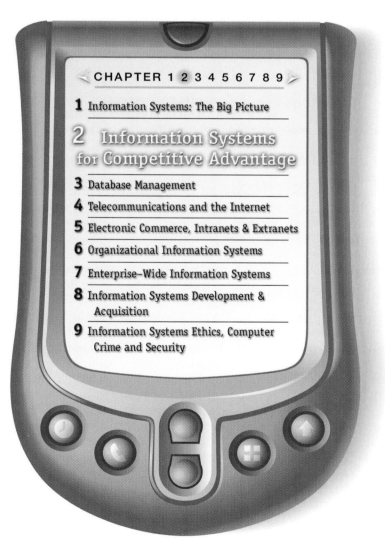

1. Discuss how organizations can use information systems for automation, organizational learning, and strategic support.

2. Describe information systems' critical, strategic importance to the success of modern organizations.

3. Formulate and present the business case for a system and understand why it is sometimes difficult to do so.

4. Explain why and how companies are continually looking for new ways to use technology for competitive advantage.

[**Figure 2.2** ➟ The Big Picture: focusing on information systems for competitive advantage.]

This chapter is the second piece of The Big Picture (see Figure 2.2). We begin by showing how and why a firm ought to use information systems to support its strategy and to enable it to gain or sustain competitive advantage over rivals. We then describe what it means to make the business case for a system and discuss why it is important that the business cases for technology-related projects be carefully developed. Next, we describe the factors you must identify and consider when building a successful business case. We then illustrate important factors to keep in mind when presenting the business case to executives and other decision makers. Making the business case for a technology investment is a business decision that should be made in a way that helps your organization achieve its strategy. Finally, we talk about the continual need to find innovative ways to succeed with and through information systems.

WHY USE INFORMATION SYSTEMS?

In the first chapter we described the strategic importance of information systems developed for the Denver International Airport and Federal Express. These systems were developed strategically to help these organizations gain or sustain some competitive advantage over rivals. For example, Denver International Airport hopes that their state-of-the-art baggage management system will not only help to make baggage handling more efficient and subsequently lower operating costs and please passengers, but that ultimately it will also help to attract airlines, airline passengers, and other business vendors to that facility. This example highlights that there are many reasons for using an information system.

Next, we describe three ways to use an information system: for automating, for organizational learning, and for achieving strategy (see Figure 2.3). These three activities are not necessarily mutually exclusive, but we believe that each reason for using an information system is progressively more useful to the firm and, thus, adds more value to the business.

The final category, strategizing, is the one in which you use information systems to support your firm's strategy and to enable your firm to gain or sustain competitive advantage over rivals.

Information Systems for Automating: Doing Things Faster

Someone with an *automating* perspective thinks of technology as a way to help complete a task within an organization faster, more cheaply, and perhaps with greater accuracy and/or consistency. Let us look at a typical example. A person with an automating mentality would take a loan application screening process and automate it by inputting the loan applications into a computer database so that those involved in decision making for the loans could process the applications faster, more easily, and with fewer errors. Such a system might also enable customers to complete the loan application online. A transition from a manual to an automated loan application process might enable the organization to deploy employees more efficiently, leading to further cost savings.

To illustrate the benefits of automating with an information system, in Table 2.1 we compare three different loan application processes. In the first example, everything is done by hand. In the second example, a technology-supported process, potential customers fill out applications by hand, and then an employee inputs them into a computer system. The third example is a completely automated process, whereby potential customers input loan applications directly online via the Web, and then the system automatically receives these applications into a database and processes them.

The real time savings with the fully automated system come into play with the applications for loans under $250,000, which typically comprise the bulk of applications received. Conversely, one common thread across all three scenarios is that it takes the executive committee over two full weeks to make decisions on applications for loans over $250,000. Automation can do only so much!

Although many significant gains from computing in organizations have come from automating previously manual processes, computing solely for automation is a bit shortsighted. In the next section, we will explain how technology can be used more effectively.

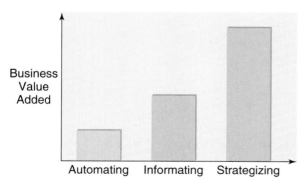

[**Figure 2.3** ➡ The business value added from automating, learning, and supporting strategy with IS.]

Primary Activities of Loan Processing	Manual Loan Process (Time)	Technology-Supported Process (Time)	Fully Automated Process (Time)
1. Complete and submit loan application	Customer takes the application home, completes it, returns it (1.5 days)	Customer takes the application home, completes it, returns it (1.5 days)	Customer fills out application from home via the Web (1 hour)
2. Check application for errors	Employee does this in batches (2.5 days)	Employee does this in batches (2.5 days)	Computer does this as it is being completed (3.5 seconds)
3. Input data from application into information system	Applications kept in paper form, although there is handling time involved (1 hour)	Employee does this in batches (2.5 days)	Done as part of the online application process (no extra time needed)
4. Assess loan applications under $250,000 to determine whether to fund them	Employee does this completely by hand (15 days)	Employee does with the help of the computer (1 hour)	Computer does this automatically (1 second)
5. Committee decides on any loan over $250,000	(15 days)	(15 days)	(15 days)
6. Applicant notified	Employee generates letters manually in batches (1 week)	Employee generates letters with the help of the computer (1 day)	System notifies applicant via e-mail (3.5 seconds)
Total Time:	Anywhere from **25 to 40 days**, depending on size of loan	Anywhere from **5 to 20 days**, depending on size of loan	Anywhere from **1 hour to 15 days**, depending on size of loan[1]

[Table 2.1] *Activities involved under three different loan application processes and the average time for each activity.*

[1]Note that many online loan application services can now give you instant "tentative" approval pending verification of data you report in your online application.

The Advanced Technology Development Center at the Georgia Institute of Technology, along with CAMotion Inc., has recently developed software algorithms that help in automating routine tasks such as inspection and quality control using robotics in manufacturing plants. According to the chairman of CAMotion, most manufacturing plants have difficulty in finding and retaining people for these routine tasks, and this often keeps U.S. manufacturing firms from being competitive. The automation of these tasks will hence ease many of the problems of manufacturers. The software algorithms that have been developed enable off-the-shelf robotic equipment to conduct routine tasks such as assembly operations or inspection of products for quality control. The Vulcan Group of Alabama has already implemented two of these systems, which they are regularly using for inspecting automobile roof racks and for stacking completed parts inside a shipping container. A robot creates different images of the same part and then inspects it against some laid-down quality standards. The software consists of three primary algorithms: a vibration-control algorithm that avoids any redundant oscillations, a learning algorithm that helps the system improve its own performance, and finally, a position-estimation algorithm that helps the robot ascertain its current position with respect to its target task. The entire system uses only one software package and hence is more cost-effective than other alternatives. In manufacturing and in other areas of operations management, you will likely find yourself relying heavily on information systems.

Career Implications:

Operations Management

[Adapted from "Motion Control Software Automates Inspection," *Manufacturing Engineering* 126, no. 5 (May 2001): 52–55.]

Information Systems for Organizational Learning: Doing Things Better

We can also use information systems to learn and improve. This was described by Shoshana Zuboff (1988) as ***informating***[2]. Zuboff explained that a technology informates when it provides information about its operation and the underlying work process that it supports. The system helps us not only to automate a business process but also to learn to improve the day-to-day activities within that process.

The learning mentality builds on the automating mentality because it recognizes that information systems can be used as a vehicle for ***organizational learning*** and change as well as for automation. In a 1993 *Harvard Business Review* article, David Garvin described a ***learning organization*** as one that is "skilled at creating, acquiring, and transferring knowledge, and at modifying its behavior to reflect new knowledge and insights."

To illustrate a learning mentality, let us think again about our loan-processing exam-

ple. Figure 2.4 shows how a computer-based loan processing system tracks types of loan applications by date, month, and season. The manager easily sees the trends and can plan for the timely ordering of blank application forms and the staffing and training of personnel in the loan department. The manager can also more efficiently manage the funds used to fulfill loans.

A learning approach allows people to track and learn about the types of applications filed by certain types of people at certain times of the year (e.g., more auto loan applications in the fall, mostly from men in their 20s and 30s), the patterns of the loan decisions made, or the subsequent performance of those loans. This new system creates data about the underlying business process that can be used to better monitor, control, and change that process. In other words, you learn from this information system about loan applications and approvals and, as a result, you can do a better job at evaluating loan applications.

A combined automating and learning approach, in the long run, is more effective than an automating approach alone. If the underlying business process supported by

[2]The concept of informating is also very closely related to Argyris' term, *double loop learning*, in which individuals learn and as a result subsequently change their thinking and/or behavior, C. Argyris. 1993. *On Organizational Learning*. Cambridge, MA: Blackwell.

Web Search

WEB SEARCH OPPORTUNITY:

Visit the homepage for the Society for Organizational Learning at **http://www.solonline.org/** and investigate this phenomenon further. How did this organization first begin? What is its purpose?

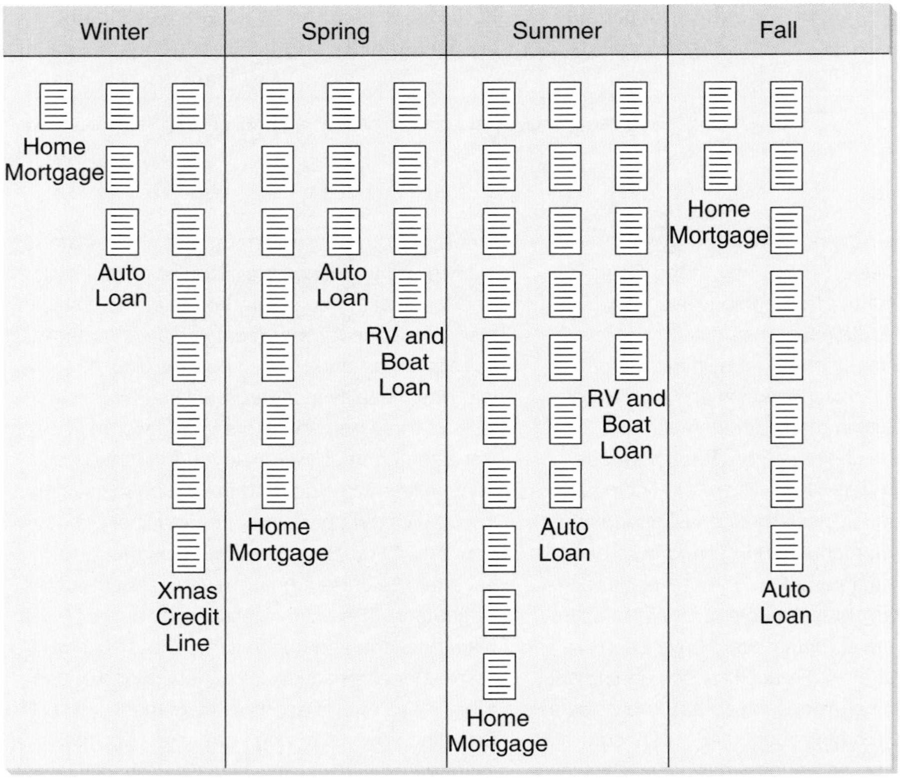

[**Figure 2.4** ➡ A computer-based loan processing system informs the bank manager of which types of loans are highest during each season.]

technology is inherently flawed, a learning use of the technology might help you detect the problems with the process and change it. For instance, in our loan processing example, a learning use of technology may help us uncover a pattern among the loans accepted that enables us to distinguish between low- and high-performing loans over their lives and, subsequently, change the criteria for loan acceptance.

If, however, the underlying business process is bad, and you are using technology only for automating (i.e., you would not uncover the data that would tell you this process is bad), you are more likely to continue with a flawed or less-than-optimal business process. In fact, such an automating use of the technology may mask the process problems.

For example, with a bad underlying set of loan acceptance criteria (i.e., the rules would allow you to approve a loan for someone who had a high level of debt as long as they had not been late on any payments recently), a person might manually review four applications in a day and, because of the problematic criteria used, inadvertently accept two "bad" applications per week on average. If you automated the same faulty process, with no learning aspects built in, the system might help a person review 12 applications per day, with six "bad" applications accepted per week on average. The technology would serve only to magnify the existing business problems. Without

learning, it is more difficult to uncover bad business processes underlying the information system.

Using Information Systems to Support Total Quality Management

Organizations that use information systems to support a **total quality management (TQM)** initiative are more than likely using these systems with a learning approach. As part of a TQM approach, people within the organization are constantly monitoring what they do to find ways to improve quality of operations, products, services, and everything else about the firm. Information systems might be used to accomplish this end through the use of computer-based statistical analysis to determine the exact procedures and materials to use in a manufacturing process in order to achieve the highest levels of quality output. In this way, people use an information system to understand a business process better and, as a result, make changes to improve that process.

Information Systems for Supporting Strategy: Doing Things Smarter

Using information systems to automate or improve processes has advantages, as described above. In most cases, however, the best way to use an information system is to support the organization's strategy in a way that enables the firm to gain or sustain competitive advantage over rivals. To understand

---

Metropolitan Life Insurance Company (MetLife) has $1.7 trillion in active life-insurance policies and provides group insurance and retirement-savings products and services to about 64,000 companies and institutions. MetLife must keep track of more than 9 million active, important customers, but with data about them stored in 30 different information systems across the firm. Executives at MetLife decided that they wanted to take better care of customers by keeping better track of their data and, as a result, grow MetLife's customer base to 100 million by 2010. In short, they wanted to shift the company's strategy to be more customer-focused and use information systems as the tool to achieve this end.

MetLife now stores all data on every MetLife customer in one place and makes it available to anyone who needs it (and has the right to see it). The new system has enabled MetLife to better track and store customer data in one location and

make that data available to people throughout the firm.

On some level it is odd to think that we are using something as impersonal as computers to build better, stronger, more intimate relationships with customers. You would think that the best way to get to know your customer better is to throw out the computer and go talk to your customer. Well, if your firm had only a handful of customers, then this approach might work well. On the other hand, if you are like MetLife and you have millions of customers, you will need those computers to keep track of everyone. It would be nice to be able to call up on your notebook computer a full record of your customer just before you walk into their office. You could instantly know their history, what they ordered last time, what they like and dislike, when their child's birthday is, and the status of their last order. If you want to give yourself and your firm a competitive edge, you need to be able to use information systems for marketing, sales, and service.

Career Implications:

Marketing

why, think about **organizational strategy** and how it relates to information systems. When senior managers conduct **strategic planning**, they form a vision of where the organization needs to head, convert that vision into measurable objectives and performance targets, and craft a strategy to achieve the desired results. In Figure 2.5, we show some common organizational strategies. An organization might decide to pursue a **low-cost leadership strategy**, as do Target and Dell, by which it offers the best prices in its industry on its goods and/or services. Alternatively, an organization might decide to pursue a **differentiation strategy**, whereby it tries to provide better products or services than its competitors, as do Porsche, Nordstrom, and IBM. A company might aim that differentiation broadly at many different types of consumers, or it might target a particular segment of consumers as Apple did for many years with its focus on high-quality computers to home and educational markets. Still other organizations might pursue a middle-of-the-road strategy of being the **best-cost provider**, offering products or services of reasonably good quality at competitive prices, as does Wal-Mart.

A person with a strategic mentality toward information systems goes beyond mere automating and learning and instead tries to find ways to use information systems to achieve the organization's chosen strategy. This individual wants the benefits of automating and learning but also looks for some strategic, competitive advantage from the system.

INFORMATION SYSTEMS FOR COMPETITIVE ADVANTAGE

Sources of Competitive Advantage

How do business firms typically get competitive advantage? An organization has competitive advantage whenever it has an edge over rivals in attracting customers and defending against competitive forces (Porter, 1985, 2001). In order to be successful, a business must have a clear vision, one that focuses investments in resources such as information systems and technologies to help achieve competitive advantage. Some sources of competitive advantage include the following:

- Having the best-made product on the market
- Delivering superior customer service
- Achieving lower costs than rivals
- Having a proprietary manufacturing technology
- Having shorter lead times in developing and testing new products
- Having a well-known brand name and reputation
- Providing customers with more value for their money

Companies can gain or sustain each of these sources of competitive advantage through the effective use of information systems. For example, rental car agencies compete fiercely with each other to provide the best cars, the best service, and the best rates. Companies find it difficult to differentiate themselves, so they discover innovative ways to use information systems to improve customer service.

Not all uses of information systems for competitive advantage are necessarily as

Type of Competitive Advantage Being Pursued

[**Figure 2.5** ➡ Five general types of organizational strategy: broad differentiation, focused differentiation, focused low-cost, overall low-cost leadership, and best-cost provider.]

Courtesy Thompson, A.A. and Strickland, A.J. III, 1995. *Strategic Management: Concepts and Cases*, 8th Edition, Homewood: Richard D. Irwin, Inc.

Brief Case: **Avis Rent A Car**

In order to sustain a competitive advantage over rivals in the area of customer service, Avis Rent A Car customer service representatives wait for the customer out in the lot, armed with specially designed, hand-held computers and printers either strapped around their waists or over their shoulders. With this "Avis Roving Rapid Return" service (shown in Figure 2.6), the representative inputs the license number of the car on the portable computer when he sees the customer driving in to return a car. Inputting this information brings up the cus-

tomer's rental contract. As the customer gets out of the car, the representative inputs the mileage and the fuel level, while a second attendant retrieves the customer's luggage and places it on the curb. By the time the customer has gotten out of the car and stood next to her luggage, the representative has already printed her receipt. The service encounter for the customer is fast and pleasant. That is using technology for competitive advantage! In Table 2.2, we show how Avis' computer-supported process compares with the traditional rental car service encounter. Notice that the computer-based service encounter (in the right column) takes significantly less time than the traditional approach.

[**Figure 2.6** ➡ Avis Roving Rapid Return.]
©PhotoEdit

[Table 2.2] *The Avis airport computer-supported service encounter versus the traditional airport rental car service encounter.*

	Traditional Rental Car Return Service Encounter	**Avis' Computer-Based Service Encounter**
	Return car to lot attendant, get bags from another attendant, walk inside and wait in line to settle contract with another attendant, walk out, and board a shuttle.	Return car to lot attendant, grab receipt and bags, and board shuttle.
Elapsed time	5–20 minutes	5–20 seconds
Number of people to interact with	2–3 people	1–2 people
Average number of footsteps customer takes	60–75 steps	5–10 steps
Relative efficiency	Low	High

Human Resource Management

As information systems continue to become an integral part of any business, top management is rethinking the structure of the IS organization in terms of how it should operate and how it should be aligned to other units of the business. Most companies have opted to keep IS closely aligned with the parent organization. A recent trend among most companies is a decentralized and dispersed IS organization, where IS staff members are located within multiple business units of the company. One such organization is Mitre Corp., whose primary business is to develop IS projects for various units of the government, ranging from the Air Force to the CIA. The company's IS staff belong to various business units. In other words, its IS department does not have any permanent staff apart from the CIO. Whenever a new project is undertaken, technical workers are brought in from various business units to work on the project. They report both to the CIO and to the individual business units to which they originally belonged. This brings about a greater amount of synergy between the IS organization and the other business units. This type of culture seems to be the norm rather than the exception within organizations. Other methods of handling IS functions are also becoming popular, such as outsourcing, third-party contractors, and application service providers. However, these new strategies do not indicate the extinction of the IS organization. Instead, IS is taking on even bigger responsibilities supporting the business requirements of the organizations. With all the information systems initiatives and new demands on firms, managing the IS staff in organizations is increasingly becoming even more critical to overall business success.

[Adapted from Diane Rezendes Khirallah, "The Changing Face of IT," **www.informationweek.com** (July 31, 2001).]

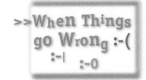

eBay Web Site Shut Down for 11 Hours

Imagine that your firm's entire strategy and success rely on the effective use of information systems. If these systems go down, so does your firm. That is exactly what happened to eBay, the successful online auctioneer (see Figure 2.7). Their critical systems were down for nearly 11 hours, grinding the company and its customers to a screeching halt.

At 11:34 A.M. PST one day, there was a hardware failure in a disk backup system, and so the outage began. Technicians attempted to fix the problem, but when they tried to restart everything they encountered further problems in both the primary and secondary systems. They brought a third backup system online at 2:45 P.M. PST, which worked for nearly 40 minutes, but that failed too. The Web site was finally fully restored by about 10 P.M. that evening.

People at eBay knew that some of their systems had potential problems, but they were waiting until after the current busy holiday season before they made the necessary changes, which would likely have slowed operations and potentially have annoyed users.

eBay took a chance with their important, strategic information systems, and they lost. When you rely on these systems to run your business, you have to treat them right. When your entire strategy and success rely on these systems, you better treat them like gold.

[**Figure 2.7** ➡ Web site of eBay, successful online auctioneer.]

advanced as Avis' use of hand-held computers. An organization might simply use a more common technology, such as a shared computer database, but in a strategic way. Let us return to the computer-based loan application processing example.

A person with a strategic view of information systems would choose a computer-based loan application process because it can help achieve the organization's strategic plan to process loan applications faster and better than rivals and to improve the selection criteria for loans. This process and the supporting information system add value to the organization *and* match the organization's strategy. It is, therefore, essential to the long-term survival of the organization. If, on the other hand, managers determine that the organization's strategy is to grow and generate new products and services, the computer-based loan application process and underlying system might not be an efficient, effective use of resources, even though the system could provide automating and learning benefits.

Information Systems and Value Chain Analysis

Managers use **value chain analysis** to identify opportunities to use information systems for competitive advantage (Porter, 1985, 2001; Shank and Govindarajan, 1993). Think of an organization as a big input/output process. At one end, supplies are purchased and brought into the organization (see Figure 2.8). The organization integrates those supplies to create products and services, which it markets, sells, and then distributes to customers. The organization provides customer service after the sale of these products and services. Throughout this process, there are opportunities for people to add value to the organiza-

tion by acquiring supplies in a more effective manner, improving products, and selling more products. This process of adding value throughout the organization is known as the **value chain** within an organization.

Value chain analysis is the process of analyzing an organization's activities to determine where value is added to products and/or services and the costs that are incurred for doing so. Because IS can automate many activities along the value chain, value chain analysis has become a popular tool for applying IS for competitive advantage. In value chain analysis, you first draw the value chain for your organization by fleshing out each of the activities, functions, and processes where value is or should be added. Next, determine the costs—and the factors that drive costs or cause them to fluctuate—within each of the areas in your value chain diagram. You then benchmark (compare) your value chain and associated costs with those of your competitors. You can then make changes and improvements in your value chain to either gain or sustain competitive advantage.

The Role of Information Systems in Value Chain Analysis

The use of information systems has become one of the primary ways that organizations improve their value chains. In Figure 2.9 we show a sample value chain and some ways that information systems can be used to improve productivity within it. For example, many organizations use the Internet to connect businesses with one another electronically so that they can exchange orders, invoices, and receipts online in real time. Using the Internet has become a popular method for improving the front end of the organizational value chain. In fact, many firms now use the

Web Search

WEB SEARCH OPPORTUNITY: Visit the Avis homepage at **www.avis.com** and investigate other ways that Avis is using technology to gain or sustain competitive advantage.

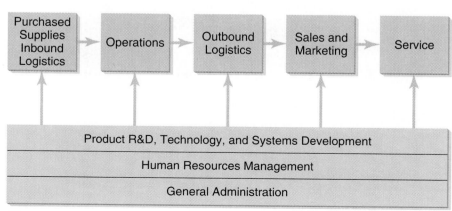

[**Figure 2.8** ➡ A sample generic organizational value chain.]

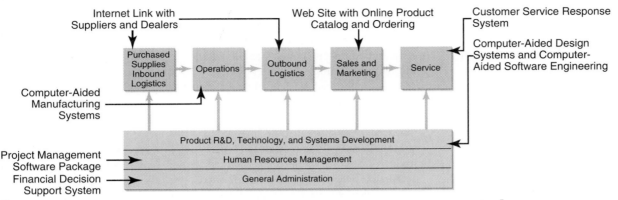

[**Figure 2.9** ➡ Sample value chain and corresponding sample uses of information systems to add value.]

Internet for such business-to-business interactions; these systems are called ***Extranets*** (described in greater detail in Chapter 5).

An innovative way to use information systems to improve the back end of the value chain, the service after the sale, is to provide online customer service. For example, owners of McLaren's $850,000 F1 Supercar (see Figure 2.10) plug a modem into the car and into a phone line and then let McLaren engineers diagnose the car and make adjustments to it over the phone lines in real time. That may sound exotic and restricted to those few individuals who can afford an $850,000 automobile, but computer companies such as IBM and Sun also use this method to diagnose and maintain their customers' products remotely and, in some cases, to download new software products.

The Technology/Strategy Fit

You might be asking, if any information system helps do things faster and better and helps save money, who cares whether or not it matches the company's strategy? Good question. If money grew on trees, you probably would build and use just about every information system you could imagine. Organizations could build many different, valuable systems but are constrained by time and money to build only those that add the most value: those that help automate and learn, as well as have strategic value. In most cases, you do not want systems that do not match the strategy, even if they offer automating and learning benefits.

You probably do not want a system that helps differentiate your products based on high

[**Figure 2.10** ➡ The McLaren F1 Supercar.]
©Getty Images, Inc.

quality when the organizational strategy is to be the overall industry low-cost leader. For example, if managers of a firm were trying to make the firm a low-cost leader, would they want to buy or build an expensive **computer-aided design** system that enabled them to use high-powered computers to design very state-of-the-art, high-quality products? They probably would not choose to do that given that such a system would most likely add exorbitant costs to the design and manufacturing process and would likely defeat the strategy of spending less in the production of products and, subsequently, selling products at the lowest possible prices.

We should also caution that merely choosing and implementing an emerging information system is not sufficient to gain or sustain competitive advantage. In any significant information systems implementation there must be commensurate, significant organizational change. This typically comes in the form of business process reengineering (BPR) and other similar methods of improving the functioning of the organization as opposed to merely dropping in an information system with no attempts at changing and improving the organization. We will talk more in Chapter 7 about the role of BPR in enterprise-wide information systems implementations.

MAKING THE BUSINESS CASE FOR A SYSTEM

Given that money does not grow on trees, people in organizations are constantly trying to justify having to spend money on anything, especially information systems. Before people are willing to spend money to build a new information system or spend more money on an existing system, they want to be convinced that this will be a good investment. Will the system provide automating, learning, and/or strategic benefits? The phrase that is used to describe the process of identifying the value provided by an information system is **making the business case**.

What does making the business case for an information system mean? Think for a moment about what defense lawyers do in court trials. They carefully build a strong, integrated set of arguments and evidence to prove that their clients are innocent. In short, they build and present their case to those who will pass judgment on their clients. In much the same way, people in business often have to build a strong, integrated set of arguments and evidence to prove that an information system is adding

value to the organization or its constituents. For better or for worse, the business lingo that people use to refer to this process of building and presenting the rationale for a system is "making the business case" for a system.

As a business professional, you will be called on to make the business case for systems and other capital investments. As a finance, accounting, marketing, or management professional, you are likely to be involved in this process and will need to know how to make the business case for a system effectively, as well as understand the relevant organizational issues involved. It will be in the organization's best interest, and in your own, to ferret out systems that are not adding value. In these cases, you will either need to improve the systems or replace them.

Making the business case is as important for proposed systems as it is for existing systems. For a proposed system, the case will be used to determine whether the new system is a "go" or a "no go." For an existing system, the case determines whether the company will continue to fund the system. Whether a new system or an existing one is being considered, your goal is to make sure that the system adds value, that it helps the firm to achieve its strategy and competitive advantage over its rivals, and that money is being spent wisely.

The Productivity Paradox

Unfortunately, while it is easy to quantify the costs associated with developing an information system, it is often difficult to quantify tangible productivity gains from the use of an information system. Recently, the press has given a lot of attention to computer systems' impact or lack of impact on worker productivity. In many cases, IS expenditures, salaries, and the number of people on the IS staff have all been rising, but results from these investments have been disappointing. For example, it is estimated that technology-related spending by organizations increased fivefold from the 1980s to the 1990s (Hagendorf, 1998). As a result, justifying the costs for information technology has been a hot topic among senior managers at many firms. In particular, "white-collar" productivity, especially in the service sector, has not increased at the rate one might expect, given the billions of dollars spent on office information systems (Leibs and Carrillo, 1997).

Why has it been difficult to show that these vast expenditures on information technology have led to productivity gains? Have

Team Work

Pizza, Anyone?

Compare with your classmates your experiences with ordering pizza over the phone for delivery to your home. When you call to order the pizza, do you have to give them your full name, address, and phone number *every* time you call them, or do they merely ask your phone number and then automatically know who you are and where you live? If it is the latter, then they are using an information system to keep track of you so that they do not continually have to annoy you by asking you for your name, address, and phone number every time you call. How important is this to you and your classmates? Is this giving the pizza company a competitive advantage? Is it as important as the price of the pizza or how fast it is delivered to you?

Using IS to Manage Global Customer Service at Unilever

Have you ever eaten a Dove bar, drunk some Lipton tea, or used a bar of Dove soap? You might not realize it, but Unilever provides these and other everyday products for consumers all over the world (see Figure 2.11). With sales well into the billions of dollars annually, with nearly 300,000 employees worldwide, and with products sold in 150 countries in categories such as washing powder, shampoo and toothpaste, teas, ice cream, and oils and spreads, it is amazing that Unilever can keep track of it all.

Even more amazing is that, with millions of customers spread across 150 countries, Unilever's competitive advantage is based on providing excellent customer service. Unilever prides itself on not only responding to consumers' needs but also anticipating their future demands.

In order to provide the best customer service in its Philippines operation, in early 2002 Unilever successfully implemented mySAP™ Customer Relationship Management software. The mySAP CRM software now helps improve Unilever's call center capability and boost the productivity of its customer service and consumer advisory representatives.

The implementation, dubbed "Project Polaris," automates the help desk processes of Unilever's two call centers: customer service and consumer advisory. Unilever Philippines commercial director Efren Samonte, who served as the project sponsor for the implementation, said, "mySAP CRM enabled faster response time to queries and needs raised by consumers, provided for effective maintenance of our customer database, and gave the company easy access to customer information for analysis and strategy development."

Samonte added that, "Prior to the implementation, our customer and consumer care officers browsed through thick books, brochures, various online databases, and reports to answer customer inquiries. Now, they can click on any Unilever product on their computer screen, and data about the particular item automatically comes up. This significantly enhances our agents' ability to respond to customer inquiries fast, accurately, and completely."

Easy data access resulted in substantial productivity gains, according to Samonte. "Previously, monthly calls peaked at 3,000," he said. "mySAP CRM increased the company's call center capability immediately to 5,000 calls per month."

"The ability to access product information quickly and efficiently is the foundation for providing effective customer relationship management," said Carol Burch, senior vice president, Global CRM, SAP AG. "Unilever Philippines is now in the position to provide their customers with superior service than in the past, and will be able to handle more customer inquiries than ever before."

[Adapted in part from, "Unilever Goes Live with mySAP™ Customer Relationship Management," **www.sap.com/company/press/** (April 1, 2002).]

[**Figure 2.11** ➡ Unilever uses information systems to provide the best global customer service possible for products such as ice tea and soap.]
©Getty Images, Inc.

information systems somehow failed us, promising increases in performance and productivity and then failing to deliver on that promise? Determining the answer is not easy. Information systems may have increased productivity, but other forces may have simultaneously worked to reduce it, the end result being no visible change. Factors such as government regulation, more complex tax codes, and more complex products can all have major impacts on a firm's productivity.

It is also true that information systems built with the best intentions may have had unintended consequences—employees spending excessive amounts of time surfing the Web to check sports scores on the ESPN Web site, volumes of electronic junk mail being sent by Internet marketing companies or from personal friends, and company PCs being used to download and play software games. In these situations, information technology can result in less efficient and effective communication among employees and less productive uses of employee time than before the IS was implemented. Does this kind of employee behavior affect productivity figures? You bet it does. Still, in general, sound IS investments should increase organizational productivity. If this is so, why have organizations not been able to show this increased productivity? A number of reasons have been given for the apparent "productivity paradox" of IS investments.

Measurement Problems

In many cases, the benefits of information technology are difficult to pinpoint because firms may be measuring the wrong things. Often, the biggest increases in productivity result from increased **system effectiveness**. Unfortunately, many business metrics focus on **system efficiency**. Although information systems may have real benefits, those benefits may not be detected. Effectiveness improvements are sometimes difficult to measure. Also, expected benefits from IS are not always defined in advance, so they are never "seen." After all, in order to "see" something, you usually have to know what to look for. Measurement problems are not limited to traditional office information systems either. All types of systems have potential measurement problems. Consider the following:

End-user development. Because end-user developed systems are often designed for individual users or individual needs, those individuals do not often meticulously track costs

and benefits in order to measure impact. In addition, end users in one business unit may be tracking and analyzing a system's benefits and costs in ways that are quite different from the methods used by end users in other units.

Decision support systems (DSSs). By definition, DSSs are designed to improve decision making. The problem is, how do we measure their impact? To quantify the results of a DSS, we would need to measure the differences between decisions made with the DSS and the decisions that would have been made if no DSS had been in place. This kind of comparison is difficult to make in a business setting. Furthermore, it is not clear what constitutes adding value in this context. Does adding value mean making decisions that result in better outcomes, improving the decision-making process, having the capability to make more decisions, being able to justify a decision more effectively, making people feel better about the decision outcomes and/or the decision-making process, or some combination of these and other factors? Until it becomes clearer how to measure the benefits of a DSS easily and effectively, making the business case for a DSS will continue to be difficult.

Strategic systems. Ideally, IS managers could point to strategic information systems as having a tremendous impact on the firm's financial performance. However, the intent of strategic systems is often to help the organization enter a new market, gain or maintain market share, better serve customers, and so on. As we have said, traditional financial measures of system benefits—time/money saved or return on investment—do not adequately indicate whether these strategic systems have been successful. Better serving customers may be vitally important in a competitive environment. However, this may not easily translate into impressive-looking productivity figures for an information system in the short run.

A good example of measurement problems associated with IS investment is the use of automatic teller machines (ATMs). How much have ATMs contributed to banking productivity? Traditional statistics might look at the number of transactions or output as some multiple of the labor input needed to produce that output (for example, a transaction). However, such statistics do not work well for the ATM example. The number of checks written may actually decrease with ATMs, making productivity statistics appear lower. On the other hand, can you imagine a bank staying competitive without offering ATM services? The value added for the customer in terms of improved delivery of services almost dictates that banks offer a wide range of ATM services in today's competitive market. Deploying these information systems has become a strategic necessity.

Time Lags

A second explanation for why productivity is difficult to demonstrate for IS investment is that a significant time lag may occur from when a company makes the IS investment until that investment is translated into improvement in the bottom line. Brynjolfsson (1993) reports that lags of two to three years are typical before strong organizational impacts of IS investment are felt.

The explanation for lags is fairly simple. At one level, it takes time for people to become proficient at using new technologies. Remember the first time you ever used a computer? It probably seemed difficult and cryptic to use. It may have taken you more time to figure out how to use the computer than it would have to complete the task manually. Nonetheless, the computer probably became easier to use as you became more proficient with it. If you multiply this learning curve over everyone in an organization who may be using a given technology, you can see that until a firm has some experience in using a technology, the benefits associated with using it may be deferred. Everyone must become proficient with that technology in order to gain the benefits from its use.

It may also take some time before the tangible benefits of a new information system can be felt. Let us return to our ATM example. It may take years from the first implementation of this new system before the benefits may be felt. The system must first be implemented, which could take years in a large, distributed financial institution. Then the system must be fine-tuned to operate optimally and must be tied into all of the necessary subsystems. Employees and customers must be trained in how to use the system properly, and it may take years before they truly become proficient and comfortable with using it.

When the system is working well, and people are using it efficiently, productivity gains may be measured. It takes time for the system to produce any labor savings within the organization and for customers' satisfac-

tion levels to rise. Given that the ATMs have become a strategic necessity, perhaps one of their benefits is that they enable banks to gain, or simply keep, customers. It can take years for a financial institution to feel the effects of its deployment of ATM machines.

If time lags are the reason IS investments do not show up in productivity figures, then eventually IS managers should be able to report some very good news about organizational return on IS investment. Still, for managers faced with the day-to-day pressures of coming up with a demonstrable impact on firm performance, the issue of time lags may not be very helpful or comforting.

Redistribution

A third possible explanation for why IS productivity figures are not easy to find is that IS may be beneficial for individual firms, but not for a particular industry or the economy as a whole. Particularly in competitive situations, IS may be used to redistribute the pieces of the pie rather than making the whole pie bigger. In other words, strategic information systems may help one firm to increase its market share; however, this may come at the expense of another firm, which loses its market share as consumers transfer to the first firm. The result for the industry or economy as a whole is a wash—that is, the same number of products is being sold and the same number of dollars is being spent across all the firms. The only difference is that now one firm is getting a larger share of the business, while another firm is getting a smaller share.

While such an explanation may be feasible for some markets and industries, it does not fully explain why productivity figures would be stagnant at the level of one individual firm. Shouldn't each organization be more productive than before? Part of the problem is that our expectations of performance are somewhat biased. We tend to take for granted that technology fundamentally enables people to do things that would otherwise be nearly impossible. In effect, we continue to "raise the bar" with our expectations of what people can accomplish when supported by technology. For example, you might wonder whether the electronic spreadsheet on the PC on your desk is really helping you do your job better. To best answer this, you should think back to what it was like to create a spreadsheet by hand. It was a much slower process, was far more likely to produce errors, and left people significantly less time to work on other, more important tasks.

Mismanagement

A fourth explanation is that IS has not been implemented and managed well. Some believe that people often simply build bad systems, implement them poorly, and rely on technology fixes when the organization has problems that require a joint technology/process solution. Rather than increasing outputs or profits, IS investments might merely be a Band-Aid and may serve to mask or even increase organizational slack and inefficiency.

Similarly, the rapid decrease in processing time enabled by IS can result in unanticipated bottlenecks. For example, if automation has increased the potential output of a system, but part of that system is reliant on human input, then the system can operate only as fast as the human can feed input into or through that system. Eli Goldratt very aptly showed how this happens in his best-selling book, *The Goal*, in which he uses the format of a novel to show how people can think logically and consistently about organizational problems in order to determine true "cause and effect" relationships between their actions and the results. In the novel, the characters do this so well they save their manufacturing plant and make it successful. Spending money on IS does not help increase the firm's productivity until all of the bottlenecks are addressed. From a management standpoint, this means that managers must be sure that they evaluate the entire process being automated, making changes as necessary to old processes in order to truly benefit from IS investment. If managers simply overlay new technology on old processes, sometimes known as "paving the cow path," then they will likely be disappointed in the meager productivity gains reaped from their investment.

If it is so difficult to quantify the benefits of information systems for individual firms and for entire industries, why do managers continue to invest in information systems? There are two answers. First, competitive pressures force managers to invest in information systems whether they like it or not. Second, some managers are getting better at making the business case for information systems.

Making a Successful Business Case

There a number of types of arguments that people make in their business cases for information systems. When managers make the business case for an information system they typically base their arguments on **F**aith, **F**ear, and/or **F**acts (Wheeler, 2002a)[3]. Table 2.3 shows examples of these three types of arguments.

Do not assume that you must base your business case on facts only. It is entirely appropriate to base the business case on faith,

---

[3]Wheeler also adds a fourth F, that being for Fiction, and notes that, unfortunately, managers sometimes base their arguments on pure fiction, which is not only bad for their careers but is not at all healthy for their firms either.

Type of Argument	Description	Example
Faith	Arguments based on beliefs about organizational strategy, competitive advantage, industry forces, customer perceptions, market share, and so on.	"I know I don't have good data to back this up, but I'm convinced that having this Customer Relationship Management system will enable us to serve our customers significantly better than do our competitors and, as a result, we'll beat the competition.... You just have to take it on faith."
Fear	Arguments based on the notion that if the system is not implemented, the firm will lose out to the competition or, worse, go out of business.	"If we don't implement this Enterprise Resource Planning system we'll get killed by our competitors because they're all implementing these kinds of systems.... We either do this or we die."
Fact	Arguments based on data, quantitative analysis, and/or indisputable factors.	"This analysis shows that implementing the inventory control system will help us reduce errors by 50%, reduce operating costs by 15% a year, increase production by 5% a year, and will pay for itself within 18 months."

[Table 2.3] *Three types of arguments commonly made in the business case for an information system.*

fear, or facts. Indeed, the strongest and most comprehensive business case will include a little of each type of argument. In the following sections, we talk about each of these types of arguments for the business case.

Business Case Arguments Based on Faith

In some situations arguments based on faith (or fear) are the most compelling and are what drive the decision to invest in an information system despite the lack of any data on system costs or even in the face of some data that say that the dollar costs for the system will be high. Arguments based on faith often hold that an information system *must* be implemented in order to achieve the organization's strategy effectively and to gain or sustain a competitive advantage over rivals, despite the dollar costs associated with that system. Given the power of modern information systems, their rapid evolution, and their pervasiveness in business today, information systems have become a common tool for enabling business strategy. Consequently, the business cases for systems are frequently grounded in strategic arguments.

An example would be that a firm has set as its strategy that it will be the dominant, global force in its industry. As a result, this firm cannot escape that it will have to adopt a global telecommunications network and a variety of collaboration technologies such as e-mail, desktop video conferencing, and groupware tools, in order to enable employees from different parts of the globe to work together effectively and efficiently. Similarly, a firm that has set as its strategy that it will

have a broad scope—producing products and services across a wide range of consumer needs—cannot escape that it will have to adopt some form of an Enterprise Resource Planning system to coordinate business activities across its diverse product lines. For example, Procter & Gamble produces dozens of household products that are consumed under various brand names—Noxzema, Folgers Coffee, Tide laundry detergent, Cover Girl cosmetics, Crest toothpaste, and Pringles potato chips, to name a few. Integration across various product lines and divisions is a key goal for IS investments. Such integration allows Procter & Gamble to streamline inventory, thus improving efficiency. In short, successful business case arguments based on faith should clearly describe the firm's mission and objectives, the strategy for achieving them, and the types of information systems that are needed in order to enact the strategy.

Business Case Arguments Based on Fear

There are several different factors to take into account when making a business case in which you will provide arguments based on fear. These include a number of factors involving competition and other elements of the industry in which the firm operates, which are shown in Figure 2.12 (Harris and Katz, 1991).

Industry Factors
The nature of the industry can often determine what types of information systems would be most effective. Furthermore, many different types of industry factors can affect the business value of different systems. A system that

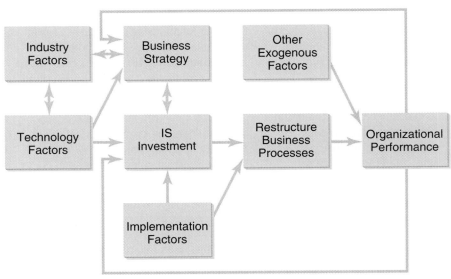

[Figure 2.12 ➡ Factors in IS investment decisions.]

may have a very positive impact on a firm in one industry may have little or no impact on a firm in another industry.

Stage of maturity. The stage of maturity for a given industry can have an important influence on IS investment. For example, a mature and stable industry, such as the automotive industry, may need IS simply to maintain the current pace of operations. While having the newest IS available may be nice, it may not be needed to stay in business. However, a company in a newer, more volatile industry, such as the cellular phone industry, may find it more important to be on the leading edge of technology in order to compete effectively in the marketplace. In fact, it may be a strategic necessity in some industries to deploy newer technologies, even though the tangible benefits of deploying these technologies may be difficult to demonstrate.

Regulation. Some industries are more highly regulated than others. In some cases, companies can use IS to control processes and ensure compliance with appropriate regulations. For example, the aircraft industry is highly regulated. Information technology can provide sophisticated engineering and modeling tools to designers who can test various designs for reactions to gravity forces (G-forces) and turbulence before aircraft prototypes are built. The designer can then understand which designs may not comply with regulatory requirements. Similar applications exist (and are often mandated) across other highly regulated industries, such as the radio and television broadcasting industries. The argument for the business case here would be something like, "If we do not implement this information system we run the risk of being sued or, worse, being thrown in jail."

Nature of competition or rivalry. Probably the most important industry factor that can affect IS investment is the nature of competition or rivalry in the industry. For example, when competition in an industry is high and use of information systems is rampant, as it is in the personal computer industry, strategic necessity more than anything else forces firms to adopt information systems. Given how tight profit margins are in the PC industry, Dell and other manufacturers must use inventory control systems, Web-based purchasing and customer service, and a host of other systems that help them to be more effective and effi-

cient. If they do not adopt these information systems, they will likely go out of business. One framework often used to analyze the competition within an industry is Porter's notion of the five primary competitive forces (Porter, 1979): 1) the rivalry among competing sellers in your industry, 2) the threat of potential new entrants into your industry, 3) the bargaining power that customers have within your industry, 4) the bargaining power that suppliers have within your industry, and 5) the potential for substitute products from other industries. Table 2.4 provides examples of how IS can have an impact on the various competitive forces in an industry.

Porter's Five Forces model of competition can be used in this way to help you determine which specific technologies will be more or less useful depending on the nature of your industry. You can then use these as the bases for your arguments as to whether or not to invest in new or existing information systems. This kind of industry-based business case might not enable you to attach specific, monetary benefits to particular information systems, but it can be used to show you and others that specific uses of particular systems are necessary to compete in your markets. Business case arguments formulated this way sound something like, "If we do not implement this information system, our competitors are going to beat us on price, we will lose market share, and we will go out of business."

Business Case Arguments Based on Fact

Many people, including most Chief Financial Officers, want to see the business case for an information system be based on some convincing, quantitative analysis that proves beyond a shadow of doubt that the benefits of the system will outweigh the costs. The most common way to prove this is to provide a detailed cost-benefit analysis of the information system. Although this step is critical, the manager must remember that there are inherent difficulties in and limits to cost-benefit analysis for information systems, as described previously.

Cost-Benefit Analysis for a Web-Based System

In this section we are going to discuss the cost-benefit analysis for an information system and show how that analysis would be part of a business case based on fact. Let us consider the development of a Web-based order entry system for a relatively small firm.

[Table 2.4] *IS impact on competitive forces.*

Competitive Force	Implication for Firm	Potential Use of IS to Combat Competitive Force
Traditional rivals within your industry	Competition in price, product distribution, and service	Implement Enterprise Resource Planning system to reduce costs and be able to act and react more quickly
		Implement Web site to offer better service to customers
Threat of new entrants into your market	Increased capacity in the industry	Better Web site to reach customers and differentiate product
	Reduced prices	Inventory Control System to lower costs and better manage excess capacity
	Decreased market share	
Customers' bargaining power	Reduced prices	Implement Customer Relationship Management system to serve customers better
	Increased quality	
	Demand for more services	Implement computer-aided design and/or computer-aided manufacturing system to improve product quality
Suppliers' bargaining power	Prices raised	Use Internet to establish closer electronic ties with suppliers and to create relationships with new suppliers located far away
	Reduced quality	
Threat of substitute products from other industries	Potential returns on products	Use Decision Support System and customer purchase database to assess trends and customer needs better
	Decreased market share	
	Losing customers for life	Use computer-aided design systems to redefine products

[Adapted from Applegate and McFarlan. *Corporate Information Systems Management: Text and Cases*, 5th ed. (Columbus, Ohio: McGraw-Hill/Irwin, 1999).]

Brief Case: Competition and IS Investments: Domino's Pizza Delivers

Most of you have experienced the intense competition in the pizza restaurant industry, especially in and around college towns. This competition has forced many smaller companies to go out of business, although plenty are still around to compete with the big names of Pizza Hut, Domino's, Little Caesar's, and Papa John's. As a result, even these large companies are using technology to stay ahead of the competition. Domino's Pizza Incorporated, headquartered in Ann Arbor, Michigan, is a prime example. Domino's inventory system automatically deducts the proper quantities of toppings (based on preset standards) from inventory files every time an order is placed (Dragoon, 1998). A nightly report is then produced showing the store manager what to reorder. Soon, the reordering process will be online, and within the next year, distribution centers will automatically check store inventories and place orders as necessary without the involvement of management. Similar advances are occurring in the delivery market. Domino's stores employ a custom software package that combines Caller ID with their order database to display the customer's name, address, phone number, and most recent order to the employee. The system can even display special delivery instructions to save time. All customers need to do is call up, say they want the same order as last time, and that is it. The production and delivery processes are automatically set into motion, and the inventory system prepares the reorder report based on the order. So, although the pizza is made in 15 minutes and the driver reaches your home in another 10, a lot more is going on behind the scenes to make the process work and to keep the restaurant competitive.

In a cost-benefit analysis, costs can usually be divided into two categories, **nonrecurring costs** and **recurring costs.** Nonrecurring costs are one-time costs that are not expected to continue after the system is implemented. These include costs for things such as the Web server, telecommunications equipment, Web server software, HTML editors, Java, PhotoShop, and other tools. These one-time costs also include the costs of attracting and training a Webmaster, renovating some office space to serve as the location of the Web server, and paying analysts and programmers to develop the system.

Recurring costs are ongoing costs that occur throughout the life cycle of systems development, implementation, and maintenance. Recurring costs include the salary and benefits of the Webmaster and any other personnel assigned to maintain the system, upgrades and maintenance for the system components, monthly fees paid to a local Internet service provider, and the continuing costs for the space in which the Webmaster works and the server resides. Personnel costs are usually the largest recurring costs, and the Web-based system is no exception in this regard. These recurring expenses can go well beyond the Webmaster to include expenses for help desk personnel, maintenance programmers, IS management, and data entry personnel.

The sample costs described thus far have been fairly **tangible costs**, which are easy to identify. Some **intangible costs** ought to be accounted for as well, even though they will not fit neatly into the quantitative analysis. These might include the costs of reducing traditional sales, losing some customers that are not "Web ready," or losing customers if the Web application is poorly designed or not on par with competitors' sites. We can choose either to quantify these in some way (that is, determine the cost of losing a customer) or simply to reserve these as important costs to consider outside of, but along with, the quantitative cost-benefit analysis.

Next we determine both **tangible benefits** and **intangible benefits.** Some tangible benefits are relatively easy to determine. For example, we can estimate that the increased customer reach of the new Web-based system will result in at least a modest increase in sales. Based on evidence from similar projects you might estimate, say, a five percent increase in sales the first year, a 10 percent increase the second year, and a 15 percent increase the

third year. In addition, we might also include as tangible benefits the reduction of order entry errors because orders will now be tracked electronically and shipped automatically. We could calculate the money previously lost on faulty and lost orders, along with the salaries and wages of personnel assigned to fix and find these orders, and then consider the reduction of these costs as a quantifiable benefit of the new system. Cost avoidance is a legitimate, quantifiable benefit of an information system. Similarly, the new system may enable the company to use fewer order entry clerks or redeploy these personnel to other, more important functions within the company. We could consider these cost reductions as benefits of the new system.

Our Web-based system has intangible benefits as well. Some intangible benefits of this new system might include faster turnaround on fulfilling orders and resulting improvements in customer service. These are real benefits, but they might be hard to quantify with confidence. Perhaps an even more intangible benefit would be the overall improved perception of the firm. Customers might consider it more progressive and customer-service oriented than its rivals, and, in addition to attracting new customers, this might increase the value of the firm's stock if it were a publicly traded firm. Another intangible benefit might be simply that it was a strategic necessity to offer Web-based ordering to customers to keep pace with rivals. While these intangibles are difficult to quantify, they must be considered along with the more quantitative analysis of benefits. In fact, the intangible benefits of this Web-based system might be so important that they could carry the day despite an inconclusive or even negative cost-benefit analysis.

An example of a simplified cost-benefit analysis with tangible costs and benefits is presented in Figure 2.13. You will notice the fairly large investment up front, with another significant outlay in the fifth year for a system upgrade. We could now use the net costs/benefits for each year as the basis of our conclusion about this system. Alternatively, we could perform a break-even analysis (break even occurs early in the second year of the system's life) or a more formal net present value analysis of the relevant cash flow streams associated with the system. In any event, this cost-benefit analysis helps us make the business case for this proposed Web-based order fulfillment system. It clearly shows that

		2002	2003	2004	2005	2006
Costs						
Non-recurring						
Hardware		$ 20,000				
Software		$ 7,500				
Networking		$ 4,500				
Infrastructure		$ 7,500				
Personnel		$100,000				
Recurring						
Hardware			$ 500	$ 1,000	$ 2,500	$ 15,000
Software			$ 500	$ 500	$ 1,000	$ 2,500
Networking			$ 250	$ 250	$ 500	$ 1,000
Service Fees			$ 250	$ 250	$ 250	$ 500
Infrastructure				$ 250	$ 500	$ 1,500
Personnel			$ 60,000	$ 62,500	$ 70,000	$ 90,000
Total Costs		$139,500	$ 61,500	$ 64,750	$ 74,750	$110,500
Benefits						
Increased Sales		$ 20,000	$ 50,000	$ 80,000	$115,000	$175,000
Error Reduction		$ 15,000	$ 15,000	$ 15,000	$ 15,000	$ 15,000
Cost Reduction		$100,000	$100,000	$100,000	$100,000	$100,000
Total Benefits		$135,000	$165,000	$195,000	$230,000	$290,000
Net Costs/Benefit		$ (4,500)	$103,500	$130,250	$155,250	$179,500

[**Figure 2.13** ➡ Worksheet showing simplified cost-benefit analysis for the Web-based order fulfillment system.]

the investment for this system is relatively small, and we can fairly quickly recapture the investment. In addition, there appear to be intangible, strategic benefits to deploying this system. This analysis, and the accompanying arguments and evidence, go a long way toward convincing senior managers in the firm that this new system makes sense.

Career Implications:

Accounting and Finance

If you find yourself working in the field of accounting and/or finance, you will likely be asked to prepare or evaluate a proposal for an information system given your expertise with numbers. As noted in this chapter, it will be relatively easy for you to determine and report the costs of the information system, but it will be more difficult for you to quantify the benefits of the system. In some cases you will be able to quantify the benefits in terms of cost savings or increased sales, but in many cases you will not be able to quantify clear, tangible benefits. Does that mean you should recommend against implementing such systems? Not necessarily. It means that there ought to be clear, compelling reasons for implementing these systems in the absence of hard numbers. You might be a bit scared about having to help with such an important, complex decision, but do not worry. It is exciting to think that right out of college you will soon find yourself involved in such critical, strategic decisions in the business world.

Measuring the value of IS and justifying that value to various stakeholders in the organization has become one of the most important aspects of information systems projects. In many cases, the value of IS has been justified if the CIO has been able to prove that a new information system will enable the company to cut costs and increase efficiency. Financial or tangible measures of return on investment thus have often been used as a measure of the value of an information systems project. However, such a measure is useful only in the case of projects where the benefits are tangible, such as the implementation of a new processing system that will clearly decrease the time taken to process orders (and thus cut costs demonstrably). However, many other important IS projects have less tangible outcomes and return on investment (ROI), and hence ROI is becoming a controversial measure of the value of IS. For different types of IS projects, companies are switching to alternate measures of their value, including evaluating the strategic value of that project to the organization. For example, while justifying e-business projects, CEOs are evaluating how they may enhance the competitive edge of the organization, open up new marketing channels for the company, or lead to higher customer satisfaction, rather than focusing only on the dollar amount of the return the system will provide. Similarly, for intranet projects, factors such as increased employee morale and higher levels of collaboration are taking precedence over how much money the project will cost or will help save. As a systems analyst, systems consultant, or systems project manager, you will be asked to make the business case for information systems. You are quite likely to find yourself in the middle of this debate about quantitative versus qualitative measurement of the value of information systems.

[Adapted from "Rethinking ROI," **www.informationweek.com** (May 24, 1999).]

PRESENTING THE BUSINESS CASE

Up to this point, we have discussed the key issues to consider as you prepare to make the business case for a system. We have also shown you some tools for determining the value that a system adds to an organization. Now you are actually ready to make the case, to present your arguments and evidence to the decision makers in the firm. This task is much like that of a lawyer presenting a persuasive written and oral argument to win a judgment in her client's favor. Making a business case for IS really is not much different. You are simply trying to persuade the boss, steering committee, or board of directors to invest money in something you think is important to the business. Your job is to persuade them that you are right!

Know the Audience Matters!

Depending on the firm, a number of people might be involved in the decision-making process. In the following sections, we describe the typical decision makers and their perspectives when evaluating a business case.

The IS Manager

Obviously, as the head of the information systems department, the IS manager has overall responsibility for managing IS development, implementation, and maintenance. They should be in the best position to make recommendations to decision makers, given their expertise in applying IS to business problems. The IS manager may also rely on experts in particular areas within IS to help analyze and present useful information to decision makers. For example, a networking expert may provide detailed technical information about cost, speed, and installation procedures.

Company Executives (Vice Presidents and Higher)

Often, executives act as the decision-making body for the firm's large investment projects. They typically represent various stakeholders or interest groups within the organization, and they may have their own agendas at stake when making decisions about expenses. For example, approving a large IS investment may mean that a new, expensive marketing idea gets delayed. Understanding the political implications of the approval process can be just as important as demonstrating a solid impact on the firm's bottom line.

Steering Committee

Sometimes, a firm uses a steering committee made up of representatives or managers from each of the functional areas within the firm. The IS manager may make her case to this steering committee on which projects should be pursued and why. The steering committee then makes its recommendation to the CEO or corporate staff. In other cases, the steering

Brief Case: **Making the Most of Executive Support at In Focus**

Not only do company executives make many of the decisions regarding large investment projects for a company, but many times they are also the ones the employees look to for guidance. Therefore, it is extremely important for large IS projects to have executive support. That way, IS projects have a sponsor outside of IS to keep the project on track and to rally the employees behind it if necessary. An extreme example of this occurred in 1993 at In Focus Systems Incorporated, a manufacturer of data and video projectors (Slater, 1998). In Focus competes with much larger companies such as Sony, Toshiba, and Panasonic. In order to stay competitive and to keep their jobs, the executives realized that they had to incorporate a cultural change into an organization that is constantly

improving itself and its business processes. The executives decided that an information infrastructure was necessary to support these changes. For the project to succeed, the employees had to believe in the change and adopt it into their work. To make this happen, the executives, especially Mike Yonker (CFO) and John Harker (CEO), became active and vocal supporters of the new culture and the new information system. Employees who were quick to adopt were given salary rewards, and other incentives helped the remainder of the employees with the change. During the entire process, Yonker and Harker were staunch supporters, and everyone knew it. As it turns out, In Focus has experienced a 40 percent drop in operating expenses and an increase of 26 percent in market share. Everyone at In Focus agrees that without Yonker and Harper, the changes would have failed.

committee may have approval authority, depending on its makeup. It may, for example, include the CEO, senior vice presidents, or other influential people in the organization.

The goal of a steering committee is to get an organization's leaders, who have different interests and agendas, to share the responsibilities and risks that come with aligning IS initiatives with broader business aims. Many organizations utilize a steering committee for some aspect of their IS management. Citizens Communications (formerly Citizens Utilities Company), a provider of natural gas, electricity, water, and wastewater treatment to 1.7 million customers in the northeast United States, is one such example (Pearson, 1998). Citizens organizes its management into numerous steering committees. All of these committees report to the Operating Team, which is led by the president of the company. The IS steering committee, which is known as the Operating Technology Team (OTT), includes the CIO, Nicholas Ioli; the general managers of communications and public service; and the vice presidents of finance, human resources, and regulatory affairs. A recent decision to implement an enterprise-wide Lotus Notes system had the full support of the OTT and passed through the Operating Team with no problems. Ioli notes that without the OTT's support, the implementation would have had a much lower chance of being approved. In fact, Ioli feels strongly that without the OTT, the implementation would never have happened in the first place, due to the lack of team

unity and overall business support from the other leaders involved. The OTT enables Ioli to lead Citizens into the future with the necessary support and commitment from the other top-level managers.

Convert Benefits to Monetary Terms

Try to translate all benefits into monetary terms. For example, if a new system saves department managers an hour per day, try to quantify that savings in terms of dollars. Figure 2.14 shows how you might convert time savings into dollar figures. While merely explaining this benefit as "saving managers time" makes it sound useful, managers may not consider it a significant enough inducement to warrant spending a significant amount of money. Justifying a $50,000 system because it will "save time" may not be persuasive enough. However, an annual savings of $90,000 is more likely to capture the attention of firm managers and is more likely to result in project approval. Senior managers can easily rationalize a $50,000 expense for a $90,000 savings and can easily see why they should approve such a request. They can also more easily rationalize their decision later on if something goes wrong with the system.

Devise Proxy Variables

The situation presented in Figure 2.14 is fairly straightforward. Anyone can see that a $50,000 investment is a good idea because the return on that investment is $90,000 the first

Benefit:

New system saves at least one hour per day for 12 mid-level managers.

Quantified as:

Manager's Salary (per Hour)	$30.00
Number of Managers Affected	12
Daily Savings (One Hour Saved *12 Managers)	$360.00
Weekly Saving (Daily Saving *5)	$1800.00
Annual Savings (Weekly Savings *50)	$90000.00

[Figure 2.14 ➥ Converting time savings into dollar figures.]

year. Unfortunately, not all cases are this clear-cut. In cases in which it is not as easy to quantify the impact of an investment, you can come up with **proxy variables** to help clarify what the impact on the firm will be. Proxy variables can be used to measure changes in terms of their perceived value to the organization. For example, if mundane administrative tasks are seen as a low value (perhaps a 1 on a five-point scale), while direct contact with customers is seen as a high value (a 5), you can use these perceptions to indicate how new systems will add value to the organization. In this example, you can show that a new system will allow personnel to have more contact with customers, while at the same time reducing the administrative workload. Senior managers can quickly see that individual workload is being shifted from low-value to high-value activities.

Alternatively, you can create a customer contact scale from 1 to 5, with 1 representing very low customer contact and 5 representing very high customer contact. You can argue that currently your firm rates a 2 on the customer contact scale and that with the new information system, your firm will rate a significantly higher number on the scale.

You can communicate these differences using percentages, increases or decreases, and so on—whatever best conveys the idea that the new system is creating changes in work, in performance, and in the way people think about their work. This gives senior firm management some relatively solid data upon which to base their decision. They typically like numbers. Why not make them happy?

Develop a Work Profile Matrix

Sassone and Schwartz (1986) developed a model that has also been used to measure the benefits of information systems directly. As suggested earlier in the chapter, productivity gains have been notoriously difficult to measure with respect to information technology. Sassone and Schwartz use a two-step method to help quantify productivity benefits.

First, a **work profile matrix** is developed. The matrix, which consists of job categories and work categories, shows how much time is spent on each of the job categories and each of the different types of work. Figure 2.15 shows an example of a work profile matrix. To design a work profile matrix, you must first have participants fill out an activity log. Every two hours over several weeks, the activity log asks participants to indicate how much time they have spent in each category over the last

Work Categories	Managers	Senior Professionals (or Senior Clerks)	Junior Professionals (or Junior Clerks)	Administrators & Technicians	Secretaries
Managerial	30%	2%	1%	0%	0%
Senior Professional	16	35	10	0	0
Junior Professional	13	26	50	1	0
Administrative	16	13	13	58	10
Clerical	7	12	14	27	76
Nonproductive*	18	12	12	14	14

*Necessary but not useful activities, such as walking to a meeting or waiting to use a photocopier or fax

[Figure 2.15 ➥ A sample work profile matrix.]

two hours. This information is summarized and indicated on the matrix. The results provide you with a snapshot view of how human resources are being allocated.

Second, as in Figure 2.15, you calculate the amount of money each department is spending on each type of work using salary figures. You compile this information into a "before system" figure. Then you make an estimate of how the new system will change the amount of time each job category spends on each type of activity. This can help quantify how a new system will change the balance of time spent by various workgroups on different activities and can make work shifts associated with the new system more salient to senior managers in terms of actual dollar savings or shifts.

Measure What Is Important to Management

One of the most important things you can do to show the benefits of a system is one of the simplest: Measure what senior managers think is important. You may think this is trivial advice, but you would be surprised how often people calculate impressive-looking statistics in terms of downtime, reliability, and so on, only to find that senior managers disregard or only briefly skim over those figures. You should concentrate on the issues senior business managers care about. The "hot button" issues with senior firm managers should be easy to discover, and they are not always financial reports. Hot issues with senior managers could include cycle time (how long it takes to process an order), customer feedback, or employee morale. By focusing on what senior business managers believe to be important, you can make the business case for systems in a way that is more meaningful for those managers, which makes selling systems to decision makers much easier. Managers are more likely to buy in to the importance of systems if they can see the impact on areas that are important to them.

Making a Good Case at Conoco

Lloyd Belcher, manager of Executive Information Systems (EIS) at Conoco, and Hugh Watson at the University of Georgia, outlined a methodology that was used to establish the value of Conoco's EIS (Belcher and Watson, 1993). Conoco, based in Houston, Texas, is a global energy company with oil and natural gas refineries, as well as retail gasoline outlets. The EIS at Conoco was initially developed in the early 1980s but has grown significantly to include thousands of users worldwide. The IS group at Conoco was charged with conducting a complete review of the existing EIS in order to determine its value for the firm.

The IS group interviewed users of the current system from all departments, and they dis-

---

EIS Application Benefits Worksheets

Application: _____ *Industry Statistical Data* _____

Improved Productivity

A. Decreased Information Creation Cost Savings:	$ 41,000
B. New Information Creation Cost Savings:	0
C. Reduced Information Access Time Savings:	

    (1) Average Access Time Reduction: *1 Minute*
    (2) Average Number of Accesses: *108/Week*
    (3) Employee Cost: *$1.00/Minute*
    (4) Savings Per Year: *1 * 108 * 1 * 52* $ 5,615

Improved Decision Making   0

Information Distribution Cost Savings

    (1) Cost of Document: *$2.00*
    (2) Average Number of Copies: *60/Week*
    (3) Savings per Year: *2 * 60 * 52* $ 6,240

Services Replacement Cost Savings   0

Total Tangible Benefits $ 52,856

[Figure 2.16 ➡ A sample EIS application benefits worksheet.]

cussed the results with each of the respective department heads. The summaries included details about the amount of usage and which parts of the system were actually used by each department. They completed a review for each of these parts of the system to determine the purpose, costs, savings, and improvements in decision making for each department, as well as any intangible improvements gained. They combined costs and benefits of using the system into a single worksheet to show a bottom line for each part of the system (see Figure 2.16 for an example). When they completed these assessments for all applications and for all departments, they summarized the results across all departments into a single corporate report.

Using conservative assessments that focused primarily on tangible benefits and ignored most intangible benefits, Belcher and Watson were able to show that the benefits of Conoco's EIS were four to five times greater than the costs of the system. However, the analysis did show that parts of the system were not being used. As a result, these pieces

of the system were eliminated while, overall, the system proved its worth and was kept.

Changing Mindsets About Information Systems

Perhaps the most significant change in the information systems field has been in mindsets about technology rather than in technology itself. The old way for managers to think about information systems was that information systems are a necessary service, a necessary evil, a necessary, distasteful expense that is to be minimized. Managers cannot afford to think this way anymore. Successful managers now think of information systems as a competitive asset to be nurtured and invested in. Does this mean that managers should not require a sound business case for every information systems investment? No! Does this mean that managers do not need to have facts as part of a business case for a system? No! This means that managers have to stop thinking about systems as an expense and start thinking about systems as

Web Search

WEB SEARCH OPPORTUNITY: Visit **http://www.3m.com/ meetingnetwork/presen- tations/delivering.html** and find tips on giving presentations. How can this Web site help you find other ways to effectively make the business case for an information system?

USING INFORMATION SYSTEMS IN THE MILITARY

Perhaps nothing demonstrates better the ability to use information systems for competitive advantage than the uses of modern information technologies in the military. We all know that soldiers now use high-tech equipment and weapons (see Figure 2.17). However, these types of uses of technology in war are fast becoming less important than the use of sophisticated information systems in what is being called "information warfare."

Information warfare involves the use of information systems to eavesdrop on, confuse, or subvert the enemy and other stakeholders in an attempt to either win or avoid war. One example is intercepting enemy communication in order to know what they are thinking and doing. This is known as "signals intelligence" and is a huge part of the armed forces of every developed country.

Another example of information warfare is feeding the enemy false information that would cause them to take a misstep such as being at the wrong place at the wrong time or bombing the wrong targets. A subtler alternative is the use of information systems to destabilize the economies and governments of enemy countries by spreading false information.

[**Figure 2.17** ➡ Use of high-tech equipment has become a first step in warfare.]
©AP/Wide World Photos

One thing is clear; information warfare is on the rise. Indeed, as a result of this reliance on technology, the all-important first step in battle has now become to take out the enemies' communications and networking infrastructure. Ironically, as information warfare becomes more prevalent, it will appear to us that there are fewer "wars." Think about it. In conventional warfare it is painfully obvious that there has been an attack when a bomb has been dropped. On the other hand, with information warfare it will be very difficult for us to see the various forms of digital attack that occur. Chances are that the enemy that is being attacked will not even notice it or will pass it off as a systems error!

an asset. Managers have to become strategic about information systems and think of them as an enabler of opportunities.

COMPETITIVE ADVANTAGE IN BEING AT THE CUTTING EDGE

To differentiate itself, an organization often must deploy new, state-of-the-art technologies to do things even better, faster, and more cheaply than rivals that are using older technologies. Although firms can continually upgrade contemporary organizational information systems, such as mainframe-based transaction processing, these improvements can at best give only a short-lived competitive edge. To gain and sustain significant competitive advantage, firms must often deploy the latest technologies or deploy existing technologies in clever, new ways.

Imagine, for example, that a manager decides to implement a local area network within a department to automate the operations of the office workers and to enable them to share peripheral devices, such as laser printers. This local area network is implemented using a personal computer with a Pentium III® microprocessor with 256MB of RAM as a server for the network. This may seem like state-of-the-art computing to the office workers, but it is likely that rival firms have already been doing this for years. The manager might upgrade the server to a Pentium IV® microprocessor with nearly a gigabyte of RAM. Chances are that this would make the local area network run a bit faster, but would this necessarily give the firm a clear advantage over rivals, and what would be the result of rivals upgrading their own networks with faster, more powerful servers?

Consider another example. A firm implements a relational database management system for sales and inventory, giving it an edge over rivals in fulfilling orders faster and more accurately. Competitors soon do the same thing and it becomes necessary to improve to stay ahead. The firm could improve the system and gain a relatively small, short-lived advantage over rivals. Even better, the firm could extend this idea and implement similar database applications for all of its business processes and then integrate these applications with one another. Perhaps the firm could go one step further and enable customers and suppliers to access these systems directly. There is nearly always a better way to do things, along with new technologies to help you do these things better. Clearly, if you choose to use information technology as a source of competitive advantage, you must choose to use emerging technologies in innovative ways. As they say, the best never rest.

But with the plethora of new information technologies and systems being developed, how can you possibly choose winners? Indeed, how can you even keep track of all the new breakthroughs, new products, new versions, and new ways of using technologies? For example, in Figure 2.18 we present a small subset of some new information technologies and systems, ranging from some that are here now and currently being used to some that are easily a decade away from being a reality. Which one is important for you? Which one will make or break your business? Does this list even include the one that you need to be concerned about?

The Need for Constant IS Innovation

Sir John Maddox, a physicist and the editor for 22 years of the influential scientific journal, *Nature*, was quoted in *Scientific American* in 1999 as saying, "The most important dis-

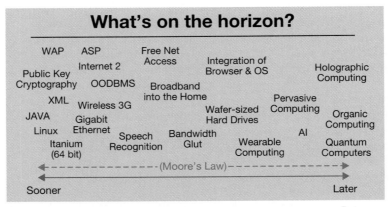

[Figure 2.18 ➨ Some new information technologies on the horizon.]

coveries of the next 50 years are likely to be ones of which we cannot now even conceive." Think about that for a moment. Most of the important discoveries of the next 50 years are likely to be things that, at present, we have no clue about. To illustrate that point, think back just a short decade ago about what the state of the Internet was. That is difficult to do because the Internet as we now know it did not even exist then, and certainly the Internet was not on the radar screens of business organizations back at that point. Yet, look now at how the Internet has transformed modern business. How could something so transformational as the Internet not have been easier for businesses to imagine or predict a decade ago? Well, it is difficult to see these things coming. You have to work at it.

Executives today who are serious about using information technology in innovative ways have made it a point to have their people be continually on the lookout for new information technologies that will have a significant impact on their business. Wheeler (2002b) has summarized this process nicely as the **E-Business Innovation Cycle** (see Figure 2.19). Like the term *e-commerce*, *e-business* refers to the use of information technologies and systems to support the business. Whereas

the term *e-commerce* is generally used to mean the use of the Internet and related technologies to support commerce, the term **e-business** is used more broadly to mean the use of nearly any information technologies or systems to support every part of the business. The model essentially holds that the key to success for modern organizations is the extent to which they use information technologies and systems in timely, innovative ways.

On the vertical dimension of the E-Business Innovation Cycle is the extent to which an organization derives value from a particular information technology, and on the horizontal dimension is time. The first bubble in the lower left of the graph shows that successful organizations first create jobs, groups, and processes that are all devoted to scanning the environment for new emerging and **enabling technologies** that appear to be relevant for the organization. For example, an organization might designate a small group within the MIS unit as the "Emerging Technologies" unit and charge them with looking out for new technologies that will have an impact on the business. As part of their job, this group will pore over current technology magazines, participate in Internet discussion forums on technology topics, go to technology conferences and con-

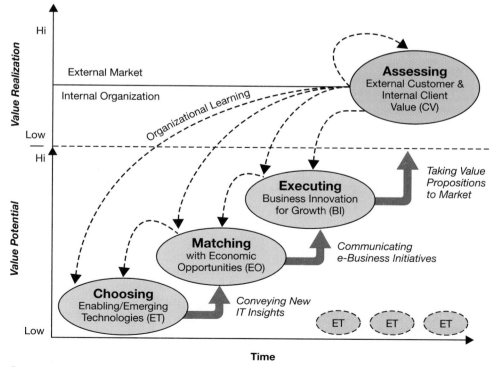

[**Figure 2.19** ➡ The E-Business Innovation Cycle.[4]]

[4]B. C. Wheeler, "The E-Business Innovation Cycle: A Capabilities Theory for Harnessing IT to Create Customer Value," forthcoming in *Information Systems Research*

ventions, and have strong, active relationships with technology researchers at universities and technology companies.

Next, in the second bubble, the organization matches the most promising new technologies with current **economic opportunities**. For example, the Emerging Technologies group might have identified advances in database management systems (and a dramatic drop in data storage costs) as a key emerging technology that now enables a massive data warehouse to be feasible. In addition, managers within the marketing function of the firm have recognized that competitors have really dropped the ball in terms of customer service and that there is an opportunity to gain customers and market share by serving customers better.

The third bubble represents the process of selecting, among myriad opportunities, to take advantage of the database and data storage advances and addressing the current opportunity to grab customers and market share. The organization decides to implement an enterprise-wide data warehouse that enables them to have at their fingertips integrated corporate-wide data and an unparalleled capability to understand, react to, and better serve customers. The fourth bubble represents the process of assessing the value of that use of technology not only to customers but to internal clients (i.e., sales representatives, marketing managers, the COO, etc.) as well.

So, what is new about this way of thinking about information technology? First, this approach says that technology is so important to strategy and to success that you have to begin with technology. Notice that the first bubble involves understanding, identifying, and choosing technologies that are important. The first bubble does not begin with strategy, as a traditional approach to running a business organization would suggest. In fact, many would argue that given the importance of technology today and how fast it changes, if you start with a strategy and then try to retrofit technology into your aging strategy, then you are doomed. This approach argues that you begin by understanding technology and develop a strategy from there. This approach is admittedly very uncomfortable for people who think in traditional ways and/or who are not comfortable with technology. We believe, however, that for many modern organizations, thinking about technology in this way is key.

The second way that this approach turns conventional wisdom on its head is that, like strategy, marketing takes a back seat to the technology. Think about it carefully and you will see that marketing does not come in to play until later in this model. A very traditional marketing-oriented approach would be to go first to your customers and find out from them what their needs are and what you ought to be doing with technology. The trouble with this approach is that, given the rapid evolution of technology, your customers are not likely to know about new technologies and their capabilities. In some sense, they are the last place you ought to be looking for ideas about new technologies and their impact on your business. Indeed, if they know about the new technology, then chances are your competitors already do too, and that technology is not one to rest your competitive advantage on.

The third way that this approach is interesting, and potentially troubling, is that the process has to be ongoing. As shown along the time dimension along the bottom of the graph, the first bubble repeats over and over again as the "emerging technologies" group is constantly on the lookout for the "next new thing" that will revolutionize the business. The rate of information technology evolution is not likely to slow down, and innovative organizations truly cannot, and do not, ever rest.

The Cutting Edge Versus the Bleeding Edge

As we hinted at above, there are limits to using emerging information systems to gain or sustain a competitive advantage. Information systems are often bought from, or built by, someone else. They are often either purchased from a vendor or developed by a consultant or outsourcing partner. In these situations, the information systems are usually not proprietary technologies owned by the organization. For example, although a soft drink company can patent the formula of a cola, or a pharmaceutical company can patent a new drug, an organization typically cannot patent its use of an information system, particularly if someone else developed it. The data in the system may be proprietary, but the information system typically is not.

Even in situations where an organization has developed an information system in-house, they usually do so with hardware, software, and networking components others can purchase. In short, rivals can copy emerging information systems, so this form of competitive advantage can be short-lived. Indeed, if use of the new system causes one organization to gain a significant advantage over others, smart rivals are quick to duplicate or improve on that use of the system.

Using emerging information systems always entails a risk. The classic example from consumer electronics is the choice of a VCR in the early days of that technology and the competing Betamax and VHS designs (see Figure 2.20). Most experts agreed that the Betamax had superior recording and playback quality, but VHS ultimately won the battle in the marketplace. People who made the "smart" choice at the time probably would have chosen a VCR with the Betamax design. Ultimately, however, that turned out to be an unfortunate choice. Other examples in the field of consumer electronics abound today. For example, when buying a stereo today, should you invest in traditional compact disc technology (such as the read-only CD-ROM), recordable compact discs, digital audiotape, an MP3 device, or some other technology? Many people have been stuck with huge collections of vinyl records, cassette tapes, or (gulp!) 8-track tapes. It is easy to make poor choices in consumer electronics, or to make choices that are good at the time but soon turn out to be poor choices.

Choosing among emerging information systems is just as difficult as choosing consumer electronics. In fact, choosing emerging systems may be far more difficult, given that the evolution of many consumer electronic technologies has stabilized, whereas the evolution of emerging information systems is just beginning to heat up. Furthermore, it is far more devastating to choose a poor information system due to the size of the investment and the mission-critical nature of the system. On the other hand, choosing a suboptimal home stereo, although disappointing, is usually not devastating.

Choosing new technologies in the information systems area is like trying to hit one of several, equally attractive, fast-moving targets. You can find examples of the difficulty of forecasting emerging technologies in the experiences that many organizations have had in forecasting the growth, use, and importance of the Internet. The 1994 Technology Forecast prepared by the major consulting firm, Price Waterhouse, mentioned the word "Internet" on only five pages of the 750-page document. The next year over 75 pages addressed the Internet. In the 1997 briefing, the Internet is a pervasive topic throughout. Back in 1994 it would have been difficult, perhaps even foolish, to forecast such pervasive, rapidly growing business use of the Internet today. Table 2.5 illustrates how many people and organizations have had difficulty making technology-related predictions.

Given the pace of research and development in the information systems and components area, staying current has been nearly impossible. Probably one of the most famous metrics of computer evolution has been "Moore's Law." Intel founder Gordon Moore predicted that the number of transistors that could be squeezed onto a silicon chip would double every 18 months, and this prediction has proven itself over the past 20 years. In fact, some computer hardware and software firms roll out new versions of their products every three months. Keeping up with this pace of change can be difficult for any organization.

Requirements for Being at the Cutting Edge

Certain types of competitive environments require that organizations remain at the cutting edge in their use of information systems. For example, consider an organization that operates within an environment with strong competitive forces (Porter, 1979). The organization has competitive pressures coming from existing rival firms or from the threat of entry of new rivals. It is critical for these organizations to do things better, faster, and more cheaply than rivals. These organizations are driven to deploy emerging information systems.

These environmental characteristics alone, however, are not enough to determine whether an organization should deploy emerging information systems. Before an organization can deploy new systems well, its people, structure, and processes must be capable of adapting well to change. An organization that has, say, a 10-month approval process for new information systems will probably have difficulty keeping up in an environment that forces organizations to decide on and deploy emerging information systems within a matter of weeks.

[**Figure 2.20** ➡ Betamax tapes were shaped differently and required different technology inside the VCR than did VHS tapes.]

©Getty Images, Inc.

[Table 2.5] *Some predictions about technology that were not quite correct. [Source: "The Past Imperfect," Time Magazine (July 15, 1996): 54.]*

Year	Source	Quote
1876	Western Union, internal memo	"This 'telephone' has too many shortcomings to be seriously considered as a means of communication. The device is inherently of no value to us."
1895	Lord Kelvin, president, Royal Society	"Heavier-than-air flying machines are impossible."
1899	C. H. Duell, commissioner, U.S. Office of Patents	"Everything that can be invented has been invented."
1927	H. M. Warner, Warner Brothers	"Who the hell wants to hear actors talk?"
1943	Thomas Watson, chairman, IBM	"I think there is a world market for maybe five computers."
1977	Ken Olsen, president, Digital Equipment Corporation	"There is no reason for any individuals to have a computer in their home."

To deploy emerging systems well, people in the organization must be willing to do whatever they can to bypass and eliminate internal bureaucracy, set aside political squabbles, and pull together for the common good. Can you imagine, for example, a firm trying to deploy a Web-based order entry system that enables customers to access inventory information directly, when people in that firm do not even share such information with each other?

Organizations deploying emerging systems must also have the human capital necessary to deploy the new systems. The organization must have enough employees available with the proper systems knowledge, skills, time, and other resources to deploy these systems. Alternatively, the organization must have resources and able systems partners available to outsource the development of such systems.

The last characteristic of an organization ready for the deployment of emerging systems is that its members must have the appropriate tolerance of risk, uncertainty, and problems to be willing to deploy and use emerging information systems that may not be as proven and pervasive as more traditional technologies. If people within the organization desire low risk in their use of information systems, then gambling on cutting-edge systems will probably not be desirable or tolerable for them.

Predicting the New, New Thing

As you can see, using information systems toward a strategic end will be difficult to sustain. As Bakos and Treacy (1986) and others have argued, if you are using information systems to gain a competitive advantage in the area of operating efficiencies, it is likely that your rivals can just as easily adopt the same types of information systems and achieve the same gains. For example, you might set up a Web site that enables customers to check on the status of their order without requiring help from a customer service representative, and this might enable you to cut costs. Rivals could, however, easily copy this approach and match your cost reductions. The competitive advantage thus turns into strategic necessity for anyone in this industry.

On the other hand, there are ways to use information systems to gain a competitive advantage in a way that is easier to sustain. For example, Bakos and Treacy argued that if you can use information systems to make your products or services unique or to cause your customers to invest heavily in you so that their switching costs are high, then you are better able to develop competitive advantage that is sustainable over the long haul. For example, you might combine heavy investments in computer-aided design systems with very bright engineers in order to perfect your product and make it unique, something relatively difficult to copy. Alternatively, you might use a Customer Relationship Management system to build an extensive database containing the entire history of your interaction with each of your customers, and then use that system to provide very high-quality, intimate, rapid, customized service that would convince customers that if they switched to a rival it would take them years to build up that kind of relationship with the other firm.

How can you possibly predict the next wave of emerging information systems? Well, you have help. Michael Lewis wrote the best-selling, *The New, New Thing: A Silicon Valley Story* (W.W. Norton & Company, 2000), which tells the story of Jim Clark, a noted high-tech entrepreneur who is famous for the unprecedented business "hat trick" of creating three, separate billion-dollar technology companies—Silicon Graphics, Netscape, and Healtheon. As a result, Jim Clark is known as someone who is very good at knowing what the next, new, major information technology breakthrough will be. Most of us do not have that same level of business or technology acumen. Fortunately, there are Jim Clark and others like him to whom we can look and from whom we can take our cues.

In any event, while using information systems for competitive advantage has become a given for modern organizations, it can be difficult to achieve and sustain, and it can be expensive. Go forth and conquer, but do so with your eyes wide open!

KEY POINTS REVIEW

1. **Discuss how information systems can be used for automation, organizational learning, and strategic support of organizations.** Automating business activities occurs when information systems are used to do a business activity faster or more cheaply. IS can be used to help automate. It can also be used to improve aspects of an operation in order to gain dramatic improvements in the operation as a whole. When this occurs, technology is said to help us learn because it provides information about its operation and the underlying work process that it supports. Using information systems strategically occurs when the technology is used to enable organizational strategy and to help the firm gain or sustain competitive advantage over rivals

2. **Describe information systems' critical, strategic importance to the success of modern organizations.** Using information systems to automate and learn about business processes is a good start. However, information systems can add even more value to an organization if they are conceived, designed, used, and managed with a strategic approach. To apply information systems strategically, you must understand the organization's value chain and be able to identify opportunities in which you can use information systems to make changes or improvements in the value chain to gain or sustain a competitive advantage. This requires a change in mindset from thinking about information systems as an expense to be minimized to thinking of information systems as an asset to be invested in.

3. **Explain how you formulate and present the business case for a system and why it is sometimes difficult to do so.** Making the business case is the process of building and presenting the set of arguments that show that an information system is adding value to the organization and/or its constituents. It is often difficult to quantify the value that an information system provides. To formulate a business case for an information system, you must understand the nature of the industry—its stage of maturity, its regulation, and the nature of its competition or rivalry. You must also understand the particular business strategy of your organization in order to make an effective business case for systems. In short, technology investments should be closely linked to the business strategy of the organization because these investments are becoming one of the major vehicles by which organizations can achieve their strategy. After you gain an understanding of your organization's position in the marketplace, its strategy for investing in systems that add value, and firm-level implementation factors, you can quantify the relative costs and benefits of the system. Considering all of these factors simultaneously will help you formulate an effective business case. In order to make a convincing presentation, you should be specific about the benefits this investment will provide for the organization. To do this, you must convert the benefits into monetary terms, such as the amount of money saved or revenue generated. If you have difficulty identifying specific monetary measures, you should devise some proxy measures to demonstrate the benefits of the system. Alternatively, you could develop a work profile matrix to help build the business case for a system. Finally, make sure that you measure things that are important to the decision makers of the organizations. Choosing the wrong measures can yield a negative decision about a beneficial system.

4. **Explain why and how companies are continually looking for new ways to use technology for competitive advantage.** Organizations are finding clever ways to use new technologies to help them do things faster, better, and more cheaply than rivals. Being at the technological cutting edge has its disadvantages. Given that new technologies are not as stable as traditional ones, relying on emerging systems can be problematic. Because constantly upgrading to newer and better systems is expensive, relying on emerging systems can hurt a firm financially. In addition, using emerging information systems for competitive advantage can be short-lived; competitors can quickly jump on the technological bandwagon and easily mimic the same system. As a result, many organizations find themselves on the technological bleeding edge rather than the cutting edge. Not every organization should deploy emerging information systems. Those organizations that find themselves in highly competitive environments are probably most in need of deploying new technologies to stay ahead of rivals. To best deploy these new technologies, organizations must be ready for the changes that will ensue, have the resources necessary to deploy new technologies successfully, and be tolerant of the risk and problems involved in being at the cutting edge. Deploying emerging information systems is essentially a risk/return gamble: The risks are relatively high, but the potential rewards are great. Firms today have people, and in some cases special units, that scan the environment, looking out for emerging and enabling technologies that can help their firm. They then narrow down the list to technologies that match with or create economic opportunities the firm faces. Next, they choose a particular technology, or set of technologies, and implement them in a way that enables them to gain or sustain competitive advantage. Finally, they assess these technology projects in terms of their value not only to internal people and groups but externally to clients and partners. This process is ongoing, as information technologies and systems continually evolve.

KEY TERMS

automating 34

business process reengineering 43

competitive advantage 33

computer-aided design 43

e-business 59

E-Business Innovation Cycle 59

economic opportunities 60

enabling technologies 59

Extranet 42

informating 36

intangible benefits 51

intangible costs 51

learning organization 36

making the business case 43

nonrecurring costs 51

organizational learning 36

organizational strategy 38

proxy variables 55

recurring costs 51

strategic planning 38

system effectiveness 45

system efficiency 45

tangible benefits 51

tangible costs 51

total quality management 37

value chain 41

value chain analysis 41

work profile matrix 55

REVIEW QUESTIONS

1. Describe competitive advantage and list six sources.
2. Compare and contrast automating and learning.
3. Describe the attributes of a learning organization.
4. List five general types of organizational strategy.
5. What are some of the problems in measuring productivity changes?
6. What categories are typically used in a work profile matrix?

7. List the three factors you should consider when making the business case for an information system.
8. Who comprises a steering committee, and what is the purpose of the committee?
9. Define a proxy variable and give an example.
10. Describe the productivity paradox.
11. Compare and contrast tangible and intangible benefits and costs.

Answers are at the end of the Problems and Exercises.

SELF-STUDY QUESTIONS

1. _____ is using technology as a way to help complete a task within an organization faster and, perhaps, more cheaply.

   A. Automating
   B. Learning
   C. Strategizing
   D. Processing

2. Which of the following is an intangible benefit?

   A. negative benefits
   B. qualitative benefits
   C. quantitative costs
   D. positive cash flows

3. Which of the following is **not** improving the value chain?

   A. improving procurement processes
   B. increasing operating costs
   C. minimizing marketing expenditures
   D. selling more products

4. Which of the following is **not** one of the three types of arguments commonly made in the business case for an information system?

   A. Fear
   B. Fact
   C. Faith
   D. Fun

5. A company is said to have _____ when it has gained an edge over its rivals.

   A. monopoly
   B. profitability
   C. competitive advantage
   D. computer advantage

6. The IS manager has the overall responsibility for the _____ of the information systems.

   A. management, development, implementation, and maintenance
   B. development, implementation, and maintenance
   C. management, development, and maintenance
   D. management, development, and implementation

7. Many firms now use the Internet for business-to-business interactions, and these systems are called _____ .

   A. Internets
   B. Extranets
   C. Intranets
   D. Infonets

8. A _____ consists of job and work categories, along with how time is spent in each of those categories.

   A. budget
   B. work budget
   C. work profile matrix
   D. professional matrix

9. Making the _____ is the process of building and presenting the set of arguments that show that an information system is adding value to the organization.

   A. organizational chart
   B. organizational case
   C. law case
   D. business case

10. Besides business industry and strategic factors, other implementation-related factors must be considered when making the business case for systems, including the type of _____ .

A. organization
B. culture
C. political environment
D. all of the above

PROBLEMS AND EXERCISES

1. Match the following terms with the appropriate definitions:

   _____ Value chain analysis

   _____ Tangible costs

   _____ Extranet

   _____ Competitive advantage

   _____ Business case

   _____ Learning organization

   _____ Total quality management

   _____ Value chain

   _____ Work profile matrix

   _____ Proxy variable

   a. An approach in which people within an organization are constantly monitoring what they do to find ways to improve quality of operations, products, services, and everything else about the firm
   b. Costs that are quantifiable or have physical substance
   c. The set of arguments that illustrate that an information system is adding value to the organization and/or its constituents
   d. The use of the Internet by firms for business-to-business interactions
   e. A substitute variable (such as customer contact) expressed on a five-point scale from low to high that is used in place of an information system's intangible benefit, which is difficult to quantify
   f. The edge a firm has over its rivals
   g. An organization that is able to learn, grow, and manage its knowledge well
   h. A matrix consisting of job and work categories that is used to show how much time is spent by each of the job categories on different types of work
   i. Identification of opportunities to use information systems for competitive advantage
   j. The process of adding value to products/services throughout the organization

2. After reading this chapter, it should be fairly obvious why an IS professional should be able to make a business case for a given system. Why, however, is it just as important for non-IS professionals? How are they involved in this process? What is their role in information systems planning?

3. Search the World Wide Web for items related to end-user development. What information did you find? Why is end-user development difficult to track in terms of productivity? What are some of the measurement problems associated with end-user development? How can these problems be eliminated? Prepare a 10-minute presentation to the rest of the class of your group's findings.

4. Why is it important to look at industry factors when making a business case? What effect might strong competition have on IS investment and use? What effect might weak competition have on IS investment and use? Why?

5. Argue for or against the following statement: "When making the business case, you should concentrate on the 'hot buttons' of the decision makers and gloss over some of the other details."

6. What role does the organizational culture play in IS investments? Is this something that can be easily adjusted when necessary? Why or why not? Who is in control of a firm's organizational culture? Do you have personal experiences with this issue?

7. Why can it be difficult to develop an accurate cost-benefit analysis? What factors may be difficult to quantify? How can this be handled? Is this something that should just be avoided altogether? What are the consequences of that approach?

8. Have you ever rented a car over the Web? Research car rentals, including Avis Rent A Car, over the Web, and then telephone the car agency to find the following answers. What types of vehicles are available for what price and for how long? Is there a minimum age required to rent a vehicle? Is insurance a consideration? Is it difficult to rent a car in a particular area of the United States or it is easy? How do you make a car reservation?

9. Within a small group of classmates, describe any involvement you have had with making the business case for a system. To whom were you making the case? Was it a difficult sell? Why? Did you follow the guidelines set forth in this chapter? How did your business case differ from those of others in your group? Were you successful? Why or why not? Were they successful? Why or why not?

10. Consider an organization that is familiar to you or one of the Brief Cases in this chapter or in another chapter. Of the five industry factors presented in the chapter (Porter's model), which is the most significant for this organization in terms of IS investment and development? Why? Which is the least significant? Why?

11. Discuss the following in a small group of classmates or with a friend. Describe a situation from your own experience in which a system's cost-benefit analysis showed a negative result when based on tangible factors but the system was still implemented. Was the implementation decision based on intangible factors? Have these intangible factors proven themselves to be worth the investment in this system? Was it a harder sell because of these intangible factors?

12. Choose one of the Brief Cases in this chapter or another chapter. Determine the length of time it has taken for various information systems to show their productivity improvements. Was it a long time? Why did it take so long? Was it longer than expected? Why or why not? Search the Internet to find additional anecdotes about IS productivity improvements. You may want to search through CIO Magazine Online at **www.cio.com** to get started. How does this information compare with the organization you researched?

13. Why shouldn't every organization deploy cutting-edge emerging information systems? What are some of the recommended characteristics of an organization that are necessary in order for that organization to successfully deploy emerging information systems?

ANSWERS TO THE SELF-STUDY QUESTIONS

1. A   2. B   3. B   4. D   5. C   6. A   7. B   8. C   9. D   10. D

CASE 1:   *Using IS for Efficiency, Effectiveness, and Competitive Advantage*

No one can imagine a successful business organization of today not using information systems. IS is being seen as the driving force for most companies, and the primary means through which strategic advantage can be gained or sustained. Teradyne Inc. is a manufacturing company that specializes in building equipment that tests computer chips. In its zealousness to stay ahead of its competitors, the company has focused on the use of IS to lower its costs and increase its efficiency. Recently, the company installed a new virtual private network (VPN) that allows its employees to log in through its firewall, irrespective of their location in the world, by entering six digits from small palm tokens that they carry with them. These tokens generate certain random numbers, which are matched with another set of numbers generated by a computer located behind the company's firewall. Once the numbers match, Teradyne employees from any part of the world can log into the system and perform a variety of functions, such as conducting performance evaluations with their supervisors, who may be located in another city or country, or modifying their benefit packages. The company also installed some new software that enables it to service the equipment of its customers by remotely logging into the customer's server and conducting repairs.

Staples, Inc. has also focused on using information systems to enhance its customer service. New software now enables Staples' customer service representatives to chat directly with shoppers using an online chat tool. The company is also installing kiosks in each of its stores, which will enable customers to go directly to the Staples Web site and browse through its large inventory if they cannot find a certain product in store.

L.L. Bean, on the other hand, is focusing on using IS for increasing its Internet sales. It has recently acquired software to track who visits its site and which banners or links on its site are most commonly clicked on. The ultimate goal of L.L. Bean is to transform the "clicks to sales."

Kompass has shown that in addition to adopting a new information system, you also have to undergo other corresponding changes within the firm as well. Kompass is a mid-sized company in Ireland whose primary business is to provide a directory of Irish businesses. Its primary purpose is to link buyers and sellers. Kompass links buyers accurately to the products of their choice and helps sellers to target their potential clients. Initially, the company published its directory on paper, but with the advent of new technology, it now offers a fully developed search engine over the Web. In the late 1990s, the company realized that the Web technology may provide it with the opportunity to deliver its directory of Irish businesses to a global market. Unlike many other companies, Kompass realized that in order to adopt this new technology, the company would have to go through significant remodeling and repositioning. At first, the company conducted a detailed evaluation of the strategic opportunities that the Internet provided. The firm's business model, along with its position, staffing, and so on, were also evaluated. The evaluation revealed that the adoption of the new technology would help the company to position itself in a new marketplace (the digital marketplace) and would help it to increase its market share. The company executives also realized through their detailed surveys that in order to succeed, the company would have to align its new use of the Internet with the existing business strategy and structure. The alignment of this new technology took place at three levels.

At the first level, the firm aligned its Internet strategy with its business strategy. The firm decided that the Internet would become core to its business and would help it to enhance its relationship with its customers and deliver better options to them. At the second level, the firm aligned the new technology with its existing marketing approach. The firm's executives realized that in order to gain from this new technology, the Internet could not be treated just as a delivery channel, but it had to form the foundation of the organization's products. As a result, they made attempts to make the Internet central to the product development process. Finally, the firm also aligned the new technology with its human resource management processes. They decided that new human resources, specialized training, tools, and technical skills would be required to make this new venture a success. Thus, they formed a new division called Kompass Internet, whose primary responsibility was to oversee all aspects of this new business of the company.

While many other companies have attempted to use information systems to experience quick gains, such as lowered costs or increased market share, Kompass has focused on integrating the new technology into its existing business processes in order to gain long-term benefits. This is probably why today Kompass' Internet strategy is seen as one of the success stories of the business use of the Internet.

[Adapted from E. Medina, "N.E. Companies Focus on Creative Use of Technology: It's Vital to Boost Efficiency, Competitive Edge," *Boston Globe* (June 11, 2001): C2; C. O'Kelley, "Electronic Commerce: A Case Study in Competitive Advantage," *Accountancy Ireland* 31 no. 4 (August 1999): 39–40; **www.kompass.ie**]

Discussion Questions

1. Do you think that the companies mentioned in the first part of the case (Teradyne, Staples, etc.) will experience significant gains from their implementation of the new information technologies?
2. What did Kompass do differently that made the adoption of the Internet technology a success in their organization?
3. In order to gain strategically, what should an organization focus on while implementing a new information technology?

CASE 2: *Managing Change at STS Training Inc.*

STS Training Inc. is a training company located in the northwest region of the United States. The company was founded in the early 1980s. During the initial years, the company focused on providing various kinds of vocational training. They handed out certificates at the end of each of the training courses. At that time the company primarily had individual clients who were interested in furthering their careers or making changes in their current jobs through the use of these training classes. With the growth of computers and the need for computer training, STS Training Inc. realized that there was an opportunity in the area of computer training. From vocational training classes, the company slowly moved toward training on various computer applications, architectures, and networks. Along with individual clients, STS also signed annual contracts with many large companies for providing computer training to their employees and staff. At the same time STS still retained its entire range of vocational training classes, which still continued to bring in the majority of its revenue. A small number of staff taught the computer application classes. They were the primary users of computers within the organization, and most of them used it only in the classrooms. STS handled this change to computer training by hiring a new IS manager. The role of the IS manager was to provide technical and networking support to the staff members who taught computer application classes.

In recent years, the company has gone through another major change. In order to attract clients not located in the same city, the company has recently introduced online delivery, where communication and delivery often occur over the Internet. The online delivery method is not only being used by staff members who teach computer applications, but by others as well. This has led to a significant increase in the number of computers being used in the organization. The IS manager is often responsible for more than 1,500 computers that are networked and linked to the Internet. Adding to this complexity is the fact that the administrative use of computers has also significantly increased within the organization. A centralized management information system focusing on student and staff management has recently been installed within the organization. There is an increase in the diversity of software being used in the organization, and the traditional IS support department has fallen short of catering to the needs of every employee and student within the organization.

Realizing that in order to avoid chaos and breakdown within the company, drastic measures needed to be taken to manage this change, STS took some careful change management steps. The company initially conducted strategic planning to understand the organization's need for IS and other resources. The IS manager was closely involved in this process, and her foresight and knowledge regarding the changing computer environment proved valuable in making forward predictions regarding the organization's computer and other IS needs. Once the company conducted the strategic planning session and ascertained the IS needs of the organization, it established a formal asset management and support system. The goal was to provide more timely and reliable help to the ever-increasing and diverse group of users. The company hired additional support staff in the computer service department, and installed new information systems to handle the increasing volume of users. The company realized that there was a need to have open communication between the IS department and other staff members. Many of the staff members providing online delivery were not computer literate and, thus, needed extra support and patience from the computer support personnel. STS felt that the responsibility of improving and changing the communication pattern between the computer service department and the staff members should be on the IS manager. STS also felt that the IS manager should take on the additional responsibility of being involved in continuous strategic planning and staff management, along with collaborating with managers from other departments. However, the current IS manager was keen on continuing to focus on just the technical issues and was reluctant to take on any additional duties. Realizing that the IS manager would play a critical role in managing the current change within the organization, the company decided to replace the existing IS manager.

The organization also took a series of other measures at the same time. STS put specific emphasis on accurately evaluating the changing requirements of the staff members who taught online courses. This helped them not only to understand the software requirements, but also to gain an understanding regarding the functional requirements of online delivery. The new IS manager helped initiate a new form of dialogue between the teaching staff and the IS staff. The organization also encouraged the IS staff to interact more closely with the students and their computing needs, and to help them regarding their technological requirements. Finally, the organization implemented a new training program for all staff members of STS Training Inc., especially those that regularly accessed the computer networks or were involved with online delivery. The IS manager took on the responsibility of specifying the level of training required by the various staff managers.

Overall, STS Training Inc. spent a significant amount of resources and planning on managing the changes that the company was facing due to the changes in the number and the diversity of computers and software being used in the organization, along with the way they were being used.

[Adapted from "A Scenario for Change: The Impact of Online Delivery on IT Managers in VET," **www.tafe.sa.edu.au/lsrsc/one/natproj /cm/itman.htm**]

Discussion Questions

1. What were the technological and other changes facing STS Training Inc.? What role did/should strategy play in this case?
2. Do you think that the measures taken by the organization will ultimately help it successfully manage change?
3. The company visualized a new set of roles and responsibilities for its IS manager. What, in your opinion, should be the ideal role of an IS manager, especially in the context of change management?

Database Management

Chapter 3

OPENING: Using a Customer Database to Keep the Hard Rock Cafe Rockin'!

With more than 100 locations around the world, the Hard Rock Cafe is one of the most easily recognized restaurants in the world (see Figure 3.1). Known for its laid-back atmosphere and American cuisine, not to mention its rock and roll music and memorabilia, the Hard Rock offers a very special experience for its customers. With more than 60,000 pieces of rock and roll memorabilia, a collection that is rotated from restaurant to restaurant, the Hard Rock provides the world's most comprehensive visual history of rock and roll. The collection includes guitars and instruments, posters, costumes, music and lyric sheets, gold and platinum LPs, and photos.

With millions of customers per year, the HRC did not really know much about its customers. To rectify this, the company recently installed a customer-tracking database in order to understand how often customers visited, what they purchased, and how they felt about their dining experience. With the help of this system, the Hard Rock Cafe can keep in close contact with its 5,500 most loyal customers, called Pin Collectors, in order to keep their best customers coming back. Pin Collectors receive preferred seating and a 10 percent discount on all purchases. The company also tracks less-frequent visitors, called All Access Members, and provides them with discounts for dining and merchandise purchases. Using the tracking system that is also linked to the company's Web site, the company can send e-mail messages to all preferred customers to inform them of upcoming events such as a live musical performance at a local Cafe or the availability of new merchandise. One recent e-mail campaign netted more than $150,000 in merchandise sales.

Keeping track of its loyal customers had been impossible prior to acquiring the customer database system. Executives report that the system had a nine-month payback and believe that the system will be the key to improved revenue and heightened customer loyalty. Database technology is the foundation for most information systems, from tracking customers to keeping track of student grades at your university. More than any single information systems technology, the database is truly the heart of most systems.

[Adapted from **www.hardrock.com**; E. Colkin, "Hard Rock Finds More Ways to Keep Customers Happy," **www.informationweek.com** (December 24, 2001).]

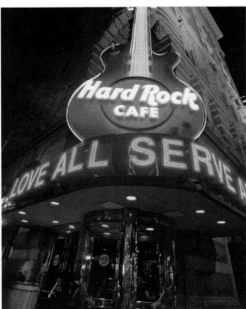

[**Figure 3.1** ➡ The Hard Rock Cafe is using database technology to keep track of its best customers.]

© CORBIS

In the last chapter, you learned how organizations are using information systems for competitive advantage. In this chapter, we will discuss how a very important category of information system, databases and database management systems, allow organizations to store and manipulate their key information easily.

People in organizations rely on information about customers, products, invoices, suppliers, markets, transactions, and competitors. In large organizations, this information is stored in databases that can be billions (giga-) or trillions (tera-) of bytes in size. If an organization lost this data, it would have difficulty pricing and selling its products or services, cutting payroll checks for its employees, and even sending out mail. After reading this chapter, you will be able to do the following:

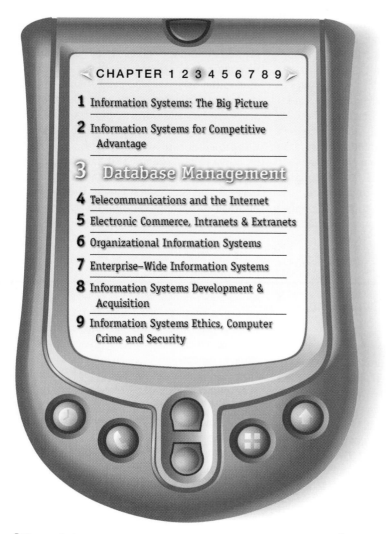

1. Describe why databases have become so important to modern organizations.

2. Describe what databases and database management systems are and how they work.

3. Explain how organizations are getting the most from their investment in database technologies.

[Figure 3.2 ➡ The Big Picture: focusing on database management.]

In terms of our guiding framework—The Big Picture—this chapter focuses on one of the essential elements of "information" systems (see Figure 3.2). We begin by discussing the importance of database technology for the success of organizations. The chapter continues by describing the key activities involved in designing and using modern databases. We conclude by examining how organizations are utilizing this stored information for competitive advantage.

DATABASE MANAGEMENT FOR STRATEGIC ADVANTAGE

Database technology, a collection of related data organized in a way to facilitate data searches, is vital to an organization's success. Increasingly, we are living in an information age. Information once taken for granted or never collected at all is now used to make organizations more productive and competitive. Stock prices in the market, potential customers who meet a company's criteria for its products' target audience, and the credit rating of wholesalers and customers are all types of information. Think about this book you are reading, which is in itself information. The publisher had to know available authors capable of writing this book. The publisher also had to have information on you, the target audience, in order to determine that writing this book was worthwhile and to suggest a writing style and collection of topics. The publisher had to use market information to set a price for the book, along with information on reliable wholesalers and distribution partners to get the books from the publisher to you, the consumer.

In addition to using databases to create this book, the publisher also uses databases to keep track of the book's sales, to determine royalties for the authors, to set salaries and wages for employees, to pay employees, to prospect for new book opportunities, to pay bills, and to perform nearly every other function in the business. For example, to determine royalties for authors on books sold, the publisher must collect information from hundreds of bookstores and consolidate it into a single report. Large publishers, such as Prentice Hall/Pearson Education, rely on computer databases to perform these tasks.

Other organizations also make use of the database process used to create and sell this book. For example, Lands' End uses databases to design and produce its clothing catalog and market and sell products. Companies such as Lands' End also use databases to gather and store information about customers and their purchasing behavior. Companies such as Nordstrom and Eddie Bauer even produce tailor-made catalogs and other mailings for specific individuals based on the purchasing information stored in corporate databases.

Given these examples, it should be no surprise that database management systems have become an integral part of the total information systems solution for many organizations. Database management systems

---

Brief Case: Fast, Easy, and Cheap Textbook Buying

One of the big headaches of being a college student is buying textbooks. The drudgery of standing in line, paying high prices, and then lugging the books home is probably a vivid memory. With the advent of the Web, you now have options other than your local campus bookstore. One site in particular, **ecampus.com**, is focusing on making the life of college students a little easier. The largest college and university textbook store in the world, **ecampus.com** has more than 3,000,000 items for sale, including all books in print (both new and used), clothing with school insignias for both men and women, electronic gadgets, and various school supplies. Like your local bookstore, **ecampus.com** also has a buyback program for your old textbooks. In short, **ecampus.com** is attempting to provide all the services you have come to expect from your campus bookstore … well, less the latte bar. At the heart of **ecampus.com** is a massive database that keeps track of all the inventory and customer orders. In fact, without database technology, it would be impossible for sites like **ecampus.com** to exist; database technology is needed to organize the vast amounts of information about products as well as to keep customers and their orders straight.

[Adapted from **www.oracle.com/**]

allow organizations to retrieve, store, and analyze information easily. Next we examine some basic concepts, advantages of the database approach, and how databases are managed.

The Database Approach: Foundation Concepts

The database approach now dominates nearly all of the computer-based information systems used today. To understand databases, we must familiarize ourselves with some terminology.

In Figure 3.3, we compare database terminology (middle column) with equivalents in a library (left column) and a business office (right column). We use **database management systems (DBMSs)** to interact with the data in databases. A DBMS is a software application with which you create, store, organize, and retrieve data from a single database or several databases. Microsoft Access is an example of a popular DBMS for personal computers. In the DBMS, the individual database is a collection of related attributes about entities. An **entity** is something you collect data about, such as people or classes (see Figure 3.4). We often think of entities as **tables**, where each row is a **record** and each column is an **attribute** (also referred to as field). A record is a collection of related attributes

about a single entity. Each record typically consists of many attributes, which are individual pieces of information. For example, a name and social security number are attributes about a person.

Advantages of the Database Approach

Before there were DBMSs, organizations used the file processing approach to store and manipulate data electronically. Data were usually kept in a long, sequential computer file, which was often stored on tape. Information about entities often appeared in several different places throughout the information system, and the data was often stored along with, and sometimes embedded within, the programming code that used the data. People had not yet envisioned the concept of separately storing information about entities in nonredundant databases, so files often had repetitive data about a customer, supplier, or another entity. When someone's address changed, it had to be changed in every file where that information occurred, an often tedious process. Similarly, if programmers changed the code, they typically had to change the corresponding data along with it. This was often no better than the pen-and-paper approach to storing data.

[**Figure 3.3** ➡ Computers make the process of storing and managing data much easier.]

Attribute
Types

ID Number	Last Name	First Name	Street Address	City	State	Zip code	Major
209345	Vance	James	1242 N. Maple	Bloomington	Indiana	47401	Recreation
213009	Haggarty	Joe	3400 E. Longvi	Bloomington	Indiana	47405	Business Management
345987	Borden	Chris	367 Ridge Roa	Bloomington	Indiana	47405	Aeronautical Engineering
457838	Jessup	Mike	12 Long Lake	Bloomington	Indiana	47401	Computer Science
459987	Chan	Virginia	8009 Walnut	Bloomington	Indiana	47405	Sociology
466711	Monroe	Lisa	234 Jamie Lan	Bloomington	Indiana	47401	Pre-Medicine
512678	Austin	John	3837 Wood's E	Bloomington	Indiana	47401	Law
691112	Sherwin	Jordan	988 Woodbridg	Bloomington	Indiana	47404	Political Science
910234	Moore	Larry	1234 S. Grant	Bloomington	Indiana	47403	Civil Engineering
979776	Dunn	Pat	109 Hoosier Av	Bloomington	Indiana	47404	Psychology
983445	Pickett	Steve	989 College	Bloomington	Indiana	47401	Sports Science

Attribute

Record
(One Row)

[**Figure 3.4** ➥ This sample data table for the entity Student includes eight attributes and 11 records.]

It is possible for a database to consist of only a single file or table. However, most databases managed under a DBMS consist of several files, tables, or entities. A DBMS can manage hundreds, or even thousands, of tables simultaneously by linking the tables as part of a single system. The DBMS helps us manage the tremendous volume and complexity of interrelated data so that we can be sure that a change is automatically made for every instance of that data. For example, if a student or customer address is changed, that change is made through all parts of the system where that data might occur. Using the DBMS pre-

[Table 3.1] *Advantages of the database approach.*

Advantages	Description
Program–data independence	Much easier to evolve and alter software to changing business needs when data and programs are independent.
Minimal data redundancy	Single copy of data assures that data storage is minimized.
Improved data consistency	Eliminating redundancy greatly reduces the opportunities for inconsistency.
Improved data sharing	Easier to deploy and control data access using a centralized system.
Increased productivity of application development	Data standards make it easier to build and modify applications.
Enforcement of standards	A centralized system makes it much easier to enforce standards and rules for data creation, modification, naming, and deletion.
Improved data quality	Centralized control, minimized redundancy, and improved data consistency help to enhance the quality of data.
Improved data accessibility	Centralized system makes it easier to provide access for new personnel within or outside organizational boundaries.
Reduced program maintenance	Information changed in the central database is replicated seamlessly throughout all applications.

vents unnecessary and problematic redundancies of the data, and the data are kept separate from the programming code in applications. The database need not be changed if a change is made to the code in any of the applications. Consequently, there are numerous advantages to using a database approach to managing organizational data, and these are summarized in Table 3.1. Of course, moving to the database approach comes with some costs and risks that must be recognized and managed (see Table 3.2). Nonetheless, most organizations have embraced the database approach because most feel that the advantages far exceed the risks or costs.

Effective Management of Databases

Now that we have outlined why databases are important to organizations, we can talk about how organizational databases can be managed effectively. The **database administrator (DBA)** is responsible for the development and management of the organization's databases. The DBA works with the systems analysts (described in Chapter 8) and programmers to design and implement the database. The DBA must also work with users and managers of the firm to establish policies for managing an organization's databases. The DBA implements security features for the database, such as designating who can look at the database and who is authorized to make changes. The DBA should not make these decisions unilaterally; rather, the DBA merely implements the business decisions made by organizational managers. A good DBA is fundamental to adequately leveraging the investment in database technology.

Cost or Risk	Description
New, specialized personnel	Conversion to the database approach may require hiring additional personnel.
Installation and management cost and complexity	Database approach has higher up-front costs and complexity in order to gain long-term benefits.
Conversion costs	Extensive costs are common when converting existing systems, often referred to as *legacy systems,* to the database approach.
Need for explicit backup and recovery	A shared corporate data resource must be accurate and available at all times.
Organizational conflict	Ownership—creation, naming, modification, and deletion—of data can cause organizational conflict.

[Table 3.2] *Costs and risks of the database approach.*

Database Problems Halt FBI Background Checks

To assure that criminals and convicted felons cannot purchase guns, the FBI maintains a complex database for checking the backgrounds of potential gun buyers. Federal law maintains that the FBI must complete a background check of a potential buyer within three days; if it fails to complete the check within three days, the merchant is free to make the sale. A report published by the General Accounting Office (GAO) in 2000 concluded that more than 2,500 gun sales have been made to criminals because checks were not completed on time. Needless to say, this database must be working at all times because, without it, it is impossible for the FBI to process and adequately investigate all pending requests in a timely manner. Unfortunately, the system recently failed for 66 hours. Although the FBI will not confirm the number of pending background checks that may have resulted in gun sales to unqualified buyers, most insiders believe that at least some criminals were able to buy guns during the outage.

[Adapted from C. McGeever, "FBI Database Problem Halts Gun Checks," **www.comptuerworld.com**, *Computerworld* (May 22, 2000).]

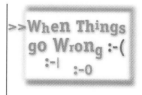
>>When Things go Wrong :-(
:-| :-0

KEY DATABASE ACTIVITIES

In this section, we describe the key activities involved in the design, creation, use, and management of databases (for more information, see Hoffer, Prescott, and McFadden, 2002). We start by describing how people use databases, beginning with the entry of data.

Entering and Querying Data

DBMS software enables end users to create and manage their own database applications. At some point, data must be entered into the database.

A clerk or other data entry professional creates records in the database by entering data. This data may come from telephone conversations, preprinted forms that must be filled out, historical records, or electronic files (see Figure 3.5A). Most applications enable us to use a graphical user interface (GUI) (see Figure 3.5B) to create a **form**, which typically has blanks where the user can enter the information or make choices, each of which represents an attribute within a database record. This form presents the information to the user in an intuitive way so that the user can easily see and enter the data. The form might be online or printed, and the data could even be entered directly by the customer rather than by a data entry clerk. Forms can be used to add, modify, and delete data from the database.

To retrieve information from a database we use a **query**. **Structured Query Language (SQL)** is the most common language used to interface with databases. Figure 3.6 is an example of an SQL statement used to find students who earned an "A" in a particular course. These grades are sorted by student ID number.

Writing SQL statements requires time and practice, especially when you are dealing with complex databases with many entities or when you are writing complex queries with multiple integrated criteria—such as adding numbers while sorting on two different attributes. Many DBMS packages have a simpler way of interfacing with the databases—using a con-

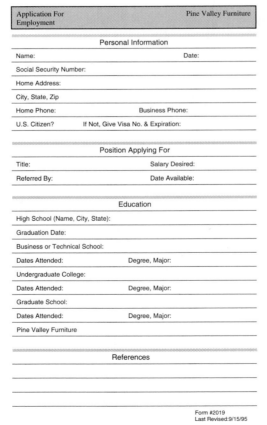

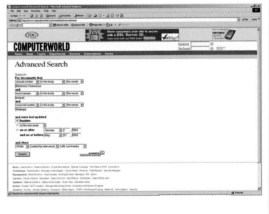

[**Figure 3.5** ➡ A. A preprinted form used for gathering information that could be stored in a database. B. A computer-based form used for gathering information that could be stored in a database.]
Benjamin/Cummings Pub. [3.5A] **www.computerworld.com** [3.5B]

```
SELECT DISTINCTROW STUDENT_ID, GRADE
FROM GRADES
WHERE GRADE="A"
ORDER BY STUDENT_ID;
```

[Figure 3.6 ➡ This sample SQL statement would be used to find students who earned an "A" in a particular course and to sort that information by student ID number.]

cept called *query by example (QBE)*. QBE capabilities in a database enable us to fill out a grid, or template, in order to construct a sample or description of the data we would like to see. Modern DBMS packages, such as Microsoft Access, let us take advantage of the drag-and-drop features of a GUI to create a query quickly and easily. Conducting queries in this manner is much easier than typing the corresponding SQL commands. In Figure 3.7, we provide an example of the QBE grid from Microsoft Access' desktop DBMS package.

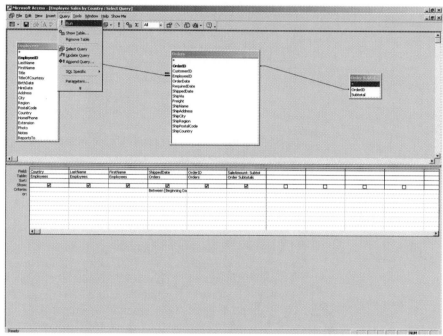

[Figure 3.7 ➡ Query by example allows you to fill out a form to define what information you want to see.] Microsoft

Small businesses often require the use of databases to manage their accounting and financial information. However, due to issues related to cost and lack of skilled personnel, they often shy away from developing and implementing databases in-house, or acquiring them from outside vendors. Now, a new Web database service called QuickBase is making it affordable and possible for small businesses to implement and use databases. This service from software maker Intuit enables small business owners to easily create a database from scratch or from templates provided by the system. It also enables the small businesses to import data from other files or applications. The databases are all hosted on the servers of Intuit, which saves the small businesses the hassle and costs of buying, implementing, and maintaining the servers. The Web-based feature of the database enables small business employees to access data irrespective of their location, just by using a browser. Additionally, the databases are extremely secure, protected using secure sockets layer technology. The service allows users to use three databases for free, and up to 15 databases for approximately $15 a month. Many small businesses, such as Michael Rosenfield Architects in Massachusetts, are already using this service and are extremely pleased with the system.

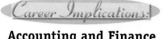

Accounting and Finance

[Adapted from Gopika Vaidya, "Intuit Unveils Web-Based Database Tool," **www.pcworld.com** (December 11, 2000).]

Creating Database Reports

DBMS packages include a report generation feature. A *report* is a compilation of data from the database that is organized and produced in printed format. Reports are typically produced on paper, but they can be presented to users on-screen as well. *Report generators* retrieve data from the database and manipulate (aggregate, transform, or group) and display it in a useful format.

An example of a report is a quarterly sales report for a restaurant. Adding the daily sales totals, grouping them into quarterly totals, and displaying the results in a table of totals creates a quarterly sales report. Reports are not limited to text and numbers. Report writers enable us to create reports using any data in the databases at whatever level we choose. For example, we could add to the restaurant report breakdowns of the data that show the average daily sales totals by days of the week. We could also show the quarterly sales totals in a bar chart, as shown in Figure 3.8. Each of these reports could be presented to the user either on paper or online. We could create automatic links between the underlying sales data located in the database and the attributes on the report in which the underlying data is used so that the reports could be updated automatically.

Database Design

The best database in the world is no better than the data it holds. Conversely, all the data in the world will do you no good if they are not organized in a manner in which there are few or no redundancies and in which you can retrieve, analyze, and understand them. The two key elements of an organizational database are the data and the structure of that data.

Let us refer back to the library example in Figure 3.3 to understand the structure of data. We know that we can find books in the library by using the card catalog. The card catalog is a structure for finding books. Each book has three cards, one each for the title, the author, and the subject. These classifications—title, author, subject—are a model, or representation, of the data in this system. Likewise, we must have a data model for databases. A *data model* is a map or diagram that represents entities and their relationships.

Much of the work of creating an effective organizational database is in the modeling. If the model is not accurate, the database will not be effective. A poor data model will result in data that is inaccurate, redundant, or difficult to search. If the database is relatively small, the effects of a poor design might not be too severe. In a corporate database, however, there are many entities, perhaps hundreds or thousands. In this case, the implications of a poor data model can be catastrophic. A poorly organized database is difficult to maintain and process—thus defeating the purpose of having a database management system in the first place. Undoubtedly, your school maintains databases with a variety of entity types—for example, students and grades—with both of these entities having several attributes. Attributes of a Student

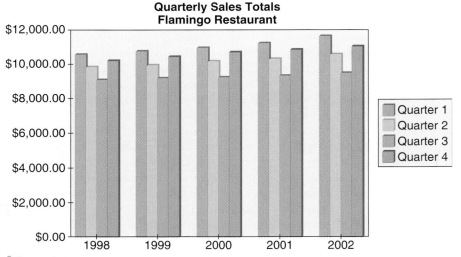

[**Figure 3.8** ➡ The quarterly sales report could show either text and numbers or a bar chart and could include the level of detail captured by the database data.]

entity might be Student ID, Name, Campus Address, Major, and Phone. Attributes of a Grades entity might include Student ID, Course ID, Section Number, Term, and Grade (see Figure 3.9).

For the DBMS to distinguish between records correctly, each instance of an entity must have one unique identifier. For example, each student has a unique Student ID. Note that using the student name, or most other attributes, would not be adequate because students may have the exact same name, live at the same address, or have the same phone number. Consequently, when designing a data-

base, we must always create and use a unique identifier called a ***primary key*** for each type of entity, in order to store and retrieve data accurately. In some instances, the primary key can also be a combination of two or more attributes, in which case it is called a ***combination primary key***. An example of this is the Grades entity shown in Figure 3.9, where the combination of Student ID, Course ID, Section Number, and Term uniquely refers to the grade of an individual student, in a particular class (section number), from a particular term.

Attributes not used as the primary key can be referred to as ***secondary keys*** when

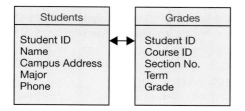

Students

Student ID	Name	Campus Address	Major	Phone
555-39-3232	Joe Jones	123 Any Avenue	Finance	335-2211
289-42-8776	Sally Carter	1200 Wolf Street #12	Marketing	335-8702

Grades

Student ID	Course ID	Section No.	Term	Grade
555-39-3232	MIS 250	2	F'00	D+
555-39-3232	MIS 250	1	F'01	A–
289-42-8776	MIS 250	3	S'02	B+

[**Figure 3.9** ➡ The attributes for and links between two entities—students and grades.]

The Venetian Hotel in Las Vegas is a 3,000-room hotel with a casino and conference center, often holding multiple conferences in a single day. One of the problems that the company has been facing is long check-in lines, which often get out of control, leading to increased customer dissatisfaction. The company has recently decided to implement a new wireless system that will enable customers to check in to the hotel with hotel clerks at any of the hotel's multiple entrances (including the car drop-off area), just by showing a credit card. The clerks will be able to check the reservations in the hotel's main reservation database using a wireless local area network (LAN) connection, and then encode

a room key for the customer. The hotel clerks are using handheld computers running the Palm OS operating system. These handhelds have magnetic stripes for reading credit cards and are connected to another device located on the clerk's belt, which encodes room keys. The handhelds are connected to the encoding device by a short-range radio connection, instead of a coiled cord. The handheld computers are passive information capture and display devices, whereas the database is the brains of the system, providing all data validation and processing. If you find yourself working in the hotel industry, you are likely to be using these wireless technologies someday.

Operations Management

[Adapted from Matt Hamblem, "Las Vegas Hotel to Try Wireless Check-In," *Computerworld* (May 24, 2001); **www.thestandard.com**, *The Industry Standard* (October 9, 2001).]

they are used to identify one or more records within a table that share a common value. For example, a secondary key in the Student entity shown in Figure 3.9 would be Major when used to find all students who share a particular major.

Associations

To retrieve information from a database, it is necessary to associate or relate information from separate tables. The three types of associations among entities are one-to-one, one-to-many, and many-to-many. Table 3.3 summarizes each of these three associations and how they should be handled in database design for a basketball league.

To understand how associations work, consider Figure 3.10, which shows four tables—Home Stadium, Team, Player, and Games—for keeping track of the information for a basketball league. The Home Stadium table lists the Stadium ID, Stadium Name, Capacity, and Location, with the primary key underlined. The Team table contains two attributes, Team ID and Team Name, but nothing about the Stadium where the team plays. If we wanted to have such information, we could gain it only by making an association between the Home Stadium and Team tables. For example, if each team has only one

home stadium, and each home stadium has only one team, we have a one-to-one relationship between the team and the home stadium entities. In situations in which we have one-to-one relationships between entities, we place the primary key from one table in the table for the other entity and refer to this attribute as a foreign key. In other words, a *foreign key* refers to an attribute that appears as a nonprimary key attribute in one entity and as a primary key attribute (or part of a primary key) in another entity. By sharing this common—but unique—value, entities can be linked, or associated, together. We can choose in which of these tables to place the foreign key of the other. After adding the primary key of the Home Stadium entity to the Team entity, we can identify which stadium is the home for a particular team and find all the details about that stadium (see section A in Figure 3.11).

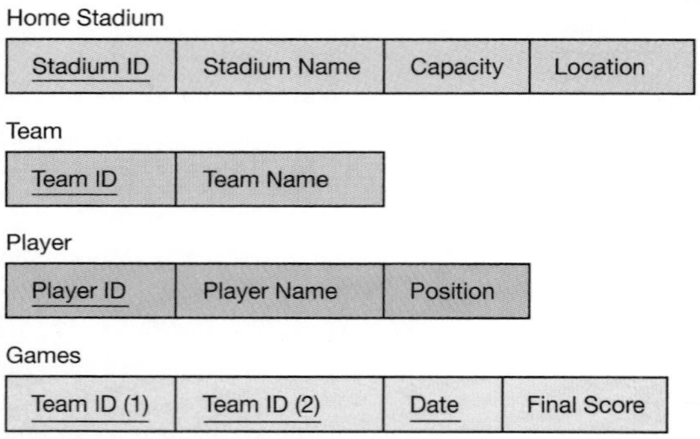

When we find a one-to-many relationship—for example, each player plays for only one team, but each team has many players—we place the primary key from the entity on the one side of the relationship, the team entity, as a foreign key in the table for the entity on the many side of the relationship, the player entity (see section B in Figure 3.11). In essence, we take from the one and give to the many, a Robin Hood strategy.

When we find a many-to-many relationship (for example, each player plays in many games, and each game has many players), we create a third, new entity—in this case, the Player Statistics entity and corresponding table. We then place the primary keys from each of the original entities together into the

[Figure 3.10 ➡ Tables used for storing information about several basketball teams, with *no* attributes added so that associations cannot be made.]

[Table 3.3] *Rules for expressing associations among entities and their corresponding data structures.*

Relationship	Example	Instructions
One-to-One	Each team has only one home stadium, and each home stadium has only one team.	Place the primary key from each table in the table for the other entity as a forein key.
One-to-Many	Each player is on only one team, but each team has many players.	Place the primary key from the entity on the one side of the relationship as a foreign key in the table for the entity on the many side of the relationship.
Many-to-Many	Each player participates in games, and each game has many players.	Create a third entity/table and place the primary keys from each of the original entities together in the third table as a combination primary key.

A. One-to-one relationship: Each team has only one home stadium, and each home stadium has only one team.

Team

Team ID	Team Name	Stadium ID

B. One-to-many relationship: Each player is on only one team, but each team has many players

Player

Player ID	Player Name	Position	Team ID

C. Many-to-many relationship: Each player participates in many games, and each game has many players.

Player Statistics

Team 1	Team 2	Date	Player ID	Points	Minutes	Fouls

[**Figure 3.11** ➡ Tables used for storing information about several basketball teams, with attributes added in order to make associations.]

third, new table as a new, combination primary key (see section C in Figure 3.11).

You may have noticed that by placing the primary key from one entity in the table of another entity, we are creating a bit of redundancy. We are repeating the data in different places. We are willing to live with this bit of redundancy, however, because it enables us to keep track of the interrelationships among the many pieces of important organizational data that are stored in different tables. By keeping track of these relationships, we can quickly answer questions such as, "Which players on the SuperSonics played in the game on February 16 and scored more than 10 points?" In a business setting, the question might be, "Which customers purchased the 2003 forest green Ford Escape from Thom Roberts at the Roberts' Ford dealership in Bloomington, Indiana, during the first quarter of 2003, and how much did each pay?" This kind of question would be useful in calculating the bonus money Thom should receive for that quarter or in recalling those specific vehicles in the event of a recall by the manufacturer.

Team Work

Is using a database always the fastest?

As a group, argue for and against the following statement: Using a database is faster than manually searching for information. Is this statement always true or always false? Provide clear reasons and/or examples for your arguments. What conclusions can you draw from this discussion?

Brief Case: **Streamlining Procurement at Xerox**

Xerox Corporation, headquartered in Stamford, Connecticut, is a leader in the global document management market. It provides color and monochrome digital printers, copiers, and related document-processing equipment. In addition, Xerox also delivers solutions, services, software, and supplies so that people everywhere, from home offices to production-printing environments, can create, manage, and share ideas through paper or digital documents. Xerox has nearly 100,000 employees worldwide and annual revenues of almost $20 billion.

Throughout its global operations, Xerox spends billions of dollars each year on nonproduction goods and services such as office supplies, computer hardware and software, employee travel, and equipment repair and maintenance. When executives studied the buying patterns for goods and services, it became very clear that Xerox was not benefiting from its tremendous buying power. To address this problem, Xerox adopted an Internet-based procurement application from Oracle Corporation that helped to dramatically improve and streamline Xerox's largely manual purchasing processes. The procurement software not only automated the procurement process, it centralized the product sourcing, approval routing, and payments, while it decentralized requisitioning and receiving. By integrating product catalogs and individual procurement transactions into a single automated database management system, Xerox was able to better analyze supplier performance and to establish better supplier relationships. As a result of the new procurement system, Xerox expects to achieve a 400 percent internal rate of return and save more than $10 million annually. ⬤

[Adapted from **www.xerox.com**; **www.oracle.com**.]

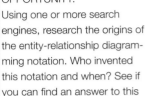

Entity-Relationship Diagramming

A diagramming technique called an *entity-relationship diagram (ERD)* is commonly used when designing databases, especially when showing associations between entities. To create an ERD, you draw entities as boxes and draw lines between entities to show relationships. Each relationship can be labeled on the diagram to give additional meaning to the diagram. For example, Figure 3.12 shows an ERD for the basketball league data previously discussed. From this diagram, you can see the following associations:

▌ Each Home Stadium has a Team.

▌ Each Team has Players.

▌ Each Team participates in Games.

▌ For each Player and Game there are Game Statistics.

When designing a complex database, with numerous entities and relationships, ERDs are very useful. They allow the designer to talk with people throughout the organization to make sure that all entities and relationships have been found.

The Relational Model

Now that we have discussed data, data models, and the storage of data, we need a mechanism for joining entities that have natural relationships with one another. For example, there are several relationships among the four entities we described previously—students, instructors, classes, and grades. Students are enrolled in classes. Likewise, instructors teach multiple classes and have many students in their classes in a semester. It is important to keep track of these relationships. We might, for example, want to know which courses a student is enrolled in so that we can notify her instructors that she will miss courses because of an illness. The primary DBMS approach, or model, for keeping track of these relationships among data entities is the relational model.

Other models are also used to join entities with commercial DBMSs—the hierarchical, network, and object-oriented models—but this is beyond the scope of our discussion (see Hoffer, Prescott, and McFadden, 2002).

The most common DBMS approach in use today is the *relational database model*. A DBMS package using this approach is referred to as a relational DBMS, or RDBMS. With this approach, the DBMS views and presents entities as two-dimensional tables, with records as rows and attributes as columns. Tables can be joined when there are common columns in the tables. The uniqueness of the primary key, as mentioned earlier, tells the DBMS which records should be joined with others in the corresponding tables. This structure supports very powerful data manipulation capabilities and linking of interrelated data. Database files in the relational model are three-dimensional: a database has rows (one dimension) and columns (a second dimension), and can contain a row of data in common with another file (a third dimension). This three-dimensional database is potentially much more powerful and useful than traditional, two-dimensional, "flat file" databases (see Figure 3.13).

A good relational database design eliminates unnecessary data duplications and is easy to maintain. To design a database with clear, nonredundant relationships, you perform a process called normalization.

Normalization

To be effective, databases must be efficient. Developed in the 1970s, *normalization* is a technique to make complex databases more efficient and more easily handled by the DBMS (Date, 1995). To understand the normalization process, let us return to the scenario in the beginning of this chapter. Think about your report card. It looks like nearly any other form or invoice. Your personal information is usually at the top, and each of your classes is listed, along with an instructor, a class day

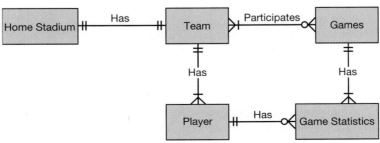

[**Figure 3.12** ➡ An entity-relationship diagram showing the relationships between entities in a basketball league database.]

Department Records

Department No	Dept Name	Location	Dean
Dept A			
Dept B			
Dept C			

Instructor Records

Instructor No	Inst Name	Title	Salary	Dept No
Inst 1				
Inst 2				
Inst 3				
Inst 4				

[Figure 3.13 ➡ With the relational model, we represent these two entities, department and instructor, as two separate tables and capture the relationship between them with a common column in each table.]

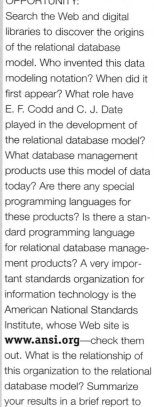

Web Search

WEB SEARCH OPPORTUNITY: Search the Web and digital libraries to discover the origins of the relational database model. Who invented this data modeling notation? When did it first appear? What role have E. F. Codd and C. J. Date played in the development of the relational database model? What database management products use this model of data today? Are there any special programming languages for these products? Is there a standard programming language for relational database management products? A very important standards organization for information technology is the American National Standards Institute, whose Web site is **www.ansi.org**—check them out. What is the relationship of this organization to the relational database model? Summarize your results in a brief report to submit to your instructor.

and time, the number of credit hours, and a location. Now think about how this data is stored in a database. Imagine that this database is organized so that in each row of the database, the student's identification number is listed on the far left. To the right of the student ID are the student's name, local address, major, phone number, course and instructor information, and a final course grade (see Figure 3.14). Notice that there is redundant data for students, courses, and instructors in each row of this database. This redundancy means that this database is not well organized. If, for example, we want to change the phone number of an instructor who has hundreds of students, we have to change this number hundreds of times.

Elimination of data redundancy is a major goal and benefit of using data normalization techniques. After the normalization process, the student data is organized into five separate tables (see Figure 3.15). This reorganization helps simplify the ongoing use and maintenance of the database and any associated analysis programs.

Data Dictionary

Each attribute in the database needs to be of a certain type. For example, an attribute may contain text, numbers, or dates. This *data type* helps the DBMS organize and sort the data, complete calculations, and allocate storage space.

Student ID#	Student Name	Campus Address	Major	Phone	Course ID	Course Title	Instructor Name	Instructor Location	Instructor Phone	Term	Grade
A121	Joy Egbert	100 N. State Street	MIS	555-7771	MIS 350	Intro. MIS	Van Deventer	T240C	555-2222	F'02	A
A121	Joy Egbert	100 N. State Street	MIS	555-7771	MIS 372	Database	Hann	T240F	555-2224	F'02	B
A121	Joy Egbert	100 N. State Street	MIS	555-7771	MIS 375	Elec. Comm.	Chatterjee	T240D	555-2228	F'02	B+
A121	Joy Egbert	100 N. State Street	MIS	555-7771	MIS 448	Strategic MIS	Chatterjee	T240D	555-2228	F'02	A-
A121	Joy Egbert	100 N. State Street	MIS	555-7771	MIS 474	Telecomm	Gilson	T240E	555-2226	F'02	C+
A123	Larry Mueller	123 S. State Street	MIS	555-1235	MIS 350	Intro. MIS	Van Deventer	T240C	555-2222	F'02	A
A123	Larry Mueller	123 S. State Street	MIS	555-1235	MIS 372	Database	Hann	T240F	555-2224	F'02	B-
A123	Larry Mueller	123 S. State Street	MIS	555-1235	MIS 375	Elec. Comm.	Chatterjee	T240D	555-2228	F'02	A-
A123	Larry Mueller	123 S. State Street	MIS	555-1235	MIS 448	Strategic MIS	Chatterjee	T240D	555-2228	F'02	C+
A124	Mike Guon	125 S. Elm	MGT	555-2214	MIS 350	Intro. MIS	Van Deventer	T240C	555-2222	F'02	A-
A124	Mike Guon	125 S. Elm	MGT	555-2214	MIS 372	Database	Hann	T240F	555-2224	F'02	A-
A124	Mike Guon	125 S. Elm	MGT	555-2214	MIS 375	Elec. Comm.	Chatterjee	T240D	555-2228	F'02	B+
A124	Mike Guon	125 S. Elm	MGT	555-2214	MIS 474	Telecomm	Gilson	T240E	555-2226	F'02	B
A126	Jackie Judson	224 S. Sixth Street	MKT	555-1245	MIS 350	Intro. MIS	Van Deventer	T240C	555-2222	F'02	A
A126	Jackie Judson	224 S. Sixth Street	MKT	555-1245	MIS 372	Database	Hann	T240F	555-2224	F'02	B+
A126	Jackie Judson	224 S. Sixth Street	MKT	555-1245	MIS 375	Elec. Comm.	Chatterjee	T240D	555-2228	F'02	B+
A126	Jackie Judson	224 S. Sixth Street	MKT	555-1245	MIS 474	Telecomm	Gilson	T240E	555-2226	F'02	A-
...	...	...	...	...	...	...	...	...	...	...	...

[Figure 3.14 ➡ Database of students, courses, instructors, and grades with redundant data.]

Student Table

Student ID#	Student Name	Campus Address	Major	Phone
A121	Joy Egbert	100 N. State Street	MIS	555-7771
A123	Larry Mueller	123 S. State Street	MIS	555-1235
A124	Mike Guon	125 S. Elm	MGT	555-2214
A126	Jackie Judson	224 S. Sixth Street	MKT	555-1245
...	...	...	...	...

Class Table

Course ID	Course Title
MIS 350	Intro. MIS
MIS 372	Database
MIS 375	Elec. Comm.
MIS 448	Strategic MIS
MIS 474	Telecomm
...	...

Teaching Assignment

Course ID	Term	Instructor Name
MIS 350	F'02	Van Deventer
MIS 372	F'02	Hann
MIS 375	F'02	Chatterjee
MIS 448	F'02	Chatterjee
MIS 474	F'02	Gilson
...	...	...

Instructor Table

Instructor Name	Instructor Location	Instructor Phone
Chatterjee	T240D	555-2228
Gilson	T240E	555-2226
Hann	T240F	555-2224
Van Deventer	T240C	555-2222

Enrolled Table

Student ID#	Course ID	Term	Grade
A121	MIS 350	F'02	A
A121	MIS 372	F'02	B
A121	MIS 375	F'02	B+
A121	MIS 448	F'02	A-
A121	MIS 474	F'02	C+
A123	MIS 350	F'02	A
A123	MIS 372	F'02	B-
A123	MIS 375	F'02	A-
A123	MIS 448	F'02	C+
A124	MIS 350	F'02	A-
A124	MIS 372	F'02	A-
A124	MIS 375	F'02	B+
A124	MIS 474	F'02	B
A126	MIS 350	F'02	A
A126	MIS 372	F'02	B+
A126	MIS 375	F'02	B+
A126	MIS 474	F'02	A-
...	...	...	...

[Figure 3.15 ➦ Organization of information on students, courses, instructors, and grades after normalization.]

Once the data model is created, a format is needed to enter the data in the database. A *data dictionary* is a document prepared by the database designers to help individuals enter data. The data dictionary explains several pieces of information for each attribute, such as its name, whether or not it is a key or part of a key, the type of data expected (dates, alphanumeric, numbers, and so on), and valid values. Data dictionaries can include information such as why the data item is needed, how often it should be updated, and on which forms and reports the data appears.

Data dictionaries can be used to enforce business rules. *Business rules*, such as who has authority to update a piece of data, are captured by the designers of the database and included in the data dictionary to prevent illegal or illogical entries from entering the database. For example, designers of a warehouse database could capture a rule in the data dictionary to prevent invalid ship dates from being entered into the database.

Organizational sales personnel are usually frequent travelers and often have to carry large volumes of data, files, and presentations regarding their company's products and clients in their travel. The sales force at Simon and Schuster (a book company) faced a great many problems in carrying huge volumes of information with them. To make the sales force more independent and mobile, the company recently provided them with laptops. However, this added further to the complexity, since now the sales personnel were required to carry information about all their bookstore buyers, along with enough data to enable them to make in-depth presentations to their clients regarding the upcoming titles, in a very modest laptop with only a 1.2GB hard drive and 32MB of RAM. This was an almost impossible task, and the IS manager of the company was constantly on the lookout for a way in which to fit all the data in the company database onto these laptops. The solution came in the form of a small footprint database, whose "selective replication features" allowed the sales personnel to input only the data that was relevant to them. These small footprint databases provide data in an easily accessible format and use very little memory (most of these databases take up no more than 2MB of RAM in a laptop). Moreover, these databases also have the flexibility to be installed in handheld devices or smartphones and can be synchronized with a central database located in the corporate offices.

[Adapted from Amy Helen Johnson, "It May Be a Small World After All," **www.cio.com**, *CIO Magazine* (February 1, 2000).]

HOW ORGANIZATIONS GET THE MOST FROM THEIR DATA

Modern organizations are said to be drowning in data but starving for information. Despite being a mixed metaphor, this statement seems to portray quite accurately the situation in many organizations. The advent of Internet-based electronic commerce has resulted in the collection of an enormous amount of customer and transactional data. How this data is collected, stored, and manipulated is a significant factor influencing the success of a commercial Internet Web site. In this section we discuss how organizations are getting the most from their data.

Linking Web Site Applications to Organizational Databases

A recent database development is the creation of links between sites on the Web and organizational databases. For example, many companies are enabling users of their Web site to view product catalogs, check inventory, and place orders—all actions that ultimately read and write to the organizations' databases.

Some Internet electronic commerce applications can receive and process millions of transactions per day. To gain the greatest understanding of customer behavior and to assure adequate system performance for customers, you must manage online data effectively. For example, **Amazon.com** is the world's largest bookstore, with more than 2.5 million titles, and is open 24 hours a day, 365 days a year with customers all over the world ordering books and a broad range of other products. Amazon's servers log millions of transactions per day. Amazon is a vast departure from a traditional physical bookstore. In fact, the largest physical bookstore carries "only" about 170,000 titles, and it would not be economically feasible to build a physical bookstore the size of Amazon; a physical bookstore that carried Amazon's 2.5 million titles would need to be the size of nearly 25 football fields! The key to effectively designing an online electronic commerce business is clearly the effective management of online data.

Data Mining

To support more effective information management, many large organizations such as Chase Manhattan Bank and Harrah's Entertainment are using data mining. **Data mining** is a method used by companies to sort and analyze information to better understand their customers, products, markets, or any other phase of their business for which data has been captured. With data mining tools, you can graphically drill down from summary data to more detailed data, sort or extract data based on certain conditions, and perform a variety of statistical analyses, such as trend analysis, correlation analysis, forecasting, and analysis of variance. The next section describes how data mining is being implemented.

Online Transaction Processing (OLTP)

Fast customer response is fundamental to having a successful Internet-based business. **Online transaction processing (OLTP)** refers to immediate automated responses to the requests of users. OLTP systems are designed specifically to handle multiple concurrent

Brief Case: **Database Technology Powers CNN Interactive**

CNN Interactive presents an example of the successful linking of a large corporate database with a Web interface. CNN Interactive provides a free, online custom news service to hundreds of thousands of subscribers around the world. Using the World Wide Web, the site delivers up-to-the-minute news from over 100 sources and offers more than 2,000 categories of customized news options, ranging from sports and health to recreation, pop culture, crime, and consumer issues. In a typical week, 20,000 new articles are stored. CNN Interactive uses an Oracle database to dynamically build personalized news pages for hundreds of thousands of daily users. These pages are updated every 15 minutes to deliver the most current information. This application is made possible only by the sophisticated database system, which manages the vast amount of changing information and automatically builds the customized Web pages.

[Adapted from **www.oracle.com**]

Global Perspective

Transborder Data Security and Privacy

Apart from technical and human resource–related challenges, some cultural issues also pose significant challenges for organizations. The most important of these issues is that of the general rules and regulations existing in different nations regarding information systems and transborder data flow. One of the most prominent examples of rules and regulations on transborder data flow is the European Union Data Protection Directive, which went into effect in October 1998. The data protection laws according to this directive limit how personal data may be used within Europe. While some European countries, such as France, have had data protection laws for a long time, the laws passed by the directive are stricter. Contrary to many of the regulations in the United States, the directive suggests that personal data collected in Europe may be used for only the purposes for which it has been collected. For all other purposes, a consent form needs to be obtained from the consumer. Frequent flyer mile information, for example, cannot include information about the passenger. This directive has had severe implications for the airline industry. Moreover, Article 25 of the directive argues that no personal data can be transferred from Europe to countries that have less stringent privacy policies, including the United States. This article has posed severe challenges for U.S. organizations that conduct business with European companies. There is hope that a single unified treaty on data security and privacy might be developed. In the meantime, organizations will expend considerable resources complying with the different rules in different countries.

---

transactions from customers. Typically, these transactions have a fixed number of inputs, such as customer name and address, and a specified output, such as total order price or order tracking number. Common transactions include receiving user information, processing orders, and generating sales receipts. Consequently, OLTP is a big part of interactive electronic commerce applications on the Internet. Since customers can be located virtually anywhere in the world, it is critical that transactions be processed efficiently (see Figure 3.16). The speed with which database management systems can process transactions is, therefore, an important design decision when building Internet systems. In addition to which technology is chosen to process the transactions, how the data is organized is also a major factor in determining system performance. Although the database operations behind most transactions are relatively simple, designers often spend considerable time making adjustments to the database design in order to "tune" processing for optimal system performance. Once an organization has all this data, it must design ways to gain the greatest value from its collection; online analytical processing is one method being used to analyze these vast amounts of data.

Online Analytical Processing (OLAP)

Online analytical processing (OLAP) refers to graphical software tools that provide complex analysis of data stored in a database. The chief component of an OLAP system is the **OLAP server**, which understands how data is organized in the database and has special functions for analyzing the data. OLAP tools enable users to analyze different dimensions of data, beyond data summary and data aggregations of normal database queries. For example, OLAP can provide time series and trend analysis views of data, data drill-downs to deeper levels of consolidation, and the ability

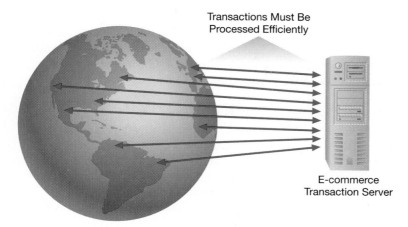

Transactions Must Be
Processed Efficiently

E-commerce
Transaction Server

[**Figure 3.16** ➡ Global customers require that online transactions be processed efficiently.]

to answer "what if" and "why" questions. An OLAP query for **Amazon.com** might be: "What would be the effect on profits if wholesale book prices increased by 10 percent and transportation costs decreased by five percent?" Managers use the complex query capabilities of an OLAP system to answer questions within executive information systems (EISs), decision support systems (DSSs), and Enterprise Resource Planning (ERP) systems (each of these systems is described in a later chapter). Given the high volume of transactions within Internet-based systems, analysts must provide extensive OLAP capabilities to managers in order to gain the greatest business value.

Merging Transaction and Analytical Processing

The requirements for designing and supporting transactional and analytical systems are quite different. In a distributed online environment, performing real-time analytical processing diminishes the performance of transaction processing. For example, complex analytical queries from an OLAP system require the locking of data resources for extended periods of execution time, whereas transactional events—data insertions and simple queries from customers—are fast and can often occur simultaneously. Thus, a well-tuned and responsive transaction system may have uneven performance for customers while analytical processing occurs. As a result, many organizations replicate all transactions on a second database server, so that analytical processing does not slow customer transaction processing performance. This replication typically occurs in batches during off-peak hours when site traffic volumes are at a minimum.

The consultants at Accenture (previously known as Anderson Consulting), one of the leading global consulting firms, depend on a knowledge management system on a regular basis. This system, known as Knowledge Xchange, is an online system, and consultants are required to be connected to the network in order to access it. Due to the fact that most of the consultants spend much of their time on planes and at hotels, they often run into difficulty connecting and thus fail to access the knowledge management (KM) system. To add to the complexity, the KM system had grown to over 100 gigabytes of data, and accessing the database easily and quickly had become a problem. To ease these problems, Accenture's IT staff designed and developed a new application system called Pocket Xchange, which operates on a Microsoft SQL Server database and is installed on Microsoft Windows NT Server. Pocket Xchange accesses data from a Microsoft Access database using Data Access Objects (DAO) and displays the data in a document view. The Access database is populated with data retrieved from a set of Lotus Notes databases. This application is loaded on the consultants' machines and enables them to access the data without being connected to the network. Some Accenture consultants have reported that the new software has saved them at least as much time as one day a week.

Human Resource Management

[Adapted from **www.microsoft.com/business/casestudies/bi/accenture.asp**.]

The systems that are used to interact with customers and run a business in real time are called the *operational systems*. Examples of operational systems are sales order processing and reservation systems. The systems designed to support decision making based on stable point-in-time or historical data are called *informational systems*. The key differences between operational and informational systems are shown in Table 3.4. Increasingly, data from informational systems is being consolidated with other organizational data into a comprehensive data warehouse, where OLAP tools can be used to extract the greatest and broadest understanding from the data.

Data Warehousing

Large organizations such as Wal-Mart, Target, and Sears have built *data warehouses*, which integrate multiple large databases and other information sources into a single repository. This repository is suitable for direct querying, analysis, or processing. Much like a physical warehouse for products and components, the data warehouse stores and distributes data on computer-based information systems. The data warehouse is a user's virtual storehouse of valuable data from the organization's disparate information systems and external sources. It supports the online analysis of sales, inventory, and other vital business data that has been culled from operational systems. The purpose of a data warehouse is to put key business information into the hands of more decision makers. Table 3.5 lists sample industry uses of data warehouses. Data warehouses can take up hundreds of gigabytes, even terabytes, of data. They usually run on fairly powerful mainframe computers and can cost millions of dollars.

Data warehouses represent more than just big databases. An organization that successfully deploys a data warehouse has committed to pulling together, integrating, and sharing critical corporate data throughout the firm.

Data Marts

Rather than storing all enterprise data in one data warehouse, many organizations have created multiple data marts, each containing a subset of the data for a single aspect of a company's business—for example, finance, inventory, or personnel. A *data mart* is a data warehouse that is limited in scope. It contains selected information from the data warehouse, such that each separate data mart is customized for the decision support applications of a particular end-user group. For example, an organization may have several data marts that are customized for a particular type of user, such as a marketing data mart or a finance data mart. Data marts have been popular among small and medium-sized businesses and among departments within larger organizations, all of which were previously prohibited from developing their own data warehouses due to the high costs involved.

For example, Merck-Medco Managed Care is a mail-order business that sells drugs to the country's largest health care providers: Blue Cross and Blue Shield state organizations, large HMOs, U.S. corporations, and state governments. Using both data warehouses and data marts, Merck-Medco is mining its data to uncover hidden links between illnesses and known drug treatments, spotting trends that help pinpoint which drugs are the most effective for what types of patients. The results are more effective treatments that are also less costly. Merck-Medco's data mining project has

[Table 3.4] *Comparison of operational and informational systems.*

Characteristic	Operational System	Informational System
Primary purpose	Run the business on a current basis	Support managerial decision making
Type of data	Current representation of state of the business	Historical or point-in-time (snapshot)
Primary users	Online customers, clerks, salespersons, administrators	Managers, business analysts, customers (checking status, history)
Scope of usage	Narrow vs. simple updates and queries	Broad vs. complex queries and analysis
Design goal	Performance	Ease of access and use

Uses of Data Warehousing	Representative Companies
Retail	
Analysis of scanner checkout data	Wal-Mart
Tracking, analysis, and tuning of sales	Target
promotions and coupons	Sears
Inventory analysis and redeployment	Osco/Savon Drugs
Price reduction modeling to "move" the product	Casino Supermarkets
Negotiating leverage with suppliers	W.H. Smith Books
Frequent buyer program management	Otto Versand Mail Order
Profitability analysis	
Product selections or granular market segmentation	
Telecommunications	
Analysis of the following:	AT&T
Call volumes	Ameritech
Equipment sales	Belgacom
Customer profitability	British Telecom
Costs	Telestra Australia
Inventory	Telecom Ireland
Purchasing leverage with supliers	Telecom Italia
Frequent buyer program management	
Banking and Financing	
Relationship banking	Bank of America
Cross-segment marketing	Bank One
Risk and credit analysis	Merrill Lynch
Merger and acquisition analysis	CBOE
Customer profiles	CNA
Branch performance	

[Table 3.5] *Sample industry uses of data warehousing (adapted from Boar, 1998).*

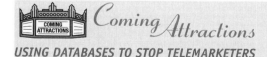

Coming Attractions

USING DATABASES TO STOP TELEMARKETERS

Most people do not enjoy getting phone solicitations from telemarketers, especially during dinnertime or a favorite television show. As a result, more than 20 states have established, or are planning to establish, "do not call" databases; most believe that if the government does not create a single unified database, there soon will be 50 separate databases, making it extremely difficult for telemarketers to maintain accurate call databases. Consequently, the Federal Trade Commission (FTC) wants to create a "unified" national do not call registry that would make it illegal for telemarketers to call anyone on that list. Consumers would be able to call an 800 number or sign up over the Web to add themselves to the database. The telemarketing industry is greatly opposed to this plan because of the increased costs associated with maintaining accurate databases and the fear that a large part of the population would want to be listed in the database. For example, Connecticut recently established its own system and had the majority of the households listed on the do not call list within the first year. Although the FTC plans to seek public comment and hold numerous public forums on the pros and cons of such a system, most feel that such a system will eventually be established.

[Adapted from P. Thibodeau, "FTC Wants National 'Do Not Call' List to Stop Telemarketers," **www.computerworld.com** (January 22, 2002).]

helped customers save an average of 10 to 15 percent on prescription costs.

Data marts typically contain tens of gigabytes of data, as opposed to the hundreds of gigabytes in data warehouses. Therefore, data marts can be deployed on less powerful hardware. The differences in costs between differ-

ent types of data marts and data warehouses can be significant. The cost to develop a data mart is typically less than $1 million, while the cost for a data warehouse can exceed $10 million. Clearly, organizations committed to getting the most out of their data must make a large investment in database technology.

Information Systems

Effective decision making requires that data be consolidated into useful information. Unfortunately, most companies store data in a wide variety of databases and files, making the dissemination of useful information to decision makers within the organization a key concern of most IT departments. Today, different collaborative tools and communications technologies such as e-mail can help in achieving information sharing and dissemination. However, increasingly, companies are realizing that it is not enough to disseminate the information; it is also important to enable users to analyze data, gain insights from it, and use it effectively. To facilitate better decision making, many organizations are

switching to virtual data warehouses that enable both efficient information dissemination and improved decision making. Virtual data warehouses enable users to retrieve the most relevant data from legacy applications, without the time, cost, and risk associated with traditional data warehousing. In fact, one of the key benefits of a virtual data warehouse is that it allows the retrieval of data via easy-to-use applications and environments (for instance, a Web browser). As a result, there is a vast need for people who are skilled at extracting data from disparate systems and transforming them into a format that is easy to use by decision makers.

[Adapted from Paul Holland, "Virtues of a Virtual Data Warehouse," **itmanagement.earthweb.com/article/ 0,,10454_621401,00.html**.]

KEY POINTS REVIEW

1. **Describe why databases have become so important to modern organizations.** Databases often house mission-critical organizational data, so proper design and management of the databases is critical. If they are designed and managed well, the databases can be used to transform raw data into information that helps people do their jobs faster, better, and more cheaply, which ultimately helps customers and makes the firm more competitive.

2. **Describe what databases and database management systems are and how they work.** A database is a collection of related data organized in a way that facilitates data searches. A database contains entities, attributes, records, and tables. Entities are things about which we collect data, such as people, courses, customers, or products. Attributes are the individual pieces of information about an entity, such as a person's last name or social security number, that are stored in a database record. A record is the collection of related attributes about an entity; usually, a record is displayed as a database row. A table is a collection of related records about an entity type; each row in the table is a record, and each column is an attribute. A database management system is a software application with which you create, store, organize, and retrieve data from a single database or several databases. Data is typically entered into a database through the use of a specially formatted form. Data is retrieved from a data-

base through the use of queries and reports. The data within a database must be adequately organized so that it is possible to store and retrieve information effectively. The main approach for structuring the relationships among data entities is the relational database model. Normalization is a technique to transform complex databases into a more efficient form, allowing them to be more easily maintained and manipulated.

3. **Explain how organizations are getting the most from their investment in database technologies.** Many organizations are allowing employees and customers to access corporate database management systems via the World Wide Web. This capability allows greater flexibility and innovative products and services. Data mining is a popular application of database technologies in which information stored in organizational databases, data warehouses, or data marts is sorted and analyzed to improve organizational decision making and performance. A data warehouse is the integration of multiple large databases and other information sources into a single repository or access point that is suitable for direct querying, analysis, or processing. A data mart is a small-scale data warehouse that contains a subset of the data for a single aspect of a company's business—for example, finance, inventory, or personnel.

KEY TERMS

attribute 71

business rules 82

combination primary key 77

data dictionary 82

data mart 86

data mining 83

data model 76

data type 81

data warehouse 86

database 70

database administrator (DBA) 73

database management system (DBMS) 71

entity 71

entity-relationship diagram (ERD) 80

form 74

foreign key 78

informational system 86

normalization 80

online analytical processing (OLAP) 84

online transaction processing (OLTP) 83

OLAP server 84

operational systems 86

primary key 77

query 74

query by example (QBE) 75

record 71

relational database model 80

report 76

report generator 76

secondary key 77

Structured Query Language (SQL) 74

table 71

REVIEW QUESTIONS

1. Explain the difference between a database and a database management system.
2. List some reasons that record keeping with physical filing systems is less efficient than using a database on a computer.
3. Describe how the following terms are related: entity, attribute, record, and table.
4. Compare and contrast the primary key, combination key, and foreign key within an entity.
5. How do Structured Query Language (SQL) and query by example (QBE) relate to each other?

6. What is the purpose of normalization?
7. Explain how organizations are getting the most from their investment in database technologies.
8. How are databases used with a World Wide Web interface? Who has access to the database?
9. Compare and contrast a data warehouse and a data mart.
10. Describe why databases have become so important to modern organizations.

SELF-STUDY QUESTIONS

1. A database comprises _____ .

   A. attributes
   B. records
   C. organized data for querying
   D. all of the above

2. A database is used to collect, organize, and query information. Which of the following is least likely to use a database as a fundamental part of their job?

   A. airline reservations agent
   B. university registrar
   C. Social Security Administration
   D. Security Guard

3. A _____ is a unique identifier that can be a combination of two or more attributes.

   A. secondary key
   B. primary key
   C. tertiary key
   D. elementary key

Answers are at the end of the Problems and Exercises.

4. Which of the following is **not true** in regard to the relational database model?

   A. Entities are viewed as tables, with records as rows and attributes as columns.
   B. Tables use keys and redundant data in different tables in order to link interrelated data.
   C. Entities are viewed as children of higher level attributes.
   D. A properly designed table has a unique identifier that may be one or more attributes.

5. Each team has only one home stadium, and each home stadium has only one team. This is an example of which of the following relationships?

   A. one-to-one
   B. one-to-many
   C. many-to-many
   D. many-to-one

6. Data warehousing refers to _____.
   A. the secure storage of corporate data in a fire proof vault.
   B. the integration of multiple large databases into a single repository.
   C. a concept that is no longer practical due to the pace of technological change.
   D. none of the above.

7. Which of the following statements about databases is **false**?
   A. Databases are becoming more popular.
   B. Minimal planning is required since the software is so advanced.
   C. A data warehouse utilizes a database.
   D. A database administrator is responsible for the development and management of a database.

8. Databases are used for _____ .
   A. data mining
   B. data marts
   C. expert systems
   D. all of the above

9. _____ is a technique to make a complex database more efficient by eliminating redundancy.
   A. Data depository
   B. Associating
   C. Normalization
   D. Standardization

10. Which of the following is a document, sometimes published as an online interactive application, prepared by the designers of the database to aid individuals in data entry?
    A. data dictionary
    B. database
    C. normalization
    D. data model

PROBLEMS AND EXERCISES

1. Match the following terms with the appropriate definitions:

   ____ Database

   ____ Database management system

   ____ Data mart

   ____ Query by example

   ____ Data mining

   ____ Data warehouse

   ____ Data dictionary

   ____ Relational model

   ____ Normalization

   ____ Entity-relationship diagram

   a. A data warehouse that is limited in scope and contains selected information that is customized for the decision support applications of a particular end-user group
   b. A diagramming technique commonly used when designing databases, especially when showing associations between entities
   c. A collection of related data organized in a way that facilitates data searches
   d. A method used to sort and analyze information to better understand data captured in normal business activities
   e. A software application with which you can create, store, organize, and retrieve data for one or many databases
   f. A technique used to simplify complex databases so that they are more efficient and easier to maintain
   g. The capability of a DBMS to enable us to request data by simply providing a sample or a description of the types of data we would like to see
   h. A DBMS approach in which entities are presented as two-dimensional tables that can be joined together with common columns
   i. A single repository that integrates multiple large databases and other information sources
   j. A document, sometimes published as an online interactive application, prepared by the designers of the database to aid individuals in data entry

2. You see an announcement for a job as a database administrator for a large corporation but are unclear about what this title means. Research this on the World Wide Web and obtain a specific job announcement.

3. How and why are organizations without extensive databases falling behind in competitiveness and growth? Is this simply a database problem that can be fixed easily with some software purchases? Search the World Wide Web for stories or news articles that deal with the issue of staying competitive by successfully managing data. How are these stories similar to each other? How are they different? Prepare a 10-minute presentation to the class on your findings.

4. What are six advantages of databases and three costs or risks of a database system? Why are databases becoming more popular?

5. Why would it matter what data type is used for the attributes within a database? How does this relate to programming? How does this relate to queries and calculations? Does the size of the database matter?

6. Discuss the issue of data accuracy, based on what you have learned from this chapter. Does a computer database handle accuracy issues better than a filing system? Who (or what) is ultimately responsible for data accuracy?

7. List three different database software applications. Compare and contrast the advantages and disadvantages, including price, program size, and other pertinent factors.

8. Have several classmates interview database administrators within organizations with which they are familiar. To whom do these people report? How many employees report to these people? Is there a big variance in the responsibilities across organizations? Why or why not?

9. Go to the **ecampus.com** site on the Web, and search for a couple of textbooks that you either have bought or intend to purchase. What is the selection of books available, and what is the delivery time? Are shipping costs added to the cost of the books? How does this compare with the campus bookstore? Is it more convenient?

10. On the World Wide Web find data warehouses and data marts. What companies are currently using them? How do they differ in size, implementation time, scope, cost, and so on?

11. Based on your understanding of a primary key and the following sample grades table, determine the best choice of attribute(s) for a primary key.

STUDENT ID	COURSE	GRADE
100013	Visual Programming	A-
000117	Telesystems	A
000117	Introduction to MIS	A

12. In the Brief Case about Xerox, what did streamlining procurement encompass? What functions did it affect? What application was implemented? Was this a good software investment? Are other companies upgrading their software with a Web interface?

13. Search the World Wide Web for an organization with a homepage that utilizes a link between the homepage and the organization's own database. Describe the data that the browser enters and the organization's possible uses for this data. Can you retrieve company information, or can you only send information to the company? How are the data displayed on the homepage?

14. Select an organization with which you are familiar that utilizes flat file databases for their database management. Determine whether the organization should move to a relational database. Why would you make this recommendation? Is it feasible to do so? Why or why not?

15. What databases are used at your educational institution? Have you filled out a lot of paperwork that was then entered by someone else? Did you actually do some of the data entry for your account? What kind of information were you able to retrieve about your account? From where was the database administered? Were you able to access it online?

ANSWERS TO THE SELF-STUDY QUESTIONS

1. D   2. D   3. B   4. C   5. A   6. C   7. B   8. D   9. C   10. A

CASE 1: *American Leak Detection: Lessons for Selecting the Perfect Data Management System*

American Leak Detection is a worldwide leader in detection of leakage for water and sewer systems. The company was founded in 1974 in Hemet, California. Its initial focus was on the detection of leaks in swimming pools and spas. However, over the last many years, due to advancement in technology, the company has diversified into leak detection in cold climates and in international locations as well. The company currently provides leak detection services for all types of residential, commercial, municipal, and industrial settings. The mission statement of the company (as shown on their Web site) is to "find leaks in a manner that is noninvasive, efficient, and environmentally sound." The company operates primarily through franchises, and today it comprises approximately 170 team members working out of 307 offices in 38 states within the United States and 10 other countries. Over the last few years, the company had been facing a lot of problems related to its data management. The fact that it is a franchise company further added to the complexity of data management. There were mounds of data coming

in from different locations, often belonging to heterogeneous systems. Data from all these disparate systems needed to be integrated. To add to the problems, the company had recently grown, almost doubling the number of spreadsheets and computer files to deal with. Many times, employees would find themselves recreating old documents, primarily because no one was sure where the last person who handled that file had kept it. As a result of these recreations, multiple files dealing with similar information were kept by different people, and no one seemed to know which one was the most current. The data management problem at American Leak Detection had grown to be so huge that it was seriously affecting the efficiency and performance of the organization.

The company wanted to implement a system that would enable its employees to enter team member data only once, whereby the data would populate all the areas so that different applications could draw on it. Its requirements also included being able to review team conversations, retrieve financial information, check whether the team mem-

bers were current on their royalties, and send customized e-mail messages. For three years, the company explored different options—from building in-house, to evaluating products of other vendors, and even to partnering with other data management solution provider companies—but none of the ventures ended successfully. The company increasingly realized that while every franchisor needed franchise data management, no one seemed to provide a solution that would take care of it. Hence, even after a search and several efforts spanning a few years, half of American Leak Detection's data were not integrated, and the company was still on the lookout for the appropriate solution.

The solution finally arrived in the form of NeoCom, a company based in California that provides data management solutions, especially to franchisors. After the first demo of the software, American Leak Detection realized that, while customization was still required for it to meet the needs of the company, NeoCom's software was at least 75 percent of what they had been looking for over the years. The software had several modules that were well suited for franchisors and enabled customers to roll out implementations whenever they wanted. Without any further delay, American Leak Detection hired NeoCom, who immediately started work on customizing and implementing the data management software at the site of their client. The current system enables American Leak Detection to conduct a single search on the company's system and get all the relevant information that it needs. Moreover, the system also incorporates all of the team member data, including the contact information, compliance data, financial information, and all other types of support documents. The system also enables the company to connect all the customer survey cards to team member data. This further facilitates its customer service program. The data are also accessible by sales personnel, even when they are in remote locations, which helps them in tracking prospective customers and provides benefits for future sales. Finally, one of the last modules of the system enables the company to upload royalty reports and other statistical data, which can now be efficiently used for planning and projecting future sales and number of team members.

After searching fruitlessly for almost three years, the company finally found a solution in NeoCom. From this experience, American Leak Detection has learned not only that data management is important, and that an all-in-one-solution is available for franchisors, but has also learned a few things about selecting the right data management solution and the perfect data management solution provider. The vice president of corporate operations of American Leak Detection argues that some of the success factors for a data management project are selecting the right solution, conducting and implementing good beta groups, implementing a good rollout program, and, finally, selecting the best solution provider. In fact, the company has openly acknowledged that the key to any data management issue is finding the right partner and provider, which they found in NeoCom. The company feels that a data management partner should be one who is willing to work on a project for several years, and not just view their customer as a one-time contract. Any information technology implementation takes time, and if the provider is willing to give that time, the chances of project success are much higher. American Leak Detection also feels that in order to solve a data management problem, the solution provider should be well aware of the business that the customer is in and, hence, be able to better understand the client's data needs and requirements. NeoCom provided solutions primarily for franchisors and, hence, was very well able to understand American Leak Detection's needs. Finally, it is important to have a data management solution provider who meets deadlines and budgets. American Leak Detection found it in NeoCom, who had met every challenge that they were given.

[Adapted from **www.leakbusters.com/**; N. Bigley, "Files, Files, Everywhere Files: Managing Data Management," *Franchising World* 33, no. 5 (2001): 32–33.]

Discussion Questions

1. Outline American Leak Detection's primary data management problems.
2. Why had the company been unsuccessful in finding an appropriate data management solution, even after searching intensely for over three years?
3. Summarize the benefits to American Leak Detection of having a successful data management system.
4. Briefly discuss 10 factors that are key to solving a data management problem successfully. Be sure to include a few that were not implied in the case.

CASE 2: *Data Warehouse Project Failure at Close Call Corp.*

Close Call Corp. is a teleservices company that was founded about three decades ago. Over the years, the company has grown steadily and has a current net worth of approximately $100 million. The founder and CEO of the company realized that it was time to make some significant changes to the organization, especially on the technology front. Close Call still relied on some old antiquated information systems, which were extremely ill-equipped to handle the company's recent growth and expansion. The thought of a major technological change became even more deeply ingrained in the CEO's mind when he met a software vendor at a social event. The vendor promised him some customized solutions that would help integrate the company's data.

Close Call had two primary units: an outbound telemarketing unit and an inbound catalog sales unit. Both these units operated independently of each other. Recently, however, the company was working toward integrating them, which required a significant amount of integration of the relevant data and information. In addition, the company was also planning some significant growth strategies whereby its number of call centers would be increased from six to 116. There were also plans to implement new open switching systems in the call centers that would enable automatic dialing and call forwarding. Plans were also in place to implement new human resources and ledger software. The vendor assured the CEO that the building of a data warehouse would be the company's solution for effectively managing its expansion plans and the new software. Convinced by the vendor, the CEO decided to go forward with the idea. He allocated a budget of $250,000, and the plan was to implement a 500GB data warehouse. Since most of the internal IS staff were not comfortable in handling a data warehouse and were already swamped with other IS projects, some new personnel, such as a manager of the data warehousing project and an MIS director, were hired from outside the company. The time span given for this project was approximately four months.

An initial project team was assembled, consisting of the MIS director, the project manager, and a couple of users, among others. The project manager attempted to push back the deadlines, to make the project more realistic, but the CEO was insistent on staying with the original plan. Ultimately, the CEO agreed to the implementation of a pilot project after five months, before the rollout of the actual data warehouse. Although it was envisioned by the CEO that the data warehouse would serve the needs of multiple departments, the project team members were at a loss to understand the real importance of the data warehouse. In fact, because the company never felt the need for a data warehouse in the past, the business objectives of this project were unclear to the team. Nonetheless, the project team remained optimistic and started the second phase of the project, namely the collection of user requirements. The team scheduled lengthy interviews with potential users throughout the organization and asked them to talk in depth about their job requirements, day-to-day activities, technology needs, and so on. Hence, the user requirement phase was relatively long (about three months).

The project team members also focused on defining the business dimensions, attributes, relationships, and so on, for the design of the data warehouse. Since there were multiple departments, there were many conflicting needs and definitions, all of which needed to be integrated. At the end of this stage, the project team realized that the business requirements of each of the units were too inconsistent. All of the business managers had their own customized spreadsheets, which they used to create their respective reports. These individual spreadsheets were based on the managers' own set of assumptions and had no synergy with each other. The project team had to spend an enormous amount of time just sorting through these inconsistent definitions in order to find some coherence among them, which ended up delaying the project time frame to a great extent (which was not anticipated earlier). To add to the existing troubles of the data warehousing project team, roughly around this time, the team also realized that there were no appropriate data to enter into the data warehouse. Some of the data were captured in the company's old proprietary systems, and extraction of the data from those systems would become costly and time consuming. The only solution was to upgrade the systems of the six existing call centers to open technology. The existing IS department refused to cooperate with the team, since they were threatened by the data warehousing project and viewed it as reducing their importance to the organization.

The data warehousing project team attempted to salvage the situation by gathering some data from the existing reports and manually entering them into the pilot data warehouse. However, they still knew that, without significant changes to the existing systems, the actual data warehouse could not be implemented. Yet, plans for the pilot went ahead as scheduled. When the pilot data warehouse was finally installed, the situation became even worse. The users refused to use it, claiming that it did not add anything to their existing capabilities and was difficult to use. Instead of the originally planned five months, the pilot development and installation had taken over eight months. In addition, it incurred an estimated cost of $750,000, significantly over the CEO's budget.

At the time the pilot failed, there were some structural changes in the organization as well, including new directors of MIS and technology. The data warehousing project manager built a new plan that estimated that the data warehousing project could be delivered within two years. However, by this time most of the company executives, including the CEO, had grown tired of it, and the project was officially closed within a short period of time.

[Adapted from Lauren Gibbons Paul, "Anatomy of Failure," **www.cio.com**, *CIO Enterprise Magazine* (November 15, 1997).]

Discussion Questions

1. Based on your knowledge of the information systems development process, what would you consider to be the factors that contributed to the failure of the data warehousing project at Close Call Corp.?
2. What would you do differently if you were the CEO of Close Call?
3. What would you do differently if you were the project manager of the data warehousing project?
4. Briefly describe five lessons that you learned from this case. Include both technology-related lessons and other social issues–related lessons.

Telecommunications and the Internet

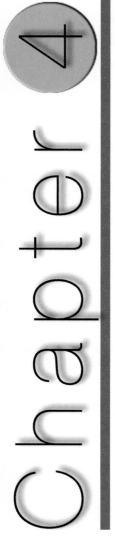

OPENING: New York Pilot Testing a Telecommunications Network to Combat Terrorism

As a result of the September 11, 2001 terrorist attacks, state and federal agencies in the United States are finding innovative ways to use information technology to ensure safety and security. For example, the state of New York will soon have a new weapon to use in the war on terrorism. The state is developing a new, secure telecommunications network that will let the state's law-enforcement agencies share critical intelligence with each other instantaneously in order to better combat terrorism.

The system was designed by IBM and codeveloped by the state's Office of Public Safety in consultation with other state police associations. A prototype system, which cost $100,000 and supports 16 law-enforcement zones, was launched and initially allows electronic alerts to be sent via a secure telecommunications network to recipients using stand-alone flat-screen PCs. Even better, the next phase of the project will enable two-way communication between any and all of the state's 543 law-enforcement agencies and police departments. The total cost of the network is estimated to be about $2 million.

Upon completion, the system will enable law-enforcement personnel across the state of New York to communicate with one another instantly and, as a result, act quickly and effectively to protect and serve people living, working, and visiting the Empire State. What better way to use new telecommunications technologies than to help people to be safe and secure?

[Adapted from Marianne Kolbasuk McGee, "NY Piloting Counter-Terrorism Network," *InformationWeek* (January 31, 2002). **http://www. informationweek.com/story/ IWK20020131S0015**]

[Figure 4.1 ➥ Combating terrorism on the 'net in New York.]
© CORBIS

rganizations need to bring products to a global market quickly and be closely integrated with their customers and suppliers. These and related demands have driven the rapid development of telecommunications technologies. These technologies enable people and enterprises to share information across time and distance, and they can lower boundaries between markets and cultures. The telecommunications revolution is changing the way we live and work, and how we communicate with each other. This chapter introduces key telecommunications concepts, technologies, and applications, including how the Internet works and is being used in and across business organizations. This discussion provides you with a solid foundation for understanding how computers are connected across a room or across the world.

After reading this chapter, you will be able to do the following:

1. Understand the role of telecommunications in organizations.

2. Describe the evolution of and types of computer networks.

3. Describe the Internet and how it works.

4. Describe the basic Internet services and the use of the World Wide Web.

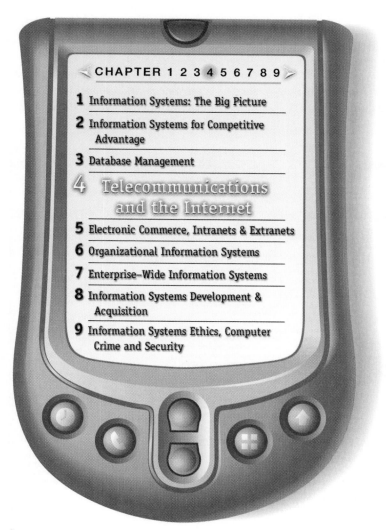

◄ CHAPTER 1 2 3 **4** 5 6 7 8 9 ►

1 Information Systems: The Big Picture

2 Information Systems for Competitive Advantage

3 Database Management

4 Telecommunications and the Internet

5 Electronic Commerce, Intranets & Extranets

6 Organizational Information Systems

7 Enterprise–Wide Information Systems

8 Information Systems Development & Acquisition

9 Information Systems Ethics, Computer Crime and Security

[Figure 4.2 ➦ The Big Picture: focusing on telecommunications.]

Preview

Telecommunications technologies are becoming more and more important in our lives. Understanding how these technologies work and can be leveraged for success is essential to your overall understanding of The Big Picture (see Figure 4.2). This chapter begins with a discussion of the expanding role that telecommunications is playing in organizations.

THE ROLE OF TELECOMMUNICATIONS AND NETWORKS IN ORGANIZATIONS

> **Web Search**
>
> WEB SEARCH OPPORTUNITY: check your Internet connection speed at **http://computingcentral.msn.com/internet/speedtest.asp**.

People in organizations around the world are finding that telecommunications and networks are highly effective tools for communication, coordination, and collaboration across and among enterprises and people. ***Telecommunications*** refers to the transmission of all forms of information, including digital data, voice, fax, sound, and video, from one location to another over some type of network. A ***network*** is a group of computers and associated peripheral devices connected by a communication channel capable of sharing information and other resources (e.g., a printer) among users. ***Bandwidth***, or the carrying capacity of telecommunications networks, has increased to the point that any digitized data, from photographs, to art, to movies, to complicated business records, can be quickly transmitted via a network.

Powerful new technologies are giving networks the bandwidth needed to handle rich content, such as movies, medical records, or great works of art. These networks also work at speeds great enough to support interaction between users. In the next section, we offer some examples of how digital content and high-powered networks are changing interpersonal communication and business applications.

Interpersonal Communication Applications

The most remarkable feature of networking computers is not that computers can speak to each other, but that the people who use the computers can communicate with each other through their machines. Just as telephones let users communicate over long and short distances, networked computers allow users to send messages across the office, across town, across the country, or around the world.

Electronic Mail (E-Mail)

One of the most pervasive uses of networks is sending ***electronic mail***, or e-mail (see Figure 4.3). The benefits of e-mail are that it nearly

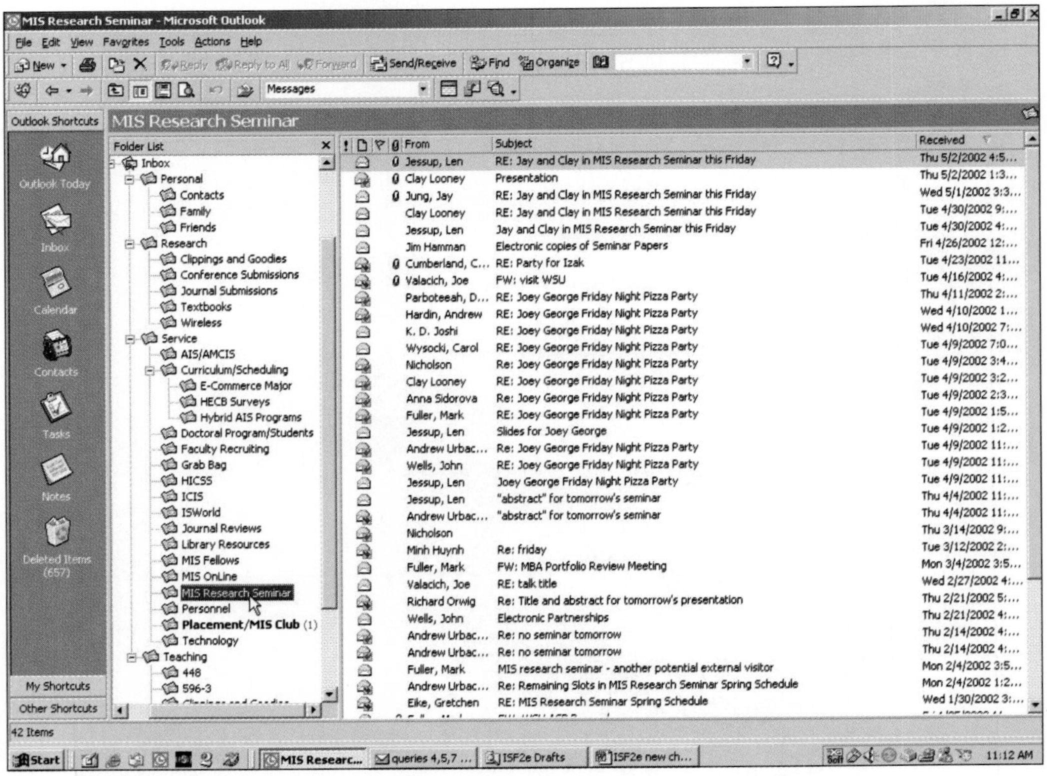

[**Figure 4.3** ➡ Electronic mail is one of the most popular network applications.]

eliminates "telephone tag" and that it enables widespread work groups to ignore time zones and office hours. The greater the number of people in an organization who use e-mail, with its capability to store information and deliver it when a recipient is ready to receive it, the less they are controlled by the constraints of real-time communication.

Later in this chapter we will describe in more detail how the Internet works. For now, realize that people everywhere use the Internet to easily exchange information using a variety of tools. *Newsgroups*, also called computer-based discussion groups, allow individuals and organizations to participate in discussions on almost any subject. There are now thousands of newsgroups, on every topic imaginable. Companies are using discussion groups as an easy way to share information with customers who want to discuss topics such as product applications or customer support.

Mailing lists, also known as listservs, let you use e-mail to participate in discussion groups on topics of special interest to you. Lists can be small and regional, or they can include participants from all over the world. Companies often create mailing lists for customers in order to send a single e-mail message to thousands of customers simultaneously.

Internet Relay Chat (IRC)

Internet Relay Chat (IRC) lets you have conversations with others in real time on the Internet (also referred to as real-time messaging). The process is somewhat like talking on the telephone, although you must type your comments instead of speaking them. You can converse with others as long as they are online and using the same messaging service you are using. Companies are using IRC as a way to have interactive conversations with colleagues and customers throughout the world (see Figure 4.4).

Facsimile (Fax)

Facsimile or fax machines digitize images, such as letters, memos, newspaper and magazine articles, photos, contracts, even handwritten notes, so that they can be transmitted to other fax machines over telephone lines. The receiving fax machine translates the material from digital data back to the original image. Facsimile machines are stand-alone desktop peripherals that send and receive printed information. More and more, organizations are using a PC as a fax machine, where the fax is sent and received like an e-mail message.

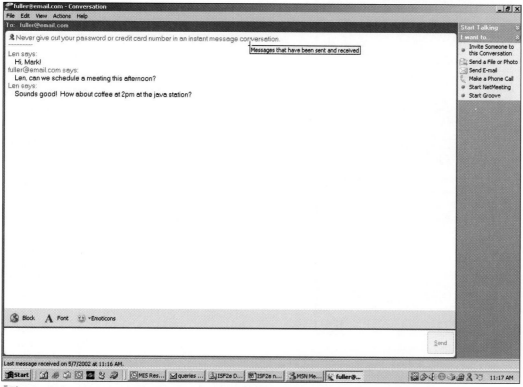

[**Figure 4.4** ➥ The Internet allows distributed people to have text-based conversations.]

Source Microsoft Instant Messenger

Voice Mail

In addition to e-mail, you may also have access to a voice mail system, either at work or through your PC at home or school, since many PC fax applications allow users to set up a voice mail system. **Voice mail** allows callers to leave voice messages in a voice mailbox, much like leaving a message on an answering machine. Unlike an answering machine, however, voice mail digitizes voice messages so that they can be stored on the computer.

Videoconferencing

Videoconferencing lets groups of people in the same office or at diverse locations meet online, rather than gathering together in one meeting room or traveling across the country to see one another in person (see Figure 4.5). A combination of software and hardware, including video cameras, microphones, and speakers, allows people in diverse locations to get together online to share information, discuss projects, and otherwise conduct business. Some videoconferencing systems let remote participants share applications and data and jointly make changes to documents and other information shown on-screen.

[**Figure 4.5** ➡ Videoconferencing allows people to see each other, to talk, and to collaborate on the same document from two or more different locations.]

Courtesy of Microsoft Corporation

Common Business Applications

Today companies around the world consider networks to be essential tools for daily business communication. In addition to supporting interpersonal communication, networks support other types of telecommunication used to exchange business information, including electronic commerce, electronic data interchange, telecommuting, and electronic fund transfer. In this section, we will briefly describe these and other business examples.

Electronic Commerce (EC or E-Commerce)

Electronic Commerce (EC or e-commerce) refers to the use of the Internet to support a variety of business activities, such as streamlining operations, selling products and providing customer support, connecting to suppliers, and many other business-related activities. E-commerce has become such an important aspect of business communication that most organizations—both small and large—now have a presence on the World Wide Web and many use the Internet to conduct day-to-day business.

Business **Web sites** range from simple, just-the-facts pages that resemble printed brochures or data sheets to more sophisticated, interactive productions where customers can do everything from ordering products to taking a virtual tour through manufacturing facilities (see Figure 4.6). Chapter 5, "Electronic Commerce, Intranets, and Extranets," describes in more detail how businesses utilize electronic commerce.

Electronic Data Interchange (EDI)

Electronic Data Interchange (EDI) is another form of electronic commerce. It involves the use of telecommunications technology to transfer business information between organizations, thus cutting down on paperwork. With computers linked via a network, businesses using EDI can quickly transfer purchase orders to a supplier or invoices to affiliated stores, as well as other information that would take much longer to reach destinations if sent through regular mail services and would require paperwork at both ends of the transaction. For example, a company such as General Motors or Dow Chemicals may use EDI to send an electronic purchase order to a supplier, rather than a paper request. Some businesses use private proprietary networks that are not subject to traffic and security problems common with Internet use. Other firms use the Internet but use encryption software to keep financial data private.

[**Figure 4.6 ➡** Internet-based shopping is growing rapidly.]
www.Amazon.com

Home Depot first began implementing an electronic data interchange network in 1992; today, 85 percent of all the company's dealings with suppliers—from ordering to invoicing—are conducted electronically. Home Depot is working with suppliers to bring consumers into an electronic network, thereby completing the loop among supplier, retailer, and customer. For instance, the company is linking its e-commerce engine to marketing sites operated by manufacturers. Shoppers browsing small-engine manufacturer Briggs & Stratton Corp.'s Web site, for example, are dropped directly into Home Depot's checkout page if they click the "Find a merchant" button; they can buy from the site if there is a store in their area. We will describe EDI in more detail in Chapter 5.

Telecommuting

Telecommuting is the act of working at home or from another remote location and "commuting" to the office via computing and networking technologies (see Figure 4.7). Many recent television advertisements tout the advantages of doing business online by showing a home worker dressed for a teleconference in a no-nonsense business suit—from the waist up. Below the waist, the happy telecommuter wears pajama bottoms and bunny slippers. Other ads show the at-home worker cheerfully bouncing a small child while at the same time performing routine workday business at the computer. Telecommuting can let workers live where they choose, while being employed by a company in a distant location. The advantages of such an arrangement are

---

Brief Case: EDI at Walgreens

Walgreens Corporation has found a way to save time and money. Using EDI, Walgreens Corporation can easily combine the invoices from more than 2,100 of their specialty and drug stores into a single statement and forward this to a supplier such as Hallmark Corporation. In a recent exchange, Walgreens sent an invoice containing more than 66,000 records with payment authorizations to Hallmark. When Hallmark received the invoice, its EDI system not only verified the correctness and completeness of the order, but also was able to notify Walgreens' bank that it needed to transfer payment to Hallmark's bank. This transaction was verified, and payment was exchanged in a matter of minutes. Before EDI, the processing of 66,000 records would have taken several weeks (if not months) to prepare, verify, send, and resolve. It is easy to see that telecommunications applications like EDI have the potential to radically change the way organizations are able to do business. ⬤

[Figure 4.7 ➡ Telecommuting allows people to work from home using computing and networking technologies.]
© Getty Images, Inc.

[Figure 4.8 ➡ Automated teller machines are connected to networks, allowing people to access their bank accounts throughout the world.]
© CORBIS

obvious for disabled and ill employees, as well. Benefits for employers include increased worker satisfaction and productivity and decreased travel and on-site office maintenance costs.

Electronic Fund Transfer (EFT)

Electronic fund transfer (EFT) is another aspect of e-commerce. It involves transferring funds from one financial account to another via computer. For example, instead of receiving paychecks or Social Security checks in the mail and depositing them in the bank, many people have such checks sent directly from the source to their bank accounts. No money or paper changes hands, and the transfer occurs in the same day because checks do not have to be mailed from one destination to another. Many people also authorize the paying of bills electronically from their bank accounts. Automated teller machines (ATMs) are another visible means of electronic fund transfer that allow ATM card users to make deposits or withdraw cash quickly from machines placed in handy locations (see Figure 4.8). Companies, banks, and other financial institutions worldwide also use EFT to transfer funds among themselves.

Distance Learning

Distance learning is the process of providing instruction to students who are physically separated from instructors through the use of some sort of communication technologies including videoconferencing, Internet chatting, and various Web-based tools. As computer literacy and the availability of high-speed Internet access continue to increase, distance learning is gaining in popularity, and teaching methods are rapidly improving.

Telemedicine

Telemedicine is the exchange of medical information from one location to another via a computer network. This allows remote patients to be examined by the best medical doctors, regardless of where the doctors are located. When doctors are connected to a remote location, they can examine medical images and monitor patients effectively.

Now that you have seen some sample uses of telecommunications and networks, we will next describe how these technologies work and how they have evolved.

EVOLUTION OF COMPUTER NETWORKING

Human communication involves the sharing of information and messages between senders and receivers. The sender of a message forms the message in his brain and codes the message into a form that can be communicated to the receiver—through voice, for example. The message is then transmitted along a communication pathway to the receiver. The receiver, using her ears and brain, then attempts to decode the message, as shown in Figure 4.9. This basic model of human communication helps us to understand telecommunications or computer networking.

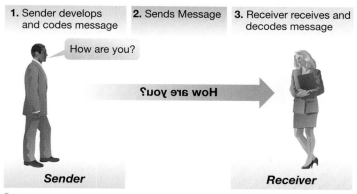

1. Sender develops and codes message

2. Sends Message

3. Receiver receives and decodes message

How are you?

How are you?

Sender

Receiver

[**Figure 4.9** ➡ Communication requires senders and receivers.]

Messages, Senders, and Receivers

Computer networking is the sharing of information or services. As with human communication, all computer networks require three things:

▮ Senders and receivers that have something to share

▮ A pathway or transmission medium, such as a cable, to send the message

▮ Rules or protocols dictating communication between senders and receivers

The easiest way to understand computer networking is through the human communication model. Suppose you are planning to study abroad in Europe for a semester. You need information about schools that accept exchange students. The first requirement for a network—information to share—has now been met. You start your search by writing a letter (coding your message) and faxing it to several schools. You have met the second requirement—a means of transmitting the coded message. The fax system is the pathway or transmission medium used to contact the receiver. *Transmission media* refers to the physical cable(s) used to carry network information. At this point, you may run into some difficulties. Not all the receivers of your fax may understand what you have written—decode your message—because they speak other languages. Although you have contacted the receiver, you and the receiver of your message must meet the third requirement for a successful network: You must establish a language of communication—the rules or protocols governing your communication. *Protocols* define the procedures that different computers follow when they transmit and receive data. You both might decide that one communication protocol will be that you communicate in English. This communication session is illustrated in Figure 4.10.

Computer Networks

A fundamental difference between human and computer communication is that human communication consists of words, whereas computer communication consists of bits, the fundamental information units of computers, as depicted in Figure 4.11. Virtually all types

1. Coding Your Message

2. Sending Your Message

3. Decoding and Receiving Message

Is this English? I speak only French.

[**Figure 4.10** ➡ Coding, sending, and decoding a message.]

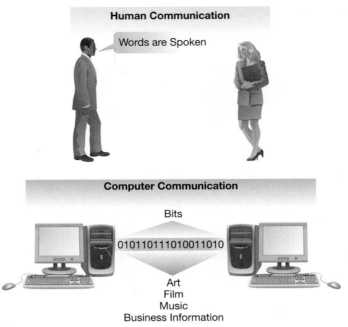

[Figure 4.11 ➡ In human communication, words are spoken and transmitted in the air. In computer communication, digital data is transmitted over some type of communication medium.]

of information can be transmitted on a computer network—documents, art, music, film—although each type of information has vastly different requirements for effective transmission. For example, a single screen of text is approximately 10KB of data, whereas a photograph-quality picture could be larger than 200MB of data (see Table 4.1). The process of converting a photograph or a song into digital information, or bits, is called *digitizing*. After information is converted into bits, it can travel across a network. To transmit either the screen of text or the picture in a timely manner from one location to another, adequate bandwidth is needed. For example, using a 56KB *modem*—a modem that transmits approximately 56KB of data in a second—a single screen of text would be transferred in under one second, while a high-quality photograph could take more than four seconds. Hence, different types of information have different communication bandwidth requirements.

Now that you understand the basic elements of networks, we will talk about how they have evolved. Since the beginning of the Information Age in the 1950s, people and enterprises have used computers to process data and information. Over the years, however, computer networks have gotten better and better.

Centralized Computing

Centralized computing, depicted in Figure 4.12, remained largely unchanged through the 1970s. In this model, large centralized computers, called mainframes, were used to process and store data. During the mainframe era (beginning in the 1940s), people entered data on mainframes through the use of local input devices called *terminals*. These devices were called "dumb" terminals because they did not conduct any processing or "smart" activities. The centralized computing model is not a true network

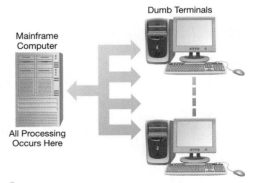

[Figure 4.12 ➡ In the centralized computing model, all processing occurs in one central mainframe.]

Type of Information	Raw Size	Compressed Size
Voice		
Telephone	64 Kbps	16–32 Kbps
Teleconference	96 Kbps	32–64 Kbps
Compact disc	1.41 Mbps	63–128 Kbps
Data		
Single screen of text	14.4KB	4.8–7.2KB
Typed page, single-spaced	28.8KB	9.6–14.4KB
Faxed page (low to high resolution)	1.68–3.36MB	130–336KB
Super VGA screen image	6.3MB	315–630KB
Digital X-ray	50.3MB	16.8–25.1MB
Publication-quality photograph	230.4MB	23–46MB
Video		
Video telephony	9.3 Mbps	64–384 Kbps
Video teleconferencing	37.3 Mbps	384 Kbps–1.92 Mbps
CCITT multimedia	166 Mbps	1.7 Mbps
High definition television	1.33 Gbps	20–50 Mbps

[Table 4.1]
Communication and storage/bandwidth requirements for different types of information.

Note: KB = Kilobytes, Kbps = Kilobytes per second; MB = Megabyte; Mbps = Megabytes per second; Gbps = Gigabytes per second.

Source: Table adapted from Business Data Communications, Second Edition by Stallings/VanSlyke. © 1997. Reprinted by permission of Prentice-Hall, Inc., Upper Saddle River, NJ.

because there is no sharing of information and capabilities. The mainframe provides all the capabilities, and the terminals are only input/output devices. Computer networks evolved in the 1980s when organizations needed separate, independent computers to communicate with each other.

Distributed Computing

The introduction of personal computers in the late 1970s and early 1980s gave individuals control over their own computing. Organizations also realized that they could use multiple small computers to achieve many of the same processing goals of a single large computer. People could work on subsets of tasks on separate computers rather than using one mainframe to perform all the processing. Achieving the goal of separate processing required computer networks so that information and services could be easily shared between these distributed computers. The 1980s were characterized by an evolution to a computing model called ***distributed computing***, shown in Figure 4.13, in which multiple

types of computers are networked together to share information and services.

Collaborative Computing

In the 1990s, a new computing model, called ***collaborative computing***, emerged. Collaborative computing is a synergistic form of distributed computing, in which two or more networked computers are used to accomplish a common processing task. That is, in this model of computing, computers are not simply communicating data but are sharing processing capabilities. For example, one computer may be used to store a large employee database. A second computer may be used to process and update individual employee records selected from this database. The two computers collaborate to keep the company's employee records current, as depicted in Figure 4.14.

Types of Networks

Computing networks today include all three computing models: centralized, distributed, and collaborative. The emergence of new computing

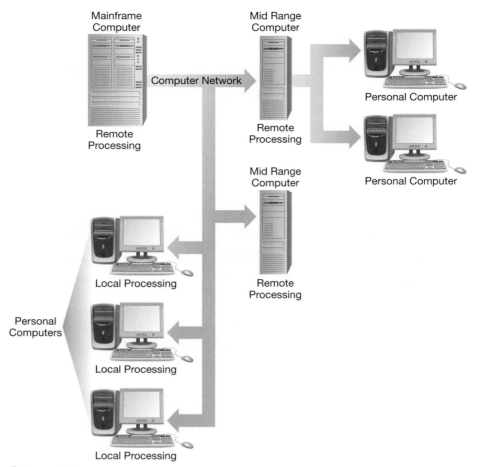

[**Figure 4.13** ➡ In the distributed computing model, separate computers work on subsets of tasks and then pool their results by communicating over a network.]

[**Figure 4.14** ➡ In the collaborative computing model, two or more networked computers are used to accomplish a common processing task.]

models did not mean that organizations completely discarded older technologies. Rather, a typical computer network includes mainframes, minicomputers, personal computers, and a variety of other devices. Computer networks are commonly classified by size, distance covered, and structure. The most commonly used classifications are a private branch exchange (PBX), local area network (LAN), wide area network (WAN), metropolitan area network (MAN), and personal area network (PAN). Each is described in the following sections.

Private Branch Exchange (PBX)

A *private branch exchange (PBX)* is a telephone system that serves a particular location, such as a business (see Figure 4.15). It connects one telephone extension to another within the system and connects the PBX to the outside telephone network. It can also connect computers within the system to other PBX systems, to an outside network, or to various office devices such as fax machines or photocopiers. Since they use ordinary tele-

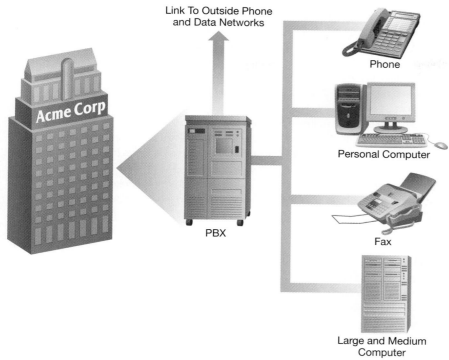

Link To Outside Phone
and Data Networks

Phone

Personal Computer

Fax

Large and Medium
Computer

PBX

Acme Corp

[**Figure 4.15** ➡ A private branch exchange (PBX) supports local phone and data communications, as well as links to outside phone and data networks.]

phone lines, PBX systems have limited bandwidth. This prevents them from transmitting such forms of information as interactive video, digital music, or high-resolution photos. Using PBX technology, a business requires few outside phone lines but has to purchase or lease the PBX equipment.

Local Area Network (LAN)

A *local area network (LAN)*, shown in Figure 4.16, is a computer network that spans a rela-

tively small area, allowing all computer users to connect with each other to share information and peripheral devices, such as a printer. LAN-based communications may involve the sharing of data, software applications, or other resources between several users. LANs typically do not exceed tens of kilometers in size, and are typically contained within a single building or a limited geographical area. They typically use only one kind of transmission medium or cabling such as twisted-pair wire or coaxial cable. There are also *wireless*

[**Figure 4.16** ➡ A local area network (LAN) allows multiple computers located near each other to communicate directly with each other and to share peripheral devices, such as a printer.]

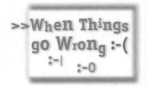

Worrying About Wireless LANs

John Montgomery, chief technical officer at Embarcadero Systems Corp. in Alameda, California, said he is working to improve the security of 802.11b wireless local area networks (LANs) that the company has installed at nine West Coast ports. Those wireless LAN infrastructures support container inventory control at the ports. They also track movement and dispatch operations. Cranes and lifts communicate data read from smart tags on cargo boxes to a central database.

When Embarcadero, a division of Oakland, California–based Marine Terminals Corp., installed the wireless LANs, "the issues about security were not well known or publicized," Montgomery said. After the September 11, 2001, terrorist attacks on the United States and the resulting heightened concerns over security, he "commissioned a security audit, which detected numerous holes." For example, signals sent out over a wireless LAN can often easily be intercepted and, in the right hands, can be decoded. In addition, in some cases people can gain access to wireless LANs and use them as a gateway into other networks and computers.

Brian Ruf, an information assurance scientist at CACI International Inc., in Arlington, Virginia, said that in his view, running an insecure wireless LAN is "essentially the same as running a wire from your network out to the street and leaving the jack loose for anyone to plug in."

To address the problems, Embarcadero hired a staff dedicated to cybersecurity, installed firewalls on its routers, and is working with third-party software vendors to provide additional encryption software.

Similarly, the U.S. Department of Energy's Lawrence Livermore National Laboratory in Livermore, California, recently put a temporary ban on wireless LANs, which had been installed in non-classified areas. Ted Michels, the lab's acting CIO and principal deputy director for computation, said in a recent version of the lab's newsletter that "wireless networks and their built-in security features have been found under testing to be very insecure. For this reason, the lab has decided to control the deployment of wireless technologies until solutions can be found to address their security vulnerabilities."

Lawrence Livermore spokesman David Schwoegler said the lab would keep its wireless LANs shut down "as long as it takes to get it right." He added that because of these security concerns, the DOE has a long-standing policy against the use of wireless LANs in classified areas.

David Halasz, manager of software development in the wireless networking business unit at Cisco Systems Inc. and chairman of IEEE 802 Task Group I, which is working on wireless LAN security enhancements, said enterprises already have some robust wireless security tools to choose from. They will have even better tools later this year and next when vendors start adding the hard-to-crack Advanced Encryption Standard to their defensive arsenal.

Dennis Eaton, chairman of the Wireless Ethernet Compatibility Alliance, said he believes that although it is prudent for organizations such as Lawrence Livermore to demand tight security, other enterprises can comfortably operate wireless LANs with today's 40-bit Wired Equivalent Privacy security.

[Adapted from Bob Brewin, "Wireless LAN Worries Mount," *Computerworld* (February 4, 2002).]

local area network products available as well. These are very popular because they are relatively easy to set up and enable you to have a network without any network cables strewn around your home or office.

Wide Area Network (WAN)

A *wide area network (WAN)* is a computer network that spans a relatively large geographical area. WANs are typically used to connect two or more LANs. Different hardware and transmission media are often used in WANs because they must cover large distances efficiently. Used by multinational companies, WANs transmit and receive information across cities and countries. Four specific types of WANs—global networks, enterprise networks, value-added networks, and metropolitan area networks—are discussed below.

Global Networks

A *global network* spans multiple countries and may include the networks of several organizations. The Internet is an example of a global network. The Internet is the world's largest computer network, consisting of thousands of individual networks supporting millions of computers and users in over 60 countries. Later in this chapter we will provide a more detailed discussion of the Internet.

Brief Case: Pepsi's Enterprise Network

An enterprise network connects all the LANs of a single organization that may, for example, have locations across the United States, as shown in Figure 4.17. When consumers reach for a Pepsi beverage on a store shelf, they may not give much thought to how it got there. Little do consumers know that delivering a Pepsi product to the consumer is a complex and information-intensive activity, with data collected at multiple points in the manufacturing and distribution processes. For Pepsi, like any consumer-goods company, a critical business challenge is to ensure that these processes deliver the right products to the right place at the right time. Pepsi's enterprise network connects nearly 330 manufacturing, distribution, and sales sites around the United States and Canada. The Pepsi enterprise network transports sales data that help marketing managers identify buying trends and make faster decisions regarding product distribution. For example, sales data help managers identify regions where certain products are not selling well, and move any excess inventory to areas where those products are in demand. Sales data also help Pepsi managers make decisions about products before they reach the freshness date and must be pulled from the shelf and discarded. Who would have thought that all this was happening behind the shelves with those cans and bottles of Pepsi?

Enterprise Networks

An **enterprise network** is a WAN that is the result of connecting disparate networks of a single organization into a single network (see Figure 4.17).

Value-Added Networks

Medium-speed WANs, called **value-added networks (VANs)**, are private, third-party managed networks that are economical because they are shared by multiple organizations. Customers lease communication lines rather than investing in dedicated network equipment. The "added value" provided by VANs can include network management, e-mail, EDI, security, and other special capabilities. Consequently, VANs can be more expensive than generic communication lines leased from a common telecommunication company like AT&T or Sprint, but they provide valuable services for customers.

Metropolitan Area Networks

A **metropolitan area network (MAN)** is a computer network of limited geographic scope, typically a city-wide area, that combines both LAN and high-speed fiber-optic technologies. MANs are attractive to organizations that need high-speed data transmission within a limited geographic area.

Personal Area Networks

A final type of computer network, called a **personal area network (PAN)**, is an emerging technology that uses wireless communication to exchange data between computing devices using short-range radio communication, typically within an area of 10 meters. The enabling technology for PAN is called **Bluetooth**, a specification for personal networking of desktop computers, peripheral devices, mobile phones, pagers, portable stereos, and other handheld devices. Bluetooth's founding members include Ericsson, IBM, Intel, Nokia, and Toshiba. Although Bluetooth is a relatively new concept, it is very likely that you will hear a lot more about this important new type of network.

Although there are many different types of networks, all networks are very similar in how they are designed and function. In the next section, we examine in more detail the Internet, one of the largest and most widely used networks.

Web Search

WEB SEARCH OPPORTUNITY:
To find out more about Bluetooth technologies and applications, see the Web site at **http://www.bluetooth.com**.

[**Figure 4.17** ➡ An enterprise network allows an organization to connect distributed locations into a single network.]

Information Systems

Video, voice, and data are three types of information that are most commonly shared between individuals and organizations. To date, these three types of information had been shared across separate network lines, adding to telecommunications redundancies and increased cost for companies. Data has been primarily shared through the use of the local area network, while voice communications had depended on the use of the private branch exchange (PBX). Similarly, video communications had primarily occurred through the use of dedicated links, such as T1, or circuit-switched telephone lines, such as the Integrated Services Digital Network (ISDN). However, modern day technologies are now making the integration of these three forms of communication a reality. Many companies are now moving their telephony services to the LAN, eliminating the costs associated with additional voice cabling networks. This integration is also enabling employees to shift seamlessly between voice and data during their communication. The current Ethernet LANs usually have a bandwidth of 10 Mbps and easily enable the transmission of voice, which requires only a bandwidth of 64 Kbps. The data and voice integrated LANs support various applications such as voice-enabled groupware, conversion of electronic mail into voice messages, and so on. The next step is to integrate video with data and voice. Lack of industry standards and high bandwidth requirements have so far prevented the widespread adoption of video LAN. However, with the emergence of the new standard H.323, which describes equipment and services for integrating real-time voice, data, and video into networked PCs and workstations, the problem related to standards is slowly being eliminated. H.323 is also compatible with current-generation LAN cards, hubs, switches, and routers, and is bringing a new promise to the integration of voice, video, and data. Newer ATM technologies are also enabling the transmission of video at faster speeds through PCs. If you plan on going into the field of information systems, you had better know something about this and other emerging standards for networking.

[Adapted from John Edwards, "Data and Telecommunications Convergence," **http://www.cio.com**, *CIO Magazine* (February 15, 1997).]

Brief Case: Remotely Managing AFS's Network

To give you an idea of what a network operating system (NOS) can do, consider AFS-USA, a nongovernmental, nonprofit organization that manages an international exchange program for high school students. Overseeing more than 10,000 volunteers from coast to coast and a paid staff of 100 in New York City, AFS-USA uses Novell NetWare to manage its local area network. To match students with sponsor families effectively, AFS-USA needs up-to-the-minute information. Unfortunately, when AFS decided to interconnect its computers via a network, it did not have an information systems staff. Given its nonprofit status and the attendant responsibility to keep its overhead low, AFS-USA did not want to hire network professionals to manage its network. Consequently, AFS-USA hired Quality Technology Solutions, Inc. (QTS), in South Orange, New Jersey, to manage the network. Using Novell's remote network-management features in the NOS, QTS could remotely manage the AFS-USA network from its New Jersey offices, enabling AFS-USA to focus on its primary mission of facilitating student exchange programs, not on its network, and keep its overhead to a minimum.

THE INTERNET

The name *Internet* is derived from the concept of *internetworking*, which means connecting host computers and their networks together to form even larger networks. The Internet is a large worldwide collection of networks that use a common protocol to communicate with each other.

How Did the Internet Get Started?

You can trace the roots of the Internet back to the late 1960s when the U.S. *Defense Advanced Research Projects Agency (DARPA)* began to study ways to interconnect networks of various kinds. This research effort produced *ARPANET* (Advanced Research Projects Agency Network), a large wide area network that linked many universities and research centers. The first two nodes on ARPANET were UCLA and the Stanford Research Institute, followed by the University of Utah.

ARPANET quickly evolved and was combined with other networks. For example, in 1986, the U.S. *National Science Foundation (NSF)* initiated the development of the NSFNET

(National Science Foundation Network), which became a major component of the Internet. Other networks throughout the United States and the rest of the world were interconnected and/or morphed into the growing "Internet." Among these were BITNET, CSNET, NSINET, ESNET, and NORDUNET. Throughout the world, support for the Internet has come from a combination of federal and state governments, universities, national and international research organizations, and industry.

The Internet Uses Packet-Switching Technology

The Internet relies on **packet-switching** technology to deliver data and information across networks. Packet switching enables millions of users to send large and small chunks of data across the Internet concurrently. Packet switching is based on the concept of turn taking. To minimize delays, network technologies limit the amount of data that a computer can transfer on each turn. Consider a conveyor belt as a comparison. Suppose that the conveyor belt connects a warehouse and customer storeroom. When a customer places an order, it is sent to the warehouse, where a clerk assembles the items in the order. The items are placed on the conveyor belt and delivered to the storeroom. In most situations, clerks finish sending items from one order before proceeding to send items from another order. This process works well when orders are small, but when a large order with many items is placed, sharing a conveyor belt can introduce delays for others. Consider waiting in the storeroom for your one item while another order with 50 items is being filled.

LANs, WANs, and the Internet all use packet-switching technologies so that users can share the communication channel and minimize delivery delays. Figure 4.18 illustrates how computers use packet switching.

Computer A wants to send a message to computer C; similarly, computer B wants to send a message to computer D. For example, computer A is trying to send an e-mail message to computer C, while computer B is trying to send a word processing file to computer D. The outgoing messages are divided into smaller packets of data, and then each sending computer (A and B) takes turns sending the packets over the transmission media. The incoming packets are reassembled at their respective destinations using previously identified packet sequence numbers.

For packet switching to work, each packet being sent across a network must be labeled with a header. This header contains the network address of the source (sending computer) and the network address of the destination (receiving computer). Each computer attached to a network has a unique network address. As packets are sent, network hardware detects whether a particular packet is destined for a local machine. Packet-switching systems adapt instantly to changes in network traffic. If only one computer needs to use the network, it can send data continuously. As soon as another computer needs to send data, packet switching, or turn taking, begins. Now, let us see how the Internet handles this packet switching.

Transmission Control Protocol/ Internet Protocol (TCP/IP)

Organizations use diverse network technologies that may or may not be compatible with the technologies of other organizations. Because so many different networks are interconnected nowadays, they must have a common language, or **protocol**, to communicate. The protocol of the Internet is called **TCP/IP (Transmission Control Protocol/Internet Protocol)**. The first part, TCP, breaks information into small chunks called data packets and manages the transfer of those packets from

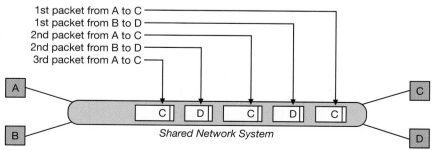

[Figure 4.18 ➡ Using packet switching to send messages from files on computers A and B to computers C and D.]

Comer, Douglas E. The Internet Book, 2/e, 1997; Prentice Hall.

computer to computer (via packet switching, as described above). For example, as described above, a single document may be broken into several packets, each containing several hundred characters, as well as a destination address, which is the IP part of the protocol. The IP defines how a data packet must be formed and to where a router must forward each packet. Packets travel independently to their destination, sometimes following different paths and arriving out of order. The destination computer reassembles all the packets based on their identification and sequencing information. Together, TCP and IP provide a reliable and efficient way to send data across the Internet.

A data packet that conforms to the IP specification is called an *IP datagram*. Datagram routing and delivery are possible because, as previously mentioned, every computer and router connected to the Internet is assigned a unique IP address. When an organization connects to the Internet, it obtains a set of IP addresses that it can assign to its computers. TCP helps IP guarantee delivery of datagrams by performing three main tasks. First, it automatically checks for datagrams that may have been lost en route from their source to their destination. Second, TCP collects the incoming datagrams and puts them in the correct order to recreate the original message. Finally, TCP discards any duplicate copies of datagrams that may have been created by network hardware.

Connecting Independent Networks

Now that you understand how computers share a transmission path, we can examine how packet-switching networks are interconnected to form the Internet. The Internet uses special-purpose computers, called *routers*, to interconnect independent networks. For example, Figure 4.19 illustrates a router that connects Network 1 and Network 2. A router, like a conventional computer, has a central processor, memory, and network interfaces. However, routers do not use conventional software, nor are they used to run applications. Their only job is to interconnect networks and forward data packets from one network to another. For example, in Figure 4.19, computers A and F are connected to independent networks. If computer A generates a data packet destined for computer F, the packet is sent to the router that interconnects the two networks. The router forwards the packet onto Network 2, where it is delivered to its destination at computer F.

Routers are the fundamental building blocks of the Internet because they connect thousands of LANs and WANs. LANs are connected to backbone WANs, as depicted in Figure 4.20. A *backbone network* manages the bulk of network traffic and typically uses a higher-speed protocol than the individual LAN segments. For example, a backbone network might use fiber-optic cabling, which can transfer data at a rate of 2 Gbps, whereas a LAN connected to the backbone may use Ethernet cabling, transferring data at a rate of 10 Mbps. To gain access to the Internet, an organization connects a router between one of its own networks and the closest Internet site. Business organizations typically connect to the Internet not only with personal computers but with Web servers, or hosts, as well.

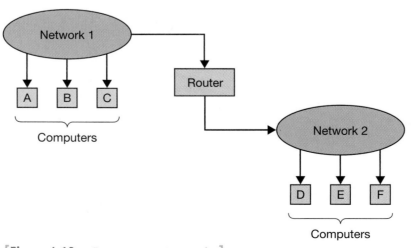

[**Figure 4.19** ➡ Routers connect networks.]

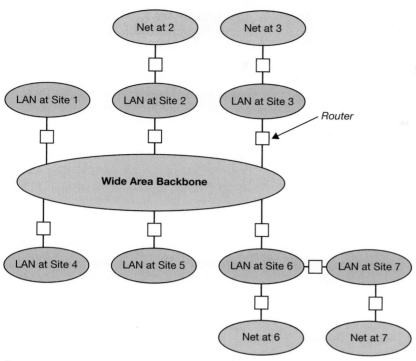

[Figure 4.20 ➡ LANs connect to wide area backbones.]
Comer, Douglas, E. The Internet Book, 2/e, 1997; Prentice Hall.

Increasing bandwidth at a reasonable cost seems to be the primary telecommunications and networking concern for most companies. The Federal Home Loan Mortgage Corp., or Freddie Mac, (buyer and reseller of mortgage packages) also had a similar concern for a long time. Today, due to the availability of modern technology, the company is finally able to increase its bandwidth by a factor of at least 20, though it is paying only half the price it was paying before. The company, which is based in Virginia, previously had a 100 Mbps metropolitan area network connecting its offices in Virginia and Washington, D.C. However, this network was running close to its capacity, thus affecting the company's business, especially its e-commerce initiatives. Freddie Mac finally found the solution in the new fiber-optic technology called MetroMedia Fiber Networks' WaveChannel service. This service uses Nortel Networks' Optera dense wavelength-division multiplexing (DWDM) equipment and connects the multiple offices through optical fibers by linking them on a ring. The DWDM technology allows a single strand of fiber to carry voice, video, and data on separate wavelengths. The ability of this technology to enable transmissions from multiple networks through a single fiber significantly cuts costs and makes network management an easier task.

[Adapted from Bob Wallace, "Freddie Mac Runs Multiple Networks on a Single Fiber," **http://www. informationweek.com** (May 8, 2000).]

Career Implications:

Accounting and Finance

Web Domain Names and Addresses

Each of the hosts or Web sites that you visit on the Internet is assigned a *domain name*. Domain names are used in *Uniform Resource Locators (URLs)* to identify particular *Web pages*. For example, in the URL **www. pcWebopedia.com/index.html**, the domain name is pcWebopedia.com.

The prefix of every domain name is a term that helps people recognize the company or person that domain name represents. For example, Microsoft's domain name is microsoft. com. The prefix, microsoft, lets you know that it is very likely that this domain name will lead you to the Web site of Microsoft Corporation. Domain names also have a suffix that indicates which ***top-level domain*** they belong to. For example the "com" suffix is reserved for commercial organizations.

- edu—educational institutions
- org—organizations (nonprofit)
- mil—military
- com—commercial business
- net—network organizations
- ca—Canada
- th—Thailand

Domain names ending with .com, .net, or .org can be registered through many different companies (known as "registrars") that compete with one another. An alphabetical listing of these registrars is provided in the InterNIC Registrar Directory on the InterNIC site at **http://www.internic.net/regist.html**. Given the proliferation of domain names, more of these top-level domain categories are being added, such as .aero for the air transport industry, .coop for business industry cooperatives, and .museum for museums.

Each of these domain names is associated with one or more ***IP addresses***. For example, the domain name microsoft.com represents about a dozen underlying IP addresses. IP addresses serve to identify all the computers or devices on the Internet (or on any TCP/IP network). The IP address serves as the destination address of that computer or device and enables the network to route messages to the proper destination. The format of an IP address is a 32-bit numeric address written as four numbers separated by periods. Each of the four numbers can be any number between zero and 255. For example, 1.160.10.240 could be an IP address. You could set up a private network using the TCP/IP protocol and assign your own domain names and IP addresses for computers and other devices on that network. On the other hand, if you wish to connect to the Internet, you must use registered IP addresses.

Who Manages the Internet?

So, who keeps track of these IP addresses on the Internet? A number of national and international standing committees and task forces have been used to manage the development and use of the Internet. Among these is the Coordinating Committee for Intercontinental Networks (CCIRN), which has helped to coordinate government-sponsored research in this area. The Internet Society (ISOC) is a professional membership society, with over 150

organizational and 6,000 individual members around the world, that helps to shape the future of the Internet and is home for the Internet Engineering Task Force (IETF) and the Internet Architecture Board (IAB). These groups help manage Internet standards. For example, the IAB has guided the evolution of the TCP/IP Protocol Suite. The Internet Assigned Numbers Authority (IANA) has provided the recording of system identifiers on the Internet and has helped to manage an Internet Registry that acts as a central repository for Internet-related information and which provides central allocation of network system identifiers. The ***Internet Registry*** also provides central maintenance of the ***Domain Name System (DNS)*** root database, which points to distributed DNS servers replicated throughout the Internet. This database is used to associate Internet host names with their Internet IP addresses.

In 1993 the NSF created ***InterNIC***, a government–industry collaboration, to manage directory and database services, domain registration services, and other information services on the Internet. In the late 1990s, this Internet oversight was transitioned more fully out into industry when InterNIC morphed into the ***Internet Corporation for Assigned Names and Numbers (ICANN)***, a nonprofit corporation that assumed responsibility for managing IP addresses, domain names, and root server system management. Specifically, the ***InterNIC Registration Service*** now assigns Internet addresses. The number of unassigned Internet addresses is running out, so new classes of addresses are being added as we adopt ***IPv6***, the latest version of the Internet Protocol.

How Do You Connect to the Internet?

Now you can see how the Internet works and how it is managed. How do you connect to the Internet? For personal use (i.e., from home) we typically connect to the Internet through ***Internet Service Providers (ISPs)***, also called Internet Access Providers. For a monthly fee, these ISPs will give you a username, password, and access phone number (and in some cases specialized access software). With your personal computer and a modem, you can then log on through the ISP's servers to access the Internet and browse the World Wide Web and Usenet, and send and receive e-mail. ISPs serve not only individuals like you, but they also serve large companies by providing them with a direct connection from the company's networks to the Internet.

Many organizations are utilizing telecommunications and networking technologies to improve their human resource management practices. For example, NASA is in the process of implementing NASA STARS, an automated, Web-based Staffing and Recruitment System. As each NASA center implements NASA STARS, vacancy announcements for that center will direct applicants to an Online Resume Builder (part of NASA STARS) to submit an electronic resume. As each NASA center comes onboard with NASA STARS, when it posts a vacancy announcement for an open position, the announcement will notify applicants that the position is being filled using NASA STARS. Applicants can then apply for these jobs only if

they go on the Web and use the resume builder and other components of NASA STARS.

The Online Resume Builder allows you to provide required information about yourself in a standard resume format. With the Online Resume Builder you can create, edit, view, and print your resume. You will also have the option to paste a text copy of your resume. This will not only enable NASA to handle more resumes and applicants, but will help to standardize processes, documents, and decisions in the hiring process. This will enable NASA to make better hiring decisions. If you would like to find out more about NASA STARS, or if you would like to apply for a job at NASA, check out its Web site at **http://resume.nasa.gov/**.

Human Resource Management

ISPs connect to one another through **Network Access Points (NAPs)**. Much like railway stations, these NAPs serve as access points for ISPs and are an exchange point for Internet traffic. They determine how traffic is routed and are often the points of most Internet congestion. NAPs are a key component of the **Internet backbone**, which is the collection of main network connections and telecommunications lines comprising the Internet (see Figure 4.21).

The Internet follows a hierarchical structure, similar to the interstate highway system. High-speed central network lines are like interstate highways, enabling traffic from midlevel networks to get on and off. Think of midlevel networks as city streets which, in turn, accept traffic from their neighborhood

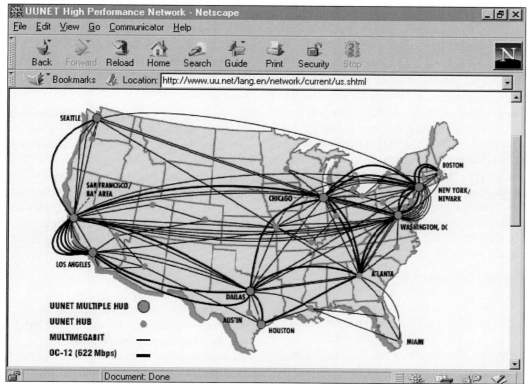

[**Figure 4.21** ➡ The Internet backbone.]
UUNet Technologies

streets or member networks. However, you cannot just get on an interstate or city street whenever you want to. You have to share the highway and follow traffic control signs to arrive safely at your destination. The same holds true for traffic on the Internet.

How Fast Is Your Connection to the Internet?

There are a number of ways that people can connect to the Internet. In addition to traditional connections through plain old telephones and modems, there are a number of high-speed alternatives. This section briefly describes several different ways that people connect to the Internet from home, office, and beyond.

Plain Old Telephone Service

Many of us connect to the Internet through a telephone line at our home or work. The term we use for standard telephone lines is *plain old telephone service (POTS)*. The speed, or bandwidth, of POTS is generally about 52 Kbps (52,000 bits per second). The POTS system is also called the *public switched telephone network (PSTN)*.

Integrated Services Digital Network (ISDN)

Integrated Services Digital Network (ISDN) is a standard for worldwide digital communications. ISDN is intended to replace all analog systems, such as most telephone connections in the United States, with a completely digital transmission system. ISDN uses existing twisted-pair telephone wires to provide high-speed data service. ISDN systems can transmit voice, video, and data. Because ISDN is a purely digital network, you can connect your PC to the Internet without the use of a modem[1]. Removing the analog-to-digital conversion for sending information and the digital-to-analog conversion for receiving information greatly increases the data transfer rate. Consequently, people and organizations wanting high-speed access to the Internet are rapidly switching their phone systems to ISDN.

Digital Subscriber Line (DSL)

One popular alternative now available from telephone service providers around the world is the use of *Digital Subscriber Lines (DSL)*. DSL uses special modulation schemes to fit more data onto copper wires. Both ISDN and

DSL are referred to as "last-mile" solutions because they are used only for connections from a telephone switching station to a home or office, and they generally are not used between telephone switching stations. DSL and ISDN are similar in that they both use existing copper telephone lines and they both require relatively short runs to a central telephone office (typically less than 20,000 feet). DSL has relatively high speeds of up to 32 Mbps when receiving data (i.e., for downstream traffic), and from 32 Kbps to over 1 Mbps when sending data (i.e., for upstream traffic).

The acronym DSL is used to refer collectively to ADSL, SDSL, and other forms of DSL. ADSL and SDSL enable more data to be sent over existing copper telephone lines. ADSL is short for *Asymmetric Digital Subscriber Line*. ADSL speeds range from 1.5 to 9 Mbps downstream and from 16 to 640 Kbps upstream. Like ISDN, ADSL requires a special ADSL modem-like device. SDSL is short for *Symmetric Digital Subscriber Line*. SDSL is said to be symmetric because it supports the same data rates for upstream and downstream traffic. SDSL supports data rates up to 3 Mbps and works by sending digital pulses in the high-frequency area of telephone wires. Given that these high frequencies are not used by normal voice communications, SDSL enables your computer to operate simultaneously with voice connections over the same wires. Like ADSL, SDSL requires a special modem-like device. ADSL is most popular in North America, whereas SDSL is being developed primarily in Europe.

Cable Modems

In some areas the company that provides cable television service also provides Internet service. With this type of service, a special *cable modem* is designed to operate over cable TV lines. Coaxial cable used for cable TV provides much greater bandwidth than telephone lines, and millions of homes in the United States are already wired for cable TV, so cable modems are a fast, popular method for accessing the Internet. Cable modems offer speeds up to 2 Mbps.

Satellite Connections

In many regions of the world people can now access the Internet via *satellite*, referred to as *Internet over Satellite (IoS)*. IoS technologies allow users to access the Internet via satellites that are placed in fixed positions above the earth's surface in what is known as a *geostationary* or *geosynchronous* orbit

---

[1]Some special equipment, however, like a modem, is often needed when using an ISDN-based service.

(i.e., the satellite moves along with the earth). With these services, your PC is connected to a satellite dish hanging out on the side of your home or placed out on a pole (much like satellite services for your television) and is able to maintain a reliable connection to the satellite in the sky because the satellite orbits the earth at the exact speed of the earth's rotation. Given the vast distance that signals must travel from the earth up to the satellite and back again, IoS is slower than high-speed terrestrial (i.e., land-based) connections to the Internet over copper or fiber-optic cables.

In remote regions of the world, IoS is the only option available because installing the cables necessary for Internet connection is not economically feasible or in many cases is just not physically possible. For example, at Len's home high up on Paradise Ridge in Moscow, Idaho, he cannot get any high-speed data services from the phone company and, similarly, cable modems and cable television are not available that far out of town. As a result, he purchased the new Starband Internet over Satellite service offered jointly by Starband, Microsoft, and Radio Shack. With that service he can access the Internet at speeds of up to 900 Kbps downstream and up to 100 Kbps upstream. Joe lives over on the other side of town, high up on Moscow Mountain, and he faced the same constraints in getting high-speed Internet access. He chose to acquire a wireless service whereby he has a dish that is much like Len's satellite dish except that Joe's is pointed down into town rather than up into the sky. Joe's dish sends data to, and receives data from, a transceiver mounted on a pole in downtown Moscow that is connected to a land-based DSL line.

So, whose Internet service is faster? Joe's or Len's? Well, Len's service is truly satellite based, and so his data signals have to go all the way up to the Starband satellite in the sky and then back down again[2], while Joe's travel only a short distance into town, so Joe's service should be much faster, right? It turns out that is not the case. The reality is that Joe shares his service with other people on Moscow Mountain and, thus, when they are all

on the system at the same time they are sharing the same land-based DSL connection. As a result, there are times when Joe's connection to the Internet is faster than Len's, and there are times when Joe's connection is slower.

In addition to these *fixed wireless* approaches for connecting to the Internet, there are also many new *mobile wireless* approaches for connecting to the Internet. For example, there are Internet-enabled *cellular phones* from Sprint and others, and small palm-top computers from Palm and others, that give you Internet access nearly anywhere. With a special network adapter card you can use your notebook computer, tablet PC, or personal digital assistant and enjoy the freedom of wireless mobility. The beauty of these systems is that as long as you are in the coverage area you have access to the Internet (much like coverage with cellular phones). One other option for wireless access to the Internet is to use a wireless Ethernet network adapter card in any of these computing devices, but with this type of equipment you would have to be located near a transceiver on the network. You would be free to roam around your office or building, but that would be it. With these other technologies you would be able to wander freely around your network, or cellular, coverage area.

Up until now we have talked about ways that individuals rather than organizations typically access the Internet. In the following section we talk more about ways that organizations typically access the Internet—although an individual with high amounts of discretionary income could certainly access the Internet in these same ways!

T1 Lines

To gain adequate access to the Internet, organizations are turning to long-distance carriers to lease a dedicated *T1 line* for digital transmissions. The T1 line was developed by AT&T as a dedicated digital transmission line that can carry 1.544 Mbps of information. In the United States, companies such as BrandX that sell long-distance services are called interexchange carriers because their circuits carry service between the major telephone exchanges. As previously mentioned, a T1 line can carry 1.544 Mbps and usually traverses hundreds or thousands of miles over leased long-distance facilities.

AT&T and other carriers charge anywhere from $500 to several thousands of dollars per month for a dedicated T1 circuit spanning

Team Work

Who Is Faster?

Sit in a small group with members of your class and, one-by-one, tell how you connect to the Internet from your homes, dorm rooms, and/or apartments. Which of the connections described above are you each using? Which of your connections is fastest? Who pays the least? Does this information make any of you want to change the way you connect?

---

[2]In addition, traveling up to the satellite in the sky and back again, the signals from Len's system are a bit more sensitive to weather and atmospheric conditions than are the signals to and from Joe's system, which travel on a much shorter, lower path from the mountaintop down into town and back again.

1,000 miles. If you need an even faster link, you might choose a *T3 line*. T3 provides about 45 Mbps of service at about 10 times the cost of leasing a T1 line. Alternatively, organizations often choose to use two or more T1 lines simultaneously rather than jump to the more expensive T3 line. Higher speeds than the T3 are also available but are not typically used for normal business activity. See Table 4.2 for a summary of communication line capacities.

Asynchronous Transfer Mode (ATM)
Asynchronous Transfer Mode (ATM) is a method of transmitting voice, video, and data over high-speed LANs at speeds of up to 2.2 GBps (gigabits per second). ATM has found wide acceptance in the LAN and WAN arenas as a solution to integrating disparate networks over large geographic distances. ATM uses a form of packet transmission in which data is sent over a packet-switched network in a fixed-length, 53-byte cell. Although it is based on packet-switching technology, ATM has the potential to do away with routers, allocated bandwidth, and contention for com-

munications media. Organizations in the movie and entertainment industries that need to deliver synchronized video and sound, for example, are particularly interested in ATM.

Security in the Internet Age

As use of the Internet and other types of technologies and systems has become more pervasive, the need for security has increased dramatically. Concerns have risen over the accuracy and privacy of personal data, and organizations now demand that their information systems be reliable and secure. A number of techniques have arisen to secure systems that are Internet related. **Encryption** is a technique whereby key data are encoded with a special secret key when being stored or transmitted. **Firewalls**, consisting of specialized hardware and software, keep unwanted users out of a system, or let users in with restricted access and privileges. A variety of means of **authentication** are used to verify who users are and what they are allowed to do once they are inside a system or a database. These and other security tools and issues will

[Table 4.2] *Capacity of communication lines.*

Type of Line	Data Rate (Mbps)	Equivalent Number of Voice Lines
T1	1.544	24
T3	44.736	672

Career Implications:
Operations Management

In today's fast-paced world, the transmission and access speed of voice, video, and data over the Internet is critical for the efficiency of organizations, including small businesses. However, until recently, most small businesses relied on DSL or cable modems for access, due to the huge costs involved in adopting other forms of access. New fiber-optic cables are now the high-speed solution for the small business. Until even a couple of years ago, fiber-optic cables had been affordable only for large enterprises. However, a recent dramatic price decrease in fiber-optic cabling (due to a surplus of construction) is now making it possible for even smaller businesses to acquire them without incurring any significant increases in cost. For example, InSors, a small company based in Illinois, recently realized that they had to pay only a $1000 monthly

fee for fiber optics and network speeds of 100 megabits per second, instead of up to $1500 for a T1 line with a speed of 1.5 Mbps. Similarly, NxTier, a small business based in Massachusetts, is paying only $4000 per month for high-speed access, which is only marginally higher than their previous Internet access costs. NxTier is using this new telecommunication capability to offer a comprehensive customer, supply-chain, and distribution management system. From the moment a customer places an order to the moment the delivery is made, NxTier uses telecommunications to provide the infrastructure to move information and products accurately, rapidly, and efficiently. These new fiber-optic capabilities enable NxTier and other small businesses to easily handle large volumes of data, including voice and video, through very thin cables composed of glass.

[Adapted from Tom Spring, "Broadband: Beyond DSL and Cable," **http://www.pcworld.com**, *PC World Magazine* (September 2001).]

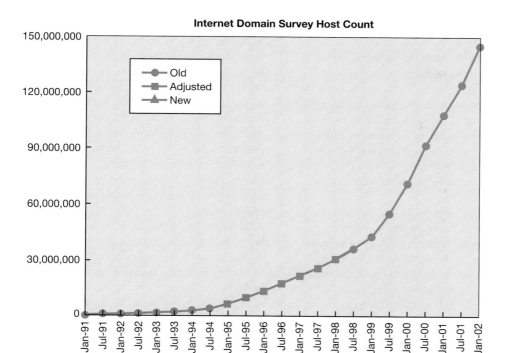

Internet Domain Survey Host Count

[**Figure 4.22** ➡ Growth in Internet servers (hosts).]
Reprinted by permission of Network Wizards.

be covered in detail in Chapter 9, which is devoted to the topic.

State of the Internet

The Internet is now the most prominent global network. More than a billion people worldwide have access to the Internet. A recent study found that the profile of the average U.S. Internet user now mirrors that of the average U.S. adult (InsightExpress, 2001). For example, today 51 percent of Internet users are female, as are 51 percent of U.S. adults. The average household income of Internet users has dropped from $62,700 in 1996 to $49,800, which is much closer to the overall average household income of $40,816. Back in 1996, 88 percent of Internet users were between ages 18 and 49, but that has dropped to 76 percent, much closer to the overall average of 63 percent. Finally, the number of people over 50 years of age online has increased in the past five years from 12 percent to 24 percent, which is much closer to the overall figure of 37 percent. The Internet is clearly being used by more people and by a more diverse audience. It is becoming more a part of the mainstream.[3]

[3]See InsightExpress, "Net Population Mirrors Overall Population," July 23, 2001, at **Web.insightexpress. com/news/index.asp**

One other way to measure the rapid growth of the Internet, in addition to the number of users, is to examine the growth in the number of Internet hosts, that is, computers working as servers on the Internet, as shown in Figure 4.22.

What Are People Doing on the Internet?

The Internet enables people to access a wide range of data, including text, video, audio, graphics, databases, maps, and other data types. The Internet is more, however, than just access to data. The Internet also enables people not only to access data but to connect with each other. In the last couple of years, with increases in bandwidth and decreases in prices for computers and Internet access, there have been substantial changes in the ways people are using the Internet. For example, recent advancements in communication technologies and increasingly high transmission speeds have made interactivity—real time collaboration between people—possible over the Internet.

A range of ways that people use, and have used, the Internet are summarized in Table 4.3. Essentially, these involve ways to access data and to communicate with other people via text either through real-time chat or via electronic mail. Perhaps the most significant use of the Internet has been for electronic mail.

Web Search

WEB SEARCH OPPORTUNITY: Investigate the American National Standards Institute at its Web site, **http://www. ansi.org/**, and then investigate the International Organization for Standardization at its Web site, **http://www.iso. ch/iso/en/ISOOnline. frontpage**. See what you can learn about these organizations and their interaction.

Technology-Related Challenges for Global Telecommunications

The primary technological challenges faced by organizations when operating across national boundaries are related to telecommunications infrastructure. The price, quality, and speed of telecommunications support can vary from country to country. For example, in Greece only half of the telecommunication networks are digital, whereas the networks in Finland are 100 percent digital. You cannot assume you will find the same kind of telecommunications infrastructure and performance when you move from one country to the next.

In some cases, the differences are merely in terms of performance (e.g., one country has a faster telecommunications infrastructure for businesses than does another country). Worse, however, are situations in which one country uses a different telecommunications standard than does another country, because then businesses may face compatibility and other problems as they move from one country to the next. For example, a company headquartered in Hong Kong recently expanded its operations to Thailand, only to realize that the manufacturing facilities were located in an area that had no telecommunications connections available using the X.25 standard. As a result, given the network infrastructure that the parent firm was using and assuming, the subsidiary was not easily able to interact electronically with its headquarters located in Hong Kong (Sarker and Sarker, 2000).

Differences in telecommunications standards across the planet pose serious challenges for organizations, and these differences are more the norm than the exception. For example, in the United States, most people prefer to use network standards produced by the American National Standards Institute (e.g., ANSI X.12), whereas in Europe people more commonly use network standards produced by the International Organization for Standardization (e.g., the OSI model for networks). Moreover, within Europe itself one can witness a variety of different standards due to the lack of political unification.

Similarly, the hardware platforms used in different countries are also different, causing further, significant integration problems. For example, the United States has seen a predominance of the use of IBM mainframes and Windows-based servers and PCs, whereas in Europe UNIX is much more popular. The preferences for software are also different. European nations, such as Norway, prefer to use "pdf" files, whereas in the United States there is a predominance of files created using Microsoft Office software products. This, too, causes serious problems in data sharing and data transfer.

The proliferation of the Internet and platform-independent programming languages such as Java has helped, but it is still very difficult to develop a seamless global telecommunications infrastructure for an organization.

Electronic Mail

As described earlier in this chapter, **electronic mail**, or e-mail, is the transmission of messages over computer networks. Most organizations now use **gateways** to connect their internal computer systems and networks to the Internet, enabling people to send electronic mail over the Internet to and from nearly anywhere in the world.

All Internet Service Providers offer e-mail, and nearly all of them provide gateways so that you can exchange mail across the Internet with users of other systems. In business organizations, some popular e-mail systems include Microsoft Exchange, Lotus Notes, and Novel GroupWise. Hotmail is a free, Web-based e-mail system that requires only access to the Internet and use of a Web browser. Companies typically use e-mail extensively because it is a fast, flexible, reliable, and relatively inexpensive way for people to communicate with each other.

Although different e-mail systems look and behave differently, there are some emerging standards that enable users on different systems to exchange messages. MAPI, IMAP, POP, MIME, and SMTP are all examples of standards used to manage the exchange of e-mail across different systems. Given how good e-mail systems have gotten, and how popular e-mail has become, estimates are that billions and billions of e-mail messages are sent each year.

While the Internet is an amazing collection of technologies, the real power of the Internet was not realized until the early 1990s with the invention of the World Wide Web and the Web browser. The Web and the Web browser have essentially given us a graphical user interface with which to use the Internet and, as a result, have made the Internet much more accessible and easy to use, and opened the door for some very innovative uses of the Internet, as described on page 120.

What Is Next for the Internet?

In the mid-1990s, many researchers at universities became frustrated with the increased personal and business use of the Internet. The

Internet Tool	Description
E-mail	Enables users to send messages to each other.
Telnet	Enables users to connect, or log in, to any computer on the Internet.
File transfer	Enables users to connect to a remote computer solely for the purpose of transferring files; either uploading (sending to the remote machine) or downloading (obtaining from the remote machine) files and data; using File Transfer Protocol (FTP).
Listserv, **short for "mailing list server"**	Enables groups of people with common interests to send messages to each other. Interested people subscribe to a discussion group, which is essentially a mailing list. When a subscriber sends a message to the list, the message is sent to all other subscribers.
Usenet	Enables groups of people with common interests to send messages or other binary information to each other. Unlike listserv, Usenet has no master list of subscribers. Rather, anyone with access to Usenet may use a newsreader program to post and read articles from the group.
Archie	Enables users to search FTP sites for their contents. For example, if you were looking for a particular file, perhaps a software application or game, you could use Archie to search FTP sites. Using the results of the Archie search, you can determine which FTP site has the desired files and then use FTP to download them.
WAIS **(Wide Area Information Server)**	Enables users to locate information by indexing electronic data using standard keywords.
Gopher	A text-based, menu-driven interface that enables users to access a large number of varied Internet resources as if they were in folders and menus on their own computers. Menu choices on a Gopher server include text files, graphic images, sounds, software, or even another menu.
Voice over IP	A collection of hardware and software that enables the use of the Internet as the transmission medium for telephone calls.

[Table 4.3] *Internet tools past and present.*

Internet had previously been a network primarily for researchers from universities and other organizations, and all of a sudden shortly after 1995 (note that this is the year Netscape went public and Microsoft turned its attention squarely to the Internet), the Internet was quickly being overrun with all types of nonresearch-oriented traffic. As a result, in 1996 thirty-four U.S. research universities began working on **Internet2**, a faster, private alternative to the public Internet (**www.internet2.edu**). In 1997, the University Corporation for Advanced Internet Development (UCAID) was created to help manage Internet2. Researchers now use Internet2 as a testing-ground network to develop advanced Internet technologies and applications. Internet2 requires state-of-the-art infrastructure,

so Internet2 universities are connected to the **Abilene network backbone**, which uses regional network aggregation points called **gigaPoPs** and very high-speed network equipment and facilities.

The term gigaPoP is short for gigabit Point of Presence, a network access point that supports data transfer rates of at least 1 Gbps. Each university that connects to Internet2 must do so through a gigaPoP, which connects the university's networks with Internet2. For comparison, the point-of-presence facilities maintained by regular ISPs are designed to allow low-speed modems to connect to the Internet, while these gigaPoPs are designed for fast access to a high-speed network like Internet2.

There are over 180 Internet2 member universities and over 60 participating companies.

Marketing

Applying for a mortgage is often a tiresome experience for customers. It includes filling out lengthy forms with a wide array of financial and credit information, multiple trips to the bank, and long waiting periods to get approval. All of this often results in frustration for customers and diminished profits for the mortgage companies. Chris Larsen and Janina Pawlowski, who owned a small brokerage firm in Palo Alto, California, realized this problem and wanted to do something about it. In their quest to make customers more satisfied and cut down on loan agents (who act as middlemen and add to the time required to get an approval) and related fees, they realized that they could use the Internet to ease their problems. With the technical expertise they had gained at NASA and Xerox, they designed an online loan application system that enabled customers to search for more than 50,000 mortgage products from 70 lenders and then allowed them to submit and track loan applications online. They also transformed their physical organization to a virtual one (naming it E-Loan), thus providing more flexibility and access to customers. One of the pioneers in the online mortgage industry, today the company is the leader of online mortgages, just ahead of Quicken Loans. The company is now working toward adding two more features to its online system: 1) an ability to provide human customer service, a feature that most mortgage consumers desire, and 2) an ability to provide home equity loans, which are not yet offered by E-Loan, Inc. Whether you go to work for one of these entrepreneurial Internet firms or for a more traditional bank or other financial institution, you will likely be working with just such an online system. If you are headed out into one of these related industries, you should check out the Web sites of these firms: **http://quickenloans.quicken.com/** and **http://www.eloan.com/**

[Adapted from Constantin Von Hoffman, "Mouse-Click Mortgages," *CIO Web Business Magazine* (October 1, 1999).]

Internet2 operates at speeds up to 2.4 gigabits per second, 45,000 times faster than a typical modem. Will you ever surf Internet2, as you now do the Internet? Not likely, unless you embark on a career in IS research! The good news is that Internet2 is now a fast, private place for researchers to come up with new, Internet-related discoveries and technologies, and these will eventually migrate over onto the public Internet.

One other program that might potentially help the Internet to develop further is the Next Generation Internet Initiative. This is a U.S. program that is designed to fund and coordinate federal agencies and academia in the design and development of the next generation of Internet technologies and services. This program was first proposed by President Clinton in 1996 and has not yet been formally specified or funded by Congress. One other similar initiative is vBNS+, which stands for very high-speed Backbone Network Service, which is a cooperative agreement between WorldCom and the National Science Foundation and is aimed at developing high-performance, high-bandwidth Internet-related technologies and applications. Given these initiatives and the tens of thousands of corporate and academic researchers pursuing new Internet technologies and applications, one thing is for sure: The Internet will continue to get better and faster!

WORLD WIDE WEB

One of the most powerful uses of the Internet is something that you have no doubt heard a great deal about—the *World Wide Web*. More than likely, you have probably browsed the Web using Netscape Navigator, Microsoft's Internet Explorer, or some other popular *Web browser*, as shown in Figure 4.23. A Web browser is a software application that can be used to locate and display Web pages including text, graphics, and multimedia content. Browsers are fast becoming a standard Internet tool. As previously mentioned, the Web is a graphical user interface to the Internet and provides users with a simple, consistent interface to a wide variety of information.

Prior to the invention of the Web by Tim Berners-Lee in 1991, content posted on the Internet could be accessed through the Internet tool, Gopher, previously described. Gopher provides a menu-driven, hierarchical interface to organize files stored on servers, providing a way to tie together related files from different Internet servers across the world. The Web took Gopher one step further by introducing *hypertext*. A hypertext document, otherwise known as a Web page, contains not only information, but also references or links to other documents that contain related information. These links are known as *hyperlinks*. The Web also introduced the *Hypertext Markup Lan-*

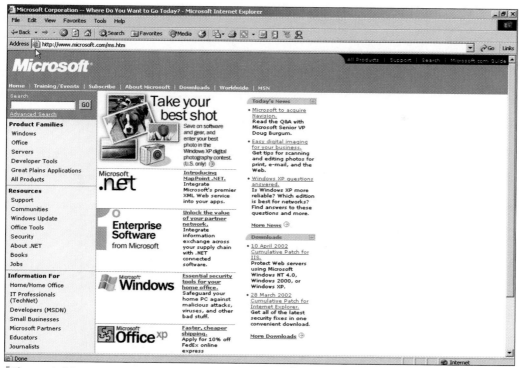

[**Figure 4.23** ➡ Microsoft's Internet Explorer Web browser.]

Source www.microsoft.com

guage, or HTML, which is the standard method of specifying the format of Web pages. Specific content within each Web page is enclosed within codes, or markup tags, which stipulate how the content should appear to the user. Web pages are stored on **Web servers**, which process user requests for pages using the **Hypertext Transfer Protocol**, or HTTP. Web servers typically host a collection of interlinked Web pages created by the same author, which is known as a Web site. Web sites and specific Web pages within those sites have a unique Internet address called a URL, or **Uniform Resource Locator**. A user who wants to access a Web site enters the URL, and the Web server hosting the Web site retrieves the desired page and delivers it to the user.

The introduction of the Web was the first of three events that led to its proliferation. The second event was the Information Infrastructure Act (Berghel, 1996), passed by the U.S. government in 1992, which opened the Web for commercial purposes. Prior to this legislation, universities and governmental agencies were the Web's predominant users. The third event was the arrival of a graphical Web browser, Mosaic, which quickly transcended Gopher by adding a graphical front end to the Web. Mosaic's graphical interface allowed Web pages to be constructed to deliver an extended range of content, including images, audio, video, and other multimedia, all of which could be included and displayed within the same Web page. Mosaic was the predecessor to Netscape's Navigator.

World Wide Web Architecture

The Web uses Web browsers, Web servers, and the TCP/IP networking protocol to facilitate the transmission of Web pages over the Internet. Figure 4.24 depicts the architecture of the Web. To access information on the Web, a Web browser, as well as the TCP/IP protocol, must be installed on a user's computer. Users can access Web pages by entering into their Web browser the URL of the Web page. Once the user enters the URL in the Web browser, TCP/IP breaks the request into packets and routes them over the Internet to the Web server where the requested Web page is stored. When the packets reach their destination, TCP/IP reassembles them and passes the request to the Web server. The Web server understands that the user is requesting a Web page (indicated by the http:// prefix in the URL) and retrieves the Web page, which is packetized by TCP/IP and transmitted over the Internet back to the Web browser. TCP/IP reassembles the packets at the destination and

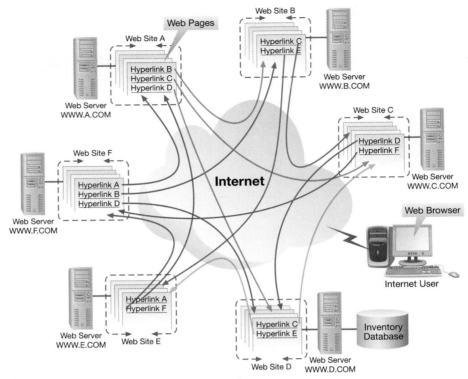

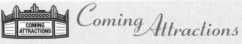

[Figure 4.24 ➡ World Wide Web architecture.]

Coming Attractions

"FILL 'ER UP WITH WIRELESS DATA, PLEASE!"

Imagine filling up your car not with fuel but with data, and doing it without stopping the vehicle! Well, the folks in the research division of Mercedes-Benz have built a C320 sedan equipped with what many people believe will be the "next big thing" in technology for vehicles. This car uses next-generation high-speed wireless LAN technology that can send and receive large amounts of data in spurts.

The equipment in the Mercedes test car, which is part of its DriveBy InfoFueling project, is based on the emerging 802.11a wireless LAN standard. Mercedes USA gave a demonstration at a recent Comdex convention. The Mercedes system sent and received data from a moving vehicle at 54 Mbps in tests—many times faster than the data-transfer rates of cell-phone frequencies or even standard wireless local area networks. The 802.11a standard has the potential to accommodate wireless LANs at speeds up to 100 Mbps.

The DriveBy InfoFueling system involves sending data in bursts as vehicles pass transceiver sites with limited range. For example, a car would send and receive data as it sped past a transceiver and would not be able to send or receive again until it passed another base station.

"We've set up a network that has wireless hot spots the car can use to download large amounts of data as it drives by at highway speeds," says Wieland Holfelder, manager of smart vehicles research at DaimlerChrysler Research and Technology North America Inc. in Palo Alto, California. DaimlerChrysler is Mercedes-Benz USA's parent.

Potential uses include downloading maps, traffic data, and digital music or video without stopping or slowing down, Holfelder says. It could also be used to send data from a moving car to another vehicle or to a person connected to a conventional LAN or the Internet.

[Adapted from John Rendleman, "Fill 'Er Up With Wireless Data, Please," *Information Week* (November 19, 2001).]

delivers the Web page to the Web browser. In turn, the Web browser translates the HTML code contained in the Web page, formats its physical appearance, and displays the results. If the Web page contains a hyperlink, the user can click on it and the process repeats itself.

World Wide Web Applications

Considering that the powerful and relatively inexpensive Web platform is extremely well suited for disseminating information on a global basis, organizations are constantly trying to devise innovative applications for the Web. Over the years, many organizations have become very sophisticated users of Web technologies. The first wave of Web-based commerce occurred around 1994, when new businesses brought product marketing to the Web, pioneering an explosion of commercial activity that will continue into the foreseeable future (Looney and Chatterjee, 2002).

There are a number of ways in which companies can utilize the Web to support business activities. For example, very many companies use the Web to at least disseminate sales and marketing information—what is referred to as the *electronic brochure*. Many companies also now use the Web for *online ordering*, which means that they enable customers to order and, in many cases, actually pay for products and services online. Still other firms, such as eBay, create *electronic marketplaces*, bringing multiple sellers and multiple buyers together and providing a vehicle for them to trade with each other online. Many firms also use the Web to provide *online customer service*, or at least to enhance their traditional customer service. We will talk about each of these uses of the Web in detail in Chapter 5, "Electronic Commerce, Intranets, and Extranets."

KEY POINTS REVIEW

1. **Understand the role of telecommunications in organizations.** Applications such as electronic mail, newsgroups, mailing lists (listservs), Internet Relay Chat, facsimile, voice mail, and videoconferencing are rapidly changing business and interpersonal communication. Global computer networks allow organizations to streamline business operations in ways never before possible. Telecommunications technologies are becoming fundamental, not only for supporting day-to-day activities within most organizations, but also for playing a growing role in the competitive strategy of more and more organizations. Business applications that are particularly important include electronic commerce, Electronic Data Interchange, telecommuting, electronic fund transfers, distance learning, and telemedicine. More than ever before, managers must understand these technologies to ride the information systems wave and to apply the right solutions to the right problems.

2. **Describe the evolution of and types of computer networks.** Since the 1950s, three models of computing have been used. First, from the 1950s until the 1970s, the centralized computing model was dominant. In the centralized computing model, all processing occurs at a large central computer, and users interact with the system through the use of terminals. From the late 1970s until the late 1980s, a distributed computing model was dominant. In this model, separate computers work on subsets of tasks and then pool their results by communicating via a network. In the 1990s, the collaborative computing model emerged. In this model, two or more networked computers work together to accomplish a common processing task. There are several types of computer networks. A private branch exchange (PBX) is a private telephone exchange, located in a single facility, which pro-

vides both voice and data communication. A local area network (LAN) is a group of computers at one location that share hardware and software resources. A wide area network (WAN) refers to two or more LANs from different locations that are linked together. There are four general types of WANs: global networks, enterprise networks, value-added networks, and metropolitan area networks (MANs). A global network is a WAN that spans multiple countries and may include the networks of several organizations. An enterprise network is a WAN that connects all the LANs of a single location. Value-added networks are private, third party–managed networks that are shared by multiple organizations. Metropolitan area networks span a limited geographic scope, typically a city-wide area with both LAN and high-speed fiber-optic technologies. A final type of computer network, called a personal area network (PAN), is an emerging technology that uses wireless communication to exchange data between computing devices using short-range radio communication, typically within an area of 10 meters.

3. **Describe the Internet and how it works.** The Internet is composed of networks that are developed and maintained by many different entities, and follows a hierarchical structure, similar to the interstate highway system. High-speed central networks called backbones are like interstate highways, enabling traffic from midlevel networks to get on and off. The Internet relies on packet-switching technology to deliver data and information across networks. Routers are used to interconnect independent networks. Because so many different networks are connected to the Internet, they use a common communication protocol (TCP/IP). TCP/IP is divided into two parts. TCP breaks information into small chunks, called data packets, which are transferred from computer to com-

puter. IP defines how a data packet must be formed and how a router must forward each packet. All computers, including routers, are assigned unique IP addresses. Data routing and delivery are possible due to the unique addressing of every computer attached to the Internet. Together, TCP and IP provide a reliable and efficient way to send data across the Internet.

4. Describe the basic Internet services and the use of the World Wide Web. A collection of Internet tools enables you to

exchange messages, share information, or connect to remote computers. These tools include electronic mail, Telnet, file transfer protocol, listserv, Usenet, Archie, WAIS, Gopher, and voice over IP. The most powerful tool today is the World Wide Web, which binds together the various tools used on the Internet, providing users with a simple, consistent interface to a wide variety of information through the use of Web browsers.

KEY TERMS

Abilene network backbone 119
Archie 119
ARPANET 108
Asymmetric Digital Subscriber Line (ADSL) 114
Asynchronous Transfer Mode (ATM) 116
authentication 116
backbone network 110
bandwidth 96
Bluetooth 107
cable modem 114
cellular phone 115
centralized computing 102
collaborative computing 103
Defense Advanced Research Projects Agency (DARPA) 108
Digital Subscriber Line 114
digitizing 102
distance learning 100
distributed computing 103
domain name 111
Domain Name System 112
electronic brochure 123
electronic commerce 98
Electronic Data Interchange (EDI) 98
electronic fund transfer 100
electronic mail 96, 118
electronic marketplace 123
encryption 116
enterprise network 107
facsimile or fax machine 97
file transfer 119
firewall 116
fixed wireless 115
gateway 118
geostationary 114
geosynchronous 114
gigaPoP 119

global network 106
Gopher 119
Hypertext Markup Language (HTML) 120
Hypertext Transfer Protocol (HTTP) 121
hyperlink 120
hypertext 120
Integrated Services Digital Network (ISDN) 114
Internet 108
Internet backbone 113
Internet Corporation for Assigned Names and Numbers (ICANN) 112
Internet over Satellite 114
Internet Registry 112
Internet Relay Chat (IRC) 97
Internet Service Provider (ISPs) 112
Internet2 119
internetworking 108
InterNIC 112
InterNIC Registration Service 112
IP address 112
IP datagram 110
IPv6 112
listserv 119
local area network (LAN) 105
mailing lists 97
metropolitan area network (MAN) 107
mobile wireless 115
modem 102
National Science Foundation 108
network 96
Network Access Point 113
newsgroups 97
National Science Foundation Network (NSFNET) 109
online customer service 123
online ordering 123

packet switching 109
personal area network (PAN) 107
plain old telephone service (POTS) 114
private branch exchange (PBX) 104
protocols 101, 109
public switched telephone network (PSTN) 114
router 110
satellite 114
Symmetric Digital Subscriber Line (SDSL) 114
T1 line 115
T3 line 116
telecommunications 96
telecommuting 99
telemedicine 100
Telnet 119
terminals 102
top-level domain 112
Transmission Control Protocol/Internet Protocol (TCP/IP) 109
transmission media 101
Uniform Resource Locator 111, 121
Usenet 119
value-added network (VAN) 107
very high-speed Backbone Network Service (vBNS+) 120
videoconferencing 98
voice mail 98
voice over IP 119
WAIS 119
Web browser 120
Web page 111
Web server 121
Web site 98
wide area network (WAN) 106
wireless local area network 105
World Wide Web (Web) 120

REVIEW QUESTIONS

1. List and describe three types of interpersonal communication applications for telecommunications.
2. List and describe three common business applications of telecommunications.
3. Compare and contrast centralized, distributed, and collaborative computing.
4. How are local area networks, wide area networks, enterprise networks, and global networks related to each other?
5. What is the Internet, and why was it created?

6. What are packet switching and TCP/IP?
7. What organization is responsible for managing IP addresses, domain names, and root server systems?
8. Other than the telephone, what are three alternatives for connecting to the Internet?
9. List and describe five major tools for and/or uses of the Internet.
10. What is the World Wide Web, and what is its relationship to the Internet?

SELF-STUDY QUESTIONS

Answers are at the end of the Problems and Exercises.

1. Telecommunications refers to the transmission of all forms of information including ____, from one location to another over a network.
   - A. digital data
   - B. voice and sound
   - C. fax and video
   - D. all of the above

2. ____ allows conversations with others in real time on the Internet.
   - A. Voice mail
   - B. Newsgroups
   - C. E-mail
   - D. Internet Relay Chat

3. All of the following are applications of telecommunications except ____
   - A. electronic commerce
   - B. telemedicine
   - C. distance learning
   - D. transmission media

4. The process of converting a photograph or a song into digital information, or bits, is called ____. After information is converted into bits, it can travel across a network.
   - A. digitizing
   - B. analyzing
   - C. converting
   - D. importing

5. A ____ is a private, third party–managed network that can be shared by multiple organizations.
   - A. local area network
   - B. wide area network
   - C. value-added network
   - D. personal area network

6. All of the following are correct domain suffix pairs except ____.
   - A. edu—educational institutions
   - B. mil—military
   - C. neto—network organizations
   - D. com—commercial businesses

7. Which of the following is faster and becoming more popular than the standard telephone as a way to connect to the Internet?
   - A. DSL
   - B. ISDN
   - C. cable
   - D. all of the above

8. The Internet is being used by ____.
   - A. more users than ever before
   - B. young and old people
   - C. companies and universities
   - D. all of the above

9. ____ enables a person to send one e-mail message and have it simultaneously reach a group of people.
   - A. Archie
   - B. Listserv
   - C. Usenet
   - D. WAIS

10. Web sites and specific Web pages within those sites have a unique Internet address called a URL, or ____.
   - A. Universal Resource Login
   - B. Universal Router Locator
   - C. Uniform Resource Locator
   - D. Uniform Resource Language

PROBLEMS AND EXERCISES

1. Match the following terms to the appropriate definitions:

   ____ Distributed computing

   ____ Internet Relay Chat

   ____ Router

   ____ Internet Service Provider

   ____ Web browser

   ____ Telecommuting

   ____ Desktop videoconferencing

   ____ Domain name

   ____ Firewall

   ____ Hypertext

   a. Specialized hardware and software that are used to keep unwanted users out of a system, or to let users in with restricted access and privileges

   b. Used in Uniform Resource Locators (URLs) to identify a source or host entity on the Internet

   c. Text in a Web document that is highlighted and, when clicked on by the user, evokes an embedded command that goes to another specified file or location and brings up that file or location on the user's screen

   d. A software application that can be used to locate and display Web pages including text, graphics, and multimedia content

   e. A computing model in which computers are networked together to share information and services

   f. The process of working at home or at another remote location and "commuting" to the office via computing and networking technologies

   g. An application that allows conversations with others in real time on the Internet

   h. An intelligent device used to connect and route data traffic across two or more individual networks

   i. Allows people to use their desktop computers together with specialized software and hardware (including cameras) to speak with and see other people online

   j. An individual or organization who enables other individuals and organizations to connect to the Internet

2. Discuss the differences between PBX networks and LANs. What are the advantages of each? What are possible disadvantages of each? When would you recommend one over the other?

3. Have you taken a distance or online course at your university? What did you like and dislike? If you have not taken a course in this medium, investigate a course that you would be interested in taking. What are the pros and cons of a course without a regular classroom time?

4. How many types of communication tools do you use each day, such as e-mail, voice mail, fax, desktop videoconferencing, electronic fund transfers, pagers, and cellular phones? What is happening to the speed of communication today?

5. Do you feel that desktop videoconferencing, as described in the opening to this chapter, will continue to rise in popularity? Why or why not? What about the face-to-face, in-person meetings that have existed for centuries? Are certain industries or products more conducive to desktop videoconferencing?

6. In the Brief Case about Remotely Managing AFS's Network, what are the problem and the solution? What software package is utilized? Is this a viable long-term solution? How does it affect costs?

7. Do you know of anyone telecommuting full- or part-time? What are the positive and the negative aspects of this type of commuting?

8. Scan the popular press and search the World Wide Web for clues concerning emerging technologies for telecommunications. This may include new uses for current technologies or new technologies altogether. Discuss as a group the "hot" issues. Do you feel they will become a reality in the near future? Why or why not? Prepare a 10-minute presentation to the class of your findings?

9. Reread the Brief Case about Pepsi's Enterprise Network. How many sites does it connect? How has this system affected inventory and helped management with the decision-making process?

10. Explain in simple language how the Internet works. Be sure to talk about backbones, packet switching, networks, routers, TCP/IP, and Internet services. What technologies, hardware, and software do you utilize when using the Internet? What else is available?

11. How long, on average, are you willing to wait for a Web page to load in your browser on your computer? Under what conditions would you be willing to wait longer for a page to come up in your browser? Based on your answers, what are the implications for Web site design? Do you wait longer if you know what you will be seeing, that is, if you are loading a page at a site you have been to in the past?

12. Search through recent articles in your favorite IS publication—whether print or online. What are some of the issues being discussed that relate to the Internet and/or the World Wide Web in particular? Have you experienced any of these technologies or applications? What is your opinion about them? How will they affect your life and career? Prepare a 10-minute presentation to the class of your findings?

13. Research projects can now be accomplished by using the Internet as the sole source of information. Conduct such a research project using solely the Internet for source information, and answer the following questions: 1) what is the history of the Internet, 2) what are the demographics of the users of the Internet, and 3) what are the historic growth and the projected growth of the Internet? Remember, use only the Internet itself to research and write this short paper?

ANSWERS TO THE SELF-STUDY QUESTIONS

1. D   2. D   3. D   4. A   5. C   6. C   7. D   8. D   9. B   10. C

CASE 1: *Telemedicine*

Telemedicine is quickly becoming a viable option for residents who are located in remote areas. This new form of providing state-of-the-art and timely medical help to underserved areas has a significant potential for reducing some of the health-care disparities that exist in remote locations (Sands and Bauer, 2001). Many states that have a large rural population that is spread over large areas have consistently faced the challenge of making leading-edge health-care facilities available to the residents. They are discovering that telemedicine is their solution.

Arizona is one such state. Until recently, it had significant problems in providing health care to all its residents. For a majority of the state's residents, premier health-care facilities are located at least 150 miles away. The state's population is spread over 113,000 square miles and is served by only one academic medical school at the University of Arizona, and a couple of academic specialty facilities available at Tucson and Phoenix. To add to this problem, many people in remote residential areas did not even have electricity in their homes.

The state was also faced with the challenge of providing appropriate health care to its correctional inmates. The inmates at the state's various correctional institutions had to be transferred to outside physicians and specialists, which were often located at sites that were far away. The average cost of these referrals would be in the neighborhood of $500, resulting in the state incurring high costs for medical care of its inmates. Given that all these existing problems had been plaguing the state for a long time, Arizona was on the lookout for a viable solution.

The solution came in the form of telemedicine, where telecommunications and networking technologies would enable the state to provide premier and sufficient health care to remote and underserved regions, and encourage medical professionals to increase their rural services.

After lobbying by multiple groups and organizations, legislation for telemedicine was passed in Arizona in 1996, which resulted in the creation of the Arizona Rural Telecommunications Network (ARTN). The leaders of the telemedicine program wanted to set up a network such that specialists at the University of Arizona's medical centers could be easily connected with the small rural hospitals. They could consult with the local physicians or the patients directly depending on the need. The vision was to enable teleradiology as well, such that local physicians could send reports such as CT scans and x-rays over the network for referral by a specialist located at the university centers. The project leaders also wanted to ensure that the network to be built had sufficient bandwidth, such that it would be able to support a large volume of users and their communication.

After the initial plan was formulated, the next phase involved the building and the development of the network that would support the telemedicine program. The architects considered ISDN lines, but many of the participating locations throughout the state did not have access to high-speed phone services such as ISDN. They deployed an ATM network because they determined that it was the most cost effective. In addition to cost benefits, the ATM network also ensured high quality, reliability, and the ability to send multiple types of information (e.g., text, voice, pictures, etc.) quickly. They developed a distributed backbone network with switches located at Northern Arizona University and two other sites. After a lot of evaluation, they selected for the backbone the ASX-1000 switches from a company called Marconi, based in Pittsburgh. Each of the rural sites would then link to its nearest backbone switch.

Since the initial implementation of the network, the network architecture has gone through some significant changes. ATM inverse multiplexing was installed recently to support the increasing traffic on certain routes. This new technology has significantly reduced the work of many network administrators. They no longer have to assign traffic flows to specific connections. This is now done automatically. Four new ISDN circuits have also been added to the ARTN network. This now enables smoother videoconferencing over the Internet between some of the remote locations and the central offices. The next step is to implement IP video, which would enable the use of Internet technologies to provide videoconferencing facilities to a larger group of users at a significantly lower cost.

Today, more than 90 physicians from various areas such as radiology, neurology, psychiatry, and cardiology have seen more than 11,000 patients through the telemedicine program. The program has also helped in reducing risky travel for patients with unstable conditions. The average cost of a rural patient's visit to an urban medical center has gone from $500 down to about $100. Similarly, the cost of transferring correctional inmates to medical facilities has also gone down from about $500 to about $150. Costs related to air evacuations of patients have also been significantly reduced. As of this writing, 23 institutions and treatment centers in Arizona are linked through this network, with many more to be added in the near future.

[Adapted from Ronald S. Weinstein and Kevin M. McNeill, "Powering the Arizona Telemedicine Program," *Health Management Technology* 22(6): 46–47.]

Discussion Questions

1. Do you think that the telemedicine program in Arizona has successfully taken care of the state's primary medical challenges and can be considered a success? Why or why not?
2. Do you think that something as important as medical care can be provided successfully through a telecommunications network? What does this system lack?
3. Currently, the telemedicine program enables only patient consultancy. What other related capabilities could be included?
4. What might health care of the future be like if we used more telecommunications and computer networks?

CASE 2:   *The Downfall Of Cisco*

Cisco is one of the worldwide leaders in Internet networking and has experienced steady growth over the last many years. Cisco's Internet Protocol–based networking solutions are the foundation of the Internet and most corporate, education, and government networks around the world (**www. cisco.com**). Cisco was founded in 1984 by a group of computer scientists from Stanford University, and since its inception, it has risen significantly above all other networking companies. Cisco is dedicated to manufacturing products and technologies that will make the Internet more dynamic in the future. Among some of Cisco's key technologies are advanced routing and switching, voice and video over IP, optical networking, wireless technologies, storage networking, security, and broadband. Cisco went public in 1990, and the growth of the company has never stopped. The company's executives have witnessed an increase in its revenues from millions to billions to tens of billions of dollars. In fact, the New York Stock Exchange once announced Cisco as the most valued company in the world, over GE, with a half-trillion–dollar market capitalization. The company had witnessed growth for 40 straight consecutive quarters, and in the last few quarters had even witnessed extreme growth (around 66 percent).

Given this phenomenal growth, it was puzzling to the Cisco executives and the industry experts when Cisco suddenly experienced its first negative quarter. Sales plunged down to 30 percent of what they had been, and the company's stock sank down to $13 from $82. The company had to write off $2.2 billion worth of inventory and impose dramatic layoffs to reduce its costs.

Many have argued that one of the primary reasons for Cisco's sudden downturn was the overreliance of the company on its forecasting system. Cisco had always attributed its competitive advantage to the use of its forecasting tool, which enabled it to use real operating data stored in a massive database to forecast growth and sales in various regions. It was this software that helped the company to predict the slowdown in the Japanese economy ahead of its competitors. Cisco was able to take advantage of this prediction and "garner half of the switching market there." The system made forecasting significantly faster and easier for the Cisco executives. The Cisco executives have always stood by the system, arguing that it is one of the best of its kind.

The question to be asked, then, is, if the system is as good as it is claimed to be, why was it not able to accurately predict the growth in the United States? Most of the other networking companies (Cisco's competitors), who used less sophisticated systems, had already seen the downturn coming and had downgraded their forecasts. Cisco at the same time continued to predict further growth. Other companies saw a decline in demand and cut down on their inventory, while Cisco continued to increase inventory, claiming that demand was rising. Industry experts also claim that there was ample evidence that the system prevented the executives at Cisco from accurately judging the environment, and overreliance of the company on its technology lead the company down the wrong path. They further claim that the superiority of the system was just hype, and that it was not designed to model forecasts if one of the software's critical assumptions (growth) was removed. As a result, the executives at Cisco continued to supply growth figures, and the system continued to paint pretty pictures for them.

Still others claim that it is incorrect to blame the system, or overreliance of the company on it, for Cisco's decline. Cisco's executives continue to defend its use and argue that the reason for the company's sudden downturn is the economy and not their forecasting tool. Others claim that bad carpenters always blames their tools, and the problem lies not in the system, but in the people who used it. A database and forecasting system, they claim, is only as good as the data and assumptions put into it, and the Cisco system was actually pretty good. Moreover, they argue that the information produced by the system is dependent on the data that was entered by managers and analysts. If the Cisco employees entered incorrect figures, then the forecasting would also be inaccurate, and it was, therefore, incorrect to blame the system. Other analysts also seem to agree that overrated numbers may have been entered into the Cisco database. The CEO of a Silicon Valley–based company argued that salespeople often do not like to be caught without supply, and hence they always forecast more sales than expected. If these hyped numbers are entered into the system, growth rate will seem much higher than the actual rate.

Analysts also claim that the strategy of demand forecasting is itself very flawed. Reports from salespeople and inventory managers (which along with formal estimates may include figures that emerge during informal coffee breaks) are integrated with actual sales data and trends and are fed into the software. These data are then used by the software to run complex statistical algorithms and generate growth numbers. As one industry expert claims, the system does not know what is in the manager's heart. If a certain number is reported to it, the system cannot intuitively understand what the manager's strategy is. It just takes that number and runs models on it.

Meanwhile, Cisco still continues to see declining sales. At the same time, the debate continues as to who is to blame. Cisco continues to argue that the recent problems were due to unprecedented events, and without their forecasting system, things could have been worse. Others claim that the overreliance on the system clouded the managers' judgment and intuition. The ability to look away from the computer screen could have helped them foresee the situation. According to these critics, while it is important to rely on the technology, equal importance should also be given to the business conditions surrounding a company. Still others claim that the problem lies in the system itself. If factors such as debt levels, economic spending, interest rates, the bond market, and so forth, are ignored, and if instead the system relies solely on overrated growth numbers, this will cause it to be unable to accurately foresee a downturn in demand.

[Adapted from **http://www.cisco.com**; Scott Berinato, "What Went Wrong at Cisco," **http://www.cio.com**, *CIO Magazine* (August 1, 2001); "Did Forecasting Technology Do Cisco In?" **http://www.cio.com**, *CIO Magazine* (August 1, 2001).]

Discussion Questions

1. Fundamentally, what drives demand for Cisco's products?
2. What do you think is the primary cause of Cisco's sudden downturn: the overreliance on the technology, changing customer needs for telecommunications equipment, the overall economic slowdown, the inability of the executives to look at the environment, or problems with the forecasting software itself?
3. Could the forecasting software be designed better in order to enable the company to better predict growth and sales of telecommunications equipment? If so, how?
4. How best can/should a company like Cisco predict demand for its products?

Electronic Commerce, Intranets, and Extranets

OPENING: Amazon Turns a Profit!

Internet skeptics have for many years pointed to the fact that online retail pioneer Amazon.com (see Figure 5.1) had not yet turned a profit as evidence that doing business over the Internet was not yet for real. Well, early in the first business quarter of 2002, Amazon.com announced its first profit ever. Amazon beat Wall Street expectations and reported a net income of $5 million for the business quarter just ended, or one cent per share, on revenue of $1.12 billion, up 15 percent year-over-year. Looks like those skeptics will have to get on board the Internet bandwagon or else find another Internet company to pick on.

Amazon CEO Jeff Bezos had for years strategically plowed revenue back into the company in order to grow and strengthen the firm, and only recently had he promised anything remotely resembling a profit. Warren Jenson, chief financial officer at Amazon, attributed the strong showing mainly to running a tighter ship, saying, "We just ran better and much more smoothly." In fact, operating expenses were down 24 percent from a year ago.

The milestone could mean Internet-based electronic commerce is stabilizing. While e-tailers like Pets.com and Webvan are gone, others like Drugstore.com and GSI Commerce, Inc. are flourishing. As further evidence of the strength of electronic commerce, U.S. online retail spending topped $53 billion last year (as estimated by research firm ComScore Networks).

"It appears that consumers have become more sophisticated about using the Web to compare products and make buys," says Dan Hess, vice president of ComScore Networks. In addition, Amazon and others appear to have honed their operations. For example, Drugstore.com recently said it expects to turn a profit from retailing operations, excluding some costs, next year.

What is next for Amazon? It plans to continue to lure shoppers by cutting prices and adding perks. For example, it recently announced free shipping on some orders of $99 or more. Sounds like Amazon is getting down to business and doing so in a profitable way.

[Adapted from Byron Acohido, "Amazon.com Turns its First Profit Ever," *USA Today* (January 23, 2002).]

[Figure 5.1 ➡ Amazon.com pioneered online retailing using the Internet.]
Source: AP/Wide World Photos

Source: **www.Amazon.com**

This chapter focuses on how companies are conducting business electronically with their customers, business partners, and suppliers, which is referred to as electronic commerce (e-commerce or EC). The Internet and World Wide Web are extremely well suited for conducting business electronically on a global basis. Web-based EC has introduced unprecedented opportunities for the marketing of products, accompanied by features, functionality, and innovative methods to serve and support consumers.

After reading this chapter, you will be able to do the following:

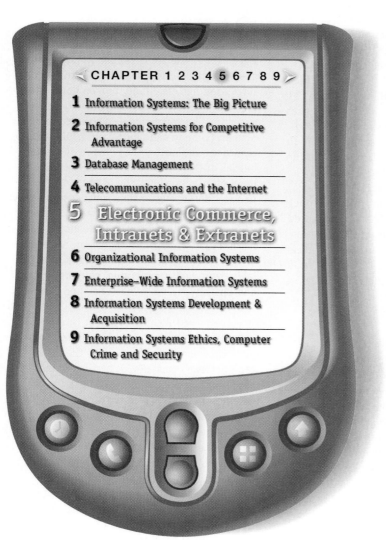

◄ CHAPTER 1 2 3 4 5 6 7 8 9 ►

1 Information Systems: The Big Picture

2 Information Systems for Competitive Advantage

3 Database Management

4 Telecommunications and the Internet

5 Electronic Commerce, Intranets & Extranets

6 Organizational Information Systems

7 Enterprise-Wide Information Systems

8 Information Systems Development & Acquisition

9 Information Systems Ethics, Computer Crime and Security

1. Describe electronic commerce and how it has evolved.

2. Describe the strategies that companies are adopting to compete in cyberspace.

3. Explain the differences between intranets and extranets.

4. Describe the difference between consumer-focused and business-focused electronic commerce.

5. Understand the keys to successful electronic commerce applications.

[Figure 5.2 ➡ The Big Picture: focusing on electronic commerce, intranets, and extranets.]

Chapter 5's place within The Big Picture is shown in Figure 5.2. With EC projected to soon represent approximately 5 percent of the nation's gross domestic product, an understanding of EC can be a powerful tool in your arsenal. People with EC skills are in high demand in the marketplace and, therefore, the more you know about EC, the more valuable you will become!

ELECTRONIC COMMERCE DEFINED

The Internet now provides a set of interconnected networks for individuals and businesses to complete transactions electronically. We define *electronic commerce* very broadly as the online exchange of goods, services, and money[1] between firms, and between firms and their customers. It was estimated that in 2002 over $327 billion in revenues was to be generated through EC, representing 2.3 percent of the nation's Gross Domestic Product (Rockwell, 1999). With this much money at stake, it is little wonder that no other information systems issue has captured as much attention as has EC. Although EC was being used as far back as 1948 during the Berlin Airlift (Zwass, 1996), the emergence of the Internet and World Wide Web (Web) has fueled a revolution in the manner in which products and services are marketed and sold. Their far-reaching effects have led to the creation of an electronic marketplace where a virtually limitless array of new services, features, and functionality can be offered. As a result, a presence on the Web has become a strategic necessity for companies.

Contrary to popular belief, EC goes beyond merely buying and selling products online. EC can involve the events leading up to the purchase of a product, as well as customer service after the sale. Furthermore, EC is not limited to transactions between businesses and consumers, which is known as *business-to-consumer* EC (B2C) and vice versa. EC is also used to conduct business with business partners such as suppliers and intermediaries. This form of EC is commonly referred to as *business-to-business* EC (B2B). Some companies choose to operate in both arenas, such as the clothing and home furnishing retailer Eddie Bauer, while other firms concentrate solely in B2C or B2B. Some forms of EC happen

between businesses and their employees and are referred to as *business-to-employee* (B2E). Some forms of EC do not even involve business firms, as would be the case with an online textbook exchange service for students at a university or an online trading Web site such as eBay.com; these forms of EC are referred to as *consumer-to-consumer* (C2C).

Furthermore, there is a wide variety of ways to conduct business in each arena. In the following section, we examine the reasons that Web-based EC is revolutionizing the way business is being done. This is followed by an in-depth analysis of how companies are utilizing EC in their daily operations.

Internet and World Wide Web Capabilities

Technological forces are driving business, and the Internet and Web emerged as a strong new agent of change. The resulting technological revolution has essentially broken down the barriers to entry, leveled the playing field, and propelled commerce into the electronic domain (Looney and Chatterjee, 2002). Companies are exploiting one or more of the capabilities of the Web to reach a wider customer base, offer a broader range of products, and develop closer relationships with customers by striving to meet their unique needs. These wide-ranging capabilities include global information dissemination, integration, mass customization, interactive communication, collaboration, and transactional support (Looney and Chatterjee, 2002; Chatterjee and Sambamurthy, 1999).

The powerful combination of Internet and Web technologies has given rise to a global platform where firms from across the world can effectively compete for customers and gain access to new markets. EC has wide geographical potential given that many countries have at least some type of Internet access. The global connectivity of the Internet provides a relatively economical medium for marketing products over vast distances. This increased geographical reach has been facilitated by storefronts located on every Web-enabled computer in the world. Unlike traditional storefronts, time limitations are not a factor, allowing firms to sell and service products seven days a week, 24 hours a day, 365 days a year to anyone, anywhere. A larger customer base creates increased sales volumes, which ultimately saves consumers money since firms can offer their products at lower prices (Christensen and Tedlow, 2000). In addition, parking for cus-

Web Search

WEB SEARCH OPPORTUNITY: Visit the homepage for Eddie Bauer at **www.eddiebauer. com/** and see how they do business. Visit some other clothiers on the Web and see how they compare.

---

[1]EC can also include the physical distribution of digital products such as software or digital images.

tomers is no problem, and firms can deliver the goods right to the customer's door.

Web technologies also allow integration of information via Web sites, which can be linked to corporate databases to provide real-time access to information. No longer must customers rely on old information from printed catalogs or account statements that arrive in the mail once a month. For example, when Alaska Airlines (**www.alaskaair.com**) updates fare information in their corporate database, customers can access the revisions as they occur simply by browsing the company's Web site. As with nearly every other major airline, the Web allows Alaska Airlines to disseminate real-time fare pricing. This is particularly important for companies operating in highly competitive environments such as the airline industry. Furthermore, Alaska Airlines offers their valued customers the ability to check the balances of their frequent flier accounts, linking customers to information stored on the firm's corporate database (see Figure 5.3). Customers do not have to wait for monthly statements to see if they are eligible for travel benefits and awards.

Web technologies are also helping firms realize their goal of mass customization. Mass customization helps firms tailor their products and services to meet a customer's particular needs. For instance, clothing retailer Lands' End (**http://www.landsend.com**) has developed an application called My Virtual Model™, which allows customers to create a virtual person to model clothing for them (see Figure 5.4). Customers can configure the virtual model based on a number of criteria such as gender, height, weight, build, complexion, and hair color. Once customers have created a virtual model, they can dress the model in clothing to see how it will look on them. The virtual model application also assists Lands' End in tracking customers' preferred clothing styles and colors, allowing them to target marketing efforts to individual customers.

Interactive communication via the Web enables firms to build customer loyalty by providing immediate communication and feedback to/from customers, which can dramatically improve the firm's image through demonstrated responsiveness. Many firms are augmenting telephone-based ordering and customer support with Web-based applications and electronic mail. In some cases, online chat applications are provided to allow customers to communicate with a customer service representative in real time through the corporate Web site. The online brokerage firm E*Trade (**www.etrade.com**) has implemented such a feature. Should a question arise during the

CONTENTS   WHAT'S HOT   TRAVEL   MILEAGE PLAN   VACATIONS   CARGO   COMPANY   MYALASKAAIR

Alaska Airlines / Horizon Air

Alaska - home to over 17,000 Reindeer

Join Now   About Mileage Plan   Alaska Visa   Bonus Miles   Mileage Partners   Airline Partners   Partners Guide
Mileage Plan Q & A   Program Guidelines   Traveler Newsletter   Buy Miles   Check Your Account   More...

Mileage Plan Account Activity

Member Number: 123456789
Member Name: JOHN Q. PUBLIC
Mileage Plan Status: ACTIVE
Current Balance:* 12,789

---

* Please Note: Depending on the partnership, activity will appear on your account 30-60 days after you have earned miles. If you do not see activity after 60 days, contact Mileage Plan.

All Activity in the past 3 months, sorted by Activity Date.

Activity Date	Activity Type	Flight	Miles	Bonus	Total	Posted
6/23/2002	Seattle to Los Angeles	0036	1,233	0	1,233	6/30/2002
5/23/2002	Portland to San Jose	0551	819	0	819	5/31/2002
5/23/2002	Bonus Miles	0000	1,000	1,000	1,000	5/31/2002

[**Figure 5.3** ➡ Alaska Airlines' Mileage Plan Web site.]
Source: **www.alaskaair.com**

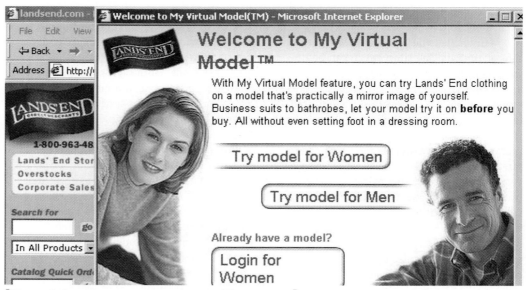

[Figure 5.4 ➡ Lands' End's *My Virtual Model*™ application.]
Source: **www.landsend.com**

placement of an order, customers can click a button that opens a chat application, connecting them in real time to a customer service representative. The customer can type questions into a window and receive immediate responses from the representative. This feature allows the customer service agent to walk the customer through the ordering process step-by-step while the customer is entering the transaction. Customers never have to leave E*Trade's Web site or terminate their Internet connection to get their business done. This customer-driven approach far outdistances traditional, nonelectronic means in terms of tailoring and timeliness.

Web technologies can also enable collaboration. As an example, E*Trade maintains a community for investors who regularly share opinions concerning companies, news, rumors, and investment strategies through an E*Trade sponsored forum. The community exposes investors to a wide array of information that would otherwise be unavailable through traditional channels. IBM Microelectronics uses the Web to collaborate with its custom-logic chip customers. A Java-enabled Web browser allows users to share product information, access design specifications, and download software tools from the Web site. The application provides interactive, or two-way, communications, helping IBM engineers pinpoint design issues and provide personalized support to better serve customers (Alexander, 2001).

By providing ways for clients and firms to conduct business online without human assistance, the Internet and Web have greatly

reduced transaction costs while enhancing operational efficiency. Many companies, such as Dell Computer Corporation, are utilizing the Web to provide automated transaction support. Dell began selling computers on the Web in mid-1996. By early 1998, Dell was experiencing around $3 million in online sales per day. Dell derives about 90 percent of its overall revenues from sales to medium and large businesses, yet more than half of its Web-based sales have been from individuals and small businesses, who typically buy one computer at a time. As a result, Dell is experiencing significant cost savings per sale by reducing the demand for phone representatives on the smaller purchases. Individual customers can access product information at any time from anywhere, empowering customers to service themselves. This benefits not only the end consumer but Dell as well. Customer service representatives can focus on lucrative corporate customers, reducing labor costs involved in servicing small-ticket items. By streamlining operations and greatly increasing sales through both online and traditional channels, Dell has grown into one of the world's largest personal computer manufacturers, with sales well in excess of $10 billion annually. This phenomenon of cutting out the "middleman" and reaching customers more directly and efficiently is known as *disintermediation*.

Electronic Commerce Business Strategies

The Web has transformed traditional business operations into a hyper-competitive electronic marketplace. Companies must strategically

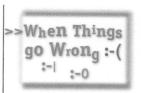

Alleged Flaw in Browser Can Potentially Threaten Electronic Commerce

An independent security researcher who refers to himself as ThePull recently reported to Microsoft Corporation an alleged flaw in recent versions of its browser, Internet Explorer (IE). The alleged flaw could potentially allow hackers to enter Web sites undercover and steal cookies and related information from those Web sites or even from the computers of individual browser users.

David Ahmad, moderator of Bugtraq, a mailing list on which ThePull first posted details of the alleged flaw, says the vulnerability is the result of Microsoft's failure to abide by an industry-standard browser security rule known as the same-origin policy. This policy ensures that when one Web site is used to open another Web site in a separate pop-up window, no information from the first site should be able to affect the information or properties on the other site.

Microsoft's Security Response Center reported that they are investigating the issue. In the meantime, an advisory put out by San Mateo, California–based SecurityFocus.com recommended that anyone concerned simply turn off JavaScript capabilities in the properties of their browser software until the alleged flaw is either proved to be false or is fixed. The happy ending to this story is that according to Microsoft Security Bulletin MS02-047 this is fixed in the latest cumulative patch for IE.

Check Microsoft's TechNet at **http://www.microsoft.com/technet/default.asp** for the latest on this issue.

[Adapted from Jaikumar Vijayan, "Microsoft Investigates Alleged Flaw in Browser: Experts Say Standard Security Rule Ignored," *Computerworld* (January 14, 2002).]

position themselves to compete in the new EC environment. At one extreme, companies following a **brick-and-mortar** approach choose to operate solely in the traditional, physical markets. These companies approach business activities in a traditional manner by operating physical locations such as department stores, business offices, and manufacturing plants. In other words, the brick-and-mortar business strategy does not include EC. In contrast, **click-only** (also referred to as **virtual, or "pure play") companies** conduct business electronically in cyberspace. These firms have no physical locations, allowing them to focus purely on EC. An example of a click-only company might be the popular eBay.com trading and exchange Web site, which does not have a physical storefront in the classic sense. Other firms choose to straddle the two environments, operating in both physical and virtual arenas. These firms operate under the **click-and-mortar** business model. The three general business models are depicted in Figure 5.5 (Looney and Chatterjee, 2002).

The greatest impact of the Web-based EC revolution has occurred in companies adopting the click-and-mortar approach. Click-and-mortars continue to operate their physical locations and have added the EC component to their business activities. With transactions occurring in both physical and virtual environments, it is imperative that click-and-mortars learn how to fully maximize commercial opportunities in both domains. Conducting physical and virtual operations presents special challenges for these firms, as business activities must be tailored to each of these different environments in order for the firms to compete effectively.

Another challenge for click-and-mortars involves increasing information system complexity. Design and development of complex

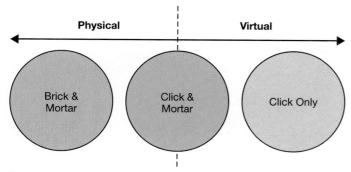

[**Figure 5.5** ➥ General approaches to electronic commerce.]

computing systems are required to support each aspect of the click-and-mortar approach (Looney and Chatterjee, 2002). Furthermore, different skills are necessary to support Web-based computing, requiring substantial resource investments. Companies must design, develop, and deploy systems and applications to accommodate an open computing architecture that must be globally and persistently available. For instance, over the course of 18 months, the click-and-mortar brokerage firm Charles Schwab increased its full-time IS staff more than 50 percent, or 700 employees. In addition, the organization could no longer accurately predict usage trends of computing resources. Schwab experienced increased volatility in online transactions as compared with offline transactions, prompting the need to increase computing capacity to 32 mainframe computers in order to handle the increased volume (Tempest, 1999).

Click-only companies can compete effectively on price since they do not need to support the physical aspects of the click-and-mortar approach. Thus, these companies can reduce prices to rock-bottom levels. On the other hand, a relatively small click-only firm may not sell enough products and/or may not order enough from suppliers to be able to realize economies of scale and thus reduce prices. Click-only firms also tend to be highly adept with technology and can innovate very rapidly as new technologies become available. This can enable them to stay one step ahead of their competition. However, conducting business in cyberspace can be problematic in some respects. For example, it is much more difficult for a customer to return a product to a purely online company than simply to return it to a local department store. In addition, some consumers may not be comfortable making purchases online. Individuals may be leery about the security of giving credit card numbers to a *virtual company*.

As you can see, there are a variety of ways that firms can and have conducted EC. In the next section we describe in greater detail how firms have evolved toward using the Internet and Web to support internal operations and to interact with each other.

BUSINESS-TO-BUSINESS ELECTRONIC COMMERCE

Prior to the introduction of the Internet and Web, business-to-business EC was facilitated using *Electronic Data Interchange (EDI)*. These systems are generally limited to large corporations who can afford the associated expenses. The Internet and Web have provided an economical medium over which information can be transmitted, enabling small to midsized enterprises to participate in B2B markets. Companies have devised a number of innovative ways to facilitate B2B transactions using these technologies. Web-based B2B systems range from simple extranet applications to complex trading exchanges where multiple buyers and sellers come together to conduct business. In the following sections, we examine the stages under which modern B2B EC is done, shedding light on the different approaches and their suitability for different business requirements. Figure 5.6 provides a high-level overview of how B2B architectures typically evolve.

How Electronic Data Interchange Works

Electronic Data Interchange (EDI) is the forefather of modern B2B EC and continues to maintain a stronghold in B2B computing. Giga Information Group estimates that U.S. companies buy about $500 billion worth of goods and services electronically each year via EDI networks. EDI refers to the digital, or electronic, transmission of business documents and related data between organizations via telecommunications networks. More specifically, these telecommunications networks commonly take the form of *value-added networks (VANs)*, which provide a direct link over which data can be transmitted. VANs are telephone lines that are leased from telecommunications providers, creating a secure, dedicated circuit between a company and its business partners. Figure 5.7 depicts a typical EDI system architecture using VANs to connect a company with its suppliers and customers.

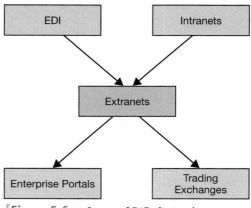

[**Figure 5.6** ➡ Stages of B2B electronic commerce.]

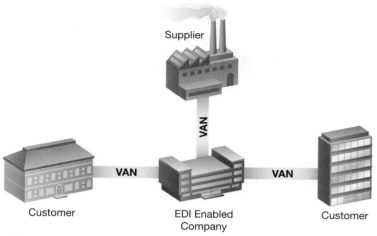

[**Figure 5.7** ➥ A typical EDI system architecture.]

Companies use EDI to exchange a wide variety of business documents, including purchase orders, invoices, shipping manifests, delivery schedules, and electronic payments. The exchange of data in EDI follows a set of formatting standards, which specifies how information is transmitted electronically. These standards are known as the ***ANSI X.12*** and ***UN/EDIFACT*** standards. Currently, over 100,000 U.S. companies are using either one or both of the standards to conduct business via EDI. ANSI X.12 and UN/EDIFACT provide a common set of guidelines that business partners adhere to when designing the format of EDI-based transmissions. Figure 5.8 provides an example of an EDI transmission, in this case a purchase order document.

EDI began in the mid-1960s as an initiative to reduce paperwork. Although EDI has never totally eliminated paper, it does help reduce the number of times business documents need to be handled. EDI provides many efficiencies because it helps to streamline business processes. By reducing the number of times documents need to be handled, business partners can exchange data faster and with fewer errors. EDI shortens the time spent producing and delivering business documents from days to seconds, allowing companies to process and update information faster. Having up-to-date information at the company's dis-

posal allows it to make more accurate forecasts and decisions.

EDI helps to reduce errors by providing a single point of entry. For example, in a paper-based environment a supplier must enter an invoice into its own system, print it, and send the invoice via surface mail to its customer. When the customer receives the invoice, someone must reenter it into the customer's system so that the invoice can be processed. In this situation, errors can occur at the original point of entry in the supplier's system, as well as the point of reentry in the customer's system. EDI eliminates dual entry. By using EDI, the supplier enters the invoice into its system and transmits the invoice to the customer electronically. The customer's computer automatically receives the invoice via EDI and updates the system accordingly, eliminating reentry and a potential source of error.

EDI enabled RJR Nabisco to reduce the cost of processing a paper-based purchase order from $70 to less than $1. However, the cost associated with EDI-based systems has limited its usefulness to large companies. EDI is costly to implement and maintain. Software and hardware required to enable EDI can cost upwards of $100,000, and monthly telecommunications charges associated with VANs can approach several thousand dollar per month, depending upon the number of communication

```
51043...PO1*10*6*EA*2.98**SK*333734*ZZ*GRAY
51044...PO1*11*24*EA*.79**SK*333776*ZZ*VIOLET
EZ21406...PO1*12*6*EA*1.12**SK*333802*ZZ*MAROON
S51051...PO1*13*10*EA*.99**SK*333815*ZZ*AQUA
```

[**Figure 5.8** ➥ Transmission format for a purchase order document using the ANSI X.12 standard.]

lines necessary to connect the company with its business partners.

EDI requires skilled technicians to develop and maintain EDI systems. The ANSI X.12 and UN/EDIFACT standards can take months or years to master. As you can tell from Figure 5.9, transmission formats are difficult for humans to decipher. Developers must be able to understand what every piece of information means in order to build systems that can process the data. This issue can be exacerbated by a multitude of different transmission formats that companies must become familiar with. For example, in the grocery industry over 30 different EDI transmission formats exist (Hennessey, 2000), meaning that if a produce supplier wants to conduct business with grocery chains such as Safeway, Albertsons, and Ralph's, they may need to support three separate EDI formats.

Large enterprises can afford the enormous costs associated with EDI. They can justify the costs since EDI has created such dramatic efficiencies for their organizations. Yet EDI has proved to be beyond the reach of smaller enterprises. Before the introduction of the Internet and Web, a viable, economical alternative to EDI was unavailable, preventing small to midsized firms from participating in B2B markets. To make matters worse, some large corporations and government agencies had gone so far as to refuse business to companies that were not EDI-enabled. What small and midsized companies needed was a technology that would level the playing field, making B2B affordable and accessible. This leads us to the next generation of Internet-based B2B architectures.

The Internet Changed Everything

EDI has been used for over four decades to conduct business between organizations. However, the trend in business today is to use the public Internet and Web as the vehicle for business-to-business EC. The global accessibility and economics afforded by the Internet and Web have enabled small to midsized firms to participate in B2B markets once reserved for large corporations. With the entrance of buyers and suppliers of all shapes and sizes, the mass adoption of these technologies has propelled B2B into the forefront of modern commerce.

Just as the number of Internet business users is growing, B2B EC is exploding. AMR Research estimates that B2B EC will account for $5.7 trillion in 2004. Although these staggering

figures seem mind-boggling, they account only for the shipment of goods between businesses and do not take into consideration less tangible factors such as savings associated with process improvements and the value of accurate and timely information (Hill, 2000).

By late 1997, Cisco Systems, a leading producer of networking technologies such as routers, had shifted nearly 40 percent of its B2B sales from brick-and-mortar markets to the Web. That amounts to almost $9 million per day or more than $3 billion per year! Cisco has continued its trend toward a click-only approach, selling more than 50 percent of its products online in 1998, and 60 percent in 1999. Additionally, Cisco is letting its biggest customers, such as Qwest Communications and MCI WorldCom, connect directly into its online inventory and product ordering system through Web-based applications. Cisco's B2B initiatives have enabled customers to service themselves, resulting in a redeployment of customer service representatives to other critical areas within the company. As a result, Cisco is saving about $20 million per year related to sales transactions. These huge cost savings are being invested into the company's research and development (R&D) program—far exceeding the R&D investment of Cisco's nearest competitors such as Nortel Networks and Foundry Networks. Cisco's savings are passed on to its customers. For example, a six-person department at Sprint Communications (Sprint) buys approximately 40 routers per week for its customers. Using Cisco's B2B applications, Sprint estimates it will save as much as $200,000 per year in order-processing costs.

Using the Internet for Intranets and Extranets

Once organizations realize the advantage of using the Internet and Web to communicate public information outside corporate boundaries, Web-based technologies can also be leveraged to support proprietary, internal communications within an organization through the implementation of an *intranet*[2]. An intranet consists of an internal, private network using Web technologies to facilitate the secured transmission of proprietary infor-

---

[2]It can be argued that, on a technological level, intranets and extranets are variants of the same thing in that both employ firewalls to cordon off a select group of users. However, given that intranets and extranets have very different purposes from a business point of view, we choose to distinguish between the two.

While many companies adopted the new e-commerce technologies, the $507 billion North American chemical industry lagged far behind. Most of their transactions with the suppliers of their production goods had taken place through the traditional methods of phone calls and faxes, often costing companies $50 to $100 to process a single order. As any accountant will tell you, one of the key success factors of most businesses lies in reducing overhead costs and increasing efficiency, and the chemical companies were failing at both. The chemical companies had previously explored the concept of EDI, but lack of standards in the industry had failed to make it a success. Similarly, with the advent of the Internet, many chemical companies had built Web-based connections with their suppliers and customers. However, these systems often took a long time and a huge amount of money to build, and hence companies could not afford to build these connections with each of their suppliers. Some time ago, the chief financial officer (CFO) of Ethyl, a chemical company in Virginia, decided that the solution to this problem would be to build an electronic hub technology that would link the back-end systems of the chemical companies to the systems of all their suppliers. The hub would enable the transformation of the purchase order generated by a chemical company's Enterprise Resource Planning (ERP) system to a standard Extensible Markup Language (XML) document, which would be sent to the supplier and transformed into the format preferred by the supplier's ERP system. This would take care of the problem of lack of standards as well. Last year marked the birth of the electronic hub called Envera, which differed from other EDI systems such as Chematch.com, which only matched suppliers and buyers. Envera enables companies who already have established suppliers to transact business with them, and charges them an annual subscription fee. Today many chemical companies such as Lubrizol and Occidental are efficiently conducting business using Envera. Some months ago, Envera also extended its capabilities, and it now links many service providers such as trucking companies and rail companies (responsible for transporting the goods) to their hub. It is interesting that Envera's roots are in accounting concerns and the actions of a clever CFO.

[Adapted from Lauren Gibbons Paul, "The Right Chemistry," **http://www.cio.com**, *CIO Magazine* (March 1, 2001).]

Career Implications:

Accounting and Finance

---

mation within the organization. An intranet can be considered a private, internal Web, which limits viewing access to authorized users within the organization. Intranets take advantage of standard Internet and Web protocols to communicate information to and from authorized employees. As they do on the Web, employees access information on the intranet through a Web browser. However, this information cannot be viewed by users outside the organization and, thus, is separated from the visible, publicly accessible Web.

In order to communicate proprietary information with authorized users outside organizational boundaries, a company can implement an extended intranet, or **extranet**. An extranet enables two or more firms to use the Internet to do business together. Table 5.1 provides a comparison of characteristics between the Internet, intranet, and extranet environments.

Intranets and extranets are the fastest growing segment of Web-based technologies, and the Web, whether it be Internet-, intranet-, or extranet-based, has become the predominant method of conducting business. Aerospace giant, The Boeing Company, operates an intranet with more than one million pages registered with its internal search engine, serving over 200,000 employees. The intranet has become pervasive, impacting every department within the organization. Employees rely on the intranet to assist them in their daily business activities, ranging from tracking vacation benefits to monitoring aircraft production.

The company has also launched an extranet that can be accessed by over 1,000 authorized business partners. One of Boeing's business partners, aluminum supplier Alcoa, accesses the extranet to coordinate its shipments to Boeing, as well as to check Boeing's raw materials supply to ensure appropriate inventory levels. Customers, such as the United States Department of Defense, log in to Boeing's extranet to receive status updates on the projects Boeing is working on for them (Sullivan, 1999). Overall B2B results mirror those of Boeing. B2B conducted via extranets in 1998 surpassed $35 billion and was expected to double by 2001. A survey conducted in 1998 with Fortune 1,000 companies found that 68 percent of these companies had implemented an extranet for B2B, up 24 percent from the preceding year (Kalakota, Oliva, and Donath, 1999).

[Table 5.1] *Characteristics of the Internet, intranet, and extranet (Szuprowicz, 1998; Turban et al., 2000.)*

Focus	Type of Information	Users	Access	
The Internet	External communications	General, public, and "advertorial"	Any user with an Internet connection	Public and not restricted
Intranet	Internal communications	Specific, corporate, and proprietary	Authorized employees	Private and restricted
Extranet	External communications	Communications between business partners	Authorized business partners	Private and restricted

Intranets and extranets benefit corporations in a number of ways, so it is no surprise that firms have readily and rapidly adopted these technologies. First and foremost, intranets and extranets can dramatically improve the timeliness and accuracy of communications, reducing the number of misunderstandings within the organization, as well as with business partners and customers. In the business world, very little information is static and, therefore, information must be continually updated and disseminated as it changes. Intranets and extranets facilitate this process by providing a cost-effective, global medium over which proprietary information can be distributed. Furthermore, they allow central management of documents, thus reducing the number of versions and amount of out-of-date information that may be stored throughout the organization. While security is still thought to be better on proprietary networks, the Internet can be made to be a relatively secure medium for business.

Web-based technologies are cross-platform, meaning that disparate computing systems can communicate with each other, provided that standard Web protocols have been implemented. For example, an Apple Macintosh can request Web pages from a UNIX Web server. Even though the computers are running under different operating systems, they can communicate with each other over the Internet, provided that TCP/IP is being used by each machine. The cross-platform nature of the Web makes implementing intranets and extranets extremely attractive as a way to connect disparate computing environments.

In addition, intranets and extranets do not require large expenditures to train users on the technologies. Since many employees, customers, and business partners are familiar with the tools associated with the Internet and Web, they do not require special training to familiarize them with intranet and extranet interfaces. In other words, intranets and extranets look and act just like public Web sites and Web pages. As long as the user is familiar with a Web browser, they can utilize intranets and extranets with little difficulty.

Above all, intranets and extranets impact the company's bottom line. A company can use them to automate business transactions, reducing processing costs and achieving shortened cycle times. Intranets and extranets can also reduce errors by providing a single point of data entry, from which the information can be updated on disparate corporate computing platforms without having to rekey the data. Management can then obtain real-time information to track and analyze business activities. Intranets and extranets are incredibly powerful and intensely popular. We describe in the following sections how they work and how they are being used best (beginning with intranets).

Intranet System Architecture

An intranet looks and acts just like a publicly accessible Web site and uses the same software, hardware, and networking technologies to communicate information. However, intranets use *firewalls* to secure proprietary information stored within the corporate LAN and/or WAN. Firewalls are hardware devices with special software that are placed between the organization's LAN or WAN and the Internet, preventing unauthorized access to the proprietary information stored on the intranet. In the simplest form of an intranet, communications take place within the confines of organizational boundaries and do not travel across the Internet. Figure 5.9 depicts a typical intranet system architecture.

To enable access to an intranet, Web browsers are installed on each employee's workstation, and the TCP/IP protocol must be implemented on top of the protocols existing

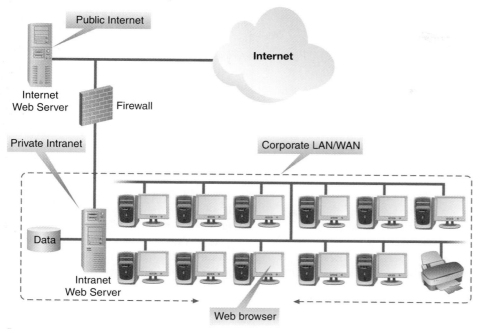

[**Figure 5.9** ➡ Intranet architecture.]

on the corporate LAN/WAN. An intranet Web server is placed behind the firewall and connected to the LAN/WAN to facilitate user requests for information. Employees may access intranet content through a Web browser by entering the URL of the main intranet Web page. Once the user enters the URL in the Web browser, TCP/IP breaks the request into data packets and routes the transmission over the LAN/WAN to the intranet Web server. When the packets reach their destination, they are reassembled and passed to the Web server. The Web server understands that the user is requesting a Web page and retrieves the information, which TCP/IP breaks into packets and transmits back to the Web browser. TCP/IP reassembles the Web page at the destination and delivers it to the Web browser. In turn, the Web browser processes the HTML code, formats the physical appearance of the Web page, and displays the results in the Web browser. It should be noted that during the intranet transaction, packets are never routed outside the corporate firewall. All transmissions travel within the bounds of the organization's private network rather than over the public Internet, eliminating potential security risks such as unauthorized access to corporate information.

Intranet Applications

Training

The Boeing Company offers over 200,000 employees training via the Center for Leader-ship and Training (CLT) intranet site. The training being delivered over Boeing's intranet opens up courses and training opportunities for employees worldwide. By using the CLT intranet, employees can choose from a wide range of course offerings, including educational programs, supervisor training, and techniques to improve quality control. CLT contains an online catalog summarizing course offerings and provides a feature that allows employees to register for courses using their Web browsers. Once registered for a course, users can access multimedia content including video lectures, presentation slides, and other course materials directly from their desktops .

Boeing's intranet-based training initiative has led to dramatic business improvements and cost reductions. The intranet helped eliminate redundant courses and standardize course material. It virtually eliminated travel costs associated with sending employees to training sites. In addition, employees can take courses on a time-permitting basis, meaning that they can learn at a pace that accommodates their work schedule. At Boeing, employee training is no longer subject to the physical and time constraints associated with traditional forms of education.

Application Integration

Many organizations have invested substantial sums of money and resources in a variety of software applications such as Enterprise

Web Search

WEB SEARCH OPPORTUNITY: Visit the Intranet Journal online at **http://www. intranetjournal.com** to further your exploration of intranets.

Resource Planning (ERP), Customer Relationship Management (CRM), Sales Force Automation (SFA), and various other packages to support internal operations. Often these disparate applications are installed on different computing platforms, where each may be running under a different operating system, using a different database management system, and/or providing a different user interface. Due to these disparate environments, it may be difficult for a user to consolidate information from these different systems into a single screen that can display all the information the user needs to make a business decision. Intranets can be used to alleviate this problem by providing application integration.

For example, salespeople may need information about the sales calls they need to make for the upcoming day, as well as information related to customers that they currently support. Data related to sales calls may be located in a SFA application running on a UNIX server, whereas the CRM application may be running on an IBM mainframe. Prior to the emergence of intranets, the workstation that a salesperson used to access the information would need to be loaded with the appropriate network operating systems and user interfaces necessary to retrieve the information from each of the disparate systems. In addition, the salesperson would need to toggle back and forth between the applications to access all the necessary information from the SFA and CRM systems.

By installing a product such as DataChannel's Enterprise Information Portal (EIP) on the intranet Web server, information from the SFA and CRM applications can be consolidated and presented to the user through a single Web browser interface (see Figure 5.10). Now, when the salesperson needs information related to sales calls and customer support activities, the request is routed to the intranet Web server running EIP, which accesses the relevant data from the SFA and CRM applications. The intranet server consolidates the information and delivers it to the salesperson, displaying all the information necessary to make business decisions in a single Web page.

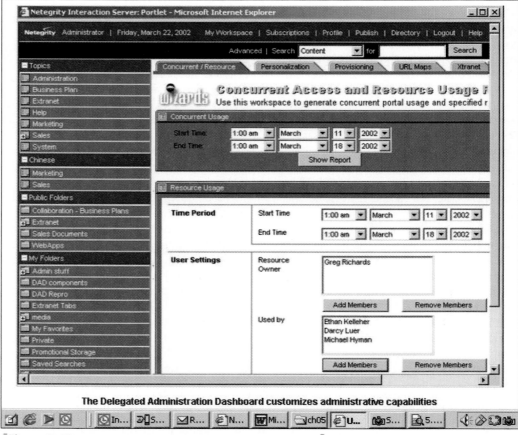

[Figure 5.10 ➥ Application integration using DataChannel's EIP.]
Source: **www.datachannel.com**

Online Entry of Information

Companies can use intranets to streamline routine business processes because an intranet provides a Web browser interface to facilitate online entry of information. Microsoft has implemented an intranet-based expense reporting application, called MSExpense, that allows employees from across the world to submit expense reports online, dramatically reducing the inefficiencies and expenses associated with paper-based expense report processing.

Prior to MSExpense, 136 different expense report templates existed within the corporation, and information such as mileage rates were often outdated. These issues cost Microsoft employees precious time and effort in locating the appropriate template and ensuring that the expenses they were submitting were accurate. With MSExpense, expense report templates and expense rates are centrally managed on the intranet Web server, where modifications can be made instantaneously as conditions change. Now, Microsoft employees submit the appropriate template electronically with the assurance that they have used the correct version and up-to-date expense rates.

The implementation of the MSExpense intranet application reduced the cost of processing employee expense reports by over $3.3 million per year, shortened expense reimbursements from three weeks to three days, and dramatically reduced error rates by providing a single point of entry (Microsoft, 2001). Furthermore, applications such as MSExpense provide management with accurate, up-to-date information to track and analyze the costs associated with key business activities, as well as a way to enforce business policies to take advantage of reduced corporate rates offered by airlines, rental car companies, and hotels.

Real-Time Access to Information

Unlike paper-based documents, which need to be continually updated and distributed to employees when changes occur, intranets make it less complicated to manage, update, distribute, and access corporate information. U.S. Steel, the nation's largest manufacturer of steel products, developed a sophisticated intranet solution to provide employees access to up-to-date personal benefits information, allowing them to make more informed decisions related to health and financial benefits offered by the company. The intranet reduces employee reliance on human resources personnel, freeing them up for other tasks. Further-

more, when benefits packages such as the 401(k) plan change, the appropriate documents can be modified and posted on the intranet Web server as they occur. Employees are notified of the change via electronic mail, and they can access the revised documents through a Web browser interface by simply clicking on the URL provided in the mail message.

Boeing disseminates corporate news using multimedia files distributed over the company's intranet. Formerly, news releases were produced on videotape, duplicated, and distributed via surface mail to each corporate office around the world. With the intranet-based solution, the company has eliminated the videotape reproduction process by allowing employees to monitor company news releases as they occur from the convenience of their desktops. Boeing can now disseminate news in a more timely fashion while, in the process, saving millions annually in distribution costs.

With intranet-based solutions such as those deployed at U.S. Steel and Boeing, up-to-date, accurate information can be easily accessed on a company-wide basis from a single source that is both efficient and user-friendly. Companies can become more flexible with resources required to create, maintain, and distribute corporate documents, while in the process, employees become more knowledgeable and current about the information that is important to them. Employees develop a sense of confidence and become self-reliant, reducing time spent dealing with employment-related issues, which allows them to focus on their work responsibilities.

Collaboration

One of the most common problems occurring in large corporations relates to the communication of business activities in a timely fashion across divisional areas of the organizations. For instance, a product engineer located at a branch office in Sydney, Australia, may need to access information from product marketing personnel located in San Francisco, California, to ensure the product will meet the needs of the market. These individuals may need to share technical information such as CAD/CAM drawings, project management reports, and information related to prevailing industry and market conditions. In other words, employees must be able to collaborate across departmental and geographical boundaries to complete project requirements in an efficient and timely manner.

Boeing uses its intranet to facilitate these collaborative efforts. Project managers disseminate daily project progress reports over the intranet to members of the project team, who may be located in any of its offices in 60 countries. Companies can also use multimedia technologies such as video-conferencing or Microsoft NetMeeting to facilitate team meetings over the intranet. Intranet-based collaboration alleviates the need for costly travel and use of less user-friendly media such as conference calling. Furthermore, three-dimensional modeling of aircraft designs can be shared between aero-space engineers. For example, an engineer can send a drawing across the intranet to another engineer at a remote location, who revises the drawing as necessary and returns the updated drawing using the intranet. The Boeing intranet provides the company with the capability of reducing product develop-ment cycles, as well as the ability to stay abreast of current project, corporate, and market conditions.

Extranet System Architecture

An extranet looks and acts just like an intranet and uses the same software, hardware, and net-working technologies to communicate informa-tion (see Figure 5.11). However, an extranet connects the intranets of two or more business partners and, thus, requires an additional com-ponent. Intranets can be connected together using a *virtual private network*, or VPN, to facilitate the secured transmission of propri-etary information between business partners. VPNs take advantage of the public nature of the Internet and its standardized protocols to communicate information by combining the global connectivity of the Internet with the security of a closed, private network. When intranets are connected via a VPN, they act as if they are directly connected as a single LAN/WAN, but in reality they are not. As the name implies, virtual private networks are vir-tual in the sense that a connection is created between the intranets when a transmission needs to take place and terminated once the transmission has been completed. In other words, the VPN exists only when it is needed. Further, a VPN is backed by the telephone ser-vice provider, which adds an increased level of trust in the network. In addition, this approach enables you to scale bandwidth up and down as needed.

To access information on an extranet, Web browsers are installed on the workstations within each intranet and the TCP/IP protocol must be implemented on top of existing net-work protocols. Authorized business partners can access extranet content through a Web browser by entering the URL of their business partner's main extranet Web page. Once the

---

Career Implications:

Marketing

A large durable goods manufacturing company ran into some problems when disseminating weekly sales reports within the organization. The company consists of approximately 60 sales employees who needed to send their weekly reports to approximately 40 people ranging from regional managers to top managers. The sales personnel were required to e-mail their weekly reports to an administrative assistant, who gath-ered all the reports together, made copies, and sent them to the relevant people. This took a long time, and often the information was not received in a timely manner. The company already had an intranet installed, and the Webmaster of the intranet, when consulted about this problem, decided that the intranet could be used for this purpose. As a result, a collaboration package was installed on the intranet. Using Sitescape Forums,

discussion forms and secured documents were created for each of the company's products. All the sales personnel and users who would be viewing the reports were registered and given proper security. A macro was written on the intranet to create a combined report from all the individual sales reports. The sales personnel are now required to connect to the intranet and upload their weekly reports. Once the reports are submitted, an administrative assistant in the sales department downloads all of them to create a combined report, then uploads it to a combined report folder. Anyone who has access to this area of the intranet can now read those reports. The intranet has been used successfully by the organi-zation to improve its internal sales communica-tion. Chances are you will be using just such a corporate intranet. If not, you might suggest that your firm build one!

[Adapted from P. G. Daly, "Using the Intranet to Improve Internal Sales Communications," **www.intranetjournal. com/articles/200011/it_11_08_00a.html**]

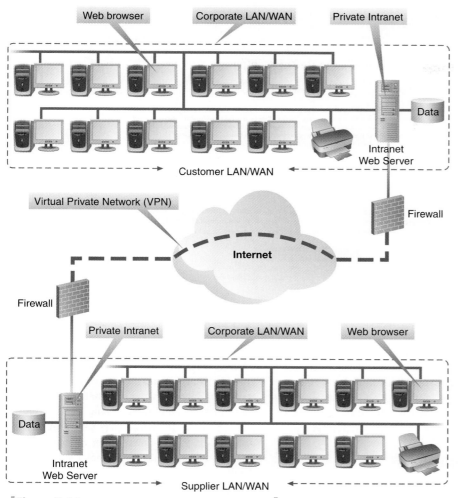

[**Figure 5.11** ➡ Typical extranet system architecture.]

user enters the URL in the Web browser, TCP/IP breaks the request into packets and routes the packets over the internal LAN/WAN to the firewall.

VPNs use a technology known as **_tunneling_** to encapsulate, encrypt, and transmit data over the Internet infrastructure, enabling business partners to exchange information in a secured, private manner between organizational firewalls. Before information can be transmitted from one intranet to the other, the VPN connecting the two firewalls is established, and a secured tunnel is created over the VPN. TCP/IP routes the encrypted packets through the firewall and through the tunnel en route to their destination. When the packets reach the business partner's firewall, each packet is verified to ensure it has been sent from an authorized business partner. After packet verification, the packets are decrypted, and TCP/IP reassembles the packets and delivers them to the intranet Web server for processing.

Extranet Web servers perform an additional security measure through a process called **_authentication_**. Authentication confirms the identity of the remote user who is attempting to access information from the Web server. The authentication process forces the remote user to supply a valid username and password before the Web server fulfills requests. Boeing has implemented authentication through the Web page depicted in Figure 5.12.

After the remote user has been authenticated, the Web server retrieves the requested information, which is packetized by TCP/IP and sent back to the firewall. At the firewall, the packets are encapsulated and encrypted and sent via TCP/IP through the tunnel across the VPN. When the packets reach the business partner's firewall, each packet is verified to ensure it has been sent from an authorized business partner. After verification, the packets are decrypted, and TCP/IP reassembles the packets and delivers them to the Web browser

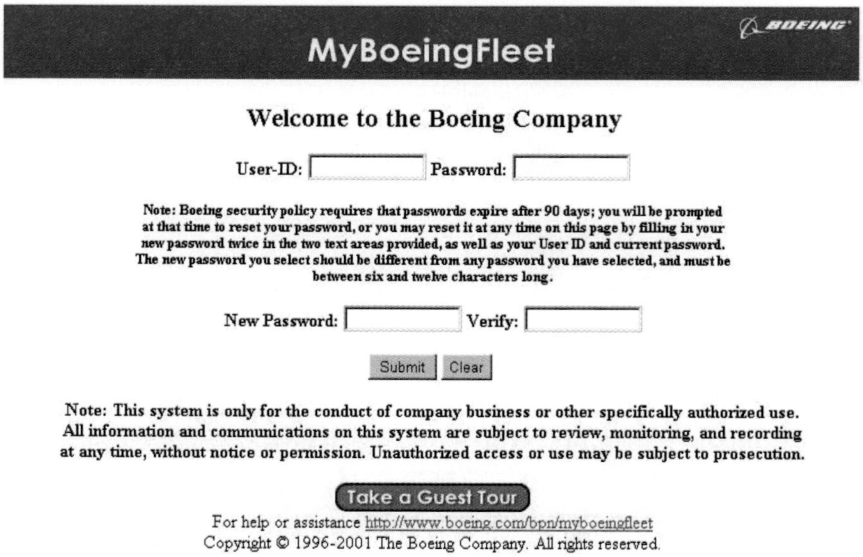

[**Figure 5.12** ➡ Boeing's extranet authentication page.]
Source: Boeing, 2001 **www.boeing.com**

that originally requested the information. The Web browser processes the HTML code, formats the physical appearance of the Web page, and displays the results in the Web browser. Once the transmission has been completed, the tunnel is discarded and the VPN is disconnected.

Web Search

WEB SEARCH OPPORTUNITY: Visit Aventail, a leading extranet service provider, at **http://www.extranet-strategist.com** to further your exploration of extranets.

Extranet Applications

Supply Chain Management

The big three U.S. automobile manufacturers, Ford, General Motors, and Chrysler, teamed up in 1997 to implement an industry-wide extranet to exchange supply and manufacturing information between customers and suppliers. Although it may seem outlandish that major competitors within an industry are teaming up for ***supply chain management***, the results have benefited everyone in the industry (Turban et al., 2000). The extranet includes features that allow participants to make online purchases, check supplier inventory levels, and transfer design specifications, as well as perform a variety of related tasks involved in business transactions. The extranet has helped reduce product manufacturing time, enabled inventory to arrive on a just-in-time basis, and compressed the turnaround time on work orders from three weeks to as little as five minutes. Overall, the extranet has achieved an industry-wide savings exceeding $1 billion per year (Turban et al., 2000).

Dell Computers, a leading supplier of personal computers and servers, has used an extranet to streamline its supply chain, reducing its number of suppliers from more than 1,000 to approximately 100. Dell's suppliers are able to predict upcoming demands by accessing data from the extranet and can pass these forecasts and orders along to their suppliers, in turn, to ensure they can meet Dell's orders. This trickle-down effect introduced by Dell's use of extranet technologies has resulted in operational efficiencies throughout its supply chain (McDougall, 2000).

Real-Time Access to Information

CSX, one of the largest railroad companies in the United States, leverages extranet technologies to facilitate real-time information access by customers and business partners. CSX developed an application, originally implemented as an intranet-based tool for the company's customer service agents, that can track train shipments from coast to coast, providing real-time status updates. CSX now offers this service to its customers and business partners through an extranet. CSX has connected its extranet with over 200 business partners, including freight shippers and forwarders, who act as intermediaries between CSX and its customers. These business partners deliver customer shipments to the railroad and deliver arriving shipments to customers on the company's behalf. CSX's business partners use the extranet's real-time information to streamline their business operations, enabling them to pick up and deliver goods at the yard on a just-in-time basis.

CSX customers can log in to see where their shipments are in transit (down to the individual package level), allowing them to identify unanticipated delays and respond to them in a timely manner. Customers also use the extranet to calculate expected shipping rates, which CSX keeps updated on a regular basis. Customers can enter purchase orders online and receive confirmations nearly instantaneously, creating great efficiencies in the order processing cycle for both companies (Turban et al., 2000).

Collaboration

Collaboration via extranets allows companies to respond proactively to the changing marketplace by working directly with their business partners, suppliers, and customers. These applications provide companies with the ability to develop products that will soon be in demand, giving them an understanding of what will be needed and when. Through extranet-based collaboration, the product development cycle can be initiated and completed faster. Companies can plan for the necessary components and communicate information with suppliers well in advance of the product coming to market. Companies can also deploy purchasing resources more effectively, transforming traditional procurement personnel into supplier relationship managers rather than transaction processors.

Caterpillar, a global manufacturer of heavy machinery, implemented an extranet to assist with customer requests for customizations to their products. Prior to the extranet, salespeople, managers, and technical staff would need to wade through a plethora of paperwork to process a request, resulting in poor response times and unsatisfactory customer service levels. With the extranet, customers can request customized components online, and the request can be forwarded to Caterpillar's product engineers and component suppliers, who can securely share the required information such as CAD/CAM drawings. In some cases, Caterpillar gains process efficiencies by acting as an intermediary between the end customer and supplier. Caterpillar can redirect requests directly to the supplier, who builds the custom component and delivers it directly to the customer (Turban et al., 2000).

Enterprise Portals

Many companies operate multiple extranets, each designed to service particular business partners with particular business requirements. A desire to integrate these stand-alone extranets has prompted the evolution of a more powerful class of extranets known as **enterprise portals**. **Portals**, in the context of B2B EC, can be defined as access points (or front doors) through which a business partner accesses secured, proprietary information from an organization. Enterprise portals provide a single point of access to this type of information, which may be dispersed throughout an organization. Enterprise portals can provide substantial productivity gains by combining multiple extranet applications to create a single point of access where the company can conduct business with any number of business partners. This can help reduce the maintenance costs associated with supporting multiple extranets and can simplify the process for end users since all the information they need to carry out business is available from a single source.

Enterprise portals come in two basic forms, **distribution portals** and **procurement portals**. Distribution portals automate the business processes involved in selling, or distributing,

---

Brief Case: Success at Dell

In addition to using the Internet to support its supply chain, Dell also uses the Internet extensively to interact with customers (**http://www.dell.com**). Dell began selling computers online in mid-1996 and continues at the eShop Dell Store at **www.eshop.com**. Dell derives about 90 percent of its overall revenues from sales to medium and large businesses, yet more than half of its Internet-based sales have been to individuals and small businesses, who typically buy one computer at a time. The Web site allows customization of a computer by listing the prices for various components and accessories. Customers can check the status of an order on the Web. Dell offers purchase assistance with information on payment solutions, taxes and shipping, catalogs, and rebate information. The extensive Web site includes a search engine.

By streamlining operations and greatly increasing sales through both online and traditional channels, Dell has grown into one of the world's largest personal computer manufacturers, with sales of more than $32 billion at the end of the year 2000. This 17-year old company passed IBM in terms of global market share two years ago and has been atop the U.S. market, the world's largest, for the last eight quarters.

Information Systems

GE has traditionally been known as a dominant player in the area of e-commerce. Recently, the company kept up with its image as an adopter of innovative technologies and methods by developing a proprietary EDI service for its vendors and suppliers in order to manage purchases and procurements within the various divisions of GE. GE first built an Internet-based information system in 1994, which reached 25,000 of its suppliers worldwide. Bids for industrial items were sent out over the Internet. Suppliers who wanted to continue supplying to GE, or those who were interested in becoming suppliers, would connect to GE's system and respond online. This Internet-based system formed the basis of GE's extranet, termed the Trading Process Network (TPN), and allowed current and future suppliers to access the procurement process without the huge costs that are usually involved in the case of proprietary systems. This extranet has helped GE realize huge cost savings and also helped the company manage inventory and track orders. In addition, the extranet has also increased GE's just-in-time practices, reduced the time taken for manufacturing, and decreased its inventory warehouse costs. GE can now send out, evaluate, and select bids within 24 hours. The extranet has also enabled the company to increase the number of quotes that it receives by enabling it to reach a larger number of suppliers. This increase in the number of supplier quotes has made the suppliers more competitive; they are now more eager to provide more comprehensive quotes and increase their level of service. Take note! GE has pioneered the use of Internet-based information systems like these.

[Adapted from **www2000.ogsm.vanderbilt.edu/Student.Projects/Extranet/extranet. html#genelec**.]

products from a single supplier to multiple buyers. On the other end of the spectrum, procurement portals automate the business processes involved in purchasing, or procuring, products between a single buyer and multiple suppliers (see Figure 5.13). Distribution and procurement portals can vary based on the number of buyers and suppliers that utilize the portal. For example, automotive industry giants Ford Motor Company, DaimlerChrysler, and General Motors have teamed up to create a procurement portal that suppliers to the big three can access. Similarly, a few companies can share distribution portals to purchase products from many suppliers. When the balance between buyers and sellers nears a point of equilibrium, these systems are classified as **trading exchanges**.

Distribution portals, procurement portals, and trading exchanges commonly service specific industries or groups of firms that rely on similar products or services. Tailoring products and services to particular companies creates a **vertical market**, or a market that services the needs of a specific sector. Vertical markets can create tremendous efficiencies for companies since they can take advantage of existing applications that already meet the requirements of other companies in their industry, eliminating the need to develop proprietary systems of their own.

Distribution Portals

Distribution portals are designed to automate the business processes that occur before, during, and after sales have been transacted between a supplier and multiple customers. In other words, distribution portals provide efficient tools for customers to manage all phases of the purchasing cycle, including product information, order entry, and customer service. Dell Computers services business customers through its distribution portal Premier Dell.com (see Figure 5.14).

Premier Dell.com goes well beyond providing its business customers with order entry and status updates. The distribution portal helps companies keep track of and manage their computing equipment through a series of online reporting tools. Need to know when a particular piece of equipment was ordered? Premier Dell.com can search Dell's corporate database and produce a report tracing the equipment purchase to a particular transaction, purchase order, and/or order number.

Customers can also obtain customized, system-specific technical information about the products they have purchased. HelpTech, an application available on Premier Dell.com, provides help desk personnel with the same information available to Dell technicians. This information includes a troubleshooting toolkit, a library of documents containing manuals and technical specifications, and a knowledge base containing searchable documentation from technicians and end users.

When placing orders, customers are taken to a personalized storefront where discounted prices are calculated depending upon rates

Web Search

WEB SEARCH OPPORTUNITY:

Visit the homepage for the U.S. Federal Government at **www.firstgov.gov/** to see what types of information and services can be found there. What type of portal is this?

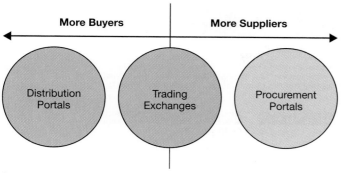

[**Figure 5.13** ➡ Distribution portals, trading exchanges, and procurement portals.]

[**Figure 5.14** ➡ Distribution portal Premier Dell.com.]
Source: **www.dell.com**

negotiated with Dell. The system immediately informs customers exactly how much an order will cost. Customers can utilize an application called E-Quote to build a purchase order online and send a copy of the quote via e-mail to a purchasing manager for approval. Once the quote has been received by the customer's purchasing department, an approved purchasing agent uses E-Quote to review the quote, approve it, and place the order with one click of the mouse. An application called Image-Watch informs Dell's customers of technological trends and changes before they impact Dell's products. This enables customers to make more educated purchasing decisions and plan ahead for technical innovations that can benefit the customer. Premier Dell.com allows Dell's business customers to take control of business needs, saving them time and money while creating management efficiencies (Dell, 2001).

Procurement Portals

Procurement portals are designed to automate the business processes that occur before, during, and after sales have been transacted between a buyer and multiple suppliers. Procurement portals provide efficient tools for suppliers to manage all phases of the distribution cycle, including dissemination of product information, purchase order processing, and customer service. Ford Motor Company has implemented a procurement portal called Ford Supplier Network (FSN; **fsn.ford.com/default. html**), where suppliers come to share information and conduct business with Ford (see Figure 5.15).

The FSN portal consists of a variety of applications addressing such issues as customer support, quality control, purchase order management, and product development. DEALIS (Distribution, Export, and Logistics Information System) is a real-time tracking

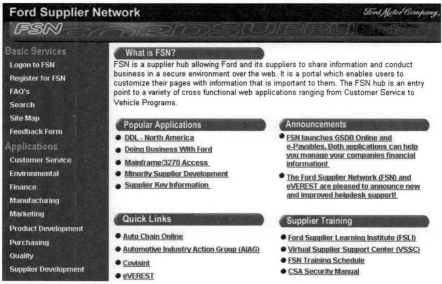

[Figure 5.15 ➥ Ford Supplier Network procurement portal.]
Source: **www.Ford.com** (word search Ford Supplier Network)

application built for FSN that provides up-to-the-minute sales and shipping information to suppliers and shippers. These business partners use DEALIS to receive updates on shipments in transit and allow users to view information based on containers, packages, or even down to specific parts. If you are a Ford supplier and need to know where that shipment of bumpers is located, DEALIS can help you find out.

The Master Part Number Registry (MPNR) is an application designed to standardize part numbers and descriptions. In an environment in which a company makes purchases from multiple suppliers, each supplier may use different nomenclature to describe the same part. Implementing a common set of part numbers and descriptions allows Ford to make more efficient purchasing decisions, since product comparisons can be based on a common set of standards. Suppliers use MPNR to verify that the product information given to Ford adheres to the company's standards. MPNR is linked to Ford's corporate databases to ensure the accuracy and consistency of part numbers and descriptions used within Ford and throughout its supply chain.

An FSN application called Supplier Direct Data Links (SDDL) provides real-time information internally as well as to suppliers concerning parts shortages. When inventory levels reach a critical or potentially critical stage, the application notifies suppliers, who can respond immediately to the issue. Suppliers can inform Ford that they are investigating the shortage and revise promised delivery dates through SDDL.

FSN is also a learning and information site. Included in the portal are applications that enable suppliers to take courses online. The FORDSTAR program helps Ford certify its dealerships, employees, and suppliers. Here, users can access training materials, online courses, and developmental resources that will help Ford and its suppliers remain competitive in the ever-changing automotive industry. The interactive system helps suppliers determine which learning opportunities would be most beneficial to the organization.

FSN also provides suppliers with information concerning Ford's key business processes and plans for the future, as well as an online tutorial to teach suppliers how to conduct business with Ford. From a supplier perspective, one of the key attractions of FSN lies in its distribution of competitive intelligence. Being aware of market trends and the activities of competitors enables Ford's suppliers to stay one step ahead of the competition.

The Ford procurement portal has created a win-win situation for the company, its suppliers, and end consumers. Ford has been able to streamline its business operations with suppliers, leading to dramatic process efficiencies and cost reductions. By using FSN, suppliers have direct access to a large company that can produce a substantial revenue stream. Suppliers also benefit from the information provided on FSN, which enables them to operate more efficiently, access Ford-sponsored

Cisco Systems is the worldwide leader in networking for the Internet. Cisco Marketplace, the Cisco Web site for online ordering, is also considered by many to be one of the most successful global distribution portals on the planet (see Figure 5.16; **www.cisco.com/pcgi-bin/marketplace/ entrance.pl**). Cisco Marketplace is a global e-commerce portal for all Cisco products, including networking equipment, training materials, literature, technical documentation, subscriptions, and Cisco apparel and gift items.

With the processing of well over $2 billion of customer orders over the Web since October 1996, Cisco has entered into a new business model that takes complete advantage of the Internet. This raises a serious question: Has this global electronic marketplace actually delivered on the promise of the Internet—a new way of making money—or is it merely a clever marketing ploy by the largest vendor in the Internet-working industry to showcase what can be done on the Internet without giving much thought to its real implications? This question is important to Cisco because they have been promoting their online sales channel as the archetypical example of what EC should become.

The site offers Cisco's 45,000 global business customers real-time information on price, availability, configuration requirements, ordering, invoice status and validation, and shipping information over the Web. Regardless of which country the customer lives in, if she can get an Internet connection, then she can check out her Cisco orders and products. Cisco also uses the site to forward procurement information to its own employees for possible modifications and approvals via e-mail. It used to take days or weeks for a salesperson to complete an order; now it takes only 15 minutes to an hour. Customers are able to join discussion forums, receive bug alerts, and download software patches directly from the Internet. The site currently claims 80,000 registered users and 3.5 million hits per day, and handles about 40 percent of Cisco's multiple billions of dollars in sales. John Chambers, CEO, states that the annualized savings to the company of $270 million is due to taking advantage of the Internet, intranet, and extranet technologies.

One analyst suggests that it is difficult to measure the actual savings on the bottom line. It is difficult to put an accurate price tag on what it would have cost Cisco to implement a physical, global sales, marketing, and distribution infrastructure. Cisco has avoided these costs while at the same time increasing revenue globally, and the site is credited for increased customer satisfaction. But efficiency does not always translate into a stronger business relationship or higher demand for products. Thus, Cisco has made it a point to carefully manage the account relationship with its customers beyond what can be done on the Web site.

As if operating one of the most successful online, global distribution portals is not enough, Cisco has also implemented the Cisco Networking Academy Program, a partnership between Cisco Systems, education, business, government, and community organizations around the world. The Networking Academy curriculum teaches students around the globe to design, build, and maintain computer networks. There are currently over 8,400 Academies enrolling nearly a quarter million students in over 130 countries.

[**Figure 5.16** ➡ Web site for Cisco Marketplace, one of the most successful global distribution portals.]
Source: **www.cisco.com**

training, and help them to remain competitive in their markets. End consumers also profit from the distribution portal. When products can be manufactured more cheaply and efficiently, consumers ultimately benefit through reduced prices and faster delivery.

Trading Exchanges

Enterprise portals tend to be beyond the reach of small to midsized businesses due to the costs involved in designing, developing, and maintaining this type of system. Many of these firms do not have the necessary monetary resources or skilled personnel to develop EC applications on their own. To service this market niche, a number of *trading exchanges*, or electronic marketplaces, have sprung up. Trading exchanges are operated by third-party vendors, meaning that they are built and maintained by a particular company. These companies generate revenue by taking a small commission for each transaction that occurs, by charging usage fees, by charging association fees, and/or by generating advertising revenues. Unlike distribution and procurement portals, trading exchanges allow many buyers and many sellers to come together, offering firms access to real-time trading with other companies in their vertical markets. This can be accomplished at a reasonable cost, making trading exchanges a competitive reality.

Many experts foresee trading exchanges as the dominant force on the B2B landscape. It is estimated that by 2004, 52 percent of all B2B EC will be conducted through trading exchanges, meaning that they will control over $3 trillion worth of commerce! (Hill, 2000). At the end of 2000, over 200 trading exchanges were in operation, with the number predicted to jump to over 10,000 by 2005 (Kalakota, Oliva, and Donath, 1999). Trading exchanges provide companies with not only transaction processing, but also information pertinent to their industries, procurement resources to compare products from various sellers, and invoicing services. Some of the most popular trading exchanges include **E-Steel.com** and **MetalSite.com** (steel), **Citadon.com** (building and construction),

PaperExchange.com (pulp and paper), and **neoforma.com** (medical equipment).

SciQuest Corporation (**http://www. SciQuest.com**) has developed a trading exchange to service the laboratory products and scientific supply industry, which represents a $36 billion vertical market (SciQuest, 2001).

With industry globalization rapidly occurring, the industry had become increasingly fragmented, producing inefficiencies in the distribution and procurement processes. Many customers purchased products from a multitude of suppliers based on outdated information in paper-based catalogs. As a result, firms were wasting time in product/supplier research and managing relationships with many more suppliers than necessary. To exacerbate matters, outside influences were exerting pressure on the industry to become more cost conscious, bring new products to market at a faster pace, and adhere to environmental legislation mandated by government agencies.

SciQuest supports the particular needs of the laboratory products and scientific supply industry in six ways, as depicted in Figure 5.17. Other trading exchanges such as E-Steel, which services the steel industry, have different support strategies since different industries have unique business requirements that the exchanges need to support.

SciQuest's SciCentral application provides a centralized repository for research articles relevant to the industry. SciCentral allows users to search thousands of scientific journals by keyword and also offers the capability to order and download research online. Trading exchange participants can also search for innovations that assist in the development of new products such as pharmaceuticals.

Once customers locate the product they are interested in, they need to source the product. Sourcing refers to finding the supplier that can provide the highest-quality product at the lowest price. SciQuest's Select-Site APA (Advanced Procurement Application) takes the customer's request and matches it with the most appropriate supplier. This eliminates the time customers spend in searching for the best supplier, since the application

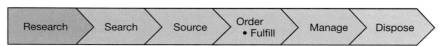

[**Figure 5.17** ➥ SciQuest supports its vertical market in six ways.]
Source: **www.SciQuest.com**

does it for them. Customers review the results from the sourcing application and choose to place the order automatically with one mouse click or reject the transaction.

SciQuest also supports the customer service aspects of the transaction by providing functions for coordinating shipping, receiving products, and tracking customer and supplier inventory levels. Furthermore, there can be a great deal of managerial overhead involved with transactions in the laboratory products and scientific supply industry. For example, certain chemical compounds, such as those used in the manufacture of illicit drugs, must be cleared through government agencies. SciQuest can assist companies in coordinating government approvals. Other chemicals must be tracked and monitored as they move throughout an organization, and SciQuest's EMAX application can perform bar-code tracking functions to locate sensitive materials. Some products used in the industry, such as chemicals that can potentially harm the environment, need to be disposed of properly once they are used. EMAX can guide customers through the disposal process by helping them locate an approved materials disposer and coordinate pickup between the two companies.

SciQuest's customers include The Dow Chemical Company, DuPont Pharmaceuticals Company, Glaxo Wellcome, Merck & Co., and The Monsanto Company, while suppliers include Alltech Associates, Ambion Biotech, Endogen, NEN Life Science Products, PerkinElmer Instruments, Pierce Chemical, QIAGEN, and Shimadzu Scientific Instruments. In other words, if you are a small company in this industry using SciQuest, you can conduct business as if you were an industry heavyweight.

BUSINESS-TO-CONSUMER ELECTRONIC COMMERCE

The Internet and Web have evolved with mind-boggling quickness, achieving mass acceptance faster than any other technology in modern history. The widespread availability and adoption of the Internet and Web, which are based on an economical, open, ubiquitous computing platform, have made Internet access affordable and practical, allowing consumers to participate in Web-based commerce. In addition, a great number of businesses have similarly benefited from the revolution and have implemented Web-based systems in their daily operations. This heightened level of participation by both consumers and producers has made the emergence of business-to-consumer (B2C) EC economically feasible. Unlike B2B, which concentrates on business-to-business relationships at the wholesale level, B2C focuses on retail transactions between a company and end consumers.

B2C revenues are expected to be approximately $10 billion this year. The major portion of B2C focuses on electronic retailing, or *e-tailing*, which provides many advantages over brick-and-mortar retailing in terms of product, place, and price. Web sites can offer a virtually unlimited number and variety of products since e-tailing is not limited by physical space restrictions. For instance, in 1999 click-only book e-tailer Amazon.com offered over 4,000,000 book titles on the Web compared with the brick-and-mortar book retailer Barnes & Noble, which could offer merely 200,000 items due to the restricted space of their physical stores. Place proves advantageous in the e-tailing environment because company storefronts exist on every computer that is connected to the Web, enabling e-tailers to compete more effectively for customers. Whereas traditional retailing can be accessed only at physical store locations during open hours, e-tailers can conduct business anywhere, at any time. E-tailers can also compete on price effectively since they can turn their inventory more often due to the sheer volume of products and customers who purchase them. Companies can sell more products, reducing prices for consumers while at the same time enhancing profits for the company (Christensen and Tedlow, 2000).

Despite all the recent hype associated with e-tailing, there are some downsides to this approach. Barring products that you can download directly such as music or an electronic magazine, e-tailing requires additional time for products to be delivered. If you have run out of ink for your printer and your research paper is due this afternoon, chances are that you will drive to your local office supply store to purchase a new ink cartridge rather than ordering it online. The ink cartridge purchased electronically needs to be packaged and shipped, delaying use of the product until it is delivered. Other issues can also arise. The credit card information that you provided online may not be approved, or the shipper may try to deliver the package when you are not home.

With the growth of B2B e-commerce, maintaining efficient supplier relationships has become increasingly important. According to Mike Brunsting (e-commerce/EDI team leader at Herman Miller), sharing timely information with suppliers is the key to many e-commerce successes. However, different factors, such as lack of technical sophistication of the suppliers and lack of foresight of the company, pose as barriers to improving these supplier relationships. Many new modern technologies, such as the portal technology, provide an efficient way to improve such relationships, as Herman Miller discovered. Herman Miller is a $1.9 billion manufacturer of office furniture headquartered in Zeeland, Michigan. For a while the company (like other office furniture makers) had a reputation of being slow-moving and unreliable. After a lot of investigation the company realized that one of the ways in which to reduce its lead times

and become reliable was to reduce its communication time with its suppliers. After exploring different options (including building in-house products), the company decided to proceed with a portal technology developed by TopTier. The technology would enable the company to establish two-way communication with their suppliers and enable the suppliers to look more deeply into Herman Miller's business online, including their prices, their payments, manufacturing lead times, materials required, engineering data, and so on. The portal technology was ultimately implemented at the company site approximately two years ago, and today it connects more than 50 percent of the company's suppliers. The company has significantly decreased its manufacturing lead times and increased its reliability (in terms of on-time shipping) to over 90 percent. As someone working in manufacturing, you will be wired!

[Adapted from Derek Slater, "Portal Potential," **http://www.cio.com**, *CIO Magazine* (September 15, 2000).]

Another problem associated with e-tailing relates to a lack of sensory information such as taste, smell, and feel. When trying on clothes with your virtual model at Lands' End, how can you be sure that you will like the feel of the material? Or what if you discover that the pair of 9 EE roller blades you just purchased online fits you like an 8 D? Other products such as fragrances and foods can also be difficult for consumers to assess via the Web. Does the strawberry cheesecake offered online actually taste as good as it looks? How do you know if you will really like the smell of a perfume without actually sampling it? Finally, e-tailing eliminates the social aspects of the purchase. Some e-tailers are having a hard time competing with shopping malls since going to the mall with some friends is a lot more fun for most people than buying online! As with B2B procurement, comparison shopping can be difficult since vendors provide product information in different ways. However, a number of comparison shopping services that focus on aggregating content are available to consumers. Some companies fulfilling this niche are BestBookBuys.com, Bizrate (**http://www.bizrate.com**), and My Simon (**http://www.mysimon.com**). These compari-

son shopping sites can literally force sellers to focus on relatively low prices in order to be successful. Either that or sellers must be able to offer better quality, better service, or some other advantage if they do not have the lowest price. These comparison shopping sites generate revenue by charging a small commission on transactions, by charging usage fees to sellers, and/or through advertising on their site.

Stages of Business-to-Consumer Electronic Commerce

With thousands of B2C-oriented Web sites in existence, Web sites range from passive to active. At one extreme are the relatively simple, passive Web sites that provide only product information and the company address and phone number, much like a traditional brochure would do. At the other extreme are the relatively sophisticated, active Web sites that enable customers to see products, services, and related real-time information and actually make purchases online. As shown in some early, pioneering research on EC (Kalakota, Olivia, and Donath, 1999; Quelch and Klein, 1996), companies usually start out with an electronic brochure and pass through a series of stages as depicted in Figure 5.18, adding additional capa-

[**Figure 5.18** ➡ Stages of business-to-consumer electronic commerce.]

bilities as they become more comfortable with EC. These stages can be classified as *e-information*, *e-integration*, and *e-transaction*.

E-Information

One of the first ways corporations utilize the Web is to promote sales and marketing information via an *electronic brochure*, or *e-brochure*. Figure 5.19 provides an example of an e-brochure developed by Italian car manufacturer Ferrari (**www.ferrari.it/cgi-bin/ fworld.dll/ferrariworld/scripts/home/home .jsp?language=ENGLISH**). The e-information stage achieves the goal of global information dissemination, allowing potential customers to access information about the company and its products. The company can disseminate this information globally in the sense that e-information can be accessed by any Internet user with access to a Web browser. Furthermore, the information is available 24 hours a day, seven days a week, 365 days a year. No matter where on earth the user is located and regardless of the time, the e-brochure is available for their review.

E-information is more flexible than traditional promotional methods such as hard-copy catalogs and print advertisements. When information needs to be updated, e-information can be modified and posted very quickly, whereas traditional methods require typesetting, printing, and/or distribution, depending on the medium. Eliminating these manual processes not only shortens cycle times but also reduces the associated labor expenses.

In the process, users are provided with the timeliest information possible. E-information may ultimately lead to a purchase. However, the e-information stage is limited because it merely provides company and product information, not the capability to customize information dynamically, which leads to the next stage of B2C—e-integration.

E-Integration

Once companies have mastered the e-information stage, they become more comfortable with EC and want to enhance their Web sites by adding additional features and functionality. The e-information stage provides a mechanism to distribute information to the general public, yet cannot accommodate requests for customized information. Customized information is dynamic, meaning that Web pages are created on-the-fly to produce tailored information that addresses the particular needs of the consumer. For instance, a banking customer may want more than information related to the bank and its products. This customer would like to access information related to her accounts, such as the balance in her checking account or the amount of interest credited to her savings account last month. In other words, customers may want information that is relevant to them rather than the general public.

In order to facilitate this type of customer request, Web sites must be integrated with corporate databases to extract and display the appropriate information. This integration

[**Figure 5.19** ➥ An e-information Web site operated by Ferrari.]
Source: **www.Ferrari.com**

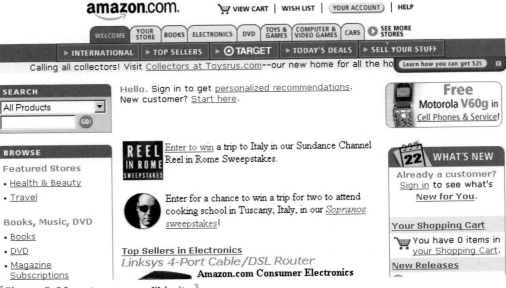

[**Figure 5.20** → Amazon.com Web site.]
Source: **www.Amazon.com**

process characterizes the e-integration phase of B2C. The e-integration stage helps companies fulfill their goals of integration and mass customization. Firms such as the insurance and financial services company, Allstate (**www.allstate.com**), provide a useful example of the e-integration approach to EC. Customers register their identity through an online form to gain access to their account. Once registered, customers can access detailed, personalized information about their auto, home, and life insurance policies online. Allstate can also identify specific groups of customers, such as those holding home insurance policies, and target marketing efforts to those individuals.

The Burlington Northern Santa Fe Railway (BNSF) (**http://www.bnsf.com**), one of the nation's largest railroads, utilizes the e-integration approach to assist with transactional support. Using a Web-based application called Custom Tracing, customers enter their shipment number and receive information about the status of their shipment. In addition, customers can use the Web site to calculate shipping rates by simply entering the source and destination locations. Companies that provide e-integration services have enabled customers to find the information they need when they want it, without having to call a customer service representative for assistance.

One drawback of the e-integration stage lies in its inability to accommodate online ordering. Although companies such as Allstate and Burlington Northern Santa Fe enable

access to customized information, when customers want to conduct a transaction, they must resort to calling the company. For instance, when an Allstate customer needs to update his life insurance policy, he must contact his agent through other means. Similarly, BNSF customers must call the railroad to schedule shipments. In the cases of Allstate and BNSF, there are strategic business reasons not to enable online ordering, yet providing the ability to place orders online can prove beneficial in most cases. The ability to conduct transactions online leads us to the next stage of B2C—e-transaction.

E-Transaction

E-transaction takes the e-integration stage one step further by adding the ability for customers to enter orders and payments online. The e-transaction stage helps companies fulfill their goals of collaboration, interactive communication, and transactional support. Many of the most well-known B2C Web sites fall into the e-transaction category, such as the click-only e-tailer Amazon.com (see Figure 5.20). Customers can not only find out product information but also make purchases, enter payments, and track the status of their orders once the sale has been made. The Amazon.com Web site has been so successful that the company has branched from selling books to offering other products such as electronic equipment, home décor, pharmaceuticals, and even cars!

E-transaction can take many forms. Virtual companies such as Priceline.com and eBay have developed innovative ways of generating revenue. Priceline.com offers consumers discounts on airline tickets, hotel rooms, rental cars, new cars, home financing, and long distance telephone service. The revolutionary aspect of the Priceline.com Web site lies in its ***reverse pricing*** system called Name Your Own Price[SM]. Customers specify the product they are looking for and how much they are willing to pay for it. This pricing scheme transcends traditional ***menu-driven pricing***, in which companies set the prices that consumers pay for products. After a user enters the product and price, the system routes the information to appropriate brand-name companies such as United Airlines and Avis Rent A Car, which either accept or reject the consumer's offer. Since Priceline.com opened its virtual doors in April 1998, it has sold over 7 million airline tickets, 2 million nights of hotel lodging, and 2 million days of rented cars! (Priceline.com, 2001).

eBay has transformed e-tailing into an ***electronic marketplace***, which is similar to B2B trading exchanges except B2C electronic marketplaces service end consumers at retail prices. Unlike e-tailers such as Lands' End and Amazon.com, where one seller services many buyers, an electronic marketplace services many buyers and sellers, who can come together to sell and purchase a wide variety of products. Items sold on eBay range from rare coins to antiques and fine art. Looking for that hard-to-find concert ticket? EBay may be the place to find it. However, you must outbid other consumers in an auction style format to get what you want. The bidding starts at a

price set by the seller and continues until a predetermined time, when the auction ends. If you are the top bidder, you are the proud owner of your prized concert ticket. But be careful, and know what you are purchasing and whom you are purchasing it from! In 1997, a series of forged signatures on baseballs, bats, and pieces of paper appeared on the eBay auction block. These included signed memorabilia from baseball greats Mickey Mantle, Joe DiMaggio, and Babe Ruth, all of whom attract high prices for their autographs (Couzin, 2000). Although the FBI eventually caught the perpetrators, electronic marketplaces are not immune to improprieties.

The e-transaction stage can also include electronic distribution of products and services. If the product or service can be digitized, it can be delivered online, as in the case of information-based products, videos, and software. ***Digitization*** creates products without tangible features, which are commonly referred to as ***virtual products***. Liquid Audio's Web-based music distribution system (see Figure 5.21) is changing how music is being purchased and delivered. The company's technology enables the music industry to use the Web as another distribution channel without fear of piracy. The system enables users to download CD-quality music that can be played only on the computer to which it was downloaded. The music is ***watermarked*** so that any illegal copy—even on cassette tapes—can be traced to the original purchaser. Electronic watermarking is similar in concept to watermarks placed on paper currency to prevent counterfeiting. Such technology works for the distribution of any type of information-based

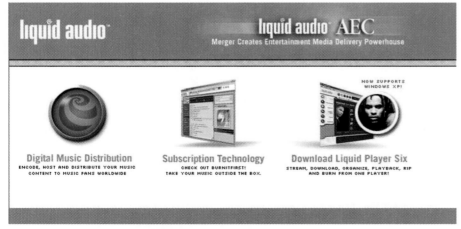

[**Figure 5.21** ➡ Liquid Audio's Web site.]
Source: **www.liquidaudio.com**

Team Work

So Many Books, So Little Time …

Have you or your classmates bought books online? Compare and contrast your experiences with your classmates. What types of books have you bought? From which Web sites? How did you like your online purchase experience? If you have not yet bought books online, visit the Web sites of Amazon.com and Barnes & Noble, as well as other such sites, and compare their offerings. What do you think?

Brief Case: Evolution of Business-to-Consumer Electronic Commerce at Federal Express

Innovative, aggressive firms such as package shipper Federal Express are finding ways to use technology to sell goods and services. FedEx generates approximately $19 billion in revenues annually in overnight package shipping and related activities. The company understands the importance of doing EC on the Web and created a long-range goal of generating 100 percent of its business online. With the multibillion dollar overnight shipping market at stake and technologically savvy competitors such as United Parcel Service (UPS) right on their heels, FedEx's financial future depended on the development of a world-class Web site that allows customers to do all their business online.

Rather than jumping into the unfamiliar Web environment, FedEx chose to implement its Web site in a step-by-step fashion. The company's Web site has undergone a series of developmental stages, starting with an e-brochure and evolving into a sophisticated Web site where customers can track shipments and arrange online for pickups. Table 5.2 shows stages of the development of the FedEx Web site (**http://www.fedex.com**). The staged approach has allowed the company to be continually innovative with their online business, mastering one facet of EC before progressing to the next. The Web site has evolved into a venue where all the necessary features are available, allowing customers to conduct business with FedEx via the corporate Web site. FedEx has become a B2C pioneer, continually inventing new ways of using Web-based EC to achieve competitive advantage.

[Table 5.2] *The stages of Web site deployment for FedEx. (Quelch and Klein, 1996)*

Stage	Focus	Activities
E-Information	Establish a corporate image and disseminate product information	Registered a domain name and created a Web site that provides information about the company and its products.
E-Integration	Information collection, market research	The company created electronic forms with which customers can register their identity and be assigned account numbers. FedEx uses customer information as a tool for conducting market research, enabling the company to get to know their customers.
	Customer support and service	Linked Web site to the company's corporate database, which allows customers to enter shipment numbers and view up-to-date information on package delivery or location.
E-Transaction	Online order entry	Created facilities that allow customers to request pickups and arrange payment options.

product. Orders of tangible products such as electronic equipment can be fulfilled by more traditional brick-and-mortar or click-and-mortar methods, but any information-based components to these products or services—such as an owner's manual—can be digitized and delivered online. It is a certainty that you will see more and more virtual products such as music, art, video, and software delivered over the Web in the near future.

THE FORMULA FOR ELECTRONIC COMMERCE SUCCESS

The basic rules of commerce are to offer valuable products and services at fair prices. These rules apply to EC as well as to any business endeavor. However, having a good product at a fair price may not be enough to compete in the EC arena. Companies that were traditionally successful in the old markets will not necessarily dominate the new electronic markets. Successful companies are found to follow a basic set of principles, or rules, related to Web-based EC[3]. These rules are:

---
[3]Please note that these rules apply mainly to how to make a Web site more successful. Realize that the underlying business model must be sound and that there are a host of similar rules that information systems personnel must follow to ensure that 1) the Web site works well, 2) it interacts properly with back-end business information systems, and 3) the site is secure.

According to Richard Dalzell (CIO of Amazon.com), one of the biggest challenges of an online retailer is taking care of the customers. The key success factors of such companies therefore lie in making their customers happy. Amazon, which is known as one of the most customer-friendly companies, realized this early on and has since focused on using technology innovatively to become known as the most customer-centric company in the world. Amazon has primarily focused on the development of a personalization technology that enables it to create a unique store that changes with every customer. The technology also helps Amazon build a real-time environment that knows who each of their customers is, and what he wants to buy on the Internet. As a result, the tool deals with a lot of real-time data, including those data provided by their customers about their purchasing interests. The database is maintained by Oracle, while most of the tools and software that run on this database are created in-house. The company has also built a new 1-Click technology that provides customers with easier navigational capabilities and makes the site much more user friendly.

Apart from the customer aspects, Dalzell argues that there are two other important factors that help in making a successful B2C e-commerce company. First, always look toward the future, and second, hire a world-class engineering team. Amazon so far has been successful in both. It is known as one of the most innovative companies, constantly reinventing the wheel in order to better align themselves to the future. It also lays great importance on having world-class professionals in the company and spends a great deal of time and money on hiring. On its Web site, Amazon claims that the top six reasons that you would want to choose to work for the company are to:

▮ Work with and learn from an unusually high proportion of smart, focused people who are passionate about their work.
▮ Work on challenging, interesting projects that have a huge impact on our success.
▮ Work in a casual but accountable environment in which hard work, initiative, and smart decisions are rewarded.
▮ Play an important part in continuing our leadership in e-commerce by bringing new ideas to the table and launching new businesses.
▮ Be rewarded with great career opportunities and the chance to participate financially in the company's long-term success.
▮ Have fun!

Indeed, Amazon sums it up very nicely by saying that their employees, "work hard, have fun, and make history."

Career Implications:

Human Resource Management

[Adapted from Susannah Patton, "Talking to Richard Dalzell," **http://www.cio.com**; **www.amazon.com**.]

Rule 1—The Web site should offer something unique.

Rule 2—The Web site must be aesthetically pleasing.

Rule 3—The Web site must be easy to use and FAST!

Rule 4—The Web site must motivate people to visit, to stay, and to return.

Rule 5—You must advertise your presence on the Web.

Rule 6—You should learn from your Web site.

Rule 1. The Web site should offer something unique. Providing visitors with information or products that they can find nowhere else leads to EC profitability. Many small firms have found success on the Web by offering hard-to-find goods to a global audience at reasonable prices. For example, Eastern Meat Farms (**www.salami.com**), an Italian market in New York, sells hard-to-find pasta, meats, cheeses, and breads over the Internet at its Web site (see Figure 5.22). Their first order came in 1995 from a customer in Japan. Although the Japanese customer paid $69 in shipping costs for the $87 order of pasta, he did not mind; he was saving $150 by not buying the Italian delicacies locally (Rebello, 1996).

Rule 2. The Web site must be aesthetically pleasing. Successful firms on the Web have sites that are nice to look at. People are more likely to visit, stay at, and return to a Web site that looks good! Creating a unique look and feel can separate a Web site from its competition. Aesthetics can include the use of color schemes, backgrounds, and high-quality images (but not too many!) Furthermore, Web sites should have a clear, concise, and consistent layout, taking care to avoid unnecessary clutter.

[**Figure 5.22** ➥ The Salami.com Web site.]
Source: **www.salami.com**

Rule 3. The Web site must be easy to use and FAST! As with nearly all software, Web sites that are easy to use are more popular. If Web surfers have trouble finding things at the site or navigating through the site's links, or have to wait for screens to download, they are not apt to stay at the site long or to return. In fact, some early studies suggest that the average length of time that a Web surfer will wait for a Web page to download on his screen is only a couple of seconds. Rather than presenting a lot of information on a single page, successful Web sites present a brief summary of the information with hyperlinks, allowing users to "drill down" to locate the details they are interested in.

[**Figure 5.23** ➥ The GardenWeb Web site.]
Source: **www.GardenWeb.com**

Rule 4. The Web site must motivate people to visit, to stay, and to return. People visit Web sites that provide useful information and links or free goods and services. One of the reasons that Microsoft's Web site is popular is because users can download free software. Other firms motivate visitors to visit their Web sites by enabling them to interact with other users who share common interests. These firms establish an online community where members can build relationships, help each other, and feel at home. For example, at GardenWeb (**www.gardenweb.com**), visitors can share suggestions and ideas with other gardeners, post requests for seeds and other items, and follow electronic links to other gardening resources. At this Web site, the participants communicate and carry out transactions with one another, returning over and over for more (see Figure 5.23).

Rule 5. You must advertise your presence on the Web. Like any other business, a Web site cannot be successful without customers. Companies must draw, or pull, visitors to their Web sites. This strategy is known as **pull marketing**. Unlike **push marketing**, which actively pushes information at the consumer whether it is wanted or not (e.g., television commercials), pull marketing is a passive method used to attract visitors to your site and away from the thousands of other sites they could be visiting. The predominant method of pull marketing involves advertising the Web site. The first way to advertise your firm's presence on the Web is to include the Web site address on all company materials, from business cards and letterheads to advertising copy. It is now common to see a company's URL listed at the end of its television commercials.

Another strategy is to register the Web site with the more popular search engines such as Lycos, Excite, Google, and Yahoo. In most cases, registering with these sites is free and fast and can be done online. Many search engines provide context-sensitive advertising, meaning that your ad will be shown only when a related keyword is entered into the search engine. For example, if you are selling sporting goods, you can have your advertisement appear when certain terms like baseball, football, basketball, and so on are entered in the search.

In addition to registering with the many search engines, a firm can advertise its Web site

---

Brief Case: Internet Advertising at Starwave

If you want to learn more about Internet-based advertising and the current fees for advertising on some of the Web's hottest sites, visit Starwave Corporation (**www.starwave.com**). Starwave has designed and developed some of the most often visited sites on the Web, such as ABCNEWS. COM, ESPN SportsZone (**www.espn.com**), and many other top Web destinations. Paul Allen (cofounder of Microsoft) and The Walt Disney Company founded Starwave in 1993. At the Starwave Web site, you can investigate advertising rates, as well as the number and demographics of the visitors to each of its online partners. Starwave shows the size and shape of online advertisements and their associated rates. Companies like Starwave, which hosts and manages company sites for ESPN and CBS, are generally referred to as Internet Service Providers (ISPs), which are dis-cussed in Chapter 4. Starwave can provide total Web site hosting, design, continuous connection services, or some subset of these services. ISPs that focus on supporting organizational Web sites typically have sophisticated backup and recovery facilities, as well as redundant servers to recover seamlessly from a system failure.

Internet advertising has become an important way to reach customers and, potentially, to generate revenue through a Web site. There are a number of approaches to advertising on a Web site, from banners that scroll across a screen, to pop-up windows, to dynamic Web pages that fill in the content based on your attributes. Similarly, there are a number of approaches for charging for advertising on Web pages, from flat fees to paying for every instance in which a user clicks on an ad. Advertising on Web sites has become very important to EC and is a very interesting area in which to work.

on other commerce sites or Web sites containing related information. Companies have made a great deal of money by enabling other companies to advertise on their Web sites. According to Jupiter Communications, Web advertising revenue totaled nearly $72 million for the first half of 1996, a figure that grew substantially from the previous year and has continued to grow. Advertising your presence on other popular Web sites, such as *USA Today* (**http://www.usatoday.com**), can cost as much as $20,000 to $30,000 per month, but they can promise that more than a million users a day will visit their sites. Given the high cost of advertising on these sites, and the fact that many of those Web surfers do not even look at the online ad, the trend in Web advertising is moving away from high, fixed, monthly charges to a "pay by the click" scheme. Under this type of pricing scheme, known as **hypermediation**, the firm

running the advertisement pays only when a Web surfer actually clicks on the advertisement (Carr, 2000).

Rule 6. You should learn from your Web site. Smart companies learn from their Web sites. A firm can track the path that visitors take through the many pages of its Web site and record the time of day, day of the week, or times throughout the year that people visit these sites. It can then use this information to improve its Web site. If 75 percent of the visitors follow links to check the company's online posting of job opportunities within the firm or check on current pricing for a particular product, then that firm can redesign its Web site to provide that information quickly and easily for visitors. Similarly, pages that go unused can be eliminated from the site, reducing maintenance and upkeep.

USING YOUR CELLULAR PHONE FOR M-COMMERCE

Mobile phones such as the new Nokia 8265, pictured in Figure 5.24, not only look great but also enable you to access the Internet. These phones include a mobile Internet browser based on the Wireless Application Protocol. With this browser you can check mail, check the news, order a pizza, or do whatever else you want to do on the Web. This new mobile form of EC is known as "m-commerce," where the "m" stands for mobile.

M-commerce opens up all kinds of possibilities for being connected to the Internet literally anytime, anywhere. In addition to letting users surf the Web using the integrated wireless Internet browser, the phone also enables two-way text messaging and picture messaging. Users of the phone will thus have many ways to access information and to keep in touch with friends, family, and colleagues.

Based on the highly successful Nokia model 8260, the new Nokia model 8265 phone is Nokia's newest entry in the "fashion" category. Users can change the cover on the phone to match their clothes or suit their mood. The company offers four different colorful covers: orange, pink, purple, and light blue. The Nokia 8265 also has space for 10 downloadable ring tones, which can be selected

[**Figure 5.24** ➡ The new Nokia 8265, stylish and ready to surf the Web.]
Source: © Nokia, **www.Nokia.com**

from an Internet site and sent over the air to the phone. As you can see, in addition to being a technical marvel, this phone can be highly personalized. E-commerce in the future is going to be fun!

———
[Source: the Nokia Web site.]

KEY POINTS REVIEW

1. **Describe electronic commerce and how it has evolved.** Electronic commerce is the online exchange of goods, services, and money between firms, and between firms and their customers. Although EC was being used as far back as 1948 during the Berlin Airlift, the emergence of the Internet and World Wide Web has fueled a revolution in the manner in which products and services are marketed and sold. Their far-reaching effects have led to the creation of an electronic marketplace that offers a virtually limitless array of new services, features, and functionality. As a result, a presence on the Internet and Web has become a strategic necessity for companies. The powerful combination of Internet and Web technologies has given rise to a global platform where firms from across the world can effectively compete for customers and gain access to new markets. EC has no geographical limitations. The global connectivity of the Internet provides a relatively economical medium for marketing products over vast distances. This increased geographical reach has been facilitated by storefronts located on every Web-enabled computer in the world. Unlike traditional storefronts, time limitations are not a factor, allowing firms to sell and service products seven days a week, 24 hours a day, 365 days a year to anyone, anywhere. A larger customer base creates increased sales volumes, which ultimately saves consumers money since firms can offer their products at lower prices. Companies are exploiting one or more of the capabilities of the Web to reach a wider customer base, offer a broader range of product offerings, and develop closer relationships with customers by striving to meet their unique needs. These wide-ranging capabilities include global information dissemination, integration, mass customization, interactive communication, collaboration, and transactional support.

2. **Describe the strategies that companies are adopting to compete in cyberspace.** The Web has transformed the traditional business operation into a hyper-competitive electronic marketplace. Companies must strategically position themselves to compete in the new EC environment. At one extreme, companies known as brick-and-mortars choose to operate solely in the traditional, physical markets. These companies approach business activities in a traditional manner by operating physical locations such as department stores, business offices, and manufacturing plants. In other words, the brick-and-mortar business strategy does not include EC. In contrast, click-only (or virtual) compa-

nies conduct business electronically in cyberspace. These firms have no physical locations, allowing them to focus purely on EC. Other firms choose to straddle the two environments, operating in both physical and virtual arenas. These firms operate under the click-and-mortar business model.

3. **Explain the differences between intranets and extranets and how they are used on the Internet.** Intranet refers to the use of the Internet within an organization to support internal business processes and activities. Examples of the types of processes or activities that might be supported include things such as training, data storage, access to information, and employee collaboration. Extranet refers to the use of the Internet between firms for things such as supply chain management and interfirm collaboration.

4. **Describe the difference between consumer-focused and business-focused electronic commerce.** Business-focused EC uses techniques such as Electronic Data Interchange to enable the online exchange and sale of goods and services between firms. While EDI uses proprietary networks, the trend in business today is to use extranets (the public Internet and Web) as the vehicle for business-to-business EC. These portals are used to support distribution, procurement, and other activities. Consumer-focused EC refers to business use of the Internet, Web, and other platforms to reach customers. Companies usually start out with an electronic brochure and pass through a series of stages, including e-information, e-integration, and e-transaction, the latter including sales and service that are conducted online.

5. **Understand the keys to successful electronic commerce applications.** The basic rules of commerce are to offer valuable products and services at fair prices. These rules apply to EC as well as to any business endeavor. However, having a good product at a fair price may not be enough to compete in the EC arena. Companies that were traditionally successful in the old markets will not necessarily dominate the new electronic markets. Successful companies are found to follow a basic set of principles, or rules, related to Web-based EC. These rules include having a Web site that offers something unique, is aesthetically pleasing, is easy to use, is fast, and that motivates people to visit, to stay, and to return. A company should also advertise its presence on the Web and should try to learn from its Web site.

KEY TERMS

ANSI X.12 137	digitization 157	Electronic Data Interchange 136
authentication 145	disintermediation 134	electronic marketplace 157
brick-and-mortar 135	distribution portal 147, 148	enterprise portal 147
business-to-business 132	e-brochure 155	extranet 139
business-to-consumer 132	e-information 155	firewall 140
business-to-employee 132	e-integration 155	hypermediation 162
click-and-mortar 135	e-tailing 153	intranet 138
click-only 135	e-transaction 155	menu-driven pricing 157
consumer-to-consumer 132	electronic commerce 132	portal 147

REVIEW QUESTIONS

1. What is electronic commerce (EC), and how has it evolved?
2. How have the Web and other technologies given rise to a global platform?
3. Compare and contrast two electronic commerce business strategies.
4. Explain the differences between the Internet, an intranet, and an extranet. What is the common bond among all three?

5. Describe two types of portals and several applications.
6. Define trading exchanges, and give a couple of examples.
7. What are the three stages of business-to-consumer electronic commerce?
8. Compare and contrast reverse pricing and menu-driven pricing.
9. What is an electronic marketplace? Give an example.
10. List and describe six elements of or rules for a good Web site.

SELF-STUDY QUESTIONS

Answers are at the end of the Problems and Exercises.

1. Electronic commerce is the online exchange of _____ between firms, and between firms and their customers.
   A. goods
   B. services
   C. money
   D. all of the above

2. _____ allow many buyers and many sellers to come together, offering firms access to real-time trading with other companies in their vertical markets.
   A. Distribution portals
   B. Procurement portals
   C. Trading exchanges
   D. E-exchanges

3. _____ are those companies that operate in the traditional, physical markets and do not conduct business electronically in cyberspace.
   A. Brick-and-mortars
   B. Click-onlys
   C. Both A and B
   D. Dot-coms

4. _____ automate the business processes involved in purchasing, or procuring, products between a single buyer and multiple suppliers.
   A. Distribution portals
   B. Procurement portals
   C. Enterprise portals
   D. Resource portals

5. According to the text, the three stages of Web sites include all of the following except _____ .
   A. e-tailing
   B. e-integration
   C. e-transaction
   D. e-information

6. The revolutionary aspect of the Priceline.com Web site lies in its _____ system called Name Your Own Price^{SM}. Customers specify the product they are looking for and how much they are willing to pay for it.
   A. immediate pricing
   B. menu-driven pricing
   C. forward pricing
   D. reverse pricing

7. Under this type of pricing scheme, known as _____ , a firm running an advertisement pays only when a Web surfer actually clicks on the advertisement.
   A. cost-effective
   B. hypermediation
   C. cost-plus
   D. pay-plus

8. _____ creates electronic forms with which customers can register their identity and be assigned account numbers. Customer information is used as a tool for conducting market research, enabling the company to get to know its customers.
   A. E-commerce
   B. E-integration
   C. E-transaction
   D. E-information

9. A Web site should _____ .
   A. be easy to use and fast
   B. offer something unique and be aesthetically pleasing
   C. motivate people to visit, to stay, and to return
   D. all of the above

PROBLEMS AND EXERCISES

1. Match the following terms with the appropriate definitions:

   ____ Electronic commerce

   ____ Hypermediation

   ____ Value-added networks

   ____ E-transaction

   ____ Electronic market

   ____ Electronic Data Interchange

   ____ Distribution portals

   ____ Vertical markets

   ____ E-integration

   ____ Digitization

   a. Online exchange of goods, services, and money between firms, and between firms and their customers
   b. The online sale of goods and services between firms with proprietary networks that the firms have developed and paid for entirely themselves
   c. A process that creates products without tangible features, which are commonly referred to as virtual products
   d. A class of extranets that automate the business processes involved in selling, or distributing, products from a single supplier to multiple buyers
   e. A pricing scheme whereby a firm running an advertisement pays only when a Web surfer actually clicks on the advertisement
   f. Telephone lines that are leased from telecommunications providers, creating a secure, dedicated circuit between a company and its business partners
   g. Markets that service the needs of a specific sector, creating tremendous efficiencies for companies since they can take advantage of existing applications that already meet the requirements of other companies in their industry, eliminating the need to develop proprietary systems of their own
   h. A stage that takes the e-integration stage one step further by adding the ability for customers to enter orders and payments online
   i. A market that allows many buyers and many sellers to come together, offering firms access to real-time trading with other companies in their vertical markets
   j. A stage in which Web pages are created on-the-fly to produce tailored information that addresses the particular needs of a consumer

2. How did Federal Express implement the development of the FedEx Web site (**http://www.fedex.com**)? Who is the company's primary competitor? How has the Web site improved Federal Express's competitive advantage?

3. Visit Alaska Airlines' Web site (**http://www.alaskaair.com**) for real-time pricing, and test the clothing model at the clothing retailer Lands' End (**http://www.landsend.com**). How have Internet technologies improved over the years?

4. Search the World Wide Web for the Web site of a company that is purely Web-based. Next find the Web site of a company that is a hybrid (i.e., they have a traditional "brick-and-mortar" business plus a presence on the Web). What are the pros and cons of dealing with each type of company?

5. Do you feel that e-commerce will help or hurt shipping companies such as FedEx and UPS? Have you purchased anything over the Internet? If so, how was it delivered?

6. Do you receive advertisements through e-mail? Are they directed toward any specific audience or product category? Do you pay much attention or just delete them? How much work is it to get off an advertising list?

7. What is it about a company's Web site that draws you to it, keeps you there on the site longer, and keeps you coming back for more? If you could summarize these answers into a set of criteria for Web sites, what would those criteria be?

8. Consider an organization with which you are familiar that maintains an e-commerce Web site. Determine the types of information and processes available on the system. Do the employees make good use of the system and its capabilities? Why or why not?

9. As described in the Global Perspective in this chapter, "Cisco Systems Online—The World's Most Successful Distribution Portal," what makes the company successful? Visit **http://www.cisco.com** on the World Wide Web to find out why.

10. Visit the following services for comparison shopping: BestBookBuys.com, Bizrate (**http://www.bizrate.com**), and My Simon (**http://www.mysimon.com**). These companies focus on aggregating content for consumers. What are the advantages of these Web sites?

11. Look at the list of your favorite bookmarks on the World Wide Web. Why have you saved these addresses? How often do you visit some of these Web sites? Is it faster to bookmark an address than to look it up again?

ANSWERS TO THE SELF-STUDY QUESTIONS

1. D   2. C   3. A   4. B   5. A   6. D   7. B   8. B   9. D

CASE 1: *Dot-Com Vs. Brick-And-Mortar: Who Will Have The Last Laugh?*

With the tremendous growth in e-commerce, dot-com retailers have enjoyed significant success. They have been successful in enticing customers with cheap prices and free shipping and have consistently taken away business from the brick-and-mortar retailers, who have been left wondering whether their business processes, which had been so successful for so many years, need serious reengineering. The dot-com retailers did not have to worry about integrating their online business with their existing business, and as a result experienced faster success. However, suddenly, the tide seems to have changed. The dominance of the dot-com retailers is on the decline. They are facing increasing competition and declining sales. To add to all this, the stock prices of the dot-com retailers have also been going down. The situation has been so bad that many dot-com retailers, such as Toysmart.com, Foofoo.com, Boo.com, and Craftshop.com, have all closed their businesses. On one hand, analysts are continually predicting a growth in the B2C e-commerce market, which is expected to grow by 85 percent and top $61 billion within a year or two. On the other hand, in spite of this predicted growth, the purely B2C Internet companies (i.e., pure plays) seem to be failing. At the same time, many of the brick-and-mortar companies are strengthening their Web initiatives and, motivated by the announcements of growth in e-commerce, are "fighting back with successful click-and-mortar strategies."

One such company is Office Depot. The company is one of the largest and most profitable office-supply retailers and has a network of 750 superstores, 30 warehouses, 2,000 trucks, $1.3 million in goods, and $250 million in sales. The company launched its Web site and started experiencing success from the very beginning. The company did not have to build any new distribution centers or products, and all it needed was a well-designed and effective Web site.

Unlike many other online retailers, the company has focused on integrating its Web operations within the very fabric of its existing operations and business processes. To start with, Office Depot has developed its Web initiatives primarily for its business-to-business customers such as Proctor and Gamble and MCI. Office Depot has built over 37,000 customizable pages for its corporate clients. These customizable pages are built in a manner such that they allow different employees in an organization to view different catalogs. For example, a storeroom clerk is only able to see products such as pencil and toner cartridges, while the CEO's assistant may be able to see the entire list of Office Depot's products. The corporate clients also can check inventory of Office Depot's nearest warehouses and stores and see which of the products are available for delivery the next day. The company has gone all out to ensure the success of its e-commerce initiative, and has used the Internet not merely to extend its business, but to "leverage their bricks and mortar."

Through the use of the Internet, Office Depot has cut down its order-processing costs by at least half. Since no customer service representative is required to enter an order, order-entry errors have been eliminated and the number of returns has also been significantly reduced. Though Web sales account for only three percent of the company's total sales, they are predicted to grow at the rate of 50 percent per quarter. Today, 20 percent of Office Depot's corporate sales are from the Web, and the company is looking to grow Web sales further in the near future.

The company is also focusing on extending its Web initiatives to small businesses and consumers. The Web sites have been designed such that each small business can set up a list of authorized users. If any employee orders products, the site automatically sends an e-mail message to the employee's supervisor and completes the order only after the supervisor sends in an approval. This initiative promises to be successful, and the site has had more than 800,000 visitors since it was recently opened.

Staples, based in Massachusetts, is another major office-supply retailer that is also experiencing significant success in the area of e-commerce. The company has invested a great deal in researching customer needs through focus groups and independent surveys. It has completely revamped its old Web site and has focused it more on customer service. The site now enables improved purchase management and checkout, and has special features to help small businesses. There is also a rebate center to further help customers. The company's current Web sales are fairly high at approximately $200 million, though this is approximately 25 percent lower than the Web sales of Office Depot. While the brick-and-mortar office-supply retailers are becoming increasingly successful, many of the online retailers such as AtYourOffice.com and onlineofficesupplies.com are slowly going out of business. In fact, onlineofficesupplies.com had less than $1 million in sales in one year.

Motivated by the success stories of many of the brick-and-mortar retailers, other retailers are also increasingly strengthening their e-commerce initiatives. JC Penney recently reengineered its plus-size apparel section on the Web. Customers can now create their body dimensions on the Web and then model their preferred clothing. Saks Fifth Avenue has also revamped its site from one that allowed customers only to request catalogs and store locations, to one that attempts to give the same shopping experience that customers would get when they walk into a physical Saks Fifth Avenue store. OfficeMax, another office-supply retailer, has also increased its e-commerce sales in the last few months.

Using their strong brand names, their extensive distribution centers, and their capability to purchase more products, these brick-and-mortar retailers are becoming serious competitors of their cyber rivals.

Discussion Questions

1. What do you think are the reasons that some of the purely online or dot-com retailers are experiencing declining sales and profitability?
2. What are some of the reasons that the brick-and-mortar retailers are experiencing great success in the area of e-commerce?
3. Who do you think will have the last laugh in the battle between the dot-com retailers and the brick-and-mortar retailers? In other words, is the new-found e-commerce success of the brick-and-mortar retailers short-lived, or is it here to stay?

References

Mottl, J. N. 2000. "Bricks 'N Mortar Vs. Dot-Com," **http://www.informationweek.com** (June 19, 2000).

Rocks, D. 1999. "Why Office Depot Loves the Net," *Business Week* 3648 (September 27, 1999): EB66–EB68.

CASE 2:   *A Portal for General Motors*

General Motors is a $161 billion corporation with over 600,000 employees worldwide. It conducts business in over 125 countries and manufactures products ranging from SUVs to satellites. Coordinating the transfer of information to so many employees had become one of the primary problems in the organization. A few years ago, the communications department at GM explored the idea of building a corporate intranet that would help GM distribute various types of information, including press releases, to its worldwide employees. At the same time, the GM finance and HR groups also became eager to build their own intranets. The company thus made a decision to form an intranet building team consisting of employees from the communications, finance, and HR departments, who would be responsible for designing and building a GM-wide intranet. This particular project received the support of the senior management, including the CIO and vice president, and the vice president of communications. However, building a company-wide standardized intranet for such a large organization was no easy task, as the intranet-building team soon realized.

The team envisioned the intranet to be a single integrated entity that would control the content of the entire company. However, there were significant obstacles to this strategy. While control was important, since it would enable the team to impose standards and structures without which the site could become chaotic, it was impossible to impose a high level of control over every site for such a large organization. As the director of Internet technology mentioned, "On the Web, you want to be fast to market, and you do not want to put up a lot of impediments." The intranet team was faced with a dilemma. They wanted to have control over each site, yet try to implement the intranet within a short period of time. They wanted to impose standards and structures, yet provide access to information that was relevant to all the departments and divisions around the world. In addition, the intranet team's meeting room had notes stuck all around the walls,

each of which reflected an intranet site that needed to be built.

In addition to the problems of control and creativity and the high number of potential sites needed, there was the additional problem of employee access. The way GM's desktop platform was structured prevented the users (employees) from downloading and installing any new software themselves. The initial task of loading the browsers onto the desktops of at least 100,000 employees would be cumbersome. This process would take time, significantly delaying the intranet implementation project.

When Michael Wiley joined as the intranet manager at GM, the intranet project had been going on for over a year, and yet nothing had been implemented. The designers were still pursuing their strategy of control, and the information systems department had just started installing browsers onto employee desktops. Wiley described the intranet team's meeting room as a "virtual war room" with the "sticky" notes still around the walls, representing the hundreds of intranet sites that needed to be built. The project was thus taking much too long, and little light could be seen at the end of the tunnel.

Wiley soon realized (from his past experience) that this strategy of control would not work. He urged the team to focus on building an intranet portal instead and using it to serve as a central directory site. This central site would provide links to locally controlled divisional and other departmental sites. He envisioned the site as one that would let users browse and search all other internal GM sites. It would provide employees with all company-wide information and at the same time help them to access particular divisional sites. In short, it would function like the Yahoo Web site in that it would serve as a directory to all GM intranet sites and link to new sites as each site was created by the departments.

The first step to implementing such a strategy was to give browser access to the employees. The information systems group took up the responsibility of installing

browsers on employee desktops. At the same time, the intranet team worked out a deal through which some employees would be able to buy the browser and install it themselves, thus facilitating the process.

The second step was to make it easy for the departments and other divisions to develop and maintain their sites. For this, the intranet team offered free server space to many divisions that were already beginning to work on an intranet site. They also imposed few constraints and guidelines for building the site, making it much more flexible for the individual departments.

Soon, the intranet portal was launched. It was called "Socrates," a name that would be easily recognizable in any part of the world. At the time of its launch, it linked to only 40 internal sites. However, today, the site links to more than 500 sites and reaches over 100,000 employees worldwide. It provides access to a wide range of sophisticated information such as a catalog of GM University's online classes, online forms for signing up for classes or training programs, approval and posting of new press releases, requests for graphical services, best practices at GM, posting of jobs, and so on. Socrates functions like a full portal. It enables users to access the information via a search engine, an alphabetical list of sites, and by top-level channels and categories. It has been described as the company's Yahoo and has been the recipient of the CIO Web Business 50/50 site award.

However, even today, the majority of GM's employees do not have access to Socrates, primarily due to the fact that they work in manufacturing plants and do not have the necessary computer equipment. The intranet team is currently working on installing intranet-connected computer kiosks on the shop floors. The team is also working on launching region-specific variants of Socrates that would function exactly like the region-specific Yahoo sites.

[Adapted from Sari Kalin, "Overdrive," *CIO Web Business Magazine* (July 1, 1999).]

Discussion Questions

1. Do you think that the intranet portal implemented at GM that provided only a "skin-deep" level of user-interface consistency violated the rules of a corporate portal? If so, is this necessarily a problem?
2. Will the intranet team's plan of launching region-specific variants of Socrates make the intranet chaotic and difficult to manage?
3. Derive three "lessons learned" from this intranet portal implementation case, and describe how you would apply them in a summer internship.

Organizational Information Systems

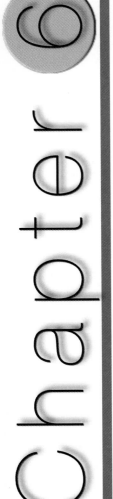

OPENING: Automating Web Purchase Returns at J.Crew

As more people use the Web to shop and purchase all kinds of products, the number of returned orders also increases. Online retailers have two ways to reduce the costs of handling returns. They can either refuse to accept returns or try to automate the return process. The first option is not a viable one since most customers will simply bypass those merchants who refuse to accept returns. Automating the return process will be a key capability for long-term profitability for most online merchants. In fact, market researchers estimate that 73 percent of the cost of processing a return can be saved through an efficient automated return process.

To address this issue, many companies are developing or acquiring systems to expedite the handling of returned items. For example, J.Crew (see Figure 6.1) recently began using a system called the ReturnValet by Newgistics, which is being used by several other successful online retailers including Lillian Vernon, Spiegel, and Eddie Bauer. Using the ReturnValet, shoppers receive a preauthorized United States Postal Service label with barcoded information. A shopper who wants to return a product simply goes to an authorized independent mail center such as Pak Mail or Post Net, where the bar-coded information is scanned and sent via an Internet connection to notify J.Crew that a return is on its way. By getting the notification by the independent mail center that the product is on its way, J.Crew will have a better idea of return volume and can speed the process of providing a refund.

Because all returned merchandise must be inspected before a refund can be authorized, the best method is for customers to return items to retail outlets. This is the fastest way for the company to inspect the product and return the purchase price. Unfortunately, that is not an easy or even a viable option for many online customers. Consequently, providing an easy way for customers not only to purchase online, but also to return items, will be a requirement as online shopping matures. With the ReturnValet, J.Crew is positioning itself to be a major player in the online retailing industry.

[Adapted from C. Heun, "JCrew Automates Returns to Save Money," **http://www.informationweek. com** (January 14, 2002).]

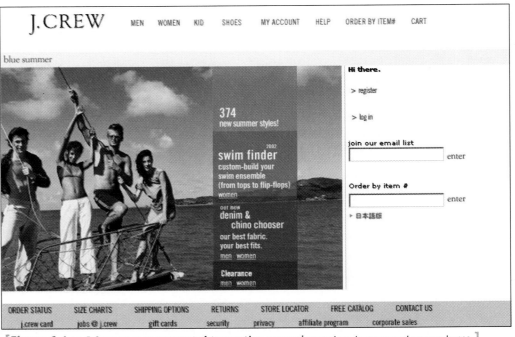

[**Figure 6.1** ➡ J.Crew uses an automated transaction processing system to ease customer returns.]
Source: **www.jcrew.com**

This chapter describes several types of information systems and where and how each is used in organizations. Some of the systems described are relatively new, while others have been mainstays in organizations since the 1960s.

After reading this chapter you will be able to do the following:

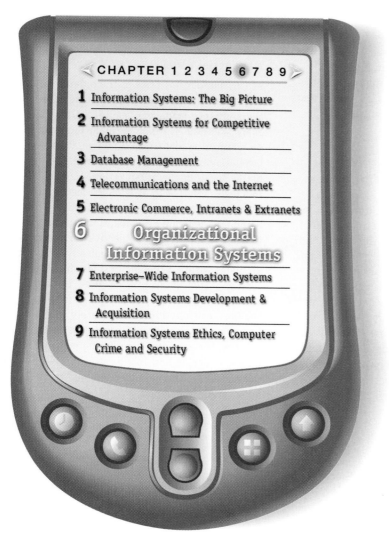

CHAPTER 1 2 3 4 5 6 7 8 9

1 Information Systems: The Big Picture

2 Information Systems for Competitive Advantage

3 Database Management

4 Telecommunications and the Internet

5 Electronic Commerce, Intranets & Extranets

6 Organizational Information Systems

7 Enterprise–Wide Information Systems

8 Information Systems Development & Acquisition

9 Information Systems Ethics, Computer Crime and Security

[Figure 6.2 ➡ The Big Picture: focusing on organizational information systems.]

1. Describe the characteristics that differentiate the operational, managerial, and executive levels of an organization.

2. Explain the characteristics of the three information systems designed to support each unique level of an organization: transaction processing systems, management information systems, and executive information systems.

3. Describe the characteristics of six information systems that span the organizational, managerial, and executive levels: decision support systems, expert systems, office automation systems, collaboration technologies, functional area information systems, and global information systems.

This chapter focuses on how organizations are using and applying information systems (see Figure 6.2). In the next chapter we discuss an additional class of organizational information system, the enterprise-wide information system. The next section describes the different types of information required at various levels of organizations. This is followed by a discussion of the general types of information systems used to span organizational boundaries.

DECISION-MAKING LEVELS OF AN ORGANIZATION

Every organization is composed of decision-making levels, as illustrated in Figure 6.3. Each level of an organization has different responsibilities and, therefore, different informational needs. In this section, we describe each of these levels.

Operational Level

At the *operational level* of a firm, the routine, day-to-day business processes and interaction with customers occur. Information systems at this level are designed to automate repetitive activities, such as sales transaction processing, and improve the efficiency of business processes and the customer interface. Managers at the operational level, such as foremen or supervisors, make day-to-day decisions that are highly structured and recurring. *Structured decisions* are those in which the procedures to follow for a given situation can be specified in advance. For example, a supervisor may decide when to reorder supplies or how best to allocate personnel for the comple-

tion of a project. Because structured decisions are relatively straightforward, they can be programmed directly into operational information systems so that they can be made with little or no human intervention. For example, an inventory management system for a shoe store in the mall could keep track of inventory and issue an order for additional inventory when levels drop below a specified level. Operational managers within the store would simply need to confirm with the inventory management system that the order for additional shoes was needed. Figure 6.4 summarizes the general characteristics of the operational level.

Managerial Level

At the *managerial level* of the organization, functional managers (e.g., marketing managers, finance managers, manufacturing managers, and human resources managers) focus on monitoring and controlling operational-level activities and providing information to higher levels of the organization. Managers at this level, referred to as midlevel managers or functional managers, focus on effectively utilizing and deploying organizational resources to achieve the strategic objectives of the organization. Midlevel managers typically focus on problems within a specific business function, such as marketing or finance. Here, the scope of the decision usually is contained within the business function, is moderately complex, and has a time horizon of a few days to a few months. For example, a marketing manager at Nike may decide how to allocate the advertising budget for the next business quarter or some fixed time period.

[**Figure 6.3** ➥ Organizations are composed of levels, with each using information technology to automate activities or assist in decision making.]

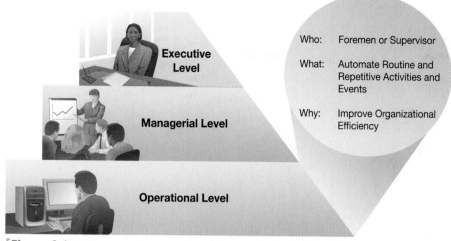

Who: Foremen or Supervisor

What: Automate Routine and Repetitive Activities and Events

Why: Improve Organizational Efficiency

[Figure 6.4 ➡ The operational level of an organization uses information systems to improve efficiency by automating routine and repetitive activities.]

Managerial-level decision making is not nearly as structured or routine as operational-level decision making. Managerial-level decision making is referred to as semistructured decision making because solutions and problems are not clear-cut and often require judgment and expertise. For *semistructured decisions*, some procedures to follow for a given situation can be specified in advance, but not to the extent where a specific recommendation can be made. For example, an information system could provide a production manager at Nike with summary information about sales forecasts for multiple product lines, inventory levels, and overall production capacity. The manager could use this information to create multiple production schedules.

With these schedules, the manager could examine inventory levels and potential sales profitability, depending upon the order in which manufacturing resources were used to produce each type of product. Figure 6.5 summarizes the general characteristics of the managerial level.

Executive Level

At the *executive level* of the organization, managers focus on long-term strategic issues facing the organization, such as which products to produce, which countries to compete in, and what organizational strategy to follow. Managers at this level include the president and chief executive officer (CEO), vice presidents,

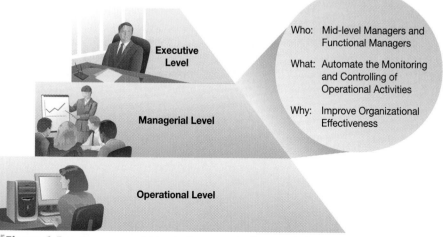

Who: Mid-level Managers and Functional Managers

What: Automate the Monitoring and Controlling of Operational Activities

Why: Improve Organizational Effectiveness

[Figure 6.5 ➡ The managerial level of an organization uses information systems to improve effectiveness by automating the monitoring and control of organizational activities.]

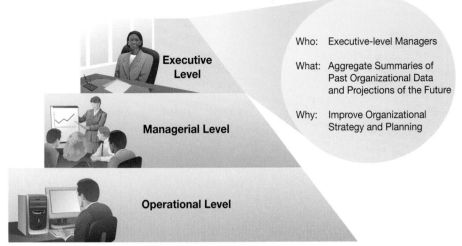

[**Figure 6.6** ➡ The executive level of an organization uses information systems to improve strategy and planning by providing summaries of past data and projections of the future.]

and possibly the board of directors, and are referred to as "executives." Executive-level decisions deal with complex problems with broad and long-term ramifications for the organization. Executive-level decisions are referred to as unstructured decision making because the problems are relatively complex and nonroutine. In addition, executives must consider the ramifications of their decisions in terms of the overall organization. For **unstructured decisions**, few or no procedures to follow for a given situation can be specified in advance. For example, top managers may decide to develop a new product or discontinue an existing one. Such a decision may have vast, long-term effects on the organization's levels of employment and profitability. To assist executive-level decision making, information systems are used to obtain aggregate summaries of trends and projections of the future. Figure 6.6 summarizes the general characteristics of the executive level.

In summary, most organizations have three general levels: operational, managerial, and executive. Each level has unique activities, and each requires different types of information. The next section examines various types of information systems designed to support each organizational level.

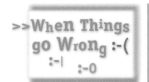

Online-Only Banks Struggle and Fail

Online banking is starting to catch on with consumers, with nearly 20 percent of U.S. households banking online. Online banks had more than 14 million visitors in the month of July 2001, an increase of over 100 percent from the prior year. For online-only banks, however, the number of visitors slightly declined over the same period. The vision for online-only banks was to have very low overhead costs relative to banks that had physical facilities and branches, in order to pass on savings to customers. The banks intend to offer low-interest credit cards and inexpensive online bill-payment services. Unfortunately, this vision has not proved to be a reality. In fact, in early 2002, Phoenix-based NextBank NA was the first Internet-only bank to fail when government regulators shut down the bank for having operated in an "unsafe and unsound manner." Research has shown that as consumers get more comfortable with online commerce, they prefer banks that have both a physical and online presence in order to have physical access to money and personal customer service. It remains to be seen what the final outcome will be for the online-only bank, but industry experts feel that as online banking becomes more of a commodity, with little or no charge for online services, the long-term prognosis for the online-only bank is not a good one.

[Adapted from L. Mearian, "Brick-and-Click Bank Sites Outpacing Online-Only Banks," **http://www. computerworld.com**, *Computerworld* (September 3, 2001); S. Machlis, "Feds Shut Down $700M Internet Bank," **http://www.computerworld.com**, *Computerworld* (February 8, 2002).]

GENERAL TYPES OF INFORMATION SYSTEMS

An easy way to understand how all information systems work is to use an input, process, and output model—the basic systems model (see Checkland, 1981 for a thorough discussion). Figure 6.7 shows the basic systems model that can be used to describe virtually all types of systems. As an example, Figure 6.8 shows elements of a payroll system decomposed into input, process, and output elements. The inputs to a payroll system include time cards and employee lists, as well as wage and salary information. Processing transforms the inputs into outputs that include paychecks, management reports, and updated account balances. The remainder of this section uses the basic systems model to describe various information systems.

Transaction Processing Systems

Many organizations deal with repetitive activities. Grocery stores scan groceries at the checkout counter. Banks process checks drawn on customer accounts. Fast food restaurants process customer orders. All these repetitive activities are examples of **transactions** that occur as a regular part of a business's day-to-day operations. ***Transaction processing systems (TPSs)*** are a special class of information systems designed to process business events and transactions. Consequently, TPSs often reside close to customers, at the operational level of the organization, as illustrated in Figure 6.9. The goal of transaction processing systems is to automate repetitive information-processing activities within organizations to increase speed and accuracy and to lower the cost of processing each transaction—that is, to make the organization more efficient. Because TPSs are used to process large volumes of information, organizations have spent considerable resources designing them. A TPS can reduce or eliminate people from the process, thereby reducing transaction costs and reducing the likelihood of data entry errors. Examples of the types of activities supported by TPS include:

▌ Payroll processing

▌ Sales and order processing

▌ Inventory management

▌ Product purchasing, receiving, and shipping

▌ Accounts payable and receivable

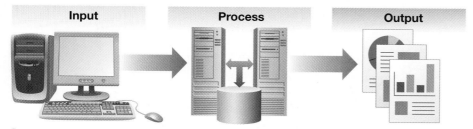

[**Figure 6.7** ➡ The basic systems model can be used to describe all types of information systems.]

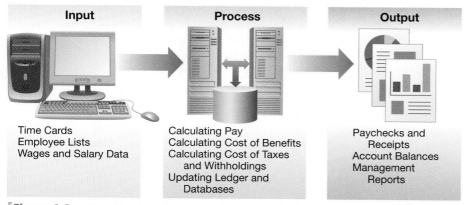

Time Cards
Employee Lists
Wages and Salary Data

Calculating Pay
Calculating Cost of Benefits
Calculating Cost of Taxes
and Withholdings
Updating Ledger and
Databases

Paychecks and
Receipts
Account Balances
Management
Reports

[**Figure 6.8** ➡ Payroll system shown as an instance of the basic systems model.]

[**Figure 6.9** ➥ Transaction processing systems are used to improve operational-level decision making.]

Architecture of a Transaction Processing System

The basic model of a TPS is shown in Figure 6.10. When a business transaction occurs, source documents describing the transaction are created. *Source documents*, paper or electronic, serve as a stimulus to a TPS from some external source. For example, when you fill out a driver's license application, it serves as a source document for a TPS that records and stores all licensed drivers in a state. Source documents can be processed as they are cre-

ated—referred to as online processing—or they can be processed in batches—referred to as batch processing. *Online processing* of transactions provides immediate results to the system operator or customer. For example, an interactive class registration system that immediately notifies you of your success or failure to register for a class is an example of an online TPS. *Batch processing* of transactions occurs when transactions are collected and then processed together as a "batch" at some later time. Banks often use batch proc-

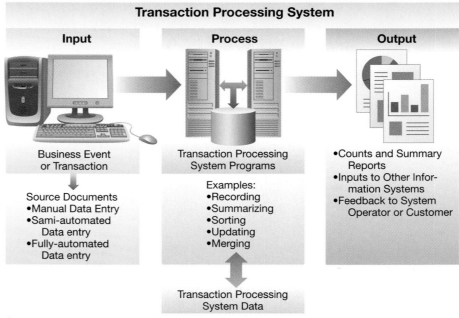

[**Figure 6.10** ➥ Architecture of a transaction processing system using the basic systems model.]

essing when reconciling checks drawn on customer accounts. Likewise, your university uses batch processing to process end-of-term grade reports—all inputs must be periodically processed in batches to calculate your grade point average. Online processing is used when customers need immediate notification of the success or failure of a transaction. Batch processing is used when immediate notification is not needed or is not practical. Table 6.1 lists several examples of online and batch transaction processing systems.

Information can be entered into a TPS in one of three ways: manually, semiautomated, or fully automated. *Manual data entry* refers to having a person enter the source document information by hand into the TPS. For example, when you apply for a new driver's license, a clerk manually enters information about you into a Driver's License Recording System, often

Online TPS	Batch TPS
University class registration processing	Students final grade processing
Airline reservation processing	Payroll processing
Concert/sporting event ticket reservation processing	Customer order processing (for example, insurance forms)
Grocery store checkout processing	Bank check processing

[Table 6.1] *Examples of online and batch transaction processing systems.*

Brief Case: Processing Web Requests at Ford

Ford Motor Company uses an online TPS on the Web to post information about their products and dealers. Figure 6.11 shows a screen from Ford's Web site in which customers can locate their nearest dealer. The inputs to this system are zip codes—or other geographic information—entered by customers. Processing occurs at Ford in Dearborn, Michigan, where a TPS matches the customer's zip code with one in a database containing all dealers. When the TPS makes a match, the output of the system is a report provided to the customer giving the names, addresses, and phone numbers of the closest dealers. In creating this online TPS, Ford has provided a valuable customer service with no human intervention. The cost to Ford of processing this transaction is virtually negligible. Alternatively, if a customer calls Ford on an 800 number requesting the same information, Ford pays for the phone call and for the personnel answering the customer's question—a much higher transaction cost. Remember that the goal of TPS is to increase the speed and accuracy and lower the cost of processing for each transaction. Ford achieved all three goals with the creation of the "Dealer Locator" feature on its Web site.

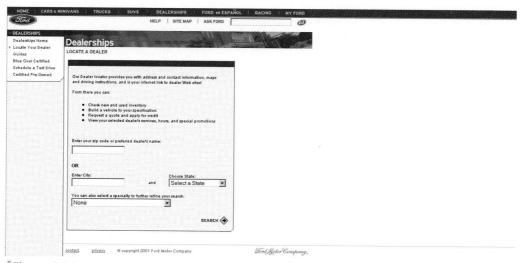

[Figure 6.11 ➥ Ford's Dealer Locator system on the Web.]
Courtesy Ford Motor Company. **www.ford.com**

copying the information from a form that you filled out.

In a *semiautomated data entry* system, a data capture device such as a grocery store checkout scanner speeds the entry and processing of the transaction. The checkout scanner speeds the checkout for the customer and also provides accurate and detailed data directly to many types of information systems. Another example of a semiautomated TPS is an electronic shopping mall on the Web. In this mall, customers enter their purchase requests, which go directly to an order fulfillment system without any additional human intervention.

Fully automated data entry does not require any human intervention. Two computers "talk" to each other via a computer network. For example, for automobiles built at Ford Motor Company, each part used in the manufacturing process represents a transaction in the inventory management system. When the inventory of windshields runs low, the inventory management system automatically contacts the supplier's computer system via a computer network to request more windshields. An electronic link between computers to share data related to business operations is referred to as Electronic Data Interchange (EDI) and was discussed in detail in Chapter 4, "Telecommunications and the Internet." Many organizations spend considerable effort with their suppliers and customers working on EDI standards—both how to communicate over the network and how data is to be formatted—so that more and more information can be exchanged without human intervention.

The characteristics of a TPS are summarized in Table 6.2. Inputs to a TPS are business events or transactions. The processing activities of a TPS include recording, summarizing, sorting, updating, and merging transaction information with organizational databases. Outputs from a TPS include summary reports, inputs to other systems, and operator notification of processing completion. People who are very close to day-to-day operations most often use TPSs. For example, a checkout clerk at the grocery store uses a TPS to record your purchases. Supervisors may review transaction summary reports to control inventory, to manage operations personnel, or to provide customer service. Additionally, inventory man-

[Table 6.2] *Characteristics of a transaction processing system.*

Inputs	Business events and transactions
Processing	Recording, summarizing, sorting, updating, merging
Outputs	Counts and summary reports of activity inputs to other information systems; feedback to system operators or customers
Typical Users	Operational personnel and supervisors

Career Implications:

Information Systems

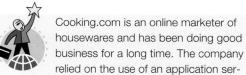

Cooking.com is an online marketer of housewares and has been doing good business for a long time. The company relied on the use of an application service provider (ASP) for online payment processing and credit card authorization. In addition, the system also provided the company with order confirmation, and it did not require heavy investment into IT resources. However, in recent times, before a holiday season, the company realized that its transactions had increased significantly, and the old ASP environment was falling short of handling the volume. The company was also concerned about security and reliability, in addition to speed. The company finally decided to buy server-based payment processing and authorization software from ClearCommerce, based in Austin, Texas. The software allowed the company to conduct real-time authorization and processing, even when the transaction volume was very high. The new software was installed on a new Sun Solaris server, at great expense to the company. There was a flat fee of $75,000, as opposed to the nominal charges of the ASP. In addition, the company also had to set up a direct link to the credit card processor, First Data Merchant Service, using a Frame Relay line, to ensure a dedicated connection all the time. In spite of these additional costs, Cooking.com felt that its investment on this new transaction processing system was justified. According to the company, it was more important to ensure real-time processing and authorization, even in times of high volume, than reduction of costs.

[Adapted from L. Goff, "The Lowdown on ... Payment Processing Systems," *Catalog Age* (February 2001).]

agement systems may monitor transaction activity and use this information to manage inventory reordering. This is an example of the output from a TPS being the input to another system.

Management Information Systems

Management information system (MIS) is a term with two meanings. It describes the field of study that encompasses the development, use, management, and study of computer-based information systems in organizations. It also refers to a specific type of organizational information system. A management information system is used to produce scheduled and ad hoc reports to support the ongoing, recurring decision-making activities associated with managing an entire business or a functional area within a business. Consequently, an MIS often resides at the managerial level of the organization, as shown in Figure 6.12. We will discuss the reports produced by an MIS later in this section.

Whereas transaction processing systems automate repetitive information-processing activities to increase efficiency, a management information system helps midlevel managers make more effective decisions. MISs are designed to get the right information to the right people in the right format at the right time to help them make better decisions. MISs can be found throughout the organization. For example, a marketing manager for Nike may have an MIS that contrasts sales revenue and marketing expenses by geographic region so that she can better understand how regional marketing for the "Tiger Woods Golf" promotions are performing. Examples of the types of activities supported by MISs include:

- Sales forecasting
- Financial management and forecasting
- Manufacturing planning and scheduling
- Inventory management and planning
- Advertising and product pricing

Architecture of a Management Information System

The basic architecture of an MIS is shown in Figure 6.13. At regular intervals, managers need to review summary information of some organizational activity. For example, a sales manager at a Ford dealership may review the weekly performance of all his sales staff. To aid his review, an MIS summarizes the total sales volume of each salesperson in a report. This report may provide a plethora of information about each person, including the following:

- What are this salesperson's year-to-date sales totals?
- How do this year's sales figures compare with last year's?
- What is the average amount per sale?
- How do sales change by the day of the week?

Imagine the difficulty of producing these weekly reports manually for an organization that has 50 salespeople, 500 salespeople, or even 5,000 salespeople! It would be very difficult, if not impossible, to create these detailed reports on each salesperson without an MIS.

An MIS combines information from multiple data sources into a structured report that allows managers to monitor and manage the organization better. Reports produced at predefined intervals—daily, weekly, or monthly—to support the routine informational needs of

[**Figure 6.12** ➡ Management information systems are used to improve managerial-level decision making.]

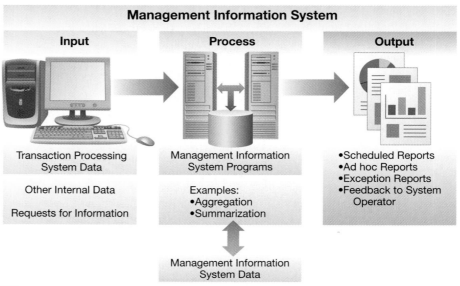

Management Information System

Input	Process	Output

Input: Transaction Processing System Data; Other Internal Data; Requests for Information

Process: Management Information System Programs; Examples: •Aggregation •Summarization

Output: •Scheduled Reports •Ad hoc Reports •Exception Reports •Feedback to System Operator

Management Information System Data

[**Figure 6.13** ➡ Architecture of a management information system using the basic systems model.]

managerial-level decision making are called *scheduled reports* (e.g., a weekly inventory level report). These reports can provide summaries of all types of information but most often provide information related to key indicators. A *key-indicator report* provides a summary of critical information on a recurring schedule. Key-indicator reports provide high-level summaries so that a manager can quickly see if all important activities are operating as planned. MISs can also be used to produce *exception reports* that highlight situations that are out of the normal range. For example, a manager with a large number of sales personnel can produce an exception report highlighting those not achieving minimum sales goals. By focusing the manager's attention on specific information, the MIS helps the organization take a first step in making better decisions. When managers want greater detail as to why a key indicator or exception is not at an appropriate level, they request that a *drill-down report* be produced. In essence, drill-down reports provide details behind the summary values on a key-indicator or exception report.

Managers can also use an MIS to make ad hoc requests for information. *Ad hoc reports*

refer to unplanned information requests in which information is gathered to support a nonroutine decision (e.g., world events precipitate an unforeseen demand for a product). For example, if a particular product at the dealership, such as the Ford Escape, is not selling as well as forecasts predicted, the manager can request a report showing which salespeople are selling the product effectively and which are not. The manager could use this information to examine reasons that this is occurring and investigate ways to intervene before the problem gets out of hand.

The characteristics of an MIS are summarized in Table 6.3. In general, inputs to an MIS are transaction processing data produced by a TPS; other internal data, such as sales promotion expenses; and ad hoc requests for special reports or summaries. The processing aspect of an MIS system focuses on data aggregation and summary. Outputs are formatted reports that provide scheduled and nonrecurring information to a midlevel manager. For example, a store manager can use an MIS to review sales information to identify products that are not selling and are in need of special promotion.

[Table 6.3] *Characteristics of a management information system.*

Inputs	Transaction processing data and other internal data; scheduled and ad hoc requests for information
Processing	Aggregation and summary of data
Outputs	Scheduled and exception reports; feedback to system operator
Typical Users	Midlevel managers

Brief Case: Tracking Enrollment at Washington State University

All universities track class enrollments during student registration periods. The faculty and administrators at Washington State University are using an example of one such system—the course enrollment system called Metro, shown in Figure 6.14 (**http://www.metro.wsu.edu**). Using Metro, students can enroll in classes, check grades, request degree audits, and request countless other student services. During the registration period, students and administrators can track which classes are filling up and which are not. This allows administrators to add more sections of a particularly popular class, while removing courses that fail to attract students. This enables administrators to move faculty resources to where the demand is and, in essence, more effectively manage university resources. Students can see which classes are full prior to trying to register, saving both time and frustration.

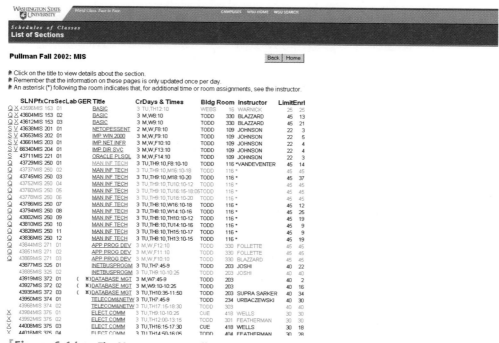

[Figure 6.14 ➡ The Metro course enrollment system provides students and university administrators with up-to-date information.]

Source: **www.metro.wsu.edu**

Executive Information Systems

In addition to operational personnel and midlevel managers, top-level managers or executives can use information technology to support day-to-day activities such as cash and investment management, resource allocation, or contract negotiation. Information systems designed to support the highest organizational managers are called *executive information systems (EIS)*. An EIS (sometimes referred to as an executive support system—ES) consists of technology (hardware, software, data, and procedures) and the people needed to consolidate information and support users to assist executive-level decision making (see Figure 6.15). An EIS provides information to executives in a very highly aggregated form so that they can scan information quickly for trends and anomalies. For example, executives may track various market conditions—like the Dow Jones Industrial Average—to assist in making investment decisions. Although EISs are not as widely used as other types of information systems, this trend is rapidly changing because more and more executives are becoming comfortable with information technology and because an EIS can provide substantial benefits to the executive. Activities supported by an EIS include:

- Executive-level decision making
- Long-range and strategic planning
- Monitoring of internal and external events and resources
- Crisis management
- Staffing and labor relations

Web Search

WEB SEARCH OPPORTUNITY: Go to Big Charts, **http://www.bigcharts.com**, the world's most comprehensive investment research Web site, to look up and provide a report on a stock of your interest for the past 30 days.

[Figure 6.15 ➡ Executive information systems are used to improve executive-level decision making.]

An EIS can deliver both "soft" and "hard" data to the executive decision maker. *Soft data* include textual news stories or other nonanalytical information. *Hard data* include facts and numbers. Lower-level TPSs and MISs generate much of the hard data provided by an EIS. Providing timely soft information to executive decision makers has been much more of a challenge. For example, deciding how to get the late-breaking news stories and information to the system in a format consistent with the EIS philosophy was a significant challenge to organizations. Many investment organizations, for example, subscribe to online services such as Dow Jones as a source for their stock market data. However, executives typically want to view only data that is aggregated and summarized in a user-friendly format. To get the right information into the hands of the executives, personnel or specially designed systems select appropriate information and translate the information into a user-friendly format.

The Internet has made it much easier to gather soft data to support executive decision making. The use of numerous Web-based news portals like **cnn.com**, **abcnews.com**, and **msnbc.com** allow users to easily customize news content so that information can be quickly summarized and evaluated by assistants for viewing by executives. In addition, a product on the Web called Infogate has radically changed how many executives gain soft information by offering a customized and user-friendly environment (**www.infogate.com**). Infogate provides information on almost any subject or industry, virtually as it hits the news

wires. Figure 6.16 shows a typical screen from a computer desktop with Infogate installed. Information is arranged as a banner bar across the top of the screens, with topics such as headline news, sports, weather, and financial information on a specific industry, company, or country. Information is drawn from *The New York Times*, Reuters, AccuWeather, E! Online, MarketWatch, and CBS Sportsline. See Table 6.4 for a summary of the types of information available from Infogate. Two very powerful features of Infogate make it particularly attractive for gathering soft data. First, Infogate can be customized to filter information so that it delivers only the information deemed relevant to the executive. For example, if an executive is interested in the software, Internet/online, and telecommunications industries, these industries can be selected to be tracked. Infogate will present stories related to these industries; all others will be ignored. Second, Infogate will deliver this information to virtually any device, literally tracking you until you receive the message. For example, you can customize Infogate so that important messages are sent to a computer (using e-mail or instant messaging), a cell phone or even a pager. The goal of Infogate is to get the right information to a customer using the most convenient medium.

Architecture of an Executive Information System

The architecture of an EIS is shown in Figure 6.17. Inputs to an EIS are all internal data sources and systems; external data sources like Dow Jones and CNN that contain information on competitors, financial markets, news

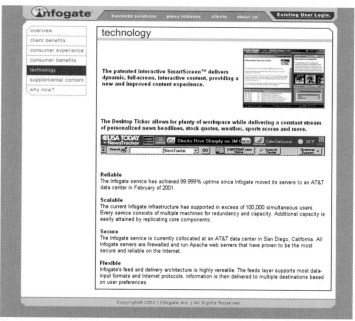

[Figure 6.16 ➥ Infogate provides up-to-the-minute information on a variety of topics and on a variety of devices.]
Source: **http://newstracker.usatoday.com**

Information	Description
News Alerts	Track national, international, political, and business news as soon as it happens
Stock Alerts	Track stock price changes, volume, and news of companies traded on the AMEX, NASDAQ, and NYSE
Weather Alerts	Track weather information for most national and international cites, as well as provide graphic weather maps for the continental United States, Europe, and Asia
Sports Scores	Track news stories, team standings, schedules, and scores for professional and college sports
Entertainment Alerts	Track deals and gossip within the music, film, and television industries

[Table 6.4] *Categories of information available through Infogate.*

(local, national, and international); and any other information deemed important by the executive in making day-to-day decisions. An EIS could "overload" the executive with too much information from too many sources. Systems designers use filtering software to customize the EIS so that only key information is provided in its most effective form to executives. Also, system designers provide output information to executives in a highly aggregated form, often using graphical icons to make selections and bar and line charts to summarize data, trends, and simulations. Large monitors are often used to display the information so that it is easier to view. The characteristics of an EIS are summarized in Table 6.5.

Although data are provided in a very highly aggregated form, the executive also has the capability to drill down and see the details if necessary. For example, suppose an EIS summarizes employee absenteeism and the system shows that today's numbers are significantly higher than normal. The executive can see this information in a running line chart, as illustrated in Figure 6.18. If the executive wants to understand why absenteeism is so high, a selection on the screen can provide

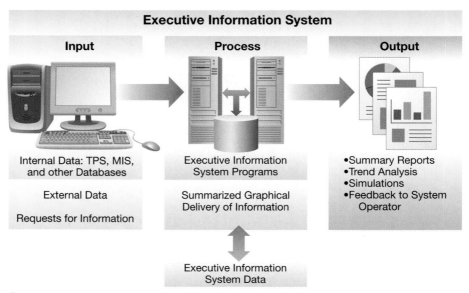

[Figure 6.17 ➡ Architecture of an executive information system using the basic systems model.]

[Table 6.5] *Characteristics of an executive information system.*

Inputs	Aggregate internal and external data
Processing	Summarizing, graphical interpreting
Outputs	Summary reports, trends, and simulations; feedback to system operator
Typical Users	Executive-level managers

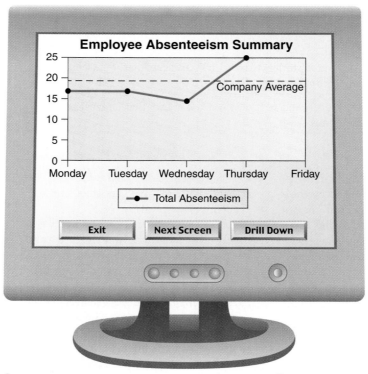

[Figure 6.18 ➡ Total employee absenteeism line chart.]

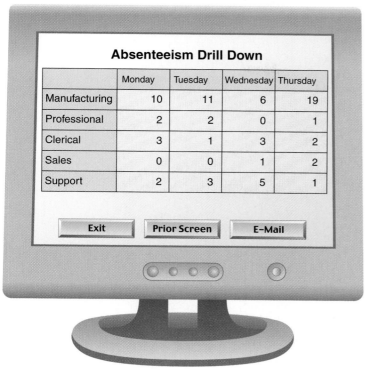

Absenteeism Drill Down

	Monday	Tuesday	Wednesday	Thursday
Manufacturing	10	11	6	19
Professional	2	2	0	1
Clerical	3	1	3	2
Sales	0	0	1	2
Support	2	3	5	1

Exit   Prior Screen   E-Mail

[Figure 6.19 ➥ Drill-down numbers for employee absenteeism.]

the details behind the aggregate numbers, as shown in Figure 6.19. By drilling down into the data, the executive can see that the spike in absenteeism was centered in the manufacturing area. An EIS also can connect the data in the system to the organization's internal communication systems (e.g., electronic or voice mail) so that the executive can quickly send a message to the appropriate managers to discuss solutions to the problem she discovered in the drill-down.

INFORMATION SYSTEMS THAT SPAN ORGANIZATIONAL BOUNDARIES

The preceding section examined three general classes of information systems within specific hierarchical levels in the organization. There are also systems that span all levels of the organization (see Figure 6.20). Six types of boundary-spanning systems are:

▌ Decision support systems

▌ Expert systems

▌ Office automation systems

▌ Collaboration technologies

▌ Functional area information systems

▌ Global information systems

This section describes each of these in more detail. One additional form of organiza-

tional-spanning system, enterprise-wide information systems, is discussed in the following chapter.

Decision Support Systems

Decision support systems (DSS) are special-purpose information systems designed to support organizational decision making. A DSS is designed to support the decision making related to a particular recurring problem in the organization through the combination of hardware, software, data, and procedures. DSSs are typically used by managerial-level employees to help them solve semistructured problems such as sales and resource forecasting, yet a DSS can be used to support decisions at virtually all levels of the organization. With a DSS, the manager uses decision analysis tools such as Microsoft Excel—the most commonly used DSS environment—to either analyze or create meaningful data to support the decision making related to nonroutine problems. A DSS is designed to be an "interactive" decision aid, whereas people use the systems described previously—TPS, MIS, and EIS—primarily in a passive way by simply reviewing the output from the system.

A DSS augments human decision-making performance and problem solving by enabling users to examine alternative solutions to a problem via "what-if" analyses. ***What-if***

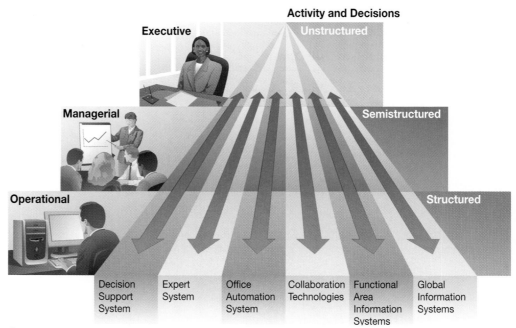

[Figure 6.20 ➡ Organizational boundary–spanning information systems.]

analysis allows you to make hypothetical changes to the data associated with a problem (e.g., loan duration, interest rate) and observe how these changes influence the results. For example, a cash manager for a bank could examine what-if scenarios of the effect of various interest rates on cash availability. Results are displayed in both textual and graphical formats.

Architecture of a Decision Support System
Like the architecture of all systems, a DSS consists of input, process, and output components as illustrated in Figure 6.21 (Sprage, 1980). Within the process component, models and data are utilized. The DSS uses *Models* to manipulate data. For example, if you have some historic sales data, you can use many different types of models to create a forecast of

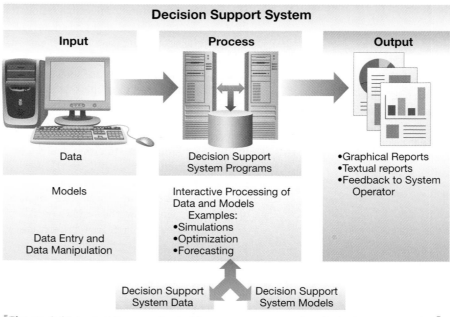

[Figure 6.21 ➡ Architecture of a decision support system using the basic systems model.]

future sales. One technique is to take an average of the past sales. The formula you would use to calculate the average is the model. A more complicated forecasting model might use time-series analysis or linear regression. See Table 6.6 for a summary of the models used to support decision making in organizations. Data for the DSS can come from many sources, including a TPS or MIS. The user interface is the way in which the DSS interacts with the user by collecting inputs and displaying output and results.

Table 6.7 summarizes the characteristics of a DSS. Inputs are data and models. Processing supports the merging of data with models so that decision makers can examine alterna-

tive solution scenarios. Outputs are graphs and textual reports. The next section discusses an example of a DSS that you might use at home.

Using a Decision Support System to Buy a Car

When you buy a new car, you must decide how to pay for it. Will you pay cash? Will you finance most or part of the purchase price? Organizations face the same decisions every day when purchasing supplies, raw materials, and capital equipment: Should they pay cash or finance these purchases? What information do they need to make this decision? The tools that organizations use are relatively simple

Area	Common DSS Models
Accounting	Cost analysis, discriminant analysis, break-even analysis, auditing, tax computation and analysis, depreciation methods, budgeting
Corporate Level	Corporate planning, venture analysis, mergers and acquisitions
Finance	Discounted cash flow analysis, return on investment, buy or lease, capital budgeting, bond refinancing, stock portfolio management, compound interest, after-tax yield, foreign exchange values
Marketing	Product demand forecast, advertising strategy analysis, pricing strategies, market share analysis, sales growth evaluation, sales performance
Personnel	Labor negotiations, labor market analysis, personnel skills assessment, employee business expense, fringe benefit computations, payroll and deductions
Production	Product design, production scheduling, transportation analysis, product-mix inventory level, quality control, learning curve, plant location, material allocation, maintenance analysis, machine replacement, job assignment, material requirement planning
Management Science	Linear programming, decision trees, simulation, project evaluation and planning, queuing, dynamic programming, network analysis
Statistics	Regression and correlation analysis, exponential smoothing, sampling, time-series analysis, hypothesis testing

[Table 6.6] *Common DSS models for specific organizational areas.*

Inputs	Data and models; data entry and data manipulation commands (via user interface)
Processing	Interactive processing of data and models; simulations, optimization, forecasts
Outputs	Graphs and textual reports; feedback to system operator (via user interface)
Typical Users	Midlevel managers (although a DSS could be used at any level of the organization)

[Table 6.7] *Characteristics of a decision support system.*

[Table 6.8] *Interest rates and loan duration.*

Interest Rate	Loan Duration
7% per year	3 years
10% per year	4 years
12% per year	5 years

and readily available to you. After going through the car purchasing example, you will have a better understanding of how organizations use decision support technology to help their employees make day-to-day decisions.

Assume that the selling price of the car you decide to purchase is $20,000 and that you make a $2,500 down payment, leaving you with a monthly payment of about $400. You want to see how different financing options from your credit union might influence your monthly payments. As you can see from Table 6.8, interest rates vary depending upon the duration of your loan—lower rates for a shorter duration, higher rates for a longer duration. You now have all the information you need to analyze your financing options.

To conduct this analysis, you can use Microsoft Excel's loan analysis template (Excel uses the term "template" to refer to models). In this template, you enter the loan amount, annual interest rate, and length of the loan, as shown in Figure 6.22. With this information, the loan analysis DSS automatically calculates your monthly payment, the total

amount paid, and the amount of interest paid over the life of the loan. You can change any of the input amounts to examine what-if scenarios—"What if I finance the loan over four years rather than five?" This is exactly how your college or university examines its financing options when it makes capital equipment purchases. Using this DSS tool, you decide to purchase your new vehicle over five years (see Table 6.9 for a loan analysis summary). The next section discusses expert systems, a type of organizational information system that is closely related to decision support systems.

Expert Systems

An *expert system (ES)* is a special type of information system that uses reasoning methods based on knowledge about a specific problem domain in order to provide advice, much like a human expert. Expert systems are used to mimic human expertise by manipulating knowledge (understanding acquired through experience and extensive learning) rather than simply information (see Turban and Aronson, 2001 for more information). Human knowledge can be represented in an ES by

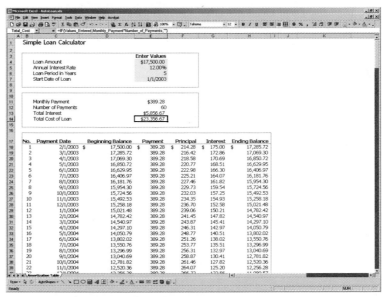

[Figure 6.22 ➡ Loan analysis template in Microsoft Excel.]

Reprinted by permission from Microsoft Corporation.

Interest Rate	Loan Duration	Monthly Payment	Total Paid	Total Interest	Feasible Payment
7% per year	3 years	$540.35	$19,452.57	$1,952.57	No
10% per year	4 years	$443.85	$21,304.57	$3,804.57	No
12% per year	5 years	$389.28	$23,356.67	$5,856.67	Yes

[Table 6.9] *Loan analysis summary.*

Marketing

Client-server versions of decision support tools providing data analysis were founded in the early 1990s and began a new era in the world of DSS. Previously, such tools were housed in mainframes. The new version of tools enabled analysts to query databases and then synthesize all the information from multiple sources and dimensions. In the last two years, newer types of decision support tools have made data analysis even easier. Data analysis tools are now manufactured in Web-enabled versions and can often be deployed over the Web. The Web versions are making it easier to send the results of analysis to a wider audience base at a lower cost. The new versions have multidimensional analysis capabilities, and the results can easily be shared across an organization. Ernex Marketing Technologies uses such a tool to find trends in its marketing data. The company is able to share the results of its analysis with its clients by providing access to real-time data. Thus, clients can gain first-hand experience regarding the effectiveness of the company's marketing efforts. The Web-based data analysis tools can also be easily integrated with the company's core business applications and eliminate any possibility of incompatibility.

[Adapted from Peggy King, "Decision Support Grows Up ... and Out," **http://www.cio.com**, *CIO Magazine* (November 15, 1999).]

facts and rules about a problem coded in a form that can be manipulated by a computer. When you use an ES, the system asks you a series of questions, much as a human expert would. It continues to ask questions, and each new question is determined by your response to the preceding question. The ES matches the responses with the defined facts and rules until the responses point the system to a solution. A *rule* is a way of encoding knowledge, such as a recommendation, after collecting information from a user. Rules are typically expressed using an IF-THEN format. For example, a rule in an expert system for assisting with decisions related to the approval of automobile loans for individuals could be represented as follows:

> IF personal income is $50,000 or more, THEN approve the loan.

The most difficult part of building an ES is acquiring the knowledge from the expert and gathering and compiling it into a consistent and complete form capable of making recommendations. ESs are used when expertise for a particular problem is rare or expensive, such as in the case of a complex machine repair or medical diagnosis. ESs are also used when knowledge about a problem will be incomplete—in other words, when judgment will be used to make a decision with incomplete information, such as designing an investment portfolio or troubleshooting a computer system. Examples of the types of activities that can be supported by expert systems include the following:

- Medical diagnosis
- Machine configuration
- Automobile diagnosis
- Financial planning
- Train and container loading
- Computer user help desk
- Software application assistance (for example, Microsoft Help "Wizards")

Architecture of an Expert System

As with other information systems, the architecture of an expert system can be described using the basic systems model (see Figure 6.23). Inputs to the system are questions and answers from the user. Processing is the matching of user questions and answers to information in the knowledge base. The processing in an expert system is called *inferencing*, which consists of matching facts and rules, determining the sequence of questions presented to the user, and drawing a conclusion. The output from an expert system

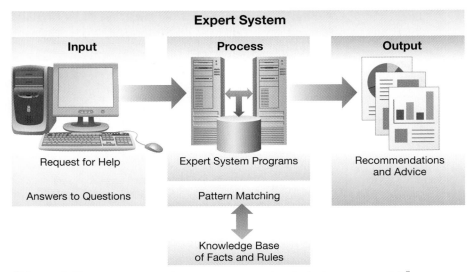

[**Figure 6.23 ➡** Architecture of an expert system using the basic systems model.]

Web Search

WEB SEARCH
OPPORTUNITY:
Explore an online health expert
system for common aliments at
http://easydiagnosis.com/.

is a recommendation. The general characteristics of an expert system are summarized in Table 6.10.

An Expert System on the Web
Historically, expert systems have been stand-alone applications that ran on personal computers. With the advent of the Internet, EXSYS, a leading producer of expert system technology, provides an expert system development environment that allows expert systems to be delivered via the Web. At the EXSYS Web site (**http://www.exsys.com**), you can test several demonstration expert systems. One system, for example, helps you select the right restaurant in Albuquerque, New Mexico (see Figure 6.24); another provides advice on selecting the right camcorder. A system that helps to troubleshoot and repair the Cessna Citation airplane—lighting and engine starting—is a particularly sophisticated example. The system analyzes a user's response to several questions and presents specific repair or troubleshooting advice. This system also explains why it came to the conclusion that it did or why it is asking certain questions. This is a very powerful feature for training personnel and for helping users have confidence in the system's recommendation.

Office Automation Systems

The *office automation system (OAS)* is the third type of system that spans organizational levels. OASs are a collection of software and hardware for developing documents, scheduling resources, and communicating. Document development tools include word processing and desktop publishing software, as well as the hardware for printing and producing documents. Scheduling tools include electronic calendars that help manage human and other resources, such as equipment and rooms. For example, "smart" electronic calendars can examine multiple schedules to find the first opportunity when all resources (people, rooms, equipment) are available. Communication technologies include electronic mail, voice mail, fax, videoconferencing, and groupware. Examples of the types of activities supported by an OAS include the following:

▌ Communication and scheduling

▌ Document preparation

▌ Analyzing and merging data

▌ Consolidating information

[Table 6.10]
*Characteristics of an
expert system.*

Inputs	Request for help, answers to questions
Processing	Pattern matching
Outputs	Recommendation or advice
Typical Users	Midlevel managers (although an expert system could be used at any level of the organization)

CORVID Restaurant Selection Expert System

The following Restaurant Selection system is a small demonstration that displays some of Exsys CORVID's features. CORVID expert systems can advise among a group of possible competing alternatives even if the user's requests may not exactly match any of the possible options. In this case, the system advises on where to go to dinner based on occasion, atmosphere, and food preferences.

The CORVID system interacts with you by asking initial questions to obtain data on your preferences. More focused queries are then made by the system based on information you have already provided. Unnecessary questions are not asked, but when your answer indicates more details are needed in a specific area, the system asks follow-up questions. Recommended restaurants are presented, along with specific comments on potential disadvantages the restaurant might present for the occasion (e.g. too noisy, not private, etc.).

Run this CORVID Applet to select the best restaurant for dinner in Albuquerque, NM:

How It Works:

This example system selects from a group of Albuquerque restaurants. These are restaurants with widely differing food types, atmosphere and prices.

The system asks the user questions on the occasion and what type of food is desired. Data is applied to a spreadsheet of information on the various restaurants. The system's analysis creates a probabilistic ranking of the restaurants related to the customer's needs. The system automatically "weights" various factors based on the occasion. The top 5 restaurants that best meet the user's requests are displayed. Comments on the suitability of the restaurant are also displayed with the results. CORVID image maps are used to ask the questions enabling a simple graphic end user interface.

All of the decision-making logic is kept separate from the restaurant data which is stored in an easily maintained spreadsheet. Generic restaurant selection logic is converted to rules using CORVID's development environment. These rules are applied to data on the specific restaurants stored in the spreadsheet. Including a new restaurant is as simple as adding it to the spreadsheet. If a restaurant changes its price, menu, or decor, it is also just edited in the spreadsheet.

(This system does not imply any use or endorsement of Exsys CORVID by the restaurants, or any endorsement of the restaurants by EXSYS Inc.
...though Ribs has really yummy key lime pie.)

[Figure 6.24 ➡ EXSYS Web-based expert system.]
Source: **www.exsys.com.**

Brief Case: Expert System to Advise Students on Class Selection

Great student advising for class selection and registration has been shown to help retain students. Advising is a time-consuming activity for faculty involved in the process and is particularly important for incoming freshmen and transfer students. Also, it is particularly difficult to schedule advising sessions with part-time students with busy work schedules. Unfortunately, with shrinking budgets, many schools have too few advisors and too many students, especially for popular majors. California State University created an expert system to help students select classes (EXSYS, 2002). Because the system is accessible on the Web, it is available on virtually any computer with a browser. The system links to the university-wide database of student records so that it can consider a list of all completed courses as well as student interests when making recommendations. The advisor makes course suggestions while considering degree requirements, prerequisites, availability, and, of course, student interests. The system knows when courses will be offered, which is particularly important when designing programs of study involving courses that are not offered each semester. In addition, the system can analyze the transcripts of transfer students and reconcile them with existing degree requirements so that appropriate substitutions and credit are given. The goal of the system is to mimic the expertise of faculty and professional advisors. In many ways, however, the system is better than the human "experts" because it has a comprehensive knowledge of the entire problem. The system is a big success, and more and more schools are adopting a similar expert advising system. ⬤

Architecture of an Office Automation System

The architecture of an OAS is shown in Figure 6.25. The inputs to an OAS are documents, schedules, and data. The processing of this information involves storing, merging, calculating, and transporting these data. Outputs include messages, reports, and schedules. The general characteristics of an OAS are summarized in Table 6.11.

Automating Your Daily Calendar

A powerful tool for helping you get to class on time is Microsoft Outlook's Calendar. At the beginning of the semester, you can enter your class meeting times into the system. After they are entered, you can make these appointments recur automatically as long as you like, as illustrated in Figure 6.26.

Additionally, you can set an alarm to notify you that class will begin in a few

Operations Management

Expert systems were introduced in the mid-1980s and promised to "capture the expertise of skilled humans and then codify that expertise into a program." However, in spite of this hype, expert systems never reached their full potential and were often discarded after being implemented company-wide. Incompatibility with a company's overall environment, along with requirements of experts to operate it, were cited as some of the primary reasons for an expert system's failure. However, after many years, expert systems are slowly growing in prominence. In the current age, expert systems are integrated into and embedded within many computer products. A new type of expert system, called online expert systems, is increasingly being used by organizations. Ebara Manufacturing is a Japanese pump manufacturer, which specializes in several different kinds of pumps for a wide variety of industries. In the traditional system, the customers of Ebara would just request a pump, and the sales personnel in the company would have to figure out what kind of pump would be suitable for them. This system worked initially; however, as Ebara's product range increased and the products became more sophisticated, it became difficult for the company's employees to choose the most appropriate pump for a client. This caused problems for managing inventories and scheduling production. The company found the solution in an online expert system. The system now takes customers through a series of questions. Based on their responses to the questions (which primarily capture the customers' needs), the expert system decides on the appropriate product, often in less than a minute, cutting down on transaction time and increasing customer service. If you choose a career in operations management, you may find expert systems to be a valuable tool.

[Adapted from Fred Hapgood, "Embedded Logic: Overhyped, Then Much Maligned, Expert Systems Find Their Niche Inside Web Applications," **http://www.cio.com**, *CIO Magazine* (May 1, 2000).]

[Table 6.11]
Characteristics of an office automation system.

Inputs	Documents, schedules, data
Processing	Storing, merging, calculating, transporting
Outputs	Messages, reports, schedules
Typical Users	All organizational personnel

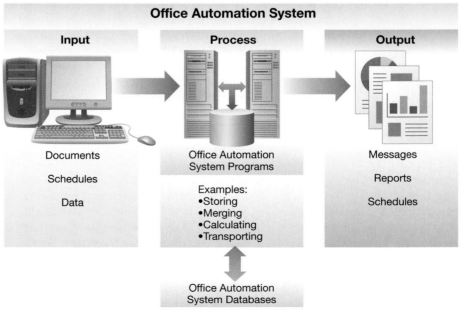

[Figure 6.25 ➥ Architecture of an office automation system using the basic systems model.]

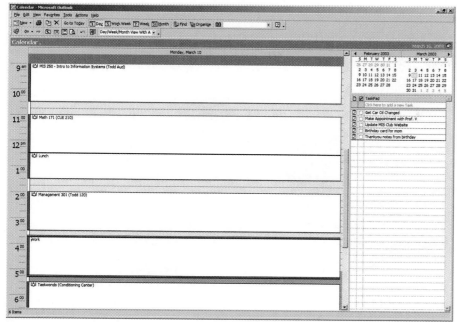

minutes. You can also use the alarm feature to remind you of meetings or appointments. Busy executives use this reminder feature to make sure they stay on schedule and do not miss any important meetings.

Collaboration Technologies

To be competitive, organizations constantly need to bring together the right combinations of people who, together, have the appropriate set of knowledge, skills, information, and authority to solve problems quickly and easily. Traditionally, organizations have used task forces, which are temporary work groups with a finite task and life cycle, to solve problems that cannot be solved well by existing work groups. Unfortunately, traditional task forces, like traditional organizational structures, cannot always solve problems quickly. Structure and logistical problems often get in the way of people trying to get things done quickly.

Organizations need flexible teams that can be assembled quickly and can solve problems effectively and efficiently. Time is of the essence. Membership on these **virtual teams** is fluid, with teams forming and disbanding as needed, with team size fluctuating as necessary, and with team members coming and going as they are needed. Employees may, at times, find themselves on multiple teams, and the life of a team may be very short. In addition, team members must have easy, flexible access to other team members, meeting con-

texts, and information. Think of these virtual teams as dynamic task forces.

Traditional office technologies, such as telephones and pagers, are of some use to members of virtual teams but are not well suited to support the types of collaboration described previously. Telephones and pagers are not useful for rich, rapid, multiple-person team collaboration. This technology is best suited for person-to-person communication. E-mail is a useful technology for teams, but it does not provide the structure needed for effective multiperson interactive problem solving. Companies need technologies that enable team members to interact through a set of media either at the same place and time or at different times and in different locations, with structure to aid in interactive problem solving and access to software tools and information. A number of technologies, described in the following sections, fit the bill.

Videoconferencing

In the 1960s, at Disneyland and other theme parks and special events, the picturephone was first being demonstrated to large audiences. The phone company estimated that we would be able to see a live picture with our phone calls in the near future. It took another 30 years, but that prediction has come true within many organizations. Many organizations are conducting **videoconferencing**, and the demand for videoconferencing equipment

[Figure 6.27 ➥ PictureTel is a leading supplier of high-end videoconferencing technology.]
©PictureTel

[Figure 6.28 ➥ Logitech's popular QuickCam.]
©Logitech Inc.

Team Work

Video conferencing and the Future of Travel

Do you think that the use of videoconferencing technologies will increase or decrease the need and demand for airline travel? Why?

is growing quickly. For example, sales for PictureTel, a leading videoconferencing company, grew from $37 million in total revenue in 1990 to almost $100 million in revenue in only the first half of 2001. Figure 6.27 shows a videoconference being conducted with a textile manufacturing company.

Stand-alone videoconferencing products are relatively large, expensive units (approximately $20,000 and up) that have video quality similar to that of broadcast television and are used primarily to connect groups of people.

Desktop videoconferencing represents a second generation of video communication that has been enabled by the growing power of processors powering personal computers. A desktop system usually comprises a fast personal computer, a small camera (often with fixed focus, though zooming and panning features are available), a speaker telephone or separate microphone, videoconferencing software, and a special video board installed inside the computer. Using the Internet or a high-speed phone line, desktop videoconferencing is a much less expensive option than stand-alone videoconferencing, but the quality of the video and audio is not as good. For example, for under $100 you can purchase one of a number of cameras, such as a QuickCam, which plugs directly into the USB port on your personal computer (see Figure 6.28). You can then use desktop videoconferencing software, such as Microsoft's NetMeeting, available for free

from Microsoft's Web site, and conduct desktop videoconferencing sessions with friends, family, and colleagues through the Internet. For the audio portion, you need a multimedia PC with a sound card and speakers. You speak into the microphone plugged into your sound card and hear other people through the speakers that are plugged into your sound card.

Groupware

The term *groupware* refers to a class of software that enables people to work together more effectively. Lotus Development put groupware in the mainstream when it introduced the Notes software product in 1989. In recent years, many new groupware products have emerged, several of which work through or with the Internet. One industry sector that has come to rely on groupware products quite a bit is consulting. For example, PricewaterhouseCoopers and Accenture are two of the biggest Notes users in the country. Chicago-based Accenture uses Notes as the basis for its internal information management system that enables consultants to exchange data with each other. With well over 30,000 people now working for the company all over the world in different time zones, it is very difficult to locate and contact the experts within the company for advice. All the large consulting firms are experiencing this problem and are using groupware like Lotus Notes to help solve this problem (see Figure 6.31 on page 194).

FUTURE OF DESKTOP VIDEOCONFERENCING

As computer components and fast connections to the Internet get less and less expensive, you can expect to see more desktop videoconferencing performed with personal computers. In fact, many notebook computers are now manufactured and sold with video cameras built in (see Figure 6.29). However, one of the most intriguing new technologies for desktop videoconferencing that we have seen is the omni-directional camera. Developed at Microsoft Research, the camera provides a 360 degree panoramic view, as well as motion- and sound-sensing capabilities (see Figure 6.30). This unit includes four tiny cameras and connects to a standard personal computer. Using a fast network connection, the unit can enable multiple people sitting around a table at one location to communicate with multiple people sitting around a table at another location. Each camera can sense sound and, if a person is talking, will focus on that person. The camera can also detect motion and can find and focus on moving people's faces, whether they are sitting at or standing around the table. This technology is in the research stage and is not currently being sold, although it works quite well. This type of videoconferencing unit opens up all kinds of possibilities and does so at a fraction of the cost of other videoconferencing units.

[Adapted from Rui, Gupta, and Cadiz, "Viewing Meetings Captured by an Omni-Directional Camera," Collaboration and Multimedia Systems Group, Microsoft Research, **http://www.research.microsoft.com/ research/coet/Camera/chi2001/ Omnidirectional/paper.doc**.]

[Figure 6.29 ➥ The Sony Vaio Picturebook is one of many notebook computers that can be purchased with an integrated camera for both still pictures and video images.]
©Sony Electronics

[Figure 6.30 ➥ Microsoft Research has developed this omni-directional, motion- and sound-detecting camera for desktop videoconferencing in which multiple people are involved.]

Electronic Meeting Software

Although many forms of groupware can be used to help groups work more effectively, one category of groupware focuses on helping groups have better meetings. These systems are commonly referred to as *electronic meeting systems (EMSs)*. An EMS is essentially a collection of personal computers networked together with sophisticated software tools to help group members solve problems and make decisions through interactive, electronic idea generation, evaluation, and voting. Some typical uses for an EMS include strategic planning sessions, marketing focus groups, brainstorming sessions for system requirements definition, business process reengineering, and quality improvement. EMSs have traditionally been housed within a dedicated meeting facility, as shown in Figure 6.32 on page 195. However, EMSs are also being implemented with notebook computers so that the systems can be taken on the road. Additionally, Web-based implementations are supporting distributed meetings in which group members access the EMS software from their computers in their offices or from home. While EMS and related software have been around for quite some time, organizations are still discovering new and useful ways to use these tools to support e-meetings and other forms of group work.

Functional Area Information Systems

Functional area information systems are cross-organizational-level information systems designed to support a specific functional area (see Figure 6.33 on page 195).

**Human Resource
Management**

Organizations are often using video-conferencing to imitate face-to-face interaction, especially where organizational members are not located in the same place. However, one of the primary problems most companies face related to videoconferencing is the time needed for system setup. Consequently, vendors of videoconferencing equipment are working on a new generation of products that are both easy to use and easy to set up. For example, new products from Sony have a built-in Ethernet port and software that enables users to connect to them from a remote computer. Additionally, the systems can be operated and maintained remotely through an Internet browser–based control center. Once a meeting has been scheduled, meeting reminders are sent automatically to participants via e-mail. Also, before the start of the meeting, the videoconferencing system calls up the other participating devices. This way, the system is ready to start when the users arrive. The system also allows pictures and graphics to be integrated easily into the meeting. Ease of configuration and use is the trend for all types of information technology devices. As a result, videoconferencing is becoming very popular in a variety of human resource management, contexts including executive training and employee recruitment. In fact, no matter what career you pursue, it is likely that videoconferencing will be a valuable tool for you in all types of meeting situations. The good news is that you will be able to use videoconferencing easily, without frustration or the need for a technology guru.

[Adapted from **http://www.sel.sony.com/news**.]

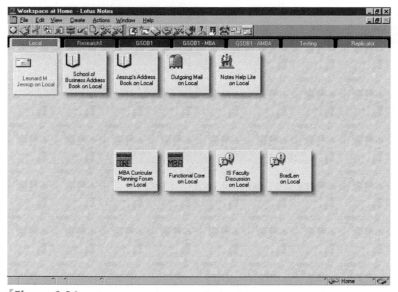

[**Figure 6.31** ➥ Lotus Notes is an award-winning groupware application with an installed base of millions of users worldwide.]

These systems may be any of the types described previously—TPS, MIS, EIS, DSS, ES, and OAS. A functional area represents a discrete area of an organization that focuses on a specific set of activities. For example, people in the marketing function focus on the activities that promote the organization and its products in a way that attracts and retains customers. People in accounting and finance focus on managing and controlling capital assets and financial resources of the organiza-tion. Table 6.12 lists various organizational functions, describes the focus of each one, and lists examples of the types of information systems used in each functional area.

Global Information Systems

Organizations use a variety of system configurations in order to manage global operations more effectively. For example, Nestle, one of the world's largest food producers, is considered to be one of the world's largest global companies,

[**Figure 6.32** ➥ A computer-supported meeting facility, complete with networked PCs and Electronic Meeting System software.]

Courtesy of Ventanna Medical Systems Inc.

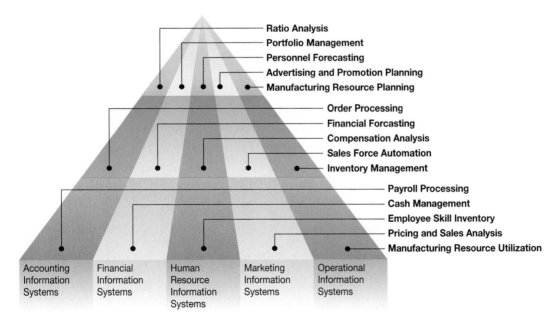

Ratio Analysis
Portfolio Management
Personnel Forecasting
Advertising and Promotion Planning
Manufacturing Resource Planning

Order Processing
Financial Forcasting
Compensation Analysis
Sales Force Automation
Inventory Management

Payroll Processing
Cash Management
Employee Skill Inventory
Pricing and Sales Analysis
Manufacturing Resource Utilization

Accounting Information Systems   Financial Information Systems   Human Resource Information Systems   Marketing Information Systems   Operational Information Systems

[**Figure 6.33** ➥ Functional area information systems.]

with over 500 factories and operations in more than 70 countries. According to (Roche, 1992), firms like Nestle, which are operating in multiple nations, can have five distinct types of global information systems: 1) international information systems, 2) transnational information systems, 3) multinational information systems, 4) global information systems, and 5) collaborative information systems (see Table 6.13). We describe each in this section.

[Table 6.12]
Organizational functions and representative information systems.

Functional Area	Information System	Examples of Typical Systems
Accounting and Finance	Systems used for managing, controlling, and auditing the financial resources of the organization	▌ Inventory management ▌ Accounts payable ▌ Expense accounts ▌ Cash management ▌ Payroll processing
Human Resources	Systems used for managing, controlling, and auditing the human resources of the organization	▌ Recruiting and hiring ▌ Education and training ▌ Benefits management ▌ Employee termination ▌ Workforce planning
Marketing	Systems used for managing new product development, distribution, pricing, promotional effectiveness, and sales forecasting of the products and services offered by the organization	▌ Market research and analysis ▌ New product development ▌ Promotion and advertising ▌ Pricing and sales analysis ▌ Product location analysis
Production and Operations	Systems used for managing, controlling, and auditing the production and operations resources of the organization	▌ Inventory management ▌ Cost and quality tracking ▌ Materials and resource planning ▌ Customer service tracking ▌ Customer problem tracking ▌ Job costing ▌ Resource utilization

[Table 6.13] *Types of global information systems.*

Type of Information System	Definition	Example
International Information System	System that supports transactions that may originate in one nation and end in another nation	Xerox's copier machine tracking system
Transnational Information System	International "transactional" space allowing people from different parts of the world to conduct transactions simultaneously	Foreign exchange systems that allow traders from different parts of the world to interact with each other
Multinational Information System	A loose confederacy of various local information systems	Nestle's 140 financial systems used at different locations in the world
Global Information System	Centralized network with an even distribution of integrated applications to all the nations	General Motors global inventory management system that consolidates all inventory information from around the world
Collaborative Information System	System that integrates different applications but is not specific to any given user	The International Airline Reservation System funded jointly by many airline companies

There are several things you can do to improve the management of human resources in global organizations. First, it is important to hire individuals who are experienced in working in cross-cultural teams, who can speak different languages, and who have the necessary cultural sensitivity to empathize with other cultures. In addition to the general IS staff, it is also important to hire the proper IS leader or CIO. Global companies argue that the ideal quality required for a CIO is the ability both to understand the global strategies of the company, and at the same time be able to collaborate successfully with the regional offices to implement those global strategies. Beyond personnel, the organizational reward system should be designed to reward individuals for their global initiatives, rather than base rewards solely on the local information systems' goals within the organization. Additionally, the organizational culture needs to be modified to fit the needs of local employees. For example, Fujitsu recently is making a breakthrough in the international market (especially in Internet and multimedia products), after years of overseas failure. To better deal with these new markets, it has changed its culture significantly to fit the local needs. There has been a relaxation in the strict Japanese standards of dress and conduct, introduction of flexible working hours, and the hiring of young, talented individuals representing a diverse set of cultures. Finally, the organization as a whole should also be extremely sensitive to the various cultural issues and political problems that exist between people from different countries when they are involved in cross-cultural IS operations. Such sensitivity and awareness can be developed through careful and in-depth research and also by having a diverse mix of employees representing different cultures.

Global Perspective

Managing Human Resources in a Global Organization

International information systems are a general class of information systems that support transactions that cross national boundaries. In other words, these systems support transactions that may originate in one nation and end in another nation. These types of systems can have either a centralized or a decentralized structure. Xerox Corporation uses a centralized information system that keeps track of all its copier machines that are placed in different customer locations around the world. This way it maintains strong control over all maintenance and billing issues regarding its copier machines. *Transnational information systems*, on the other hand, are not specific to any country or any particular organization. They exist as separate entities and as an international "transactional" space allowing people from different parts of the world to conduct transactions simultaneously. An example of such an information system is the foreign exchange systems that allow traders from different parts of the world (connected through decentralized networks) to interact with each other.

Next, are the *multinational information systems*, used often by multinational companies. These information systems act as a loose confederacy of various different local information systems. The existence of different types of rules and regulations on international data transfer and telecommunications has made this type of network very popular among multinational companies. This way, companies are able to retain the decentralized local data processing centers that are responsive to local needs and regulations, and at the same time use information technology to integrate them loosely into the framework of the parent organization. Up until a few years ago, Nestle had such an information system structure. It had over 140 financial systems that were being used around the world. However, the increasing globalization of the market and the recent advances in telecommunications and networks has caused a transition from multinational information systems to *global information systems*. Such networks are used especially when a single transaction requires the input of data from multiple data centers located across more than one nation. These networks are usually centralized, and there is an even distribution of integrated applications to all the nations. As a result, data can be accessed irrespective of its location. After some major consolidation efforts, Nestle has moved toward a global information system, namely through the implementation of an enterprise-wide information system (see Chapter 7). It has cut down its number of financial systems to just a few, with the objective of relying on just one in the future.

Finally, there are the *collaborative information systems* that integrate different applications but are not specific to any given user. For example, international airline reservation systems such as Galileo or Apollo have been funded by different airline companies and allow a multitude of airlines and travel agents to execute transactions, irrespective of their geographic location. These systems support the operational collaboration of major airline companies and travel agents.

Career Implications:

Accounting and Finance

Avon Products was founded over 100 years ago, and from the time of its initiation it focused on a direct-sales strategy whereby its sales force went from door to door in parts of the United States. However, in recent times, due to the emergence of new markets across the globe, the company has followed an expansion strategy. According to the company executives, the implementation of a globally integrated financial management system along with high-quality analysis and reporting tools have significantly helped in its expansion strategy. The company required an integrated and standardized financial management system that could serve as an operation management tool, not merely as a tool for reporting the company's profit and loss. At the same time, since the company was expanding into unknown markets, the tool had to be flexible enough to be easily customizable for local requirements. After evaluating many products, Avon chose Integrated Accounting System by CODA (based in Harrogate, England, and having U.S. headquarters in Manchester, New Hampshire), to build the Avon Standard Accounting System (ASAS), which is a global financial reporting system. Initially implemented at 40 sites around the globe, the tool helps to capture critical information that helps executives make strategic decisions. Later, the tool was connected to data warehouses to store financial and operational information, both at a global and at a local level. The global financial system allows the company to deal easily with the different tax and accounting requirements existing around the globe. At the same time, the system enables executives to develop standardized interfaces, which can be easily modified for the many overseas regional sites, based on local needs and differences related to language, culture, currency rates, and tax and accounting regulations.

[Adapted from Peter Fabris, "Global Market Scents," **http://www.cio.com**, *CIO Magazine* (September 1, 1995).]

KEY POINTS REVIEW

1. **Describe the characteristics that differentiate the operational, managerial, and executive levels of an organization.** At the operational level of the firm, the routine day-to-day business processes and interaction with customers occur, and information systems are designed to automate repetitive activities, such as sales transaction processing. Operational-level managers such as foremen or supervisors make day-to-day decisions that are highly structured and recurring. At the managerial level of the organization, functional managers focus on monitoring and controlling operational-level activities and providing information to higher levels of the organization. Midlevel or functional managers focus on effectively utilizing and deploying organizational resources to achieve the strategic objectives of the organization. At this level, the scope of the decision usually is contained within the business function, is moderately complex, and has a time horizon of a few days to a few months. At the executive level of the organization, decisions are often very complex problems with broad and long-term ramifications for the organization. Executive-level decisions are often referred to as being messy or ill-structured because executives must consider the ramifications of the overall organization.

2. **Explain the characteristics of the three information systems designed to support each of the unique levels of an organization: transaction processing systems, management information systems, and executive information systems.** Transaction processing systems (TPSs) are designed to process business events and transactions and reside close to customers at the operational level of the organization. These systems are used to automate repetitive information-processing activities to increase speed and accuracy and to lower the cost of processing each transaction—that is, to make the organization more efficient. Management information systems (MISs) reside at the managerial level and are designed to produce regular and ad hoc reports to support the ongoing, recurring decision-making activities associated with managing an entire business or a functional area within a business. These systems are used to help midlevel managers make more effective decisions. Executive information systems (EISs) are used to provide information to executives in a very highly aggregate form so that information can be scanned quickly for trends and anomalies. Executives use these systems to provide a one-stop shop for a lot of their informational needs.

3. **Describe the characteristics of the three information systems that span the organizational, managerial, and executive levels: decision support systems, expert systems, and office automation systems.** Decision support systems (DSS) support organizational decision making and are typically designed to solve a particular recurring problem in the organization. DSSs are most commonly used to support semistructured problems that are addressed by managerial-level employees. A DSS is designed to be an interactive decision aid. An expert system (ES) is a special type of information system that uses knowledge within some topic area to solve problems or provide advice. Expert systems are used to mimic human expertise by manipulating knowledge

(understanding acquired through experience and extensive learning) rather than simply information. ESs are used when expertise for a particular problem is rare or expensive. In this way, organizations hope to replicate the human expertise more easily and inexpensively. Office automation systems (OASs) are technologies for developing documents, scheduling resources, and communicating. Collaboration technologies such as videoconferencing, groupware, and electronic meeting systems are used to support the communication and teamwork of virtual teams. Functional areas represent discrete areas of organizations and typically include accounting and finance, human resource management, marketing, and production and operations management. Functional area information systems are designed to support the unique requirements of specific business functions. Finally, global information systems are used to support international activities of global organizations. There are five distinct types of global information systems: 1) international information systems, 2) transnational information systems, 3) multinational information systems, 4) global information systems, and 5) collaborative information systems. Each type of global information system has distinct characteristics to best support a given international information-processing situation.

KEY TERMS

ad hoc reports 178

batch processing 174

collaborative information system 198

decision support system (DSS) 183

desktop videoconferencing 192

drill-down report 178

electronic meeting system (EMS) 193

exception report 178

executive information system (EIS) 179

executive level 171

expert system (ES) 186

fully automated data entry 176

functional area information system 194

global information system 197

groupware 192

hard data 180

inferencing 187

international information system 195

key-indicator report 178

management information system (MIS) 177

managerial level 170

manual data entry 175

models 184

multinational information system 195

office automation system (OAS) 188

online processing 174

operational level 170

rule 187

scheduled reports 178

semiautomated data entry 176

semistructured decisions 171

soft data 180

source documents 174

structured decisions 170

transactions 173

transaction processing system (TPS) 173

transnational information system 195

unstructured decisions 172

videoconferencing 191

virtual teams 191

what-if analysis 183

REVIEW QUESTIONS

1. Compare and contrast the characteristics of the operational, managerial, and executive levels of an organization.
2. What is the difference between "hard" and "soft" data?
3. Describe the differences between online processing and batch processing. Give examples of each.
4. What are the three methods used for inputting data into a transaction processing system? Provide examples of each.
5. List three different types of reports and where or how the information from each is used.
6. How does a management information system differ from a transaction processing system in terms of purpose, target users, capabilities, and so forth?
7. Describe and give examples of two types of data entry.
8. How does an executive information system "drill down" into the data?
9. What are the three types of information systems that traditionally span the boundaries of organizational levels?
10. Explain the purpose of a model within a decision support system.
11. What is the difference between a decision support system and an expert system?
12. What is groupware, and what are the different types?
13. Compare and contrast stand-alone videoconferencing and desktop videoconferencing.
14. Provide some examples of functionally specific information systems and needs within an organization.
15. Define and contrast five types of global information systems.

SELF-STUDY QUESTIONS

1. At the _____ level of the organization, functional managers (e.g., marketing managers, finance managers, manufacturing managers, and human resources managers) focus on monitoring and controlling operational-level activities and providing information to higher levels of the organization.
   A. operational
   B. managerial
   C. organizational
   D. executive

2. Examples of the types of activities supported by management information systems include all of the following except _____ .
   A. inventory management and planning
   B. manufacturing planning and scheduling
   C. financial management and forecasting
   D. sales and order processing

3. A _____ report provides a summary of critical information on a recurring schedule.
   A. scheduled
   B. exception
   C. key-indicator
   D. drill-down

4. Examples of the types of activities that can be supported by expert systems include all of the following except _____ .
   A. payroll calculations
   B. financial planning
   C. machine configuration
   D. medical diagnosis

5. A supervisor having to decide when to reorder supplies or how best to allocate personnel for the completion of a project is an example of a _____ decision.
   A. structured
   B. unstructured
   C. automated
   D. delegated

Answers are at the end of the Problems and Exercises.

6. The types of boundary-spanning systems include all of the following except _____ .
   A. decision support systems
   B. resource planning systems
   C. office automation systems
   D. expert systems

7. _____ processing of transactions provides immediate results to the system operator or customer.
   A. Online
   B. Batch
   C. Fully automated
   D. Semiautomated

8. A marketing manager for Nike may have a(n) _____ system that contrasts sales revenue and marketing expenses by geographic region so that she can better understand how regional marketing for the "Tiger Woods Golf" promotions are performing.
   A. transaction
   B. expert
   C. office automated
   D. management information

9. In a(n) _____ data entry system, a data capture device such as a grocery store checkout scanner speeds the entry and processing of the transaction.
   A. manual
   B. semiautomated
   C. fully automated
   D. expert

10. A(n) _____ information system is defined as a loose confederacy of various different local information systems.
   A. international
   B. multinational
   C. collaborative
   D. transnational

PROBLEMS AND EXERCISES

1. Match the following terms with the appropriate definitions:
   _____ Operational level
   _____ Transactions
   _____ Virtual teams
   _____ Source document
   _____ Online processing
   _____ Management information system
   _____ Expert system
   _____ Inferencing
   _____ Transaction processing system
   _____ Decision support system

   a. An information system designed to process day-to-day business event data at the operational level of an organization
   b. A special-purpose information system designed to mimic human expertise by manipulating knowledge (understanding acquired through experience and extensive learning) rather than simply information
   c. The bottom level of an organization, where the routine day-to-day interaction with customers occurs
   d. A special-purpose information system designed to support organizational decision making primarily at the managerial level of an organization
   e. Processing of information immediately as it occurs
   f. Repetitive events in organizations that occur as a regular part of conducting day-to-day operations

g. An information system designed to support the management of organizational functions at the managerial level of the organization

h. A document created when a business event or transaction occurs

i. The matching of facts and rules, as well as determining the sequence of questions presented to the user, and drawing a conclusion

j. Teams forming and disbanding as needed, with team size fluctuating as necessary, and with team members coming and going as they are needed

2. Visit (**http://www.infogate.com**) on the Web. Infogate provides information on almost any subject or industry, virtually as it hits the news wires. Information is arranged as a banner bar across the top of the screen where general topics such as headline news, sports, and weather, as well as news and financial information on a specific industry, company, or country are provided. Information is drawn from *The New York Times*, Reuters, AccuWeather, E! Online, MarketWatch and CBS Sportsline. What types of "hard" and "soft" data can you find?

3. Do you feel that, as much as possible, transaction processing systems should replace human roles and activities within organizations? Why or why not? How much cost savings will there be if these humans are still needed to run the systems? What if you were the person being replaced? Will all errors necessarily be eliminated? Why or why not?

4. Imagine that your boss has asked you to build an inventory transaction system that would enable the receiving and shipping clerks to enter inventory amounts for purchases and sales, respectively. Discuss the pros and cons of building this system as an online processing system versus a batch processing system. Which would you recommend to your boss?

5. The national sales manager for ABC Corp. is interested in purchasing a software package that will be capable of providing "accurate" sales forecasts for the short term and long term. She has asked you to recommend the best type of system for this purpose. What would you recommend? Do you have any reservations about such a system? Why or why not?

6. Visit **http://moneycentral.msn.com/investor/calcs/ n_expect/main.asp** on the Web to determine your life expectancy using a decision support system. What did you learn? Is there a difference between life expectancies for different genders? If you browse Moneycentral, what other interesting stuff do you find? Also check out **http://www.bigcharts.com**.

7. Interview a top-level executive within an organization with which you are familiar or within one of the companies from the Brief Cases. Determine the extent to which the organization utilizes

executive information systems. Does this individual utilize an EIS in any way? Why or why not? Which executives do utilize an EIS?

8. Based on your experiences with transaction processing systems (in everyday life and/or in the workplace), which ones use online processing and which use batch processing? Do these choices fit the system, the information, and the environment? Would you make any adjustments? Why or why not?

9. Using any program you choose, or using the Web site **http:// www.Moneycentral.com**, find or create a template that you could use in the future to determine monthly payments on car or home loans. Compare your template with the one at **carpoint. msn.com/LoanCalc**. Would you have categorized the program you used to create this template as a decision support system before doing this exercise?

10. Describe your experiences with expert systems, or look up **http://www.exsys.com** on the Web. In what situations did you encounter expert systems, and what is their future? Did you actually use the system or did another individual use it on your behalf?

11. Choose an organization with which you are familiar that utilizes office automation systems. Which systems does it use? Which functions have been automated, and which have not been? Why have some functions not been automated? Who decides which office automation system to implement?

12. Have you seen or used ad hoc, exception, key-indicator, and/or drill-down reports? What is the purpose of each report? Who produces and who uses the reports? Do any of these reports look or sound familiar from your work experience?

13. Interview an IS manager within an organization at a university or workplace. Of the three categories of information systems—transaction processing, management, and executive—which do people utilize most in this organization? Why? Have any of these areas experienced an increase or decrease in the last few years? What predictions does this manager have regarding the future of traditional information systems? Do you agree? Prepare a 10-minute presentation to the class on your findings.

14. Describe how various systems described in this chapter might enable workers to work from home rather than at the company's office. What technologies in particular might these workers utilize and how? Will companies look favorably on this use of technology? Why or why not?

15. Interview an IS professional, and ask about travel and assignments outside of the United States. Do global assignments contribute to promotion? What is the length of an average assignment?

ANSWERS TO THE SELF-STUDY QUESTIONS

1. B   2. D   3. C   4. A   5. A   6. B   7. A   8. D   9. B   10. B

CASE 1: *Automated Work Flow Implementation Reduces Transaction Processing at Pacific Century Trust*

Pacific Century Trust is a division of the Bank of Hawaii and is the largest trust department in the state. The company oversees more than $13 billion in client assets. One of its primary focuses is on investment management, which accounts for $7 billion of the total client assets it oversees. The company is a corporate trustee and manages the majority of personal trust and government funds in the state of Hawaii. In addition, Pacific Century Trust manages corporate pension and profit sharing plans. Among the many services provided by the company are 401(k) plans, professional trustee services, estate services, corporate money management and custody services, and so on. One of the most common processes in the organization is generating a cash transaction on behalf of a client. For the most part, these transactions consist of paying bills for a client, but other services such as money movement are also done as part of these processes. On average, an administrative staff processes about 300 such transactions on a given day, in response to client requests. For a long time, the company relied on a paper-based system for these transactions. Depending on a staff member's location (whether in the headquarters or in a remote location), the request was usually initiated by logging into the company's trust accounting system or by faxing in a copy of the authorization form to the staff member who initiated the request. A form that carried all the details of the transaction was then printed out. Next, the report was carried by hand to the staff members who were in charge of approving the transaction. Once it was approved, another staff member carried it to the floor where the operations department was housed. This department was responsible for actually processing the transaction. This paper-based system became increasingly expensive for the organization. Apart from requiring a large number of staff members, the transaction often took a long time, leading to delays in

fulfilling customer requests. The average time required just to fill out a form was approximately 10 minutes. In addition, it was often difficult to locate an individual who would approve the transaction, and oftentimes, staff members who were authorized to approve transactions had to be interrupted during their regular work hours to process such transactions. On average, the cash transaction processes at Pacific Century Trust took about 86 person-hours per week to be completed.

Realizing this, the company's primary concern was to find an appropriate way to automate its transaction processing, improve its customer service significantly, and reduce the number of errors in its system (which was not significantly high). In its quest for a solution, the company came across a software application called AddVantage Connect from SunGuard Asset Management Systems. This software consists of form design and work flow process management, and provides an environment that allows for easy streamlining of work flows. A team was immediately set up at Pacific Century Trust that was responsible for implementing this new transaction processing system in the company. The team used the graphical tools of the software to design the forms required for initiating and approving a check request and used other task-specific tools to redefine the workflow processes. The result was a dramatic change in the entire process.

The whole process was made Web-enabled. A staff member can just use a Web browser to download an electronic form for initiating a customer request. The form consists of only a few fields and can easily be filled out. Once the form is submitted, the underlying business logic of the information system routes the form for approval based on the type and the size of the request. Usually, the system routes the form to any staff member who is authorized to give approval. Once the approval is given, the system automati-

cally routes the form to the operations department, where the transaction is processed in the next batch. The system has brought about a dramatic reduction in the time taken for transaction processing at Pacific Century Trust. Forms can now be filled out and approved within two minutes, which is significantly faster than the older paper-based method at the organization. Also, staff members no longer need to be interrupted for approval. All approval requests are sent to their in baskets, and they can approve them in a batch whenever they get the time.

Overall, the primary advantage of this system has been increased customer service. Apart from reducing the transaction time, the system has achieved a few more improvements. First, it has reduced the number of errors in transactions, primarily by allowing the staff member who receives the request to fill in the form. Second, the form was designed in a way to restrict the user to only a few options, providing default values wherever possible, thus reducing the chance for errors. Finally, the amount of paperwork was also significantly reduced, thus letting staff members focus more on customer service.

The Web-based environment of the system has also helped staff members in remote locations to process transactions at no extra cost or time. This eliminated delays in transaction processing that usually occurred for all branch office requests in the days of the paper-based method. The Web-based system also enabled Pacific Century Trust to open operations in other states such as California and Arizona, without incurring huge costs of setting up information systems in those offices. Staff members in those locations can log into the company's system using a browser and process transactions just as staff members in the head office and other branch offices can.

[Case adapted from M. O'Brien, "Electronic Workflow Reduces Daily Transaction Processing," *Trusts and Estates* 139, no. 1: 18–21.]

Discussion Questions

1. What were the information systems needs at Pacific Century Trust? Was a transaction processing system the appropriate solution for the information system requirements?
2. What advantages did the new transaction processing system provide to Pacific Century Trust?
3. Of the different types of organizational information systems covered in this chapter, could any other type of information system solve Pacific Century Trust's problems? Why or why not?
4. Which of the several advantages that the system provided was the most important? Why?

CASE 2: *Ernst & Young Deploys Lotus Notes Throughout Its Large, Global Enterprise*

Ernst & Young is one of the world's leading consulting organizations. Its mission is to help businesses around the world "identify and capitalize on business opportunities" (www.ey.com). It is a decentralized organization of some 130 national firms around the world that work together to provide seamless cross-border service to multinational businesses. It has over 70,000 employees in more than 650 locations. The company offers a wide range of solutions, including delivering leading-edge assurance, advisory, tax, and consulting services that help corporations achieve their business goals. Given the fact that it is such a large organization, one of the primary challenges the company faces is enabling the sharing of information and data amongst the company's tens of thousands of employees around the globe. The capability of its people to communicate, collaborate, and share knowledge—within local and multinational teams, within service lines, and across national boundaries—has become essential to maintaining and sharpening Ernst & Young's competitive edge in the global marketplace. In other words, the key to the success of this company lies in its ability to effectively manage and share information across the entire company. "We deliver our client solutions through multidisciplinary, and often multinational, teams working together in person or through connectivity to apply their combined skills and our organization's expertise to our clients' problems and needs. This is the core of our business," says John Whyte, CIO of Ernst & Young International.

The company began to search for a solution to take care of its information-sharing problem. The company's objective was to implement a stable infrastructure that would also provide quality service. After a lot of searching, the company finally decided to use a Lotus Notes infrastructure for messaging and sharing information and knowledge across the many member firms. Soon, Ernst & Young–member firms adopted Lotus Notes as their standard tool for collaborative working and knowledge management. This decision was made against a clean technology slate, so to speak; there were no legacy systems. Lotus Consulting helped the company in designing the internal Notes network and also provided system support, which included the assignment of a special Lotus Notes account manager, dedicated only to Ernst & Young. Within six months, member firms located in at least 12 countries in Asia Pacific were making use of the Notes infrastructure and communicating and collaborating with each other through the system. These member firms were primarily connecting through the company's hub located in Singapore. Ernst & Young then introduced two new hubs, one in New Jersey and one in London. Within the next two years, there were over 100 Ernst & Young virtual teams communicating and interacting from locations around the world using their Domino/Notes Engagement Team Data Base to serve multinational clients. Even more teams were using Notes applications to manage projects and share work products and ideas within country boundaries. All but one country had migrated to Lotus Mail by the end of the second year—an outstanding achievement for a decentralized organization of Ernst & Young's size, geographical spread, and diversity. International e-mail traffic alone (that is, excluding in-country electronic messages, which, in fact, total even more) rose from 6,000 messages per month to 400,000 per month within a span of only one year. The number of e-mail messages rose to about 800,000 per month in three years. The effective implementation of the Notes infrastructure requirement was possible due to the excellent support of Lotus Consulting, which had taken the effort to satisfy the requirements of its client and help them at every step of the way.

"Notes enabled us to scale up to a global enterprise system that provides mission-critical connectivity among our people, within our teams, to our clients, and to internal and external knowledge stores," Whyte says. Two years after Notes was implemented, Ernst & Young's worldwide revenues grew by 17 percent. Whyte says, "Some of that global growth is certainly due to being able to do work without barriers and have this high level of communication and knowledge-sharing capability."

Today, the company's focus is on making significant extensions to the existing system. The Notes infrastructure provides the company with the ability to build applications and add Internet/intranet capabilities without investing heavily in new software or hardware. Ernst & Young is now focusing on using the Internet along with the Notes/Domino messaging system and has already implemented the EYI InnerSpace, which is a global Domino-based intranet system.

[Adapted from "Success Story," **www.lotus. com/home.nsf/welcome/stories**; "Ernst and Young: Global Messaging and Knowledge Management Improve Consultancy Services," **www. lotus.com/home.nsf/welcome/stories**; and **www.ey.com**. ©2001 Lotus Development Corporation. Used with permission of Lotus Development Corporation. Lotus and Lotus Notes are registered trademarks of Lotus Development Corporation.]

Discussion Questions

1. How are collaboration technologies and knowledge management useful to Ernst & Young?
2. How important is it to a firm such as Ernst & Young to use collaboration technologies such as Notes successfully? Why? How would it look if a leading IS/IT consultant were not deploying emerging technologies successfully?
3. Is the process of knowledge management using Notes useful only to consulting firms such as Ernst & Young? Why or why not?
4. What do you think is the role of the technology development/consulting firm in ensuring the successful implementation of an emerging technology within an organization?

Enterprise-Wide Information Systems

OPENING: Hop to It, with ERP Systems

John I. Haas, established in 1914, is a privately owned agricultural company that grows, processes, and trades hops and hop products worldwide. Hops are a key ingredient for the making of beer, and Haas hops find their way to microbreweries around the world. The company owns and operates extensive hop farms, pellet plants, cold-storage warehouses, CO_2 facilities, and further refinement plants in the Pacific Northwest of the United States. John I. Haas is at the forefront of research and development of hop-based products for applications in brewing and other industries.

Haas is also at the forefront in its use of Enterprise Resource Planning systems. Haas wanted to enable owners and managers of microbreweries to order hops and related products directly from the Haas Web site (see Figure 7.1), so the company recently upgraded to Oracle's 11i E-Business Suite so it could add Web tools for customers and suppliers. "The recession set the priority for us," says Kyle Lambert, vice president of information solutions. "We had to get closer to our customers and suppliers."

The Oracle software also enabled Haas to more easily integrate its front-office applications with its back-office systems. The company decided that a single suite, rather than a best-of-breed strategy, would eliminate potential integration headaches, a serious consideration for nearly every business organization. If you are of drinking age, the next time you sip a beer at, or from, a microbrewery, think about the information systems that helped to brew and deliver it to you.

[Adapted from Steve Konicki, "Companies Consolidate, Replace, or Rewrite Apps to Improve Efficiencies," *InformationWeek* (February 4, 2002); **http://www.john-i-haas.com/**.]

[**Figure 7.1** ➡ Enterprise-wide information systems are used to produce some of the finest beers in the world.]
Source: ©Getty Images, Inc.

This chapter describes how companies are deploying enterprise-wide information systems to support and integrate their various business activities, to streamline and better manage interactions with customers, and to coordinate better with their suppliers in order to meet changing customer demands more efficiently and effectively.

After reading this chapter you will be able to do the following:

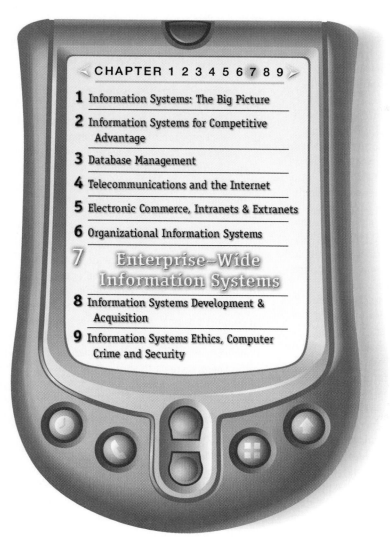

1. Explain how organizations support business activities by using information technologies.

2. Describe what enterprise systems are and how they have evolved.

3. Explain the differences between internally and externally focused software applications.

4. Understand and utilize the keys to successfully implementing enterprise systems.

[Figure 7.2 ➡ The Big Picture: focusing on enterprise systems.]

Figure 7.2 shows how this chapter fits within The Big Picture. With enterprise systems sales projected at over $100 billion by 2005 (Shah, 2001), it is apparent that companies are viewing these systems as a strategic necessity. An understanding of enterprise systems is critical to succeed in today's competitive and ever-changing world. People with enterprise systems skills are in high demand and, therefore, the more you know about enterprise systems, the more you will be in demand in the employment marketplace!

ENTERPRISE SYSTEMS

Companies use information systems to support their various business processes and activities for internal operations such as manufacturing, order processing, and human resource management. Companies can also use information systems to support external interactions with customers, suppliers, and business partners. Businesses have leveraged information systems to support business processes and activities for decades, beginning with the installation of applications to assist companies with specific business tasks such as issuing paychecks. Oftentimes, these systems were built on different computing platforms such as mainframes and minicomputers, each operating in unique hardware and software environments. Applications running on different computing platforms are difficult to integrate, as custom interfaces are required in order for one system to communicate with another.

Running different applications on separate computing platforms can create tremendous inefficiencies within organizations because data cannot readily be shared between the systems. Information must be reentered from one system to the next and the same pieces of data may be stored in several versions throughout the organization. *Enterprise-wide information systems* (a.k.a. *enterprise systems*), thus, are information systems that allow companies to integrate information across operations on a company-wide basis. Rather than storing information in separate places throughout the organization, enterprise systems provide a central repository common to all corporate users. This, along with a common user interface, allows personnel to share information seamlessly no matter where the data is located or who is using the application.

The emergence of the Internet and Web has resulted in the globalization of customer and supplier networks, opening up new opportunities and methods to conduct business. Customers have an increasing number of options available to them, so they are demanding more sophisticated products that are customized to their unique needs. They also expect higher levels of customer service. If companies cannot keep their customers satisfied, the customers will not hesitate to do business with a competitor (Grosvenor and Austin, 2001). Companies need to provide quality customer service and develop products faster and more efficiently to compete in global markets. Enterprise systems can be extended to streamline communications with customers and suppliers. Rather than focusing only on internal operations, these systems can also focus on business activities that occur outside organizational boundaries. Enterprise systems can help companies find innovative ways to increase accurate on-time shipments, avoid (or at least anticipate) surprises, minimize costs, and ultimately increase customer satisfaction and the overall profitability of the company.

Enterprise systems come in a variety of shapes and sizes, each providing a unique set of features and functionality. When deciding to implement enterprise solutions, there are a number of issues that managers need to be aware of. One of the most important factors involves selecting and implementing applications that meet the requirements of the business, as well as its customers and suppliers. In the following sections, we examine the ways in which information systems can be leveraged to support business activities. This is followed by an in-depth analysis of how enterprise systems have evolved and how companies are using these systems to support their internal and external operations.

Supporting Business Activities

As we talked about in Chapter 2, information systems can be used to increase competitive advantage by supporting and/or streamlining business activities (Porter and Millar, 1985). For example, an information system could be used to support a billing process in such a way that it helps to reduce the use of paper and, more important, the handling of paper, thus reducing material and labor costs. This same system can help managers keep track of that same billing process more effectively because they will have more accurate, up-to-date information about the billing process, enabling them to make smart, timely business decisions.

Information systems can be used to support either internally or externally focused business processes. Internally focused systems

The Wells Fargo Education Financial Services (EFS) is based in Sioux Falls, South Dakota, and specializes in providing student loans to different types of clients ranging from parents of kindergartners to postgraduate students. The company also works closely with financial aid officers from different schools. Traditionally, the company maintained all of its customer information in paper files that were tucked away in desks and drawers across multiple departments. Often these files would be missing or at least very hard to find. Applying for loans was hence a very frustrating process, since customers often had to wait for long periods for approval due to the mismanagement of the paper files and other paperwork. Wells Fargo often acknowledged that while it was not yet losing business, the chaotic structure was giving customers very little reason to come to Wells Fargo. As you know, in recent times, attracting new and repeat customers has been key to remaining competitive, and companies have often relied on the use of information technology for

this. Wells Fargo, too, moved toward the use of information technology to solve its customer service problems. The company first installed a state-of-the-art work-flow and imaging system from Paragon systems to automate its business processes. Now customer service representatives no longer have to hunt for files; they can access any customer information with nothing more than a mouse click. The sophisticated new software now speeds up loan processing and approval. Customers can also get their loans approved online in minutes. The amount of student loans provided by the company increased from $800 million in 1994 to $2.1 billion in 2000. The student loan division has also become one of the five core areas of business at Wells Fargo. Satisfied customers are now not only purchasing loans from Wells Fargo, but are also coming back to purchase other types of products from the company as well. The company has shown how Customer Relationship Management systems can be used well to manage customers in the loan application and management process.

[Adapted from Rebecca Lynch, "Paperless Tigers," **http://www.cio.com**, *CIO Magazine* (February 15, 2001).]

Career Implications:
Accounting and Finance

support functional areas, processes, or activities within the organization. These activities can be viewed as a series of links in a chain along which information flows within the organization. At each stage (or link) in the process, value is added in the form of the work performed by people associated with that process, and new, useful information is generated. Information begins to accumulate at the point of entry (i.e., a customer sends an order to the company) and flows through the various links, or processes within the organization, progressing through the organization with new, useful information being added every step of the way. For example, when a customer places an order, the order is entered into an order-entry application. The information containing the order is sent to the fulfillment department, which picks the items from inventory, packages them for distribution, and produces an additional piece of information called a packing list, which specifies the items contained within the package. The package, along with the packing list, is forwarded to the shipping department, which coordinates the shipment, produces an additional piece of information in the form of an invoice, and sends the package with its associated invoice to the customer. Each link in the process has a unique set of information inputs and outputs, as depicted in Figure 7.3.

In contrast with internally focused applications, which coordinate functions inside organizational boundaries, externally focused systems coordinate business activities with customers, suppliers, business partners, and others who operate outside the organization's boundaries. Systems that communicate across organizational boundaries are sometimes referred to as *interorganizational systems (IOSs)* (Kumar and Crook, 1999). The key purpose of an IOS is to streamline the flow of information from one company's operations to another's. This type of application could be used, for example, to coordinate the flow of information from a company to its potential or existing customers who exist outside the organization, and vice versa.

Competitive advantage can be accomplished here by integrating multiple business processes in ways that enable firm(s) to meet a wide range of unique customer needs. Sharing information between organizations helps companies to adapt more quickly to changing market conditions. For instance, should consumers demand an additional component to be added to a product, a company can gain this information from its information systems that support sales and pass it along to its component suppliers in real time. Information allows the company and its suppliers to satisfy the needs of customers efficiently

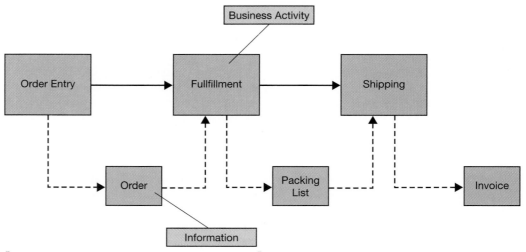

[**Figure 7.3** ➥ Information flow for a typical order.]

since changes can be identified and managed immediately, creating a competitive advantage for companies that can respond quickly.

We can view processes and information flows across organizations just as we previously viewed the processes and information flows within an organization. At each stage (or link) in the process, value is added by the work performed and new, useful information is generated and exchanged between organizations (see Figure 7.4). Using IOS, one company creates information and transmits it electronically to another company.

For example, when a company places an order for components with a supplier, the supplier processes the order as shown in Figure 7.4. The supplier performs the shipping activity, which results in the delivery of a physical package and the electronic transmission of the associated invoice to the customer. At this point, the information crosses corporate boundaries from the supplier's organization to the customer's (the organization that ordered the component from the supplier). The customer's receiving department takes delivery of the supplier's package and verifies the invoice that was transmitted to ensure the order is complete. When the customer has accounted for the components, it stocks the items in inventory and updates inventory levels on its internal system accordingly.

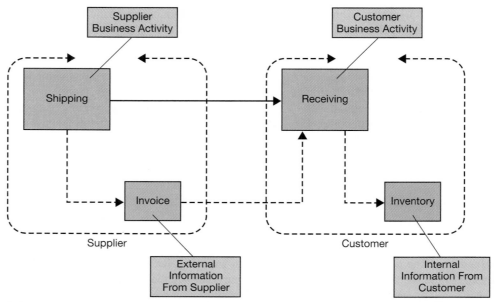

[**Figure 7.4** ➥ Information flow for a typical shipment across organizational boundaries.]

Internally Focused Applications

Because companies within certain industries operate their businesses differently, one of the first challenges an organization must face is to understand how it can use information systems to support its unique internal business activities. Generally, the flow of information through a set of business activities is referred to as a *value chain* (Porter and Millar, 1985), in which information flows through functional areas that facilitate the internal activities of the business. Figure 7.5 depicts the value chain framework. In Chapter 2 we spoke of the strategic value of analyzing a value chain. We now show you how to use value chain analysis to implement enterprise systems.

Functional areas can be broken down into primary and support activities. Primary activities are functional areas within an organization that process inputs and produce outputs. Support activities are those activities that enable primary activities to take place. In the following sections, we focus on primary activities and then turn our attention to the support activities that make them possible.

Primary Activities

Primary activities include inbound logistics, operations and manufacturing, outbound logistics, marketing and sales, and customer service. These activities may differ widely based on the unique requirements of the industry in which a company operates, although the basic concepts hold in most organizations. Inbound logistics involves the business activities associated with receiving and stocking raw materials, parts, and products. For example, inbound logistics at Cisco Systems involves the receipt of electronic components that go into making their end products such as routers. Shippers deliver elec-

tronic components to Cisco, at which time employees unwrap the packages and stock the components in the company's inventory. Cisco can automatically update inventory levels at the point of delivery, allowing purchasing managers to access real-time information related to inventory levels and reorder points.

Once the components have been stocked in inventory, the functional area of operations takes over. Operations can involve such activities as processing orders and/or manufacturing processes that transform raw materials and/or component parts into end products. As discussed in Chapter 5, Dell utilizes Web-based information systems to allow customers to enter orders online. This information is used to coordinate the manufacturing of a customized personal computer, in which the component parts are gathered and assembled to create the end product. During this process, inventory levels from inbound logistics are verified and, if the appropriate inventory exists, workers pick the components from existing supplies and build the product to the customer's specifications. When components are picked, items are deducted from inventory; once the product is assembled, inventory levels for the final product are updated.

The functional area of outbound logistics mirrors that of inbound logistics. Instead of involving the receipt of raw materials, parts, and products, outbound logistics focuses on the distribution of end products. For example, outbound logistics at Amazon.com involves the delivery of books that customers have ordered. Orders that have been processed by the operations area are forwarded to outbound logistics, which picks the products from inventory and coordinates delivery to the customer. At that point, items are packaged and deducted from the company's inventory, and

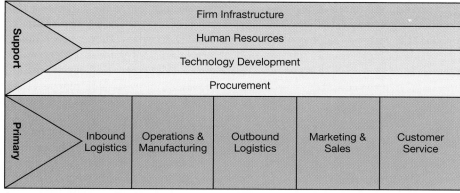

[**Figure 7.5** ➡ Value chain framework.]
Porter and Millar, 1985

an invoice is created that will be sent to the customer. Amazon.com can automatically update sales information at the point of distribution, allowing managers to view inventory and revenue information in real time.

The marketing and sales functional area facilitates the presales activities of the company. These include such things as the creation of marketing literature, communicating with potential and existing customers, and pricing goods and services. As discussed in Chapter 5, many companies support the business activity of marketing and sales by creating an e-brochure. Other companies such as Amtrak, a U.S. passenger train service, use information systems to update pricing information and schedules. This information is entered directly into the pricing and scheduling systems, which becomes immediately accessible throughout the organization and to end consumers through the corporation's Web site.

Whereas marketing and sales focus on presales activities, the customer service functional area focuses on the postsales activities of the company. Customers may have questions and need help from a customer service representative. Many companies, such as Hewlett-Packard (HP), are utilizing information systems to provide customer service. These applications allow customers to search for and download information related to the products that they have purchased. For example, HP customers may need to install drivers for the printers they have just purchased. Rather than calling a customer service representative, customers can help themselves through a self-service customer support application.

Companies can use information systems to track service requests. When a customer calls in for repairs to a product, customer service representatives can access a bevy of information related to the customer. For instance, an agent can access technical information concerning the specific product, as well as review any problems the customer has encountered in the past. This enables customer service representatives to react quickly to customer concerns, improving the customer service experience.

Support Activities

Support activities are business activities that enable the primary activities to take place. Support activities include infrastructure, human resources, technology development, and procurement. Infrastructure refers to the hardware and software that must be implemented to support the applications that the primary activities use. An order entry application requires that employees who enter orders have a computer and the necessary software to accomplish their business objective. In turn, the computer must be connected via the network to a database containing the order information so that the order can be saved and recalled later for processing. Infrastructure provides the necessary components to facilitate the order entry process.

Human resources involves the business activities associated with employee management, such as hiring, interview scheduling, payroll, and benefits management. Human resources is classified as a support activity since the primary activities cannot be accomplished without the employees to perform them. In other words, all the primary activities use the human resources business activity. For example, if a company needs a new customer service representative to serve the growing volume of customers, the request is processed through the human resources function, which creates the job description and locates the appropriate person to fill the job.

Technology includes the design and development of applications that support the primary business activities. If you are planning on pursuing a career in the management information systems field, the technology business activity is likely where you will find a job. Technology can involve a wide array of responsibilities such as the selection of packaged software or the design and development of a custom application to meet a particular business need. Many companies are leveraging the technology business activity to build Internet, intranet, and extranet applications for these purposes. As seen in previous chapters, companies use these systems to support a wide variety of primary business activities.

Procurement refers to the purchasing of goods and services that are required as inputs to the primary activities. Allowing each functional area to send out purchase orders can create problems for companies, such as maintaining relationships with more suppliers than necessary and not taking advantage of volume discounts. The procurement business activity can leverage information systems by accumulating purchase orders from the different functional areas within the corporation. By having this information at their disposal, procurement personnel can combine multiple purchase orders containing the same item into a single purchase order. Ordering larger volumes from its suppliers means that the company can achieve dramatic cost savings through volume discounts. Procurement receives, approves, and processes requests for goods and services from the primary activities and coordinates the purchase of those items. This allows the primary activities to concentrate on running the business rather than adding to their workload.

Externally Focused Applications

The flow of information can be streamlined not only within a company but outside organizational boundaries as well. A company can create additional value by integrating internal applications with suppliers, business partners, and customers. Companies accomplish this by connecting their internal value chains as a *value system* (Porter and Millar, 1985), in which information flows from one company's value chain to another company's value chain. Figure 7.6 depicts the value system framework. In this diagram, three companies are aligning their value chains to form a value system. First, company A processes information through its value chain and forwards the information along to its customer, company B, which processes the information through its value chain and sends the information along to its customer, company C, which processes the information through its value chain. Adding additional suppliers, business partners, and customers can create complex value systems. However, for our purposes, we simply view an organization's information systems as a value chain that interacts with the value chains of other organizations.

Externally focused systems can be used to coordinate a company's value chain with another company's value chain or with consumers (such as in business-to-consumer (B2C) electronic commerce). Any information that feeds into a company's value chain, whether its source is another company's value chain or an end consumer, is considered to be part of the value system. In other words, the value system for a particular organization acts like a vacuum cleaner, gathering information from the outside world.

The value system can be viewed as a river of information that flows from a source to an ultimate destination. Like a river, at any particular point there is a flow coming from upstream and progressing downstream. Value systems comprise **upstream** and **downstream** information flows. An upstream information flow consists of information that is received from another organization, whereas a downstream information flow relates to the information that is produced by a company and sent along to another organization. For instance, using the value system depicted in Figure 7.6 as an example, the upstream and downstream information flows for company B become quite evident. In this case, company B receives information from its upstream supplier, processes the information through its internal value chain, and subsequently passes information downstream to its distributors and/or customers. It is these flows of external information into and from a company that can be leveraged to create additional value and competitive advantage. Next, we will look at the enterprise systems used to support the processes and information flows we have talked about so far.

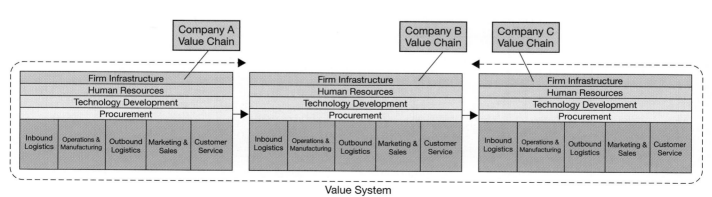

[Figure 7.6 ➡ Value system framework.]
Porter and Millar, 1985

TYPES OF ENTERPRISE SYSTEMS

Enterprise systems come in two forms—packaged and custom. *Packaged applications* are software programs written by third-party vendors, whereas *custom applications* are software programs that are designed and developed by company personnel. Packaged applications that you are likely familiar with are Microsoft Money and Quicken, which allow users to purchase software off-the-shelf to help them with their financial matters. Packaged systems are highly useful for standardized, repetitive tasks such as making entries in a check register. They can be quite cost effective since the vendor that builds the software application can spread out development costs through selling to a large number of users.

Yet, packaged applications may not be well suited for tasks that are unique to a particular business. In these cases, companies may prefer to develop (or have developed for them) custom applications that can accommodate their particular business needs. The development costs of custom systems are much higher than packaged applications due to the time, money, and resources that are required to design and develop them. Furthermore, applications need to be maintained internally when changes are required. With packaged applications, the vendor makes the changes and distributes new versions to its customers. In all, there are trade-offs when choosing between the packaged and custom application routes. Managers must consider whether packaged applications can meet the business requirements and, if not, conduct a cost-benefit analysis to ensure that taking the custom application approach will prove worthwhile to the company.

Figure 7.7 provides a high-level overview of how enterprise systems typically evolve. As companies begin to leverage information systems applications, they typically start out by fulfilling the needs of particular business activities in a particular department within the organization. Systems that focus on the specific needs of individual departments are not designed to communicate with other systems in the organization and are, therefore, referred to as *stand-alone applications*. Stand-alone applications usually run on a variety of computing hardware platforms such as mainframes and minicomputers. Together, stand-alone applications and the computers they run on are often referred to as *legacy systems*, given that they are typically older systems that are either fast approaching or beyond the end of their useful life within the

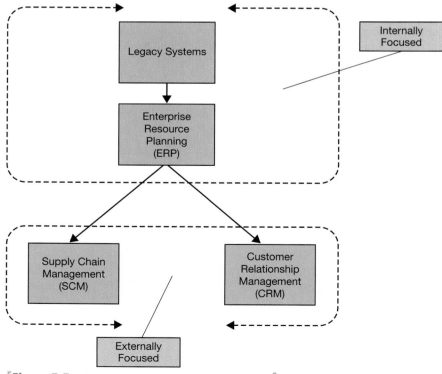

[**Figure 7.7** ➥ Stages of enterprise systems evolution.]

organization. Legacy systems tend to require substantial resources to maintain them to accommodate emerging business needs (O'Leary, 2000).

Companies can gain several advantages by integrating and converting legacy systems so that information stored on separate computing platforms can be consolidated to provide a centralized point of access. The process of **conversion** transfers information stored on legacy systems to a new, integrated computing platform, which typically comes in the form of **Enterprise Resource Planning (ERP)** applications. Although ERP applications do an excellent job of serving the needs of internal business operations on an organization-wide basis, they are not designed to completely accommodate the communication of information outside the organization's boundaries.

Systems that facilitate interorganizational communications focus on either the upstream or downstream information flows. Since these systems coordinate business activities across organizational boundaries, they are classified as externally focused applications. **Supply Chain Management (SCM)** applications operate on the upstream information flows, integrating the value chains of a company and its suppliers. In contrast, **Customer Relationship Management (CRM)** applications concentrate on the downstream information flows, inte-

grating the value chains of a company and its distributors. In some cases, companies deal directly with end consumers rather than selling products through distributors. CRM applications can also accommodate this scenario.

Legacy Systems

When companies first use information systems to support business activities, they usually begin by implementing systems in various departments rather than starting with a single application that can accommodate all aspects of the business. Each department implements applications to assist it with its daily business activities, which are optimized for its unique needs and the manner in which personnel in a particular unit accomplish job tasks. These applications tend to be infrastructure-specific, meaning that they run on particular hardware and software platforms. As a result, each department normally has its own computing system that runs its necessary applications. Although departmental systems are greatly beneficial in enabling departments to conduct their daily business activities efficiently, these systems often are not very helpful when people from one part of the firm need information from another part of the firm (e.g., people in manufacturing need forecasts from sales).

Enterprise Resource Planning (ERP) implementations usually incur huge costs and take a long period of time. As a result, only large, established companies were able to afford them. However, in recent times, advanced ERP applications are enabling even small businesses to implement and take advantage of ERP systems. Georgia-based eCompanyStore is a company that specializes in providing promotional products for its clients. It felt the need to implement a company-wide information system in order to be scalable and realized that it did not have the money, the time, or the information systems personnel to implement a large-scale ERP package. It found its solution in fast-track ERP, a technology that provides the same functionalities to small businesses as the large ERP packages do to the Fortune 500 companies. The CIO of eCompanyStore partnered with SAP of Germany to implement the R/3 system within the organization. This system had several modules, including those

enabling materials management, functional planning, an online store, and finance. The implementation stayed within intended costs and was more or less completed within a couple of months. The fast-track ERP systems are built in a way very similar to the large ERP applications, and are usually based on best-practices templates. The templates are designed so as to provide maximum efficiency and effectiveness, and are helping many small businesses to streamline their business processes. The only downside to these fast-track systems is the fact that they enable very limited customization. On the other hand, that simplifies things for people within the company's information systems group. In addition, this lack of customization capabilities saves companies a lot of time and money, since consultants now do not have to spend the bulk of their time tailoring these systems. If you find yourself working in information systems for a small business, you may still find yourself implementing an ERP package!

Information Systems

[Adapted from Lee Pender, "Faster, Cheaper ERP," **http://www.cio.com**, *CIO Magazine* (May 15, 2001).]

As previously described, given that these older systems are not designed to communicate with other applications beyond departmental boundaries, they are classified as "legacy" systems, or systems that operate within the confines of a particular business need. Legacy systems and their associated stand-alone applications can prove problematic when information from multiple departmental systems is required to make business decisions (as is often the case). For example, if the applications for inbound logistics and operations are not integrated, companies will lose valuable time in accessing information related to inventory levels. When an order is placed through operations, personnel need to verify that the components are available in inventory before the order can be processed. If the inventory and order-entry systems are not integrated, personnel must have access to two separate applications. Further, if these applications reside on different computing platforms, personnel must have two separate pieces of hardware on their desks in order to accomplish their duties. Figure 7.8 provides an example of how information flows through legacy systems within an organization.

As the diagram depicts, information is generated by the inbound logistics business activity, but it does not flow through to the next business activity, in this case operations. Since the inbound logistics and operations departments use different legacy systems, information cannot readily flow from one business activity to another. Understandably, this creates a highly inefficient process for operations personnel, who must have access to two systems in order to get both the order entry

and inventory information. For instance, if the inventory application is running on an IBM mainframe systems and the order entry application is running on a UNIX-based minicomputer, operations personnel must have access to both the IBM mainframe and UNIX systems. This may mean installing two separate terminals at an employee's desk so the employee can view the information from both systems at the same time. In some cases, inventory information may be stored on both systems, creating the potential for inaccuracies. Should data be updated in one system but not the other, the data becomes outdated and inaccurate. In addition, there are further, unnecessary costs associated with entering, storing, and updating data redundantly.

Enterprise Resource Planning

When companies realize that legacy systems can create dramatic inefficiencies within their organizations, the next step is to integrate legacy information on a company-wide basis. As previously described, applications that integrate business activities across departmental boundaries are often referred to as Enterprise Resource Planning (ERP) systems. In the 1990s there was a push by companies to implement integrated applications, as exhibited by ERP sales forecasts that are expected to reach approximately $50 billion annually. Readers should be cautioned that the terms *resource* and *planning* are somewhat misnomers, meaning that they do not accurately describe the purpose of ERP since these applications do very little in the way of planning or managing resources (Koch, Slater, and

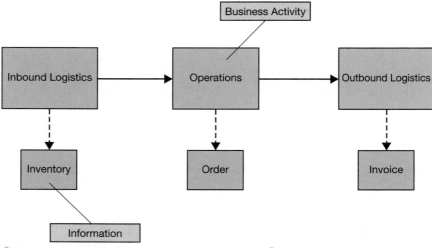

[Figure 7.8 ➡ Information flow using legacy systems.]

Baatz, 2000). The reason for the term Enterprise Resource Planning is that these systems evolved in part during the 1990s from material requirements planning (a.k.a. MRP) packages. Do not get hung up on the words *resource* and *planning*. The key word to remember from the acronym ERP is *enterprise*.

ERP takes stand-alone applications a step further by providing a common data warehouse and similar application interfaces that service the entire enterprise rather than portions of it. Information stored on legacy systems is converted into large, centralized data repositories known as **data warehouses**. Data warehouses are databases that store information related to the various business activities of an organization. Data warehouses alleviate the problems associated with multiple computing platforms by providing a single place where all information relevant to the company and particular departments can be stored and accessed, as depicted in Figure 7.9.

In contrast to legacy systems, where it is difficult to share information between business activities, ERP applications make accessing information easier by providing a central information repository. By using an ERP solution, both inbound logistics and operations have access to inventory data since both business activities have access to the same pieces of information. Rather than having information

flow from one department to the next, data can be accessed and updated at will, meaning that the next business activity can access information in the data warehouse whenever it needs to. This provides personnel access to accurate, real-time information. The beauty of ERP lies in the fact that information can be shared throughout the organization. For example, inventory information is accessible not only to inbound logistics and operations, but also to accounting and customer service personnel. If a customer calls in wondering about the status of an order, customer service representatives can find out by accessing the data warehouse through the ERP application. Prior to the emergence of ERP, customer service representatives may have had to retrieve information from two or more separate computing systems, making their job extremely difficult while potentially resulting in dissatisfied customers. Storing data in a single place and making it available to everyone within the organization empowers everyone in the organization to be aware of the current state of business and to perform their jobs better.

ERP applications that access the data warehouse are designed to have the same look and feel, regardless of the unique needs of a particular department. Inbound logistics and operations personnel will use a common user interface to access the same pieces of information

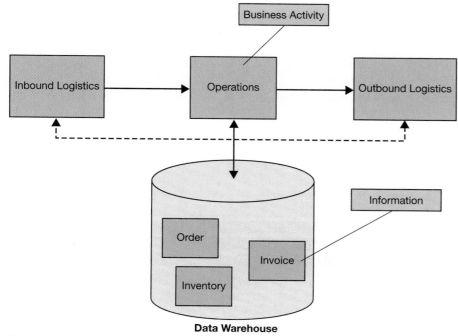

Data Warehouse

[**Figure 7.9** ➡ Information storage using an ERP solution.]

from the data warehouse. Although the inbound logistics screens and the operations screens will have different features tailored to the unique needs of the business activity, the screens will look comparable, with similar designs, screen layouts, menu options, and so on. The Microsoft Office products provide a useful analogy. Microsoft Word and Microsoft Excel are designed to serve separate functions (word processing and spreadsheets, respectively), but overall the products look and feel very similar to one another. Word and Excel have similar user interfaces and simply differ in the features and functionality that each application offers.

ERP systems are packaged applications that are purchased from software vendors. ERP vendors include BAAN, Oracle, PeopleSoft, SAP, and J.D. Edwards among others (O'Leary, 2000). SAP (see Figure 7.10) holds the largest market share with over 36 percent and has become the fourth largest software supplier in the world behind software behemoths Microsoft, Oracle, and Computer Associates (Herrera, 1999). In 1999, SAP had implemented over 9,000 copies of its ERP packages (known as R/3) at 6,000 companies, with a total of 2,500,000 users (O'Leary, 2000). Oracle, the world's second largest software supplier in the world, started out in 1977 as a database vendor and grew into an ERP vendor by developing integrated applications that access information stored in the data warehouse. Interestingly, Oracle not only sells

ERP software, but is also continues to sell its popular database management software, which serves as the database engine underlying many of the other ERP products. In recent years, Oracle has held a 10 percent share of the ERP market with revenues from ERP sales in excess of $2.4 billion. J.D. Edwards, PeopleSoft, and BAAN accounted for seven percent, six percent, and five percent of the ERP market, respectively.

When selecting an appropriate ERP application for a company, management needs to take many factors into careful consideration. ERP applications come as packaged software, which means a one-size-fits-all strategy. However, businesses have unique needs even within their own industries. In other words, like snowflakes, no two companies are exactly alike. Management must carefully select an ERP application that will meet the unique requirements of the particular company. There are a number of factors that companies must consider in the ERP selection. Among the most prevalent issues facing management are control, business requirements, and best practices (Ptak, 2000).

Control refers to the locus of control over the computing systems and decision making regarding these systems. Companies typically either opt for centralized control or allow particular business units to govern themselves. In the context of ERP, these decisions are based on the level of detail in the information that

[Figure 7.10 ⇒ SAP is one of the most popular ERP products worldwide.]
Source: SAP software **www.sap.com**

With 90,000 employees spread around the globe, Hewlett-Packard works hard at human resource management. Unfortunately, HP's human resource information systems were getting in the way. For example, there were four different HR-related information systems operating within HP around the globe, and getting them to work together was difficult. HP knew it needed a new, better technology solution for HR.

Spending money on an expensive system was just not in the cards, however. Management at Hewlett-Packard had just asked employees to reduce costs by $1 billion within two years. HR decided to find a new technology solution that would not only help it to manage human resources more effectively but would also help save money.

HP's HR department decided on a global implementation of PeopleSoft's human resource software product, PeopleSoft 8 HRMS. This new HR solution gave HP one global, enterprise-wide

human resource information system that enabled universal access to anyone within HP, from anywhere, with any Web browser.

The new system not only helped employees to have better HR data and make better HR-related decisions, but the system saved money too. The HR department went from 25 servers to 10, and from the four geographic HR systems to one. They realized $3 million in annual savings from just the reduced hardware, software, databases, and maintenance.

"In PeopleSoft 8 HRMS, HR found a technology platform that would provide better service at a lower cost," says Steve Rice, director of HR global enterprise programs and technology at HP. "PeopleSoft 8 gives us a Web-based architecture that will be deployed globally to streamline HR operations around the world. It's a cornerstone of how we're going to improve value and decrease costs for our organization. This upgrade will standardize HR processes in eight different languages for all of our 90,000 employees in over 120 countries."

Human Resource Management

[Adapted from **http://www.peoplesoft.com/media/en/pdf/hp_hrms.pdf**]

---

must be provided to management. Some corporations want to have as much detail as possible made available at the executive level, whereas other companies do not require such access. For instance, an accountant in one company may want the ability to view costs down to the level of individuals' transactions, while an accountant in another company may want only summary information. Another area related to control involves the consistency of policies and procedures. Some companies prefer that policies and procedures remain consistent throughout an organization. Other companies want to allow each business unit to develop its own policies and procedures to accommodate the unique ways that they do business. ERP applications vary widely in their allowance for control, typically assuming either a corporate or business-unit locus of control. Some ERP applications allow users to select or customize the locus of control. In either case, management must consider the ERP's stance on control to ensure it will meet the business requirements of the company.

Because all companies are different, no packaged software application will exactly fit the unique requirements of a particular business. ERP applications come in a variety of shapes and sizes, each designed to accommodate certain transaction volumes and business

activities. For example, Oracle's ERP application can accommodate over 1,000 users, SAP R/3 can be scaled from 25 to 1,000 users, and PeopleSoft can handle from 10 to 500 users. As far as supporting various business activities is concerned, ERP systems can include a wide variety of features and functionality. Each function is classified as a component, and components are often bundled together to form software **modules**. The ERP modules provided by each ERP vendor vary in the specific functions that they provide, as well as how they are referred to. Tables 7.1 and 7.2 provide a comparison between some of the ERP modules provided by SAP and Oracle.

As evidenced by Tables 7.1 and 7.2, it is critical for managers to understand the vendors' naming conventions and software modules to gain an understanding of how these features can be implemented to meet the requirements of the business's activities. The features and modules that the ERP comes with out of the box are referred to as the **vanilla** version. If the vanilla version does not support a certain business process, the software may require **customizations** to accommodate it. Customizations involve additional software that is integrated with the ERP or direct changes to the vanilla ERP application itself. SAP, for example, includes

[Table 7.1] *SAP R/3 modules.*

Module	Functionality
FI (financial accounting)	GL—General Ledger AR—Accounts Receivable AP—Accounts Payable LC—Legal Consolidations
HR (human resources)	PA—Personnel Administration PD—Planning and Development
MM (materials management)	IM—Inventory Management IV—Invoice Verification WM—Warehouse Management
PP (production planning)	SOP—Sales & Operations Planning MRP—Material Requirements Planning CRP—Capacity Requirements Planning
SD (sales & distribution)	OE—Order Entry FUL—Fulfillment SH—Shipping

[Table 7.2] *Oracle ERP modules.*

Module	Functionality
Demand	Order Entry Accounts Receivable Inventory Management
Supply	Bill of Materials Materials Requirements Planning Work-in-process Management Purchasing
Finance	General Ledger Accounts Payable Cost Management

literally thousands of elements in their ERP software that can be customized, and also offers many industry-specific versions of their software that have already been customized for a particular industry based on SAP's perceptions of the best way to do things in that industry (i.e., best practices). Companies must take special care when dealing with customization issues. Customizations can be costly, and maintaining and upgrading customizations can be troublesome. For example, a customization made to the vanilla version will need to be reprogrammed when a new release of the ERP is implemented. This is due to the fact that subsequent releases of the ERP do not contain the necessary logic embedded in the customizations. In other words, new vanilla versions must be continually upgraded to accommodate the customization. This process can involve a substantial investment of time and resources.

One of the major hurdles posed to companies that implement ERP applications involves changing business processes to accommodate the manner in which the software works. ERP implementations are often used as a catalyst for overall improvement of underlying business processes. ERP applications are designed to operate according to industry-standard business processes, known as *best practices*. Many ERP vendors build best practices into their applications to provide guidelines to management to identify business activities within their organizations that need to be streamlined. Implementations will go more smoothly when companies change their business practices to fit the way the ERP software operates.

Altering the way in which business processes are conducted is known as *business process reengineering (BPR)*. Many organizations have spent many years developing business practices that provide them with a competitive advantage in the marketplace. Adopting their industry's best practices may force these companies to abandon their unique ways of doing business, putting them on par with their industry competitors. In other words, companies can potentially lose their competitive advantages by adapting the "best practices" within their industry. Best practices is an area that managers must carefully consider before selecting an ERP application. Some ERP vendors tightly integrate best practices into the software, and companies that reject best practices are in for a long and time-consuming implementation. Other vendors provide a series of options that companies select before implementing the software, allowing them some (but not complete) flexibility in reengineering their business processes to accommodate the ERP application.

There is also a growing, useful body of research evidence on ERP implementations that suggests that these business process reengineering and related organizational issues are just as important as are the ERP technical implementation issues (Kumar and Van Hillegersberg, 2000; Markus and Tanis, 2000). Indeed, in order to be successful, in some situations managers must literally choose between either making the ERP system

Brief Case: SAP Implementation at Microsoft

Prior to implementing ERP in the mid-1990s, Microsoft Corporation, the world's leading supplier of software applications, used a variety of legacy systems and stand-alone applications to support its internal operations. Some of these applications had been custom built internally, whereas others had been purchased as packaged software from outside vendors. All of the applications ran on mainframe or midrange computing platforms. At the time, Microsoft maintained over 400 applications that used specialized user interfaces to access data from the various legacy systems. Integrating legacy systems in this way proved problematic for the company. As the applications grew more complex to accommodate the company's spectacular growth, integration became extremely difficult and expensive to maintain. Changes made to one legacy system commonly required extensive overhauls to the other legacy systems that were integrated with it. Furthermore, as the systems grew in complexity, the company found it more and more difficult to produce timely information to management, resulting in unacceptable delays during decision-making processes. Microsoft clearly needed an alternative approach to the manner in which it was supporting its internal business activities.

Seeing the need for an integrated, enterprise-wide solution, in 1992 Microsoft started to evaluate a number of ERP applications. During the next two years, the company proceeded down the ERP path, yet did not have executive buy-in for the project, resulting in a number of delays. Management buy-in came in 1994 when then vice president of sales and support, Steve Ballmer, visited Wal-Mart, which was well respected in implementing information systems to support its internal business processes. Soon after, Microsoft selected SAP as its ERP vendor.

The first phase of the ERP implementation was to convert legacy systems supporting the company's financial activities to the new ERP software. SAP's FI (financial accounting) module would be put to use to streamline Microsoft's financial processes, from initiating a transaction such as a purchase order to producing corporate financial statements. After realizing that some of its internal practices had become dated, the company decided to implement the FI module without customizations. This would require some reengineering to the company's financial business activities, but Microsoft wanted to experience the benefits of best practices that SAP had built into the ERP application. Plus, by choosing not to customize the ERP, the company sidestepped many of the maintenance issues they had encountered with their custom legacy applications.

The ERP implementation was completed in 1996 and serves thousands of users at the company's headquarters in Redmond, Washington. Whereas it took Microsoft three weeks to put together its monthly financial statements when using its legacy systems, with the aid of the ERP package it took just three days to prepare the same statements. The time involved in processing payments to vendors was shortened dramatically, saving the company enormous sums of money while creating happy suppliers. Once the ERP was accepted at corporate headquarters, the system was rolled out over a twelve-month period to thousands more financial users worldwide. Due to the success of the SAP FI implementation, Microsoft decided to install SAP's HR (human resources) module, and other modules are planned to go online in the near future (O'Leary, 2000).

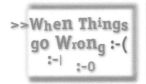

ERP Woes Hurt Grainger

Chicago-based W.W. Grainger recently experienced less-than-expected earnings that were caused in part by the installation of SAP R/3, its new ERP system. How could this happen? Grainger officials said that at times a physical count of inventory showed that the ERP software was counting more products than were actually on hand in the company's warehouses.

The "inventory shrinkage," which was blamed on transaction-processing failures during the rollout of the new system, required a downward adjustment in the inventory figures. That affected earnings, and Grainger said salary and employee benefit costs were also higher than expected due to costs associated with installing the ERP system and doing the inventory count.

How bad was the hit on earnings? Grainger estimates that the system has cost them $19 million in lost sales and $23 million in reduced earnings during the latter half of the 1999 fiscal year alone.

David Dobrin, an analyst at Benchmarking Partners in Cambridge, Massachusetts, said installing an ERP system can be an especially thorny task for a distribution-oriented company such as Grainger. "There's such an enormous number of things they sell, and they have an extremely complicated business model and lots of [facilities]," Dobrin said. "It's the sort of thing that puts a lot of pressure on anybody's ERP system, not just SAP's."

Hasso Plattner, SAP's co-CEO, mentioned Grainger's struggles after a press conference in November, while suggesting that some users could avoid major problems with their R/3 rollouts by calling SAP for help earlier in the projects. Plattner took some of the blame for the situation himself, acknowledging that SAP has not "developed as close relationships [with users] in the U.S. market as we have in Europe."

Grainger is one of several high-profile users that have had difficulties with new R/3-based systems in the past few months. Hershey Foods Corp. and Whirlpool Corp. both said last fall that they were also having trouble processing orders through their systems. But SAP is not the only ERP vendor that is being stung by problem rollouts—for example, Oracle Corp. and PeopleSoft also recently had users who ran into trouble with installations of their applications.

Grainger CEO Richard Keyser said in a statement that the company has taken steps to correct its transaction-processing problems and has now installed the ERP system at all of its six distribution centers and 370 branch offices.

[Adapted from Craig Stedman, "ERP Woes Cut Grainger Profits," *Computerworld* (January 7, 2000).]

---

fit the organization or making the organization fit the ERP system (Soh, Sia, and Tay-Yap, 2000). Others have suggested that for the ERP system to help you transform the organization and gain new competitive capabilities, a full organizational and operational change process is required (Willcocks and Sykes, 2000). Finally, there is some evidence that, in order to be successful, managers must in fact first transform the organization and then implement the ERP system (Sarker and Lee, 2000). In any event, the evidence suggests that these organizational change issues are very important in implementations of ERP and other enterprise-wide information systems.

While ERP helps companies to integrate systems across the organization, ERP falls short in communicating across organizational boundaries (Larson and Rogers, 1998). Since ERP applications are designed to service internal business activities, they tend not to be well suited for managing value system activities. Companies wanting to integrate their value chains with the business activities of their suppliers, business partners, and customers typically choose to implement systems other than ERP to manage the upstream and/or downstream flow of information. These types of applications are designed to coordinate activities outside organizational boundaries and are discussed in the following sections.

Customer Relationship Management

With the changes introduced by the Web, in most industries a company's competition is simply a mouse click away. It is increasingly important for companies not only to generate new business, but to attract repeat business as well. This means that companies must keep their customers satisfied to remain competitive. In today's highly competitive markets, customers hold the balance of power because, if they become dissatisfied with the levels of customer service they are receiving, there are many alternatives readily available to them. The global nature of the Web has affected companies worldwide and infected a wide swath of industries. An economic transformation is taking place, shifting the emphasis from conducting business transactions to managing relationships. Vendors such as Siebel[1] argue that the cost of trying to get back customers that have gone elsewhere can be up to 50 to 100 times as much as keeping a current one satisfied. Companies are finding it imperative to develop and maintain customer satisfaction and develop deeper relationships with their customers in order to compete effectively in their markets.

Applications focusing on downstream information flows have two main objectives in mind—to attract potential customers and create customer loyalty. The process of attracting potential customers, or prospects, can be streamlined by implementing *Sales Force Automation (SFA)* applications, which mainly focus on contact management and scheduling. SFA applications provide salespeople with computerized support tools to assist them in their daily routines. SFA focuses on presales marketing and sales functions, whereas *Customer Relationship Management (CRM)* applications go beyond SFA by offering postsales support activities as well. CRM offers a completely integrated approach to customer management. CRM suites typically include SFA modules, as well as the ability to track activities related to customers throughout the entire organization. CRM helps close the loop once the sale has been made. For example, once a sale has been made, CRM can retrieve information related to a customer's order, such as identifying where the order is in the pipeline, whether it be in manufacturing, in the warehouse, or in the process of being shipped. CRM also integrates the multiple ways that companies interact with customers, such as electronic mail and call centers. By providing exactly the information the customer requests, CRM can help build customer loyalty through demonstrated responsiveness.

The appropriate CRM technology combined with reengineering of sales-related business processes can have a tremendous impact on a company's bottom line. Siebel Systems argues that improving customer satisfaction by one percent a year over a five-year period can result in increases of more than 10 percent in return on investment over the period. To pursue customer satisfaction as a basis for

achieving competitive advantage, organizations must be able to access information and track customer interactions throughout the organization, regardless of where, when, or how the interaction occurs. This means that companies need to have an integrated system that captures information from retail stores, Web sites, call centers, and various other ways that organizations communicate downstream within their value chain. More important, managers need the capability to monitor and analyze factors that drive customer satisfaction as changes occur according to prevailing market conditions.

CRM applications come in the form of packaged software that is purchased from software vendors. CRM applications are commonly integrated with ERP to leverage internal and external information to serve customers. CRM vendors include E.Piphany, FirePond, Onyx Software, and Siebel Systems. According to AMR Research, the market for CRM applications is expected to grow from $10.6 billion in 2000 to $37.8 billion in 2005 (Shah, 2001). With billions of dollars at stake, ERP vendors such as Oracle, PeopleSoft, and SAP are entering the CRM fray, enhancing their ERP solutions to include CRM. Like ERP, CRM applications come with various features and modules. Management must carefully select a CRM application that will meet the unique requirements of their particular company. In general, CRM applications are modularized along two lines—sales and service. Sales modules include SFA functions, which are designed to assist companies with the presales (i.e., before the sale) aspects of the business activities, such as marketing and prospecting. Service modules help companies with the postsales (i.e., after the sale) customer service aspects of their business.

BlueCross BlueShield of Minnesota, a large provider of health-care services, has used FirePond's CRM solution to streamline presales activities throughout the organization. The CRM application replaces a paper-based system with an interactive application that provides a comprehensive view of customer-related information. Prior to the implementation, product information was mainly limited to paper-based documents and brochures. Sales agents had difficulty locating the proper marketing materials and forms and had to fill them out by hand in order to provide prospects with a quote. The FirePond CRM application (see Figure 7.11) allowed BlueCross agents to access a wide variety of product information

Web Search

WEB SEARCH OPPORTUNITY: Visit the Siebel Systems Web site at **www.siebel.com/** to see what the company is up to. What is it currently offering in the way of CRM capabilities? What other types of software and/or services does Siebel offer?

[1]See Siebel Systems, "CRM Case Studies," **www. siebel.com**.

Marketing

IBM Global Systems, Accenture, and Siebel Systems have the strongest CRM brands, according to a study by the Information Technology Services Marketing Association (ITSMA). Intriguingly, the study, "Customer Relationship Management Services: Understanding Brand Awareness and Positioning in the CRM Services Market," found that nearly half the respondents could not name a single provider of CRM services.

Only IBM Global Services, Accenture, and Siebel registered any sort of significant unaided awareness. In surveying 400 key decision makers from Fortune 1,000 companies and government entities, ITSMA found that awareness of CRM service providers is extremely low. IBM Global Services was recognized most frequently as a CRM services company, capturing just 12 percent

unaided awareness. Accenture and Siebel, which led the CRM software awareness category, each garnered nine percent. The Big Five professional services firms followed next.

The survey also revealed that Oracle, Siebel, IBM Global Services, PricewaterhouseCoopers, and Deloitte Consulting had the highest favorability ratings among CRM solution providers.

The most important attributes in selecting providers of CRM services were reputation and financial stability, agility and responsiveness, and ability to integrate new CRM systems with existing systems.

In any event, it appears that vendors within the CRM space need to do some basic marketing to build better brand awareness. Now there is an opportunity for a marketing major with interests in technology.

[Adapted from "CRM Companies Lack Brand Identity," *CRM Forum* (February 13, 2002). www.crm-forum.com/cgi-bin/item.cgi?id=72040]

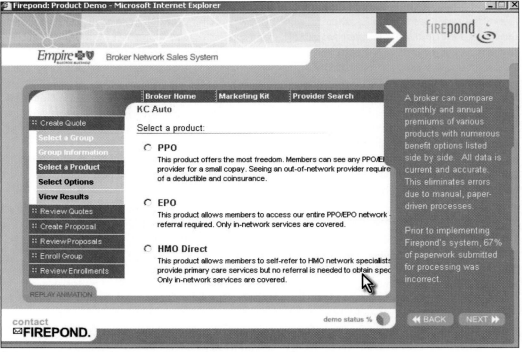

[Figure 7.11 ➥ Screen shot of FirePond's CRM application.]
Source: FirePond, 2001

from a single source, which could be tailored to the unique needs of the individual in real time. In addition, the system allowed Blue-Cross to give side-by-side comparisons of the different services the organization offered, facilitating faster decision making on the part of the potential customer. Agents can also build what-if scenarios, which allow prospects

to compare the advantages of the company's different health-care plans.

The National Basketball Association (NBA) uses E.Piphany's CRM application to gather information about basketball fans from around the world, including the United States, Europe, Asia, and Australia. This information allows the NBA to personalize promotions that are directly targeted to fan desires. By implementing CRM, the NBA can maximize overall value per customer and eliminate wasted marketing efforts, creating profits for both the league and its teams through one-to-one marketing. CRM products have helped organizations like BlueCross and the NBA identify who their customers are, gain an understanding of what they want, and provide products and services to meet their unique needs.

The service side of CRM brings with it many opportunities to gain competitive advantage by providing customized, individual attention to existing customers. However, facilitating premium customer service requires a great deal of coordination since customers can interact with a company across multiple channels and through different personnel within the organization. MGM Mirage, which operates The Mirage, MGM Grand, Bellagio, Treasure Island, Golden Nugget, and Beau Rivage casinos and resorts, has deployed CRM to help it design marketing campaigns, such as seasonal promotions and special events, for its existing customers. With the gaming industry growing exponentially, the market has become highly competitive, and MGM Mirage needed an advantage. Customer information—including gambling activities, lodging preferences, and purchase histories—from all of its properties can be consolidated, providing management with a comprehensive, real-time view of market conditions. With accurate, real-time information, management can make decisions more efficiently than their competitors and design targeted marketing campaigns that work. Similarly, American Airlines, one of the nation's largest commercial airline carriers, uses CRM to personalize products and services for their most loyal frequent flyers by giving them rewards for their patronage and increasing repeat business with their most profitable customers.

Marriott International, one of the world's largest hotel and resort corporations, built its marketing philosophy around creating a superior experience for its customers. The company implemented Siebel Systems' CRM solution to accomplish just that. One way that Marriott achieved this goal was through the development of a program called Personal Planning Service, which allowed the company to create personalized vacation itineraries for guests at the time a reservation is made. When a customer returns for a visit to any one of Marriott's properties, an itinerary is built, based on customer requests and preference information stored in the CRM application. For example, when a customer arrives at one of Marriott's resorts, the company has scheduled client activities such as tee times, dinner reservations, and tours well in advance of the customer's stay. Marriott's CRM success has resulted in higher customer satisfaction and an increase of $100 per visitor in service revenues beyond the room rate.

Companies that have successfully implemented CRM can experience greater customer satisfaction and increase productivity in their sales and service personnel, translating into dramatic enhancements to the company's profitability. CRM allows organizations to focus on driving revenue as well as streamlining costs, as opposed to emphasizing cost cutting alone. Cost cutting tends to have a lower limit because there are only so many costs that companies can streamline, whereas revenue generation strategies are bound only by the size of the market itself. The National Quality Research Center estimates that a one percent increase in customer satisfaction can lead to a threefold increase in a company's market capitalization. That is significant!

Supply Chain Management

In the previous section we looked downstream at CRM applications. Now we turn our attention upstream. Getting the raw materials and components that a company uses in its daily operations is an important key to business success. When deliveries from suppliers are accurate and timely, companies can convert them to finished products more efficiently. Coordinating this effort with suppliers has become a central part of companies' overall business strategies, as it can help them reduce costs associated with inventory levels and get new products to market more quickly. Ultimately, this helps companies drive profitability and improve their customer service since they can react to changing market conditions swiftly. Collaborating, or sharing information, with suppliers has become a strategic necessity for business success. By developing and maintaining stronger, more integrated relationships with suppliers, companies can more effectively compete in their markets through cost reductions and responsiveness to market demands.

The term *supply chain* is commonly used to refer to the producers of supplies that a company uses. Companies use many different suppliers to procure specific raw materials and components. These suppliers, in turn, work

Team Work

ERP, CRM, and SCM

Work in a small group with classmates and use a search engine like Google to search the Web for sites with information on ERP, CRM, and SCM. What types of Web sites are you finding? In what ways are the sites portraying these systems? Most likely you are finding corporate and vendor sites and related information. Now search for articles on these systems at an online magazine such as *InformationWeek* or *Computerworld*. What new information can you learn from these articles?

Brief Case: Siebel Implementation at Quick & Reilly

Quick & Reilly, the nation's first discount brokerage firm, maintains 118 investor centers nationwide, and more than 900 brokers service more than 1 million accounts per year. As the company grew, their Marketing Database & Fulfillment System (MDFS), a homegrown legacy system, could no longer meet the information needs of brokers and investors. Although MDFS provided the company with many of the customer marketing capabilities that it required, the company found it difficult to aggregate marketing information, sales information, and customer service assistance in a single source that brokers and customers could access.

The presales side of the business suffered because the legacy system was capturing only 40 percent of incoming inquiries, resulting in low overall rates of converting prospects to customers. Inquiries were coming into the business through a variety of channels such as call centers, retail operations, electronic mail, and the company's Web site. The legacy system, built prior to the emergence of the Internet and Web, was designed to handle traditional forms of communication and was, therefore, not well suited to handle the new channels through which prospects were now contacting the company. In addition, much of the information related to prospects consisted of handwritten notes that people rarely entered into the system, preventing the sharing of information with the rest of the organization.

Quick & Reilly also experienced issues surrounding the customer service aspects of its business. Many brokers found it difficult to build customized investment strategies for investors since they had to retrieve information stored on MDFS, wade through paper files, and sort through records stored on microfiche. The brokers' jobs had become highly inefficient, and the company realized that it needed to put all the information that brokers require at their fingertips.

Quick & Reilly formalized a corporate goal of 100 percent customer satisfaction as a core value throughout the company. The company needed the right tools to increase prospect conversion rates, serve customers more effectively, and ultimately build stronger relationships with its clients. It conducted a search for CRM applications and selected Siebel Systems as its CRM vendor. Siebel's CRM promised to play a key role in the company's ability to attract and retain customers by providing a single repository of marketing, prospect, and customer information to brokers throughout the organization. The data warehousing approach would allow the company to market, sell, and service customers across multiple channels such as cell centers, retail, electronic mail, and the Web. Furthermore, Siebel's CRM could assist the company in tailoring products and services to the unique needs of individual investors more efficiently than the MDFS legacy system.

Quick & Reilly hired consulting firm PricewaterhouseCoopers to assist it with the implementation. The consultants provided the company with project management, technical services, and end-user training, which proved invaluable to the organization. The new system, known as Socrates, was rolled out throughout the organization's 118 offices in less than eight months. After the CRM application went live, the company discovered that it could open up more accounts by converting more inquiries to actual sales. Conversion rates climbed 15 percent to 20 percent on an annual basis. By streamlining the presales process, brokers found it easier to concentrate on servicing existing customers, communicating with them more often, and helping them meet their financial objectives. The results were clear—when prospects can be converted to customers more efficiently, and when personnel could better meet the needs of current customers, the company's revenues and profitability increased throughout the organization.

Socrates provided Quick & Reilly with other benefits. The application gave brokers more control over marketing campaigns, allowing them to profile customers and keep track of their activities across multiple channels. For instance, a broker could retrieve a comprehensive view of a particular client's activity, including detailed accounts of inquiries that he had made and trades he had executed, regardless of the channel that he used (e.g., call center or Web site). This information helps brokers identify trends and investor preferences, allowing them to design and propose customized investment strategies for individual investors. Existing customers can also access information on Socrates related to their specific accounts. Socrates is linked to a Web browser interface, where customers can serve themselves. Prospects can open an account in a single step, while existing customers can maintain their accounts, view their portfolios, and enter transactions, all through a single interface.

From a management perspective, Socrates has opened a window through which managers can access productivity information related to the efficiencies of brokers and branch offices. Managers can analyze where leads are coming from and tailor marketing campaigns to the most profitable market segments. Socrates also enables management to explore productivity by providing information on prospect conversions. This information helps them determine in real time which brokers, offices, and territories are most productive, enabling timely decision making based on current market trends. Prior to the Socrates implementation, brokers were compensated mainly for opening new accounts. Socrates has prompted an enhancement to the company's compensation policy by rewarding brokers for the growth of assets in investor accounts and providing quality customer service to existing customers. Siebel argues that the new compensation plan focuses on the activities that create lasting customer relationships and the associated rewards focus personnel on both the presales and postsales aspects of the business.

Customer Relationship Management software is sweeping across the continent as European companies look for ways to better understand and serve their customers. Europe has come relatively late to CRM. British consulting firm Hewson Group says that Europe accounted for just $1.7 billion of the $7.6 billion global CRM market last year, a small percentage compared with the United States, which leads in CRM use. That is changing, however, Hewson founder, Nick Hewson, says. "CRM vendors are seeing a significantly increased proportion of their business out of Europe," he says. Europe is one of the fastest-growing CRM markets, with the growth there expected to continue at 80 percent to 100 percent over the next three years, on par with or ahead of growth in the U.S. market.

It is not only a question of faster growth. According to some, European CRM implementations are typically more costly than those in the United States. PricewaterhouseCoopers says the average implementation cost for its European clients is $7 million. That is significantly more than the $4 million its clients spend on CRM in the United States, says Denis Collart, the consulting firm's CRM director for Europe. The difference, Collart says, is that Europeans tend to plan implementations more extensively and deploy them more broadly. "The major difference is that European companies get to CRM [by] starting with the business case," he says. "The United States takes a tactical approach, but in Europe, it's more strategic." While U.S. projects often focus on a particular aspect of the business, Europeans tend to look at their CRM needs across the entire organization.

Europeans also often take their time on software deployments. An average European CRM project takes 12 to 15 months, while a U.S. CRM project takes six to nine months, according to PricewaterhouseCoopers. This approach may be grounded in a more reserved European business culture. "It's related to the speed of change in the marketplace," Collart says.

European organizations, less swayed by technology fads than U.S. counterparts, may have been slower to adopt CRM. On the other hand, their ambitious, thorough CRM implementations—and the urgency with which deployments are made—indicate that Europe is waking up to the importance of the customer.

[Adapted from Jeff Sweat, "A New Appreciation for the Customer Is Sweeping Across Europe as More of the Continent's Businesses Invest Billions of Dollars in CRM Software," *InformationWeek* (May 21, 2001).]

with their suppliers to obtain goods; their suppliers work with additional suppliers, and so forth. The further out in the supply chain one looks, the more and more suppliers are involved. As a result, the term *chain* becomes somewhat of a misnomer since it implies one-to-one relationships facilitating a chain of events flowing from the first supplier to the second to the third, and so on. A more descriptive term to describe the flow of materials from suppliers to a company is **supply network** because multiple suppliers are involved in the process of servicing a single organization. Figure 7.12 depicts a hypothetical supply network.

Several problems can arise when firms within a supply network do not collaborate effectively. Information can easily become distorted as it moves from one company down through the supply network, causing a great deal of inefficiency. Problems such as excessive inventories, inaccurate manufacturing capacity plans, and missed production schedules can run rampant. These issues can lead to degradations in profitability and poor customer service. Implementing software applications to manage a company's activities with its supply network can help alleviate these barriers to competitiveness.

Applications focusing on upstream information flows have two main objectives in mind—to accelerate product development and to reduce costs associated with procuring raw materials, components, and services from

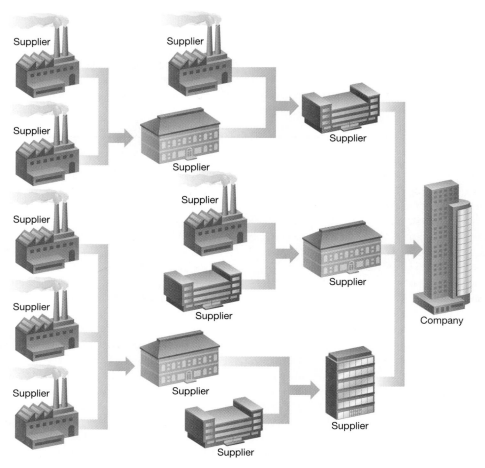

[**Figure 7.12** ➡ A typical supply network.]

suppliers. *Supply Chain Management (SCM)* applications are designed to assist companies in streamlining these areas. SCM applications are commonly integrated with ERP to leverage internal and external information to collaborate with suppliers. According to AMR Research, the market for SCM applications is expected to grow from $5.2 billion in 2000 to $21.1 billion in 2005 (Shah, 2001). Most SCM applications come in the form of packaged software, which can be purchased from some of the leading SCM software vendors such as Agile Software, Ariba (see Figure 7.13), Commerce One, i2 Technologies, and Manugistics. ERP vendors including BAAN, J.D. Edwards, Oracle, and SAP also offer SCM solutions that are integrated with their ERP applications (Butler, 2001).

Like ERP and CRM applications, SCM packages are delivered in the form of modules (see Table 7.3), which companies select and implement according to their business requirements.

The appropriate SCM technology, combined with the coordination of business processes with the supply network, can provide substantial paybacks for companies. SCM solutions help streamline work flow and enhance employee productivity. Companies can more efficiently manage business travel, time, and expenses, and collaborate with suppliers in real time. Up to $95 billion in operational savings is expected to be generated by implementing SCM in the U.S. manufacturing economy alone (Manugistics, 2001). To pursue supplier collaboration as a basis to achieve competitive advantage, organizations must be able to access information and track activities throughout the supply network. This means that companies need to have an integrated system that captures information from the various methods they use to communicate upstream with their suppliers. More important, managers need the capability to monitor and analyze factors that drive supplier productivity to ensure they can meet demands based on prevailing market conditions.

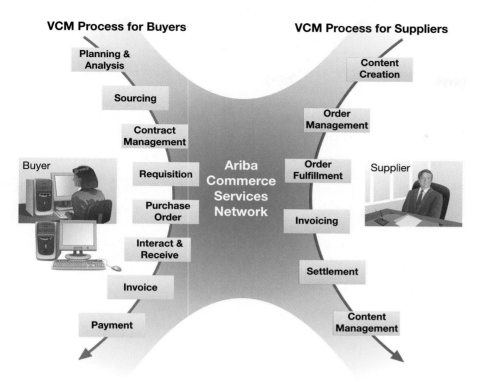

VCM Process for Buyers

- Planning & Analysis
- Sourcing
- Contract Management
- Requisition
- Purchase Order
- Interact & Receive
- Invoice
- Payment

Buyer

Ariba Commerce Services Network

VCM Process for Suppliers

- Content Creation
- Order Management
- Order Fulfillment
- Invoicing
- Settlement
- Content Management

Supplier

[Figure 7.13 ➥ An overview of Ariba's value chain management solution—Commerce Services Network.]
Source: **www.ariba.com**

Many companies utilize SCM applications to accelerate product development. The ability to swiftly react to changing market conditions can provide companies with the competitive advantage of bringing products to market more quickly than their competition. Oceaneering International helps locate shipwrecks and perform emergency equipment repairs in hazardous environments. In this company's line of business, time is of the essence. To win business, personnel and equipment need to be deployed at the right time to the right location more quickly than the competition can deliver. Many of Oceaneering's products and services require a great deal of customization to accommodate the unique requirements of projects. Oceaneering chose Agile Software's SCM application to achieve this goal, enabling the company to collaborate across their supply network in real time on the materials and products they needed for projects. Once the SCM application had been installed, Oceaneering found that it could locate the appropriate personnel, materials, and knowledge dispersed throughout its supply chain in a timelier manner, allowing them to react more quickly to customer needs. For instance, SCM helped the company streamline communications with suppliers, sharing draw-

ings for customizations and using information from past experiences that utilized similar equipment and procedures. This information could be brought to bear more quickly, which enhanced productivity, increased revenues, and produced satisfied customers.

The other major reason that SCM applications are becoming widely used is based on the fact that they can help companies streamline costs and create efficiencies across their supply networks. Dell uses Ariba's SCM application to automate its formerly paper-based purchasing process, shorten the time it takes to obtain goods and services from suppliers, and lower overall purchasing costs. Dell's SCM connected to its broad supplier network and integrated the company's purchasing activities with its existing ERP solution. Ariba SCM provides Dell with data to identify inefficiencies within its supply network and negotiate key contracts for goods and services, resulting in significant volume purchasing discounts. Ariba[3] showed that by automating and streamlining its procurement processes, Dell achieved

---

[3]See "Ariba Customer Success Stories" at **www.ariba.com**

[Table 7.3] *Functions that optimize the supply network.*[2]

Module	Key Uses
Supply chain collaboration	Share information and integrate processes up and down the supply chain Provide Internet-enabled processes such as collaborative planning, forecasting, and replenishment (CPFR) and vendor-managed inventory
Collaborative design	Streamline product design processes across supply chain partners to reduce time to market React quickly to changing market conditions, such as product launches and new customer segments
Collaborative fulfillment	Commit to delivery dates in real time Fulfill orders from channels on time with order management, transportation planning, and vehicle scheduling Support the entire logistics process, including picking, packing, shipping, and international activities
Collaborative demand and supply planning	Develop a one-number forecast of customer demand by sharing demand and supply forecasts instantaneously across multiple tiers Enable suppliers and vendors to use shared forecasts and real-time demand signals to replenish stock automatically
Collaborative procurement	Provide global visibility into direct material spending Allow partners to leverage buying clout and reduce ad hoc buying
Production planning	Support both discrete and process manufacturing Optimize plans and schedules while considering resource, material, and dependency constraints
Supply chain event management	Monitor every stage of the supply chain process, from price quotation to the moment the customer receives the product, and issue alerts when problems arise Capture data from carriers, vehicle on-board computers, GPS systems, and more
Supply chain exchange	Create an online supply chain community that enables partners to collaborate on design, procurement, demand and supply management, and other supply chain activities
Supply chain performance management	Report key measurements in the supply chain, such as filling rates, order cycle times, and capacity use Integrate planning and execution functions with competitive information and market trends

[2] See SAP's product literature at **www.sap.com.**

Web Search

WEB SEARCH OPPORTUNITY: Visit the Manugistics Web site at **http://www.manugistics.com/** to see what the company is currently offering. What is it currently offering in the way of Supply Chain Management capabilities? What other types of software and/or services does Manugistics offer?

over 60 percent reductions in procurement cycles and cost per purchase order.

Southwest Airlines, the nation's fourth largest commercial airline, chose i2 Technologies as its SCM vendor to streamline its maintenance, repair, and overhaul operations. Operating over 2,500 flights per day to more than 50 destinations makes it very challeng-ing to schedule its planes for service. Southwest needed an application to coordinate spare parts inventory for its fleet to ensure the parts were available when needed. The company needed to store excess parts for immediate repairs, yet wanted to optimize inventory levels since storing large quantities in inventory can prove costly to a company's

Brief Case: Manugistics Implementation at Cisco Systems

Cisco Systems, the world's leading supplier of routers, is well known for innovative approaches to Supply Chain Management. Cisco had been using an extranet extensively to collaborate with its first-tier suppliers (those that deal directly with the company), enabling its suppliers to directly access Cisco's proprietary information, such as manufacturing forecasts, inventory levels, and competitive market data. The extranet allowed its suppliers to interact with Cisco as if they were part of the company. By utilizing the extranet for Supply Chain Management, Cisco had reduced inventory levels by 45 percent, cut purchasing cycle times (order to delivery) by 70 percent, and increased productivity for purchasing personnel. In the year 2000, Cisco achieved financial benefits in excess of $695 million as a result of this approach.

Although Cisco received many benefits from its extranet implementation, the company still experienced a number of problems. In dealing with only its first-tier suppliers, the company was unable to view information throughout the total supply network, causing distortions between the information Cisco kept internally and the information provided from deep within its supply network. The company experienced high levels of variability in supply forecasts, making it difficult for it to plan manufacturing activities. Since the company could not synchronize the incoming data from its multilayered supply network, Cisco had difficulty identifying potential problems and exceptional conditions. For example, Cisco internal records could indicate a product delivery date of six weeks, in accordance with its first-tier supplier. However, when Cisco's first-tier supplier had lead times of four weeks and eight weeks from its suppliers, the parts Cisco's first-tier suppliers needed to manufacture a component would actually take eight weeks (the longest lead time) rather than six. This led to a number of inefficiencies in procuring goods and services that were critical for Cisco to meet customer demands.

Cisco wanted to integrate its entire supply network, which consisted of over 2,000 suppliers, distributors, and contract electronics manufacturers. The company went through a detailed selection process of SCM applications and chose Manugistics as its SCM vendor. Manugistics promised to fundamentally change the manner in which Cisco had been managing its supply network, while reducing costs, bringing products to market more quickly, and enhancing the company's profitability. One of the keys to the company's successful SCM implementation stemmed from the fact that the company asked several of its strategic suppliers such as Altera, Flextronics, and Motorola to participate in defining the features and functionality required of the new application. Cisco also enlisted the support of top-level management and put together a small team of business, technical, and procurement specialists to manage the project.

Manugistic's SCM application enabled Cisco to view inventory availability from throughout its multi-tiered supply chain. By opening up visibility to the entire supply network, Cisco could react, alter production, and commit to customer orders in real time. This resulted in superior response to customer demands. The company was also able to reduce the procurement cycle from weeks to days and, in some cases, even hours. ●

---

bottom line. The i2 SCM solution gives Southwest the ability to monitor its maintenance inventory supply network, identifying potential bottlenecks in parts deliveries and providing a tool to control its stockpile of parts. The application allows Southwest to manage its parts inventory more efficiently by using real-time information to produce inventory forecasts. This ensures that parts will be available when needed and reduces Southwest's inventory levels. Airplanes cannot make any money while they are on the ground, so SCM provides a tool to maximize the time planes are in the air while minimizing the time the planes are on the ground being repaired. By implementing i2's SCM application, Southwest has reduced costs in its supply chain and increased the company's profitability.

THE FORMULA FOR ENTERPRISE SYSTEM SUCCESS

To summarize, the main objective of enterprise systems is to create competitive advantage by streamlining business activities within and outside a company. However, many implementations are more costly and time consuming than originally envisioned. It is not uncommon to have projects that run over budget, meaning that identifying common problems

Operations Management

Coordinating with one's suppliers has become a central part of the business process of most companies. This coordination is critical for companies since it enables them to reduce inventory costs and send finished products to the market faster. A&P (the Great Atlantic and Pacific Tea Co.), the "granddaddy of grocery chains," is a 142-year-old grocery chain that has been lacking in this coordination. Its supply chain is in shambles, and the company still relies on legacy systems that are at least 12 to 15 years old. There is a tremendous information gulf within the organization. The distribution system is disjointed. No one has a clear idea of which products are being sold in the stores, and thus replenishment and inventory management have become a problem. Once one of the leading groceries in the country, in recent years the company has struggled to remain competitive with other grocery chains such as Kroger and Safeway and has failed miserably. It has hence made a decision to invest heavily in IT to turn its

business around and has allocated approximately $250 million toward this new project. A&P has partnered with IBM and a software company called Retek for this venture. Retek is in charge of building applications for purchasing, merchandising, and inventory management. The system will also include a data warehouse and some forecasting tools, which will be integrated with a warehouse management system, a transportation system, and a store system. A&P will use Oracle for managing human resources and some financial issues. The transportation system has already been implemented and is running successfully. The company is also looking toward building a completely Web-enabled Supply Chain Management system in the next two or three years. Initial results seem to suggest that the investment in IT has successfully changed the nature of A&P's Supply Chain Management and is giving a new image to this grocery veteran. Who would have thought that all of this was going on behind the scenes as you grab that loaf of bread off the shelf?

[Adapted from Susannah Patton, "Can I.T. Save A&P?" **http://www.cio.com**, *CIO Magazine* (February 15, 2001).]

and devising methods for dealing with these issues can prove invaluable to management. A recent survey suggested that 40 to 60 percent of companies that undertake enterprise system implementations do not fully realize the results that they had hoped (Langenwalter, 2000). Companies that have successfully installed enterprise systems are found to follow a basic set of recommendations related to enterprise system implementations (Koch, Slater, and Baatz, 2000). Although the following list is not meant to be comprehensive, these recommendations will provide an understanding of some of the challenges involved in implementing enterprise systems:

Recommendation 1—Secure executive sponsorship.

Recommendation 2—Get help from outside experts.

Recommendation 3—Thoroughly train users.

Recommendation 4—Take a multidisciplinary approach to implementations.

Secure executive sponsorship. The primary reason that enterprise system implementa-

tions fail is believed to be a direct result of lack of top-level management support (O'Leary, 2000). Although executives do not necessarily need to make decisions concerning the enterprise system, it is critical that they buy into the decisions made by project managers. Many problems can arise if projects fail to grab the attention of top-level management. In most companies, executives have the ultimate authority regarding the availability and distribution of resources within the organization. If executives do not understand the importance of the enterprise system, this will likely result in delays or stoppages because the necessary resources may not be available when they are needed.

A second problem that may arise deals with top-level management's ability to authorize changes to the way the company does business. When business processes need to be changed to incorporate best practices, these modifications need to be completed. Otherwise the company will have a piece of software on its hands that does not fit the way people accomplish their business tasks. Lack of executive sponsorship can also have a trickle-down effect within the organization. If users and midlevel management perceive the enterprise system to be unimportant, they are not likely to view it as a priority. Enterprise systems require a concentrated effort, and executive sponsorship can propel or stifle the implementation. Executive management can obliterate any obstacles that arise.

Get help from outside experts. Enterprise systems are complex. Even the most talented information systems departments can struggle in coming to grips with ERP, CRM, and SCM applications. Most vendors have trained project managers and consultants to assist companies with installing enterprise systems. Vendors such as Siebel Systems work with consulting firms such as Accenture and PricewaterhouseCoopers rather than maintaining a huge, internal implementation division. Consultants can give companies a head start since they are already trained on the package being implemented. They also have experience in helping other companies implement the software, making them keenly aware of potential problem areas that may arise during the implementation. Many consulting organizations have developed tried and trusted methodologies that help companies develop an appropriate project plan to guide them through the installation process.

Using consultants tends to move companies through the implementation more quickly and tends to help companies train their personnel on the applications more effectively. However, companies should not rely too heavily on consultants and should plan for the consultants leaving once the implementation is complete. When consultants are physically present, company personnel tend to rely on them for assistance. Once the application goes live and the consultants are no longer there, users have to do the job themselves. A key focus should be facilitating user learning.

Thoroughly train users. Training is often the most overlooked, underestimated, and poorly budgeted expense involved in planning enterprise system implementations. Enterprise systems are much more complicated to learn than stand-alone systems. Learning a single application requires users to become accustomed to a new software interface, but enterprise system users regularly need to learn a new set of business processes as well. Once

enterprise systems go live, many companies experience a dramatic drop-off in productivity. In a survey of 64 Fortune 500 companies that have implemented enterprise systems, 25 percent have experienced productivity problems after going live. The most common reason that performance problems arise is that the applications and processes are different from the previous system (Shah, 2001). Users that have not mastered the new system will not be able to perform effectively. This issue can potentially lead to heightened levels of dissatisfaction among users, as they prefer to accomplish their business activities in a familiar manner rather than doing things the new way. By training users before the system goes live and giving them sufficient opportunities to learn the new system, a company can allay fears and mitigate potential productivity issues.

Take a multidisciplinary approach to implementations. Enterprise systems affect the entire organization and, thus, companies should include personnel from different levels and departments in the implementation project (Kumar and Crook, 1999). In CRM and SCM environments in which other organizations are participating in the implementation, it is critical to enlist the support of personnel in their organizations as well. Project managers need to include in the implementation personnel from midlevel management, the information systems department, external consultants, and, most important, end users.

Failing to include the appropriate people in the day-to-day activities of the project can prove problematic in many respects. From a needs analysis standpoint, it is critical that all the business requirements be sufficiently captured before selecting an enterprise solution. Since end users are involved in every aspect of daily business activities, their insights can be invaluable. For instance, an end user might make salient a feature that no one on the project team had thought of. Having an application that does not meet all the business's requirements can result in poorly fitting software or customizations. Another peril in leaving out key personnel involves the threat of alienation. Departments and/or personnel that do not feel included may develop a sense of animosity toward the new system and view it in a negative light. In extreme cases, users will refuse to use the new application, resulting in conflicts and inefficiencies within the organization.

Although these expansive enterprise system implementations are often cumbersome and difficult, the potential payoff is huge. As a result, organizations are compelled to implement these systems. Further, given the popularity and necessity of such systems, you are likely to find yourself involved in the implementation and/or use of such a system. We are confident that after reading this chapter you will be better able to understand and help with the development and use of such systems.

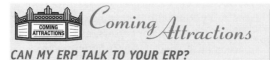

CAN MY ERP TALK TO YOUR ERP?

SAP recently unveiled an upgrade to its business-intelligence system that shows the company is slowly opening up the software used for collecting and analyzing customer, financial, and supply chain data to other vendors' business applications. The software maker said the latest version of mySAP Business Intelligence will include reporting software from Crystal Decisions that lets companies draw data from other business systems.

In addition, the company revealed at its Conference on Business Intelligence and Enterprise Portals, held recently in Leipzig, Germany, that mySAP BI will include the company's enterprise portal software and the option of integrating with Ascential Software's (formerly Informix) tools and linking to non-SAP data warehouses.

Crystal's reporting software will be embedded in the data-warehouse component of mySAP, providing 1,800 predefined reports for analyzing customer data, such as sales opportunities and deal sizes, as well as human-resource, supply chain, financial, and product life-cycle data. Under the seller agreement, customers of SAP's Business Information Warehouse can generate up to 500 different reports. Those who want more report templates or want to customize reports will have to buy a separate license.

While Crystal's software is capable of drawing data from non-SAP systems, only 20 of the 500 reports covered in the seller agreement can access other software, says Michael Schiff, an analyst at Current Analysis. "SAP is trying to move out of its closed environment and be perceived as open," he says. "But the real test will be to see if anyone not using SAP R/3 uses the business-intelligence tools." SAP R/3 is the company's flagship Enterprise Resource Planning system. "SAP has come a long way toward easing customer complaints that its ERP system, once referred to as an 'SAP jailhouse,' was too closed," Schiff says. In addition, the company has improved business-intelligence tools with each release.

[Adapted from Antone Gonsalves, "SAP Takes Step Toward More Open System," *InformationWeek* (January 30, 2002).]

KEY POINTS REVIEW

1. **Explain how organizations support business activities by using information technologies.** Organizations use information systems to better perform all of the various business processes (and activities within these processes) throughout each of the functional areas of the firm. Whether it be taking an order for a product, manufacturing a product, securing supplies from another firm, shipping a product to a customer, or providing service after the sale, companies can use information systems to make each of these processes and activities more effective and efficient. More important, companies can use information systems to integrate these processes and activities and to accumulate and use wisely the information that is generated each step of the way.

2. **Describe what enterprise systems are and how they have evolved.** Enterprise systems are information systems that span the entire organization and can be used to integrate business processes, activities, and information across all the functional areas of a firm. Enterprise systems can be either prepackaged software or custom-made applications. One popular, powerful type of enterprise system is the Enterprise Resource Planning system, from vendors such as SAP and Oracle. These ERP packages evolved from "material requirements planning" systems during the 1990s and are, for the most part, used to support internal business processes.

3. **Explain the differences between internally and externally focused software applications.** Internally focused software applications are generally used to support business processes and activities that occur within the boundaries of a firm. Examples are the manufacturing of a product or the management of inventories. ERP packages are commonly used to support these types of processes and activities. External software applications are generally used to support business processes and activities that occur across organizational boundaries. Examples are taking product orders from customers and receiving supplies from other firms. Supply Chain Management packages, such as those from Manugistics, enable a firm to interact more effectively and efficiently with upstream business partners. Customer Relationship Management packages, such as those from Siebel Systems, enable a firm to interact more effectively and efficiently downstream with customers.

4. **List the keys to successfully implementing an enterprise system.** Experience with enterprise system implementations suggest that there are some common problems that can be avoided and/or should be managed carefully. These include 1) securing executive sponsorship, 2) getting necessary help from outside experts (i.e., consultants such as Accenture), 3) thoroughly training users, and 4) taking a multidisciplinary approach to implementations.

KEY TERMS

best practices 218

conversion 213

custom application 212

Customer Relationship Management 213, 221

customization 217

data warehouse 215

downstream 211

Enterprise Resource Planning 213

enterprise systems 206

interorganizational systems 207

legacy system 212

modules 217

packaged application 212

Sales Force Automation 221

stand-alone application 212

supply chain 223

Supply Chain Management 213, 226

supply network 225

upstream 211

value chain 209

value system 211

vanilla 217

REVIEW QUESTIONS

1. Describe what enterprise systems are and how they have evolved.
2. What are the advantages and disadvantages of enterprise systems?
3. What are the primary and support activities of a value chain?
4. Give an example of upstream and downstream information flows in a value system.
5. Compare and contrast customized and packaged applications.
6. How does customer relationship management differ from supply chain management?
7. Explain a data warehouse and the types of data that flow in and out of the warehouse.
8. Describe business process reengineering and give an example.
9. What are the four components of financial software modules?
10. What are the keys to successfully implementing an enterprise system?

SELF-STUDY QUESTIONS

Answers are at the end of the Problems and Exercises.

1. _____ are information systems that allow companies to integrate information support operations on a company-wide basis.
   A. Customer Relationship Management systems
   B. Enterprise systems
   C. WANs
   D. Interorganizational systems

2. Which of the following is a primary activity according to the value chain model?
   A. firm infrastructure
   B. customer service
   C. human resources
   D. procurement

3. According to the value chain model, which of the following is a support function?
   A. technology development
   B. marketing and sales
   C. inbound logistics
   D. operations and manufacturing

4. All of the following are true about legacy systems **except** _____ .

   A. they are stand-alone systems
   B. they are older software systems
   C. they are Enterprise Resource Planning systems
   D. they may be difficult to integrate into other systems

5. _____ is a component of the production planning module.

   A. sales and operations planning
   B. material requirements planning
   C. capacity requirements planning
   D. all of the above

6. Which of the following companies produces ERP systems?

   A. Microsoft
   B. Oracle
   C. Computer Associates and SAP
   D. all of the above

7. All of the following are components of financial accounting software modules **except** _____ .

   A. general ledger
   B. personnel administration

   C. accounts payable
   D. accounts receivable

8. Which of the following is commonly used to refer to the producers of supplies that a company uses?

   A. procurement
   B. sales force
   C. supply network
   D. customers

9. _____ is global visibility into direct material spending and allows partners to leverage buying clout and reduce ad hoc buying.

   A. Collaborative procurement
   B. Collaborative fulfillment
   C. Production planning
   D. Supply chain exchange

10. _____ are databases that store information related to the various business activities of an organization.

   A. Information stores
   B. Data warehouses
   C. Web marts
   D. Specialty databases

PROBLEMS AND EXERCISES

1. Match the following terms with the appropriate definitions:

   ____ Enterprise systems

   ____ Legacy systems

   ____ Data warehouses

   ____ Supply chain

   ____ Customer Relationship Management

   ____ Value chain

   ____ Supply Chain Management

   ____ Business process reengineering

   ____ Collaborative design

   ____ Upstream information flow

   a. An information flow that consists of information received from another organization
   b. Older systems that are not designed to communicate with other applications beyond departmental boundaries
   c. Information systems that allow companies to integrate information support operations on a company-wide basis
   d. Databases that store information related to the various business activities of an organization
   e. Applications that concentrate on downstream information flows, integrating the value chains of a company and its distributors
   f. Commonly used to refer to the producers of supplies that a company uses
   g. Streamlining product design processes across supply chain partners to reduce time to market and react quickly to changing market conditions, such as product launches and new customer segments
   h. The flow of information through a set of business activities
   i. Applications that operate on upstream information flows, integrating the value chains of a company and its suppliers
   j. Altering the way in which business processes are conducted

2. Find an organization that you are familiar with (or use one of the Brief Cases in the textbook), and determine how many software applications it is utilizing concurrently. Is the company's information system cohesive, or does it need updating and streamlining?

3. What part does training users in an ERP system play, and how important is it in software satisfaction? What productivity problems can result in an ERP implementation?

4. What are the payoffs in taking a multidisciplinary approach to an ERP implementation? What departments are affected, and what is the typical time frame? Research one of the Brief Cases in this chapter or find a company that has recently implemented an ERP system. What could the company have done better, and what did it do right?

5. Describe collaborative demand and supply planning, and find an example or two of companies applying this concept. What are the advantages and disadvantages? Is it cost effective? What were some of the challenges of implementation? What improvements could be made?

6. In the Brief Case in this chapter about Manugistics implementation at Cisco, what are the advantages and disadvantages of an extranet? How did the Supply Chain Management software affect the inventory and ultimately the customers and sales? What was the final result of the implementation of the Manugistics software?

7. What companies are using data warehouses? Research this question, and determine the cost and size of a data warehouse. What are the advantages and disadvantages of data warehouses? What is the typical time frame for implementation?

8. Look on the World Wide Web and find Microsoft, Oracle, Computer Associates, PeopleSoft, J.D. Edwards, and SAP. What are some of the different applications offered and their prices? What are the differences in Web sites? What can you find out about software implementation?

9. In the Brief Case about Siebel implementation at Quick & Reilly, what are the advantages of the new system? Does it have any Web interface? What has been the response from the customers and the account representatives? How has the new system affected management at Quick & Reilly? What was the outcome of this implementation? Was it successful or not?

10. Based on your own experiences with applications, have you used customized or off-the-shelf applications? What is the difference, and how good was the system documentation?

11. Read the Brief Case in this chapter about SAP implementation at Microsoft. How many applications were combined into the ERP system? What was the time frame? Is there a disadvantage of this system, and, if so, what is it?

12. Go through the job ads in the newspaper or on the Web and find a position that you would like to have in the future. Make an appointment to visit the company and ask questions of the human resources and information systems departments. Determine who hires for this position and what the qualifications are for the position. Find out exactly what the daily duties of the position are. You might even consider investigating an internship.

13. Choose an organization from one of the Brief Cases in the textbook or an organization with which you are familiar that utilizes Customer Relationship Management. Who within the organization is most involved in this process, and who benefits?

ANSWERS TO THE SELF-STUDY QUESTIONS

1. B   2. B   3. A   4. C   5. D   6. D   7. B   8. C   9. A   10. B

CASE 1: *ERP Implementation at Manco*

Enterprise Resource Planning (ERP) systems are considered to be critical to the success of any business. However, many ERP implementations fail because certain social aspects are ignored. In this case, we narrate the experiences of a company named MANCO (a pseudoname), which realized that there was more to an ERP implementation than the technology itself. MANCO was cofounded in 1966 by two engineers who had seen the increasing demand for "high-quality air purification equipment worldwide." The company started off in the garage of one of the cofounders but had grown to be a large, well-established organization with worldwide sales of more than $25 million by the late 1990s. The company is headquartered in a large city located in the Midwest region of the United States but also has regional offices in other parts of the United States and a few subsidiary offices in the United Kingdom, Germany, and Australia. The company sells air purification equipment to commercial customers such as offices, bars, restaurants, bowling alleys, and so on, and also to industrial manufacturers of metal and

chemical products. Most of the equipment is manufactured in its primary plant located in the Midwest. MANCO employs mixed-mode manufacturing strategies, including made-to-stock, assemble-to-order, and so on. Over a period of time, the company has earned considerable repute in the air purification equipment market, and the future seemed promising enough for MANCO.

However, in the recent past, things did not seem to go as the CEO had planned. There were growing problems in the organization, which threatened not only its stability but also its very existence. There were increasing customer complaints. The sales department was promising customers delivery dates that were unachievable. It was often booking orders without accurate specifications, which was delaying the engineering design and the actual production of the equipment. There were often errors and problems in the design and the design modifications, which led to a lot of wasted time. The problems often arose due to a lack of coordination between the mechanical and the electrical engineering groups within the organization, in addition

to a lot of unnecessary paperwork and exchange of information between them. The lack of coordination, excessive information exchange, and other territorial disputes between the various departments were leading to unreasonable lead times, questionable product quality, and ultimately tremendous customer dissatisfaction. The information technology at MANCO was doing little to help ameliorate these increasing problems. MANCO's primary computer system was a Quantel minicomputer, acquired about 15 years ago, with a Quantel package QMRP 6.31 running on it that helped with inventory control, product structure, purchasing and receiving, order entry, invoice processing, Kanban replenishment, and so on. The minicomputer served 60 terminals and 20 printers, and supported flat files. It did not, however, have any relational DBMS capabilities, which affected the company's ability to produce any meaningful reports. Because production of a single piece of air purification equipment required incredible coordination and exchange of information (e.g., memos and reports between MANCO's various departments, from sales to engineering to manufacturing), the inability to run efficient reports was hindering the business significantly. In addition, MANCO had some IBM PC–compatible systems that were running CAD/CAM applications, supporting contact management, customer complaints tracking, human resource applications, and so on. In short, MANCO had several systems, each of which had little coordination or connectivity with the others. This led to a lot of redundant paperwork, ultimately slowing down the company's business processes. The CEO (in consultation with the MIS department) realized that a radical change was required in MANCO's information technology.

The company decided that the new system to be selected should have a Windows-based client-server platform that would support relational databases. This would enable users to make changes quickly to data and procedures being used by different departments. In addition, such a network would allow everyone to view information from other departments, tearing down some of the existing territorial barriers, and also allow users to view real-time data as opposed to batch data. MANCO found the solution in a particular ERP package that was a fully integrated business management system designed especially for manufacturers. The system had several modules that handled

financial analysis, capacity management, shop-floor control, order processing, and so on. In addition, the system supported CAD, EDI, external payroll, data collection, and generation of standard reports, query reports, custom reports, and executive reports (all of which were initially generated by separate systems, and often by hand). The system allowed the existing bills of materials (BOMs) to be quickly copied and modified. The CAD interface also automated the design processes and enabled BOM items to be fed directly into the system from other third-party CAD packages. All in all, it was a system that satisfied each of the information technology needs of the company.

However, before the system could be installed, the CEO realized that some critical organizational changes were required at MANCO. MANCO was struggling not only because of its archaic information technology, but (as discussed earlier) because of the lack of coordination and territorial attitudes between and within each of the company's departments, which, according to the CEO, had to be eliminated or at least reduced. The first step toward this goal was the dismissal of the three vice presidents (sales, operations, and engineering) who were harboring the territorial attitudes within the organization, and the appointment of a single senior VP of operations who would be in charge of

all these departments (the coordination among these three departments was most critical to the organization's success). Next, there was an attempt to change the culture of the company by building the principles of quality into the employee psyche and also introducing a profit-sharing scheme. The company made a sincere effort to make employees put quality at the forefront of production. The profit-sharing scheme also helped employees realize that manufacturing the product and delivering it swiftly to the customer was critical to their own, and the company's, success. This speeded up the business processes, reduced redundancy, and opened up informal lines of communication.

After making the initial organizational changes, the company implemented the ERP package in six stages, which included some pilot implementations (to iron out any difficulties that might have arisen) and training sessions. After a few months, the system was fully functional at MANCO, and today it continues to handle most of the company's operations. In general, management is satisfied with the outcome, and MANCO has begun to regain some of its old glory.

[Adapted from S. Sarker and A. Lee, "Using a Case Study to Test the Role of Three Key Social Enablers in ERP Implementation," Proceedings of *International Conference on Information Systems* (Brisbane, Australia, 2000): 414–425.]

Discussion Questions

1. What were some of the information technology problems at MANCO?
2. From your knowledge of Enterprise Resource Planning systems, do you think that the company was correct in selecting an ERP package to solve its IT problems?
3. What were some of the factors that led to the success of the ERP implementation at MANCO?
4. Would the ERP implementation at MANCO be successful even if it were not accompanied by some of the organizational structure and cultural changes?

CASE 2: *CRM in the Banking Industry*

Having come into some money, Ronnie Marshak paid off her home equity loan from Fleet Bank. Marshak had some funds left over, so she asked the customer service representative at Fleet where she could invest the extra money. When he suggested that she refinance her mortgage, Marshak asked about the bank's mortgage rates. "He couldn't tell me," recalls Marshak, a consultant with the Patricia Seybold Group. "So I just put the money into my checking account, and they didn't get my business."

Fleet's insistence on separating its services into distinct silos may make sense operationally, but from a big-picture view, it

is a terrible way to run a bank. And while Fleet has a notorious reputation for customer service, it is not the only institution that is behind the curve on CRM. Other local and regional banks are similarly out of it.

"Financial institutions are still organized internally around different products rather than around the customers," says Judy Bigesse, an analyst with AMR Research. "But competition is much fiercer today, so if banks are not figuring out who their most profitable customers are and reorganizing their business to a more customer-centric approach, they're losing out on a big opportunity."

Bigesse's warning is echoed by other industry watchers who agree that banks are facing stiffer competition from each other as well as from other institutions, like insurance companies, that are bent on becoming full-service financial organizations. Just recently, for instance, MetLife announced it would be consolidating customer data from more than 30 business systems owned by companies that it has acquired in recent years.

MetLife intends to create a "holistic view" of its 100 million customers, and that, the experts say, is exactly what banks of all sizes should be doing. Adopting an integrated approach to customer needs would not only build loyalty and business, it would also allow banks to offer their customers the additional services they might really want.

Cross-selling is a huge untapped opportunity for financial institutions, agrees Barton Goldenberg, president and founder of ISM, a consulting firm in Bethesda, Maryland. If banks want to survive today, they have to offer a broad range of services. "Say you open up a savings account for the child of a current customer; you want to give that kid a debit card, a credit card, and eventually that child grows up and wants an equity loan for college, a mortgage, bigger credit cards,"

Goldenberg says. "You can't do [that] without fusing your customer data."

The problem, according to Goldenberg and others, is that banking is an old-fashioned business. Whether it is out of concern for customer privacy or a nostalgia for tradition, many bank executives still shy away from the idea of integrating and exploiting customer data. Yet banks that do not do that will not survive.

One financial institution that has learned this lesson is Bank One, the $270 billion bank holding and credit card company headquartered in Chicago. In December 2001,

Bank One announced that it was hiring 600 new IT employees to integrate the many customer databases it acquired during its merger spree.

"Fleet and banks in general have got to make some changes, and Bank One is just reminding people of that," Goldenberg says. "The banks who pull their customer data together now are the ones who will win tomorrow."

[Adapted from, Alison Bass, "Banking on Good Customer Data," *CIO Magazine* (January 14, 2002).]

Discussion Questions

1. Why have banks evolved so that their different functional areas are like disconnected "silos"?
2. What implications does this have for the implementation of CRM and other enterprise-wide information systems?
3. What advice would you give to Bank One so that they can overcome this hurdle, integrate business units and systems, and successfully implement a new enterprise-wide system?
4. What might successful banks of the future look like, and in what ways will they use information systems?

Information Systems Development and Acquisition

OPENING: Tower Records Powers Web Site with Innovative Software Design

Tower Records (see Figure 8.1) is a fixture in most cities, with hundreds of stores around the world. Founded in 1960 in Sacramento, California, Tower Records has established itself as one of the most influential music and video retailers in the world. With its 9:00 A.M. till midnight, 365 days a year, operating hours, Tower Records has become a place not only to shop but to meet people or just hang out. Today, Tower Records is much more than just music, with movies, books, clothing, collectables, and music accessories.

In 1996, TowerRecords.com was established with a goal of being innovative and fun, much like its physical stores. For example, Tower-Records.com was one of the first to offer used CDs on the Web. In order to stay focused on selling its products, Tower Records is working with numerous partners to bring innova-

tive products and services to the Internet. One such partner is Endeca Technologies, which is known for providing robust infrastructure software for simplifying how users search, navigate, and analyze large amounts of data, that is typical of a large product catalog. Hence, the heart of TowerRecords.com is Endeca's InFront navigation engine, which provides users with clear feedback and provides only relevant choices when making selections.

When users browse Tower-Records.com, the InFront navigation engine turns the act of browsing into a search. To do this, the software presents TowerRecords.com as an entertainment portal. A portal is a Web site—like **www.msn.com**—that offers a broad array of resources, such as e-mail, chat rooms, search engines, and shopping malls. When a user chooses a particular area to shop, say music, the page turns into a music portal. When a user chooses a particular artist or genre of music, the page turns into a more specific portal for

this choice. Unlike generic portals like MSN, AOL, or Yahoo!, Tower-Records.com portals and subportals link only to Tower Records products and information resources. In the first 16 weeks that the company used this new portal-based interface to its Web site, video sales increased 29 percent, conversion rates (how many visitors become actual buyers) jumped 8.5 percent, and the average customer order size increased 28 percent. Tower Records pays a monthly fee for using the InFront navigation engine and is reporting that its use pays for itself by the end of the first day of every month! With a return on investment like that, it is a good bet that Tower Records will continue to maintain its leadership position in the music and entertainment industry.

Adapted from T. Kontzer, "Tower Reaps Fruits of Search-Powered Browsing," **http://www.informationweek.com**; **www.towerfranchises.com** *InformationWeek* (2002).

[**Figure 8.1** ➡ Tower Records continues to innovate using specially designed software.]
©Corbis/Sygma

As you have read throughout this book and have experienced in your own life, information systems are of many different types, including decision support systems, executive information systems, group support systems, and Internet commerce systems. Just as there are different types of systems, different approaches have been found to be more appropriate for developing some types of systems and less appropriate for others. Learning all possible ways to develop or acquire a system and, more important, how to identify the optimal approach, takes years of study and experience. Toward this end, this chapter, has several objectives.

After reading this chapter, you will be able to do the following:

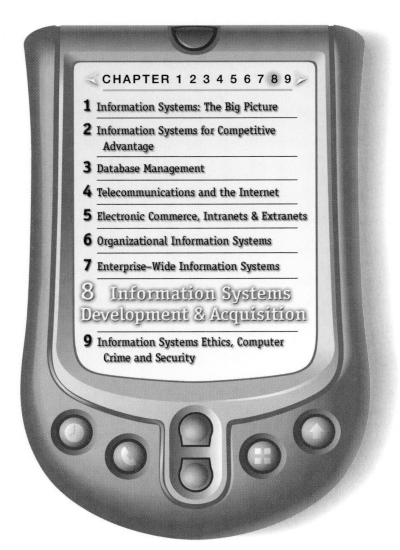

CHAPTER 1 2 3 4 5 6 7 8 9

1 Information Systems: The Big Picture

2 Information Systems for Competitive Advantage

3 Database Management

4 Telecommunications and the Internet

5 Electronic Commerce, Intranets & Extranets

6 Organizational Information Systems

7 Enterprise–Wide Information Systems

8 Information Systems Development & Acquisition

9 Information Systems Ethics, Computer Crime and Security

[Figure 8.2 ➡ The Big Picture: focusing on information systems development and acquisition.]

1. Understand the process used by organizations to manage the development of information systems.

2. Describe each major phase of the systems development life cycle: systems identification, selection, and planning; system analysis; system design; system implementation; and system maintenance.

3. Describe prototyping, rapid application development, object-oriented analysis and design methods of systems development, along with each approach's strengths and weaknesses.

4. Understand the factors involved in building a system in-house, along with situations in which it is not feasible.

5. Explain three alternative systems development options: external acquisition, outsourcing, and end-user development.

If you are a typical business student, you might be wondering why we have a chapter on building and acquiring information systems. The answer is simple: No matter what area of an organization you are in—such as marketing, finance, accounting, human resources, or operations—you will be involved in the systems development process. In fact, research indicates that the IS spending in most organizations is controlled by specific business functions. What this means is that even if your career interests are in something other than IS, it is very likely that you will be involved in the IS development process. Understanding all available options is important to your future success and an important part of your understanding of The Big Picture (see Figure 8.2).

THE NEED FOR STRUCTURED SYSTEMS DEVELOPMENT

The process of designing, building, and maintaining information systems is often referred to as *systems analysis and design*. Likewise, the individual who performs this task is referred to as a *systems analyst*. (This chapter uses *systems analyst* and *programmer* interchangeably.) Because few organizations can exist without effectively utilizing information and computing technology, the demand for systems analysts far outpaces the supply. Organizations want to hire systems analysts because they possess a unique blend of both managerial and technical expertise—systems analysts are not just "techies." In fact, systems analysts are in hot demand precisely due to their unique blend of technical and managerial expertise, but it was not always this way.

The Evolution of Information Systems Development

In the early days of computing, systems development and programming was considered an art that only a few technical "gurus" could master. Unfortunately, the techniques used to construct systems varied greatly from individual to individual. This variation made it difficult to integrate large organizational information systems. Furthermore, many systems were not easily maintainable after the original programmer left the organization. As a result, organizations were often left with systems that were very difficult and expensive to maintain. Many organizations, therefore, underutilized these technology investments and failed to realize all possible benefits from their systems.

To address this problem, information systems professionals concluded that system development needed to become an engineering-like discipline (Nunamaker, 1992). Common methods, techniques, and tools had to be developed to create a disciplined approach for constructing information systems. This evolution from an "art" to a "discipline" led to the use of the term *software engineering* to help define what systems analysts and programmers do. Transforming information systems development into a formal discipline would provide numerous benefits. First, it would be much easier to train programmers and analysts if common techniques were widely used. In essence, if all systems analysts had similar training, it would make them more interchangeable and more skilled at working on the systems developed by other analysts. Second, systems built with commonly used techniques would be more maintainable. Both industry and academic researchers have pursued the quest for new and better approaches for building information systems.

Options for Obtaining Information Systems

Organizations can obtain new information systems in many ways. One option, of course, is for the members of the organization to build the information system themselves. Organizations can also buy a prepackaged system from a software development company or consulting firm. Some information systems that are commonly used in many organizations can be purchased for much less money than what it would cost to build a new one. Purchasing a prepackaged system is a good option as long as its features meet the needs of the organization. For example, a payroll system is an example of a prepackaged system that is often purchased rather than developed by an organization because tax laws, wage calculations, check printing, and accounting activities are highly standardized. Figure 8.3 outlines several sources for information systems.

A third option is to have an outside organization or consultant custom build a system to an organization's specifications. This is generally referred to as having the development outsourced. This is a good option when an organization does not have adequate systems development resources or expertise. A final option is to let individual users and departments build their own custom systems to support their individual needs. This is referred to as end-user development. Most organizations allow end-user development to be used to construct only a limited range of systems. For example, systems that span organizational boundaries or perform complex changes to cor-

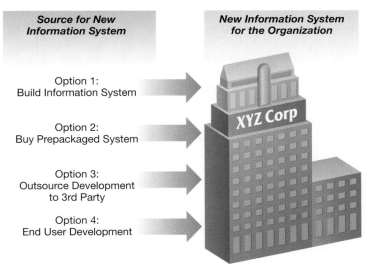

[**Figure 8.3** ➥ There are a variety of sources for information systems.]

porate databases are typically not candidates for end-user development. Alternatively, a common application that might be constructed using end-user development is a data analysis system using a spreadsheet application such as Microsoft Excel. Regardless of the source of the new information system, the primary role of managers and users in the organization is to make sure that any new system will meet the organization's business needs. This means that managers and users must understand the systems development process to ensure that the system will meet their needs.

Information Systems Development in Action

The tools and techniques used to develop information systems are continually evolving with the rapid changes in information systems hardware and software. As you will see, the information systems development approach is a very structured process that moves from step to step. Systems analysts become adept at decomposing large, complex problems into many small, simple problems. They can then easily solve each simple problem by writing a relatively short computer program. The goal of the systems analyst is to build the final system by piecing together the many small programs into one comprehensive system. This process of decomposing a problem is outlined in Figure 8.4. An easy way to think about this is to think about using Lego blocks for building a model house. When together, the blocks can create a large and very complex design. Apart, each block is a small, simple piece that is nothing without the others.

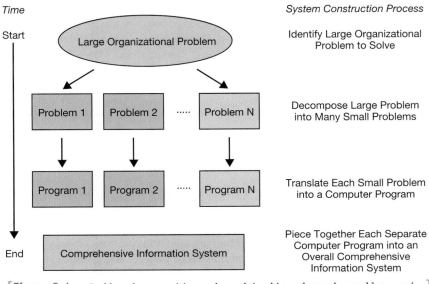

[**Figure 8.4** ➥ Problem decomposition makes solving big and complex problems easier.]

When systems are built in this manner, they are much easier to design, program, and, most important, maintain.

The Role of Users in the Systems Development Process

Most organizations have a huge investment in transaction processing and management information systems. These systems are most often designed, constructed, and maintained by systems analysts and programmers within the organization using a variety of methods. When building and maintaining information systems, systems analysts rely on information provided by system users, who are involved in all phases of the system's development process. To effectively participate in the process, it is important for all members of the organization to understand what is meant by systems development and what activities occur. A close and mutually respectful working relationship between analysts and users is a key to project success. Now that you understand the history and need for systems development, it is time to consider some of the relevant techniques that are used in systems development.

STEPS IN THE SYSTEMS DEVELOPMENT PROCESS

Just as the products that a firm produces and sells follow a life cycle, so do organizational information systems. For example, a new type of tennis shoe follows a life cycle of being introduced to the market, being accepted into the market, maturing, declining in popularity, and ultimately being retired. The term *systems development life cycle (SDLC)* is used to describe the life of an information system from conception to retirement (Hoffer, George, and Valacich, 2002). The SDLC has five primary phases:

1. System identification, selection, and planning
2. System analysis
3. System design
4. System implementation
5. System maintenance

Figure 8.5 is a graphical representation of the SDLC. The SDLC is represented as four boxes connected by arrows. Within the SDLC, arrows flow in both directions from the top box

---

Brief Case: The SDLC at NASA

Organizations modify the basic SDLC slightly to fit their specific needs. For example, the National Aeronautics and Space Administration (NASA) follows an eight-step approach (NASA, 2002). High-quality software is a key component of NASA's success. The organization uses software to control countless earth-based systems such as those used to track, guide, and communicate with the space shuttles and space-based systems that control the functioning of orbiting satellites. It is easy to imagine that a system failure could have catastrophic results! Consequently, NASA, like many other organizations, has chosen to follow a formal SDLC to help assure software and system quality and, more important, to help protect the lives and safety of its

astronauts. The value of having standard procedures and steps such as the SDLC when building software not only speeds the development process, but it also ensures the creation of high-quality and reliable systems. As shown in Figure 8.6, the NASA SDLC comprises eight phases that are essentially the same as the five-step, generic process described in this chapter. Within every step of the NASA SDLC, guidelines have been developed for accepting and ensuring the quality of work products created. These guidelines are used to make sure that all work products meet specifications and are error-free before developers move to the next phase of the SDLC. The remainder of this section describes each phase of the SDLC.

[Adapted from NASA, http://www.nasa.gov. Information verified February 10, 2002.]

(System Identification, Selection, and Planning) to the bottom box (System Implementation). Arrows flowing down represent that the flow of information produced in one phase is being used to seed the activities of the next. Arrows flowing up represent the possibility of returning to a prior phase, if needed. The System Maintenance arrow connecting the last phase to the first is what makes the SDLC a cycle.

Phase 1: System Identification, Selection, and Planning

The first phase of the systems development life cycle is *system identification, selection, and planning*, as shown in Figure 8.7. Given that an organization can work on only a limited number of projects at a given time due to limited resources, care must be taken so

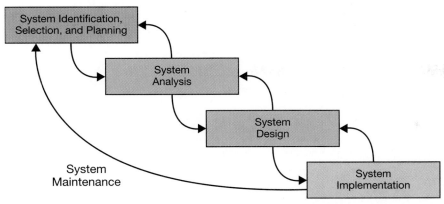

[**Figure 8.5** ➥ The systems development life cycle defines the typical process for building systems.]

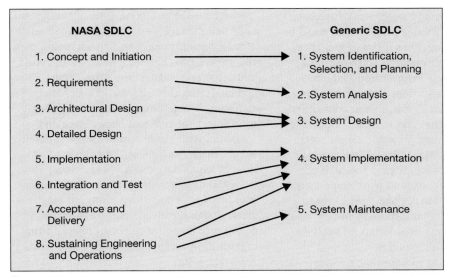

[**Figure 8.6** ➥ NASA's systems development life cycle as compared with the generic life cycle.]

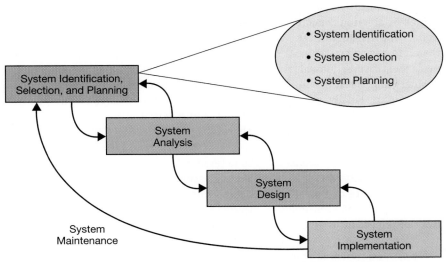

[**Figure 8.7** ➥ SDLC with Phase 1—System Identification, Selection, and Planning—highlighted.]

	Project Source	Primary Focus
[Table 8.1] *Sources of systems development projects and their likely focus. (Adapted from McKeen, Guimaraes, and Wetherbe, 1994.)*	Top management	Broad strategic focus
	Steering committee	Cross-functional focus
	Individual departments and business units	Narrow, tactical focus
	Systems development group	Integration with existing information system focus

Source Adapted from McKeen, Guimaraes, and Wetherbe. 1994.

that only those projects that are critical to enabling the organization's mission, goals, and objectives are undertaken. Consequently, the goal of system identification and selection is simply to identify and select a development project from all possible projects that could be performed. Organizations differ in how they identify and select projects. Some organizations have a formal *information systems planning* process whereby a senior manager, a business group, an IS manager, or a steering committee identifies and assesses all possible systems development projects that an organization could undertake. Others follow a more ad hoc process for identifying potential projects. Nonetheless, after all possible projects are identified, those deemed most likely to yield significant organizational benefits, given available resources, are selected for subsequent development activities.

It is important to note that different approaches for identifying and selecting projects are likely to yield different organizational outcomes (see Table 8.1). For example, projects identified by top management more often have a strategic organizational focus, and projects identified by steering committees more often reflect the diversity of the committee and therefore have a cross-functional focus. Projects identified by individual departments or business units most often have a narrow, tactical focus. Finally, the typical focus of projects identified by the development group is the ease with which existing hardware and systems can be integrated with the proposed project. Other factors—such as project cost, duration, complexity, and risk—are also influenced by the source of a given project. The source of projects has been found to be a key indicator of project focus and success.

Just as there are often differences in the source of systems projects within organizations, there are often different evaluation criteria used within organizations when classifying and ranking potential projects. During project planning, the analyst works with the customers—the potential users of the system and their managers—to collect a broad range of information to gain an understanding of the project size, potential benefits and costs, and other relevant factors. After collecting and analyzing this information, the analyst can bring it together into a summary planning document that can be reviewed and compared with other possible projects. Table 8.2 provides a sample of the criteria often used by organizations. When reviewing a potential development project, organizations may focus on a single criterion, but most often examine multiple criteria to make a decision to accept or reject a project. If the organization accepts the project, system analysis begins.

Phase 2: System Analysis

The second phase of the systems development life cycle is called *system analysis*, as highlighted in Figure 8.8. One purpose of the system analysis phase is for designers to gain a thorough understanding of an organization's current way of doing things in the area for which the new information system will be constructed. The process of conducting an analysis requires that many tasks, or subphases, be performed. The first subphase focuses on determining system requirements. To determine the requirements, an analyst works closely with users to determine what is needed from the proposed system. After collecting the requirements, analysts organize this information using data, process, and logic modeling tools. These elements will be illustrated and discussed later in the chapter (see Figure 8.12).

Evaluation Criteria	Description
Strategic alignment	The extent to which the project is viewed as helping the organization achieve its strategic objectives and long-term goals.
Potential benefits	The extent to which the project is viewed as improving profits, customer service, and so forth, and the duration of these benefits.
Potential costs and resource availability	The number and types of resources the project requires and their availability.
Project size / duration	The number of individuals and the length of time needed to complete the project.
Technical difficulty / risks	The level of technical difficulty involved in successfully completing the project within a given time and resource constraint.

[Table 8.2] *Possible evaluation criteria for classifying and ranking projects. (Source: Hoffer, George, and Valacich, 2002.)*

Source: Adapted from Hoffer, George, and Valacich. 2002. *Modern Systems Analysis and Design,* 3rd ed. Prentice Hall.

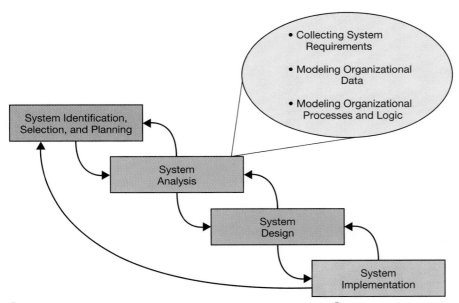

[**Figure 8.8** ➡ SDLC with Phase 2—System Analysis—highlighted.]

Collecting System Requirements

The collection and structuring of system requirements is arguably the most important activity in the systems development process because how well the information system requirements are defined influences all subsequent activities. The old saying, "garbage in, garbage out," very much applies to the system building process. ***Requirements collection*** is the process of gathering and organizing information from users, managers, business processes, and documents to understand how a proposed information system should function.

Systems analysts use a variety of techniques for collecting system requirements, including (Hoffer, George, and Valacich, 2002):

▌ *Interviews*. Analysts interview people informed about the operation and issues of the current or proposed system.

▌ *Questionnaires*. Analysts design and administer surveys to gather opinions from people informed about the operation and issues of the current or proposed system.

▌ *Observations*. Analysts observe workers at selected times to see how data are handled and what information people need to do their jobs.

▌ *Document analysis.* Analysts study business documents to discover issues, policies, and rules, as
well as concrete examples of the use of data and
information in the organization.

In addition to these techniques, there are
contemporary approaches for collecting system
requirements that include:

▌ *Critical Success Factors methodology.* A Critical
Success Factor, or CSF, is something that must go
well to ensure success for a manager, department,
division, or organization. To understand an organization's CSFs, a systems analyst interviews
people throughout the organization and asks
each person to define her own personal CSFs.
After the analyst collects these individual CSFs,
he can merge, consolidate, and refine them to
identify a broad set of organization-wide CSFs, as
shown in Figure 8.9. Table 8.3 summarizes the
strengths and weaknesses of the CSF approach.

▌ *Joint Application Design (JAD).* A JAD is a special
type of a group meeting in which all (or most)
users meet with the analyst at the same time.

During this meeting, the users jointly define and
agree upon system requirements or designs. This
process has resulted in dramatic reductions in
the length of time needed to collect requirements
or specify designs. The JAD meeting can be held
in a normal conference room or special-purpose
JAD room (see Figure 8.10). Table 8.4 summarizes the strengths and weaknesses of the JAD
approach.

Modeling Organizational Data

Data are facts that describe people, objects, or
events. A lot of different facts can be used to
describe a person: name, age, gender, race, and
occupation. To construct an information system, systems analysts must understand what
data the information system needs in order to
accomplish the intended tasks. To do this,
they use data modeling tools to collect and
describe the data to users, so as to confirm
that all needed data are known and presented
to users as useful information. Figure 8.11
shows an entity-relationship diagram (ERD), a

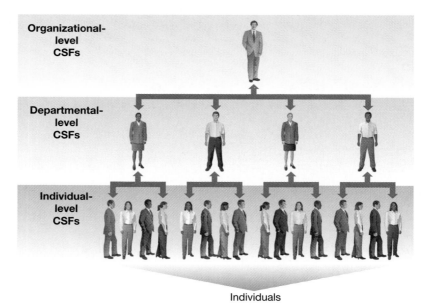

**Organizational-
level
CSFs**

**Departmental-
level
CSFs**

**Individual-
level
CSFs**

Individuals

[Figure 8.9 ➡ Merging individual CSFs to represent organization-wide CSFs.]

[Table 8.3] *Strengths and
weaknesses of the CSF
approach. (Boynton and
Zmud, 1994)*

Strengths	Weaknesses
Senior managers intuitively understand the approach and support its usage	High-level focus can lead to an oversimplification of a complex situation
Provides a method for understanding the information needs of the organization in order to make effective decisions	Difficulty in finding analysts trained to perform the CSF process that requires both understanding information systems and being able to communicate effectively with senior executives
	Method is not user-centered, but analyst focused

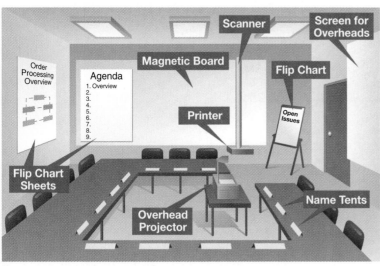

[**Figure 8.10** ➡ A JAD room.]

Adapted from J. Wood and D. Silver. *Joint Application Design*. John Wiley & Sons. 1989.

Strengths	Weaknesses
Group-based process enables more people to be involved in the development effort without adversely slowing the process	Very difficult to get all relevant users to the same place at the same time to hold a JAD meeting
Group-based process can lead to higher levels of system acceptance and quality	Requires high-level executive sponsor to ensure that adequate resources are available in order to allow widespread participation
Group involvement in the design and development process helps to ease implementation, user training, and ongoing support	

[Table 8.4] *Strengths and weaknesses of the JAD approach.*

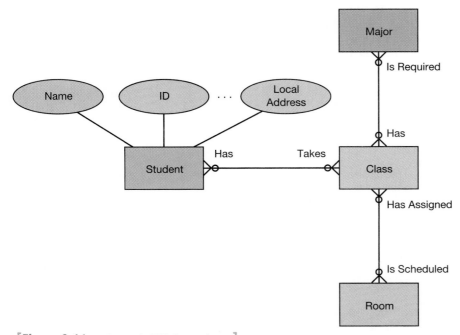

[**Figure 8.11** ➡ A sample ERD for students.]

Requirements

Data

Name	Class	GPA
Patty Nicholls	Senior	3.7
Brett Williams	Grad	2.9
Mary Shide	Fresh	3.2

Data Flows

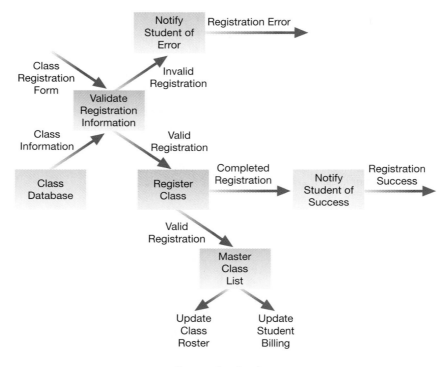

Processing Logic

```
i = read (number_of_classes)
total_hours = 0
total_grade = 0
total_gpa = 0
for j = 1 to i do
        begin
                read (course [ j ], hours [ j ], grade [ j ])
                total_hours = total_hours + hours [ j ]
                total_grade = total_grade + (hours [ j ] * grade [ j ])
        end
current_gpa = total_grade / total hours
```

[**Figure 8.12** ➡ Four key elements to development of a system: Requirements, Data, Data Flows, and Processing Logic.]

type of data model, describing students, classes, majors, and classrooms at a university. Each box in the diagram is referred to as a data entity. Each data entity may have one or more attributes that describe it. For example, a "student" entity may have attributes such as: ID, Name, and Local Address. Additionally, each data entity may be "related" to other data entities. For example, because students take classes, there is a relationship between students and classes: "Student Takes Class" and "Class Has Student." Relationships are represented in the diagram by lines drawn between related entities. Data modeling tools enable the systems analyst to represent data in a form that is easy for users to understand and critique. For more information on databases and data modeling, see Chapter 3, "Database Management."

Modeling Organizational Processes and Logic

As the name implies, **data flows** represent the movement of data through an organization or within an information system. For example, your registration for a class may be captured in a registration form on paper or on a computer terminal. After it is filled out, this form probably *flows* through several processes to validate and record the class registration, as shown as "Data Flows" in Figure 8.12. After all students have been registered, a repository of all registration information can be processed for developing class rosters or for generating

student billing information, which is shown as "Data" in Figure 8.12. **Processing logic** represents the way in which data are transformed. For example, processing logic is used to calculate students' grade point averages at the conclusion of a term, as shown in the "Processing Logic" section in Figure 8.12.

After the data, data flow, and processing logic requirements for the proposed system have been identified, analysts develop one or many possible overall approaches—sometimes called *designs*—for the information system. For example, one approach for the system may possess only basic functionality but have the advantage of being relatively easy and inexpensive to build. An analyst might also propose a more elaborate approach for the system, but it may be more difficult and more costly to build. Analysts evaluate alternative system approaches with the knowledge that different solutions yield different benefits and different costs. After a system approach is selected, then details of that particular system approach can be defined.

Phase 3: System Design

The third phase of the systems development life cycle is **system design**, as shown in Figure 8.13. As its name implies, it is during this phase that the proposed system is designed; that is, the details of the chosen approach are developed. As with analysis, many different activities must occur during system design.

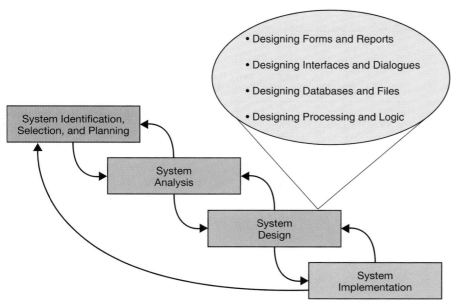

[**Figure 8.13** ➥ SDLC with Phase 3—System Design—highlighted.]

The elements that must be designed when building an information system include:

■ Forms and reports

■ Interfaces and dialogues

■ Databases and files

■ Processing and logic

Designing Forms and Reports

A *form* is a business document containing some predefined data and often including some areas where additional data can be filled in. Figure 8.14 shows a computer-based form taken from the Web homepage of Microsoft.

Using this form, users can search for a wide variety of product and service information.

A *report* is a business document containing only predefined data. In other words, reports are static documents that are used to summarize information for reading or viewing. For example, Figure 8.15 shows a report summarizing regional sales performance for several salespeople.

Designing Interfaces and Dialogues

Just as people have different ways of interacting with other people, information systems can have different ways of interacting with people.

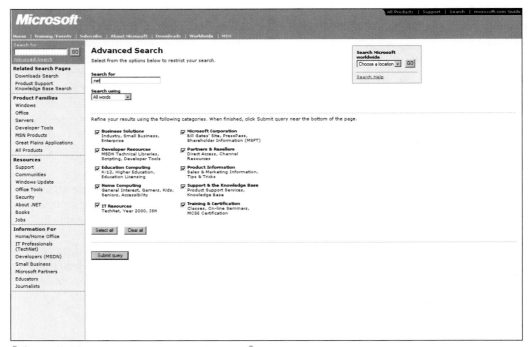

[Figure 8.14 ➥ Microsoft Web site search form.]

Ascend Systems Incorporated
SALESPERSON ANNUAL SUMMARY REPORT 2002

REGION	SALESPERSON	SSN	QUARTERLY ACTUAL SALES			
			FIRST	SECOND	THIRD	FOURT
Northwest and Mountain						
	Wachter	999-99-9999	16,500	18,600	24,300	18,0(
	Mennecke	999-99-9999	22,000	15,500	17,300	19,8(
	Wheeler	999-99-9999	19,000	12,500	22,000	28,0(
Midwest and Mid-Atlantic						
	Spurrier	999-99-9999	14,000	16,000	19,000	21,0(
	Powell	999-99-9999	7,500	16,600	10,000	8,0(
	Topi	999-99-9999	12,000	19,800	17,000	19,0(
New England						
	Speier	999-99-9999	18,000	18,000	20,000	27,0(
	Morris	999-99-9999	28,000	29,000	19,000	31,0(

[Figure 8.15 ➥ Sales summary report.]

A system interface might be text-based, communicating with you through text and forcing you to communicate with it the same way. Alternatively, a system interface could use graphics and color as a way to interact with you, providing you with color-coded windows and special icons. A system dialogue could be developed such that it does nothing and waits for you to type in a command. Or it could ask you questions to which you respond by typing in commands, or present you with menus of choices from which you select your desired options. It could even do all these things. Over the past several years, standards for user interfaces and dialogues have emerged, making things easier for both designers and users. For example, both the Macintosh and Windows operating systems are standards that are generally referred to as being **graphical user interfaces** (Figure 8.16). (See Appendix B, "Information Systems Software," for more on GUIs.)

Designing Databases and Files

To design databases and files, a systems analyst must have a thorough understanding of an organization's data and informational needs. As described previously, a systems analyst often uses data modeling tools to first gain a comprehensive understanding of all the data used by a proposed system. After the conceptual data model has been completed, typically using an entity-relationship diagram, it can be easily translated into a physical data model in a database management system. For example, Figure 8.17 shows a physical data model to keep track of student information in Microsoft Access. The physical data model is more complete (shows more information about the student) and more detailed (shows how the information is formatted) than a conceptual data model. For example, contrast Figure 8.17 with the conceptual model in Figure 8.12 that contains student information.

Designing Processing and Logic

The processing and logic operations of an information system are the steps and procedures that transform raw data inputs into new or modified information. For example, when calculating your GPA, your school needs to perform the following steps:

1. Obtain the prior grade point average, credit hours earned, and list of prior courses
2. Obtain the list of each current course, final grade, and course credit hours

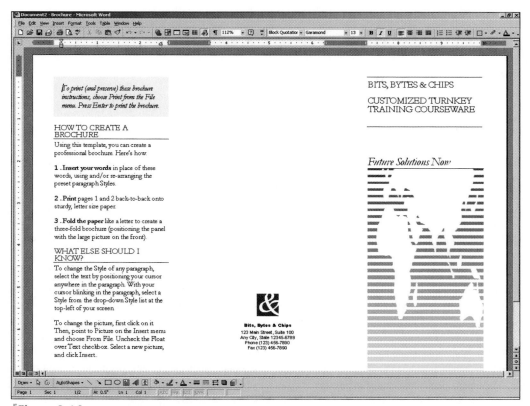

[**Figure 8.16** ➥ Most Windows-based programs follow a standard that governs the naming and placement of menus that makes it easier for users and for designers.]

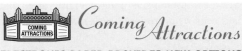

ELECTRONIC PAPER PROVIDES NEW OPTIONS FOR DESIGNING THE COMPUTER INTERFACE

One of the drawbacks of mobile computing is the small screen size and the high power requirements of traditional flat-panel displays; power requirements are particularly high for color-based displays. For years, many futurists have envisioned a day when computer displays would be lightweight, thin, and flexible like paper, as well as be inexpensive and require no external power to retain an image. Sound impossible? Well, researchers originally associated with the Massachusetts Institute of Technology (MIT) and the Xerox Palo Alto Research Center (PARC) have developed competing versions of "electronic" paper that hold most of the properties of the technology visionaries. Both versions of electronic paper use microscopic beads that change color (and retain this image indefinitely) in response to small electrical charges. The beads are encased between very thin sheets of flexible material. Current pages are about four times thicker than paper, with thinner version under development. Prototypes are impressive, and there are countless applications for electronic paper including electronic signs (that can be automatically updated by a wireless network), infinitely reusable newspapers and magazines, and improved displays for mobile phones and handheld computers. Additionally, it is projected that in the not too distant future, it will be possible to make a single book with several hundred bound pages of electronic paper (researchers believe that having pages to flip through will be the desired interface for electronic books) with enough memory in the book's spine to store the entire contents of the Library of Congress. Clearly, this is an exciting development in the history of computing technology, but it is an even more exciting development for man.

[Adapted from S. Ditlea, "The Electronic Paper Chase," **http://www.sciam.com**, *Scientific American* (November 2001).]

```
C:\MSOFFICCE\ACCESS\STUDENT.MDB                        Sunday, June 23, 2002
Table: Students                                                    Page: 1
```

Properties

Date Created:	6/23/02 10:35:41 PM	Def. Updatable:	Yes
Last Updated:	6/23/02 10:35:43 PM	Record Count:	0

Columns

Name	Type	Size
StudentID	Number (Long)	4
FirstName	Text	50
MiddleName	Text	30
LastName	Text	50
ParentsNames	Text	255
Address	Text	255
City	Text	50
State	Text	50
Region	Text	50
PostalCode	Text	20
PhoneNumber	Text	30
EmailName	Text	50
Major	Text	50
Note	Memo	-

[**Figure 8.17** ➡ An Access database that shows the physical data model for student information.]

3. Combine the prior and current credit hours into aggregate sums

4. Calculate the new grade point average

The logic and steps needed to make this calculation can be represented many ways. One method, referred to as writing pseudocode—a textual notation for describing programming code—enables the systems analyst to describe the processing steps in a manner that is similar to how a programmer might implement the steps in an actual programming language. The

Obafemi Awolowo University (OAU) in Ile-Ife is a teaching hospital located in the southwestern region of Nigeria in Western Africa, which is inhabited primarily by the Yoruba people. A few years ago, Finland and Nigeria undertook a joint collaborative project to build a low-cost patient information system for the hospital. The project team, however, faced many challenges (related primarily to culture and the context in which Yorubaland was situated) that provided important lessons for IT developers as to the difficulties one may face when trying to develop and implement an information system in a foreign land. Politically, Yoruba had a kingship and a hierarchical model. Culturally, there was a significant gender difference in the society, and the traditional religion had a "pantheon of named gods." However, more than the culture, it was the context that caused significant problems for the IT developers. The climate in Yoruba was hot and humid, which led to technical problems with computers. There was a significant lack of infrastructure in terms of electrical supply, telecommunications availability, finance, and trans-portation. To add to this problem, there was a "lack of awareness" among the hospital staff as to the necessity of an information system. Moreover, the hardware and software vendors in the region had a "sell and run" strategy—it was difficult to find anyone to provide after-sales support and maintenance. The systems development team realized that in order to be successful in such an environment, it was important to be extremely sensitive to the cultural and contextual issues. Instead of adopting western systems development methodologies and information systems to the context of Yoruba, they focused on building a new systems development methodology and information system that was fit for the Nigerian context and so far have achieved success.

[Adapted from G. Walsham, *Making a World of Difference: IS in a Global Context*, Chichester: John Wiley & Sons, Ltd., 2001; M. Korpela, "Traditional Culture or Political Economy? On the Root Causes of Organizational Obstacles of IT in Developing Countries," *Information Technology for Development* 7, no. 1 (1996): 29–42.]

Global Perspective

The Difficulty of Managing International Development Teams

"Processing Logic" in Figure 8.12 is an example of pseudocode. Other tools used by systems analysts during this activity include structure charts and decision trees. Converting pseudocode, structure charts, and decision trees into actual program code during system implementation is a very straightforward process.

Phase 4: System Implementation

Many separate activities occur during *system implementation*, the fourth phase of the systems development life cycle, as highlighted in Figure 8.18. One group of activities focuses on transforming the system design into a working information system that can be used by the organization. These activities include software programming and testing. A second group of activities focuses on preparing the organization for using the new information systems. These activities include system conversion, documentation, user training, and support. This section briefly describes what occurs during system implementation.

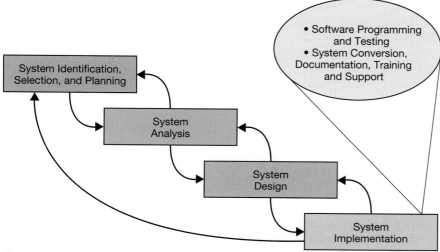

[**Figure 8.18** ➥ SDLC with Phase 4—System Implementation—highlighted.]

Software Programming and Testing

Programming is the process of transforming the system design into a working computer system. During this transformation, both processing and testing should occur in parallel. As you might expect, a broad range of tests are conducted before a system is complete, including developmental, alpha, and beta testing (see Table 8.5).

System Conversion, Documentation, Training, and Support

System conversion is the process of decommissioning the current system (automated or manual) and installing the new system in the organization. Effective conversion of a system requires not only that the new software be installed, but also that users be effectively trained and supported. System conversion can be performed in at least four ways, as shown in Figure 8.19.

Many types of documentation must be produced for an information system. Program-mers develop system documentation that details the inner workings of the system to ease future maintenance. A second type of documentation is user-related documentation, which is not typically written by programmers or analysts, but by users or professional technical writers. The range of documents can include the following:

- User and reference guides
- User training and tutorials
- Installation procedures and troubleshooting suggestions

In addition to documentation, users may also need training and ongoing support to use a new system effectively. Different types of training and support require different levels of investment by the organization. Self-paced training and tutorials are the least expensive options, and one-on-one training is the most expensive. Table 8.6 summarizes various user training options.

[Table 8.5] *General testing types, their focus, and who performs them.*

Testing Type	Focus	Performed by
Developmental	Testing the correctness of individual modules and the integration of multiple modules	Programmer
Alpha	Testing of overall system to see whether it meets design requirements	Software tester
Beta	Testing of the capabilities of the system in the user environment with actual data	Actual system users

Brief Case: Profile of a Software Tester

A software tester spends most of his time trying to break software (Software Testing Institute, 2002). Breaking software is referred to in the computer industry as "finding bugs." A bug is a programming error, design flaw, or anything else that results in the computer program not running as intended. Software testers spend countless hours trying to identify problems, typically long before the software is released to a widespread audience. Most software testers work, as you would guess, for software and computer companies such as Microsoft, IBM, or Netscape Communications. Software testers also work for companies in banking, insurance, and literally any other company devoted to developing high-quality software. In most cases, software testers are not systems developers, but many know how to program. Organizations have discovered that testers find more errors if the people testing the software are separate from the development group. Many times, companies give cash bonuses to testers for each bug found to give them a strong motivation to find these pesky errors. Because testers must not only find errors but also describe them after they are found, software testers must also have good communication skills and be detail-oriented, patient, self-motivated, and creative. In addition to looking for bugs, software testers are often assigned to provide customer support and training because of their intricate knowledge of how a new system works. Creating high-quality software requires a cooperative team of system designers, programmers, and testers. Good software testers are in high demand. So, if you like breaking things, and getting paid for it, maybe you would be a good software tester.

[Adapted from Software Testing Institute, **http://www.ondaweb.com/sti/** (2002).]

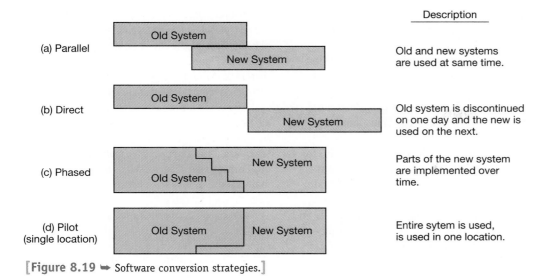

Description

(a) Parallel — Old System / New System — Old and new systems are used at same time.

(b) Direct — Old System / New System — Old system is discontinued on one day and the new is used on the next.

(c) Phased — New System / Old System — Parts of the new system are implemented over time.

(d) Pilot (single location) — Old System / New System — Entire sytem is used, is used in one location.

[**Figure 8.19** ➡ Software conversion strategies.]

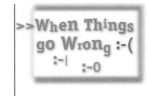

Nike Software Failure Costs the Company Millions

Developing software is a tough business, and most companies anguish over the development or acquisition process. A recent industry survey reports that almost 75 percent of all software projects had a significant cost or time overrun, were completed with fewer features than promised, or were a total failure (Berinato, 2001). For example, Nike recently accused its supply-chain software provider of providing low-quality software (Konicki, 2001). The $400 million software system placed multiple orders for shoes in some instances and completely lost orders in others. The software vender accused Nike of failing to follow its recommendations for deploying the system—to deploy it cautiously in stages to minimize risk and assure that everything was working as planned. Instead, Nike went live with the system all at once with thousands of distributors and suppliers. Nike estimates that the software glitch cost the company between $80 and $100 million in sales in early 2001, and that is a lot of shoes!

[Adapted from S. Konicki, "Nike Just Didn't Do It Right, Says I2 Technologies," **http://www. informationweek.com**, *InformationWeek* (March 5, 2001); S. Berinato, "The Secret to Software Success," **http://www.cio.com**, *CIO Magazine* (July 1, 2001).]

Training Option	Description
Tutorial	One person taught at one time by a human or by paper-based exercises
Course	Several people taught at one time
Computer-aided instruction	One person taught at one time by the computer system
Interactive training manuals	Combination of tutorials and computer-aided instruction
Resident expert	Expert on call to assist users as needed
Software help components	Built-in system components designed to train and troubleshoot problems
External sources	Vendors and training providers to provide tutorials, courses, and other training activities

[**Table 8.6**] *User training options.*

In addition to training, providing ongoing education and problem-solving assistance for users is also necessary. This is commonly referred to as system support, which is often provided by a special group of people in the organization who make up an information center or help desk. Support personnel must have strong communication skills and be good problem solvers, in addition to being expert users of the system. An alternative option for a system not developed internally is to outsource support activities to a vendor specializing in technical system support and training. Regardless of how support is provided, it is an ongoing issue that must be managed effectively for the company to realize the maximum benefits of a system.

Phase 5: System Maintenance

After an information system is installed, it is essentially in the maintenance phase of the SDLC. In the maintenance phase, one person within the systems development group is responsible for collecting maintenance requests from system users. After they are collected, requests are analyzed so that the developer can better understand how the proposed change might alter the system and what business benefits and necessities might result from such a change. If the change request is approved, a system change is designed and then implemented. As with the initial development of the system, implemented changes are formally reviewed and tested before installation into operational systems. The *system maintenance* process parallels the process used for the initial development of the information system, as shown in Figure 8.20. Interestingly, it is during system maintenance that the largest part of the system development effort occurs.

The question must be, then, why does all this maintenance occur? It is not as if software wears out in the physical manner that cars, buildings, or other physical goods do. Correct? Yes, but software must still be maintained. The types of maintenance are summarized in Table 8.7.

As with adaptive maintenance, both perfective and preventive maintenance are typically a much lower priority than corrective maintenance. Over the life of a system, corrective maintenance is most likely to occur after initial system installation or after major system changes. This means that adaptive, perfective, and preventive maintenance activities can lead to corrective maintenance activities if they are not carefully designed and implemented.

As you can see, there is more to system maintenance than you might think. Lots of time, effort, and money are spent in this final phase of a system's development, and it is important to follow prescribed, structured steps. In fact, the approach to systems development described in this chapter, from the initial phase of identifying, selecting, and planning for systems, to the final phase of system maintenance, is a very structured and systematic

Human Resource Management

Once an information system has been implemented, many companies opt to outsource the support of the system to outside organizations. The reason for outsourcing is often to avoid costs and complexities associated with hiring skilled IT professionals for supporting the information systems. Burger King recently outsourced its information systems support. The company announced that it has signed a contract with Perot Systems, which will be providing IT services for its most critical business information systems. One of the primary responsibilities of Perot Systems will be to provide help desk support, enterprise system management, data management, and global information system management for Burger King's many information systems. Perot Systems will also be involved in decentralizing Burger King's information systems from those of its parent company, Diageo, plc. As part of the contract, Perot Systems will not only provide support, but will also make several enhancements to the company's existing information systems, which will significantly increase efficiency and flexibility within Burger King. By drawing on the technological innovations and expertise of Perot Systems, Burger King will be able to optimize its IT environment and keep its operating costs down. At the same time, the company will be able to keep its labor costs from rising. The efficiency and flexibility will enable Burger King to adapt smoothly to the changing and fast-paced business world of fast food.

[Adapted from "Burger King Corporation to Outsource Information Technology (IT) Support to Perot Systems: Latest Move Toward Separation From Parent Company," **http://www.perotsystems.com/frmbase.asp?URL=/Content/newsandevents/news/Sept_5_2001.html**.]

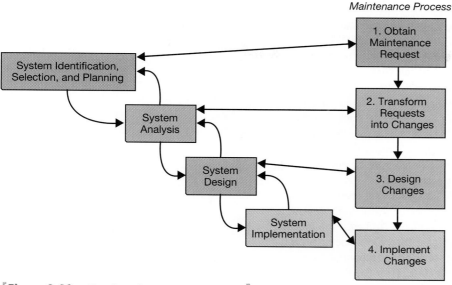

Maintenance Process

[**Figure 8.20** ➥ Mapping of maintenance to SDLC.]

Maintenance Type	Description
Corrective maintenance	Making changes to an information system to repair flaws in the design, coding, or implementation
Adaptive maintenance	Making changes to an information system to evolve its functionality to accommodate changing business needs or to migrate it to a different operating environment
Perfective maintenance	Making enhancements to improve processing performance or interface usability, or adding desired, but not necessarily required, system features (in other words, "bells and whistles")
Preventive maintenance	Making changes to a system to reduce the chance of future system failure

[Table 8.7] *Types of software maintenance.*

process. Each phase is fairly well prescribed and requires active involvement by systems people, users, and managers. It is likely that you will have numerous opportunities to participate in the acquisition or development of a new system for an organization for which you currently work or will work in the future. Now that you have an understanding of the process, you should be better equipped to make a positive contribution to the success of any systems development project.

OTHER APPROACHES TO DESIGNING AND BUILDING SYSTEMS

The systems development life cycle is one approach to managing the development process and is a very good approach to follow when

the requirements for the information system are highly structured and straightforward— for example, for a payroll or inventory system. Today, organizations need a broad variety of information systems, not just payroll and inventory systems, for which requirements are either very hard to specify in advance or are constantly changing. For example, an organization's Web site is likely to be an information system with constantly changing requirements. How many Web sites have you visited in which the content or layout seemed to change almost every day? For this type of system, the SDLC might work as a development approach, but it would not be optimal. In this section, we describe three approaches for developing flexible information systems: prototyping, rapid application development, and object-oriented analysis and design.

Prototyping

Prototyping is a systems development methodology that uses a "trial and error" approach for discovering how a system should operate. You may think that this does not sound like a process at all; however, you probably use prototyping all the time in many of your day-to-day activities, but you just do not know it! For example, when you buy new clothes you likely use prototyping—that is, trial and error—by trying on several shirts before making a selection.

Figure 8.21 diagrams the prototyping process when applied to identifying/determining system requirements. To begin the process, the system designer interviews one or several users of the system, either individually or as a group, using a JAD. After the designer gains a general understanding of what the users want, he develops a prototype of the new system as quickly as possible to share with the users. The users may like what they see or ask for changes. If the users request changes, the designer modifies the prototype and again shares it with them. This process of sharing and refinement continues until the users approve the functionality of the system.

Rapid Application Development (RAD)

Rapid application development (RAD) is a four-phase systems development methodology that combines prototyping, computer-based development tools, special management practices, and close user involvement. (Hoffer,

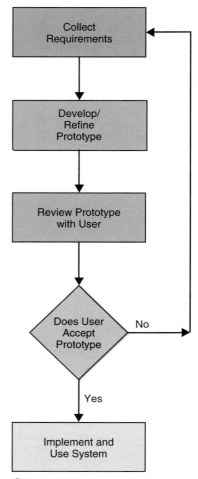

[**Figure 8.21** ➡ The prototyping process uses a trial-and-error approach to discovering how a system should operate.]

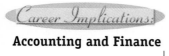

Accounting and Finance

Requirements analysis is one of the critical aspects of prototyping, since the quality of the prototype depends a great deal on the type and quality of information assimilated from the users. Various tools have now been marketed that make the requirements analysis phase a lot easier for system designers and developers. Montana State Fund was looking for a requirements analysis and management tool that was going to be easy to implement and cost effective, yet robust enough to handle all the complexities of its information systems project. The company found the solution in Analyst Pro from Goda Software. The company did not have the money or the time to invest in large-scale products, so it was looking for something that was going to provide quick and easy solutions. The Analyst Pro tool met most of its business needs. It is known to be a "hassle-free" tool that provides software requirements management, tracing, specification, and analysis, and can be effectively used in any phase of the systems development life cycle. It has an integrated workflow management feature that allowed the accounting and finance personnel to efficiently communicate all the requirements to the systems development team members. The tool has an added feature that is extremely helpful. It is designed in such a way that the application requirements model is separated from the business/process requirements model in the initial stages, but can be integrated later. This separation enables users to focus on these two critical aspects of systems design separately, instead of confusing them together.

[Adapted from **http://www.analysttool.com**, copyright 2000–2001 Goda Software.]

George, and Valacich, 2002; McConnell, 1996; Martin, 1991). RAD has four phases: 1) requirements planning, 2) user design, 3) construction, and 4) the move to the new system. Phase 1, requirements planning, is similar to the first two phases of the SDLC, in which the system is planned and requirements are analyzed. To gain intensive user involvement, the RAD methodology encourages the use of JAD sessions to collect requirements. Where RAD becomes radical is during Phase 2, in which users of the information system become intensively involved in the design process. Computer-aided software engineering (CASE) and other advanced development tools (see Appendix B, "Information Systems Software") are used to structure requirements and develop prototypes quickly. As prototypes are developed and refined, they are continually reviewed with users in additional JAD sessions. Like prototyping, RAD is a process in which requirements, designs, and the system itself are developed via iterative refinement, as shown in Figure 8.22. In a sense, with the RAD approach the people building the system and the users of that system keep cycling back and forth between Phase 2 (user design) and Phase 3 (construction) until the system is finished. As a result, RAD requires close cooperation between users and designers to be successful. This means that management must

actively support the development project and make it a priority for everyone involved.

Object-Oriented Analysis and Design

Object-oriented analysis and design (OOA&D) is very similar to other analysis and design approaches (Booch, 1990; Coad and Yourdon, 1991; Halladay and Wiebel, 1993; Hoffer, George, and Valacich, 2002). For example, when using the SDLC approach, systems analysts primarily follow a top-down process in which the system requirements are broken down into smaller and smaller pieces until specific programming modules can be defined, programmed, and pieced together to yield a system. Similarly, data and their interrelationships are modeled by the analysts, and these conceptual models are turned over to a programmer who actually implements these data models in a database management system. In most instances, a systems analyst develops a high-level design for the data and the processing and provides this design to programmers, who actually implement the design in programming code and databases. The analyst often never does any coding. This is different with the OOA&D approach, due to the tight coupling between the methods and data and between the conceptual model of the system

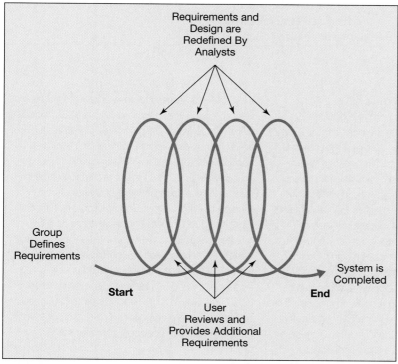

[**Figure 8.22** ➡ Iterative refinement is a key to the success of RAD.]

and its actual implementation. OOA&D can turn every programmer into an analyst and every analyst into a programmer. What this means is that the analyst using an OOA&D approach can be thinking simultaneously right from the start about the "what" (the data) and the "how" (the operations to be performed) as he defines all the relevant objects that the system entails. Furthermore, if an object-oriented programming language is being used, it enables the design and implementation of the objects to happen quickly and simultaneously. In sum, OOA&D is a more integrative prototyping process than the SDLC approach, in which data and operations on the data are modeled separately and at a concep-

tual level and are later implemented and brought together in a subsequent phase of the systems development process.

This section has described other popular information systems development approaches beyond the SDLC. Although each of these approaches has been discussed separately, the wise organization and skilled analyst often utilize multiple methods when developing a single system. What should be clear to you is that no approach is perfect and that all have strengths and weaknesses (see Table 8.8). To put this another way, a skilled systems developer is much like a skilled craftsman, with many tools at his disposal. The skilled craftsman chooses the most appropriate tool and

[Table 8.8] *Strengths and weaknesses of prototyping, RAD, and object-oriented analysis and design approaches.*

Approach	Strengths	Weaknesses
Prototyping	Develops close working relationship between designer and users; works well for messy and hard-to-define problems	Not practical with a large number of users; system may be built too quickly, which could result in lower quality
Rapid Application Development	Active user involvement in design process; easier implementation due to user involvement	Systems are often narrowly focused—limits future evolution; system may be built too quickly, which could result in lower quality
Object-Oriented Analysis and Design	Integration of data and processing during design should lead to higher-quality systems; reuse of common modules makes development and maintenance easier	Very difficult to train analysts and programmers on the object-oriented approach; limited use of common modules

Information Systems

Many software gurus are predicting that Linux will become a popular systems software in the near future. The primary reason is the fact that Linux is an open-source software, and hence its source code is available for free over the Internet, making it easy to modify it. Linux is now also available for different types of hardware such as PCs and mainframes. However, the primary reason that many organizations are contemplating switching to Linux is the fact that it can save a lot of money. For example, a company can just buy a single copy of Linux for $159 and then make as many copies as required without incurring any additional costs. The same company, if interested in installing Windows, will have to pay $2400 for the Windows software and $150 for each PC that will be connected to

the Windows server. However, software gurus are asking organizations to be cautious about installing Linux. Since it is an open-source software, it is not controlled by one vendor. Moreover, many of the applications required by an organization may not be available on Linux. Finally, technology staff in many organizations may not be experienced in running Linux systems. So far, companies that have installed Linux are happy with its performance. Weather.com (based in Atlanta) runs its Weather Channel Web site on Linux and is extremely satisfied with its performance. As long as proper testing has been conducted, and companies are aware of the downsides of Linux, this operating system can definitely become one of the most popular and cheapest systems software in the future.

[Adapted from Sari Kalin, "Free Lunch, Anyone?" **http://www.darwinmag.com** (December 2000).]

approach for the task at hand. Using one systems development approach or tool for all systems and problems is akin to using only a hammer to build a house. Building a house with just a hammer might be possible, but it would probably be a strange-looking house!

NEED FOR ALTERNATIVES TO BUILDING SYSTEMS YOURSELF

Building systems in-house with the IS staff is always an option to consider. Many times, however, this is not a feasible solution. The following are four situations in which you might need to consider alternative development strategies.

Situation 1: Limited IS Staff

Often, an organization does not have the capability to build a system itself. Perhaps its IS staff is small or deployed on other activities such as maintaining a small network and helping users with problems on a day-to-day basis. This limited staff may simply not have the capability to take on an in-house development project without hiring several analysts or programmers, which is very expensive in today's labor market.

Situation 2: IS Staff Has Limited Skill Set

In other situations, the IS staff may not have the skills needed to develop a particular kind of system. This has been especially true with the explosion of the Web; many organizations are having outside groups manage their sites. For example, Walt Disney contracted the development and management of its Web site and the sites of many of its subsidiaries, including ABC News and ESPN, to a company called Starwave.com. Starwave was founded by Paul Allen, one of Bill Gates's initial partners at Microsoft and owner of the Portland Trailblazers, Seattle Seahawks, and numerous other companies (**http://www.paulallen.com**). This relationship continued until 1998 when Disney purchased Starwave and transformed it into the Walt Disney Internet Group (Court, 1998). In essence, Disney did not initially have the right set of skills to move onto the Internet so it had an outside organization develop and manage its Web sites. Once it realized the strategic importance of the Internet, Disney purchased this expertise by buying Starwave. In sum, although the existing IS staff at Disney was highly skilled at producing and managing traditional applications, the sudden call

for Web-based systems required that Disney seek outside help. It is not as if the IS director can tell Mr. Eisner—the CEO of Walt Disney—that Disney cannot build a new Web site because the IS staff does not have the necessary skills to build it! Fortunately, there are alternatives to having the IS staff build the system; the IS director can simply tap into specialized skills not present within the existing IS staff that are available on the open market.

Situation 3: IS Staff Is Overworked

In some organizations, the IS staff may simply not have the time to work on all the systems that are required or desired by the organization. Obviously, the number of people dedicated to new development is not infinite. Therefore, you must have ways to prioritize development projects. In most cases, systems that are of strategic importance or that affect the whole organization are likely to receive a higher priority than those that offer only minor benefits or affect only one department or a couple of people in a department. Nonetheless, the IS manager must find a way to support all users, even when the IS staff may be tied up with other "higher-priority" projects.

Situation 4: Problems with Performance of IS Staff

Earlier in this book we discussed how and why systems development projects could sometimes be risky. Often the efforts of IS departments are derailed due to staff turnover, changing requirements, shifts in technology, or budget constraints. Regardless of the reason, the result is the same: another failed (or flawed) system. Given the large expenditures in staff time and training as well as the high risk associated with systems development efforts, the prudent manager tries to limit the risk of any project as much as possible. What if it were possible to see the completed system to know what it looked like before development began? Being able to see into the future would certainly help you learn more about the system and whether it would meet your needs, and it would help to lower the risk of a project. When building a system in-house, it is obviously not possible to see into the future. However, using some of the alternative methods described in this chapter, you can, in fact, see what a completed system might look like. These methods will enable you to know what you are buying, which greatly lowers the risk of a project.

Team Work

When and which development approach to employ?

Is it managerially possible (feasible) to employ all the systems analysis and design techniques and methodologies discussed in this chapter? Is that too much to handle? Why? If it is feasible, under what conditions would you advise it, and under what conditions would you recommend employing only some of the methodologies?

COMMON ALTERNATIVES TO IN-HOUSE SYSTEMS DEVELOPMENT

Any project has at least four different systems development options. Previously, we discussed the first option: building the system in-house with your IS staff. The other options are:

▌ External acquisition

▌ Outsourcing

▌ End-user development

The following sections examine each of these options in closer detail to see how one or more of them might fit the four situations described in the preceding section.

External Acquisition

Purchasing an existing system from an outside vendor such as IBM, EDS, or Accenture is referred to as *external acquisition*. How does external acquisition of an information system work? Think about the process that you might use when buying a car. Do you simply walk into the first dealership you see, tell them you need a car, and see what they try to sell you? You had better not. Probably you have done some up-front analysis and know how much money you can afford to spend and what your needs are. If you have done your homework, you probably have an idea of what you want and which dealership can provide the type of car you desire (see Figure 8.23).

This up-front analysis of your needs can be extremely helpful in narrowing your options and can save you a lot of time. Understanding your needs can also help you sift through the salesmen's hype that you are likely to encounter from one dealer to the next as each tries to sell you on why his model is perfect for you. After getting some information, you may want to take a couple of promising models for a test drive, whereby you actually get behind the wheel and see how well the car fits you and your driving habits. You might even talk to other people who have owned this type of car to see how they feel about it. Ultimately, you are the one who has to evaluate all the different cars to see which one is best for you. They may all be good cars; however, one may fit your needs just a little better than the others.

The external acquisition of an information system is very similar to the purchase of a car. When you acquire an IS you should do some analysis of your specific needs. For example, how much can you afford to spend, what basic functionality is required, and approximately how many people will use the system? Next, you can begin to "shop" for the new system by asking potential vendors to provide information about the systems that they have to offer. After evaluating this information, it may become clear that several vendors have systems that are worth considering. You may ask those vendors to come to your

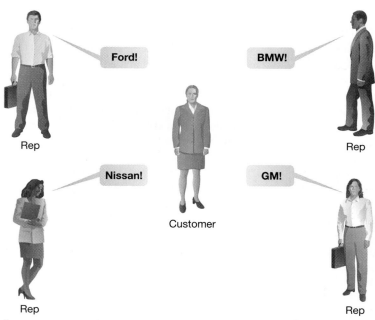

Rep

Ford!

BMW!

Rep

Nissan!

GM!

Rep

Customer

Rep

[Figure 8.23 ➡ A prospective car buyer with a "wish list."]

organization and set up their systems so that you and your colleagues are able to "test drive" them. Seeing how people react to the systems and seeing how each system performs in the organizational environment can help you "see" exactly what you are buying. By seeing the actual system and how it performs with real users, with real or simulated data, you can get a much clearer idea of whether that system fits your needs. When you take a car for a test drive, you learn how the car meets your needs. By seeing how the system meets your needs before you buy, you can greatly reduce the risk associated with acquiring that system.

Steps in External Acquisition

In many cases, your organization will use a competitive bid process for making an external acquisition. In the competitive bid process, vendors are given an opportunity to propose systems that meet the organization's needs. The goal of the competitive process is to help the organization ensure that it gets the best system at the lowest possible price. Most competitive external acquisition processes have at least five general steps:

1. System identification, selection, and planning
2. Systems analysis
3. Development of a Request for Proposal (RFP)
4. Proposal evaluation
5. Vendor selection

You have already learned about the first two steps because they apply when you build a system yourself, as well as when you purchase a system through an external vendor. Step 3, development of a Request for Proposal, is where the external acquisition process differs significantly from in-house development.

Development of a Request for Proposal (RFP)

A **Request for Proposal**, or RFP, is simply a report that is used to tell vendors what your requirements are and to invite them to provide information about how they might be able to meet those requirements (see Figure 8.24). An RFP is sent to vendors who might potentially be interested in providing hardware and/or software for the system.

Among the areas that may be covered in an RFP are:

▌ A summary of existing systems and applications

▌ Reliability, backup, and service requirements

▌ Requirements for system performance and features

▌ The criteria that will be used to evaluate proposals

▌ Timetable and budget constraints (how much you can spend)

The RFP is then sent to prospective vendors along with an invitation to present their bids for the project. Eventually, you will likely receive a number of proposals to evaluate. If, on the other hand, you do not receive many proposals, it may be necessary to rethink the requirements—perhaps the requirements are greater than the budget limitations, or the timetable is too short. In some situations, you may first need to send out a preliminary Request for Information simply to gather information from prospective vendors. This will help you determine whether, indeed, the desired system is feasible or even possible. If you determine that it is, you can then send out an RFP.

Proposal Evaluation

The fourth step in external acquisition is to evaluate proposals received from vendors. This evaluation may include viewing system demonstrations, evaluating the performance of those systems, and examining criteria important to the organization and judging how the proposed systems "stack up" to those criteria. Demonstrations are a good way to get a feel for the different systems' capabilities. Just as you can go to the showroom to look over a new car and get a feel for whether it meets your needs, it is also possible to screen various systems through a demonstration from the vendor. During a demonstration, a sales team from the vendor presents an oral presentation about their system, its features, and cost, followed by a demonstration of the actual system. In some cases this may take place at your location; other times, it may take place at the vendor's facility or at one of the vendor's clients, particularly when the system is not easily transportable. Although such demonstrations are often useful in helping you understand the features of different systems being proposed, they are rarely enough in and of themselves to warrant purchasing the system without further evaluation.

One of the ways you can better evaluate a proposed system is through **systems benchmarking**. Benchmark programs are sample programs or jobs that simulate your computer workload. You can have benchmarks designed to test portions of the system that are most critical to your needs based on your systems analysis. A benchmark might test how long it takes to calculate a set of numbers, how long

[Figure 8.24 ➥ Sample RFP document for an information systems project.]

it takes to access a set of records in a database, or how long it would take to access certain information given a certain number of concurrent users. Some common system benchmarks include:

- Response time given a specified number of users
- Time to sort records
- Time to retrieve a set of records
- Time to produce a given report
- Time to read in a set of data

In addition, vendors may also supply benchmarks that you can use, although you should not rely solely on vendor information. For popular systems, you may be able to rely on system benchmarks published in computer trade journals such as *PC Magazine* or *PC Week*. However, in most cases, demos and benchmarks alone do not provide all the information you need to make a purchase. The systems analysis phase should have revealed some specific requirements for the new system. These requirements may be listed as criteria that the organization can use to further evaluate vendor proposals. Depending upon what you are purchasing—hardware, software, or both—the criteria you use will change. Table 8.9 provides examples of commonly used evaluation criteria.

Vendor Selection

In most cases, more than one system will meet your needs, just as more than one car will usually meet your needs. However, some probably "fit" better than others. In these cases, you should have a way of prioritizing or ranking competing proposals. One way of doing this is by devising a scoring system for each of the criteria and benchmarking results. For example, an organization might create a scoring system in which benchmarking results might be worth 100 total points, while online help features are worth only 50 points. All the points for each criterion are then summed to give an overall score for each system. Then the system with the highest score (or one of the systems among several with the highest scores) is selected. Figure 8.25 shows an example of a form that could be used to evaluate systems and choose a vendor using this method.

In the example shown in Figure 8.25, System A looks like the best solution because it scored highest. Using such an evaluation method, it is possible that scoring low on a given criterion might exclude otherwise outstanding systems from being purchased. You can see that Systems B and C fared very poorly on the Vendor Support criterion. It is possible

[Table 8.9] *Commonly used evaluation criteria.*

Hardware Criteria	Software Criteria	Other Criteria
Clock speed of CPU	Memory requirements	Installation
Memory requirements	Help features	Testing
Secondary storage (including capacity, access time, and so on)	Usability	Price
	Learnability	
Video display size	Number of features supported	
Printer speed	Training and documentation	
	Maintenance and repair	

Criterion	Max Points (or weight)	Systems Being Evaluated (Score)		
		A	**B**	**C**
Disk capacity	20	10	17	12
Compatibility	50	45	30	25
Usability	30	12	30	20
Vendor Support	35	27	16	5
Benchmark Results	50	40	28	30
(add as needed...)				
Total	185	134	121	92

[Figure 8.25 ➥ Sample system evaluation form with subset of criteria.]

that those systems do not have very good vendor support. However, it is also possible that the vendor did not adequately communicate its commitment to support, perhaps because it did not realize it was such an important issue. Therefore, it is very important for you to communicate with vendors about the evaluation process and which criteria you value most highly.

Companies may use other less-formalized approaches to evaluate vendors. Sometimes they use simple checklists; other times they use a more subjective process. Regardless of the mechanism, eventually a company completes the evaluation stage and selects a vendor, ending the external acquisition process.

Outsourcing

A related, but different, alternative to purchasing an existing system is outsourcing. With the external acquisition option, an organization typically purchases a single system from an outside vendor. **Outsourcing** is the practice of turning over responsibility of some to all of an organization's information systems development and operations to an outside firm. Outsourcing includes a variety of working relationships. The outside firm, or service provider, may develop your information systems applications and house them within their organization, they may run your applications on their computers, or they may develop systems to run on existing computers within your organization. Anything is fair game in an outsourcing arrangement.

In recent years, outsourcing has become a very popular option for organizations. For example, the worldwide market for computing services is projected to grow from $439 billion in 2001 to more than $700 billion by 2005 (CIO, 2001). Of these amounts, spending on outsourcing is projected to be around $56 billion in 2000 and over $100 billion in 2005 (Mosquera, 2001). In a recent A.T. Kearney study, 90 percent of the 26 multinational companies it surveyed had outsourced at least some of its operations (Caldwell, 1996). Clearly, outsourcing is big business.

Why Outsourcing?

There are many reasons that a firm might outsource some (or all) of its information systems services. Some of these are old reasons, but some are new to today's environment (Applegate and McFarlan, 1999):

■ *Cost and quality concerns*: In many cases it is possible to achieve higher-quality systems at a lower price through economies of scale, better management of hardware, lower labor costs, and better software licenses on the part of a service provider.

■ *Problems in IS performance*: IS departments may have problems meeting acceptable service standards due to cost overruns, delayed systems, underutilized systems, or poorly performing systems. In such cases, organizational management may attempt to increase reliability through outsourcing.

■ *Supplier pressures*: Perhaps not surprisingly, some of the largest service providers are also the largest suppliers of computer equipment: IBM, Hewlett-Packard, and Compaq. In some cases, the aggressive sales forces of these suppliers are able to convince senior managers at other organizations to outsource their IS functions.

■ *Simplifying, downsizing, and reengineering*: Organizations under competitive pressure often attempt to focus on only their "core competencies."

Sales and marketing personnel are often swamped with a large volume of business cards from their customers and other contacts. In the past, people developed their own methods—address books, spreadsheets, and personal databases—for dealing with all this information. Unfortunately, most approaches were very inefficient. A new technology being purchased by many corporations is now available for making the life of many sales and marketing personnel a lot easier. The Corex CardScan Executive 600c/V6 is a small color scanner that converts business cards into a contact database which can be connected to one's PDA, cell phone, or e-mail address books. The scanner is portable and can be used to update and share contact information over the Web, which has proved to be extremely useful for sales personnel who travel frequently. The scanner also has software that can be installed on a user's portable computer. With the help of the software, a user can select an address in the database, and a MapQuest map can be generated for it on the user's browser. The CardScan can scan up to 100 business cards in less than five minutes. Today, it is being recognized as a tremendous productivity booster for all business users, especially sales and marketing personnel.

Career Implications:

Marketing

[Adapted from **http://www.zdnet.com/supercenter/stories/review/**.]

Web Search

WEB SEARCH OPPORTUNITY: Outsourcing has become very popular. Many observers believe that outsourcing will continue to grow as a way for organizations to develop and operate their information systems. Search the Web sites of some popular information systems trade magazines to find out the latest news and predictions about outsourcing. Start with **http://www.computerworld.com** and **http://www.infoworld.com**. Then you might want to look at **http://www.outsourcing-center.com** for a host of materials on outsourcing. Prepare a five-page report on outsourcing for your instructor that analyzes current outsourcing practices and provides forecasts for the future of outsourcing.

In many cases, organizations simply decide that running information systems is not one of their "core competencies" and decide to outsource this function to companies such as IBM and EDS, whose primary competency is developing and maintaining information systems.

- *Financial factors*: When firms turn over their information systems to a service provider, they can sometimes strengthen their balance sheets by liquefying their IT assets. Also, if users perceive that they are actually paying for their IT services rather than simply having them provided by an in-house staff, they may use those services more wisely and perceive them to be of greater value.

- *Organizational culture*: Political or organizational problems are often difficult for an IS group to overcome. However, an external service provider often brings enough clout, devoid of any organizational or functional ties, to streamline IS operations as needed.

- *Internal irritants*: Tension between end-users and the IS staff is sometimes difficult to eliminate. At times this tension can intrude on the daily operations of the organization, and the idea of a remote, external, relatively neutral IS group can be appealing. Whether or not the tension between users and the IS staff (or service provider) is really eliminated is open to question; however, simply having the IS group external to the organization can remove a lingering thorn in management's side.

Managing the IS Outsourcing Relationship

McFarlan and Nolan (1995) argue that the ongoing management of an outsourcing alliance is the single most important aspect of the outsourcing project's success. Their recommendations for the best management are:

1. A strong, active CIO and staff should continually manage the legal and professional relationship with the outsourcing firm.

2. Clear, realistic performance measurements of the systems and of the outsourcing arrangement, such as tangible and intangible costs and benefits, should be developed.

3. The interface between the customer and the outsourcer should have multiple levels (for example, links to deal with policy and relationship issues, and links to deal with operational and tactical issues).

Managing outsourcing alliances in this way has important implications for the success of the relationship. For example, in addition to making sure a firm has a strong CIO and staff, McFarlan and Nolan recommend that firms assign full-time relationship managers and coordinating groups lower in the organization to "manage" the IS outsourcing project. This means that as people within the IS function are pulled away from traditional IS tasks such

---

Brief Case: A Strategic Outsourcing Relationship for DuPont

An example of a strategic outsourcing relationship in which all parties are sharing risks and rewards is among the chemical giant DuPont, Accenture, and Computer Sciences Corporation (CSC) (Verity, 1997; Accenture, 2001; Computer Sciences Corporation, 2001). In this 10-year, $4 billion-plus deal, DuPont is hoping to reduce spending on IS by as much as 10 percent. In this agreement, CSC and Accenture are developing new products and services that are being used internally by DuPont and being sold to DuPont's subsidiaries in other countries. Some of these products are also being sold to DuPont's competitors in the chemical and energy industries. As part of the deal, CSC took over 13 of DuPont's data centers and hired 2,600 of its 4,200 data processing employees, while Accenture hired 500. The fees that CSC and Accenture are receiving from DuPont are proportional to the measurable improvements in shareholder value. This relationship divides both the risks and rewards among these strategic partners.

Strategic relationships require partners to work together rather than compete against each other or point fingers at each other. They learn from each other, and their pay is based in part on the success of the partners. This is a far cry from the days when outsourcing vendors competed with each other, were secretive, and were quite legalistic, adhering strictly to the letter of the contract and not willing to do or spend any more than they had to. The promise of mutually beneficial outsourcing partnerships appears to be great, both for client organizations and for vendors. It will be interesting to see where this new form of outsourcing takes us and what the next new form of outsourcing will be. The decision of whether or not to outsource is obviously not an easy one. However, it is one option that you should be aware of and consider, depending on a whole range of different factors including organizational style, access to service providers, geographic area, or scope of operations.

[Adapted from **http://www.accenture.com** (2001); **http://www.csc.com** (2001); J. W. Verity, "Megadeals March On," **http://www.computerworld.com**, *Computerworld* (July 28, 1997).]

as systems development, they are moved toward new roles and organized into new groups. The structure and nature of the internal IS activities change from exclusively building and managing systems to including managing relationships with outside firms that build and manage systems under legal contract.

Not All Outsourcing Relationships Are the Same

Most organizations no longer enter into a strictly legal contract with an outsourcing vendor, but into a mutually beneficial relationship with a strategic partner. In such a relationship, the firm and the vendor are each concerned with, and perhaps have a direct stake in, the success of the other. Yet, other types of relationships exist, which means that not all outsourcing agreements need to be structured the same way (Fryer, 1994). In fact, at least three different types of outsourcing relationships can be identified:

- Basic relationship
- Preferred relationship
- Strategic relationship

A basic relationship can best be thought of as a "cash and carry" relationship, in which you buy products and services on the basis of price and convenience. Organizations should try to have a few preferred relationships, in which the buyer and supplier set preferences and prices to the benefit of each other. For example, a supplier can provide preferred pricing to customers that do a specified volume of business. Most organizations have just a few strategic relationships, in which both sides share risks and rewards.

We have now discussed two systems development alternatives that rely on external organizations to alleviate either completely or partially the burden of managing IS development projects in-house. In some cases, however, it may not be possible or convenient to rely on agencies outside the organization for development. In these cases, organizations may rely on another option for systems development projects.

End-User Development

In many organizations, the growing sophistication of users within the organization offers IS managers a fourth alternative for systems development. This fourth alternative is ***end-user development***—having users develop their own applications. This means that the people who are actually going to use the systems are also those who will develop those systems. End-user development, then, is one way IS departments can speed up application development without relying on external entities such as vendors or service providers. However, end-user development also has risks associated with it. This section outlines the benefits of having end

---

Outsourcing is currently seen as the most viable option for developing and implementing information systems within an organization. Due to the increased cost (both in terms of technology and human resources) associated with in-house development of information systems, many organizations are looking toward outside vendors to take care of information system needs. However, managing and selecting appropriate external vendors has always been a key concern for organizations. Organizations are, therefore, figuring out newer and better ways to get the most out of their external vendors. An office of the U.S. State Department recently signed a $107.5 million contract with Computer Sciences Corp. to manage the department's telecommunications network. The responsibility of Computer Sciences Corp. will be to manage the outsourcing vendors of the State Department, such as AT&T and SBI Consulting, which will be responsible for providing services ranging from network engineering to help-desk support. This seems to be a recent trend in the world of outsourcing in which companies hire outsourcers to manage projects and operations that are being conducted by other outsourcers. Another recent trend in outsourcing is to hire multiple outsourcers to work on a single project. Companies argue that by hiring multiple outsourcers they are able to acquire diverse skills at a relatively low cost. However, using multiple outsourcers has certain downsides, such as lack of accountability and increased internal and other miscellaneous costs. Careful management is hence required in such cases, which can often be accomplished by hiring an outsourcer to manage the project, in the manner of the office of the U.S. State Department.

Operations Management

[Adapted from Elisabeth Goodridge, "When it Comes to Outsourcers, One Isn't Enough," **http://www. informationweek.com**, *InformationWeek* (October 16, 2001).]

users develop their own applications, as well as some of the drawbacks of this approach.

Benefits of End-User Development

To help you better understand the benefits of end-user development, you should quickly review some of the problems with conventional development that are suggested by the four situations presented earlier in this chapter:

▪ *Cost of labor*: Conventional systems development is labor-intensive. Over the past several decades, software costs have increased while hardware costs have declined, as shown in Figure 8.26. As you can see from the figure, it becomes much cheaper for IS managers to substitute hardware for labor by giving users their own equipment. An IS manager can significantly reduce the cost of application development simply by giving end users the tools they need and enabling them to develop their own applications. Better yet, the various departments within the organization can purchase their own equipment, and the IS staff can simply provide guidance and other services.

▪ *Long development time*: New systems can take months or even years to develop, depending on the scale and scope of the new system and the backlog of systems waiting to be developed. As a result, users' needs may significantly change between when a system is initially proposed and when it is actually implemented. In these cases, the system may be virtually obsolete before it has even been implemented! End user–developed systems can "skip" the queue of systems waiting to be developed by the IS organization, resulting in more rapidly developed systems.

▪ *Slow modification or updates of existing systems*: Related to the time it takes to develop new systems is the problem of maintaining existing systems. Often, updates to existing systems are given a lower priority than developing new systems. Unfortunately, this can result in systems that are unable to keep pace with changing business needs, becoming antiquated and underused.

▪ When end users develop their own systems, the users have the responsibility of maintaining and updating applications as needed. Also, when systems are implemented, they often cause changes to the underlying business processes. These changes may necessitate further change or modification to the application, as highlighted in Figure 8.27. Rather than rely on IS to make these changes, users are able to modify the application in a timely manner to reflect the changed business process.

▪ *Work overload*: One reason for long development times and slow modifications is that IS departments are often overloaded with work. When you leverage the talents of end-user developers, you can, in effect, increase the size of the development staff by shifting some of the workload normally handled by IS professionals to end users, as depicted in Figure 8.28.

End-user development can radically decrease the development workload in the IS department. However, such a shift may cause other areas within IS, such as a help desk, for example, to become flooded with requests for assistance. Nonetheless, end-user development can be an excellent option for organizations faced with some of the problems previously described.

Encouraging End-User Development

End-user development sounds great, but how can organizations encourage and enable users to develop their own systems? Fortunately, the availability of easy to use, fourth-generation development tools (see Appendix B) has enabled end-user development to become more practical today than in the early to mid-1980s. There are five categories of fourth-generation tools:

▪ *Personal computer tools*: Many users throughout an organization use personal computer tools, including spreadsheets, database management systems, and graphics programs. Frequently, these tools enable users to build their own appli-

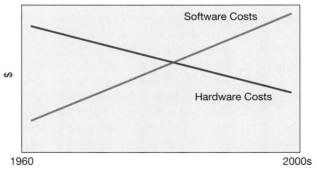

[**Figure 8.26** ➥ Rising software costs versus declining hardware costs.]

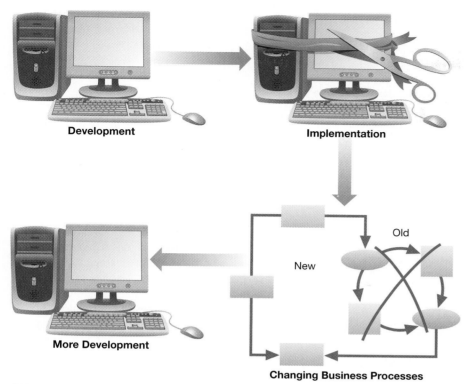

[Figure 8.27 ➡ Continuous cycle of development: a system is developed and implemented. However, it eventually becomes inadequate, and new development takes place.]

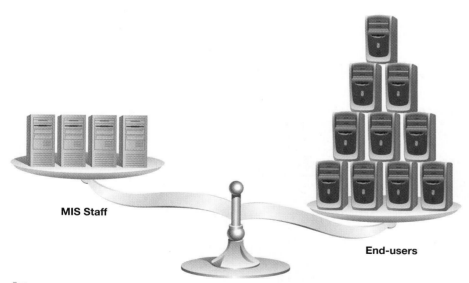

[Figure 8.28 ➡ Shifting systems development workload as end-user development has become more prevalent.]

cations using macro languages or embedded tools within the software designed to enable users to customize their own systems.

▌ *Query languages/report generators*: These tools are usually associated with database systems and enable you to search a database by entering various search criteria. Structured Query Language, or SQL, is the most common query language for

this purpose. For example, you may say "Give me the part numbers for any inventory that we have in stock whose quantity exceeds 30." A query language structures that query and presents the results of the query to the user. Report generators are similar to query languages and are designed to produce textual and tabular reports easily. Although users often use query languages independently, report generators may require some assistance from IS staff.

- *Graphics generators*: People can use these tools to extract relevant information from databases and convert that data to a graphic such as a pie chart, a line graph, or an area plot. As with report generators, users can specify many different formats.

- *Decision support or modeling tools*: Although spreadsheets can be used as decision support aids, dedicated decision support tools are often available for more complex, multidimensional models that may be too complicated to be handled easily in a spreadsheet. These tools can enable users to develop decision support systems to aid in making decisions.

- *Application generators*: Application generators are designed to automate much of the relatively tedious programming work associated with systems development. With these tools, you can specify what you want done, then the application generator decides how to accomplish that task and generates the program code. Application generators can be used to get prototypes up and

running quickly, get feedback from other potential users, and make necessary changes. Computer-aided software engineering (CASE) tools often include an application generator that end users or IS professionals can use.

End-User Development Pitfalls

This chapter has painted a pretty rosy picture of end-user development so far. However, it is important to understand that along with the benefits come some drawbacks, as depicted in Figure 8.29. The information systems and computer science professions have established software development standards and generally accepted practices that are used throughout different organizations and across different types of systems. Unfortunately, users may not be aware of these standards, such as the need for adequate documentation, built-in error checking, and testing procedures. In small, personal applications, not adhering to the standards may not present a problem. However, if the system manages or intercon-

"OK, TECHNICALLY THIS SHOULD WORK. JUDY, TYPE THE WORD, 'GOODYEAR' ALL CAPS, BOLDFACE, AT 700-POINT TYPE SIZE."

[**Figure 8.29** ➥ End-user development can sometimes be problematic.]
The 5th Wave by Rich Tennant

nects with important business data, then lack of adherence to sound principles can quickly become a *big* problem if data becomes corrupted or is not secure.

Another problem for end user–developed systems is a potential lack of continuity. Suppose James develops a new system that meets his needs perfectly. James understands the system and uses it every day. However, one day James is transferred and is replaced by Jordan, a new hire to the company. The system that was intuitive for James to use may not be so intuitive for Jordan. Jordan may quickly abandon James's system or may be forced to develop her own system. This example shows how end-user development can easily result in a lack of continuity among applications, leading to redundant development efforts and a lot of wasted productivity in the organization. In organizations where turnover is frequent, a lot of time can be lost "reinventing the wheel" simply because systems that are in place are undocumented and cannot easily be used by new employees.

Related to the continuity problem is the question of whether users and managers should be spending their time on IS development. That is, the organization has hired individuals to be financial managers, production managers, marketers, or salespeople. The organization expects these employees to add value to the organization based on the skills that they have to offer. If the time and energy of these individuals are diverted to developing new systems, then the organization loses out on the potential productivity these individuals have to offer in other ways. Also, individual motivation, morale, and performance might suffer if the employee is unable to concentrate on her area of expertise and instead spends too much of her time worrying about developing new systems.

Fortunately, organizations that have been successful in moving to end-user development are aware of many of these problems and have established some controls to avoid them. One control mechanism is an Information Center (IC), which is charged with encouraging end users to develop their own applications while at the same time providing some management oversight. The IC staff can assist or train end users in proper development techniques or standards, prevent redundancy in application development, and ensure that systems are documented properly. IC staff are often not functional-area experts but are typically experts in using the fourth-generation tools. Working together, end users and the IC staff can develop useful systems for an organization.

KEY POINTS REVIEW

1. **Understand the process used by organizations to manage the development of information systems.** The development of information systems follows a process called the systems development life cycle (SDLC). The SDLC is a process that first identifies the need for a system and then defines the processes for designing, developing, and maintaining an information system. The process is very structured and formal and requires the active involvement of managers and users.

2. **Describe each major phase of the systems development life cycle: systems identification, selection, and planning; system analysis; system design; system implementation; and system maintenance.** The SDLC has five phases: system identification, selection, and planning; system analysis; system design; system implementation; and system maintenance. Systems identification, selection, and planning is the first phase of the SDLC, in which potential projects are identified, selected, and planned. System analysis is the second phase of the SDLC, in which the current ways of doing business are studied and alternative replacement systems are proposed. System design is the third phase of the SDLC, in which all features of the proposed system are described. System implementation is the fourth phase of the SDLC, in which the information system is programmed, tested, installed, and supported. System maintenance is the fifth and final phase of the SDLC, in which an information system is systematically repaired and improved.

3. **Describe prototyping, rapid application development, and object-oriented analysis and design methods of systems development, along with each approach's strengths and weaknesses.** Prototyping is an iterative systems development process in which requirements are converted into a working system that is continually revised through a close working relationship between analysts and users. The strengths of prototyping are that it helps develop a close working relationship between designers and users and that it is a good approach for hard-to-define problems. Its weaknesses are that it is not a practical approach for a large number of users and that it can at times lead to a lower-quality system if the system is built too quickly. Rapid application development (RAD) is a systems development methodology that combines prototyping, computer-based development tools, special management practices, and close user involvement. The strength of RAD is that users are actively involved in the design process, which makes system implementation much easier. The weaknesses of RAD are

that systems are sometimes narrowly focused—which might limit future evolution—and that quality problems might result if a system is designed and built too quickly (as is the case with prototyping). Object-oriented analysis and design (OOA&D) is a systems development approach that focuses on modeling objects—data and operations bundled together—rather than on modeling these separately. The strengths of OOA&D are the integration of data and processing during the design phase, which should lead to higher-quality systems, and the reuse of common modules, which should make development and maintenance easier. The weaknesses of OOA&D are that it is very difficult to train analysts and programmers in the object-oriented approach and that analysts often recreate common modules.

4. **Explain the factors involved in building a system in-house, along with situations in which it is not feasible.** It is not feasible for an organization to build a system in-house in at least four situations. First, some organizations have limited IS staffing and, therefore, do not have the capability to build a system themselves. Second, an organization may have IS staff with a limited skill set. Existing IS staff may be highly skilled at producing traditional applications but not have the skills to build new types of systems or systems that require emerging development tools. Third, in many organizations, the IS staff does not have the time to work on all the systems that the organization desires. Fourth, some organizations have performance problems with their IS staff, whereby staff turnover, changing requirements, shifts in technology, or budget constraints have resulted

in poor results. In any of these situations, it may be advantageous to an organization to consider an alternative to in-house systems development.

5. **Explain three alternative systems development options: external acquisition, outsourcing, and end-user development.** External acquisition is the process of purchasing an existing information system from an external organization or vendor. External acquisition is a five-step process. Step 1 is system identification, selection, and planning, which focuses on determining whether a proposed system is feasible. Step 2 is systems analysis, which focuses on determining the requirements for the system. Step 3 is the development of a Request for Proposal (RFP). An RFP is a communication tool indicating an organization's requirements for a given system and requesting information from potential vendors on their ability to deliver such a system. Step 4 is proposal evaluation, which focuses on evaluating proposals received from vendors. This evaluation may include viewing system demonstrations, evaluating the performance of those systems, and examining criteria important to the organization and how the proposed systems meet those criteria. Step 5 is vendor selection, which focuses on choosing the vendor to provide the system. Outsourcing refers to the turning over of partial or entire responsibility for information systems development and management to an outside organization. End-user development is a systems development method whereby users in the organization develop, test, and maintain their own applications.

KEY TERMS

adaptive maintenance 257

alpha testing 254

beta testing 254

corrective maintenance 257

data flows 249

developmental testing 254

direct conversion 255

end-user development 267

external acquisition 262

form 250

graphical user interface (GUI) 251

information systems planning 244

object-oriented analysis and design 259

outsourcing 265

parallel conversion 255

perfective maintenance 257

phased conversion 255

pilot conversion 255

preventive maintenance 257

processing logic 249

prototyping 258

rapid application development 258

report 250

request for proposal 263

requirements collection 245

software engineering 240

system identification, selection, and planning 242

system analysis 244

system conversion 254

system design 249

system implementation 253

system maintenance 256

systems analyst 240

systems analysis and design 240

systems benchmarking 263

systems development life cycle (SDLC) 242

REVIEW QUESTIONS

1. What are the five phases of the systems development life cycle?
2. List and describe six techniques used in requirements collection.
3. What are the four major components/tasks of the system design phase of the SDLC?
4. What are the four options for system conversion? How do they differ from each other?

5. Compare and contrast the four types of system maintenance.
6. What are three alternative approaches to the SDLC for designing and building systems?
7. What are the advantages and disadvantages of prototyping?
8. List and define the four phases of rapid application development.

9. What is object-oriented analysis and design, and what are its strengths and weaknesses?

10. Define outsourcing, and list three major types.

11. What is system benchmarking, and what are some common benchmarks?

12. What are some of the reasons outsourcing is more popular than ever?

13. What are the three recommendations made in this chapter for managing an outsourcing IS relationship?

14. Describe five categories of fourth-generation tools.

15. End-user developers have what advantages and disadvantages?

SELF-STUDY QUESTIONS

Answers are at the end of the Problems and Exercises.

1. Which of the following is **not** one of the five phases of the systems development life cycle?

   A. system analysis

   B. system implementation

   C. system design

   D. systems resource acquisition

2. _____ is the process of gathering and organizing information from users, managers, business processes, and documents to understand how a proposed information system should function.

   A. Requirements collection

   B. Systems collection

   C. Systems analysis

   D. Records archiving

3. Which of the following is the correct order of phases in the systems development life cycle?

   A. maintenance, analysis, planning, design, implementation

   B. analysis, planning, design, implementation, maintenance

   C. planning, analysis, design, implementation, maintenance

   D. maintenance, planning, analysis, design, implementation

4. In the systems design phase, the elements that must be designed when building an information system include all of the following **except** _____ .

   A. reports and forms

   B. questionnaires

   C. databases and files

   D. interfaces and dialogues

5. _____ maintenance involves making enhancements to improve processing performance or interface usability, or adding desired, but not necessarily required, system features (in other words, "bells and whistles").

   A. Preventive

   B. Perfective

   C. Corrective

   D. Adaptive

6. Which of the following is an alternative to building a system in-house?

   A. external acquisition

   B. end-user development

   C. outsourcing

   D. all of the above

7. A _____ is a report that an organization uses to tell vendors what its requirements are and to invite them to provide information about how they might be able to meet those requirements.

   A. request letter

   B. vendor request

   C. Request for Proposal

   D. payables request

8. Which of the following is **not** a type of outsourcing?

   A. basic

   B. elite

   C. strategic

   D. preferred

9. Which of the following factors is a good reason to outsource?

   A. problems in IS performance

   B. supplier pressures

   C. financial factors

   D. all of the above

10. Most competitive external acquisition processes have at least five general steps. Which of the following is **not** one of those steps?

    A. vendor selection

    B. proposal evaluation

    C. development of a Request for Proposal

    D. implementation

PROBLEMS AND EXERCISES

1. Match the following terms with the appropriate definitions:

_____ Request for Proposal   _____ Systems benchmarking

_____ Alpha testing   _____ Systems development life cycle

_____ End-user development   _____ Prototyping

_____ Pilot conversion   _____ Systems analysis

_____ Outsourcing   _____ External acquisition

_____ Data flows   _____ Requirements collection

a. The movement of data through an organization or within an information system

b. Term that describes the life of an information system from conception to retirement

c. The second phase of the systems development life cycle

d. The process of gathering and organizing information from users, managers, business processes and documents to understand how a proposed information system should function

e. Performed by software testers to assess whether the entire system meets the design requirements of the users

f. When the entire system is used in one location, but not in the entire organization

g. A systems development methodology that uses a trial-and-error approach for discovering how a system should operate

h. The practice of turning over responsibility of some to all of an organization's information systems development and operations to an outside firm

i. Users developing their own applications

j. Purchasing an existing system from an outside vendor

k. A way to evaluate a proposed system by testing a portion of it with the system workload

l. A report that is used to tell vendors what your requirements are and to invite them to provide information about how they might be able to meet those requirements

2. Explain the differences between data and data flows. How might systems analysts obtain the information they need to generate the data flows of a system? How are these data flows and the accompanying processing logic used in the system design phase of the life cycle? What happens when the data and data flows are modeled incorrectly?

3. When Microsoft posts a new version of Internet Explorer on the Microsoft Web site and states that this is a beta version, what does it mean? Is this a final working version of the software, or is it still being tested? Who is doing the testing? Search the World Wide Web to find other companies that have beta versions of their products available to the public. You might try Corel at **www.corel.com/**. What other companies did you find?

4. Why is the system documentation of a new information system so important? What information does it contain? For whom is this information intended? When will the system documentation most likely be used?

5. Conduct a search on the World Wide Web for "systems development life cycle," using any browser. Check out some of the hits. Compare them with the SDLC outlined in this chapter. Do all these life cycles follow the same general path? How many phases do the ones you found on the Web contain? Is the terminology the same or different? Prepare a 10-minute presentation to the class on your findings.

6. Choose an organization with which you are familiar that develops its own information systems. Does this organization follow a systems development life cycle? If not, why not? If so, how many phases does it have? Who developed this life cycle? Was it someone within the company, or was the information system adopted from somewhere else?

7. Describe your experiences with information systems that were undergoing changes or updates. What kind of conversion procedure was being used? How did this affect your interaction with the system as a user? Who else was affected? If the system was down altogether, for how long was it down? Do you or any of your classmates have horror stories, or were the situations not that bad?

8. Compare and contrast RAD and object-oriented methodologies. What are the strengths and weaknesses of each? Visit Object Group at **http://www.oopl.com.au/** or Object FAQ at **http://www.cyberdyne-object-sys.com/oofaq2/**.

9. Conduct a search on the World Wide Web for "object-oriented analysis and design" using any browser you wish (Hint: Because people write differently, search using both "object-oriented" and "object oriented."). Check out some of the hits. You should have found numerous articles regarding OOA&D's use by IS departments. Are these articles positive or negative regarding OOA&D? Do you agree with the articles? Prepare a 10-minute presentation to the class on your findings.

10. Interview an IS manager within an organization with which you are familiar. Determine whether the organization uses methodologies such as prototyping, RAD, and/or OOA&D for system projects. Who chooses the methodology? If the organization has not used a methodology, is it due to choice, or is it due to a lack of need, understanding, or capability of using the methodology?

11. Choose an organization with which you are familiar, and determine whether it builds its applications in-house. How many IS staff members does the organization have, and how large is the organization they support?

12. Think about the requirements of a career in IS. Do IS positions generally require people to work 40 hours a week, or more if a project has a deadline? Do positions in the IS department require people skills? To find these answers, visit the IS department at your university, a local business, or **www.resumegenie.com/jobs**.

13. Find an organization, either on the Internet at **http://www.computerworld.com** or **http://www.infoworld.com** or a company you may want to work for in the future, that outsources work. What are the managerial challenges of outsourcing, and why is this a popular alternative to hiring additional staff?

ANSWERS TO THE SELF-STUDY QUESTIONS

1. D   2. A   3. C   4. B   5. B   6. D   7. C   8. B   9. D   10. D

CASE 1: *Database Outsourcing at PARTNERS*

PARTNERS National Health Plan is a 76,000-member managed-care plan located in South Bend, Indiana. Over the years, the company has gained increased recognition in the health-care industry, and in 1998, its HMO was ranked as one of the top five HMOs in Indiana. In the following year, there were further accolades in store for PARTNERS, when it received special "commendable" accreditation from the National Committee on Quality Assurance. This honor is given to only a few managed-care plans in the nation. While on one hand, the company was receiving excellent rankings and reputation for its first-class customer service, internally, the company was suffering from many information technology problems, many of which were threatening the high-quality customer service it provided. The company wanted to decrease its response time. Since it depended heavily on databases, it also wanted to make sure that in case it had a database crash, it would have a full backup, which would allow it to resume operations without any delay. Another problem that the company was facing was related to database configuration. Improper configuration meant operational inefficiencies and huge bottlenecks. Since the company had problems retaining knowledgeable staff who were capable of troubleshooting any problem, improper configuration became a huge issue. Once, the company's database crashed, and the employees realized that, due to improper configuration of the database, half of the data that the company needed was not going to be available. PARTNERS realized that it was time that it focused on a new information system, one that would be stable, and at the same time have an efficient database with proper backup systems. For the development of the new system, the company had two options. One was to hire a skilled individual to help the IT department fix the problem, which could take a long time. The other option was to outsource the entire project to an external organization that specialized in database

issues. This option could take less time and could free up PARTNERS' internal IT department for other critical projects.

Organizations often face such a dilemma regarding systems development. The decision is often critical and could significantly affect the success of the project. Hiring a single individual or developing a system in-house can cost less for a company, yet at the same time, the project may suffer due to a lack of the necessary set of skills. The project may also take a longer time than anticipated, significantly delaying it and adding more to the original budget. On the other hand, some industry experts believe that developing in-house is better than outsourcing. Ms. Donna Maxwell of CCI/Triad feels that in-house development is best since, "it is just as much work trying to get the information to your outsourcing vendor as it is to do it yourself" (Pruter, 2000). On the other hand, other IT personnel feel that outsourcing is always the best solution for software development, especially in situations in which there is no adequate staff within the organization to handle and administer a large-scale information systems project (Pruter, 2000). Deliberating between these two options, PARTNERS realized that it lacked the necessary skills in-house to handle such a critical project. Its decision was hence to outsource, and PARTNERS turned to Synertech (an application services provider (ASP) company based in Pennsylvania and a long-time outsourcer in the health-care industry). Synertech had a lot of experience in setting up and maintaining databases and knew how to increase performance and ensure proper backup. The staff of the company was also skilled at identifying potential problems and then avoiding them.

As soon as Synertech and PARTNERS signed a contract, the IT staff of Synertech were at the PARTNERS headquarters, gathering necessary requirements and conducting an in-depth analysis of the system to be built. The outsourcer prepared a report

within three days on tasks to be accomplished. In addition to the problems of performance and backup, the report suggested that PARTNERS' database was fragmented and lacked any sort of standard, which was making the database administration extremely difficult. As soon as this report was prepared, the outsourcer started working on the task of providing the solution. First, Synertech created a backup of the database and repaired it reliably. Data in the database were then grouped according to the business functions to ensure stability and make it more consistent. The database system was then defragmented. This helped in making the system faster, and, in addition, more data could be retrieved within a shorter period of time. This defragmentation helped in decrease the response time of the system, which was one of the requirements of PARTNERS. The response time was decreased so much that an accounting report that previously took several hours to complete now took only 20 to 30 minutes to complete. Synertech also saved PARTNERS the additional expense of acquiring a new server. The database was so well reconfigured that only one-third of the server was being utilized, eliminating the need for any additional servers. The backup of the system was made faster. Initially, backup would take up to 12 hours. But now, twice the amount of data could be backed up in half the time.

Synertech completed the whole project in one month. Since the outsourcer performed most of the task during the weekend or in off-peak hours, it did not disrupt the normal operation of the organization. PARTNERS was so satisfied with the performance that it has now contracted Synertech to oversee its complete database administration.

[Adapted from Anonymous, "Database Outsourcing for a Managed Care Plan," *Health Management Technology* 21, no. 11 (2000): 56–59; R. Pruter, "Case Studies Show Two Models of Flex Administration," *Employee Benefit Plan Review* 54, no. 12 (2000): 29–31.]

Discussion Questions

1. What IT-related challenges did PARTNERS face?
2. How is in-house development different from outsourcing?
3. Was PARTNERS right in its decision to outsource its database repair and maintenance to Synertech? Why?
4. Would the results of the database project have been different if PARTNERS had decided to solve the problems by using its in-house IT staff?

CASE 2: *Information Systems Failure at Integrated Solutions*

Integrated Solutions is an industrial services provider with a large global presence. The company is primarily headquartered in the United States but has large-scale operations (including offices and personnel) in most nations in Europe, Asia, South America, and Africa. The company is considered to be the market leader in its industry. In the glory days of the company, it was considered to be the most technologically sophisticated in its industry and had an excellent technological infrastructure. However, over time, the inability to keep up with the immense changes in technology had resulted in some old legacy systems, more than half of which were not properly integrated. The company's problems related to IT started in the latter half of 1996. Around that time, a lot of customers would call to check on the status of their orders. It took Integrated Solutions days to respond to most of these queries. On the other hand, some of its competitors would take only minutes to respond to such requests. Due to the global nature of the company, some of its customers would place multiple orders in different countries. Because the company's information systems were not properly integrated, such services would take even longer. Employees prepared most of these reports by hand, leading to delays and a higher risk of errors than if the process were automated. The company's pricing structure was also very complex, often requiring tremendous customization, and the existing information systems helped little in this matter as well.

Frustrated with the state of the company, Integrated Solutions decided to turn to a consulting firm to turn things around and finally contacted a consulting group to develop a long-term IT plan and to replace the existing systems. The consulting firm proposed the development and implementation of a globally integrated information system, which it believed would be the perfect solution for the company's situation. The

plan received a "go ahead" signal from the chairman, and the CIO was immediately given the responsibility to execute it. The plan also had the active involvement of the president, the CFO, and other personnel from some of its overseas regional offices. The estimated cost of the new information system was approximately $36 million.

Unfortunately, after three years very little had been accomplished on this project. Some of the regional personnel had objected to the development of the new system, and that had been the beginning of the problems associated with the project. Initially, there was a lot of debate and controversy over the choice of the development software. The consulting firm had proposed the use of Visual Basic; however, many key members of the company did not welcome this. One European executive had proposed the use of a certain tool that had met with a lot of success in Europe. Another member from another part of the world proposed yet another warehouse management tool, which he believed would fit the requirements of the firm. After some time, the European tool was selected. However, the developers in the United States were not familiar with this tool. As a result, a team was gathered in Europe and was flown to the United States to work on the development of this new system. The European team first developed a prototype of the new system. However, when the team started building the actual system, it started taking much longer than was expected. After a while, people realized that the prototype had very little functionality, and it was impossible to understand exactly what the actual global system would look like just by looking at the prototype. The company executives soon became convinced that the new system would not be the solution for the problem, and they started focusing elsewhere.

The company made the decision to acquire an outside vendor package instead of building the system in-house and selected a

vendor from Britain for this purpose. The vendor chosen was small, however, and people could put little faith in its capability to provide solutions to all the company's IT-related problems. Thus, even after many years, Integrated Solutions was unable to develop its own global information system and had to turn to a packaged solution from an outside vendor. It cost the company approximately $50 million ($14 million more than the original budget), apart from a significant delay in the completion of the project. In addition, the company suffered tremendously in the stock market (its stock price fell by 50 percent) and lost a lot of its existing market share, thus losing its position of being the market leader.

Many factors led to the failure of the development and implementation of the global information system at Integrated Solutions. More than the technology, the company's management was responsible for some of the problems with the project. Many of the overseas regional managers pushed products of their own choice and refused to accept the system as developed on a different platform. The CIO's inability to take control of the situation, along with the lack of trust and respect between the CIO and the chairman, led to the chaos surrounding the choice of the development tool. The lack of strong leadership thus led to the choice of an inappropriate development tool and a packaged solution of lower quality.

Today, the company is trying to recover its position. It is now focusing on developing a new system based on the modules of its existing information systems and is hoping that, in due time, it will be able to recover its original position as the most technologically advanced market leader in the area of industrial services.

[Adapted from James M. Spitze, "Inside a Global Systems Failure," **http://www.cio.com/ research/global/**, *CIO Magazine* (February 1, 2001).]

Discussion Questions

1. What were some of the information systems–related problems that Integrated Solutions faced?
2. Why did the global information systems implementation at Integrated Solutions fail?
3. What could Integrated Solutions have done differently to achieve a more favorable outcome?
4. Do you think Integrated Systems followed a good approach for building and acquiring the global information system? If so, why, and what did it do that was good? If not, why not, and what do you think the company could have done differently?

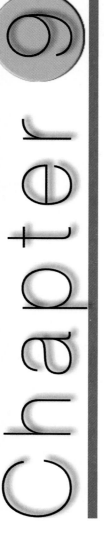

Information Systems Ethics, Computer Crime, and Security

OPENING: Microsoft Gets Hacked!

In October 2000, Microsoft released the news that the company had been the victim of a "deplorable act of corporate espionage" (see Figure 9.1). Online thieves broke into Microsoft's internal network and apparently sifted through valuable source code, examining applications in development. The company discovered the break-in on October 14, then watched the intruders at work for several days before reporting the incident to the FBI. *The Wall Street Journal* was first to report the incident, but the newspaper's claim that stolen Microsoft source code was e-mailed to St. Petersburg, Russia, could not be confirmed.

Intruders accomplished the Microsoft break-in by infecting the company's computers with a particularly hostile e-mail virus. When Microsoft employees opened the infected e-mail messages, the virus quickly spread throughout the company's networked computers. The virus supposedly allowed intruders to gain partial control of the compromised computers, allowing the techno-thieves to access stored data.

Microsoft was not the only business to report corporate espionage via computer in recent years. A survey of American corporations and government agencies conducted by the Computer Security Institute reported that of the 600 organizations responding, 25 percent said outsiders had penetrated their systems. Twenty percent reported theft of proprietary data.

Corporate security has become more difficult to ensure in recent years, primarily because most corporate computers are networked, and networks have become more complex in order to run increasingly sophisticated applications and to accommodate large numbers of employees who use the system from remote locations. The fact that millions of corporate employees worldwide exchange e-mail messages daily has also added to security risks. But as the risks have increased, the efforts of most corporations to maintain security have not. In many companies, security is "literally an afterthought," Tom Talleur, former chief of computer crime investigations for NASA, recently told *USA Today*.

The risk of security breaches to individual computer users perhaps seems not as great as it is for organizations and government agencies. But if you have ever had to straighten out a credit card bill after theft of your account number from an online source, or pay an expert to restore programs after a virus infection, you probably feel every bit as much at risk as Microsoft and other organizations.

[Figure 9.1 ➡ Microsoft, the largest and most formidable software company in the world, has been a primary target of computer criminals.]
©Corbis/Sygma

iven that computers and information systems are now a fundamental part of doing business, opportunities for misusing and abusing information, computers, and systems now abound. This new wired world we live in causes us to ask some important new ethical questions. Who owns information, particularly information about us? Who is responsible for the accuracy of information? Should guidelines be set for how business organizations and business professionals use information, computers, and information systems, and if so, what should these guidelines be? What penalties should be assessed for computer crime and abuses? How can we secure our computers and information?

After reading this chapter you will be able to:

CHAPTER 1 2 3 4 5 6 7 8 9

1 Information Systems: The Big Picture

2 Information Systems for Competitive Advantage

3 Database Management

4 Telecommunications and the Internet

5 Electronic Commerce, Intranets & Extranets

6 Organizational Information Systems

7 Enterprise-Wide Information Systems

8 Information Systems Development & Acquisition

9 Information Systems Ethics, Computer Crime & Security

1. Describe the advent of the Information Age and how computer ethics impact the use of information systems.

2. Discuss the ethical concerns associated with information privacy, accuracy, property, and accessibility.

3. Define computer crime, and list several types of computer crime.

4. Contrast what the terms computer virus, worm, Trojan horse, and logic or time bomb mean.

5. Explain what is meant by computer security and describe various methods for providing computer security.

[Figure 9.2 ➡ The Big Picture: focusing on information systems ethics, computer crime, and security.]

This chapter focuses on the last puzzle piece for seeing The Big Picture, the issues associated with information systems ethics, computer crime, and security (see Figure 9.2). The chapter is partitioned into three major sections that focus on each topic. These topics are becoming increasingly important to successfully managing information systems and living our daily lives.

INFORMATION SYSTEMS ETHICS

In his book *The Third Wave*, futurist Alvin Toffler describes three distinct phases or "waves of change" that have taken place in the past or are presently taking place within the world's civilizations (see Figure 9.3). The First Wave—a civilization based upon agriculture and handwork—was a comparatively primitive stage that began as civilizations formed and lasted for hundreds of years. The Second Wave of change—the Industrial Revolution—overlapped the First Wave. The Industrial Revolution began in Great Britain toward the end of the eighteenth century and continued over the next 150 years, moving society from a predominantly agrarian culture to the urbanized machine age. Where once families supported themselves by working the land or handcrafting items for sale or trade, now mothers, fathers, and children left home to work in factories. Steel mills, textile factories, and eventually automobile assembly lines replaced farming and handwork as the principal source of family income.

Not only did occupations change as the Industrial Revolution progressed, but so did educational, business, and social and religious institutions to accommodate the mechanized society. On an individual level, now punctuality, obedience, and the ability to perform repetitive tasks were qualities to be instilled and valued in children in public schools and, ultimately, in workers.

The Information Age Arrives

In a much shorter period of time than it took for civilization to progress past the First Wave, societies worldwide moved from the machine age into the *Information Age*—a period of change Toffler has dubbed the "Third Wave." As the Third Wave gained speed, information became the currency of the realm. For thousands of years, from primitive times through the Middle Ages, information, or the body of knowledge known to that point, was limited. It was transmitted verbally, within families, clans, and villages, from person to person, generation to generation. Then came Johann Gutenberg's invention of the printing press with movable type in 1455, and a tremendous acceleration occurred in the amount and kind of information available to populations. Now knowledge could be imparted in written form, and sometimes came from distant locations. Information could be saved, absorbed, debated, and written about in publications, thus adding to the exploding data pool.

Computer Literacy and the Digital Divide

Most modern-day high school and university students grow up in a computerized world. If by some chance they do not know how to operate a computer by the time they graduate from high school, they soon acquire computer skills, because in today's work world knowing how to use a computer—called *computer literacy* (or information literacy)—can mean the difference between being employed or unemployed. Knowing how to use a computer can also open up myriad sources of information to those who have learned how to use the computer as a device to gather, store, organize, and otherwise process information. In fact, some fear that the Information Age will not provide the same advantages to "information haves"—those computer-literate individuals who have unlimited access to information—

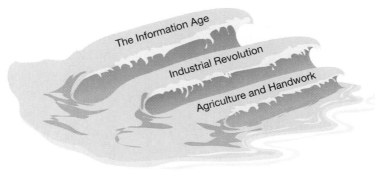

[**Figure 9.3** ➡ The Information Age is the biggest wave of change.]

and "information have-nots"—those whose computer skills and, thus, access to information, are limited.

The first computer-related occupations have evolved as computers have become more sophisticated and more widely used. Where once we thought of computer workers primarily as programmers, data entry clerks, systems analysts, or computer repairpersons, today many more job categories in virtually all industries (see Figure 9.4) involve the use of computers. In fact, today there are few occupations where computers are not somehow in use. Computers manage air traffic, perform medical tests, monitor patients during surgery, help surgeons perform operations, and more. Since they are especially adept at processing large amounts of data, they are used extensively by universities and public schools, businesses of all sizes, and in all levels and departments of government. Engineers, architects, interior designers, and artists use special computer-aided design (CAD) programs. Musicians play computerized instruments, and songs are written and recorded with the help of computers. Not only do we use computers at work, we also use them in our personal lives. We teach our children on them, manage our finances, do our taxes, compose letters and term papers, create greeting cards, send and receive electronic mail, surf the Internet, and play games on them.

Unfortunately, there are still many people in our society who are being left behind in the Information Age. The gap between those individuals in our society who are computer literate and have access to information resources like the Internet and those who do not is referred to as the *digital divide*. The digital divide is one of the major ethical challenges facing society today, when you consider the strong linkage between computer literacy and a person's ability to compete in the Information Age. For example, access to raw materials and money fueled the Industrial Revolution, "but in the informational society, the fuel, the power, is knowledge," emphasizes John Kenneth Galbraith, an American economist specializing in emerging trends in the U.S. economy. "One has now come to see a new class structure divided by those who have information and those who must function out of ignorance. This new class has its power not from money, not from land, but from knowledge."

The good news is that the digital divide in America is rapidly shrinking, but there are still major challenges to overcome. In particular, people in rural communities, the elderly, people with disabilities, and minorities lag national averages for Internet access and computer literacy. Outside the United States, the gap gets even wider and the obstacles much more difficult to overcome, particularly in the third world, where infrastructure and financial resources are lacking. Clearly, the digital divide is a major ethical concern facing the Information Age.

There is a broad range of ethical issues that have emerged through the use and proliferation of computers. *Computer ethics* is used to describe the issues and standards of conduct as they pertain to the use of information systems. In 1986, Richard O. Mason wrote a classic article on the issues central to this debate—information privacy, accuracy, property, and accessibility—and these issues are still at the forefront of most ethical debates related to how information systems store and process information (see Figure 9.5). Next, we examine each of these issues.

Information Privacy

If you use the Internet regularly, sending e-mail messages and visiting Web sites, you may have felt that your personal privacy is at risk. Several Web sites where you like to shop greet you by name and seem to know which

[Figure 9.4 ➥ Computers are used in countless types of jobs and industries.]
(9.4a) ©Getty Images, Inc. (9.4b) ©Getty Images, Inc. (9.4c) ©Getty Images, Inc. (9.4d) ©Getty Images/Eye Wire, Inc.

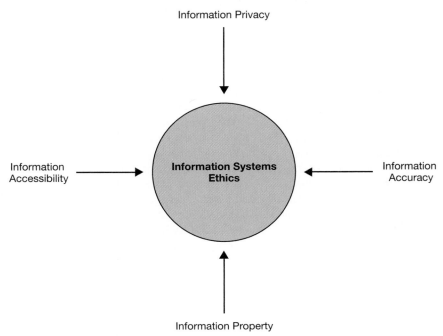

[**Figure 9.5** ➡ Information privacy, accuracy, property, and accessibility are central to most ethical concerns about information technology.]

products you are most likely to buy. Every day the in box in your browser's mail program is full to overflowing with messages urging you to buy something. As a result, you may feel as though eyes are upon you every time you log on to your ISP. **Information privacy** is concerned with what information an individual should have to reveal to others through the course of employment or through other transactions such as online shopping.

While the Information Age has brought widespread access to information, the downside is that others may now have access to personal information that you would prefer to keep private. Personal information, such as social security numbers, credit card numbers, medical histories, and even family histories, is now available on the Internet.

One of the fastest growing "information" crimes in recent years has been **identity theft**. Identity theft is the stealing of another person's social security number, credit card number, and other personal information for the purpose of using the victim's credit rating to borrow money, buy merchandise, and otherwise run up debts that are never repaid. In some cases, thieves even withdraw money directly from victims' bank accounts. Since many government and private organizations keep information about individuals in accessible databases, opportunities abound for thieves to retrieve it. Reclaiming one's identity

and restoring a good credit rating can be frustrating and time consuming for victims.

The solution to identity theft lies in the government and private sector working together to change practices used to verify a person's identity. For example, a mother's maiden name and an individual's social security number are too easily obtained. Other methods of personal identification, such as biometrics and encryption, may need to be used if the problem is to be solved. Methods of information security—including biometrics and encryption—will be discussed later in the chapter.

Before moving on, it is important to distinguish between unethical behavior and a crime. Identity theft is clearly a crime. However, many "misuses" of computers and information may not be crimes but would be considered unethical by most people. As technology moves forward and allows humans to do things not possible before, existing laws often do not apply to these emerging situations. One of the ongoing debates regarding technological innovations revolves around the question: "Just because it is not a crime, does that make it OK to do it?"

Information Accuracy

The issue of information accuracy has become highly charged in today's wired world. **Infor-**

The Social Security office in Seattle wanted to implement fire department–certified entry and exit doors in its new offices. However, when the time came for evaluating the doors, the fire officials rejected the use of dead bolts on exit doors. In order to provide security to the employees, the Seattle office contemplated installing a new key-card system that would enable employees to access the facility or move from one private office to another within the facility. The system would provide access to individuals based on their position and the day of the week and time. The system was going to replace the old cipher locks that also needed a code but, unlike the new system, did not keep track of employee movement into and within the office facilities. The new system was also designed in a manner such that the facility was protected from former employees, whose access codes were removed from the system as soon as they left the organization. This protection could not be accomplished using the old cipher locks. When the new system was being implemented, the union filed a lawsuit, claiming that the system violated employee privacy by keeping track of when a particular employee came into or left an office and could be used unfairly for disciplining employees. In order to satisfy the union, the Social Security Administration passed a new rule, which suggested that the employee information gathered by the key-card system would be kept secured and would be accessed only by supervisors on a need-to-know basis.

Human Resource Management

[Adapted from Bryant Jordan, "SSA Balances Privacy and Security," **www.fcw.com/fcw/articles/2001/ 0219/mgt-ssa-02-19-01.asp** (February 19, 2001).]

mation accuracy is concerned with the authenticity and fidelity of information, as well as identifying who is responsible for informational errors that harm people. With all the computerization that has taken place, people have come to expect to receive and retrieve information more easily and quickly than ever before. In addition, because computers "never make mistakes," we have come to expect this information to be accurate. A case in point is at the bank. The combination of automated teller machines, computerized record systems, and large, electronic client and transaction databases should provide customers with quick and accurate access to their account information. However, we continue to hear about and experience record-keeping errors at banks.

An error of a few dollars in your banking records does not seem significant. However, what if it were an error in the bank's favor of hundreds or thousands of dollars? What if the error caused one of your important payments (such as a home mortgage payment) to bounce? Bank errors can be quite important.

There are many now-infamous stories of data accuracy problems with information systems, many of which have involved banks. For example, one such case occurred in Los Angeles but has surely been repeated many times around this country and others. The basic story is as follows. Louis and Eileen Marches had bought a house in the 1950s with financing through their local bank. Louis dutifully paid the monthly payments in person and made sure that his loan book was stamped

"paid" every time, even after the bank's systems had been automated. Several years ago, the bank notified the Marches that their payments were in arrears. Louis went to the bank with his payment book, but because the account screen showed no payment, the teller, the head teller, and the bank manager refused to honor his stamped book. One month later the same thing happened again, and now two months were in arrears. The bank continued to refuse his proof of payment and based their decisions and actions solely on the computer system. Eventually, the bank foreclosed on the house, causing a near fatal stroke for Eileen. After a long lawsuit, the Marches recovered $268,000 from the bank and the following apology: "Computers make mistakes. Banks make mistakes, too." Similar stories abound about people who have found that mistakes in their credit reports have led to disastrous results.

Now, imagine how significant a data accuracy error might be in other settings. Hospitals use similar automation and computer-intensive record keeping. Imagine what would happen if prescription information appeared incorrectly on a patient's chart and the patient became deathly ill as a result of the medicine that was mistakenly dispensed to him. The significance of such a data accuracy error could be tremendous. Furthermore, it would not be clear who was to blame. Would this be the fault of the doctor, the pharmacist, the programmer, the data entry clerk, or maybe some combination of errors by the system designer, the system analyst, the system programmer, the database administrator, and the vendor? It would be too easy simply to blame the computer; some one person would need to be found at fault.

Computer-based information systems, and the data within those systems, are only as accurate and as useful as they have been made to be. The now infamous quote that "Computers make mistakes. Banks make mistakes, too" would be better restated as, "Computers never make mistakes; only humans make mistakes" (Mason, 1986). This reflects the need for better precautions and greater scrutiny when modern information systems are designed, built, and used. This means that everyone must be concerned with data integrity, from the design of the system, to the building of the system, to the person that actually enters data into the system, and to the people who use and manage the system. Perhaps more important, when data errors are found, people should not blame the computer. After all, people designed and built it, and entered data into it in the first place.

Information Property

It happens to all of us. Nearly every day in the mail, we receive unwanted solicitations from credit card companies, department stores, magazines, or charitable organizations. Many of these envelopes are never opened. We ask the same question over and over again: "How did I get on another mailing list?" Your name, address, and other personal information were most likely sold from one company to another for use in mass mailings. You probably did not give anyone permission to buy or sell information about you, but that is not a legal issue, or a matter of concern, for some firms. *Information property* focuses on who owns information about individuals and how information can be sold and exchanged.

Who owns the computerized information about people—the information that is stored in thousands of databases by retailers, credit card companies, and marketing research companies? The answer is that the company that maintains the database of customers or subscribers legally owns the information and is free to sell it. Your name, address, and other information are all legally kept in a company database to be used for the company's future mailings and solicitations. However, the company can sell its customer list or parts of it to other companies who want to send similar

mailings. This is where the problems begin. For instance, L.L. Bean, the outdoor and apparel retailer, can sell names and addresses from its customer database to companies looking for a similar customer base or buying pattern (see Figure 9.6). Of course, L.L. Bean would not sell parts of its list to competitors. The list is to be used only once and can be used again only with repayment of the initial fee. Still, many people are concerned that these companies have full ownership of this purchasing and demographic data.

There are limits, however, to what a company can do with such data. For example, if a company stated at one time that its collection of marketing data was to be used strictly internally as a gauge of its own customer base and then sold that data to a second company years later, it would be unethically and illegally breaking its original promise. Companies collect data from credit card purchases (by using a credit card, you indirectly allow this) or from surveys and questionnaires you fill out when applying for a card. They also collect data when you fill in a survey at a bar, restaurant, supermarket, or mall about service quality or product preferences. By providing this information, you are implicitly agreeing that this data can be used as the company wishes (within legal limits, of course).

What is even more problematic is the combination of this survey data with transaction data from your credit card purchases. Using the demographic data (who am I and where do I live) and the psychographic data (what are my tastes and preferences), companies can create a highly accurate profile of customers. How do you know who is accessing these databases? This is an issue that each company must address at both a strategic/ethical level (Is this something that we should be doing?) and at a tactical level (If we do this, what can we do to ensure the security and integrity of the data?). The company needs to ensure proper hiring, training, and supervision of employees who have access to the data, as well as to implement the necessary software and hardware security safeguards.

Information Accessibility

With the rapid increase in online databases containing personal information and the influx in the use of computer-based communication between individuals, who has the right to access and monitor this information has

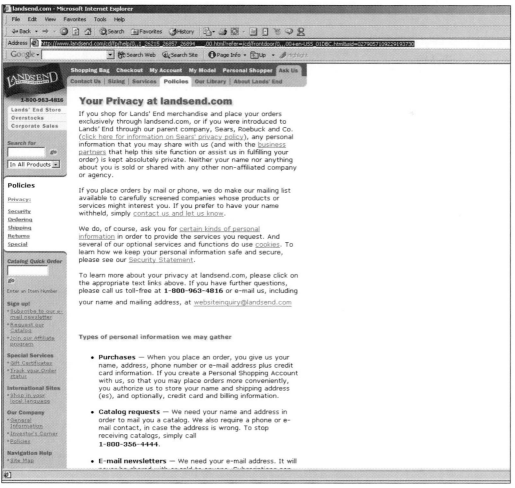

[Figure 9.6 ➡ Information privacy statement from Land's End.]

©2002 Lands' End, Inc. Used with permission.

The Improv Comedy Club in Dallas runs shows at least three times a night and needs to seat at least 260 people per show. For a while, the club depended on a low-tech and inefficient operations management technique, in which employees wrote down phone orders with a paper and pencil and noted seating arrangements on a laminated seating chart, which often led to chaos. Although the club had an old Macintosh that was used for accounting purposes only, no computer technology was used for managing operations. In order to increase efficiency in its day-to-day operations, the club decided to install a new computer system. The club's owner selected Ameranth Technology Systems' 21st Century Restaurant solution, after being impressed with its product demonstration at a restaurant trade show. The

solution implemented at Improv integrated Ameranth's software for Windows CE wireless handheld computers, Microsoft Windows NT operating system, Microsoft SQL server, a middleware, and Symbol Technologies' Wireless LAN. Customers can now book tickets online, and they can also preorder food and pay online. Customer information can be directly entered into a SQL database, which the management later uses to track sales and customers. Finally, the wireless computers (UltraPad 2700) used by the staff enable them to process customers wirelessly and also to access the database to assign customers to tables, thus making the process easier and less chaotic. The system provides enhanced customer service and smoother operations, while customers lose a bit of privacy by being tracked in a database.

Career Implications:

Operations Management

[Adapted from **http://www.microsoft.com/business/casestudies/ameranth_improv.asp**/.]

raised many ethical concerns. *Information accessibility* focuses on defining what information a person or organization has the right to obtain about others and how this information can be accessed and used.

For example, almost everyone sends and receives electronic mail, whether or not they have a PC. All that is needed to participate is access to the Internet, whether through a home PC, a school's computer lab, Web TV, wireless phone, palm PDA, or any of several other devices that provide Internet access. E-mail is one of the most popular software applications of all time, and projections are that its use will only continue to increase. That is why e-mail aficionados and privacy groups were chilled recently when the FBI under the Clinton administration demonstrated a software application named Carnivore to telecommunications industry representatives. Carnivore was designed to be connected to Internet Service Providers' computers, where it would lurk undetected by ISP subscribers, eavesdropping on all communications delivered by the ISP, including e-mail, instant messaging, chat rooms, and visits to Internet sites. If the FBI detected communications that it decided were threatening, as in, for example, activities of terrorists, members of organized crime groups, and hackers, they could unleash Carnivore (see Figure 9.7).

Carnivore provides the "surgical ability" to intercept and collect only those communications that are the subject of lawful wiretaps, explained FBI spokesman Paul Bresson in a recent *TechWeb* article (Mosquera, 2000). "There's a minimization factor built in [that] actually limits messages viewable to human eyes," he said. Despite built-in "minimization factors," Carnivore would sniff through a large percentage of ISP subscribers' activities on the Internet. "This is about the most intrusive form of search there is," countered Marc Totenberg, director of the Electronic Privacy Information Center (EPIC). Unlike police searches of cars and houses for drugs, Totenberg claimed, Carnivore would allow "dragnet fishing," while sifting through all traffic on an ISP.

After the September 11, 2001, terrorist attacks in the United States, government officials requested more leeway in deploying Carnivore in its ongoing fight against terrorism. Privacy groups are concerned that personal privacy might be eroded in a quest to provide heightened homeland security. Clearly, Carnivore and other eavesdropping technologies will be central to numerous ethical discussions.

Beyond the government accessing information, recent court cases have not supported computer privacy for employee e-mail transmissions and Internet usage. For example,

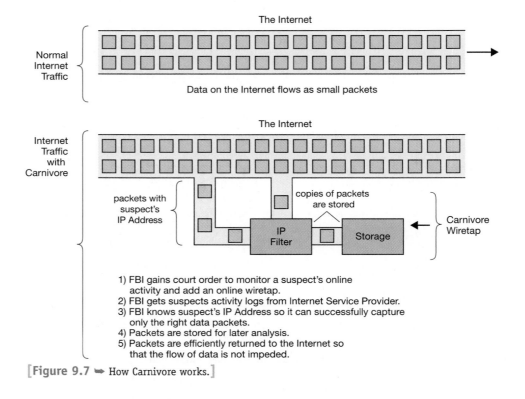

[**Figure 9.7** ➥ How Carnivore works.]

although most companies provide employees with access to the Internet and other outside e-mail systems, many periodically monitor the e-mail messages that employees send and receive. Monitoring employee behavior is nothing new, and it was to many businesses a natural extension to monitor e-mail messages. As a case in point, several recent court case judgments have upheld corporations' rights to monitor their employees' e-mail messages and Internet activity.

Surprisingly, there is little legal recourse for those who support e-mail privacy. In 1986, Congress passed the Electronic Communications Privacy Act (ECPA), but it offered far stronger support for voice mail than it did for e-mail communications. This act made it much more difficult for anyone (including the government) to eavesdrop on phone conversations. E-mail privacy is, thus, much harder to protect. In addition, no other laws at the federal or state levels protect e-mail privacy. However, some states, most notably California, have passed laws that define how companies should inform their employees of this situation and in which situations monitoring is legal. Even so, this law is more of a guideline for ethical practice than a protection of privacy (Sipior and Ward, 1995).

Fortunately, the ECPA and the court case judgments thus far on e-mail monitoring suggest that companies must be prudent and open about their monitoring of e-mail messages and Internet usage. Companies should use good judgment in monitoring e-mail and should make public their policy about monitoring messages. One primary reason that employees perceive their e-mail to be private is the fact that they are never told otherwise (Weisband and Reinig, 1995). In addition, employees should use e-mail only as appropriate, based on their company's policy and their own ethical standards. Given recent actions and rulings on the capture and usage of e-mail messages over the Internet, it appears that online privacy is in jeopardy, in and out of business organizations. As a general rule, we all need to realize that what we type and send via e-mail in and out of the workplace is likely to be read by others for whom the messages were not intended. It is wise to generate only those e-mail messages that would not embarrass us if they were made public.

The Need for a Code of Ethical Conduct

Not only has the Internet Age found government playing catch-up to pass legislation pertaining to computer crime, privacy, and security, it has also created an ethical conundrum. For instance, the technology exists to rearrange and otherwise change photographs, but is the practice ethical? After all, if photographs no longer reflect absolute reality, how can we trust published images? It may not be illegal for you to "steal" computer time from your school or place of employment to do personal business, but most people would consider this unethical. Is it ethical for companies to compile information about your shopping habits, credit history, and other aspects of your life for the purpose of selling such data to others? Should guidelines be in place to dictate how businesses and others use information and computers? If so, what should the guidelines include, and who should write them? Should there be penalties imposed for those who violate established guidelines? If so, who should enforce such penalties?

Many businesses have devised guidelines for the ethical use of information technology and computer systems, and many computer-related professional groups have also published guidelines for their members. Such organizations include the Assistive Devices Industry Association of Canada, the Association for Computing Machinery, the Australian Computer Society, the Canadian Information Processing Society, the Data Processing Management Association, the Hong Kong Computer Society, the Institute of Electrical and Electronics Engineers, the International Federation for Information Processing, the International Programmers Guild, and the National Society of Professional Engineers.

Most universities and many public school systems have written guidelines for students, faculty, and employees about the ethical use of computers. EDUCOM, a nonprofit organization of colleges and universities, has developed a policy for ethics in information technology that many universities endorse. In part, the EDUCOM statement concerning software and intellectual rights says: "Because electronic information is volatile and easily reproduced, respect for the work and personal expression of others is especially critical in computer environments. Violations of authorial integrity, including plagiarism, invasion of privacy, unauthorized access, and trade secret and copyright violations, may be grounds for sanctions against members of the academic community."

Most organization and school guidelines encourage all system users to act responsibly,

Brief Case: "Cybersquatting"

Tim Berners-Lee was once asked his opinion on "cybersquatting," or the dubious practice of registering a domain name, then trying to sell the name for big bucks to the person, company, or organization most likely to want it. He replied: "Domain names are a scarce resource—one of the few scarce resources in cyberspace. I have little sympathy for those who scoop these up with the hope of speculating on their value. This is not one of the most helpful activities on the Net. There are those who use their energy for the purposes of furthering the technology or the content or the world in some way, but just sitting on a domain name without using it in order to cash in later does not seem to me constructive."

Victims of cybersquatting include Panasonic, Hertz, Avon, and numerous other companies and individuals. Fortunately, the U.S. government passed the "Anti-Cybersquatting Consumer Protection Act" in 1999, which made registering, trafficking in, or using a domain name to profit from the goodwill of a trademark belonging to someone else a crime (Elias and Gima, 2000). Fines for cybersquatting can reach as high as $100,000 in addition to the forfeiture of the disputed domain name. As a result, recent court cases have not been kind to squatters. Many feel, however, that it is often much easier simply to pay the cybersquatter because that will likely be much cheaper and faster in the long run than to hire a lawyer and go through the legal process. Unfortunately, it seems that cybersquatting will continue to occur and those who are infringed upon will be forced to waste valuable time and resources resolving these disputes. ▬

Web Search

WEB SEARCH OPPORTUNITY: Cybersquatting is an ethical dilemma facing many famous people and companies. Use a search engine to investigate a popular entertainer who has an "official" Web site, and provide a list of domain names that are similar to those of the official site.

ethically, and legally when using computers, and to follow accepted rules of online etiquette, as well as federal and state laws.

Responsible Computer Use

The Computer Ethics Institute is a research, education, and policy study organization with members from the IT professions and from academic, corporate, and public policy communities. The group studies how advances in information technology have impacted ethics and corporate and public policy and has issued widely quoted guidelines for the ethical use of computers. The guidelines prohibit:

▌ Using a computer to harm others

▌ Interfering with other people's computer work

▌ Snooping in other people's files

▌ Using a computer to steal

▌ Using a computer to bear false witness

▌ Copying or using proprietary software without paying for it

▌ Using other people's computer resources without authorization or compensation

▌ Appropriating other people's intellectual output

The guidelines recommend:

▌ Thinking about social consequences of programs you write and systems you design

▌ Using a computer in ways that show consideration and respect for others

Responsible computer use in the Information Age includes avoiding the types of behavior mentioned above. As a computer user, when in doubt, review the ethical guidelines published by your school, place of employment, and/or professional organization.

Some users bent on illegal or unethical behavior are attracted by the anonymity they believe the Internet affords. But the fact is that we leave electronic tracks as we wander through the Web, and some perpetrators have been traced and successfully prosecuted when they thought they had hidden their trail. The fact is, too, that if you post objectionable material on the Internet and people complain about it, your ISP can ask you to remove the material or remove yourself from the service.

COMPUTER CRIME

The Microsoft incident mentioned in the chapter opening is an example of computer crime. **Computer crime** is defined as the act of using a computer to commit an illegal act. This broad definition of computer crime can include:

▌ Targeting a computer while committing an offense. For example, someone gains unauthorized entry to a computer system in order to cause damage to the computer system or to the data it contains.

▌ Using a computer to commit an offense. In such cases, computer users may steal credit card numbers from Web sites or a company's database, skim money from bank accounts, or make unauthorized electronic fund transfers from financial institutions.

▌ Using computers to support a criminal activity, despite the fact the computers are not actually targeted. For example, drug dealers and other professional criminals may use computers to store records of their illegal transactions.

The Issue of Computer Access

Traditionally, there have been two sides to the issue of computer access. On one side were liberal civil rights champions, the information industry, communications service providers, and expert computer users called hackers. This side said prosecute computer criminals under the law, but do not prevent the free exchange of information.

On the opposing side of the computer access issue were privacy advocates, government agencies, law enforcement officials, and businesses that depend on the data stored in computers. Their point of view was much stricter, advocating the free exchange of information only among those with authorization for access. Anyone who breaks into a computer is trespassing, they said, and all intruders should be subject to penalties under the law.

In today's Information Age, however, the debate has expanded, and lines between the two sides may not be as clearly drawn. The global reach of computer networks has raised concern over copyrights, privacy, and security among all user groups. Most computer users now agree that ownership rights of those who create software and other copyrighted materials disseminated over networks must be protected. And when financial or health data is collected about individuals and stored on computers, that information should not be freely available to anyone who can retrieve it. Both sides of the information access argument agree that one of the major challenges of the Internet Age will be to protect privacy and security, while at the same time allowing authorized access to digitized information.

Unauthorized Computer Access

A person who gains unauthorized access to a computer system has committed a computer crime. ***Unauthorized access*** means that the person who has gained entry to a computer system has no authority to use such access (Figure 9.8). The Microsoft intrusion described in the chapter opening is an example of unauthorized access. Here are a few additional examples from recent media reports:

- Employees steal time on company computers to do personal business.
- Intruders break into government Web sites and change the information displayed.
- Thieves steal credit card numbers and social security numbers from electronic databases, then use

the stolen information to charge thousands of dollars in merchandise to victims.

Because computer crime has increased with the increasing use of computers, there are now federal and state laws in place that expressly prohibit these crimes.

Federal and State Laws

In the United States, there are two main federal laws against computer crime: the Computer Fraud and Abuse Act of 1986 and the Electronic Communications Privacy Act of 1986. The Computer Fraud and Abuse Act of 1986 prohibits:

- Stealing or compromising data about national defense, foreign relations, atomic energy, or other restricted information
- Gaining unauthorized access to computers owned by any agency or department of the United States government
- Violating data belonging to banks or other financial institutions
- Intercepting or otherwise intruding upon communications between states or foreign countries
- Threatening to damage computer systems in order to extort money or other valuables from persons, businesses, or institutions

In 1996, the Computer Abuse Amendments Act expanded the Computer Fraud and Abuse Act of 1986 to prohibit the dissemination of computer viruses and other harmful code.

The Electronic Communications Privacy Act of 1986 makes it a crime to break into any electronic communications service, including telephone services. It prohibits the interception of any type of electronic communications. Interception, as defined by the law, includes listening in on communications without authorization and recording or otherwise taking the contents of communications.

In addition to the two main laws discussed above, other federal laws may apply to computer crime. Patent laws protect some software and computer hardware, and contract laws may protect trade secrets that are stored on computers. In 1980, the U.S. Copyright Act was amended to include computer software, making it a violation of this act to post online written compositions, photos,

© 1999 Ted Goff

"Did they have to add a sound file?"

[**Figure 9.8** ➥ Unauthorized computer access is a crime.]

©Ted Goff

sound files, and software without the permission of the copyright holder.

The Federal Bureau of Investigation (FBI) and the United States Secret Service (USSS) jointly enforce federal computer crime laws. The FBI is in charge when crimes involve espionage, terrorism, banking, organized crime, and threats to national security. The Secret Service investigates crimes against U.S. Treasury Department computers and against computers that contain information protected by the Financial Privacy Act. Information protected by the Financial Privacy Act includes credit card information, credit-reporting information, and data on bank loan applications. In some federal computer crime cases, the U.S. Customs Department, Commerce Department, or the military may have jurisdiction. In addition to federal laws against computer crime, all 50 states have passed laws prohibiting computer crime. Several foreign countries also have similar laws.

Some violations of state and federal computer crime laws are charged as misdemeanors. These violations are punishable by fines and by not more than one year in prison. Other violations are classified as felonies and are punishable by fines and by more than one year in prison. Intent can determine whether crimes are prosecuted as misdemeanors or felonies. If intruders breach computer systems with intent to do harm, they may be charged with a felony. If a break-in is classified as reckless disregard but causes no damage, the offense may be classified as a misdemeanor.

Some critics argue that laws do not go far enough to prosecute computer crimes, while others believe they should not be invoked when systems are breached but no damage is done. Even the definition of damage is debatable. For instance, has damage occurred if someone gains unauthorized access to a computer system but does not steal or change information?

There are additional difficulties in legislating and enforcing laws that affect global networks. Since many countries can be involved when break-ins and other crimes occur, who has jurisdiction? Should e-mail messages be monitored for libelous or other illegal content, and if so, who should have monitoring responsibility? Is e-mail subject to the same laws as mail delivered by the postal service, or is it more akin to telephone communications and the laws that apply to them?

Hacking and Cracking

Those individuals who are knowledgeable enough to gain access to computer systems without authorization have long been referred to as *hackers*. The name was first used in the 1960s to describe expert computer users and programmers who were students at the Massachusetts Institute of Technology (MIT). They wrote programs for the mainframes they used and freely exchanged information, but they followed unwritten rules against damaging or stealing information belonging to others. They claimed that their motives for roaming freely through computer systems were based entirely on curiosity and the desire to learn as much as possible about computers.

As computer crime became more prevalent and damaging, true hackers—those motivated by curiosity and not by a desire to do harm—objected to use of the term to describe computer criminals. Today, those who break into computer systems with the intention of doing damage or committing a crime are usually called *crackers*.

Global Perspective

Controlling Global Cybercrime

One of the difficulties in combating cybercrime is that the criminals often attack across international borders, making tracking, capturing, and punishing the culprits difficult or impossible. In late 2001, a controversial international treaty was finalized to combat cybercrime. The controversy surrounding the treaty centered on criticisms by privacy and human rights groups that feel it gives police and law enforcement agencies too much power, thereby infringing on personal privacy without adequate accountability and oversight. In addition, many Internet Service Providers are also unhappy about some of the rules in the treaty; some of the new policies in the treaty require providers to retain user account information and other data, with no provisions for cost recovery. Some believe, however, that the treaty was formulated in a way that leaves some flexibility in how rules will be enforced and interpreted because of the variations in laws and legal procedures across countries. This flexibility will provide privacy groups a position to debate how rules should be interpreted in order to protect privacy and civil liberties. Clearly, a treaty is needed to assure secure global commerce, but designing and implementing the rules to fit the situations of all countries is proving to be quite difficult.

[Adapted from R. Perera, "Controversial Cybercrime Treaty Ready for Signatures," **http://www.computerworld.com**, *Computerworld* (November 9, 2001).]

Types of Computer Criminals and Crimes

Computer crimes are almost as varied as the users who commit them (see Figure 9.9). Some involve the use of a computer to steal money or other assets, or to perpetrate a deception for money, such as advertising merchandise for sale on a Web auction site, collecting orders and payment, then sending either inferior merchandise or no merchandise at all. Other computer crimes involve stealing or altering information. Some of those thieves who steal information or disrupt a computer system have demanded a ransom from victims in exchange for returning the information or repairing the damage. Techno-terrorists have planted destructive programs in computer systems, then threatened to activate them if a ransom is not paid. Crimes in the form of electronic vandalism cause damage when offenders plant viruses, cause computer systems to crash, or deny service on a Web site.

Use of the Internet has fostered other types of criminal activity, such as the stalking of minors and others by sexual predators through newsgroups and chat rooms. Those who buy and sell pornography have also found in the Internet a new medium for carrying on their activities.

Who Commits Computer Crimes?

When you hear the term "computer hacker," you might imagine a techno-geek, someone who sits in front of her computer all day and night attempting to break the ultrasuper secret security code of one of the most sophisticated computer systems in the world, perhaps a computer for the U.S. Military, a Swiss bank, or the CIA. While this fits the traditional profile for a computer hacker, there is no clear profile today. More and more people have the skills, tools, and the motive to hack into a computer system. A modern-day hacker could be a disgruntled, middle-aged, white-collar worker sitting at a nice desk on the fourteenth floor of the headquarters building of a billion-dollar software manufacturer. Computer hackers have been around for decades. For the most part, we associate hackers with their pranks and crimes involving security systems and viruses. Hackers have caused the loss of billions of dollars' worth of stolen goods, repair bills, and lost goodwill with customers.

Surveys have shown that when businesses and other organizations are victimized, the perpetrators are most often employees or others inside the organization. For example, in a 1998 survey of 1,600 companies in 50 countries, cosponsored by PricewaterhouseCoopers and *InformationWeek*, 73 percent of the respondents reported some security breach or corporate espionage during a one-year period. Intrusions reported by survey respondents came from these groups (Figure 9.10), in order of frequency:

- Authorized employees—58 percent
- Employees who were not authorized to use a computer system—24 percent
- Outside computer hackers or terrorists—13 percent
- An organization's competitors—3 percent

Web Search

WEB SEARCH OPPORTUNITY: The article at **http://wwww.cnn.com/ TECH/specials/hackers/ primer/** describes three types of computer hackers; review this article, and prepare a short report that defines each of the three types.

© 2000 Ted Goff

"Sure, you can fire me, but I'll just hack into the HR computer and hire myself again. That's how I got this job to begin with."

[Figure 9.9 ➡ Computer crimes are as varied as the individuals who commit them.]
©Ted Goff

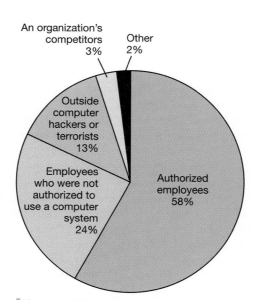

An organization's competitors 3%

Other 2%

Outside computer hackers or terrorists 13%

Employees who were not authorized to use a computer system 24%

Authorized employees 58%

[Figure 9.10 ➡ Who makes unlawful intrusions into computer systems.]

Data Diddling, Salami Slicing, and Other Techno-Crimes

As long as computers and the data they contain are an integral part of our daily lives, criminals will devise ways to take illegal advantage of the technology. Such crimes cost society billions of dollars annually. (The exact amount can only be estimated, since many businesses do not report crimes, for fear of losing customers if the offenses became public.) Over the years, colorful jargon has evolved to label the many types of computer crime, as summarized in Table 9.1.

Software Piracy

Software developers and marketers want you to buy as many copies of their products as you want, of course. But commercial software vendors do not want you or anyone else to buy one copy, then bootleg additional copies to sell or to give to others. Vendors also take a dim view of companies that buy one copy of a software application, then make many copies to distribute to employees. In fact, the practice is called *software piracy*, and it is illegal.

When you buy commercial software, it is legal for you to make one back-up copy for your own use. It is also legal to offer shareware or public domain software for free through bulletin boards and other Web sites. But warez peddling—offering stolen proprietary software for free over the Internet—is a crime. ("Warez" is the slang term for such stolen software.)

Both patent and copyright laws can apply to software. Copyright laws covering software include the 1980 Computer Software Copyright Act, a 1992 act that made software piracy a felony, and the 1997 No Electronic Theft (NET) Act, which made copyright infringement a criminal act even when no profit was involved.

Software piracy has become a problem because it is so widespread, costing the commercial software industry billions of dollars a year. The crime is difficult to trace, but some individuals and companies have been successfully prosecuted for pirating software.

Software Piracy Is a Global Business

A major international issue businesses deal with is the willingness (or unwillingness) of governments and individuals to recognize and enforce the ownership of intellectual property—in particular, software copyright. Piracy of software and other technologies is widespread internationally. The Business Software Alliance (BSA) points to countries such as Vietnam, China, Indonesia, Ukraine, and Russia as those with the highest percentages of illegal software (BSA, 2001). In these countries, more than 85 percent of the software used consists of illegal copies. Worldwide losses due to piracy were nearly $12 billion in 2000! Because technology usage varies significantly by region, average piracy levels and dollar losses greatly differ across regions (see Table 9.2).

Brief Case: Computer Criminal Hall of Fame

A few individuals with expertise in hacking and phreaking used their skills to become well-known computer criminals:

▌ John Draper, a.k.a. "Cap'n Crunch," was a notorious phone phreak who operated in the late 1960s and early 1970s. Draper discovered that the whistle that came as a prize in boxes of Cap'n Crunch cereal perfectly duplicated the 2,600-hertz tone used by the telephone company's switching system. He could blow the whistle into a telephone receiver and activate switches that allowed him to make free long distance calls. Draper was caught by the FBI and served a year and four months in prison in two separate convictions for wire fraud. Once released, Draper did not return to his old habits.

▌ Throughout his career as a phreak and cracker in the 1980s, Kevin Lee Poulsen's crimes ranged from setting up his own telephone wiretaps, to posing as a telephone directory assistance operator, to using computers to win cash and cars in radio giveaway contests. Poulsen served nearly five years in prison. After his release in 1996, he became a computer security consultant.

▌ By 1995, Kevin Mitnick had been convicted five times of various telecommunications and computer crimes. He served time in a juvenile detention center and in federal prison in California for stealing free long distance telephone service, breaking into Pentagon computers, stealing software online, and other techno-crimes. Mitnick violated terms of his probation and in 1992 was again on the run from the law. He continued to ply his trade, was captured in 1995, and was again sentenced to prison. Mitnick was released early in 2000 but was forbidden to use computers for four years after his release.

Computer Crime	Description
Data diddling	The changing of data going into or out of a computer. For example, a student breaks into his university's grade-recording system and changes the grades he earned in last semester's classes, thus raising his grade point average.
Salami slicing	A form of data diddling that occurs when a person shaves small amounts from financial accounts and deposits them in a personal account. For example, a bank employee deposits a few pennies from each of thousands of accounts into an account set up in a fictitious name. The amounts are too small to raise flags, but over time the thief collects a substantial sum.
Phreaking	Crimes committed against telephone company computers with the goal of making free long distance calls, impersonating directory assistance or other operator services, diverting calls to numbers of the perpetrator's choice, or otherwise disrupting telephone service for subscribers.
Cloning	Cellular phone fraud in which scanners are used to steal the electronic serial numbers of cellular phones, which are used for billing purposes and are broadcast as calls are made. With stolen serial numbers, clones can be made to make "free" calls that are billed to the owner of the original cell phone.
Carding	Refers to the practice of stealing credit card numbers online, to be resold or used to charge merchandise against victims' accounts.
Piggybacking or Shoulder-surfing	The act of simply standing in line behind a card user at an automated teller machine (ATM), looking over that person's shoulder, and memorizing the card's personal identification number (PIN). With the right equipment, the stolen numbers can then be placed on counterfeit access cards and used to withdraw cash from the victim's account.
Social engineering	Gaining information needed to access computers by means of tricking company employees by posing as a magazine journalist, telephone company employee, or forgetful coworker in order to persuade honest employees to reveal passwords and other information. The information is then used to break into a computer system or to steal company equipment and other contraband.
Dumpster diving	This approach requires no technical expertise, since it consists simply of going through dumpsters and garbage cans for company documents, credit card receipts, and other papers containing information that might be useful.
Spoofing	A scam used to steal passwords for legitimate accounts on computers in which the "spoofer" uses a program that duplicates an organization's login screen. When legitimate users log on to the system, the counterfeit screen responds with an error message but secretly captures the user's ID and password. The swindle lets intruders pass as legitimate users, thus allowing them to steal computer time and resources.

[Table 9.1] *Types of computer crimes.*

Region	Piracy Levels	Dollar Loss
North America	25%	$2,937,437,000
Western Europe	34%	$3,079,256,000
Asia / Pacific	51%	$4,084,061,000
Latin America	58%	$869,777,000
Mid East / Africa	55%	$376,344,000
Eastern Europe	63%	$404,491,000

[Table 9.2] *Software piracy levels and dollar losses by region. (Source: BSA, 2001)*

Is this an ethical problem? Perhaps in part, but there are other perspectives that business people must acknowledge and deal with as well. In part, the problem stems from countries' differing concepts of ownership. Many of the ideas about intellectual property ownership stem from long-standing cultural traditions. For example, the concept of individual ownership of knowledge is traditionally a strange one in many Middle Eastern countries, where knowledge is meant to be shared. Plagiarism does not exist in a country where words belong to everyone. By the same token, piracy does not exist either. This view is gradually changing; the Saudi Arabia Patent Office granted its first patents several years ago, and their piracy rates have plummeted from 79 percent in 1996 to 59 percent in 2000.

In other cases, there are political, social, and economic reasons for piracy. In many other countries, software publishers are simply not catering to the needs of consumers, who often simply do not have the funds to purchase software legitimately. This is true in many areas of South America and other regions with low per capita income. It is particularly true of students and other members of university communities, whose needs are critical in some areas.

Other factors leading to piracy or infringement of intellectual property agreements throughout the world include lack of public awareness about the issue, lack of an industrial infrastructure that can produce legitimate software, and the increasingly high demand for computer and other technology products. The United States has repeatedly pressured and threatened other countries accused of pirating. It is interesting to note, however, that despite the fact that few of these cultural and economic explanations are valid in the United States, we lead the world in the sheer volume of illegal software in use. Businesses that operate in glass offices should surely not throw stones.

Computer Viruses and Other Destructive Code

Recently, one of the popular antivirus Web sites reported that 500 new computer viruses were unleashed on computer users each month. *Viruses* are destructive programs that disrupt the normal functioning of computer systems. They differ from other types of malicious code in that they can reproduce themselves. Some viruses are intended to be harmless pranks, but more often they do damage to a computer system by erasing files on the hard drive or by slowing computer processing or otherwise compromising the system.

Viruses are planted in host computers in a number of ways (Figure 9.11). Boot sector viruses attach themselves to that section of a hard or floppy disk that lets the user boot up or start the computer. They are most often spread through use of an infected floppy disk. File infector viruses attach themselves to files with certain extensions, such as .doc or .exe. Some viruses are a combination of boot sector and file infector viruses, and many of these can change in order to fool antivirus programs. Viruses transmitted through e-mail messages became popular in the late 1990s. When an unsuspecting recipient of an e-mail message opens the message or an attachment to the message, the virus is activated. Usually such e-mail viruses can then send copies of themselves to everyone in the victim's address book, thus spreading throughout networked computers at an alarming rate.

Worms, Trojan Horses, and Other Sinister Programs

Viruses are among the most virulent forms of computer infections, but other destructive code can also be damaging. A *worm*, for example, usually does not destroy files, but, like a virus, it is designed to copy and send itself, spreading rapidly throughout networked computers. It eventually brings computers to a halt simply by clogging memory space with the outlaw code, thus preventing normal function.

Another destructive program is the *Trojan horse*. Unlike a virus, the Trojan horse does not copy itself, but like viruses it can do much damage. When a Trojan horse is planted in a computer its instructions remain hidden. The computer appears to function normally, but in fact it is performing underlying functions dictated by the intrusive code. For example, under the pretext of playing chess with an unsuspecting systems operator, a cracker group installed a Trojan horse in a Canadian mainframe. While the game appeared to be proceeding normally, the Trojan horse program was sneakily establishing a powerful unauthorized account for the future use of the intruders.

Logic or time bombs are variations of Trojan horses. They also do not reproduce themselves and are designed to operate with-

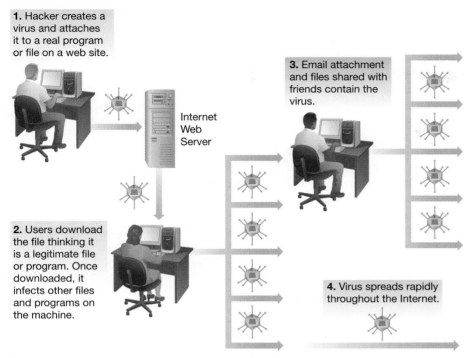

1. Hacker creates a virus and attaches it to a real program or file on a web site.

Internet Web Server

3. Email attachment and files shared with friends contain the virus.

2. Users download the file thinking it is a legitimate file or program. Once downloaded, it infects other files and programs on the machine.

4. Virus spreads rapidly throughout the Internet.

[Figure 9.11 ➡ How a computer virus is spread.]

out disrupting normal computer function. Instead, they lie in wait for unsuspecting computer users to perform a triggering operation. Time bombs are set off by specific dates, such as the birthday of a famous person. Logic bombs are set off by certain types of operations, such as entering a specific password, or adding or deleting names and other information to and from certain computer files. Disgruntled employees have planted logic and time bombs upon being fired, intending for the program to activate after they have left the company. In at least one instance in recent history, a former employee in Minnesota demanded money to deactivate the time bomb he had planted in company computers before it destroyed employee payroll records.

COMPUTER SECURITY

The rule of thumb for deciding whether computer security is at risk is simple: All computers connected to networks are vulnerable to security violations from outsiders as well as insiders, and to virus infections and other forms of computer crime. *Computer security* refers to precautions taken to keep computers and the information they contain safe from unauthorized access. Here are a few safe-

guards that can help organizations maintain a high level of computer security:

▪ Organizations should decide which computer operations are most vulnerable to break-ins by unauthorized users. They should then implement a security plan to protect those areas diligently. The information technology department is usually responsible for instituting security measures. Once an organization assesses its risks, it should formulate a plan that details what action will be taken if security is breached. Making backup copies of important files on a regular basis can help with reconstruction if a damaging security breach should occur.

▪ Organizations can prevent unauthorized access to computers by keeping stored information safe and allowing access only to those employees who need it to do their jobs. Passwords are effective only if chosen carefully and changed frequently. Besides passwords, employees may be asked to provide an ID combination, a security code sequence, or personal data such as a mother's maiden name. Employees authorized to use computer systems may also be issued keys to physically unlock a computer, photo ID cards, smart cards with digital ID, and other forms of physical devices allowing computer access.

▪ Organizations can use special software to help keep stored information secure. Access-control software, for example, may allow computer users access only to those files related to their work, and may allow read-only access, which means

Career Implications:

Marketing

In order to expedite passenger arrivals and reduce operating costs, Heathrow Airport in London is conducting a new trial, whereby iris-recognition software will be used to identify passengers at various stages of the travel process. Many passengers (especially those traveling by British Airways or Virgin Atlantic Airways) will be participating in this trial. This new form of identification process uses iris-recognition software to verify passenger identity. This kind of software identifies people by recognizing the unique patterns in the colored ring around the pupils of the eye (also known as the iris). The particular software being used by Heathrow Airport is called Jetstream Passenger Processing and was developed by a company located in McLean, Virginia. The software trans-

lates the iris pattern into a frequent-flier number or passport number. This number is then communicated to the airport and airline computers, simplifying check-in, baggage check, boarding, and passport control. In addition to simplifying operations, the software will also help in imposing stricter security controls, along with reducing the risks of errors and other forms of operating costs. Simplifying Passenger Control, the organization overseeing the implementation of this new technology, hopes to conduct a few more trials in addition to the one in Heathrow, before implementing the software on a larger scale. Enhancing security and easing the processing of frequent travelers will be an important marketing strategy; airports employing advanced technology will have a distinct advantage over those that choose not to invest.

[Adapted from **http://www.msnbc.com/news/** (July 26, 2001).]

the user can read files but cannot change them. Organizations may also use antivirus software. It does not restrict a user's access but scans files for viruses and, in many cases, eradicates them.

- Organizations may also use a form of security called **biometrics** to grant or deny access to a computer system. With biometrics, employees may be identified by fingerprints, retinal patterns in the eye, or other bodily characteristics before being granted access to use a computer (see Figure 9.12). After the hijackings and attacks on September 11, 2001, the use of better security methods became a high priority for airports, large corporate buildings, and computers. Biometrics has the promise of providing very high security and so the U.S. government and many companies are investigating how best to use this technology.

- Another way for organizations to ensure computer security is to make every effort to hire trustworthy employees. Trustworthy employees are less likely to commit offenses associated with unauthorized access.

Encryption

In any discussion of privacy and security of digitized data, the problem of unauthorized eavesdroppers arises. Organizations can use secure channels not available to computer users outside their LANs and intranets, but the Internet and public telephone lines and airwaves are not subject to the same restricted use. Most of us send e-mail around the globe; call

friends, family, and colleagues on wireless telephones; and trust our desktop and mainframe computers with all manner of personal, financial, and corporate secrets. Until recent years, we may have felt secure in our activities. Now, however, news stories about corporate spies, malicious hackers, curious neighbors and coworkers, and suspicious government agencies have us wondering if every transfer of information is somehow subject to unseen eavesdroppers.

When you do not have access to a secure channel for sending information, encryption is the best bet for keeping snoopers out. **Encryption** is the process of encoding messages before they enter the network or airwaves, then decoding them at the receiving end of the transfer, so that recipients can read or hear them (see Figure 9.13). The process works because, if you scramble messages before you send them, eavesdroppers who might intercept them cannot decipher them without the decoding key.

We now have access to encryption software that scrambles text and voice messages and also allows us to send digital signatures

```
Ciphertext letters:
JOGPSNBUJPO TZTUFNT UPEBZ
Equivalent plaintext letters:
INFORMATION SYSTEMS TODAY
```

[**Figure 9.12** ➡ Biometric devices are used to verify a person's identity.]
©AP/Wide World Photos

[**Figure 9.13** ➡ Encryption is used to encode information so that unauthorized people cannot understand it.]

Nationwide is a global insurance company based in Columbus, Ohio. The company has a complicated network of computers, including wide area networks, extranets, and other servers, and more than 50,000 users on a regular basis. In addition, the company is involved in a number of Internet businesses and maintains a wide array of business-to-business relationships. Security is hence a critical responsibility of the information systems department, and the primary concern of the company is to protect its network from unauthorized users, and "lock down its network perimeter." In spite of all its efforts, the existing technology enabled the company to take action only after a security breach had taken place. The company was always on the lookout for an application that would enable it to understand that a security problem existed even before something had happened. Nationwide found the solution in a tool provided by Vigilinx that keeps track of the operating systems, hardware, firewalls, and so on of its clients' networks. It then surveys Web sites continually to identify potential security threats, "such as viruses or software security holes," and passes the information on to its customers, who can take prompt action, even before something critical has happened. Proactive security is becoming increasingly popular among companies, and with tools from Vigilinx and other companies it is now becoming possible.

Career Implications:

Accounting and Finance

[Adapted from Karen D. Schwartz, "It's a Bad, Bad, Bad, Bad World," **http://www.cio.com**, *CIO Magazine* (April 15, 2001).]

that guarantee we are who we say we are when we send a message. You can activate the encryption function from your browser.

How Encryption Works

All encryption systems use a key—the code that scrambles, then decodes, messages. When both sender and recipient use the same key, this is called a **symmetric secret key system**. This method of encrypting messages was used for centuries. One problem with symmetric secret key encryption is that, since both sender and recipient must keep their key secret from others, key management can be a problem. If too many people use the same key, the system can soon become ineffective. If different keys are used for sending messages to different people, the number of keys can become unmanageable.

Key management problems of secret key encryption systems were eliminated with the development of **public key** technology. Public-key encryption is asymmetric, since it uses two keys—a private key and a public key (see Figure 9.14). (An eccentric former MIT hacker and researcher named Whit Diffie is credited with first envisioning the possibility of using two keys—public and private—to encrypt and decode messages. He and two coworkers published their concept in 1976.) Each person has his own key pair, a public key that is freely distributed and a private key that is kept secret. Say you want to send a message to Jane using this encryption system. First, you get Jane's public key, which is widely available, and you use it to scramble your message. Now even you cannot decode the encrypted message. When Jane receives the message she uses her private key, known only to her, to unscramble it. Public key systems also allow you to authenticate messages. If you encrypt a message using your private key, you have "signed" it. A recipient can verify that the message came from you by using your public key to decode it.

To implement public-key encryption on a large scale, such as on a busy Web site, requires a more sophisticated solution. Here, a third party, called a **certificate authority**, is used. The certificate authority acts as a trusted middleman between computers and verifies that a Web site is a trusted site. The certificate authority knows that each computer is who it says it is and provides the public keys to each computer. **Secure sockets layer (SSL)**, developed by Netscape, is a popular public-key encryption method used on the Internet.

Other Encryption Approaches

Other encryption breakthroughs followed Diffie's public–private key revelation. In 1977, three MIT professors, Ron Rivest, Adi Shamir, and Len Adleman, created RSA (named for the surname initials of the inventors), a system based on the public–private key idea. They licensed the technology to several companies, including Lotus and Microsoft, but federal laws against exporting encryption technology kept companies from incorporating RSA into their software. In 1991, Phil Zimmermann devised Pretty Good Privacy (PGP), a versatile encryption program that he gave away free to anyone who wanted to try it. It soon became the global favorite for encrypting messages.

While innovative encryption aficionados were mainstreaming the encryption concept,

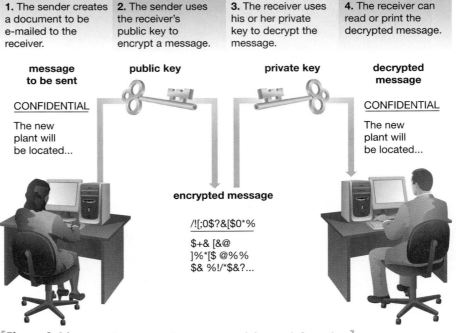

1. The sender creates a document to be e-mailed to the receiver.

2. The sender uses the receiver's public key to encrypt a message.

3. The receiver uses his or her private key to decrypt the message.

4. The receiver can read or print the decrypted message.

message to be sent

public key

private key

decrypted message

CONFIDENTIAL

The new plant will be located...

CONFIDENTIAL

The new plant will be located...

encrypted message

/![;0$?&[$0*%

$+& [&@
]%*[$ @%%
$& %!/*$&?...

[Figure 9.14 ➥ How keys are used to encrypt and decrypt information.]

the government fought to keep control over keys that would allow its agents to decode communications deemed suspicious. In 1993, then President Bill Clinton endorsed the Clipper Chip, a chip that could generate uncrackable codes. The catch was that only the government would have the key to decode any messages scrambled via the Clipper Chip. Opponents criticized the idea as a threat to personal liberty. But when a flaw was found in the chip, that under certain conditions would allow users to take advantage of the chip's strong encryption capabilities without giving the government the key, the Clipper Chip idea was scrapped before it could become reality.

The government finally loosened its control over encryption technology when, in 1999, federal regulations were written allowing the export of strong encryption programs. This paved the way for software developers to build encryption options into their products and made it easier for any computer user to take advantage of encryption technology.

While encryption cannot solve all privacy issues, such as the trading of consumer information collected on the Web, or deliberate leaking of e-mail messages the sender intended to be kept private, it is definitely effective in keeping snoopers out when both senders and receivers desire privacy. Perhaps eventually encryption will protect medical records, credit histories, credit card databases,

and other information that should be marked "keep out" to unauthorized viewers.

Internet Security

Cases like these frequently make the news: Someone breaks into a government Web site and scrambles the message displayed, adding profanity. A popular search engine's Web site is hacked and service is denied to users for several hours while the problem is corrected. Hackers add personal messages to a commercial service provider's Web page about a sports celebrity. Clearly, if you plan to publish a Web site you will want to make the site secure.

Businesses and ISPs use firewalls to keep LANs and WANs secure. A *firewall* consists of hardware or software designed to keep unauthorized users out of network systems. Firewall software can filter incoming and outgoing information and block unauthorized users and has become very popular. In fact, many individuals who have high-speed Internet access at home often purchase a *personal* firewall using software from McAfee, Zone Labs, or Symantec.

Virus Prevention

Viruses that are spread via e-mail transmitted over the Internet are also frequently in the news. Despite their colorful names—Melissa, I Love You, Naked Wife—viruses can be deadly

RSA Security owns the patent to the most popular public-key encryption algorithm. Prior to the expiration of the patent in September 2000, RSA Security released the algorithm to the public. The patent was issued in 1983 to MIT and was licensed to RSA Security. Over the last many years, the algorithm had become the standard for encryptions, especially for Internet-related applications. More than 1,000 applications, "including Microsoft Windows, Lotus Notes, and Cisco Systems routers," have been developed using the encryption algorithm from RSA Security. In spite of the popularity and the widespread use of the encryption algo-

rithm, the expiration of the patent has been widely welcomed by organizations and industry experts. With the algorithm now available publicly, software vendors will no longer have to pay a fee to RSA Security in order to use it. The integration of the "public-key infrastructure" into software applications would hence become less expensive. Industry experts feel that this will allow vendors to provide more secure applications at a cheaper price, thus making them affordable for organizations, especially for small businesses. In addition, the increased accessibility of this algorithm will help in implementing "uniform cryptographic standards."

[Adapted from Ann Harrison, "RSA Encryption Patent Released," **www.computerworld.com**, *Computerworld* (September 18, 2000).]

Information Systems

Brief Case: **The Disappearing Key**

In March 2001, Harvard professor Michael Rabin announced that he may have devised a code that is absolutely guaranteed to be unbreakable. Rabin's "hyper-encryption" is based on the idea that codes can be formed at random each time a written or spoken message is sent. It works like this: A source, perhaps a satellite or a mainframe computer, generates a stream of random bits. Jane and John select bits from the stream in a

secret, prearranged pattern. These selected bits help Jane encrypt a message to John. John uses the same bits to unscramble the message from Jane. Jane and John do not retain the random selected bits, and their computers delete them. No one else can break the code because the random stream is not stored, thus the "key" no longer exists.

Rabin claimed to have proven that total secrecy is possible, but in late 2001 his idea was not yet ready for implementation.

---

infections once contracted by your computer. Here are some precautions you can take to ensure that your computer is protected:

▌ Purchase and install antivirus software, then update frequently to be sure you are protected against new viruses. These programs can locate viruses, inform you of their presence, and, in many cases, destroy them before they do their damage. Update downloads are available, usually for a fee, at the vendor's Web site.

▌ Make a back-up disk of important applications stored on your hardware, so in worst case scenarios you can replace destroyed programs. To protect work in progress, back up files regularly.

▌ Do not use disks or shareware from unknown or suspect sources, and be equally careful when downloading material from the Internet, making sure that the source is reputable.

▌ Delete without opening any e-mail message received from an unknown source. Be especially wary of opening attachments. It is better to delete a legitimate message than to infect your computer system with a destructive germ.

▌ If your computer system contracts a virus, report the infection to your school or company's IT

department so that appropriate measures can be taken, and inform people listed in your address book, in case the virus has sent itself to everyone on your e-mail list. If forewarned, individuals listed in your address book can often delete the infectious message before it infects their computers.

How to Maintain Your Privacy Online

When you make Web purchases, vendors are not required by law to respect your privacy. In other words, a vendor can track what pages you look at, what products you examine in detail, which products you choose to buy, what method of payment you choose to use, and where you have the product delivered. After collecting all that information, unscrupulous vendors can sell it to others, resulting in more direct-mail advertising, electronic spam in your e-mail in box, or calls from telemarketers.

When surveyed about concerns related to online shopping, most consumers list issues of information privacy as a top concern. As a result, governments have pressured vendors to post their privacy policies on their Web

Web Search

WEB SEARCH OPPORTUNITY: Visit the Privacy Rights Clearinghouse, **http://www. privacyrights.org**, and learn more about how to protect your privacy. Review one of the site's numerous "fact sheets" on how to protect your privacy, and prepare a one-page report summarizing the fact sheet.

SEEING THE INVISIBLE WITH LIQUID CRYSTALS

Liquid crystals are most commonly used for making flat-panel computer displays used in notebook computers and other portable devices. Liquid crystal displays (LCDs) consist of a liquid crystal solution that is contained between two sheets of polarized material. Images and text are displayed when current is applied to the liquid, causing the crystals to align in a particular way. As light is shown through the displays, characters and images are formed. Using a method similar to the way liquid crystals are used to display information, researchers have developed pocket-sized bioweapons detectors that can process information in minutes rather than the days needed using prior techniques. For example, testing someone for anthrax using nasal

swabs in a laboratory can take up to two days. Using liquid crystal technology, a technician swipes a nasal swab onto a thin strip and inserts it into a sensor. Inside the sensor, the sample is combined with liquid crystals that contain an antibody; if the sample contains the pathogen, it binds with the liquid crystals so that when light is shown through the crystals a change in the display occurs, indicating a positive reaction. Researchers believe that that technique is capable of screening for countless bioweapons in less than five minutes. Companies are licensing this technology and developing products that will soon be available to individuals and governmental agencies for detecting airborne as well as ingested pathogens.

———

[Adapted from D. Martindale, "Seeing the Invisible: Liquid Crystals May Be Enlisted to Create Pocket Bioweapons Detectors," **http://www.sciam.com**, *Scientific American* (January 2002).]

---

sites. Unfortunately, these polices do not often protect the privacy of consumers. To protect yourself, you should always review the privacy policy of all companies you do business with and refuse to do business with those that do not have a clear policy. According to the consumer watch group at safeshopping.org, a seller's privacy policy should at least indicate:

▪ What information the seller is gathering from you

▪ How the seller will use this information

▪ Whether and how you can "opt out" of these practices

To make sure your shopping experience is a good one, you can take a few additional steps to maintain your privacy.

▪ **Choose Web sites that are monitored by independent organizations.** There are several independent organizations that monitor the privacy and business practices of Web sites. Organizations such as **http://www.epubliceye.com** and **http://www.openratings.com** provide a valuable service for consumers by monitoring the business practices of sellers and requiring conformance to standard guidelines or providing consumers a rating of a seller's practices. Choosing sites that are independently evaluated by a reputable rating company is a good way to assure your privacy.

▪ **Avoid having "cookies" left on your machine.** Many commercial Web sites are designed to leave a small file on your hard drive so that the owner of the site can monitor where you go and what you do on the site. It is possible that the site owner could obtain your e-mail address from the visit, potentially sending you unsolicited e-mail

spam. Fortunately, most Web browsers provide the ability to turn off cookies or to warn you that the site is trying to deposit a cookie on your hard drive; when configured to warn you, your browser will prompt you with a notification and ask you if you want to accept the cookie. In addition to using settings within your Web browser, you can get special "cookie management" software to help better maintain your privacy (go to **http://www.cookiecentral.com** for more on cookie management options).

▪ **Visit sites anonymously.** There are ways to visit Web sites anonymously. Using services provided by companies such as Anonymizer.com, you have total privacy from marketers, identity thieves, or even coworkers when surfing the Web. Their software blocks cookies, Java, and other tracking methods from being left on your computer; for Web sites that require cookies to be left on your machine in order for you to visit, the software allows cookies to be encrypted so that no one can trace your activity. Similarly, URL addresses are also encrypted so that anyone monitoring your activity cannot log a meaningful address.

▪ **Use caution when requesting confirming e-mail.** When you buy products online, many companies will send you a confirming e-mail message to let you know that the order was received correctly. If you use a shared computer or buy online with a computer at work where your online activity can be monitored, you should take care to protect the privacy of your purchases. A good strategy is to have a separate e-mail account, such as one that is available for viewing via a Web browser, that you use when making online purchases. For example, Hotmail, Yahoo!, Excite, and countless other Web portals provide free e-mail services that can be accessed using a standard Web browser. This allows you to keep your primary e-mail address private from unscrupulous sellers and keeps your correspondence private from anyone who has access to your computer.

Of course there are no guarantees that all your online experiences will be problem-free, but if you follow the advice provided here, you are likely to survive and thrive in the world of online electronic commerce.

Avoid Getting Conned in Cyberspace

"The Internet has changed the way consumers gather information, shop, and do business," Federal Trade Commission director of consumer protection Jodie Bernstein said in November 2000. Con artists and other lawbreakers have gone high-tech and are using the Internet to cheat consumers in a number of clever ways.

The U.S. Federal Trade Commission has compiled advice on how not to get taken by crafty con artists on the Internet (**http://www.ftc. gov/bcp/conline/pubs/online/dotcons.htm**). Among the listed "dot-cons" were offers to let you see adult images in exchange for revealing your credit card number, auction cheats, charges for a "free" Web site appearing on telephone bills, and various investment, travel and vacation, business, and health-care products scams. Table 9.3 summarizes the top ten cybercons being perpetrated on consumers using the Internet. Review this table so that you better understand what techniques con artists are using to separate you from your money. The best advice for doing business on the Internet is to follow the old adage, "if it is too good to be true, then it probably is."

Stopping Internet Fraud

The rapid and widespread adoption of the Internet has been not only a boom for business but has also become a very popular method for fraudulent behavior. According to the Internet Fraud Complaint Center, there were more than 24,000 complaints during a six-month period in 2000 (the latest released data) that were referred to law enforcement and regulatory agencies around the world. In order to create a "one-stop shopping approach" for tracking and responding to Internet-based fraud, the FBI and the National White Collar Crime Center (**http://www.nw3c.org**) have partnered to create the Internet Fraud Complaint Center (IFCC). The mission of the IFCC is to assist people who are victimized by con artists, illegal get-rich quick schemes, and bogus online auctions over the Internet. This partnership is paying

dividends with the arrest of 90 individuals involved in a host of Internet fraud schemes that involved more than 56,000 people and more than $117 million (Thibodeau, 2001). Their data show that the typical victim of fraudulent behavior is male, is in his mid-30s, and resides in one of the most populous states. They report, however, that this profile is just of the most likely victim; they have found victims from every state and every other demographic characteristic. Although the Internet has become a valuable resource to most of us, it has also provided a valuable forum for crooks and con men.

[Adapted from "Internet Fraud Complaint Center: Six-Month Data Trends Report" (May–November 2000), **http://www.ifccfbi.gov**; P. Thibodeau, "Ninety Arrested for Internet Fraud in FBI Sweep," **http:// www.computerworld.com**, *Computerworld*. (May 23, 2001).]

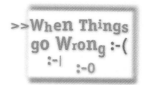

KEY POINTS REVIEW

1. **Describe the advent of the Information Age and how computer ethics impact the use of information systems.** The Information Age refers to a time in the history of civilization when information became the currency of the realm. To be successful in many careers today requires that people be computer literate, since the ability to access and effectively operate computing technology is a key part of many careers. A digital divide is said to exist between people who are computer literate and those who are not. Because computer literacy is so critical in the Information Age, a major ethical concern for society centers on who is computer literate and who is not.

2. **Discuss the ethical concerns associated with information privacy, accuracy, property, and accessibility.** Information privacy is concerned with what information an individual should have to reveal to others through the course of employment or through other transactions such as online shopping. Information accuracy is concerned with the authenticity and fidelity of information, as well as identifying who is responsible for informational errors

[Table 9.3] *Top ten list of dot-cons from the Federal Trade Commission and advice on how not to get conned. (Source: www.ftc.gov/bcp/conline/pubs/online/dotcons.htm)*

The Con	The Bait	The Switch	Advice
Internet auctions	Great deals on great products.	After sending money, consumers receive inferior item or nothing at all.	Investigate the seller carefully. Use a credit card or escrow service to pay.
Internet access service	Free money, simply for cashing a check.	After cashing "free" check, consumers are locked into long-term Web service with steep penalties for early cancellation.	Read both sides of the check, the fine print, or any documentation that comes with the check.
Credit card fraud	View online adult images for free, just for sharing your credit card number to "prove" you are over 18.	Fraudulent promoters run up unauthorized charges on consumers' cards.	Share your credit card numbers only when you are buying from a company you trust. Dispute unauthorized charges (federal law limits your liability to $50).
International modem dialing	Free access to adult material by downloading "viewer" or "dialer."	Exorbitant long-distance phone bills as the viewer or dialer reconnects to an international carrier.	Do not download programs providing "free" access without carefully reading all the fine print. Dispute unauthorized charges to your account.
Web cramming	Free custom-designed Web site for 30-day trial.	Telephone is billed even when consumers do not accept offer or agree to continue service.	Review phone bill carefully, and challenge all charges you do not recognize.
Multilevel marketing plans/ pyramids	Make money selling products you sell as well as those sold by people you recruit to sell.	Consumers are required to recruit other distributors, but products sold to distributors do not qualify for commissions.	Avoid programs that require you to recruit distributors, buy expensive inventory, or commit to a minimum sales volume.
Travel/ vacations	Great trips for bargain prices.	Low-quality accommodations and services, often with hidden charges.	Get references and the details of the trip in writing.
Business opportunities	Be your own boss, and earn a high salary.	Consumers invest in unproven or insecure ventures.	Talk with others who have made the same investment; get all promises in writing, and study the contract carefully. Consult with a lawyer or accountant.
Investments	Realize huge investment returns.	Big profits always mean big risks.	Check with state and federal securities and commodities regulators; insist on talking with other investors.
Health-care products/ services	Cure serious illness or fatal health problems.	Consumers put faith in unproven solutions and put off pursuing needed health care.	Consult with health professionals to evaluate cure-alls or promises to provide fast or easy cures.

that harm people. Information property focuses on who owns information about individuals and how information can be sold and exchanged. Information accessibility focuses on defining what information a person or organization has the right to obtain about others and how this information can be accessed and used. While the Information Age has brought widespread access to information, the downside is that others may now have access to your personal information that you would prefer to keep private. Because there are few safeguards for assuring the accuracy of information, individuals and companies can be damaged by informational errors. Additionally, because information is so easy to exchange and modify, information ownership violations readily occur. Likewise, with the rapid increase in online databases containing personal information and the increase in the use of computer-based communication between individuals, who has the right to access and monitor this information has raised many ethical concerns.

3. **Define computer crime, and list several types of computer crime.** Computer crime is defined as the act of using a computer to commit an illegal act, such as targeting a computer while committing an offense, using a computer to commit an offense, or using computers in the course of a criminal activity. A person who gains unauthorized access to a computer system has also committed a computer crime. Those individuals who are knowledgeable enough to gain access to computer systems without authorization have long been referred to as hackers. Today, those who break into computer systems with the intention of doing damage or committing a crime are usually called crackers. Hackers and crackers can commit a wide variety of computer crimes, including: data diddling, salami slicing, phreaking, cloning, carding, piggybacking or shoulder-surfing, social engineering, dumpster diving, and spoofing. Crackers are also associated with the making and distributing of computer viruses and other destructive codes. Finally, making illegal copies of software, a worldwide computer crime, is called software piracy.

4. **Contrast what is meant by the terms computer virus, worm, Trojan horse, and logic or time bomb.** Viruses are destructive programs that disrupt the normal functioning of computer systems. They differ from other types of malicious code in that they can reproduce themselves. Some viruses are intended to be harmless pranks, but more often they do damage to a computer system

by erasing files on the hard drive or by slowing computer processing or otherwise compromising the system. A worm usually does not destroy files, but, like a virus, it is designed to copy and send itself, spreading rapidly throughout networked computers. It eventually brings computers to a halt simply by clogging memory space with the outlaw code, thus preventing normal functioning. Unlike a virus, the Trojan horse does not copy itself, but like viruses it can do much damage. When a Trojan horse is planted in a computer, its instructions remain hidden. The computer appears to function normally, but in fact it is performing underlying functions dictated by the intrusive code. Finally, logic or time bombs are variations of Trojan horses. They also do not reproduce themselves and are designed to operate without disrupting normal computer function. Instead, they lie in wait for unsuspecting computer users to perform a triggering operation. Time bombs are set off by specific dates, such as the birthday of a famous person, whereas logic bombs are set off by certain types of operations, such as entering a specific password, or adding or deleting names and other information to and from certain computer files.

5. **Explain what is meant by computer security, and describe various methods for providing computer security.** Computer security refers to precautions taken to keep computers and the information they contain safe from unauthorized access. Computer security can be enhanced by keeping computers in a secure location, by keeping information stored in password-protected areas, by using special software to keep stored information secure, by using biometrics to authenticate users, and by hiring trustworthy employees. Encryption—the process of encoding messages before they enter the network or airwaves—is the best bet for keeping information secure when you do not have access to a secure channel. Firewalls can be used to keep LANs and WANs secure. Viruses can be reduced or eliminated (or at least the damage mitigated) if several steps are followed, including: installing antivirus software; backing up critical information; refusing to use disks, data, or software from unknown sources; refusing to open e-mail attachments from unknown sources; and reporting virus infections immediately to your company or school's IT department. When on the Internet you can better maintain your privacy by using only reputable Web sites, controlling the use of cookies, surfing anonymously, and being careful about who has access to your e-mail.

KEY TERMS

biometrics 296

carding 293

certificate authority 297

cloning 293

computer crime 288

computer ethics 281

computer literacy 280

computer security 295

cracker 290

data diddling 293

digital divide 281

dumpster diving 293

encryption 296

firewall 298

hacker 290

identity theft 282

information accessibility 286

information accuracy 283

information Age 280

information privacy 282

information property 284

logic or time bomb 294

piggybacking or shoulder-surfing 293

phreaking 293

public key 297

salami slicing 293

secure sockets layer (SSL) 297

social engineering 293

software piracy 292

spoofing 293

symmetric secret key system 297

trojan horse 294

unauthorized access 289

virus 294

worm 294

REVIEW QUESTIONS

1. Describe the advent of the Information Age and how computer ethics impact the use of information systems.
2. What is the difference between the digital divide and computer literacy?
3. Compare and contrast information accuracy, information privacy, and information property.
4. Define computer crime, and list several types of computer crime.
5. Explain the purpose of the Computer Fraud and Abuse Act of 1986 and the Electronic Communications Privacy Act of 1986.
6. List and describe five security precautions organizations can implement to secure their computer networks.
7. Define unauthorized access, and give several examples from recent media reports.
8. Viruses that are spread via e-mail transmitted over the Internet are also frequently in the news. What are five ways to prevent these viruses?
9. What is identity theft, and what is the solution according to this chapter?
10. Define "cybersquatting." What year did the U.S. government pass legislation to deter this action, and what is the name of the act?
11. Compare and contrast a worm, a virus, a Trojan horse, and a logic or time bomb.
12. List five dot-cons that you find interesting, and give the advice suggested for avoiding these traps.

SELF-STUDY QUESTIONS

1. Being _____ , or knowing how to use the computer as a device to gather, store, organize, and process information, can open up myriad sources of information.
   A. technology illiterate
   B. digitally divided
   C. computer literate
   D. computer illiterate

2. A broad definition of computer crime includes all of the following **except** _____ .
   A. targeting a computer while committing an offense
   B. using computers in the course of a criminal activity, despite the fact the computers are not actually targeted
   C. the act of using a computer to commit a legal act
   D. using a computer to commit an offense

3. _____ focuses on defining what information a person or organization has the right to obtain about others and how this information can be accessed and used.
   A. Information accessibility
   B. Information accuracy
   C. Information privacy
   D. Information property

4. The Computer Ethics Institute is a research, education, and policy study organization with members from the IT professions and from academic, corporate, and public policy communities. The guidelines prohibit all of the following **except** _____ .
   A. using a computer to harm others
   B. using a computer to bear false witness
   C. copying or using proprietary software without paying for it
   D. using computer resources with authorization

5. In the United States, two main federal laws have been passed against computer crime, including _____ .
   A. the Computer Fraud and Abuse Act of 1986
   B. the Electronic Communications Privacy Act of 1986
   C. the E-Commerce Internet Act of 1996
   D. answers A and B

6. Those individuals who break into computer systems with the intention of doing damage or committing a crime are usually called _____ .

A. hackers
B. crackers
C. computer geniuses
D. computer operatives

7. Which of the following copyright laws is applicable to illegal software piracy?
   A. the 1980 Computer Software Copyright Act
   B. a 1992 act that made software piracy a felony
   C. a 1997 No Electronic Theft (NET) Act, which made copyright infringement a criminal act even when no profit was involved
   D. all of the above

8. Computer security refers to precautions taken to keep computers and the information they contain safe from unauthorized access. Which of the following is **not** a safeguard that can help organizations maintain a high level of computer security?
   A. keeping stored information safe with passwords and allowing access only to those employees who need it to do their jobs
   B. using biometrics that may include fingerprints and retinal scans or other bodily characteristics
   C. making every effort to hire employees on parole
   D. utilizing special software to help keep stored information secure

9. A(n) _____ consists of hardware or software designed to keep unauthorized users out of network systems.
   A. encryption system
   B. firewall
   C. alarm system
   D. logic bomb

10. Crimes committed against telephone company computers with the goal of making free long distance calls, impersonating directory assistance or other operator services, diverting calls to numbers of the perpetrator's choice, or otherwise disrupting telephone service for subscribers is called _____ .
    A. phreaking
    B. cloning
    C. carding
    D. data diddling

PROBLEMS AND EXERCISES

1. Match the following terms with the appropriate definitions:

    _____ Digital divide

    _____ Biometrics

    _____ Information privacy

    _____ Encryption

    _____ Information accuracy

    _____ Shoulder-surfing

    _____ Identity theft

    _____ Information accessibility

    _____ Worm

    _____ Computer security

    _____ Computer ethics

    _____ Social engineering

    a. The stealing of another person's social security number, credit card number, and other personal information for the purpose of using the victim's credit rating to borrow money, buy merchandise, and otherwise run up debts that are never repaid

    b. An area concerned with what information an individual should have to reveal to others through the course of employment or through other transactions such as online shopping

    c. The gap between those individuals in our society who are computer literate and have access to information resources such as the Internet and those who do not

    d. Code that usually does not destroy files, but, like a virus, is designed to copy and send itself, spreading rapidly throughout networked computers and eventually bringing computers to a halt simply by clogging memory space with the outlaw code, thus preventing normal functioning

    e. An area concerned with the authenticity and fidelity of information, as well as identifying who is responsible for informational errors that harm people

    f. Refers to precautions taken to keep computers and the information they contain safe from unauthorized access

    g. Focuses on defining what information a person or organization has the right to obtain about others and how this information can be accessed and used

    h. The process of encoding messages before they enter the network or airwaves, then decoding them at the receiving end of the transfer, so that recipients can read or hear them

    i. The identification of employees by fingerprints, retinal patterns, or other bodily characteristics before granting them access to use a computer

    j. The issues and standards of conduct as they pertain to the use of information systems

    k. Gaining information needed to access computers by tricking company employees by means of posing as magazine journalists, telephone company employees, and forgetful coworkers in order to persuade honest employees to reveal passwords and other information

    l. The act of simply standing in line behind a card user at an automated teller machine (ATM), looking over that person's shoulder, and memorizing the card's personal identification number (PIN), then placing the stolen number on a counterfeit access card and using it to withdraw cash from the victim's account

2. The Electronic Frontier Foundation, **http://www.eff.org**, has a mission of protecting rights and promoting freedom in the "electronic frontier." The organization provides additional advice on how to protect your online privacy. Review its suggestions, and provide a summary of what you can do to protect yourself.

3. Do you consider yourself computer literate? Do you know of any friends or relatives who are not computer literate? What can you do to improve your computer literacy? Is computer literacy necessary in today's job market? Why or why not?

4. Look at the following Web sites for tips and articles on identity theft: **http://www.consumer.gov/idtheft/**, **http://www.identitytheft.org/**, and **http://www.msnbc.com/news/771662.asp**. Did you find anything that you think might help you in the future? Did you bookmark any of these tips or e-mail them to your classmates or friends?

5. Complete the computer ethics quiz at **http://web.cs.bgsu.edu/maner/xxicee/html/welcome.htm**, and visit **http://bones.cs.wcupa.edu/~epstein/social.html** for more issues on computer ethics and social implications of computing. Do ethical codes apply to all professions?

6. Find your school's guidelines for ethical computer use on the Internet and answer the following questions: Are there limitations as to the type of Web sites and material that can be viewed (i.e., pornography, etc.)? Are students allowed to change the programs on the hard drives of the lab computers or download software for their own use? Are there rules governing personal use of computers and e-mail?

7. Do you believe that there is a need for a unified information systems code of ethics? Visit **http://www.fau.edu/netiquette/net/ten.html**. What do you think of this code? Should it be expanded, or is it too general? Search the Internet for additional codes for programmers or Web developers. What did you find?

8. Visit the Consumer Sentinel, **http://www.consumer.gov/sentinel/**, to learn about how law enforcement agencies around the world work together to fight consumer fraud. The site contains statistics on consumer complaints and sorts this data in many interesting ways. Prepare a report using the most current data on the top five complaint categories.

9. Choose an organization with which you are familiar. Determine what the company's computer ethics policy is by obtaining a written copy and reviewing it. In addition, asking questions and observing several employees may provide insight into the actual application. Does this organization adhere to a strict or casual ethics policy? Prepare a 10-minute presentation to the rest of the class on your findings.

10. Visit **http://www.safeshopping.org** and prepare a summary of its top ten safe online shopping tips. Did you find these tips useful enough to share with a friend or classmate? Did you bookmark the site or e-mail it to a friend?

11. To learn more about protecting your privacy, visit **http://www.cookiecentral.com**, **http://www.epubliceye.com**, and

http://www.openratings.com. Did you learn something that will help protect your privacy? Why is privacy more important than ever?

12. When you make a withdrawal or a deposit of funds at an ATM machine, do people stand back enough so they cannot watch you, or have you had someone hover over you? Are you careful to take any receipts with you and not leave any evidence of your access code and account number?

13. Do you feel the media generates too much hype regarding hackers and crackers? Since companies such as Microsoft have been hacked into, are you concerned about your bank account or other sensitive information?

14. Review Table 9.3's list of dot-cons from the Federal Trade Commission. Have any suspicious groups contacted you or any of your friends or classmates?

15. Identity theft is a new type of theft. Visit http://www.personalidprotection.com/ and http://www.fraud.org/ to find ways to protect yourself. Search the Internet for information about identity theft, and discover what you can do to protect yourself. What are some of the losses in addition to stolen documents and additional bills to pay? Should you subscribe to a service?

16. Search the Internet for information about the damaging effects of software piracy, and/or look at the following Web sites: http://www.bsa.org/intnatl/report.phtml, http://www.microsoft. com/piracy/, and http://www.trainingabc.com/legal.htm. Is software piracy a global problem? What can you do to mitigate the problem? Give a short presentation to the class.

17. There are many brands of software firewalls, with Zone Labs's ZoneAlarm (http://www.zonealarm.com), Norton's Personal Firewall (http://www.symantec.com), McAfee's Firewall (http://www.mcafee.com), and BlackICE Defender (http://www.networkice.com) being four of the most popular. Visit one of these sites and learn more about how a firewall works and what it costs to give you this needed protection; prepare a one-page report that outlines what you have learned.

ANSWERS TO THE SELF-STUDY QUESTIONS

1. C   2. C   3. A   4. D   5. D   6. B   7. D   8. C   9. B   10. A

CASE 1: *The Ethics of IS Consulting*

Thousands of businesses, large and small, are actively participating in one of the fastest growing industry sectors of the modern world: information systems consulting services. Many large organizations, such as IBM, EDS, and Accenture, have long been successful in providing IS consulting services. New companies enter this industry on a daily basis.

As with other business endeavors, IS consulting services is an area of business that puts people into situations that test their ethics. One potentially problematic area that applies to all consulting—not just IS consulting—is the fundamental conflict between needing to secure consulting contracts to bring revenue into the consulting firm and needing not to overpromise what can be delivered and/or when it can be delivered. The pressure to bring in business to generate revenue is great. New business is, after all, the lifeblood of the consulting firm. There is natural pressure to secure a consulting contract even though it may not be absolutely clear that the firm can deliver exactly what the client wants or needs by the exact deadlines that the client has set. For IS consultants, the pressure is great to promise that the job can be done quickly using "rapid" methodologies, especially given that these methodologies are in vogue. Of course, it is in the consulting firm's long-term interests not to overpromise, but the pressure is there nonetheless.

One other potential ethical dilemma facing IS consultants is the question of whom they work for and where their loyalties lie. With Joint Application Design and the use of systems development teams in which IS consultants work closely with business users, it is sometimes difficult for consultants to determine exactly for whom they work—the client or the consulting firm. On the one hand, they are serving the client and must satisfy the client's needs. On the other hand, they work for the consulting firm. They may get pulled in two different directions, especially if the relationship between the client and the consulting firm deteriorates. The consulting firm might want the consultant to stick with the letter of the contract, to withhold certain services, or to keep her time with the client to a minimum. On the other hand, the consultant may want to go the extra distance to please the client. After all, with contemporary systems development approaches, the consultant probably spends more time with the client organization's personnel than with the consulting firm's personnel, and the client organization is likely to be doing the primary evaluation of the consultant's performance. In fact, in some cases the consultants may be housed physically and semipermanently within the client organization, may be paid directly by the client, and may enjoy other employee benefits provided by the client organization.

With increased use of Joint Application Design and other approaches to partnering with business users, comes one final, fundamental ethical dilemma that all consultants face daily. This dilemma is whether to solve problems for clients in such a way that the client learns how to solve the problems itself or to solve problems for clients in such a way that the client needs to call the consultant back in again to solve similar problems in the future. There is a natural pressure to do the latter to ensure future business.

A useful analogy for this ethical dilemma is the way that a barber cuts your hair. A barber who wants to ensure that you will have to come back to him again would give you the best possible haircut. In addition, he would have no mirrors in the shop so that you could not see what he was doing, and he would not answer any of your questions about how he was cutting and styling your hair. On the other hand, a barber who wanted you to become self-sustaining and empowered to take

care of yourself would not only give you a good haircut, but he would have mirrors all around so that you could see exactly what he was doing. He would explain exactly what he was doing at all times and answer any of your questions. Now, you would not necessarily be able to cut your own hair, but you would know how to do so and could explain this to

another person who could then cut your hair. You would not necessarily have to come back to that same barber. Good consultants do not try to generate more business for themselves in this way. They want you to ask them back because you want to have them back, not because you need to have them back.

Discussion Questions

1. How would you deal with an IS manager who was pushing you to develop a system in a time frame that was too rapid to enable you to do a good job? What if it was the client who was pushing you?
2. To whom should an IS consultant ultimately be loyal, the client or the consulting firm? Why?
3. Should IS consultants strive not only to solve clients' problems but help to teach and enable them to solve their own problems in the future? Why or why not?
4. What, in your opinion, are some of the characteristics of a good consultant? How do you think a good consultant will ensure that a client will return in the future?

CASE 2: *Electronic Mail and Employee Monitoring*

As time passes, more and more companies are providing Internet-based e-mail capabilities to their employees. Companies typically provide Internet and e-mail access to employees with the intention that it will be used for business only, or at least that nonbusiness usage will be kept to a minimum. In fact, more than 40 million employees in the United States now have e-mail access, allowing them to send e-mail to anyone in the world who has an Internet connection. It makes good business sense, for a variety of reasons, to provide these kinds of communication capabilities to employees. However, it also poses a risk for companies who fear that employees may spend valuable work time goofing off, illegally sharing important company information, or infecting the corporation with a computer virus.

As a result, many companies, such as AFLAC of Columbus, Georgia, provide e-mail and Internet access to employees, but also monitor their use and the messages that employees send (DiSabatino, 2001). Monitoring employee behavior is nothing new, and it was to many businesses a natural extension

to monitor e-mail messages. However, monitoring of employee e-mail has become quite controversial.

Messages sent and received in the workplace via e-mail often contain personal information. Most companies accept this type of interaction as healthy and necessary. However, many companies feel that because they own the systems and network that carry the e-mail, and because the e-mail is there for business purposes, they can monitor the e-mail messages of employees using the system. In fact, several recent court case judgments have upheld corporations' rights to monitor their employees' e-mail messages (Rosencrance, 2001).

Surprisingly, there is little legal recourse for those who support e-mail privacy. In 1986, Congress passed the Electronic Communications Privacy Act (ECPA), which offers far stronger support for voice mail than it does for e-mail communications. This act made it much more difficult for anyone (including the government) to eavesdrop on phone conversations. E-mail privacy is, thus, much harder to protect. In addition, no other

laws at the federal or state levels protect e-mail privacy. As a result, a recent study reports that companies monitor the e-mail and Internet usage of more than one-third of the Internet-connected workforce in the United States (more than 14 million people). Worldwide, the number grows to more than 27 million employees being monitored. It is likely that these numbers will continue to grow with the advent of very sophisticated but inexpensive monitoring tools; it is projected that the average cost of monitoring an employee for a year is $5.25, and this price is rapidly dropping (Rosencrance, 2001). In fact, new tools have been developed that allow employers not only to examine traffic, but also to remotely look through e-mail boxes, search for common words, and even delete or redirect messages without notification or detection (Costello, 2001). The monitoring of employee e-mail appears to be here to stay. However, as the technology makes it easier for companies to examine the contents of both personal and work-related messages, the debate over whether this is ethical will continue.

Discussion Questions

1. Do you believe that it is ethical to transmit personal e-mail messages over company lines?
2. Do you feel that e-mail should be protected by privacy laws such as the ECPA? Or are e-mail messages company property?
3. Now that you know that e-mail is not necessarily a private communication system, will this change your use of e-mail in any way?
4. If you were in charge of a large corporation, what would be your Internet and e-mail usage policy for your employees?

References

Costello, S. 2001. "New Software Lets Managers Search E-Mail," **http://www.computerworld.com**, *Computerworld* (August 30).

DiSabatino, J. 2001. "The Wild, Wild West," **http://www.computerworld.com**, *Computerworld* (November 12).

Rosencrance, L. 2001. "Study: Monitoring of Employee E-Mail, Web Use Escalates," **http://www.comptuerworld.com**, *Computerworld*. (July 9).

Preview

If you want to purchase a computer, you have a broad range of options. Over the years, hardware has become less expensive, making it possible for individuals and organizations of all sizes to take advantage of computer-based technologies. However, large computer systems can still cost more than a million dollars. Organizations must select the right hardware or risk making a costly mistake. To make an informed decision about IS hardware, you must understand what IS hardware is and how it works.

After reading this appendix, you will be able to do the following:

1. Describe key elements of information systems hardware.

2. List and describe the types of computers that are being used in organizations today.

Our approach in this appendix is not to bog you down with hardware facts and jargon but to provide you with an overview.

KEY ELEMENTS OF INFORMATION SYSTEMS HARDWARE

Information systems hardware is classified into three types: input, processing, and output devices (see Figure A.1). **Input devices** are used to enter information into a computer. **Processing devices** transform inputs into outputs. The **central processing unit (CPU)**, with the help of several other closely related

devices that store and recall information, is the most important processing element of a computer. We will discuss this in detail in this appendix. Finally, **output devices**, such as a computer monitor and printer, deliver information to you in a usable format. This section describes each of these three key elements of information systems hardware: input, processing, and output devices (for a more detailed discussion, see Keogh, 2002).

Input Devices

For information systems hardware to perform a task, data must be input into the system. Certain types of data can be entered more easily using one type of input device than another. For example, keyboards are currently the primary means to enter text and numbers. Alternatively, architects and engineers can use scanners to enter their designs and drawings into computers. Graphics tablets simulate the process of drawing or sketching on a sheet of paper. A great deal of research and development are conducted to identify optimal ways to input various types of information and to build and sell new input devices. To organize our discussion of input devices, we classify them into four general categories by the type of information being entered: entering text and numbers, pointing and selecting information, entering batch data, and entering audio and video. Table A.1 summarizes the fundamental characteristics of each category.

Entering Text and Numbers

The primary device used to support the entry of text and numbers into a computer is the **keyboard**. Used

[**Figure A.1** ➡ Input devices include the mouse and keyboard; output devices include the printer and monitor; the central processing unit transforms input into output.]
Courtesy of Dell Computer Corporation

[Table A.1] *Methods of providing input to an information system.*

Information Category	Representative Device(s)
Entering original text/numbers	Keyboard
Selecting and pointing	Mouse Trackball and joysticks Touch screen Light pen Touch pad
Entering batch data	Scanners Bar code/optical character readers
Entering audio and video	Microphones and speakers Video and digital cameras MIDI

first as the input method on typewriters, keyboard data entry is a mainstay of the computer industry.

Ergonomics One advance in keyboard technology is the ergonomically correct keyboard, which is designed to reduce the stress placed on the wrists, hands, and arms when typing. Figure A.2 shows a normal keyboard and the Microsoft Natural keyboard. When typing for long periods, some normal keyboard users develop aching, numbing, and tingling in their arms, wrists, or hands. These injuries are generally referred to as repetitive stress injuries. The broadened use of computers in the workplace and the associated injuries to workers, resulting in more sick days and insurance claims, has made the **ergonomics**—the design of computer hardware and work environments that minimize health risks such as repetitive stress injuries—of keyboards and employees' workstations much more important to organizations. Other ways to reduce repetitive stress injuries include:

▌ Have an ergonomically designed workplace—desk, chair, monitor size and angle, keyboard height and position.

▌ Take frequent breaks from typing. When your wrists and fingers start to ache, take a break.

▌ Maintain a straight wrist position when typing. Do not let your wrists bend up/down or left/right.

▌ Avoid resting on your wrists while typing. Keep your wrists elevated off the desk.

(a)

(b)

[**Figure A.2** ➡ Normal keyboard (a) versus the Microsoft Natural keyboard (b).]

[A.2a]Courtesy Apple Computer, Inc. [A2b] Courtesy Microsoft Corporation

▌ Use a light touch on the keys. Do not press harder than you need to on the keyboard to enter information.

▌ Maintain good health habits and exercise your arms, wrists, and hands.

Other keyboard innovations Standard keyboards connect to the back of the system unit with a cord, but you can elect to purchase a cordless keyboard. Like television remote controls, battery-operated cordless keyboards use radio frequency waves to bounce signals to the computer. One drawback is that the keyboard must be proximate to the radio frequency receiver at all times for signals to be read correctly, and it will not respond if moved too far from the transmitter.

Pointing and Selecting Information

In addition to entering text and numbers, computer users use **pointing devices** to select items from menus, to point, and to sketch or draw (see Figure A.3). You probably have used a pointing device, such as a mouse, when using a graphical operating environment (such as Microsoft Windows) or when playing a video game. Several of the most popular types of pointing devices are listed in Table A.2.

Entering Batch Data

Another category of computer-based input is batch input. **Batch input** is used when a great deal of routine information needs to be entered into the computer. **Scanners** convert printed text and images into digital data. Scanners range from a small handheld device that looks like a mouse to a large desktop box that resembles a personal photocopier, both of which are shown in Figure A.4. Rather than duplicating the image on another piece of paper, the computer translates the image into digital information that can be stored or manipulated by the computer. Special **text recognition software** can convert handwritten text into the computer-based characters that form the original letters and words. Insurance companies, universities, and other organizations that routinely process large batches of forms and documents have applied scanner technology to increase employee productivity.

When the keyboard, mouse, and typical scanner cannot handle the job of transferring data to the computer, specialized scanners may be called for. These devices include optical mark recognition (OMR) devices, optical character recognition (OCR) devices, bar code readers, and magnetic ink character readers and are summarized in Table A.3.

Smart Cards

Used in many European and Asian countries, as well as at many colleges and universities, **smart cards** are a special type of credit card with a magnetic strip, a microprocessor chip, and memory circuits.

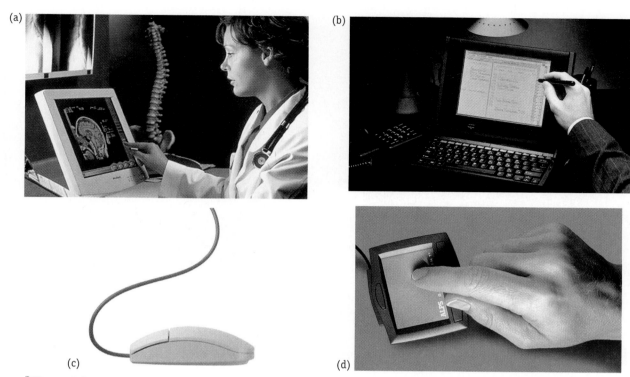

(a)   (b)   (c)   (d)

[**Figure A.3** ➥ Pointing devices: a touch screen (A.3a), a light pen (A.3b), a mouse (A.3c), and a touch pad (A.3d).]
[A.3a] Getty Images, Inc. [A.3b] Courtesy Grid Systems Coroporation. [A.3c] Getty Images, Inc. [A.3d] Apple Computer, Inc.

[Table A.2] *Selecting and pointing devices.*

Device	Description
Mouse	Pointing device that works by sliding a small box-like device on a flat surface; selections are made by pressing buttons on the mouse.
Trackball	Pointing device that works by rolling a ball that sits in a holder; selections are made by pressing buttons located near or on the holder.
Joystick	Pointing device that works by moving a small stick that sits in a holder; selections are made by pressing buttons located near or on the holder.
Touch screen	A method of input for which you use your finger; selections are made by touching the computer display.
Light pen	Pointing device that works by placing a pen-like device near a computer screen; selections are made by pressing the pen to the screen.

When issued by a school, smart cards are photo-identification cards that can also be used to unlock dormitory doors, make telephone calls, do laundry, make purchases from vending machines or student cafeterias and snack bars, and more. For making purchases, the cards are backed by funds deposited in a student account. Each time a user makes a purchase, the card keeps track of the balance remaining. Because of the microprocessor embedded in the smart card, it is much more resistant to tampering than current credit cards with magnetic strips.

Entering Audio and Video

Audio refers to sound that has been digitized for storage and replay on the computer. Audio input is helpful when a user's hands need to be free to do other tasks; it can be entered into computers via a microphone, radio, CD, or other audio device. **Video** refers to still and moving images that can be recorded, manipulated, and displayed. Video has become popular for assisting in security-related applications, such as room monitoring and employee verification. It has also gained popularity for

(a)   (b)

[**Figure A.4a** ➡ Handheld (a) and flatbed (b) scanners are a type of batch input device.]

[A.4a] Intermec Technologies Corporation. {A.4b} Courtesy of Epson America, Inc.

[**Table A.3**] *Specialized scanners for inputting information.*

Scanner	Description
Optical mark recognition (OMR)	Used to scan questionnaires and test answer forms where answer choices are circled or blocked in, using pencil or pen
Optical character recognition (OCR)	Used to read and digitize typewritten, computer-printed, and even hand-printed characters such as on sales tags on department store merchandise or patient information in hospitals
Bar code/optical character readers	Used in grocery stores and other retail businesses to record prices at the checkout counter; also used by libraries, banks, hospitals, utility companies, and so on
Magnetic ink character recognition (MICR)	Used by the banking industry to read data, account numbers, bank codes, and check numbers on preprinted checks

videoconferencing and chatting on the Internet using your PC and very inexpensive video cameras.

Voice input Perhaps one of the easiest ways to enter data into a computer is simply to speak into a microphone. With the increased interest in such applications as Internet-based telephone calls and videoconferencing, microphones have become an important component of computer systems. A process called **speech recognition** also makes it possible for your computer to understand speech. The two-step process works like this: First, you speak into a microphone connected to a speech recognition board installed in the system unit of your computer. Then special speech recognition software digitizes your spoken words and displays them on the monitor screen. Speech recognition technology is especially

helpful for physicians and other medical professionals, people with disabilities, airplane cockpit personnel, factory workers whose hands get too dirty to use keyboards, and computer users who cannot type and do not want to learn. Drawbacks are that users must pause after each word, and computers do not always hear spoken words correctly (see Figure A.5).

Other audio input Audio input devices let user enter sounds into the computer for processing. They can then analyze and manipulate the sounds via sound editing software for output to audiotapes, CDs, or other media. Here are a few examples of how audio input, other than spoken words, might be used:

▌ A musician may connect an electronic keyboard to the computer, in order to compose or manipulate music. Electronic keyboards or synthesizers are connected via

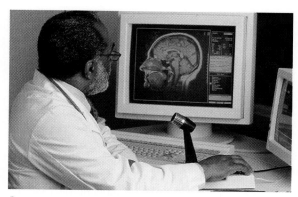

[**Figure A.5** ➡ Voice input is becoming an important way for many to interact with a computer.]

Peter Beck/Corbis/Stock Market

a **Musical Instrument Digital Interface (MIDI)** port, which can also transfer sound to the computer. MIDI is a standard for connections and communications between your computer and digital musical instruments.

▪ A scientist studying the sounds made by whales may enter those sounds into a computer to analyze pitch, volume, tone, and other patterns.

▪ Audiologists and other medical personnel may enter sounds to be played back to patients during hearing tests or therapy.

▪ Forensic scientists may use a computer to analyze a voice on a tape recorder for identification by a crime victim or witnesses.

▪ Filmmakers may manipulate sounds to serve specific story purposes.

Video input A final way in which information can be entered into a computer is through video input. Digital cameras record images, in digital form, on small, removable memory cards, rather than on film. Most cards can hold from 16 to 100 or more images. Card capacity depends upon the resolution you select and the preset capacity of the card you buy. When the camera's memory card is full, you can connect it to a port on a PC for downloading to the computer's memory (described below). Accompanying software lets you clear the memory card for later use. Some digital cameras are portable and can be used at any location. Stationary digital cameras are attached to a video board inside the PC. They allow you to record digital photos of yourself and others, documents, or products and other items. High-quality digital cameras are generally more expensive than film-based cameras, ranging in price from $400 to $10,000 or more. However, they offer two main advantages. You can store digital images without using a scanner, and you can take photographs without having film developed. Presently, photos taken with digital cameras are suitable for family albums, but for professional-quality photos, traditional cameras are still the best choice.

Video cameras, VCRs, televisions, DVDs, and other video devices can provide video input to a computer. Since huge digital files are created when video clips are put into the computer, storage requirements are demanding. That is why video segments run on PCs are usually short. A high-quality digital video camera is typically much more expensive than a comparable nondigital video recorder. These high-quality digital cameras are starting to be used in the motion picture industry and by manufacturing companies when performing quality control. For example, Ford Motor Company uses high-resolution video cameras to evaluate the quality of parts by comparing images of newly manufactured items with images stored in a database. If the images match, the part passes a quality control inspection. If the images do not match, the part can be rejected without human intervention.

However, there are also lower-quality cameras that are priced from $50 to $200 (see Figure A.6). These devices, often referred to as *cams*, have become very popular with people wanting to use the Internet for chatting with friends and family, using a program like Microsoft's NetMeeting (**http:// www.microsoft.com/netmeeting**). Unlike high-quality digital video cameras (see Figure A.7), these cams use **streaming video**, in which the camera sends a sequence of moving images in a compressed form over the Internet and the images are displayed on the receiver's screen as they arrive. **Streaming**

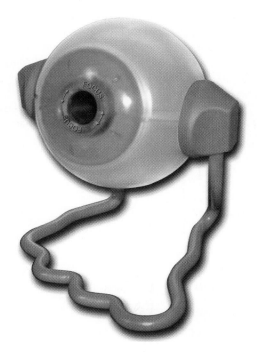

[**Figure A.6** ➡ Low-priced Web cams are popular with people who like to chat over the Internet.]

Source: ©Orange Micro, Inc.

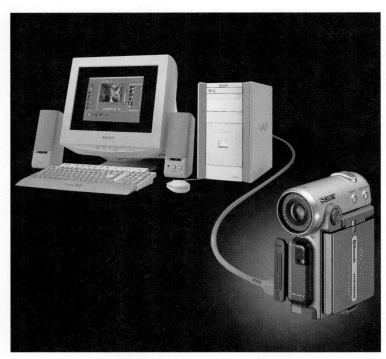

[**Figure A.7** ➡ High-quality digital video cameras can be connected directly to a computer for storing information as well as for editing and adding special effects.]
Courtesy of Sony Electronics, Inc.

media is streaming video with sound. With streaming video or streaming media, a Web user does not have to wait for the entire file to be downloaded before seeing the video or hearing the sound. Instead, the media are sent in a continuous stream that is played as it arrives. This is why *streaming* has become popular for real-time chatting and it is how live broadcasts, like the news on CNN displayed on a computer (**http://www.cnn.com**), can be viewed on the Internet.

Both audio and video are expected to increase in popularity as common input options. We have described numerous options for providing input to a computer. After information is entered into a computer, it can be processed, stored, and manipulated. In the next section, we describe the processing aspects of information systems hardware.

Processing: Transforming Inputs into Outputs

In this section we provide a brief overview of computer processing. To begin, we describe how data and information are represented within a computer. Next, we briefly describe the internal processing components of a desktop computer, focusing primarily on the central processing unit (CPU) and data storage technologies.

Binary Code

Your brain can readily process written words, photographs, music, an instructor's lecture (at least some of the time), videos, and much more. If you grew up speaking English, your brain will process incoming information in that language only. Similarly, computers can process incoming data, but only after the words, photos, music, and other information have been translated into a language they can understand. The language computers understand is called digital data or **binary code**, which simply means that all incoming data must be translated into the 1s and 0s of binary math. Binary, or base-2 math (2, 4, 8, 16, 32, and so on) is used by computers instead of the more familiar base 10, because it simplifies the way a computer's hardware works.

Binary codes make up **machine language**, the only language computers understand. The individual 1s and 0s that make up the code are called **bits**— short for binary digits. Eight bits equal a **byte**, or about one typed character, such as the letter "A", or the number "6" on the keyboard. You will often see computer storage and memory measurement terms. Table A.4 will help you make sense of them.

Future memory and storage capacities will also include petabytes (one quadrillion bytes), exabytes

[Table A.4] *Elements of computer storage.*

Measurement	No. of Bits	No. of Bytes	No. of Kilobytes	No. of Megabytes	No. of Gigabytes
Byte	8	1			
Kilobyte* (K)	8,192	1,024	1		
Megabyte (MB)	8,388,608	1,048,576	1,024	1	
Gigabyte (GB)	8,589,934,592	1,073,741,824	1,048,576	1,024	1
Terabyte (TB)	8,796,093,022,208	1,099,511,627,776	1,073,741,824	1,048,576	1,024

*A kilobyte equals a little more than 1,000 bytes, but the number is usually rounded to 1,000. The same is true for the number of kilobytes in a megabyte, and so on.

(one quintillion bytes), and brontobytes (one sextillion bytes).

The bits in the binary code are the basic instruction units for all the work the computer does. The bits represent on/off commands for tiny electric switches inside the computer's processor. When a low-voltage current is applied to a switch, it is read as a 0 and the switch is closed. A high-voltage current is read as a 1 and the switch is opened. Similarly, positive and negative magnetized locations used to store data are represented in binary notation as 0s or 1s.

One of the biggest challenges for the computer industry has been to determine how to translate all the different types of information into digital data that a computer can understand. Early computers could not translate incoming data at all. They used paper cards on which strings of 1s and 0s were represented by punched holes. Later, computers received information from a keyboard, which was the first time a translation was made to 1s and 0s from text that computer users could understand. Today's computers can translate many types of data, including words, photos, sound, and video, to binary code, then manipulate and store it. One of the main reasons computers become so quickly outdated is that newer models keep coming out that can process more and more types of information.

Programs (applications) you run on your computer contain instructions. (This is software, covered in Appendix B.) Programs may tell the computer to open a specific file, move data from one location to another, open a new window on the monitor screen, add a column of figures, and so on. Before the computer can follow program instructions, however, those instructions must be converted to machine language. The central processing unit (described below) uses a special built-in program called a language translator to translate incoming data into binary code called machine language. After the processor converts incoming data to machine language, it organizes the bits into groups—for instance, 32-bit instructions—that represent specific operations and storage locations.

Once the computer receives instructions from a program, it processes the information into a form you, the computer user, can understand. In a word processing program, for example, the letters and numbers you type are displayed on the monitor, just as they would appear on a sheet of paper if you were using an old-fashioned typewriter. But, unlike the typewriter, when you press the "L" key, for example, on the computer keyboard, the computer is actually receiving the information as a series of 1s and 0s, specifically "01001100." As you type a letter or a term paper, the data is processed, then displayed on the monitor in a form that makes sense to you. The binary code the computer actually uses is hidden

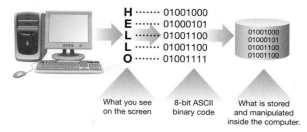

[**Figure A.8** ⇒ How computers translate information into binary code so that the computer can store and manipulate the information.]

from your view (see Figure A.8). You see words, lines, and paragraphs. After you write a document, you can then print it out on paper, store it on the computer's hard disk, or even post it to an Internet Web site.

Other binary codes are used to relay data and instructions to and from the central processing unit (CPU). For example, fixed-length binary codes such as **ASCII** (American Standard Code for Information Interchange) and **EBCDIC** (Extended Binary-Coded Decimal Interchange Code) are used to represent numbers, letters, and other characters in binary form. ASCII is the standard binary code adopted for data communications systems and is used by most microcomputers (see Table A.5). EBCDIC, developed by IBM, is used primarily on IBM mainframe computers. Both ASCII and EBCDIC use various eight-bit combinations to represent characters in the English language. Software translators are used to convert English characters in ASCII to characters in other languages such as Spanish, French, or German.

A third binary code, called **Unicode**, is better suited than either ASCII or EBCDIC for representing the letters and characters in languages other than English. This is because Unicode uses 16 bits, instead of the eight bits used by ASCII and EBCDIC to represent characters. By using 16 bits, Unicode can represent more characters than ASCII and EBCDIC and can, therefore, encode most languages.

System Unit

A computer's **system unit** is the physical box that houses all of the electronic components that do the work of the computer (see Figure A.9). Buttons on the outside, front surface of the system unit turn the machine on and off and reset the machine without turning the power off. Most PC system units include a CD-ROM drive and a diskette drive. Through ports at the back of the system unit you can connect peripheral hardware, such as a keyboard, a mouse, speakers, printers, and scanners.

The system unit contains the following:

▌ Motherboard, power supply, and fan

▌ Central processing unit (CPU)

[Table A.5] *ASCII codes for alphabet and numbers.*

Character	ASCII-8 Binary Code	Character	ASCII-8 Binary Code
A	0100 0001	S	0101 0011
B	0100 0010	T	0101 0100
C	0100 0011	U	0101 0101
D	0100 0100	V	0101 0110
E	0100 0101	W	0101 0111
F	0100 0110	X	0101 1000
G	0100 0111	Y	0101 1001
H	0100 1000	Z	0101 1010
I	0100 1001	0	0011 0000
J	0100 1010	1	0011 0001
K	0100 1011	2	0011 0010
L	0100 1100	3	0011 0011
M	0100 1101	4	0011 0100
N	0100 1110	5	0011 0101
O	0100 1111	6	0011 0110
P	0101 0000	7	0011 0111
Q	0101 0001	8	0011 1000
R	0101 0010	9	0011 1001

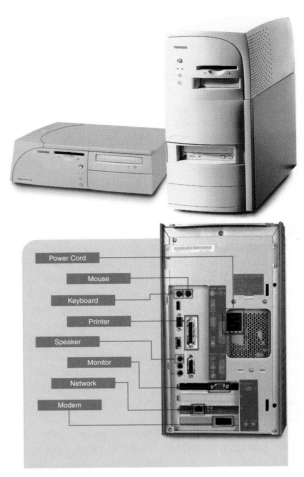

[**Figure A.9** ➥ The system unit houses all of the electronic components that do the work of the computer.]
Courtesy of Toshiba America Information Systems, Inc.

 RAM and ROM memory

▪ Hard drive, diskette drive, CD-ROM, or DVD-ROM drive

▪ Ports for plugging in peripherals and add-in slots for sound, video, internal modem, and other cards

In all types and models of computers, the main circuit board or system board, most often called the motherboard, is the heart of the system unit.

Motherboard

The **motherboard** is aptly named because it contains all of the components that do the actual processing work of the computer (see Figure A.10). It is a large printed plastic or fiberglass circuit board that holds or connects to all of the computer's electronic components. Plugged into or otherwise connected to the motherboard are the central processing unit, often referred to as the computer's brain, RAM and ROM memory, hard disk, diskette, and CD-ROM drives, all expansion slots, ports for printers and other external devices, and the power supply. All of these devices are described below.

The computer's **power supply** converts electricity from the wall socket to a lower voltage. Power can vary from 110 to 240 volts, depending upon where you are in the world, to lower voltages—5 to 12 volts DC—and the power supply adjusts voltage to prevent damage to the computer's components. The power supply also regulates the voltage to eliminate spikes and surges common in most electrical systems. For added protection against external power surges, most PC owners opt to connect their systems to a separately purchased voltage surge suppressor. The power supply includes a fan for air-cooling the electronic components inside the system unit. That low humming noise you hear while the computer is running is the fan.

Central Processing Unit

The **central processing unit (CPU)** is often called the computer's brain. It is also called a microprocessor, processor, or chip and is responsible for performing all of the operations of the computer. Its job includes loading the operating system (e.g.,

[**Figure A.10** ➥ A computer's motherboard holds or connects to all of the computer's electronic components.]

Windows) when the machine is first turned on and performing, coordinating, and managing all the calculations and instructions relayed to the CPU while the computer is running.

The CPU consists of two main sections: the **arithmetic logic unit (ALU)** and the **control unit**. The ALU performs mathematics, including all forms of addition, subtraction, multiplication, and division. It also performs logical operations, which involve comparing packets of data, then executing appropriate instructions. Combined in various ways, these functions allow the computer to perform complicated operations rapidly. The control unit works closely with the ALU by performing four primary functions:

1. *Fetching* the next program instruction from the computer's memory.

2. *Decoding* instructions, so that the computer knows what to do next. The control unit uses separate **registers** (temporary storage locations inside the CPU) to store the instructions and to store information about storage location in memory.

3. *Retrieving* the necessary data from memory and telling the ALU to *execute* the required instructions. The control unit again uses registers to store retrieved data and the action performed.

4. *Storing* results of its computations in a register or in memory.

Both the ALU and the control unit use registers because they can access them more quickly than they can access main memory, thus adding to processing speed.

The CPU is composed of millions of tiny transistors arranged in complex patterns that allow it to interpret and manipulate data. The inner workings of

a CPU are very complex. For most of us, it is easiest to think of a CPU as being a "black box" where all the processing occurs. The CPU is a small device made of silicon. For example, the Intel Pentium IV®CPU packs more than 42 million transistors into an area about the size of a dime! The Pentium IV is packaged in a container that is bigger than a dime, of course (see Figure A.11), because additional wiring is used to connect all of these transistors of the CPU to the motherboard.

The general trend in computing is toward smaller, faster, and cheaper devices. But for how long can this trend continue? In the 1970s, Dr. Gordon Moore, then a researcher at Intel, hypothesized that computer processing performance would double every 18 months. When Moore made this bold prediction, he did not limit it to any specified period of time. This prediction became known as **Moore's Law**. Interestingly, Dr. Moore has been basically correct so far. Feature size—the size of lines on the chip through which signals pass—has been reduced from

[**Figure A.11** ➥ The Intel Pentium IV microprocessor contains more than 42 million transistors.]

Source: ©Intel Corporation

about the width of a human hair in the 1960s (20 microns—a micron is equal to one millionth of a meter), to the size of a bacterium in the 1970s (5 microns), to smaller than a virus today (.13 micron—the feature size on an Intel Pentium 4). As feature size is reduced, a greater number and variety of circuits can be packed increasingly closer together. Both feature density and complexity has facilitated the continued performance increases that microprocessors have realized. Figure A.12 shows this trend. For more on Moore's Law, visit Intel's Web site (**http://www.intel.com/research/silicon/mooreslaw.htm**) or search on the Web using the phrase "Moore's Law," and you will get numerous interesting pages to review.

The number of transistors that can be packed into a modern CPU and the speed at which processing and other activities occur are remarkable. For example, the Intel Pentium IV can complete hundreds of millions of operations every second. To achieve these incredible speeds, the CPU must execute instructions very rapidly. In addition to the number of transistors on the CPU, three other factors greatly influence its speed—its system clock speed, registers, and cache memory—and these are described next.

Clock speed Within the computer, an electronic circuit generates pulses at a rapid rate, setting the pace for processing events to take place, rather like a metronome marks time for a musician. This circuit is called the **system clock**. A single pulse is a **clock tick**, and in microcomputers the processor's **clock speed** is measured in hertz (Hz). One MHz is one million clock ticks, or instruction cycles, per second. Microprocessor speeds are measured in different units, depending upon the type of computer. Personal computer speeds are most often measured in MHz or in

GHz (gigahertz, or 1 billion hertz). Microprocessor speeds improve so quickly that faster chips are on the market about every six months. Today, most new PCs operate at faster than 1 GHz. To give you an idea of how things have changed, the original IBM PC had a clock speed of 4.77 MHz.

See Table A.6 for a description of computer speeds. It takes a permanent storage device such as a hard disk (described below) about 10 milliseconds to access information. Within a CPU, however, a single transistor can be changed from a 0 to a 1 in about 10 picoseconds (one trillionth of a second). Changes inside the CPU occur about one billion times faster than they do in a fixed disk because the CPU operates only on electronic impulses, whereas the fixed disks perform both electronic and mechanical activities, such as spinning the disk and moving the read/write head (described below). Mechanical activities are extremely slow relative to electronic activities.

Registers Within the CPU itself, there are **registers** that provide temporary storage locations where data must reside while it is being processed or manipulated. For example, if two numbers are to be added together, both must reside in registers, with the result placed in a register. Consequently, one factor influencing the speed and power of a CPU is the number and size of the registers.

Cache memory A **cache** (pronounced "cash") is a small block of memory used by processors to store those instructions most recently or most often used. Just as you might keep file folders you use most in a handy location on your desktop, cache memory is located within or close to the CPU. Thanks to cache memory, before performing an operation, the proces-

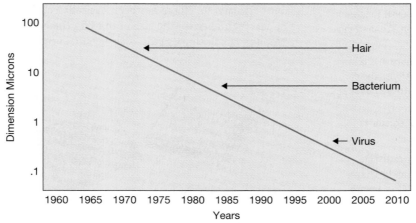

[**Figure A.12** ➡ Moore's Law predicted that computer processing performance would double every 18 months. To increase performance, feature size has had to shrink.]

[Table A.6] *Elements of computer time.*

Name	Fraction of a Second	Description	Example
Millisecond	1/1000	One thousandth of a second	Fixed disks access information in about 10–20 milliseconds.
Microsecond	1/1,000,000	One millionth of a second	A 900MHz CPU executes approximately 900 million operations in a second—or about 900 operations every microsecond.
Nanosecond	1/1,000,000,000	One billionth of a second	Most types of RAM used in PCs have access times (the time needed to read information from the RAM to the CPU) from 5–70 nanoseconds (lower is better). Most cache memory has access times of less than 20 nanoseconds.
Picosecond	1/1,000,000,000,000	One trillionth of a second	Inside a CPU, the time it takes to switch a circuit from one state to another is in the range of 5–20 picoseconds.

sor does not have to go directly to main memory, which is further from the microprocessor and takes longer to reach. Instead, it can check first to see if needed data is contained in the cache. Cache memory is another way computer engineers have increased processing speed.

Cache may be located inside the microprocessor—similar to registers—or outside of, but close to, the microprocessor. Special high-speed cache memory, called **internal cache**, is incorporated into the microprocessor's design. **External or secondary cache** is usually not built into the CPU, but is located within easy reach of the CPU on the motherboard. The more cache available to a CPU, the better the overall system performs because more information is readily available.

The CPU translates input into binary data and binary data into information that can be understood by humans. To be used by the CPU, data must be stored either temporarily or permanently. We describe this next.

Primary Storage

Primary storage is for current information. Computers need temporary storage space for current calculations, and this type of memory, measured in bytes, provides it. In addition to registers and cache, described above, examples of primary storage are random-access memory (RAM) and read-only memory (ROM). RAM and ROM are made up of chips containing thousands of electronic circuits etched on silicon wafers. These memory chips are monolithic. That is, all the circuits found on one chip comprise one inseparable unit of storage. Each circuit or switch is

either conducting an electrical current (on) or not conducting an electrical current (off).

Random-Access Memory (RAM)

Random-access memory (RAM) is the computer's main or **primary memory**. It consists of several chips mounted on a small circuit board called a **single in-line memory module (SIMM)** that plugs into the motherboard (see Figure A.13). RAM stores the programs and data currently in use. Random-access memory is so named because data stored here can easily and quickly be accessed randomly by the CPU. RAM provides temporary storage of data for the CPU; because information is stored temporarily, it is referred to as **volatile**. That is, instructions and work stored in RAM are lost when the power to the computer is turned off or when new data is placed there. So if you have been working at your computer for hours on a research paper, do not trip over the power cord or otherwise accidentally turn off the power. If you do, unless you have saved your work in progress

[Figure A.13 ➥ Random-access memory (RAM) consists of several chips mounted on a small circuit board called a SIMM.**]**

Beekman/Computer Confluence 5e, Prentice Hall, 2003

to your computer's hard disk or to a diskette (secondary storage), you will lose all your diligent work.

For the most efficient and speedy processing, the more RAM a computer has, the better. Today, the amount of RAM in most microcomputers is measured in megabytes. When this book went to print, most PC users considered 128MB of RAM essential to run available software, and many routinely opted for 256MB of RAM or more! Tomorrow's PC users will undoubtedly have some number of gigabytes, or even terabytes of RAM as an option.

Read-Only Memory (ROM)

Read-only memory (ROM) exists as a chip on the motherboard that can be read from but cannot be written to. That is, the CPU can read the information stored in ROM, but the computer user cannot change it. ROM is nonvolatile, which means that it does not lose its instructions when the power to the computer is shut off. ROM stores programs as instructions that are automatically loaded when the computer is turned on, such as the basic input/output system (BIOS).

A variation of ROM is erasable ROM, referred to as EEPROM (electrically erasable programmable read-only memory). You may have heard of EEPROM referred to by a more user-friendly term, **flash memory**. This type of memory can be repeatedly written to and erased like RAM, but, unlike RAM, it retains its information after power is turned off. Flash memory is the storage technology behind many popular consumer devices like digital cameras and MP3 players.

Secondary Storage

Secondary, nonvolatile storage is for permanently storing data to a large-capacity storage component, such as a hard disk, diskette, CD-ROM disk, or tape (see Table A.7). Nonvolatile means that data is not lost from secondary storage when the computer's power is shut off. Hard disks and diskettes are magnetic media. That is, diskettes and the disks inside a hard disk drive are coated with a magnetic material. Reading data from the disks involves converting

[Table A.7]   *Comparing methods of secondary storage.*

Type	Speed	Method of Data Access	Relative Cost/MB
Magnetic tape	Slow	Sequential	Low
Floppy disks	Slow	Direct	Low
Fixed disks	Fast	Direct	High
Compact discs	Medium	Direct	Medium
Optical disks	Fast	Direct	Medium

magnetized data to electrical impulses that can be understood by the processor. Writing to the disks is the reverse—converting electrical impulses to magnetized spots representing data.

Hard disk drives, diskette drives, and tapes are secondary storage devices with **read/write heads** that inscribe data to or retrieve data from hard disks, diskettes, and tapes. Hard disk, diskette, and tape drives are usually installed internally, but may be externally located and attached via cables to ports on the back of the system unit. Diskettes and tapes are removable secondary storage media. That is, they must be inserted into the appropriate drive (or tape reader) to be read from or written to, and are removed when these tasks are accomplished.

Hard Drives

Most of the software run on a computer, including the operating system, is stored on the **hard drive** or **hard disk**. The hard drive is a peripheral device usually located inside the system unit of a computer. It writes data and programs to a fixed disk. The storage capacity of the hard drives for today's microcomputers is now measured in gigabytes (GB), or billions of bytes. It is not unusual for PCs currently on the market to come equipped with hard drives with 20GB to 40GB storage capacities. Modern supercomputers can have millions of gigabytes of storage. Most microcomputers have one hard drive, but additional drives can usually be added, either internally or externally. To make sure critical data is not lost, some computers employ **RAID (redundant array of independent disks)** technology to store redundant copies of data on two or more hard drives. RAID is not typically used on an individual's computer, but is very common for Web servers and many business applications.

Hard drives consist of several disks, or platters, stacked on top of one another so that they do not touch (see Figure A.14). Each disk within a disk pack has an access arm with two read/write heads—one positioned close to the top surface of the disk and another positioned close to the bottom surface of the disk. (Both surfaces of each disk are used for data storage, usually with the exception of the top surface of the top disk and the bottom surface of the bottom disk.) The read/write heads do not actually touch either surface of the disks. In fact, a **head crash** occurs if the read/write head for some reason touches the disk. When this happens, data is lost. The disks inside the hard drive rotate as data is written to or read from them.

Diskette Drives and Diskettes

Most personal computers also contain diskette drives. They are separate from the hard drive, and the port for inserting diskettes is located on the outside of the system unit.

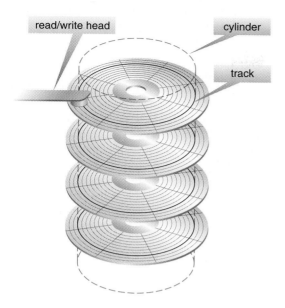

read/write head   cylinder

track

[**Figure A.14** ➡ A hard drive consists of several disks that are stacked on top of one another and read/write heads to read and write information.]

Pfaffenberger/CIYF Brief 2003, Prentice Hall, 2003

Diskettes (also called floppy disks) are 3½ inch, round, flexible Mylar devices that record data as magnetized spots on tracks on the disk surface (see Figure A.15). The actual diskette is enclosed in a nonflexible plastic jacket that fits into the diskette drive on the computer so the diskette can be read or written to. Diskettes are small enough to be easily carried home in a purse or a pocket and can be used by more than one computer. The disadvantage to using diskettes for storage is that they may not have sufficient capacity to store large amounts of data. (Typically, one diskette can store 1.4MB of data, although higher-capacity diskettes are available.)

In addition to the standard internal hard disk, some microcomputers may also have a **zip drive**®, which is a high-capacity, removable diskette drive that uses 100MB zip disks or cartridges. Zip drives® offer computer users easy-to-use additional data

[**Figure A.15** ➡ Diskettes provide low-capacity storage.]

storage that is handy for backing up information and sharing stored data with other computers.

Optical Disk Storage

Optical disks, or those using laser beam technology, have become popular as storage requirements have increased. An **optical disk**, coated with a metallic substance, is written to when a laser beam passing over the surface of the disk burns small spots into the disk surface, each one representing a data package. The data can be read when a laser scans the surface of the disk and a lens picks up various light reflections from the data spots. Some optical disks are read-only. That is, information is entered on them by a manufacturer and cannot be changed by the computer user. Nor can new information be written to the disk by the computer user. One advantage to using optical disks for storage is that they can hold much more information than diskettes: One optical disk can record the information from at least a dozen diskettes. Optical disks have made possible the huge growth in multimedia software applications for PCs.

One type of optical disk, called the **magneto-optical (MO) disk** can hold a large amount of information, as do other optical disks, but you can also write to the disk. The plastic surface of the disk contains tiny metallic crystals. To write information, a laser beam melts a small spot on the plastic surface of the disk. A magnet then rearranges the metallic crystals while the plastic is still hot and malleable. The crystals are arranged so that some reflect light while others do not. Those crystals that reflect light can later be read by a laser.

Another type of optical disk that data can be written to is the **CD-R** (compact disc—recordable) disk. Using these disks requires special software and a CD-R disk drive, distinct from a CD-ROM drive. Once written to, however, CD-R disks can be read by any CD-ROM drive.

CD-ROM Disks

The most popular type of optical disk storage is the **CD-ROM (compact disc—read-only memory)**. A CD-ROM drive is now standard equipment with most computer systems. As the name implies, CD-ROM disks can only be read; they cannot be written to. Since the typical CD-ROM disk can store up to 660MB, which is equal to about 400 diskettes, they can easily hold entire encyclopedias, plus audio and video clips, and more (see Figure A.16).

CD-RW

One of the problems with a CD-R disk is that information can only be written onto it once. A **CD-RW** disk (RW stands for rewritable) allows the disk to be written onto multiple times. Most new computers come with a CD-RW drive so that users can store and backup large amounts of information on a reusable disk.

[**Figure A.16** ➡ CD-ROM is a popular storage method because it is inexpensive, is reliable, and provides abundant storage capacity.]
©Corbis/Stock Market

DVD-ROM

Currently, **digital video disks (DVD-ROM)** have more storage space than diskettes or CD-ROM disks, because DVD-ROM drives use a shorter-wavelength laser beam, which allows more optical pits to be deposited on the disk. Single-layered disks hold about 4.7GB of information, and double-layered disks increase storage capacity to 8.5GB. The huge storage capacity of DVD-ROM disks make them ideal for movie-quality videos with state-of-the-art sound. Experts predict that the DVD will eventually replace the CD-ROM because of its increased storage capacity.

Tapes

Magnetic tapes used for storage of computer information consist of narrow plastic tape coated with a magnetic substance. Storage tapes range from one-half inch–wide wound on a reel, to one-fourth inch–wide, wound into a plastic cassette that looks much like a music cassette tape. Like on other forms of magnetic storage, data are stored in tiny magnetic spots. Storage capacity of tape is expressed as **density**, which equals the number of **characters per inch (CPI)** or **bytes per inch (BPI)**

that can be stored on the tape. Mainframe computers use tape drives called stackers that wind tape from a supply reel to a take-up reel as data are read.

Magnetic tape is still used for storing large amounts of computer information, but it is gradually being replaced by high-capacity disk storage, since disk storage is equally reliable. In fact, information stored on disks is easier to locate, because computers must scan an entire tape to find a specific data file.

Now that you understand how information is input into a computer and how it is processed, we can turn our attention to the third category of hardware—output technologies.

Output Devices

After information is input and processed, it must be presented to the user. Computers can display information on a screen, print it, or emit sound. The sections that follow discuss details about how each of these output devices operates.

Video Output

Monitors are used to display information from a computer. They consist of a cathode ray tube (CRT), which is similar to a television, but with much higher resolution. Monitors can be color, black and white, or monochrome (meaning all one color, usually green or amber). Notebooks and other portable computers use **liquid crystal display (LCD)** or plasma screens because a CRT is too bulky for a portable device, which needs a thin, lightweight monitor. The research and development of monitor technologies focuses on creating lightweight, low-cost, high-resolution devices. Because display monitors are embedded into a broad range of products and devices, such as automobiles, to display global positioning, route maps, and other relevant information, they must be sturdy, reliable, lightweight, and low in cost (see Figure A.17).

Printers and Plotters

Information can be printed in several different ways, as shown in Figure A.18. A plotter (Figure A.18a) is used for transferring engineering designs from the computer to drafting paper, which is often as big as 34" x 44". The plotter uses several pens as it draws each of the lines individually. **Dot matrix printers** (Figure A.18b) are older, electric typewriter–based technology for printing information on paper. Letters are formed using a series of small dots. Once the most commonly used type of printer, dot matrix printers are now mostly found printing voluminous batch information, such as periodic reports and forms. **Ink-jet printers** use a small cartridge to transfer ink onto paper. This process cre-

(a)

(b)

[**Figure A.17** ➡ Monitors display information from a computer: a CRT-type display (a) and an LCD-type display (b).]
Source: Courtesy of View Sonic Corporation

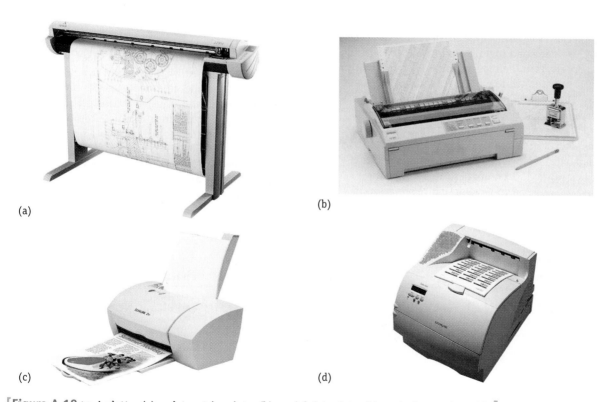

(a)

(b)

(c)

(d)

[**Figure A.18** ➡ A plotter (a), a dot matrix printer (b), an ink-jet printer (c), and a laser printer (d).]
[A.18a] Courtesy of Xerox Corporation. [A.18b] Courtesy of Epson, America, Inc. [A.18c] Lexmark International, Inc. [A.18d] Lexmark International, Inc.

ates a typewriter-like image that can initially smear because the ink is wet when it is sprayed onto the paper. Ink-jet printers (Figure A.18c) can be designed to print both black and white and color. **Laser printers** are the most commonly used printers today. They use an electrostatic process to

force ink onto the paper, literally "burning" the image onto the paper. The resulting high quality is considered necessary for almost all business letters and documents. Laser printers (Figure A.18d) can also produce color images, but high-end color laser printers can cost thousands of dollars.

Audio Output

In addition to transmitting text as output, a computer can also transmit audio as output. With the use of small specialized speakers and a **sound card**, a computer can produce stereo-quality sound. The computer translates digits into sound by sending data to a sound card that interprets these data into tones. The tones are then sent to the speakers for output. Musicians and composers often use this output to simulate a full orchestra when working on new or unfamiliar pieces of music.

Now that you understand how computer hardware works, we can discuss the types of computers that people and organizations typically use.

TYPES OF COMPUTERS

Over the last 60 years, information systems hardware has gone through many radical changes. In the 1940s, almost all business and government information systems consisted of file folders, filing cabinets, and document repositories. Huge rooms were dedicated to the storage of these records. Information was often difficult to find, and corporate knowledge and history were difficult to maintain. Only certain employees knew specific information. If or when these employees left the firm, so did all their corporate knowledge. The computer provided the solution to the information storage and retrieval problems facing organizations of the 1940s. Shifts in computing eras were facilitated by fundamental changes in the way computing technologies worked. Each of these fundamental changes is referred to as a distinct generation of computing. Table A.8 highlights the technology that defined the four generations of computing. We conclude by briefly describing the five general types of computers currently being used in organizations (see Table A.9).

Supercomputers

The most powerful and expensive computers that exist today are called **supercomputers**. Supercomputers are often used for scientific applications, solving massive computational problems that require large amounts of data. They can cost many millions of dollars. For example, Sandia National Laboratories uses a supercomputer to model the physics of nuclear explosions. This particular machine has several gigabytes of RAM and the computational horsepower of more than 9,000 Pentium processors. Pharmaceutical companies, such as Eli Lilly and Dow Chemical, use supercomputers to design and evaluate new combinations of chemical elements in order to quickly identify promising prescription drugs and treatments. IBM's "Blue Pacific" supercomputer operates 15,000 times faster than an average personal computer, with more than 5,800 processors and 2.6 trillion byes of memory. To achieve this incredible speed, supercomputers are equipped with numerous fast processors that work in parallel to execute several instructions simultaneously. An extensive staff is usually required to operate and maintain supercomputers and to support the researchers and scientists using them. Supercomputers often run only one application at a time in order to dedicate all processing capabilities to a single massive application. Figure A.19 shows a Cray supercomputer, one of the more popular com-

[Table A.8] *Generations of computing. (Freed, 1995)*

Generation	Defining Event	Computing Era	Major Characteristics/Events
1 (1946–1958)	Vacuum tubes	Mainframe era begins	ENIAC and UNIVAC were developed
2 (1958–1964)	Transistors	Mainframe era continues	UNIVAC was updated to use transistors
3 (1964–1990s)	Integrated circuits	Mainframe era ends; Minicomputer era begins and ends; Personal computer era begins	IBM 360—integrated circuits and general-purpose operating system; Microprocessor revolution: Intel, Apple Macintosh, IBM PC, MS-DOS
4 (1990s–present)	Multimedia	Personal computer era ends; Interpersonal computing era begins; Internetworking era begins	High-speed microprocessor and networks; High-capacity secondary storage; Low cost, high performance integrating video, audio, and data

Source Freed, L. 1995. The history of computing. Emeryville, CA:Ziff-Davis Press.

[Table A.9] *Characteristics of computers currently being used in organizations.*

Type of Computer	Number of Simultaneous Users	Physical Size	Typical Use	Memory	Typical Cost Range
Supercomputer	1–several	Like an automobile	Scientific research	2,000+ GB	$1,000,000 to more than $20,000,000
Mainframe	1000+	Like a refrigerator	Large general-purpose business and government	Up to 100+ GB	$1,000,000 to more than $10,000,000
Midrange	4–200	Like a file cabinet	Midsize general-purpose business	Up to 10GB	$10,000 to more than $100,000
Workstation	1	Fits on a desktop	Engineering design	512 to 2,048MB	$5,000 to more than $50,000
Microcomputer	1	Handheld to fitting on a desktop	Personal productivity	128 to 512MB	$500 to more than $5,000

puters in this class. In addition to Cray and IBM, Hitachi, NEC, and Fujitsu are leading producers of supercomputers.

Mainframes

The backbone of large corporate computing has historically been large, high-powered computers called **mainframes**. These machines can be the size of a large refrigerator (and even larger), and they often cost several million dollars to purchase. Organizations normally use mainframe computers for processing large amounts of business data, and the machines are designed to support hundreds, or even thousands,

of users simultaneously. In addition to businesses, many federal and state governments use mainframe computers to manage the massive amount of data generated by day-to-day governmental activities. Federal agencies, such as the Internal Revenue Service (IRS), have several mainframe computers to handle the massive databases related to individual and corporate payroll and tax information. Large corporations, such as Alamo Rent A Car, American Airlines, and Holiday Inn, use mainframes to perform repetitive tasks, such as processing reservations. Unisys and IBM are the largest producers of mainframes (see Figure A.20).

[Figure A.19 ➥ The Cray supercomputer.]
Cray, Inc.

[Figure A.20 ➥ IBM mainframe computer.]
Courtesy of IBM Corporate Archives

Midrange Computers

Midrange computers, often referred to as minicomputers, are scaled-down versions of mainframes that were created for companies that did not have the budgets for mainframes and did not need that amount of computing power. In the past few years, the distinction between large midrange computers and small mainframes has blurred in both performance and price. Nonetheless, midrange computers have become integral to many smaller and midsized organizations and typically cost tens to hundreds of thousands of dollars, supporting from four to 200 users simultaneously. As with mainframes, IBM is a leader in the midrange computer market, with its AS/400 model. Manufacturers such as Hewlett-Packard also service this market. The midrange market as a whole has been declining as workstations and microcomputers have become faster and have absorbed some of the functionality once required of midrange and mainframe computers.

Workstations

Workstations are a special class of microcomputer (as is your PC) designed for individuals that have the power of some midrange computers, but they fit on a desktop. Computer hardware companies, such as Silicon Graphics, Sun Microsystems, and Hewlett-Packard are leaders in this market. Workstations have an extremely fast CPU (or multiple CPUs), large capacities of RAM and secondary storage, and high-

quality video displays, costing between $5,000 and $50,000. Figure A.21 shows a Sun Sparcstation, one of the more popular computers in this class. Workstations are often used by engineers to design new products using processing-intensive applications, such as computer-aided design (CAD); by financial analysts modeling stock market fluctuations; and by researchers working with large, complex, computationally intensive applications. For example, researchers at NASA are using workstations to study the effects of global warming on ocean surface temperatures.

Microcomputers

Microcomputers, also referred to as **personal computers (PCs)**, fit on desktops, generally cost between $1,000 and $5,000, and are used in homes and offices (see Figure A.22). Microcomputers can be relatively stationary desktop models or portable, notebook-sized computers that weigh about five pounds or less. High-end microcomputers can cost more than $5,000 and rival the power and speed of low-end workstations. High-end microcomputers are often used as network and Web servers that manage shared resources such as printers or large databases, or deliver content over the Internet. In the last few years, the popularity of microcomputers has exploded. Within organizations, microcomputers are the most commonly used computing technology for knowledge workers and have become as commonplace as the telephone. In fact, more microcomputers than televisions are now sold in the United States each year. Let us delve a bit deeper into the development of microcomputers.

Network Computers

A **network computer** is a microcomputer with minimal memory and storage designed to connect to networks, especially the Internet, to use the resources provided by servers. The concept of network computing is to reduce the obsolescence and maintenance of personal computers by allowing inexpensive machines to access servers that deploy resources—software programs, printers, and so on—to all machines on

[Figure A.21 ➡ A Sun workstation is typically used by engineers.]
©Getty Images, Inc.

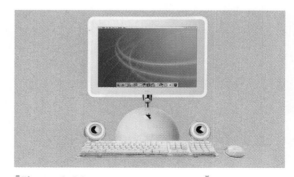

[Figure A.22 ➡ A personal computer.]
Apple Computer, Inc.

the network. Many feel that network computing is the wave of the future because the machines are less expensive than typical PCs and because they can be administered and updated from a central network server. Oracle and Sun Microsystems are two companies aggressively pushing the network-computing concept (see Figure A.23).

Portable Computers

When computers appeared that could fit on a desktop, users considered them the ultimate in lighter, smaller, handier machines. Then came laptop computers you could carry, but the first models were heavy and bulky. Next on the portable computer scene were notebook computers that could fit in a backpack or briefcase. Today battery-powered laptop and notebook computers are popular both for business and personal use (see Table A.10 for a summary of tradeoffs between desktop and portable computers). The computers are equipped with a flat display panel, fold into a small, convenient carry case, and can weigh as little as five pounds or less. With a portable computer, you can use a keyboard and a mouse, as well as a trackball, touch pad, or other built-in pointing device. Most portable computers come equipped with internal modems and USB ports and can connect to printers, scanners, or other peripherals. Many students, employees, and others now use a portable computer as their only PC, rather than buying both a desktop and a portable machine. The two most popular forms of portable computers—notebooks and handhelds—are described below.

[**Table A.10**] *Tradeoffs between desktop and portable computers.*

Desktop Computer	Portable Computer
One location for use	Mobile—any location for use
Lower price	Higher price
Expandable	Very limited expandability
Better ergonomics—full size/high resolution color screen, large keyboard, and so on	Cramped ergonomics—small screen, limited color quality, small keyboard, awkward pointing device, and so on
Relatively easy to service/repair	Hard to service/repair

Notebook computers Mobile computers once weighed twenty pounds and were portable only in the sense that they could be moved—with difficulty—from one location to another. A few years ago, machines evolved to what was referred to as a *laptop*, weighed around ten pounds, and could be folded up and carried like a briefcase. The trend has been toward smaller, lighter, yet ever more powerful **notebook computers** that weigh five pounds or less and can be easily carried in a briefcase or backpack (see Figure A.24).

(a)   (b)

(c)

[**Figure A.24** ➡ Notebook computers are very portable and typically weigh less than five pounds.]

[A.24a] Courtesy of Dell Computer Corporation, [A.24b] Courtesy of Sony Electronics [A.24c] Courtesy IBM Corporation

[**Figure A.23** ➡ A Sun Microsystems network computer.]

Sun Microsystems

Handheld computers The first handheld computers were introduced around 1994, but they failed to live up to expectations, perhaps because consumers had expected that they would replace PCs. Then in 1996, Palm introduced a handheld computer that was never intended to replace the PC but performed some essential computing tasks so well that users could often leave their laptop and notebook computers at home. Since then, billed first as information appliances, then as **personal digital assistants (PDAs)**, handheld computers have filled a niche in the portable computer market. Today, the capabilities of many PDAs are beginning to rival the functionality of desktop PCs. For example, Compaq's "Pocket PC," which runs using Microsoft's CE operating system, allows users to send and receive e-mail, work on documents and spreadsheets, surf the Web, and perform countless other activities (see Figure A.25).

As you can see, things have really evolved since the early mainframe days. In most organizations today, IS encompasses a diverse range of computing technologies, from supercomputers, mainframes, and midrange computers to workstations, personal computers, and personal digital assistants. For individuals, computers have become commonplace, with many families having several computers. Using history as a guide, it is a good bet that computing hardware will continue to evolve at a rapid pace, having some intended and unforeseen consequences for all of us.

KEY POINTS REVIEW

1. **Describe key elements of information systems hardware.** Information systems hardware is classified into three types: input, processing, and output technologies. Input hardware consists of devices used to enter information into a computer. Processing hardware transforms inputs into outputs. The central processing unit (CPU) is the device that performs this transformation with the help of several other closely related devices that store and recall information. Finally, output-related hardware focuses on delivering information in a usable format to users.

2. **List and describe the types of computers that are being used in organizations today.** Computers come in all shapes, sizes, degrees of power, and prices. The five general classes of computers are supercomputer, main-

(a)

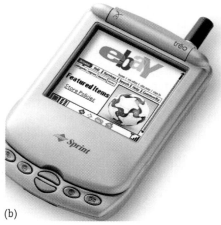

(b)

[**Figure A.25** ➥ Personal digital assistants allow you to have a very powerful computer in the palm of your hand.]

Source: [A.25a] © AP/Wide World Photos [A.25b] Courtesy of Handspring, Inc.

frame, midrange, workstation, and microcomputer. A supercomputer is the most expensive and most powerful kind of computer; it is primarily used to assist in solving massive research and scientific problems. A mainframe is a very large computer that is the main, central computing system for major corporations and governmental agencies. A midrange computer offers lower performance than mainframes but higher performance than microcomputers. Minicomputers are typically used for engineering and midsized business applications. A workstation is a very high-performance microcomputer, typically used to support individual engineers and analysts in solving highly computational problems. A microcomputer is used for personal computing, small business computing, and as a workstation attached to large computers or to other small computers on a network.

KEY TERMS

arithmetic logic unit (ALU) 317
ASCII (American Standard Code for Information Interchange) 315
audio 311
batch input 310
binary code 314
bits 314

byte 314
bytes per inch (BPI) 322
cache 318
CD-R (compact disc—recordable) 321
CD-ROM (compact disc—read-only memory) 321
CD-RW (compact disc—rewritable) 322
central processing unit (CPU) 309, 316

REVIEW QUESTIONS

1. Information systems hardware is classified into what three major types?

2. Describe various methods for entering data into and interacting with a computer.

3. Define ergonomics, and give examples of how repetitive stress injuries could be reduced.

4. How do computers represent internal information, and how is this different from the ways in which humans typically communicate information to each other?

5. Describe the system unit and its key components.

6. What determines the speed of a CPU?

7. How do a computer's primary storage, secondary storage, ROM, and RAM interact?

8. Compare and contrast the different types of secondary data storage.

9. What are output devices? Describe various methods for providing computer output.

10. Describe the different types of computers and their key distinguishing characteristics.

SELF-STUDY QUESTIONS

1. A system unit contains all of the following **except** ____ .

A. CD-ROM
B. central processing unit
C. power supply
D. monitor

2. Which of the following is **not** an input device?

A. touch pad
B. touch screen
C. sound board
D. light pen

3. Which of the following is an example of hardware?

   A. an operating system
   B. Microsoft Suite
   C. system software
   D. central processing unit

4. Which of the following is an output device?

   A. laser printer
   B. touch screen
   C. video camera
   D. keyboard

5. Which of the following could be ergonomically designed?

   A. keyboard
   B. chair
   C. monitor
   D. all of the above

6. ____ can convert handwritten text into computer-based characters.

   A. Scanners
   B. Bar code/optical character readers
   C. Text recognition software
   D. Audio video

7. A ____ card is a special credit card with a microprocessor chip and memory circuits.

   A. smart
   B. master
   C. universal
   D. proprietary

8. Which of the following has the largest storage, along with video capacity?

   A. CD-ROM
   B. floppy disk
   C. DVD-ROM
   D. cache memory

9. Which of the following type of computer is used for personal and small business usage?

   A. supercomputer
   B. microcomputer
   C. workstation
   D. mainframe

10. A ____ is the most powerful and expensive computer today.

   A. HAL
   B. mainframe
   C. personal digital assistant
   D. supercomputer

Answers are at the end of the Problems and Exercises.

PROBLEMS AND EXERCISES

1. Match the following terms with the appropriate definitions:

   ____ Cache memory   ____ DVD-ROM
   ____ Batch input   ____ Motherboard
   ____ Smart card   ____ Streaming video
   ____ Ergonomics   ____ Network computer
   ____ Audio   ____ Flash memory

   a. A special type of credit card with a magnetic strip that includes a microprocessor chip and memory circuits

   b. A small block of memory used by the central processor to store those instructions most recently or most often used

   c. An optical storage device that has more storage space than a diskette or CD-ROM disk and uses a shorter-wavelength laser beam, which allows more optical pits to be deposited on the disk

   d. A sequence of moving images, sent in a compressed form over the Internet and displayed on the receiver's screen as the images arrive

   e. The design of computer hardware and work environments that minimize health risks such as repetitive stress injuries

   f. A large printed plastic or fiberglass circuit board that contains all of the components that do the actual processing work of the computer, and holds or connects to all of the computer's electronic components

   g. A type of input for large amounts of routine information

   h. A microcomputer with minimal memory and storage designed to connect to networks to use the resources provided by servers

   i. Memory that can be repeatedly written to and erased like RAM, but unlike RAM it retains its information after power is turned off

   j. Sound that has been digitized for storage and replay on the computer

2. Imagine that you have decided it is time to purchase a new computer. Analyze your purchase options with regard to using this computer for personal productivity versus business productivity. What differences might your potential usage make on your hardware choices? Why?

3. Imagine that you have just informed your supervisor that you will need to purchase new computers for yourself and three fellow employees. Your supervisor states that she has heard in the news that computer prices are dropping constantly, and she feels that you should wait a bit before making this purchase. She adds that you can still be 100 percent effective with your current computer and software. Develop a counterargument explaining why you should make the purchase now instead of waiting. Will this be a hard sell? Why or why not?

4. Go visit a computer shop or look on the Web for mice or touch pads. What is new about how these input devices look or how they are used? What are some of the advantages and disadvantages of each device?

5. What types of printers are most common today? What is the cost of a color printer versus a black and white one? Compare and contrast laser and ink-jet printers in terms of speed, cost, and quality output. What kind of printer would you buy or have you bought?

6. What happens when a computer runs out of RAM? Can more RAM be added? Is there a limit? How does cache memory relate to RAM? Why is RAM so important in today's modern information systems world? Search the Web for RAM retailers. Compare their prices and options.

7. Do you feel that floppy disks will be obsolete sometime in the near future? Why or why not? What storage and retrieval options are available in addition to CD-ROMs and floppy disks? What are you currently using, and what would you like to purchase?

8. Back in the 1970s, rockets were sent to the moon with the amount of computing power found in today's microcomputers. Now, these microcomputers seem to be outdating themselves every two years. Will this era of continuous improvement end? Why or why not? If so, when?

9. Do you have a Palm handheld or some other type of PDA (personal digital assistant) or know of someone who does? What functions do PDAs offer? Look on the Web or go to the mall to shop for one. Are the prices decreasing? At what point do you plan to purchase one?

10. Interview an IS manager within an organization that you are familiar with. Determine what issues played a role in the latest information systems hardware purchase this person made. Other than budget, what issues do you think should be considered?

11. Based on your experiences with different input devices, which do you like the best and least? Why? Are your preferences due to the devices' design or usability, or are they based on the integration of the device with the entire information system?

12. Visit a company that utilizes several different types of computers. Which types do they use? What categories of computers are used at this company (e.g., workstations)? Does the company have any plans to expand its computer usage to another category? Why or why not?

13. In simple language, explain what happens with the keystrokes that you type into a computer using a keyboard. Be sure to discuss memory, processing, and inputs. Draw any diagrams that may help you with this explanation.

14. Check the Web for information on different types of Apple computers. What is new? What brands of IBM-compatible computers have you used or purchased? What are you currently using? What influences your computer purchasing decisions?

15. Choose a few of the computer hardware vendors that sell computers to the general public. These include Dell, Compaq, IBM, Gateway, Apple, and many lesser-known brands. Using each company's homepage on the Web, determine what options these vendors provide for input devices, processing devices, and output devices. Does it seem that this company has a broad range of choices for its customers? Is there something that you did not find available from this company? Present your findings in a 10-minute presentation to the rest of the class.

ANSWERS TO THE SELF-STUDY QUESTIONS

1. C   2. C   3. D   4. A   5. D   6. C   7. A   8. C   9. B   10. D

Preview

Software directs the functions of all computer hardware. Without software, the biggest, fastest, most powerful computer in the world is nothing more than a fancy paperweight. After reading this appendix, you will be able to do the following:

1. Describe the common functions of system software.

2. Describe the various types of application software.

3. Describe the characteristics of various types of programming languages and application development environments.

If you use an ATM to withdraw money, word processing to prepare papers, or e-mail to communicate with your classmates and professors, you rely on software to execute instructions. Software is also intertwined with all types of products and services—toys, music, appliances, health care, and countless other products. As a result, the term "software" can be confusing because it is used in many different ways. We will unravel this confusion in the next section by describing the different types of software that are used in today's organizations.

KEY INFORMATION SYSTEMS SOFTWARE COMPONENTS

Software consists of programs, or sets of instructions, that tell the computer to perform certain processing functions. Software's job is to provide instructions that allow all the hardware components in your computer system to speak to each other. The two basic types of information systems software are system software and application software. In the next section, we discuss system software and how it supports the overall operation of the computer hardware.

System Software/Operating System

System software is the collection of programs that controls the basic operations of computer hardware. System software, or the **operating system**, as it is sometimes called, coordinates the interaction between hardware devices (for example, the CPU and the monitor), peripherals (for example, printers), application software (for example, a word processing program), and users, as shown in Figure B.1.

Operating systems are often written in assembly language, a very low-level computer programming language that allows the computer to operate quickly

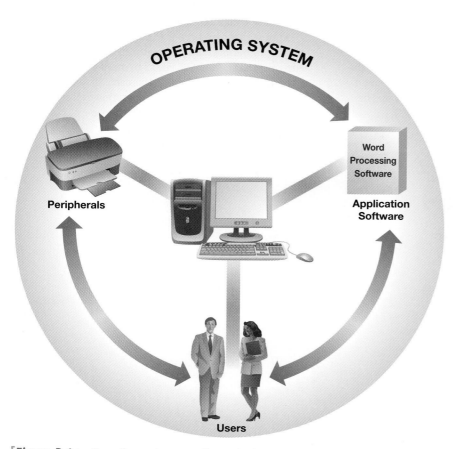

[**Figure B.1** ➡ Operating systems coordinate the interaction between users, application software, hardware, and peripherals.]

and efficiently. The operating system is designed to insulate you from this low-level language and make computer operations unobtrusive. The operating system performs all of the day-to-day operations that we often take for granted when using a computer, such as updating the system clock, printing documents, or saving information to a disk. Just as our brain and nervous system control our bodies' breathing, heartbeat, and senses without our conscious realization, the system software controls the computer's basic operations transparently.

Common System Software Functions

Many tasks are common to almost all computers. These include getting input from a keyboard or mouse, reading and/or writing data from a storage device (such as a hard disk drive), and presenting information to you via a monitor. Each of these tasks is performed by the operating system, just as a manager of a firm oversees people and processes (as depicted in Figure B.2).

For example, if you want to copy a word processing file from a floppy disk onto your computer, operating systems make this very easy for you. Using an operating system like Microsoft Windows you simply use the mouse to point at a graphic icon of the word processing file, then click and drag it onto an icon of your hard disk. That is all it takes to copy the file on the floppy disk to your hard drive. The operating system makes this process appear easy. However, underlying the icons and simple dragging operations is a complex set of coded instructions that tells the electronic components of the computer that you are transferring a set of bits and bytes located on the floppy disk to a location on your internal hard disk.

Imagine if you had to program those sets of instructions every time you wanted to copy a file from one place to another. The operating system manages and executes these types of system operations so that you can spend your time on more important tasks.

The operating system performs many different tasks, including the following:

▌ Booting (or starting) your computer

▌ Reading programs into memory and managing memory allocation

▌ Managing where programs and files are located in secondary storage

▌ Maintaining the structure of directories and subdirectories

▌ Formatting disks

▌ Controlling the computer monitor

▌ Sending documents to the printer

Interfaces: Command Versus GUI

The operating system is stored on disk, and a portion of it is transferred into temporary memory when the computer boots up. After the operating system is in memory, it begins to manage the computer and provide an **interface**. Different operating systems and application programs use different types of user interfaces, with the most typical being command, menu, or GUI. It is through this interface that you interact with the computer. The **command-based interface** requires that you type text commands into the computer to perform basic operations. You could type the command "DELETE File1" to erase the file with the name "File1." MS-DOS (Microsoft Disk Operating System) is an example of an operating system that uses a command-based user interface.

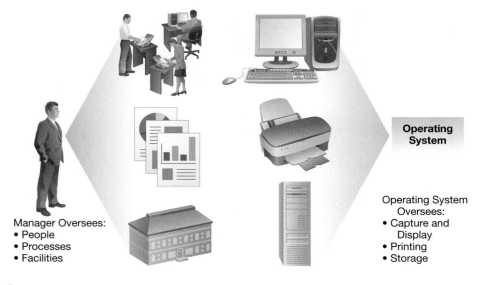

Manager Oversees:
• People
• Processes
• Facilities

Operating System

Operating System Oversees:
• Capture and Display
• Printing
• Storage

[**Figure B.2** ➥ A manager oversees organizational resources, whereas an operating system oversees computer resources.]

The most common type of interface for the PC is called a **graphical user interface (GUI)** (see Figure B.3). The GUI uses pictures, icons, and menus to send instructions from the user to the computer system. GUIs eliminate the need for users to input arcane commands into the computer and are, therefore, a popular interface. Examples of system software using a GUI are the Windows and Macintosh operating systems.

Popular Operating Systems

Just as there are many kinds of computers, there are many different kinds of operating systems (see Table B.1). In general, operating systems—whether for large mainframe computers or for small notebook computers—perform similar operations. Obviously, large multiuser supercomputers are more complex than small desktop systems; therefore, the operating system must account for and manage that complexity. However, the basic purpose of all operating systems is the same.

Utilities

Utilities or **utility programs** are designed to manage computer resources and files. Some are included in operating system software. Others must be purchased separately and installed on your computer. Table B.2 provides a sample of a few utility programs that are considered essential.

As mentioned earlier, system software (or the operating system) is only one type of software that is used to run a computer. In the next section, we discuss the second type, application software, that is used in today's information systems.

Application Software

Unlike system software, which manages the operation of the computer, **application software** lets a user perform a specific task, such as writing a business letter, processing the payroll, managing a stock portfolio, or manipulating a series of forecasts to come up with the most efficient allocation of resources for a project. The application program interacts with the system software, which, in turn, interacts with the computer hardware.

The two basic types of application software are:

- Customized, or proprietary, software—developed specifically by or for a particular organization
- Commercial software—purchased off-the-shelf and used by a variety of people and/or organizations to meet their specific needs.

These two types of software will be discussed next.

Customized Application Software

Customized application software is developed to meet the specifications of an organization. This software may be developed in-house by the company's own IS staff or it may be contracted, or outsourced,

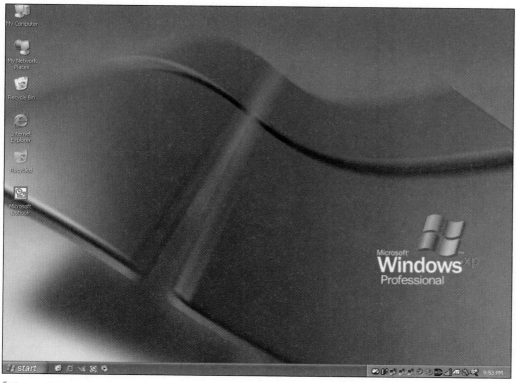

[**Figure B.3** ➡ The Windows operating environment uses a graphical user interface.]

[Table B.1] *Common operating systems.*

Operating System	Description
MVS/ESA (Multiple Virtual Storage/Enterprise Systems Architecture)	A highly reliable proprietary operating system used on large IBM mainframe computers that is being rapidly superseded by IBM's newer mainframe operating system, OS/390
UNIX	A multiuser, multitasking operating system that is available for a wide variety of computer platforms from vendors such as Sun Microsystems, Hewlett-Packard, and Silicon Graphics
MS-DOS (Microsoft Disk Operating System)	A command-based operating system used on IBM-compatible PCs that was first introduced in 1981
Windows	The most popular operating system in the world, operating on network servers, desktop PCs, notebooks, and handheld computers
OS/2	An operating system developed in 1988 by IBM for powerful PCs; can run applications written for OS/2, MS-DOS, Java, or Windows
Mac OS	The first commercially popular graphical-based operating system, making its debut in 1984, running on Apple Macintosh personal computers
Linux	An operating system designed in 1991 by a Finnish university student, it is known for its security, low price, and adaptability; by 2000, Linux powered 31% of all Web servers

[Table B.2] *Common types of computer software utilities.*

Utility	Description
Backup	Archives files from the hard disk to a diskette or to tapes
File defragmentation	Converts a fragmented file stored on your hard disk (one not stored contiguously) into one that will load and be manipulated more rapidly
Disk and data recovery	Allows the recovery of damaged or erased information from hard and floppy disks
Data compression	Compresses data by substituting a short code for frequently repeated patterns of data, much like the machine shorthand used by court reporters, allowing more data to be stored on a disk
File conversion	Translates a file from one format to another, so it can be used by an application other than the one used to create it
Antivirus	Monitors and removes viruses—lines of code designed to disrupt the computer's operation and make your life miserable
Device drivers	Allows new hardware added to your computer system, such as a game controller, printer, scanner, and so on, to function with your operating system

to a specialized vendor charged with developing the software to the company's contractual specifications. Customized application software has two primary advantages over commercial software:

1. Customizability—It can be tailored to meet unique user requirements. For example, suppose a retailer needs a kiosk in its store to help shoppers locate specific products. Many shoppers may not be familiar with computers and may be intimidated by operating a keyboard or a mouse. With customized software, the company could develop a touch screen input interface, with which users could simply point at objects in a catalog. The computer could then process this information and tell the user that, for example, women's shoes are located on the first floor in the southeast corner and provide a map of the store.

2. Problem specificity—The company pays only for the features specifically required for its users. For example,

company- or industry-specific terms or acronyms can be included in the program, as can unique types of required reports. Such specificity is not possible in off-the-shelf programs that are targeted to a general audience.

Off-the-Shelf Application Software

Although customized software has advantages, it is not automatically the best choice for an organization. **Off-the-shelf application software** is typically used to support common business processes that do not require any specific tailoring. Table B.3 summarizes advantages of the off-the-shelf application software.

Combining Customized and Off-the-Shelf Application Software

It is possible to combine the advantages of customized and off-the-shelf software. Companies can purchase off-the-shelf software and then modify it for their own use. For example, a retailer may want to purchase an off-the-shelf inventory management program and then modify it to account for the specific products, outlets, and reports it needs to conduct its day-to-day business. In some cases, the company selling the off-the-shelf software makes these customized changes for a fee. Other vendors, however, do not allow their software to be modified.

Examples of Information Systems Application Software

Application software is categorized according to its design and by the type of application or task it supports. The task-oriented categories for application software are: (1) large business systems and office automation, and (2) personal productivity tools. Applications in the business category are purchased or developed by the organization to support the central, organization-wide operations of the company. Those in the office automation or personal productivity category are tools used to support the daily work activities of individuals and small groups. We will describe and provide examples of each type of application software in the following sections.

Business Information Systems

Business information systems are applications developed to perform organization-wide operations. For example, most organizations have payroll applications to process their payrolls. A payroll application may take as inputs individual time sheets. These time sheets can be fed through an optical scanner to create a file of time sheet data, organized by employee social security numbers. The application software can look at each employee's pay rate and hours worked to calculate a gross pay figure. The application software can also calculate the federal, state, and local taxes that must be deducted from the employee's gross pay. After calculating all deductions, the application arrives at a net pay owed each employee.

Once the application has taken all time sheets, organized and sorted them by employee, and calculated gross pay, deductions, and net pay for each employee, the figures form a payroll master file. The payroll application creates the payroll master file and backs it up, perhaps on a tape drive on a mainframe computer. To process checks, the payroll application creates a check and register file that includes the date, the employee's name, the social security number, and the employee's net pay. The register file contains all of the previous elements, along with the time period, gross pay, and deductions for that time period for the employee's records. The check file is sorted by department, and checks are printed. Registers (a record of the checks printed) are also sorted and printed for distribution to employees.

This payroll process may not seem to be complex to conduct for only two or three employees. However, consider a large governmental organization, such as the Department of Defense, which must process and account for millions of employees' checks. Suddenly, a relatively simple process becomes a potential information-processing nightmare.

[Table B.3] *Advantages of off-the-shelf application software.*

Advantage	Description
Low cost	Because off-the-shelf applications are developed for general markets, development costs are distributed across a large customer base.
Faster procurement	Customized software takes a notoriously long time to develop, whereas users can simply purchase off-the-shelf software and install it.
High quality	Because off-the-shelf software typically has a large customer base, developers continuously invest in refinement and testing.
Low risk	Off-the-shelf application software is relatively easy to evaluate through in-house testing, customer feedback, or software reviews in the popular and trade press.

Application software easily manages these very large data-intensive operations.

Mega-retailers such as Sears Roebuck and Company and Lands' End must manage millions of pieces of merchandise and millions of transactions on a daily basis (Figure B.4). These businesses rely on inventory management, order processing, billing, and shipping applications to conduct their operations. Without sophisticated, large-scale business application software, these businesses could not survive.

Office Automation/Personal Productivity Application Software

The second category of application software is called **office automation** or **personal productivity software**. Individuals or groups who want to accomplish a wide range of tasks from word processing to graphics to e-mail use this type of software. Many of the large, well-known software companies, including Microsoft, Corel, Netscape, and Lotus, produce office automation software. Table B.4 outlines several popular personal productivity tools. See Chapter 6 for more information on this topic.

PROGRAMMING LANGUAGES AND DEVELOPMENT ENVIRONMENTS

Each piece of application software we have discussed in this chapter is based on some programming language. A programming language is the computer language used by the software vendor to write application programs. For application software such as spreadsheets or database management systems, the underlying programming language is invisible to the user. However, programmers in an organization's information systems group and, in some instances, end users can use programming languages to develop their own specialized applications. Many different types of programming languages exist, each with its own strengths and weaknesses. Popular languages used in businesses and industry today are summarized in Table B.5.

Compilers and Interpreters

Programs created using programming languages must be translated into code—called assembly or **machine language**—that the hardware can understand. Most programming languages are translated into machine languages through a program called a **compiler**, as depicted in Figure B.5. The compiler takes an entire program written in a programming language, such as C, and converts it into a completely new program in machine language that can be read and executed directly by the computer. Use of a compiler is a two-stage process. First, the compiler translates the computer program into machine language, and then the CPU executes the machine language program.

[Figure B.4 ➡ Large retailers manage millions of transactions per day.]
Source: **http://www.landsend.com**

[Table B.4] *Some examples of popular personal productivity tools.*

Tool	Examples
Word processor	Microsoft Word, Corel WordPerfect, Lotus AmiPro
Spreadsheet	Microsoft Excel, Lotus 1-2-3
Database management system	Borland Paradox, Microsoft Access, Borland dbase, Microsoft FoxPro
Presentation software	Microsoft PowerPoint, Software Publishing Corporation Harvard Graphics
PC-based e-mail	Lotus cc:Mail, Microsoft Mail, Novell Groupwise
Web browser	Netscape Navigator, Spyglass Mosaic, Microsoft Internet Explorer

[Table B.5] *Popular programming languages.*

Language	Application	Description
BASIC	General purpose	**B**eginner's **A**ll-Purpose **S**ymbolic **I**nteraction **C**ode. An easy-to-learn language, BASIC works well on most PCs.
C/C++	General purpose	C++ is a newer version of C. Developed at AT&T Bell Labs. Complex languages used for a wide range of system and application programming.
COBOL	Business	**Co**mmon **B**usiness-**O**riented **L**anguage. Developed in 1960. It was the first language for developing business software. COBOL is used for most business transaction processing applications on mainframes.
FORTRAN	Scientific	**FOR**mula **TRAN**slator. The first commercial high-level language, developed by IBM in the 1950s. Designed for scientific, mathematical, and engineering applications.
Pascal	Teaching structured programming	Named after mathematician Blaise Pascal. Uses a building block approach to programming. Useful in developing large programs.
HTML	World Wide Web	**H**ypertext **M**arkup Language. The most widely used language for developing Web pages. Markup languages simplify pages for transmission by using symbols that tell what document elements should look like when displayed.
Java	World Wide Web	An object-oriented programming language developed at Sun Microsystems in the early 1990s. It is a popular programming language for the Internet because it is highly transportable from one make of computer to another.
LISP	Artificial intelligence	**LIS**t **P**rocessor. Dates from the late 1950s. One of the main languages used to develop applications in artificial intelligence. Also the language for high-speed arcade graphics games.

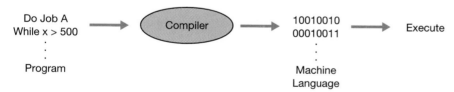

[Figure B.5 ➥ A compiler translates the entire computer program into machine language, and then the CPU executes the machine language program.]

Some programming environments do not compile the entire program into machine language. Instead, each statement of the program is converted into machine language and executed one statement at a time, as depicted in Figure B.6. The type of program that does the conversion and execution is called an **interpreter**. Programming languages can be either compiled or interpreted.

Programming Languages

Over the past few decades, software has evolved. In the early days of computing, programming languages were quite crude by today's standards. Initially used in the 1940s, the first generation of programming languages was called machine languages. Programmers wrote in binary code to instruct the computer exactly which circuits to turn on and which to turn off. As you might guess, machine language is very unsophisticated and therefore very difficult to write. Because it is so difficult, very few programs are actually written in machine language. Instead, programmers rely on higher-level languages. In the early 1950s, a more sophisticated method for programming was developed, in which the binary codes used in

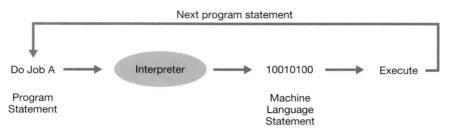

[**Figure B.6** ➥ Interpreters read, translate, and execute one line of source code at a time.]

machine language were replaced by symbols, called symbolic languages, that were a lot easier for humans to understand. Programs written in symbolic language, or any higher-level language, still need to be converted into machine language in order to run.

In the mid-1950s, the first high-level programming language, called FORTRAN, was developed by IBM. The big innovation of high-level languages was that they used English-like words to instruct the computer. Consequently, high-level languages are much easier to program in than lower-level languages. When you refer to Table B.5, you can see that some high-level languages are better suited for different applications. Programmers must fully understand the tasks that are to be accomplished when writing a new application in order to choose the best programming language for those tasks.

In the 1970s, several user-oriented languages called fourth-generation languages were created. These languages are more like English than third-generation languages in that they focus on the desired output instead of the procedures required to get that output. Fourth-generation languages (4GLs), also called outcome-oriented languages, are commonly used to write and execute queries of a database. For example, the widely used database query language called Structured Query Language (SQL) is a fourth-generation language. See Figure B.7 for several lines of SQL displayed in a sentence-like statement requesting that the LAST and FIRST names of

people in a database called CUSTOMER with credit limits equal to $100 be displayed.

More recently, fifth-generation languages (5GLs) have been developed for application within some expert system or artificial intelligence applications. 5GLs are called natural languages because they allow the user to communicate with the computer using true English sentences. For example, Hewlett-Packard and other software vendors have developed tools for document search and retrieval and database queries that let the user query the documents or database with English-like sentences. These sentences are then automatically converted into the appropriate commands (in some cases SQL) needed to query the documents or database and produce the result for the user. If the system does not understand exactly what the user wants, it can ask for clarification. The same code shown in Figure B.7 might appear as shown in Figure B.8 if a natural language were used. Although 5GL languages are not common and are still being further developed, they have been used to forecast the performance of financial portfolios, help diagnose medical problems, and estimate weather patterns.

Of course, programming languages continue to evolve. One new characteristic for describing programming languages is whether or not they are object-oriented. In addition, visual programming languages and Web development languages are rapidly gaining popularity. Next, we discuss these.

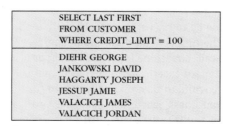

```
SELECT LAST FIRST
FROM CUSTOMER
WHERE CREDIT_LIMIT = 100

DIEHR GEORGE
JANKOWSKI DAVID
HAGGARTY JOSEPH
JESSUP JAMIE
VALACICH JAMES
VALACICH JORDAN
```

[**Figure B.7** ➥ A 4GL query using SQL that requests that the LAST and FIRST name of those that have a CREDIT_LIMIT equal to $100 be displayed from a database called CUSTOMER.]

```
BEGINNING WITH THE LAST NAME ON THE FOL-
LOWING LIST OF CUSTOMERS, FIND CUSTOMERS
WHO HAVE A CREDIT LIMIT OF $100.

DIEHR GEORGE
JANKOWSKI DAVID
HAGGARTY JOSEPH
JESSUP JAMIE
VALACICH JAMES
VALACICH JORDAN
```

[**Figure B.8** ➥ A 5GL query using natural language to request the same information as the SQL query in Figure B.7.]

Object-Oriented Languages

Object-oriented languages are the most recent in the progression of high-level programming languages. These languages allow programmers to group data and program instructions together into modules or **objects** that can be manipulated by the programmer. For example, an object might be student majors and grade point averages and a set of corresponding rules for calculating credits needed for graduation. The process of grouping pieces of data together is called **encapsulation**. When pieces of data are encapsulated, they can be isolated from other parts of the program. The programmer can then make changes in various parts of the program without having to rewrite the entire code.

A second key characteristic of object-oriented languages is **inheritance**. This means that when one class of objects is defined, all other objects with the same characteristics are automatically defined by the same terms. For example, if "student majors" is defined as an object for a search, then through inheritance, objects such as "English major," or "mathematics major" would fall under the same definition. Therefore, once an object is created, it can be plugged into several different applications. Programmers using object-oriented programming (OOP) can save time because they do not have to repeatedly write many lines of code to define the same or related objects.

In addition to being object-oriented, programs and programming languages can also be **event-driven**. Unlike a program written in a procedural programming language, a program written with the event-driven approach does not follow a sequential logic. The programmer does not determine the sequence of execution for the program. The user can press certain keys and click on various buttons and boxes presented to her. Each of these user actions can cause *events* to occur, which triggers a program procedure that the programmer has written. Object-oriented programming languages tend to be useful for designing event-driven applications. An example of an object-oriented environment that supports the development of event-driven applications is Microsoft Visual Basic. In addition, Visual Basic is also a visual programming language, which we will discuss next.

Visual Programming Languages

Just as you may have found it easier to use a computer operating system with a graphical user interface, like Windows or Mac OS, programmers using **visual programming languages** may also take advantage of the GUI. For instance, programmers can easily add a command button to a screen with a few clicks of a mouse (see Figure B.9) instead of explaining pixel-by-pixel and using many lines of code. Visual Basic

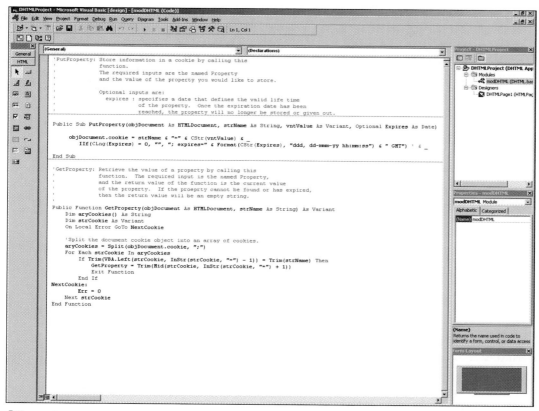

[**Figure B.9** ➡ Visual Basic, a visual programming language, is used to create standard business forms.]
Source: Microsoft Visual Basic

and Visual C++ are two popular examples of visual programming languages.

Web Development Languages

If you have been surfing the Web for a while, you probably either already have a personal Web page, or you have thought of posting one. In that event, you have some experience with using a programming language. The language you used to create your Web page is called **Hypertext Markup Language (HTML)**. HTML is a text-based file format that uses a series of codes, or tags, to set up a document. Because HTML editing programs are visually oriented and easy to use, you do not need to memorize the language to set up a Web page. The programs for creating Web pages are called **Web page builders** or **HTML editors**, and there are many on the market, including Windows Notepad, most Web browsers, and word processing programs such as Word and WordPerfect.

In HTML, the tags used to identify different elements on a page and to format the page are set apart from the text with angle brackets (< >). Specific tags are used to mark the beginning and the ending of an element or a formatting command. For example, if you want text to appear in bold type, the HTML tag to begin bolding is <b>. The tag to turn off bolding, at the end of the selected text, is </b>. The "a href" command sets up a hyperlink from a word or image on the page to another HTML document. Tags also denote document formatting commands, such as text to be used as a title, sizes of text in headings, the ends of paragraphs, underlining, italics, bolding, and where to insert pictures and sound (see Table B.6).

A good way to learn HTML is to find a Web page you like, then use the "View Source" command on your browser to see the hypertext that created the page (see Figure B.10). Once you have created your Web page and saved it to disk, you can upload it to an Internet account you have created through your ISP.

XML

Extensible Markup Language (XML) was designed both to be used as a Web page construction tool, when users want to create their own markup tags, and to build database queries. XML is a powerful language that lets users create database fields for a number of different applications. XML makes it easy for Web users to request and receive information from a variety of databases. In order to view documents created in XML, you need a browser that supports the language, commonly called an XML parser. The latest versions of Microsoft's Internet Explorer and Netscape Navigator can fill the bill.

Adding Dynamic Content to a Web Page

Markup languages such as HTML are for laying out or formatting Web pages. If you want to add animated cartoons or other dynamic content, or have users interact with your Web page other than by clicking on hypertext links, then you will need access to tools such as XML, Java, ActiveX, or a scripting language.

Java. **Java** is a programming language that was developed at Sun Microsystems in the early 1990s. It lets you spice up your Web page by adding active content such as circles that whirl and change colors, hamsters marching to a tune, forms to help users calculate car payments at various interest rates, or any

[Table B.6] *Common HTML tags.*

Tag	Description
<html> ... </html>	Creates an HTML document
<head> ... </head>	Sets off the title and other information that is not displayed on the Web page itself
<body> ... </body>	Sets off the visible portion of the document
<b> ... </b>	Creates bold text
<a href="URL"> ... </a>	Creates a hyperlink
<a href="mailto:EMAIL"> ... </a>	Creates a mailto link
<p> ... </p>	Creates a new paragraph
<table> ... </table>	Creates a table

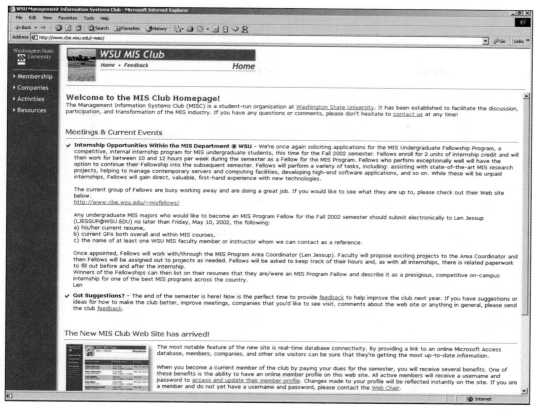

B.10a

[Figure B.10 ➡ A Web page (B.10a) and the HTML commands used to create it (B.10b).]

B.10b

other such dynamic content (see Figure B.11). You can do this in one of two ways: by learning Java or a similar language and programming the content you want, or by downloading free general-purpose **applets** from the Web. Applets are small programs that you can choose from to provide the content you want on your Web page. When a user accesses your Web page, the applets you inserted are downloaded from the server with your Web page to a Java-enabled browser running on a PC. Later, when the user leaves your Web page, the Web page and the applets disappear from his computer.

ActiveX. **ActiveX** was developed by Microsoft Corporation to perform the same function as Java. It, too, lets users program in or insert objects from any ActiveX-supported application or ActiveX-enabled Web page. ActiveX differs from Java in that it was designed to run on Windows computers and is not always supported by other platforms.

Scripting languages. **Scripting languages** can also be used to supply interactive components to a Web page. These languages let you build programs or scripts directly into HTML page code. Web page designers frequently use them to check the accuracy of user-entered information, such as names,

addresses, and credit-card numbers. You can also use them to connect freestanding applets to your HTML-created Web page. Two common scripting languages are Microsoft's VBScript and Netscape's JavaScript.

JavaScript. **JavaScript**, created by Netscape, bears little resemblance to Java. The two are similar, however, in that both Java and JavaScript are useful component software tools for creating Web pages. That is, both allow users to add or create applets that lend dynamic content to Web pages. Both are also cross-platform programs, meaning that they can typically be used by computers running Windows, Linux, Mac OS, and other operating systems.

The development of programming languages is an ongoing process of change and innovation. These changes often result in more capable and complex systems for the user. The popularity of the Internet has spurred the creation of innovative and evolving software. From the pace of change that is occurring, it is clear that many more innovations are on the horizon.

Automated Development Environments

Over the years, the tools for developing information systems have increased both in variety and in power. In the early days of systems development, a developer

[**Figure B.11** ➥ Java helps to provide dynamic content to Web pages.]

Source: Adapted from Hoffer, George, and Valacich, 1999. *Modern systems analysis and design,* Reading, MA: Addison Wesley Longman.

was left to use a pencil and paper to sketch out design ideas and program code. Computers were cumbersome to use and slow to program, and most designers worked out on paper as much of the system design as they could before moving to the computer. Today, system developers have a vast array of powerful computer-based tools at their disposal. These tools have changed forever the ways in which systems are developed. **Computer-aided software engineering (CASE)** refers to automated software tools used by systems developers to design and implement information systems. Developers can use these tools to automate or support activities throughout the systems development process, with the objective of increasing productivity and improving the overall quality of systems. The capabilities of CASE tools are continually evolving and being integrated into a variety of development environments. Below we briefly review some of the interesting characteristics of CASE.

Types of CASE Tools

Two of the primary activities when developing large-scale information systems are the creation of design documents and the management of information. Over the life of a project, thousands of documents need to be created—from screen prototypes, to database content and structure, to layouts of sample forms and reports. At the heart of all CASE environments is a repository for managing information.

CASE also helps developers represent business processes and information flows using graphical diagramming tools. By providing standard symbols to represent business processes, information flows between processes, data storage, and the organizational entities that interact with the business process, CASE eases a very tedious and error-prone activity

(see Figure B.12). The tools not only ease the drawing process but also assure that the drawing conforms to development standards and is consistent with other design documents developed by other developers.

Another powerful capability of CASE is its ability to generate program source code automatically. CASE tools keep pace with contemporary programming languages and can automatically produce programming code directly from high-level designs in languages such as Java, COBOL, BASIC, and C. In addition to diagramming tools and code generators, a broad range of other tools assists in the systems development process. The general types of CASE tools used throughout the development process are summarized in Table B.7.

The Influence of CASE on Individuals

CASE can be used to dramatically increase the speed of development and maintenance of a system, not to mention increase the quality of the system. CASE also influences the culture of an organization in many significant ways. In fact, researchers have found that people with different career orientations have different attitudes toward CASE (Orlikowski, 1989). For example, those within the development group with a managerial orientation welcome CASE because they believe it helps reduce the risk and uncertainty in managing development projects. On the other hand, people with a more technical orientation tend to resist the use of CASE because they feel threatened by the technology's capability to replace some skills they have taken years to master. Table B.8 lists several possible impacts of CASE on the roles of individuals within organizations. CASE is clearly a powerful technology that can have numerous and widespread impacts. Its adoption should be a well-thought-out and highly orchestrated activity.

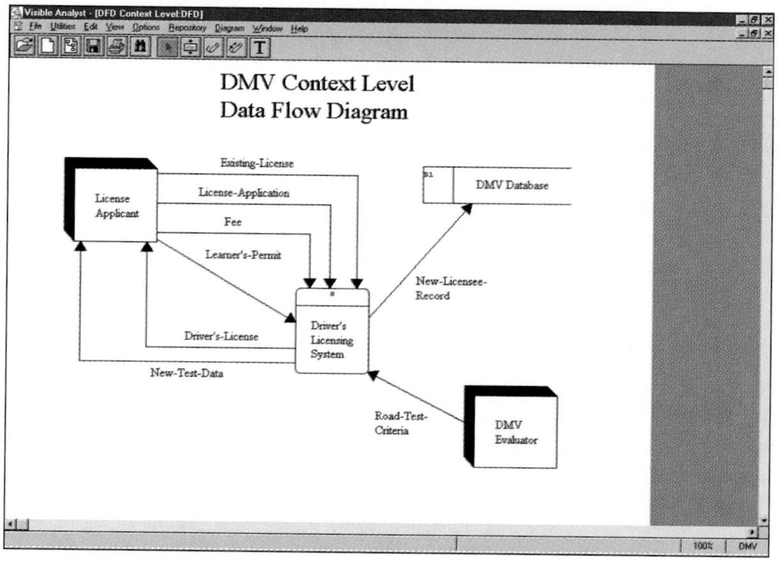

[Figure B.12 → High-level system design diagram from a CASE tool.]

Source: Visible Systems (Visible Analyst product)

[Table B.7] *General types of CASE tools.*

CASE Tool	Description
Diagramming tools	Tools that enable system process, data, and control structures to be represented graphically.
Screen and report generators	Tools that help model how systems look and feel to users. Screen and report generators also make it easier for the systems analyst to identify data requirements and relationships.
Analysis tools	Tools that automatically check for incomplete, inconsistent, or incorrect specifications in diagrams, screens, and reports.
Repository	A tool that enables the integrated storage of specifications, diagrams, reports, and project management information.
Documentation generators	Tools that help produce both technical and user documentation in standard formats.
Code generators	Tools that enable the automatic generation of program and database definition code directly from the design documents, diagrams, screens, and reports.

Source: Adapted from Hoffer, George, and Valacich. 1999. *Modern systems analysis and design,* Reading, MA: Addison Wesley Longman.

[Table B.8] *Common impacts of CASE on individuals within organizations.*

Individuals	Common Impact
Systems analysts	CASE automates many routine tasks of the analyst, making the communication skills (rather than analytical skills) of the analyst most critical.
Programmers	Will piece together objects created by code generators and fourth-generation languages. Their role will become more of maintaining designs than maintaining source code.
Users	Will be much more active in the systems development process through the use of upper CASE tools.
Top managers	Will play a more active role in setting priorities and strategic directions for IS by using CASE-based planning and through user-oriented system development methods.
Functional managers	Will play a greater role in leading development projects by using CASE to re-engineer their business processes.
IS project managers	Will have greater control over development projects and resources.

Source: Adapted from 1992. Chen and Norman.

KEY POINTS REVIEW

1. Describe the common functions of system software.
System software is the collection of programs that form the foundation for the basic operations of the computer hardware. System software, or the operating system, performs many different tasks. Some of these tasks include booting your computer, reading programs into memory, managing memory allocation to those programs, managing where programs and files are located in secondary storage, maintaining the structure of directories and sub-directories, formatting disks, controlling the computer monitor, and sending objects to the printer. The system software manages the dialogue you can have with a computer using either a command-based or graphical interface. A command-based interface requires that text commands be typed into the computer, whereas a graphical user interface (GUI) uses pictures and icons as well as menus to send instructions back and forth between the user and the computer system.

2. Describe the various types of application software. You can find a large number of computer software applications. Customized application software is developed specifically for a single organization. This kind of software is tailored to an organization's unique requirements. Off-the-shelf application software is not customized to the unique needs of one organization but is written to operate within many organizations. In general, off-the-shelf software is less costly, faster to procure, of higher quality, and less risky than customized software. Business information systems are applications developed to perform a firm's organization-wide operations, such as payroll or inventory management. Office automation or personal productivity software is designed to support activities such as word processing and electronic mail.

3. Describe the characteristics of various types of programming languages and application development environments. A programming language is the computer language used by programmers to write application programs. In order to run on a computer, programs must be translated into binary machine language. Programming languages are translated into machine languages through special types of programs, which are called compilers and interpreters. Over the past several decades, software has evolved. Early software used machine language, which told the computer exactly which circuits to turn on and which to turn off. Next, symbolic languages used "symbols" to represent a series of binary statements. This was followed by the development of high-level languages, such as FORTRAN, COBOL, C, and Java. The difference between these high-level languages and earlier languages is that the high-level languages use English-like words and commands, making it easier to write programs. Fourth-generation languages are called outcome-oriented languages because they contain even more English-like commands and tend to focus on what output is desired instead of the procedures required to get that output. Again, these languages made it even easier to program. Fifth-generation languages are called natural languages because they allow the user to communicate with the computer using true English sentences. In addition to this generational evolution, object-oriented programming, visual programming, and Web development languages are relatively new enhancements to programming languages. Object-oriented languages group together data and their corresponding instructions into manipulable objects. Visual programming languages use a graphical interface to build graphical interfaces for other programs. Web development languages are a rapidly evolving set of tools designed for constructing Internet applications and Web content. Together, object-oriented, visual programming, and Web development languages are making it easier for programmers to develop today's complex software systems, especially for modern Internet-based systems. Finally, computer-aided software engineering environments help systems developers construct large-scale systems more rapidly and with higher quality.

KEY TERMS

ActiveX 344

applets 344

application software 335

business information systems 337

command-based interface 334

compiler 338

computer-aided software engineering (CASE) 345

customized application software 335

encapsulation 341

event-driven 341

extensible markup language (XML) 342

graphical user interface (GUI) 335

hypertext markup language (HTML) 342

inheritance 341

interface 334

interpreter 339

java 342

JavaScript 344

machine language 338

object-oriented languages 341

objects 341

off-the-shelf application software 337

office automation or personal productivity software 338

operating system 333

scripting languages 344

software 333

systems software 333

utilities or utility programs 335

visual programming languages 341

web page builders or HTML editors 342

REVIEW QUESTIONS

1. Define the term software, and name several software packages and their uses.

2. Describe at least four different tasks performed by an operating system.

3. What is the difference between a command-based interface and a graphical user interface?

4. Describe the similarities and differences between at least two major operating systems in use today.

5. Name and describe four functions of utility programs.

6. Contrast using off-the-shelf application software versus customized application software.

7. Describe the evolution of programming languages as well as various contemporary programming languages in use today.

8. What is HTML, and why is it important?

9. Describe various options for adding dynamic content to a Web page.

10. What is CASE, and how can it influence individuals within organizations?

SELF-STUDY QUESTIONS

1. Which of the following is an example of an operating system?
   A. Microsoft Access
   B. Microsoft Excel
   C. Microsoft Word
   D. Microsoft Windows

2. An operating system performs which of the following tasks?
   A. booting the computer
   B. managing where programs and files are stored
   C. sending documents to the printer
   D. all of the above

3. Which of the following is a popular operating system?
   A. Noodle
   B. Linux
   C. FORTRAN
   D. PowerEdge

4. Which is **not** an advantage of off-the-shelf application software?
   A. lower cost
   B. faster to obtain
   C. easier to use
   D. higher quality due to large customer base

5. Which is **not** an example of office automation or personal productivity software?
   A. payroll system
   B. database management system
   C. Web browser
   D. word processing

6. Which of the following is **not** a tool for adding dynamic content to a Web page?
   A. Hot Coffee
   B. ActiveX
   C. scripting languages
   D. Java

7. Automated software tools used to develop information systems that can improve the overall system quality and increase programmer productivity are called _____ .
   A. computerized programming
   B. automated development
   C. computer-aided programming
   D. none of the above

8. A utility program may provide _____ .
   A. antivirus protection
   B. file conversion capability
   C. file compression and defragmentation
   D. all of the above

9. Fifth-generation languages are also referred to as _____ languages.
   A. assembly
   B. natural
   C. high-level
   D. low-level

10. What were first generation programming languages called?
    A. natural language
    B. assembly language
    C. machine language
    D. none of the above

Answers are at the end of the Problems and Exercises.

PROBLEMS AND EXERCISES

1. Match the following terms with the appropriate definitions:

   _____ Operating system
   _____ Applets
   _____ Visual programming languages
   _____ Graphical user interface
   _____ Customized application software

   _____ Scripting language
   _____ Interpreter
   _____ Business information systems
   _____ Compiler
   _____ Object-oriented programming languages

   a. Translates a computer program into machine language, which is then executed by the computer

   b. An interface that enables the user to use pictures, icons, and menus in order to send instructions to the computer

   c. Coordinates the interaction between users, applications, and hardware

   d. Applications developed to perform the organization-wide operations of a firm

e. Programming languages that provide a graphical user interface and are generally easier to use than non-GUI languages

f. Small software programs that can be used to provide special features to a Web site

g. Programming languages that group together data and their corresponding instructions into manipulable objects

h. Software developed based on specifications provided by a particular organization

i. Translates the computer program into machine language one statement at a time

j. Used to supply interactive components to a Web page by building programs or scripts directly into HTML page code

2. How do software programs affect your life? Give examples of software from areas other than desktop computers. Are the uses for software increasing over time?

3. In what situations would customized software be utilized? How does the cost compare with the benefit?

4. What are the implications for an organization of having more than one operating system? What might be the advantages? What are some of the disadvantages? Would you recommend such a situation? Can you find organizations using the World Wide Web that specifically mention their utilization of multiple operating systems in their information system architecture? Do these organizations comment on this arrangement or simply mention its existence? Prepare a 10-minute presentation to the rest of the class on your findings.

5. Imagine that you are in charge of procuring software applications for your division of a company. You are in need of a powerful business information systems software application that will control most of the accounting and bookkeeping functions. Based on your current knowledge of the intricacies of the accounting profession and its practices, would you be more likely to purchase this application as a customized software application or an off-the-shelf software application? Why did you select this choice? What would make you choose the other option?

6. What is a business information system, and what types of processing does it do? Many companies' business systems track what besides inventory? Why?

7. Based on the information within this appendix and within the chapters of this textbook, discuss the importance of a single decision to purchase one software application over another—for example, purchasing Microsoft Excel instead of Lotus 1-2-3. Who will be affected? How will they be affected? What changes might occur because of the purchase?

8. Based on your own experiences with computers and computer systems, what do you like and dislike about different operating systems that you have used? Were these uses on a professional or a personal level, or both? Who made the decision to purchase that particular operating system? Did you have any say in the purchase decision?

9. Choose an organization that utilizes a variety of different software applications. Are these software applications customized applications, off-the-shelf applications, or a combination of the two? Talk with some of the employees to determine how they feel about using customized versus off-the-shelf software applications.

10. Search the Web for organizations that specialize in creating customized software applications for their clients. What specific product categories do these organizations specialize in, if any? Were you able to find any pricing information directly from their homepages?

11. Have the off-the-shelf software applications you have used met your requirements? Were you able to perform the functions and routines that you needed? Did the software meet your expectations? Would you have bought this type of software if you knew then what you know today?

12. Find an organization that does a lot of in-house programming and utilizes a variety of different programming languages. Determine the generation level of these languages. Are the same personnel programming in most (or all) of the languages, or are different personnel programming in each of the languages? Is this assignment of programmers intentional or unintentional?

13. Imagine that you and a friend are at a local ATM getting some cash from your account to pay for a movie. The ATM does not seem to be working. It is giving you an error message every time you press any button. Is this most likely a software-related problem or a hardware-related problem? Why? Use the information in this appendix and in the previous appendix to help you make your decision.

14. Describe how you would handle the resistance to implementing CASE tools by those who feel they will be replaced by technology. From whom is this resistance most likely to come? Is this fear legitimate? Why or why not?

ANSWERS TO THE SELF-STUDY QUESTIONS

1. D   2. D   3. B   4. C   5. A   6. A   7. D   8. D   9. B   10. C

Preview

The purpose of this appendix is to introduce key networking concepts, technologies, and applications. This discussion provides you with a solid foundation for understanding how computers are connected across a room or across the world.

After reading this appendix, you will be able to do the following:

1. Understand networking fundamentals, including network services and transmission media.

2. Describe network software and hardware, including media access control, network topologies, and protocols, as well as connectivity hardware for both local area and wide area networks.

Telecommunications and networking technologies, like those described throughout this book, are taking on more and more importance as organizations rely more on computer-based information systems. Understanding how the underlying networking technologies work and where these technologies are heading will help to complete your understanding of the "essential" elements of information systems. In this appendix we describe the enabling technologies underlying computer networks, how they are used together to form networks, and how these networks are used. The discussion begins with a description of the fundamental elements of computer networking.

NETWORKING FUNDAMENTALS

Telecommunications advances have enabled individual computer networks—constructed with a variety of hardware and software—to connect together in what appears to be a single network. Networks are increasingly being used to dynamically exchange relevant, value-adding knowledge and information throughout global organizations and institutions. The following sections take a closer look at the fundamental building blocks of these complex networks and the services they provide.

Servers, Clients, and Peers

A **network** consists of three separate components: servers, clients, and peers, as depicted in Figure C.1. A **server** is any computer on the network that makes access to files, printing, communications, and other services available to users of the network. Servers only provide services. A server typically has a more advanced microprocessor, more memory, a larger cache, and more disk storage than a single-user workstation. A **client** is any computer, such as a user's workstation or PC on the network; or any software application, such as a word processing application, that uses the services provided by the server. Clients only request services. A client usually has only one user, whereas many different users share

the server. A **peer** is any computer that may both request and provide services. Whether or not a particular computer or device on the network is considered a server, client, or peer depends on the operating system that is running. The trend in business is to use **server-centric networks**, in which servers and clients have defined roles. However, **peer-to-peer networks** that enable any computer or device on the network to provide and request services can be found in small offices and homes.

Network Services

Network services are the capabilities that networked computers share through the multiple combinations of hardware and software. The most common network services are file services, print services, message services, and application services. **File services** are used to store, retrieve, and move data files in an efficient manner, as shown in Figure C.2a. An individual can use the file services of the network to move a customer file electronically to multiple recipients across the network. **Print services** are used to control and manage users' access to network printers and fax equipment, as shown in Figure C.2b. Sharing printers on a network reduces the number of printers an organization needs. **Message services** include the storing, accessing, and delivering of text, binary, graphic, digitized video, and audio data. These services are similar to file services, but they also deal with communication interactions between users and applications. Message services include electronic mail or the transfer of messages between two or more networked computers, as shown in Figure C.2c.

[Figure C.1 ➡ A server is a computer on the network that enables multiple computers (or "clients") to access data. A peer is a computer that may both request and provide services.]

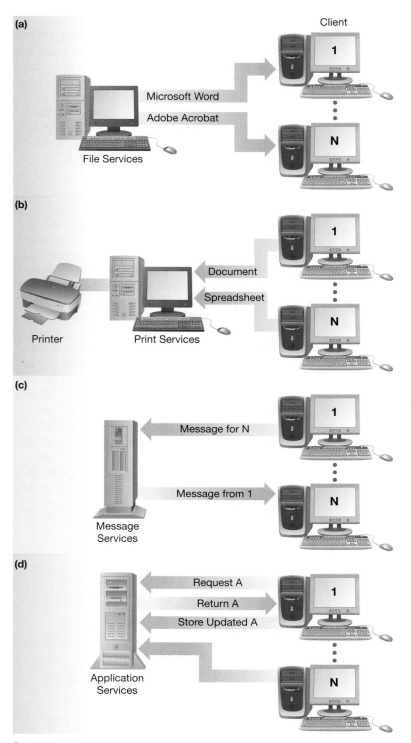

[**Figure C.2** ➥ Networks can provide file, print, message, and application services.]

Application services run software for network clients and enable computers to share processing power, as shown in Figure C.2d. Application services highlight the concept of client/server computing, in which processing is distributed between the client and server. Clients request information or services from the servers. The servers store data and applica-

tion programs. For example, the physical search of database records may take place on the server, while a much smaller database application that handles the user-interface functions runs on the client.

When an organization decides to network its computers and devices, it must decide what services will be provided and whether these services will be centralized (a server-centric approach), distributed (a peer-to-peer approach), or some combination of both. These decisions ultimately affect the choice of the network operating system. The **network operating system (NOS)** is system software that controls the network and enables computers to communicate with each other. In other words, the NOS enables network services. In most local area network (LAN) environments, the NOS consists of two parts. The first and most complex part is the system software that runs on the file server. The system software coordinates many functions, including user accounts, access information, security, and resource sharing. The second and much smaller part of the NOS runs on each workstation connected to the network. In peer-to-peer networks, usually a piece of the NOS is installed on each attached workstation and runs on top of the local operating system. A recent trend is to integrate the NOS into the workstation operating system itself. Recent versions of Windows use this approach. Examples of NOSs are Banyan Vines, Novell NetWare, Microsoft LAN Manager, and LANtastic.

Transmission Media

Every network uses some type of **transmission medium**—the physical pathway to send data and information between two or more entities on a network. To send messages, computers send energy-based signals—electric currents using electromagnetic waves—to contact each other. These electromagnetic waves can be altered by semiconductor materials and are represented in two discrete, or binary, states—the 0s and 1s of a computer, known as bits. These bits are transmitted over physical pathways, or media, as computers communicate with each other.

When deciding which type of medium to use in a network, an organization should consider bandwidth, attenuation, immunity from electromagnetic interference (EMI) and eavesdropping, the cost of the cable, and ease of installation as summarized in Table C.1. Recall that **bandwidth** is the transmission capacity of a computer or communications channel, measured in megabits per second (Mbps), and represents how much binary data can be reliably transmitted over the medium in one second. Some networks have a bandwidth of 10 Mbps; others have 100 Mbps or more. To appreciate the importance of bandwidth for speed, consider how long it would take to transmit a document the length of this book (about two million characters or 16 million bits). It would take about 1.6 seconds at 10 Mbps and .16 seconds at 100 Mbps. In contrast, using a standard PC modem that transmits data at a rate of 56K bits per second (bps), it would take nearly five minutes to transmit the same document. In addition to bandwidth, a second key issue to consider is transmission media's vulnerability to attenuation. **Attenuation** results when the power of

an electric signal weakens as it is sent over increasing distance, as shown in Figure C.3. In a network, an important concern is how far a signal can travel and still maintain its original properties or meaning. **EMI (electromagnetic interference)** occurs when fluorescent lights, weather, or other electronic signals interfere with the original signal being sent. All media differ as to how immune they are to EMI, as we will see in the next sections.

Two forms of media are used in networks: cable and wireless media. Although wireless data communications is being used increasingly, it is still in its infancy and is generally a much slower means of transmission than cable. However, the capabilities of wireless media are rapidly improving, and wireless media have many useful applications. The following sections describe the characteristics of both cable and wireless media.

Cable Media

Cable media physically link computers and other devices in a network. The most common forms of cable media are twisted pair, coaxial, and fiber-optic.

Twisted Pair Cable

Twisted pair (TP) cable is made of two or more pairs of insulated copper wires twisted together (see Figure C.4). The cable may be unshielded (UTP) or shielded (STP). Telephone wire installations use UTP cabling. UTP is rated according to its quality; category 3 (Cat 3) and Cat 5 UTP are often used in network installations. Unshielded cable is cheap, easy to install, and has a capacity from 1 to 100 Mbps at distances up to 100 meters. However, like all copper wiring, it has rapid attenuation and is very sensitive to EMI and eavesdropping—the undetected capturing of network information. Shielded twisted cable is cable wrapped in an insulation that makes it less prone to EMI and eavesdropping. Shielded twisted cable is more expensive than unshielded twisted cable, and it is more difficult to install because it requires special grounding connectors to drain EMI. STP can support bandwidths up to 500 Mbps at distances up to 100 meters. However, it is most commonly used to support networks running at 16 Mbps.

Coaxial Cable

Coaxial (or "coax") cable contains a solid inner copper conductor, surrounded by plastic insulation and

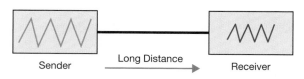

[**Figure C.3** ➡ Signals weaken when sent over increasing distances.]

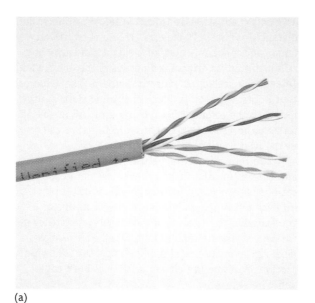

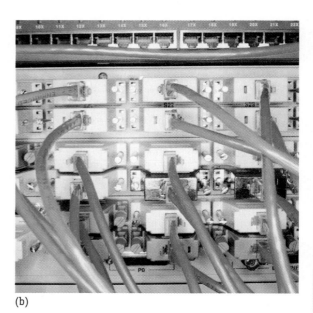

(a)   (b)

[Figure C.4 ➥ On the left is a cable spliced open showing several twisted pairs, and on the right is a sample network installation which utilizes many twisted pair cables at once.]

(a) ©Belkin Components (b) ©Getty Images, Inc.

an outer braided copper or foil shield (see Figure C.5). Coax cable comes in a variety of thicknesses—thinnet coax and thicknet coax—based on resistance to EMI. Thinnet coax is less costly than STP or Cat 5 UTP; thicknet coax, however, is more expensive than STP or Cat 3 UTP. Coax is the simplest cable to install. The cable is cut, and a connector, called a T-connector, is attached to the cable and each device. Coax cable is most commonly used for cable television installations and for networks operating at 10 Mbps. Its attenuation is lower than twisted pair cable, and it is moderately susceptible to EMI and eavesdropping.

Fiber-Optic Cable

Fiber-optic cable is made of a light-conducting glass or plastic core, surrounded by more glass, called cladding, and a tough outer sheath (see Figure C.6).

The sheath protects the fiber from changes in temperature, as well as from bending or breaking. This technology uses pulses of light sent along the optical cable to transmit data. Fiber-optic cable transmits clear and secure data because it is immune to EMI and eavesdropping. Transmission signals do not break up because fiber-optic cable has low attenuation. It can support bandwidths from 100 Mbps to greater than 2 Gbps (gigabits per second) and distances from 2 to 25 kilometers. It can transmit video and sound. Fiber-optic cable is more expensive than copper wire, due to the cost and difficulties of installation and repair. Fiber-optic cables are used for high-speed **backbones**—the high-speed central networks to which many smaller networks can be connected. A backbone may connect, for example, several different buildings in which other, smaller LANs reside.

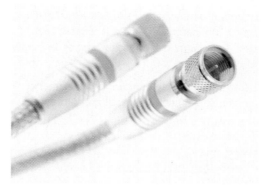

[Figure C.5 ➥ These sample coaxial cables are ready to be connected to a computer or other device.]
©Getty Images, Inc.

[Figure C.6 ➥ Fiber-optic cable consists of a light-conducting glass or plastic core, surrounded by more glass, called cladding, and a tough outer sheath.]
©Getty Images, Inc.

[Table C.1] *Key benefits and drawbacks of different cable media.*

Medium	Key Benefit(s)	Drawback(s)
Twisted Pair	Inexpensive; easy to install and reconfigure	Highly susceptible to EMI, eavesdropping, and attenuation; unsuitable for high speeds
Coaxial	Higher bandwidth than twisted pair; lower susceptibility to EMI, eavesdropping, and attenuation than twisted pair	More expensive than twisted pair; more difficult to install, reconfigure, and manage attenuation than twisted pair; bulky
Fiber-Optic	Very high bandwidth; low attenuation and immune to EMI and eavesdropping	Expensive cable and hardware; complex installation and maintenance

Wireless Media

With the popularity of cellular phones and pagers, wireless media are rapidly gaining popularity. **Wireless media** transmit and receive electromagnetic signals using methods such as infrared line of sight, high-frequency radio, and microwave systems.

Infrared Line of Sight

Infrared line of sight uses high-frequency light waves to transmit data on an unobstructed path between nodes—computers or some other device such as a printer—on a network, at a distance of up to 24.4 meters. The remote controls for most audio/visual equipment, such as your TV, stereo, and other consumer electronics equipment use infrared light. Infrared systems may be configured as either point-to-point or broadcast. For example, when you use your TV remote control, you have to be in front of the TV to have successful communication. This is an example of point-to-point infrared. Many new printers and notebooks have the capability to transmit data using infrared communication, allowing these devices to be easily connected. With broadcast infrared communication, devices do not need to be positioned directly in front of each other, but simply have to be located within some distance of each other. Infrared equipment is relatively inexpensive, but point-to-point systems require strict line-of-sight positioning. Installation and maintenance focus on ensuring proper optical alignment between nodes on the network. Point-to-point infrared systems can support up to 16 Mbps at 1 km, whereas broadcast systems support less than 1 Mbps. Attenuation and susceptibility to EMI and eavesdropping are problematic, particularly when objects obstruct the light path, or when other environmental conditions such as smoke or high-intensity light are prevalent.

High-Frequency Radio

High-frequency radio signals can transmit data at rates of up to 11 Mbps to network nodes from 12.2 up to approximately 40 kilometers apart, depending on the nature of any obstructions between them. The flexibility of the signal path makes high-frequency radio ideal for mobile transmissions. For example, most police departments use high-frequency radio signals that enable police vehicles to communicate with each other as well as with the dispatch office. This medium is expensive due to the cost of antenna towers and high-output transceivers. Installation is complex and often dangerous due to the high voltages. Although attenuation is fairly low, this medium is very susceptible to EMI and eavesdropping.

Three common applications of high-frequency radio communication are pagers, cellular phones, and wireless networks. A **pager** is a one-way, wireless messaging system. See Table C.2 for a summary of types of pagers and their advantages. In a business setting, there are countless uses for a pager. If you travel, your boss can easily contact you when you are away from the office. If you are on vacation, you can learn the outcome of an important business deal. Pagers are also popular with families for notifying others of changes in plans, notifying parents when kids need to be picked up from school, or notifying teenagers when it is time to come home!

Unlike pagers, a **cellular phone** provides two-way wireless communication. In a cellular system, for example, a city is divided into **cells** with a low-powered radio antenna/receiver in each cell; these cells are monitored and controlled by a central computer (see Figure C.7). Any given cellular network has a fixed number of radio frequencies. When a user initiates or receives a call, a unique frequency is assigned to the caller by the mobile telephone switching office for the duration of the call. As a person travels within the network, the central computer at the switching office monitors the quality of the signal and automatically assigns the call to the closest cellular antenna.

High-frequency radio-wave technology is increasingly being used to support **wireless local area networks (WLANs)**. The ease of installation has made WLANs popular for business and for home use. For example, many homes have multiple computers and have a need to share Internet access, files, or

[Table C.2] *Types of pagers.*

Pager Type	Description	Advantages
Tone-only	User is alerted with an audible tone to call a predetermined phone number for a message	Simple
Numeric display	User is alerted and number to call is displayed	Can use any phone number; phone number is stored; less chance of error or missing message.
Alphanumeric display	User is alerted and reads alphanumeric message	Same as numeric display, plus complete, accurate text message
Tone and voice	User is alerted and receives a short voice message	User gets notification and message in single event; easier for caller and user

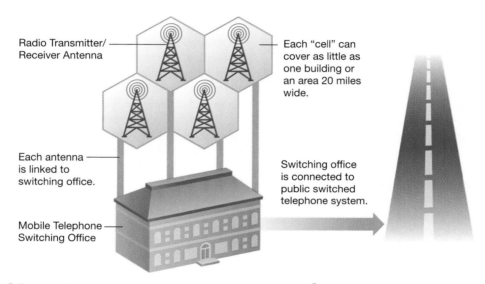

Radio Transmitter/
Receiver Antenna

Each "cell" can cover as little as one building or an area 20 miles wide.

Each antenna is linked to switching office.

Switching office is connected to public switched telephone system.

Mobile Telephone Switching Office

[Figure C.7 ➡ A cellular network divides a geographic region into cells.**]**

peripheral devices. Unfortunately, many older homes do not have a wired infrastructure to connect computers and devices, making wireless networking particularly attractive. As discussed previously, personal area networks (PANs) use low-powered Bluetooth radio-wave technology.

Microwave

Microwave transmission is a high-frequency radio signal that is sent through the air using either terrestrial (earth-based) systems or satellite systems. Both terrestrial and satellite microwave transmission require line-of-sight communications between the signal sender and the signal receiver. **Terrestrial microwave**, shown in Figure C.8, uses antennas that require an unobstructed path or line-of-sight between nodes. Terrestrial microwave systems are used to cross inaccessible terrain or to connect build-

ings where cable installation would be expensive. The cost of a terrestrial microwave system depends on the distance to be covered. Typically, businesses lease access to these microwave systems from service providers rather than invest in antenna equipment. Data may be transmitted at up to 274 Mbps. Over short distances, attenuation is not a problem, but signals can be obstructed over longer distances by environmental conditions such as high winds and heavy rain. EMI and eavesdropping are significant problems with microwave communications.

Satellite microwave, shown in Figure C.9, uses a relay station that transfers signals between antennas located on earth and satellites orbiting the earth. In other words, a **satellite** is a microwave station located in outer space. Satellite transmissions are delayed because of the distance signals must travel. Satellite communication's greatest strength is

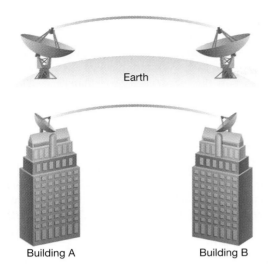

[Figure C.8 ➡ Terrestrial microwave requires a line-of-sight path between a sender and a receiver.]

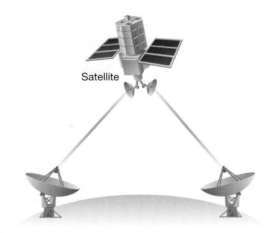

[Figure C.9 ➡ Communications satellites are relay stations that receive signals from one earth station and rebroadcast them to another.]

that it can be used to access very remote and undeveloped locations on the earth. Such systems are extremely costly because their use and installation depends on space technology. Companies such as AT&T sell satellite services with typical transmission rates ranging from <1 to 10 Mbps, but the rates can be as high as 90 Mbps. Like terrestrial microwave,

satellite systems are prone to attenuation and susceptible to EMI and eavesdropping.

As with cable media, there are key differences between the types of wireless media. Table C.3 summarizes the key benefits and drawbacks of each wireless medium. Table C.4 compares wireless media across several criteria.

[Table C.3] *Key benefits and drawbacks of different wireless media.*

Medium	Key Benefit(s)	Drawback(s)
Infrared line of sight	Easy to install and configure; inexpensive	Very limited bandwidth; line of sight required; environmental factors influence signal quality
High-frequency radio	Mobile stations; low attenuation	Frequency licensing; complex installation
Terrestrial microwave	Can access remote locations or congested areas; high bandwidth; low attenuation	Frequency licensing; complex installation; environmental factors influence signal quality
Satellite microwave	Can access remote locations; high bandwidth; earth stations can be fixed or mobile	Frequency licensing; complex installation; environmental factors influence signal quality; propagation delays

[Table C.4] *Relative comparison of wireless media.*

Medium	Expense	Speed	Attenuation	EMI	Eavesdropping
Infrared line of sight	Low	Up to 16 Mbps	High	High	High
High-frequency radio	Moderate	Up to 11 Mbps	Low	High	High
Terrestrial microwave	Moderate	Up to 274 Mbps	Low	High	High
Satellite microwave	High	Up to 90 Mbps	Moderate	High	High

NETWORK SOFTWARE AND HARDWARE

Standards play a key role in creating networks. The physical elements of networks—adapters, cables, and connectors—are defined by a set of standards that have evolved since the early 1970s. Standards ensure the interoperability and compatibility of network devices. The Institute of Electrical and Electronics Engineers (IEEE) has established a number of telecommunications standards. The three major standards for LAN cabling and media access control are Ethernet, token ring, and ARCnet. See Table C.5 for a summary of LAN standards. Each standard combines a media access control technique, network topology, and media in different ways. Software is blended with hardware to implement protocols that allow different types of computers and networks to communicate successfully. Protocols are often implemented within a computer's operating system or within a special piece of software called a network operating system. Each of these topics is described more thoroughly below.

Media Access Control

Media access control are the rules that govern how a given node or workstation gains access to the network to send or receive information. There are two general types of access control: distributed and random access. With distributed control, only a single workstation at a time has authorization to transmit its data. This authorization is transferred sequentially from workstation to workstation. Under random control, any workstation can transmit its data by checking whether the medium is available. No specific permission is required. The following sections describe each type in more detail.

Distributed Access Control

The most commonly used method of distributed access control is called token passing. **Token passing** is an access method that uses a constantly circulating electronic token, a small packet of data, to prevent collisions and give all workstations equal access to the network. A collision occurs when two or more workstations simultaneously transmit messages onto the network. A workstation must possess the token before it can transmit a message onto the network. A workstation that receives the token and wants to send a message marks the token as busy, appends a message to it, and transmits both. The message and token are passed around the ring, as depicted in Figure C.10. Each workstation copies the message and retransmits the token/message combination. When it is received back at the originating workstation, the message is removed, the token is marked as free, and it is transmitted to the next workstation on the network.

Random Access Control

The most commonly used method of random access control is called **CSMA/CD—Carrier Sense Multiple Access/Collision Detect**. In CSMA/CD each workstation "listens" to the network to determine whether a message is being transmitted. If the network is quiet, the workstation sends its message; otherwise, it waits. When a workstation gains access to the medium and sends information onto the network, messages are sent to all workstations on the network; however, only the destination with the proper address is able to "open" the message. If two or more workstations try to send a message simultaneously, all workstations detect that a collision has occurred, and all sending is ceased. After a short random period of time, the workstations again try to send their messages. When network traffic is light, there are few collisions and data is quickly transmitted. However, the speed of transmission deteriorates rapidly under heavy traffic conditions.

Network Topologies

Network topology refers to the shape of a network. The three common network topologies are star, ring, and bus.

Star Network

A **star network** is configured, as you might expect, in the shape of a star as shown in Figure C.11a. That is, all nodes or workstations are connected to a central hub or concentrator through which all messages pass. Active hubs amplify transmission signals so long cable lengths may be used. The workstations represent the points of the star. Star topologies are easy to lay out and modify. However, they are also the most costly because they require the largest amount of cabling. Although it is easy to diagnose problems at individual workstations, star networks

[Table C.5] *Summary of major LAN standards.*

Network Standards	Access Control	Topology	Typical Media	Speed
Ethernet	CSMA/CD	Bus	Coax or twisted pair	10–100 Mbps
Token ring	Token passing	Ring	Twisted pair	4–100 Mbps
ARCnet	Token passing	Star or bus	Coax or twisted pair	2.5–20 Mbps

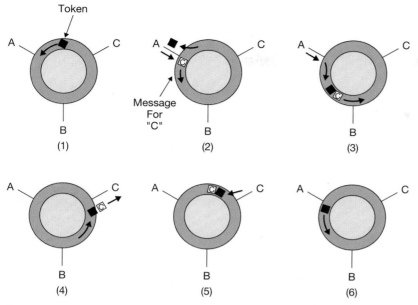

Token

Message
For
"C"

A   C   A   C   A   C

B   B   B
(1)   (2)   (3)

A   C   A   C   A   C

B   B   B
(4)   (5)   (6)

[**Figure C.10** ➥ Station A receives the token and adds a message for station C; C receives the message and token, then forwards both back to station A; station A removes the message and forwards the empty token on to the next station on the network.]

are susceptible to a single point of failure at the hub which would result in all workstations losing network access.

Ring Network

A **ring network** is configured in the shape of a closed loop or circle, with each node connecting to the next node, as shown in Figure C.11b. In ring networks, messages move in one direction around the circle. As a message moves around the circle, each workstation examines it to see whether the message is for that workstation. If not, the message is regenerated and passed on to the next node. This regeneration process enables ring networks to cover much larger distances than star or bus networks can. Relatively little cabling is required, but a failure of any node on the ring network can cause complete network failure. It is difficult to modify and reconfigure the network. Ring networks normally use some form of token passing media access control method to regulate network traffic.

Bus Network

A **bus network** is in the shape of an open-ended line, as shown in Figure C.11c and, as a result, is the easiest network to extend and has the simplest wiring layout. This topology enables all network nodes to receive the same message through the network cable at the same time. However, it is difficult to diagnose and isolate network faults. Bus networks use CSMA/CD for media access control.

Protocols

In addition to media access control and network topologies, all networks employ protocols to make sure communication between computers is successful. **Protocols** are agreed-upon formats for transmitting data between connected computers. They specify how computers should be connected to the network, how errors will be checked, what data compression method will be used, how a sending computer will signal that it has finished sending a message, and how a receiving computer will signal that it has received a message. Protocols allow packets to be correctly routed to and from their destinations. There are literally thousands of protocols for programmers to use, but a few are a lot more important than the others. In this section, we will first review the worldwide standard, called the OSI model, for implementing protocols. Next, we briefly review two of the more important network protocols: Ethernet and TCP/IP.

The OSI Model

The need of organizations to interconnect computers and networks that use different protocols has driven the industry to an open system architecture, in which different protocols can communicate with each other. The International Standards Organization (ISO) defined a networking model called the Open Systems Interconnection (OSI) that divides computer-to-computer communications into seven

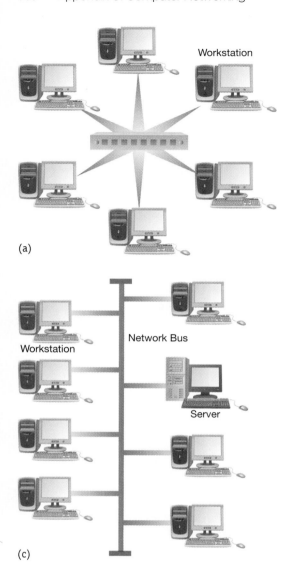

(a)

(c)

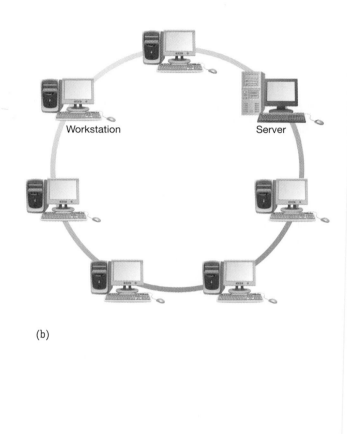

(b)

[Figure C.11 ➡ (a) The star network has several workstations connected to a central hub. (b) The ring network is configured in a closed loop, with each workstation connected to another workstation. (c) The bus network is configured in the shape of an open-ended line where each workstation receives the same message simultaneously.]

connected layers. The **OSI model** is a protocol that represents a group of specific tasks, represented in Figure C.12 as successive layers, which enable computers to communicate data. Each successively higher layer builds on the functions of the layers below. For example, suppose you are using a PC running Windows and are connected to the Internet, and you want to send a message to a friend who is connected to the Internet through a large workstation computer running UNIX—two different computers and two different operating systems. When you transmit your message, it is passed down from layer to layer in the Windows protocol environment of your system. At each layer, special bookkeeping information specific to the layer, called a header, is added to the data. Eventually, the data and head-

ers are transferred from the Windows Layer 1 to UNIX's Layer 1 over some physical medium. Upon receipt, the message is passed up through the layers in the UNIX application. At each layer, the corresponding header information is stripped away, the requested task is performed, and the remaining data package is passed on until your message arrives as you sent it, as shown in Figure C.13. In other words, protocols represent an agreement between different parts of the network about how data is to be transferred.

Ethernet
Ethernet is a local area network protocol developed by Xerox Corporation in 1976. It uses a bus or star network topology and uses random access control to send

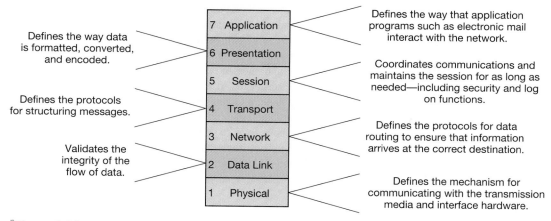

[Figure C.12 ➥ The Open Systems Interconnection (OSI) model has seven layers and provides a framework for connecting different computers with different operating systems to a network.]

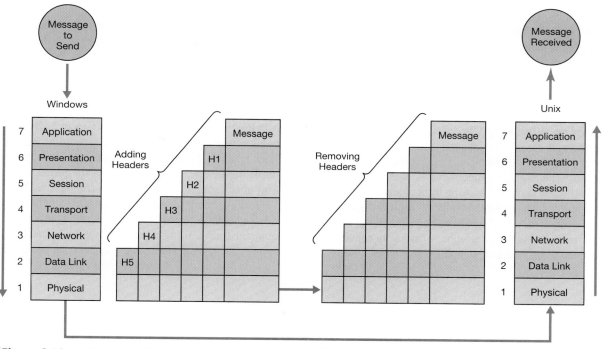

[Figure C.13 ➥ Message passing between two different computers.]

data. The original Ethernet supports data transfer rates of 10 Mbps. A later version, called 100Base-T or Fast Ethernet, supports transfer rates of 100 Mbps, and the latest version, called Gigabit Ethernet, supports transfer rates of 1 gigabit, or 1,000 megabits, per second. You need some type of Ethernet card installed in your computer to use this type of network connection.

TCP/IP

The Internet was based on the idea that individual networks could be separately designed and developed, yet still connect their users to the Internet by using their own unique interfaces. **Transmission Control Protocol/Internet Protocol (TCP/IP)**, the protocol of the Internet, allows different interconnected networks to communicate using the same language. For example, TCP/IP allows IBM, Macintosh, and Dell users to communicate despite any system differences. Computer scientist Vinton Cerf and engineer Robert Kahn defined the Internet Protocol (IP), by which packets are sent from one computer to another on their way to a destination, as part of the DARPA project. TCP/IP was discussed more thoroughly in Chapter 4.

Connectivity Hardware

Stand-alone computers can be physically connected to create different types of networks. Transmission media connectors, network interface cards, and modems are used to connect computers or devices in a network. After individual devices are connected to the network, multiple segments of transmission media can be connected to form one large network. Repeaters, hubs, bridges, and multiplexers are used to extend the range and size of the network. These devices are described below.

Transmission Media Connectors

Transmission media connectors, or simply **connectors**, are used to terminate cable in order to be plugged into a network interface card or into other network components. Connectors include T-connectors for coax cable and RJ-45 connectors (similar to a phone jack) for twisted pair cable.

Network Interface Cards

A **network interface card (NIC)** is a PC expansion board that plugs into a computer so that it can be connected to a network. Each NIC has a unique identifier (determined by the manufacturer) that is used to identify the address of the computer on the network.

Modems

A **modem** (MOdulator/DEModulator) enables computers to transmit data over telephone lines and thereby connect your PC with other PCs in a computer network. Because the dial-up telephone system was designed to pass the sound of voices in the form of analog signals, it cannot pass the electrical pulses—**digital signals**— that computers use. The only way to pass digital data over conventional voice telephone lines is to convert it to audio tones—**analog signals**—that the telephone

lines can carry. Hence, a modem converts digital signals from a computer into analog signals so that telephone lines may be used as a transmission medium to send and receive electronic information. If you send an e-mail message from your university through the Internet to a friend at another university, the modem attached to your PC converts your digital message into audio tones. The message is transmitted over the telephone lines to your university, then travels through the Internet from your university to your friend's university. Your friend also uses a modem to dial into her university to read your message, as shown in Figure C.14.

Repeaters

A **repeater** is a network device used to regenerate or replicate a signal as it weakens when traveling on a network. A repeater also moves data from one media segment to another and effectively extends the size of the network.

Hubs

A **hub** is used as a central point of connection between media segments. Like repeaters, hubs enable the network to be extended to accommodate additional workstations. Hubs are commonly used in 10Base-T networks.

Bridges

A **bridge** is used to connect two different LANs or two segments of the same LAN by forwarding network traffic between network segments. However, unlike repeaters, bridges determine the physical location of the source and destination computers. They are typically used to divide an overloaded network into separate segments, helping to minimize intersegment traffic. Bridges are also used to connect segments that use different wiring or network protocols.

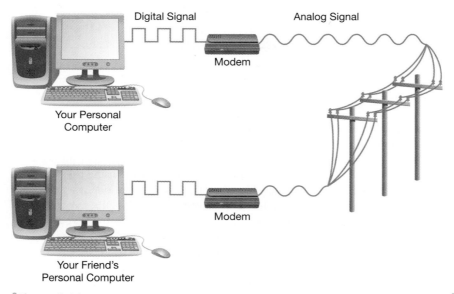

[Figure C.14 ➥ Modems convert digital signals into analog and analog signals into digital.]

Multiplexers

A **multiplexer (MUX)** is used to share a communications line or medium among a number of users. Sometimes the transmission medium provides more capacity than a single signal can occupy. To use the entire media bandwidth effectively, multiplexers are used to transmit several signals over a single channel. Multiplexers convert and combine signals from multiple users for simultaneous transmission over a single line or medium.

Organizations use these components to construct a LAN by attaching individual computers and media segments into one network. Organizations today also want to connect users and/or networks in different geographical areas. Distributed LANs, interconnected by WANs, are needed to exchange data and information across an organization. The WAN, however, appears transparent to the user because information stored in a computer at another location appears to be locally available. **Internetworking** connectivity hardware—routers, brouters, CSUs (channel service units), and gateways—provides businesses with the freedom to locate their operations in different cities or countries, while at the same time running them as integrated units. These technologies are briefly described below.

Routers

A **router** is an intelligent device used to connect two or more individual networks. When a router receives a signal, it looks at the network address and passes the signal or message on to the appropriate network.

Brouters

A **brouter** is short for *bridge router* (pronounced brau-ter) and provides the capabilities of both a bridge and a router.

Channel Service Units

A **channel service unit (CSU)** is a device that acts as a "buffer" between a LAN and a public carrier's WAN. CSUs ensure that all signals placed on the public lines from the LAN are appropriately timed and formed for the public network.

Gateways

A **gateway** performs protocol conversion so that different networks can communicate even though they "speak" different languages. For example, communications between a LAN and a large system, such as a mainframe, whose protocols are different, require a gateway.

KEY POINTS REVIEW

1. **Understand networking fundamentals, including network services and transmission media.** In networking, a distinction is made between servers, clients, and peers. A server is a computer that stores information (programs and data) and provides services to users through a network. A client is any device or software application that makes use of the information or services provided by a server. Peers are two separate computers or devices on a network that request and provide services to each other. Servers and clients are combined to create server-centric networks. Peers are combined to create peer-to-peer networks. Networks provide file, print, message, and application services that extendthe capabilities of stand-alone computers. The network operating system (NOS) is the major piece of software that controls the network. In a typical LAN, the NOS consists of two parts. The first and most complex is the system software that runs on the server. The NOS software coordinates many functions, including user accounts, access information, security, and resource sharing. The second and much smaller part of the NOS runs on each workstation connected to the LAN. Networks exchange information by using cable or wireless transmission media. Cable media include twisted pair, coaxial, and fiber-optic. Wireless media include infrared line of sight, high-frequency radio, and microwave.

2. **Describe network software and hardware, including media access control, network topologies, and protocols, as well as connectivity hardware for both local area and wide area networks.** Network access control refers to the rules that govern how a given workstation gains access to the network. There are two general types: distributed and random access. With distributed access, only a single workstation at a time has authorization to transmit its data. Under random access control, any workstation can transmit its data by checking whether the medium is available. The shape of a network can vary; the three most common topologies are star, ring, and bus configurations. Protocols are agreed-upon formats for transmitting data between connected computers. The need of organizations to interconnect devices that use different protocols has driven the industry to an open system architecture, in which different protocols can communicate with each other. The International Standards Organization (ISO) defined a networking model called the Open Systems Interconnection (OSI) that divides computer-to-computer communications into seven connected layers. Each successively higher layer builds on the functions of the layers below. Hardware and software vendors can use networking standards such as OSI to build devices that can be more easily interconnected. Ethernet is an important protocol for local area networks, whereas TCP/IP (Transmission Control Protocol/Internet Protocol) is most widely used for the world's largest WAN, the Internet. In a network, each device or computer must be connected to the medium or cable segment. To accomplish this, transmission media connectors,

network interface cards, and modems are used. After individual devices are connected to the network, multiple segments of transmission media can be connected to form one large network. Repeaters, hubs, bridges, and multiplexers are used to extend the range and size of the network. Routers, brouters, CSUs (channel service units), and gateways are used to interconnect wide area networks.

KEY TERMS

Analog signals 362

application services 352

attenuation 353

backbone 354

bandwidth 353

bridge 362

brouter 363

bus network 359

cell 355

cellular phone 355

channel service unit (CSU) 363

client 351

coaxial cable 353

connectors 362

CSMA/CD (carrier sense multiple access/collision detect) 358

digital signals 362

EMI (electromagnetic interference) 353

ethernet 360

fiber-optic cable 354

file services 351

gateway 363

high-frequency radio 355

hub 362

infrared line of sight 355

internetworking 363

media access control 358

message services 351

microwave transmission 356

modem 362

multiplexer 363

network 351

network interface card (NIC) 362

network operating system (NOS) 353

network services 351

network topology 358

OSI model 360

pager 355

peer 351

peer-to-peer networks 351

print services 351

protocols 359

repeater 362

ring network 359

router 363

satellite 356

satellite microwave 356

server 351

server-centric networks 351

star network 358

terrestrial microwave 356

token passing 358

transmission control protocol/internet protocol (TCP/IP) 361

transmission medium 353

twisted pair cable 353

wireless local area network (WLAN) 355

wireless media 355

REVIEW QUESTIONS

1. Explain the difference between servers, clients, and peers.

2. What are the major types of network services available?

3. What are three common types of transmission media that use cabling?

4. What are four common methods of wireless transmission media for networking, and how do they differ from each other?

5. What is a network topology? Describe the three common topologies that are used today.

6. What is the purpose of the OSI model?

7. What is Ethernet, and why is it so popular?

8. What is TCP/IP, and what roles does it play in the use of the Internet?

9. What are the various types of hardware used to connect computers together into networks?

10. What is a modem used for, and how does one work?

SELF-STUDY QUESTIONS

1. Which of the following is a type of computer on the network that makes access to files, printing, communications, and other services available to users of the network?

   A. server
   B. client
   C. peer
   D. pager

2. Which of the following is **not** a type of cable medium?

   A. twisted pair
   B. coaxial
   C. fiber-optic
   D. tertiary groups

3. Which of the following is a type of wireless medium?

   A. fiber-optic
   B. TCP/IP
   C. infrared
   D. microterminal

4. Which of the following are types of networks?

   A. star, ring, bus
   B. star, box, ring
   C. star, ring, triangle
   D. ring, bus, rectangle

5. All of the following are common applications of high-frequency radio communication **except** _____ .

   A. pagers
   B. cellular phones
   C. wireless networks
   D. facsimiles

6. The International Standards Organization (ISO) defined a networking model called the _____ that divides computer-to-computer communications into seven connected layers.

   A. Network Allocation System (NAS)
   B. Open Systems Network (OSN)
   C. Open Systems Interconnection (OSI)
   D. Network Transfer System (NTS)

7. Which of the following is a type of local area network protocol developed by Xerox Corporation in 1976 that typically uses a bus or star network topology and uses random access control to send data?

   A. Ethernet
   B. bridge
   C. star
   D. gateway

8. Which of the following is the protocol of the Internet, allowing different interconnected networks to communicate using the same language?

   A. Ethernet
   B. C++
   C. Transmission Control Protocol/Internet Protocol (TCP/IP)
   D. router

9. After individual devices are connected to a network, multiple segments of transmission media can be connected to form one large network. All of the following **except** _____ are used to extend the range and size of the network.

   A. bridges
   B. repeaters
   C. modems
   D. hubs

10. A _____ performs protocol conversion so that different networks can communicate even though they "speak" different languages.

    A. gateway
    B. channel service unit
    C. modem
    D. brouter

Answers are at the end of the Problems and Exercises.

PROBLEMS AND EXERCISES

1. Match the following terms with the appropriate definitions:

   _____ Pager   _____ Bus network
   _____ Token passing   _____ Peer-to-peer network
   _____ Network operat-   _____ Attenuation
          ing system
   _____ Router

   a. A decrease in the power of an electrical signal as it is sent over a distance

   b. A one-way, wireless messaging system

   c. A network access control method in which a token circulates around a ring topology and stations can trans-

   mit messages onto the network only when a nonbusy token arrives at a station

   d. A network topology in which all stations are connected to a single open-ended line

   e. A group of software programs that manages and provides network services

   f. An intelligent device used to connect two or more individual networks

   g. A network that enables any computer or device on the network to provide and request services

2. Using terms such as "digital," "analog," "dial-up telephone lines," and "modem," explain how a file is sent from your computer to your friend's computer through the regular phone system. What happens when and where?

3. Compare and contrast client-server and peer-to-peer networks. How do the computers and devices interact with each other in these networks? How does the term "client" relate to a peer-to-peer network? Under what circumstances is one type of network better than the other? Why?

4. Describe one of your experiences with a computer network. What type of topology was being used? What was the network operating system? Was the network connected to any other networks? How?

5. Scan the popular press and/or the World Wide Web for clues concerning emerging technologies for computer networking. This may include new uses for current technologies or new technologies altogether. Discuss as a group the "hot" issues. Do you feel they will become a reality in the near future? Why or why not? Prepare a 10-minute presentation of your findings to be given to the class.

6. Working in a group, have everyone describe what type of network would be most appropriate for a small office with about 10 computers, one printer, and one scanner, all within one floor in one building, and relatively close to one another. Be sure to talk about transmission media, network topology, hardware, and software. Did all group members come up with the same option? Why or why not? What else would you need to know to make a good recommendation?

7. Investigate the popular press, Web, or people you know working in companies to see to what extent firms are using twisted pair versus coaxial cable versus fiber-optic cabling. Under which circumstances is each being used, and what appear to be the trends in the use of cabling types?

8. Perform the same analysis as in Question 7, but this time check into uses of wireless networking. Which forms of wireless networking appear to be most popular and why?

9. Do some shopping on the Web and/or at a local computer store to determine what you would need, and what it would cost, to set up a wireless local area network in your home.

10. Ask questions of IS personnel at your place of work or at your school and determine which types of networks are being used in your office or classroom and how these local area networks are connected to the broader backbone network for this organization.

11. Search the Web for background information on the origin and uses of the Ethernet protocol. How did it begin, and how popular is it today?

12. Search the Web for background information on the origin and uses of the TCP/IP protocol. Why has it become so popular and powerful?

13. Investigate Cisco's Web site and determine what types of networking products the company produces and sells. Why are its products so popular, and who are its competitors?

14. Investigate the options for high-speed, broadband Internet access into your home. What options are available to you, and how much do they cost?

ANSWERS TO THE SELF-STUDY QUESTIONS

1. A   2. D   3. C   4. A   5. D   6. C   7. A   8. C   9. C   10. A

Abilene network backbone: The network which connects Internet2 universities by using regional network aggregation points called **gigaPoPs** and very high-speed network equipment and facilities.

ActiveX: Software components developed by Microsoft that provide dynamic content to a Web page in a manner similar to a Java Applet.

Ad hoc reports: Reports created due to unplanned information requests in which information is gathered to support a non-routine decision.

Adaptive maintenance: Making changes to an information system to make its functionality meet changing business needs or to migrate it to a different operating system.

Alpha testing: Testing performed by the development organization to assess whether the entire system meets the design requirements of the users.

Analog signals: Audio tones used to transmit data over conventional voice telephone lines.

ANSI X.12: One of the formatting standards used with EDI that specifies how information is transmitted electronically.

Applet: A program designed to be executed within another application such as a Web page.

Application services: Processes that run software for network clients and enable computers to share processing power.

Application software: Software used to perform a specific task that the user needs to accomplish, such as writing a business letter, processing the payroll, managing a stock portfolio, or manipulating a series of forecasts to come up with the most efficient allocation of resources for a project.

Archie: An Internet tool that enables users to search FTP sites for their contents.

Arithmetic logic unit (ALU): Part of the central processing unit (CPU) that performs mathematics, including all forms of addition, subtraction, multiplication, and division.

ARPANET: The Advanced Research Projects Agency Network, a large, wide area network that linked many universities and research centers.

ASCII (American Standard Code for Information Interchange): An 8-bit code for representing numbers, letters, and other characters in binary form.

Asymmetric Digital Subscriber Line (ADSL): A data transfer format that enables large amounts of data to be sent relatively quickly over existing copper telephone lines with speeds ranging from 1.5 to 9 Mbps downstream and from 16 to 640 Kbps upstream.

Asynchronous Transfer Mode (ATM): A method of transmitting voice, video, and data over high-speed LANs at speeds of up to 2.2 GBps.

Attenuation: The result when the power of an electric signal weakens as it is sent over increasing distance.

Attribute: Each record typically consists of many attributes, which are individual pieces of information. For example, a name and social security number are attributes about a person.

Audio: Sound that has been digitized for storage and replay on a computer.

Authentication: The process of confirming the identity of a user who is attempting to access a system or Web site

Automating: Using information systems to do an activity faster or cheaper.

Backbone: A network that manages the bulk of network traffic and typically uses a higher-speed protocol than the individual LAN segments connected to it.

Backbone network: A network that manages the bulk of network traffic and typically uses a higher-speed protocol than the individual LAN segments connected to it.

Bandwidth: The transmission capacity of a computer or communications channel, often measured in megabits per second (Mbps); it represents how much binary data can be reliably transmitted over the medium in one second.

Batch input: Methods for rapidly entering large amounts of data into a computer.

Batch processing: The processing of transactions after some quantity of transactions are collected and then processed together as a "batch" at some later time.

Best practices: Procedures and processes from business organizations that are widely accepted as being among the most effective and/or efficient

Beta testing: Testing performed by actual system users, who test the capabilities of the system with actual data in their work environment.

Binary code: Methods for representing digital data and information using sequences of zeros and ones.

Biometrics: A type of security that grants or denies access to a computer systems through the analysis of fingerprints, retinal patterns in the eye, or other bodily characteristics.

Bits: The individual 1s and 0s that make up a byte.

Bluetooth: A wireless specification for personal area networking (PAN) of desktop computers, peripheral devices, mobile phones, pagers, portable stereos, and other handheld devices.

Brick-and-mortar: Term used to identify traditional firms doing business the old-fashioned way, from a physical storefront

Bridge: Device used to connect two different LANs or two segments of the same LAN by forwarding network traffic between network segments; unlike repeaters, bridges determine the physical location of the source and destination computers.

Brouter: Short for *bridge router* (pronounced brau-ter); provides the capabilities of both a bridge and a router for managing network traffic.

Bus network: Network in the shape of an open-ended line; it is the easiest network to extend and has the simplest wiring layout.

Business information systems: Software applications that are developed to perform organization-wide operations.

Business process reengineering: Significant organizational change designed to improve the functioning of an organization as opposed to merely dropping in an information system with no attempts at changing and improving the organization.

Business rules: Rules included in data dictionaries to prevent illegal or illogical entries from entering the database.

Business-to-business: Electronic commerce that is used to conduct business with business partners such as suppliers and intermediaries.

Business-to-consumer: EC used to conduct transactions between businesses and consumers.

Business-to-employee: EC that occurs between businesses and their employees.

Byte: Typically 8 bits or about one typed character.

Bytes per inch (BPI): The numbers of bytes that can be stored on one inch of magnetic tape.

Cable modem: A specialized piece of equipment that enables a computer to access Internet service designed to operate over cable TV lines.

Cache: Pronounced "cash," it is a small block of memory used by processors to store those instructions most recently or most often used.

Carding: Refers to the practice of stealing credit card numbers online, to be resold or used to charge merchandise against victims' accounts.

CD-R (compact disc—recordable): A type of optical disk that data can be written to.

CD-ROM (compact disc—read-only memory): A type of optical disk that cannot be written to, but can only be read.

CD-RW (compact disc—rewritable): A type of optical disk that be written onto multiple times.

Cell: A geographical area containing a low-powered radio antenna/receiver for transmitting telecommunications signals within that area; monitored and controlled by a central computer.

Cellular phone: Mobile phone which uses a communications system that divides a geographic region into sections, called *cells*.

Central processing unit (CPU): Also called a microprocessor, processor, or chip, it is responsible for performing all of the operations of the computer.

Centralized computing: A system of large centralized computers, called mainframes, used to process and store data.

Certificate authority: A trusted middleman between computers that verifies that a Web sites is a trusted site and is used when implementing public-key encryption on a large scale.

Channel service unit (CSU): A device that acts as a "buffer" between a LAN and a public carrier's WAN. CSUs ensure that all signals placed on the public lines from the LAN are appropriately timed and formed for the public network.

Characters per inch (CPI): The numbers of characters that can be stored on one inch of magnetic tape.

Chief information officer: Title given to executive-level individuals who are responsible for leading the overall information systems component within their organizations and integrating new technologies into the organization's business strategy.

Click-and-mortar: Term used to identify firms doing traditional, physical business and doing business on the Internet as well.

Click-only: Term used to identify firms doing business solely on the Internet, with no physical storefront.

Client: Any computer, such as a user's workstation or PC on the network; or any software application, such as a word processing application, that requests and uses the services provided by the server.

Clock speed: The speed of the system clock, typically measured in hertz (Hz).

Clock tick: A single pulse of the system clock.

Cloning: Cellular phone fraud in which scanners are used to steal the electronic serial numbers of cellular phones as calls are made.

Coaxial cable (or "coax cable"): Contains a solid inner copper conductor, surrounded by plastic insulation and an outer braided copper or foil shield and is most commonly used for cable television installations and for networks operating at 10 Mbps. Its attenuation is lower than twisted-pair cable, and it is moderately susceptible to EMI and eavesdropping.

Collaborative computing: A synergistic form of distributed computing, in which two or more networked computers are used to accomplish a common processing task.

Collaborative information system: A type of international information system that integrates different applications and data that can be shared by different companies in different countries.

Collaboration system: An information system that enables people to communicate electronically with each other in order to solve problems, make decisions, and perform other forms of joint work.

Combination primary key: A combination of two or more attributes in a database used to uniquely identify a row in an entity.

Command-based interface: Computer interface that requires the user to enter text-based commands to instruct the computer to perform specific operations.

Competitive advantage: A firm's ability to do something better, faster, cheaper, or uniquely when compared with rival firms in the market.

Compiler: A software program that translates a programming language into machine language.

Computer-aided design: Using high-powered computers to design very state-of-the-art, high-quality products.

Computer-aided software engineering (CASE): Software tools that provide automated support for some portion of the systems development process.

Computer-based information system: A combination of hardware, software, and telecommunications networks that people build and use to collect, create, and distribute data.

Computer crime: The act of using a computer to commit an illegal act.

Computer ethics: A broad range of issues and standards of conduct that have emerged through the use and proliferation of information systems.

Computer literacy: The knowledge of how to operate a computer.

Computer security: Precautions taken to keep computers and the information they contain safe from unauthorized access.

Connectors: Also called transmission media connectors; used to terminate cable in order to be plugged into a network interface card or into other network components. Connectors include T-connectors for coax cable and RJ-45 connectors (similar to a phone jack) for twisted pair cable.

Consumer-to-consumer: A form of EC that does not even involve business firms, such as an online textbook exchange service for students at a university or an online trading Web site such as eBay.com.

Control unit: Part of the central processing unit (CPU) that works closely with the ALU (arithmetic logic unit) by fetching and decoding instructions as well as retrieving and storing data.

Conversion: The process of transferring information from a legacy system to a new computing platform.

Corrective maintenance: Making changes to an information system to repair flaws in its design, coding, or implementation.

Cracker: An individual who breaks into computer systems with the intention of doing damage or committing a crime.

CSMA/CD (Carrier Sense Multiple Access/Collision Detect): A format in which each workstation "listens" to the network to determine whether a message is being transmitted. If the network is quiet, the workstation sends its message; otherwise, it waits. When a workstation gains access to the medium and sends information onto the network, messages are sent to all workstations on the network; however, only the destination with the proper address is able to "open" the message.

Custom applications: Software programs that are designed and developed by company personnel as opposed to being bought off-the-shelf.

Customer Relationship Management: The process of managing all aspects of the relationship with customers including finding them, marketing and selling to them, servicing their needs after the sale, and so on.

Customer Relationship Management system: Information system to support interaction between the firm and its customers.

Customization: Modifying software so that it better suits user needs.

Customized application software: Software that is developed based on specifications provided by a particular organization.

Data: Recorded, unformatted information, such as words and numbers, that often has no meaning in and of itself.

Data dictionary: A document prepared by the database designers to describe the characteristics of all items in a database.

Data diddling: A type of computer crime where the data going into or out of a computer is altered.

Data flows: Data moving through an organization or within an information system.

Data mart: A data warehouse that is limited in scope and customized for the decision support applications of a particular end-user group.

Data mining: A method used by companies to sort and analyze information to better understand their customers, products, markets, or any other phase of their business for which data has been captured.

Data model: A map or diagram that represents the entities of a database and their relationships.

Data type: Each attribute in the database is a particular type such as text, number, or a date.

Data warehouse: An integration of multiple, large databases and other information sources into a single repository or access point that is suitable for direct querying, analysis, or processing.

Database: A collection of related data organized in a way to facilitate data searches.

Database administrator: A person responsible for the development and management of the organization's databases.

Database management system (DBMS): A software application with which you create, store, organize, and retrieve data from a single database or several databases.

Decision support system (DSS): A special-purpose information systems designed to support organizational decision making.

Defense Advanced Research Projects Agency (DARPA): A U.S. governmental agency that began to study ways to interconnect networks of various kinds, which lead to the development of the ARPANET (Advanced Research Projects Agency Network).

Density: The storage capacity of magnetic tape that is typically referred in either characters per inch (CPI) or bytes per inch (BPI).

Desktop videoconferencing: The use of integrated computer, telephone, video recording, and playback technologies—typically by two people—to interact with each other using their desktop computers from remote sites.

Developmental testing: Testing performed by programmers to ensure that each module is error free.

Digital divide: The gap between those individuals in our society who are computer literate and have access to information resources like the Internet and those who do not.

Digital signals: The electrical pulses that computers use to send bits of information.

Digital Subscriber Line: Or DSL uses special modulation schemes to fit more data onto traditional copper phone wires; referred to as "last-mile" solutions because they are used only for connections from a telephone switching station to a home or office, and they generally are not used between telephone switching stations.

Digitization: A process that creates products without tangible features, which are commonly referred to as virtual products.

Digitizing: The process of converting a photograph or a song into digital information, or bits, which then can travel across a network.

Direct conversion: Changing from an old to a new system by beginning the new system and discontinuing the old system at the same time.

Disintermediation: The phenomenon of cutting out the "middleman" and reaching customers more directly and efficiently.

Diskettes: Also called floppy disks, are 3½-inch, round, flexible Mylar devices that record data as magnetized spots on tracks on the disk surface.

Distance learning: The process of providing instruction to students who are physically separated from instructors through the use of some sort of communication technologies including videoconferencing, Internet chatting, and various Web-based tools.

Distributed computing: A model of using separate computers to work on subsets of tasks and then pooling their results by communicating over a network.

Distribution portals: Enterprise portals that automate the business processes involved in selling, or distributing, products from a single supplier to multiple buyers.

Domain name: Used in Uniform Resource Locators (URLs) to identify a source or host entity on the Internet.

Domain Name System: A database used to associate Internet host names with their Internet IP addresses.

Dot matrix printer: A printing technology where characters and images are formed using a series of small dots; most commonly found printing voluminous batch information, such as periodic reports and forms.

Downsizing: When companies slash costs, streamline operations, and/or let employees go.

Downstream: An information flow that relates to the information that is produced by a company and sent along to another organization such as a distributor.

Drill-down reports: Reports that provide details behind the summary values on a key-indicator or exception report.

Dumpster diving: A type of computer crime where individuals go through dumpsters and garbage cans for company documents, credit card receipts, and other papers containing information that might be useful.

DVD-ROM (digital video disk—read-only memory): A type of optical disk that uses a shorter-wavelength laser beam which allows more information to be stored on a disk than a standard CD-ROM.

E-brochure: An electronic brochure is a Web tool used to promote sales and marketing information.

E-business: Term used to refer to the use of a variety of types of information technologies and systems to support every part of the business.

E-Business Innovation Cycle: The time period and to what extent an organization derives value from a particular information technology.

E-information: The first stage of a Web site in which information about a company and its product is disseminated globally to potential customers who have access to the Internet and a Web browser.

E-integration: The second stage of a Web site in which sites containing general information about a company and its product must be integrated with corporate databases to extract and display personal customer information necessary to achieve mass customization.

E-tailing: Electronic retailing.

E-transaction: This third stage of a Web site takes the e-integration stage one step further by adding the ability for customers to enter orders and payments online.

EBCDIC (Extended Binary-Coded Decimal Interchange Code): An 8-bit code for representing numbers, letters, and other characters in binary form; typically used on mainframe computers.

Economic opportunities: Opportunities that a firm finds for making more money and/or making money in new ways.

Electronic brochure: Using the Web to disseminate sales and marketing information.

Electronic commerce: Exchanges of goods and services via the Internet among and between customers, firms, employees, business partners, suppliers, etc.

Electronic Data Interchange: (EDI) or EDI is the digital, or electronic, transmission of business documents and related data between organizations via telecommunications networks that enables the online exchange and sale of goods and services between firms.

Electronic fund transfer: The process of transferring funds from one financial account to another via computer.

Electronic mail: The transmission of messages over computer networks.

Electronic marketplace: Also called a trading exchange. A Web site built by a third party that allows buyers and sellers to come together, offering firms access to real-time trading with other companies in their vertical markets.

Electronic meeting system (EMS): An collection of personal computers networked together with sophisticated software tools to help group members solve problems and make decisions through interactive, electronic idea generation, evaluation, and voting.

EMI (electromagnetic interference): Occurs when fluorescent lights, weather, or other electronic signals interfere with the original signal being sent.

Enabling technologies: Information technologies that enable a firm to accomplish a task or goal or to gain or sustain competitive advantage in some way.

Encapsulation: The grouping of data and instructions into a single object in object-oriented programming languages.

Encryption: The process of encoding messages before they enter the network or airwaves, then decoding them at the receiving end of the transfer, so that recipients can read or hear them.

End-user development: A systems development method whereby users in the organization develop, test, and maintain their own applications.

Enterprise network: A WAN that is the result of connecting disparate networks of a single organization into a single network.

Enterprise portal: Information system that provides a single point of access to secured, proprietary information, which may be dispersed throughout an organization.

Enterprise Resource Planning: Information system that supports and integrates all facets of the business, including planning, manufacturing, sales, marketing, and so on.

Enterprise Resource Planning system: Information system that supports and integrates all facets of the business, including planning, manufacturing, sales, marketing, and so on.

Enterprise systems: Information systems that support many or all of the various parts of the firm.

Entity: Things about which we collect data, such as people or classes.

Entity-relationship diagram (ERD): A diagramming technique that is commonly used when designing databases, especially when showing associations between entities.

Ergonomics: The design of computer hardware and work environments that minimize health risks.

Ethernet: A local area network protocol developed by Xerox Corporation in 1976. It uses a bus or star network topology and uses random access control to send data. The original Ethernet supports data transfer rates of 10 Mbps. A later version, called 100Base-T or Fast Ethernet, supports transfer rates of 100 Mbps, and the latest version, called Gigabit Ethernet, supports transfer rates of 1 gigabit, or 1,000 megabits, per second. You need some type of Ethernet card installed in your computer to use this type of network connection.

Event-driven: Programming language characteristic that allows the development of programs to execute based on user-requested events rather than on a linear sequence through the program.

Exception report: Reports that highlight situations that are out of the normal operating range.

Executive information system (EIS): An information system designed to provide information in a very aggregate form so that managers at the executive level of the organization can quickly scan it for trends and anomalies.

Executive level: The top level of the organization, where executives focus on long-term strategic issues facing the organization.

Expert system (ES): A special-purpose information system designed to mimic human expertise by manipulating knowledge—understanding acquired through experience and extensive learning—rather than simply information.

Extensible Markup Language (XML): A Web programming language that allows designers to create customized features that enable data to be more easily shared between applications and organizations.

External acquisition: The process of purchasing an existing information system from an external organization or vendor.

External or secondary cache: Special high-speed cache memory that is usually not built into the CPU, but is located within easy reach of the CPU on the motherboard.

Extranet: The use of the Internet by firms and companies for business-to-business interactions.

Facsimile or fax machine: Machines that digitize images, such as letters, memos, newspaper and magazine articles, photos, contracts, even handwritten notes, so that they can be transmitted to other fax machines over telephone lines.

Fiber-optic cable: Made of a light-conducting glass or plastic core, surrounded by more glass, called cladding, and a tough outer sheath which protects the fiber from changes in temperature, as well as from bending or breaking; uses pulses of light sent along the optical cable to transmit video or sound data clearly and securely because it is immune to EMI and eavesdropping; has low attenuation; can support bandwidths from 100 Mbps to greater than 2 Gbps (gigabits per second) and distances from 2 to 25 kilometers.

File services: Processes used to store, retrieve, and move data files in an efficient manner; individuals can use the file services of the network to move a customer file electronically to multiple recipients across the network.

File transfer: The process of connecting to a remote computer in order to either upload (sending to the remote machine) or download (obtaining from the remote machine) files and data.

Firewall: Hardware or software designed to keep unauthorized users out of network systems.

Fixed wireless: A wireless solution requiring that the user's computer be stationary rather than mobile.

Flash memory: A variation of ROM that can be repeatedly written to and erased like RAM, but, unlike RAM, it retains its information after power is turned off.

Foreign key: An attribute that appears as a nonprimary key attribute in one entity and as a primary key attribute (or part of a primary key) in another entity.

Form: 1. A collection of blank entry boxes, each representing a field, that is used to enter information into a database. 2. A business document that contains some predefined data and may include some areas where additional data is to be filled in, typically for a single record.

Fully automated data entry: Data entry into an information system that does not require any human intervention.

Functional area information system: A cross-organizational-level information system designed to support a specific functional area.

Gateway: A connection between the internal computer systems and networks of a company and the Internet, enabling people to send electronic mail and other data or files over the Internet to and from nearly anywhere in the world.

Geostationary: A system of satellites that are placed in fixed positions above the earth's surface and orbit along with the earth (also called a geosynchronous orbit).

Geosynchronous: A system of satellites that are placed in fixed positions above the earth's surface and orbit along with the earth. Also called a geostationary orbit.

GigaPoP: Regional network aggregation points used in connecting different systems within a network backbone, such as the Abilene network backbone.

Global information system: A type of international information system that is used when a single transaction requires the input of data from multiple centers located in more than one nation.

Global network: Spans multiple countries and may include the networks of several organizations. The Internet is an example of a global network.

Gopher: A text-based, menu-driven interface that enables users to access a large number of varied Internet resources as if they were in folders and menus on their own computers.

Graphical user interface (GUI): Computer interface that enables the user to select pictures, icons, and menus to send instructions to the computer.

Groupware: Software that enables people to work together more effectively.

Hacker: An individual who gains unauthorized access to computer systems.

Hard data: Facts and numbers that are typically generated by transaction processing systems and management information systems.

Hard drive or hard disk: A secondary storage device usually located inside the system unit of a computer for storing data.

Hardware: Physical computer equipment, such as the computer monitor, central processing unit, or keyboard.

Head crash: A failure inside a hard disk when the read/write head touches the disk and results in the loss of the data and/or the operation of the hard disk.

High-frequency radio: Signals can transmit data at rates of up to 11 Mbps to network nodes from 12.2 to 39.6 kilometers apart.

Hub: Used as a central point of connection between media segments; like repeaters, hubs enable the network to be extended to accommodate additional workstations; commonly used in 10Base-T networks.

Hyperlink: A reference or link on a web page to other documents that contain related information.

hypermediation: A "pay by the click" pricing scheme in which the firm running the advertisement pays only when a Web surfer actually clicks on the advertisement.

Hypertext: Text in a Web document that is highlighted and, when clicked on by the user, evokes an embedded command that goes to another specified file or location and brings up that file or location on the user's screen.

Hypertext Markup Language (HTML): The standard method of specifying the format of Web pages. Specific content within each Web page is enclosed within codes, or markup tags, which stipulate how the content should appear to the user.

Hypertext Transfer Protocol (HTTP): The process by which servers process user requests for web pages.

Identity theft: Stealing of another person's social security number, credit card number, and other personal information for the purpose of using the victim's credit rating to borrow money, buy merchandise, and otherwise run up debts that are never repaid.

Inferencing: The matching of user questions and answers to information in a knowledge base within an expert system in order to make a recommendation.

Informating: The ability of information technology to provide information about the operation within a firm and/or about the underlying work process that the system supports.

Information: Data that has been formatted and/or organized in some way as to be useful to people.

Information accessibility: An ethical issue that focuses on defining what information a person or organization has the right to obtain about others and how this information can be accessed and used.

Information accuracy: An ethical issue concerned with the authenticity and fidelity of information, as well as identifying who is responsible for informational errors that harm people.

Information Age: A period of time in society where information has become a valuable or dominant currency of the realm.

Information privacy: An ethical issue that is concerned with what information an individual should have to reveal to others through the course of employment or through other transactions such as online shopping.

Information property: An ethical issue that focuses on who owns information about individuals and how information can be sold and exchanged.

Information systems: Assumed to mean computer-based information systems, which are combinations of hardware, software, and telecommunications networks that people build and use to collect, create, and distribute useful data; this term is also used to represent the field in which people develop, use, manage, and study computer-based information systems in organizations.

Information systems planning: 1. A formal organizational process for assessing the information needs of an organization in which the systems, databases, and technologies for meeting those needs are identified. 2. Planning for the investment in the deployment of information systems. This planning helps people meet organizational strategies and objectives given the organization's resource constraints.

Information technology: Refers to machine technology that is controlled by or uses information.

Informational system: The systems designed to support decision making based on stable point-in-time or historical data.

Infrared line of sight: Uses high-frequency light waves to transmit data on an unobstructed path between nodes—computers or some other device such as a printer—on a network, at a distance of up to 24.4 meters.

Inheritance: A characteristic of object-oriented programming languages that requires lower-level objects, or children, to inherit the characteristics of higher-level, or parent, objects.

Ink-jet printer: A printing technology where characters and images are formed by transferring ink onto paper.

Input devices: Hardware that is used to enter information into a computer.

Intangible benefits: A benefit of using a particular system or technology that is difficult to quantify. Examples of intangible benefits include faster turnaround on fulfilling orders and resulting improvements in customer service.

Intangible costs: A cost of using a particular system or technology that is difficult to quantify. Examples include the costs of reducing traditional sales, losing some customers that are not "Web ready," or losing customers if the Web application is poorly designed or not on par with competitors' sites.

Integrated Services Digital Network (ISDN): A standard for worldwide digital communications that is intended to replace analog systems and uses existing twisted-pair telephone wires to provide high-speed data service.

Interface: The way in which the user interacts with the computer.

Internal cache: Special high-speed cache memory that is incorporated into the microprocessor's design.

International information system: A general class of information systems that support transactions that cross national boundaries.

Internet: A term derived from the concept of internetworking, which means connecting host computers and their networks together to form even larger networks. The Internet is a large worldwide collection of networks that use a common protocol to communicate with each other.

Internet2: Developed in 1996 by leading universities as a faster, private alternative to the pubic Internet in order to be a testing-ground network to develop advanced Internet technologies and applications.

Internet backbone: The collection of main network connections and telecommunications lines comprising the Internet.

Internet Corporation for Assigned Names and Numbers: Also called ICANN, a nonprofit corporation that assumed responsibility from InterNIC for managing IP addresses, domain names, and root server system management.

Internet over Satellite (IoS): Technologies that allow users to access the Internet via satellites that are placed in fixed positions above the earth's surface in what is known as a **geostationary** or **geosynchronous** orbit (i.e., the satellite moves along with the earth).

Internet Registry: A central repository for Internet-related information and which provides central allocation of network system identifiers.

Internet Relay Chat (IRC): An application that allows typed conversations with others in real time on the Internet.

Internet Service Provider: An individual or organization that enables other individuals and organizations to connect to the Internet.

Internetworking: Connecting host computers and their networks together to form even larger networks.

InterNIC: A government–industry collaboration created by the NSF in 1993, to manage directory and database services, domain registration services, and other information services on the Internet.

InterNIC Registration Service: A service offered by InterNIC for assigning Internet addresses.

Interorganizational systems: Systems that communicate across organizational boundaries.

Interpreter: A software program that translates a programming language into machine language one statement at a time.

Intranet: An internal, private network using Web technologies to facilitate the secured transmission of proprietary information within an organization, thereby limiting the viewing access to authorized users within the organization.

IP address: An Internet Protocol address assigned to every computer and router to connect to the Internet; it serves as the destination address of that computer or device and enables the network to route messages to the proper destination.

IP datagram: A data packet that conforms to the IP specification.

IPv6:   The latest version of the Internet Protocol, also referred to as IPng, for IP next generation.

Java: An object-oriented programming language that was developed at Sun Microsystems in the early 1990s that is used in developing applications on the Web and other environments.

JavaScript: A scripting language, created by Netscape, that allows developers to add dynamic content to Web sites.

Key-indicator report: Reports that provide a summary of critical information on a recurring schedule.

Keyboard: Input device for entering text and numbers into a computer.

Knowledge: A body of governing procedures, such as guidelines or rules, which are used to organize or manipulate data to make it suitable for a given task.

Knowledge society: Term coined by Peter Drucker to refer to a society in which there is a relatively high proportion of knowledge workers, these types of people have risen in importance and leadership, and where education is the cornerstone of the society.

Knowledge worker: Term coined by Peter Drucker to refer to professionals who are relatively well educated and who create, modify, and/or synthesize knowledge as a fundamental part of their jobs.

Laser printer: A printing technology where characters and images are formed by using a laser beam.

Learning organization: Described by David Garvin as an organization that is "skilled at creating, acquiring, and transferring knowledge, and at modifying its behavior to reflect new knowledge and insights."

Legacy system: An older stand-alone computer system within an organization with older versions of applications that are either fast approaching or beyond the end of their useful life within the organization.

Liquid crystal display (LCD):   A type of computer monitor that is most commonly used on notebook and portable computers.

Listserv: A mailing list that allows individual users to participate in group discussions via e-mail.

Local area network (LAN):   A computer network that spans a relatively small area, allowing all computer users to connect with each other to share information and peripheral devices, such as a printer.

Logic or time bomb: A type of computer virus that lies in wait for unsuspecting computer users to perform a triggering operation or for a specific date before executing its instructions.

Machine language: A binary-level computer language that computer hardware understands.

Magnetic tape: A secondary storage method that consists of narrow plastic tape coated with a magnetic substance.

Magneto-optical disk (MO):   A type of optical disk that contains tiny metallic crystals where information is written to the disk using a laser beam to melt small spots on the plastic surface of the disk; once melted, a magnet then rearranges the metallic crystals while the plastic is still hot and malleable to represent specific information.

Mailing lists: Also known as listservs, let you use e-mail to participate in discussion groups on topics of special interest to you.

Mainframe computer: A very large computer that is used as the main, central computing system for many major corporations and governmental agencies.

making the business case: The process of identifying, quantifying, and presenting the value provided by an information system.

Management information system (MIS):   1. A field of study that encompasses the development, use, management, and study of computer-based information systems in organizations. 2. An information system designed to support the management of organizational functions at the managerial level of the organization.

Managerial level: The mid level of the organization, where functional managers focus on monitoring and controlling operational-level activities and providing information to higher levels of the organization.

Manual data entry: Having a person enter information by hand into an information system.

Media access control: The rules that govern how a given node or workstation gains access to the network to send or receive information; there are two general types of access control: distributed and random access.

Menu-driven pricing: A pricing system in which companies set and present the prices that consumers pay for products and these prices are non-negotiable.

Message services: The storing, accessing, and delivering of text, binary, graphic, digitized video, and audio data; similar to file services, but they also deal with communication interactions between users and applications; include electronic mail or the transfer of messages between two or more networked computers.

Metropolitan area network (MAN):   A computer network of limited geographic scope, typically a city-wide area, that combines both LAN and high-speed fiber-optic technologies. MANs are attractive to organizations that need high-speed data transmission within a limited geographic area.

Microcomputer: A category of computer that is generally used for personal computing, for small business computing, and as a workstation attached to large computers or to other small computers on a network.

Microwave transmission: A high-frequency radio signal sent through the air using either terrestrial (earth-based) systems or satellite systems.

Midrange computers: Often referred to minicomputers, these are computers whose performance is lower than that of mainframes, but higher than microcomputers.

Mobile wireless: Wireless approaches for connecting to the Internet where the computer or handheld device can be moved and will continue to connect.

Models: Conceptual, mathematical, logical, and analytical formulas used to represent or project business events or trends.

Modem: Short for modulator-demodulator; a modem is a device or program that enables a computer to transmit data over telephone lines.

Modules: In a software application, components (classified software functions) which are bundled together.

Monitor: A computer display screen.

Moore's Law: The general trend in computing is toward smaller, faster, and cheaper devices; specifically that computer processing performance would double every 18 months.

Motherboard: A large printed plastic or fiberglass circuit board that holds or connects to all of the computer's electronic components.

Multinational information system: A type of international information system that consists of a loose confederacy of various different local information systems.

Multiplexer: Used to share a communications line or medium among a number of users.

Musical Instrument Digital Interface (MIDI): A standard adopted by the electronic music industry for controlling and interconnecting musical devices and computers.

National Science Foundation: The organization in the U.S. which initiated the development of the NSFNET (National Science Foundation Network), which became a major component of the Internet.

National Science Foundation Network (NSFNET): A network developed by the U.S. in 1986 which became a major component of the Internet.

Network: A group of computers and associated peripheral devices connected by a communication channel capable of sharing information and other resources (e.g., a printer) among users.

Network Access Points: Serve as access points for ISPs and are an exchange point for Internet traffic; these access points determine how traffic is routed and are often the points of most Internet congestion.

Network computer: A microcomputer with minimal memory and storage designed to connect to networks, especially the Internet, to use the resources provided by servers.

Network interface card (NIC): An expansion board that plugs into a computer so that it can be connected to a network.

Network operating system (NOS): System software that controls the network and enables computers to communicate with each other.

Network services: Capabilities of networked computers that enable them to share files, print, send and receive messages, and to use shared software applications.

Network topology: The shape of a network; the three common network topologies are star, ring, and bus.

New economy: An economy in which information technology plays a significant role and that enables producers of both the tangible (computers, shoes, etc.) and intangible (services, ideas, etc.) to compete efficiently in global markets.

Newsgroups: Also called computer-based discussion groups; allow individuals and organizations to participate in discussions on almost any subject.

non-recurring costs: One-time costs that are not expected to continue after the system is implemented.

Normalization: A technique for converting complex databases into ones that are simple and clear.

Notebook computer: A mobile microcomputer that weighs five pounds or less.

Object-oriented analysis and design: Systems development methodologies and techniques based on objects rather than on data and processes.

Object-oriented languages: Programming languages that group together data and its corresponding instructions into manipulatable objects.

Objects: The bundling of data and programming instructions for manipulating that data into a single module.

Off-the-shelf application software: Software designed and used to support general business processes that does not require any specific tailoring to meet the organization's needs.

Office automation or personal productivity software: Information systems that span organizational levels and are used for developing documents, scheduling resources, and communicating.

Office automation system (OAS): A collection of software and hardware for developing documents, scheduling resources, and communicating.

OLAP server: The chief component of an OLAP system that understands how data is organized in the database and has special functions for analyzing the data.

Online analytical processing (OLAP): Graphical software tools that provide complex analysis of data stored in a database.

Online customer service: Assistance for customers offered over the Internet.

Online ordering: Customers visiting a company's website to order and, in many cases, actually pay for products and services over the Internet.

Online processing: Processing of information as that information occurs.

Online transaction processing (OLTP): Immediate automated responses to the requests from multiple concurrent transactions from customers.

Operational level: The bottom level of an organization, where the routine, day-to-day business processes and interaction with customers occur.

Operational systems: The systems that are used to interact with customers and run a business in real time.

Operating system: Software that coordinates the interaction between hardware devices, peripherals, application software, and users.

Optical disk: A storage disk coated with a metallic substance that is written to (or read from) when a laser beam passes over the surface of the disk.

Organizational learning: The ability of an organization to learn from past behavior and information and improve as a result.

Organizational strategy: A firm's plan to accomplish its mission and goals and to gain or sustain competitive advantage over rivals.

OSI model: Open Systems Interconnection; a protocol that represents a group of specific, successive tasks which enable computers to communicate with one another.

Output devices: Hardware devices that deliver information in a usable form.

Outsourcing: Turning over partial or entire responsibility for information systems development and management to an outside organization.

Packaged application: A software program written by third-party vendors.

Packet switching: The process of breaking information into small chunks called data packets and then managing the transfer of those packets from computer to computer via the Internet.

Pager: A one-way, wireless messaging system.

Parallel conversion: Changing over from the old to a new system by running both at the same time until the organization is sure that the new system is error free, that the users are adequately trained, and that the support procedures are in place.

Peer: Any computer that may both request and provide services.

Peer-to-peer networks: Networks that enable any computer or device on the network to provide and request services.

Perfective maintenance: Making enhancements to improve processing performance, to improve interface usability, or to add desired, but not necessarily required, system features.

Personal area network (PAN): An emerging technology that uses wireless communication to exchange data between computing devices using short-range radio communication, typically within an area of 10 meters.

Personal computer (PC): A class of computers that fit on desktops and are used in homes and offices.

Personal digital assistant (PDA): A handheld microcomputer that has somewhat limited processing and storage capabilities.

Phased conversion: Changed over from the old to a new system by utilizing parts of the new system and adding new modules and features to that new system as each part is validated as working properly. This process continues until the entire system is operating and the old system is replaced.

Phreaking: Crimes committed against telephone company computers with the goal of making free long distance calls, impersonating directory assistance or other operator services, diverting calls to numbers of the perpetrator's choice, or otherwise disrupting telephone service for subscribers.

Piggybacking or shoulder-surfing: The act of simply standing in line behind a card user at an automated teller machine (ATM), looking over that person's shoulder, and memorizing the card's personal identification number (PIN).

Pilot conversion: Changing over from the old to a new system by running the entire system in one location until it is validated as operating properly and then diffusing the system into the entire organization.

Plain old telephone service (POTS): Standard telephone lines with a speed, or bandwidth, that is generally about 52 Kbps (52,000 bits per second); also called the public switched telephone network (PSTN).

Pointing devices: Input devices for pointing at items and selecting menu items on a computer.

Portals: In the context of B2B EC, defined as access points (or front doors) through which a business partner accesses secured, proprietary information from an organization.

Power supply: A device that converts electricity from the wall socket to a lower voltage appropriate for computer components and regulates the voltage to eliminate surges common in most electrical systems.

Preventive maintenance: Making changes to a system to reduce the chance of future system failure.

Primary key: A field included in a database that assures that each instance of an entity is stored or retrieved accurately.

Primary memory: The computer's main or random access memory (RAM).

Primary storage: Temporary storage that is also referred to as random-access memory (RAM) and read-only memory (ROM).

Print services: Used to control and manage users' access to network printers and fax equipment.

Private branch exchange (PBX): A telephone system that serves a particular location, such as a business, connecting one telephone extension to another within the system and connecting the PBX to the outside telephone network.

Processing devices: Computer hardware that transforms inputs into outputs.

Processing logic: The steps by which data is transformed or moved, as well as a description of the events that trigger these steps.

Procurement portals: Enterprise portals that automate the business processes involved in purchasing, or procuring, products between a single buyer and multiple suppliers.

Protocols: Rules dictating communication between senders and receivers within a network.

Prototyping: An iterative systems development process in which requirements are converted into a working system that is continually revised through close work between analysts and users.

Proxy variables: A measurement of changes as a result a systems implementation in terms of their perceived value to the organization, particularly where it is difficult to determine and measure direct effects from a system.

Public key: A data encryption technique that uses two keys—a private key and a public key—to encrypt and decode messages.

public switched telephone network (PSTN): Also called plain old telephone service (POTS), it is a network of standard telephone lines with a speed, or bandwidth, that is generally about 52 Kbps (52,000 bits per second).

Pull marketing: A strategy by which companies must draw, or pull, visitors to their Web sites.

Push marketing: An active strategy in which the company pushes their information at the consumer whether it is wanted or not (e.g., television commercials).

Query: Method used to request information from a database.

Query by example (QBE): A capability of a DBMS that enables data to be requested by providing a sample or a description of the types of data we would like to see.

RAID (redundant array of independent disks): A secondary storage technology that makes redundant copies of data on two or more hard drives.

Random-access memory (RAM): A type of primary storage that is volatile and can be accessed randomly by the CPU.

Rapid application development: A systems development methodology that combines prototyping, computer-based development tools, special management practices, and close user involvement.

Read-only memory (ROM): A type of primary storage on which data has been prerecorded and is nonvolatile.

Read/write heads: Components that inscribe data to or retrieve data from hard disks, diskettes, and tapes.

Record: A record is a collection of related attributes about a single entity.

Recurring costs: Ongoing costs that occur throughout the life cycle of systems development, implementation, and maintenance.

Registers: Temporary storage locations inside the CPU where data must reside while it is being processed or manipulated.

Relational database model: The most common DBMS approach in which entities are presented as two-dimensional tables, with records as rows and attributes as columns.

Repeater: A network device used to regenerate or replicate a signal as it weakens when traveling on a network; also moves data from one media segment to another and effectively extends the size of the network.

Report: 1. A compilation of data from the database that is organized and produced in printed format. 2. A business document that only contains predefined data used for reading and viewing, typically for multiple records.

Report generators: Software tools for retrieving data from a database and manipulating (aggregate, transform, or group) and displaying it in a useful format.

Request for proposal: A communication tool indicating buyer requirements for a given system and requesting information from potential vendors.

Requirements collection: The process of gathering and organizing information from users, managers, business processes, and documents to understand how a proposed information system should function.

Reverse pricing: A pricing system in which customers specify the product they are looking for and how much they are willing to pay for it; this information is routed to appropriate companies, which either accept or reject the consumer's offer.

Ring network: A network that is configured in the shape of a closed loop or circle, with each node connecting to the next node.

Router: An intelligent device used to connect and route data traffic across two or more individual networks.

Rule: A way of encoding knowledge, typically expressed using an IF-THEN format, within an expert system.

Salami slicing: A form of data diddling that occurs when a person shaves small amounts from financial accounts and deposits them in a personal account.

Sales Force Automation: Or SFA, which is the system of applications which mainly focus on contact management and scheduling.

Satellite A device launched to orbit Earth and enable network communication.

Satellite microwave: The process of using relay stations that transfer high-frequency radio signals between antennas located on earth and satellites orbiting the earth.

Scanners: Input devices that convert printed text and images into digital data.

Scheduled reports: Reports produced at predefined intervals—daily, weekly, or monthly—to support the routine informational needs of managerial-level decision making.

Scripting languages: A programming technique for providing interactive components to a Web page.

Secondary key: Attributes not used as the primary that can be used to identify one or more records within a table that share a common value.

Secondary nonvolatile storage: Methods for permanently storing data to a large-capacity storage component, such as a hard disk, diskette, CD-ROM disk, or tape.

Secure sockets layer (SSL): A popular public-key encryption method used on the Internet.

Semiautomated data entry: Data entry into an information system using some type of data capture device such as a grocery store checkout scanner.

Semistructured decisions: Managerial-level decision making where solutions and problems are not clear-cut and often require judgment and expertise.

Server: Any computer on the network that enables access to files, printing, communications, and other services available to users of the network; it typically has a more advanced microprocessor, more memory, a larger cache, and more disk storage than a single-user workstation.

Server-centric networks: Networks in which servers and clients have defined roles.

Service mentality: The belief among information systems personnel that their chief goal is satisfying their systems customers within the firm while fundamentally believing that the customers, not the systems personnel, own the technology and the information.

Single in-line memory module (SIMM): A small circuit board that can hold RAM chips.

Smart card: A special type of credit card with a magnetic strip, a microprocessor chip, and memory circuits.

Social engineering: Gaining information needed to access computers by means of tricking company employees by posing as a magazine journalist, telephone company employee, or forgetful coworker in order to persuade honest employees to reveal passwords and other information.

Soft data: Textual news stories or other nonanalytical information.

Software: A program or set of programs that tell the computer to perform certain processing functions.

Software engineering: A disciplined approach for constructing information systems through the use of common methods, techniques, or tools.

Software piracy: A type of computer crime where individuals make illegal copies of software protected by copyright laws.

Sound card: A specialized circuit board that supports the ability to convert digital information into sounds that can be listened to on speakers or headphones plugged into the card; a microphone can also be plugged into the card for capturing audio for storage or processing.

Source documents: Documents describing a transaction that serve as a stimulus to a transaction processing system from some external source.

Speech recognition: Software and hardware used to convert spoken words into commands and data.

Spoofing: A scam used to steal passwords from legitimate accounts by using phony login screens.

Stand-alone application: Systems that focus on the specific needs of individual departments and are not designed to communicate with other systems in the organization.

Star network: A network with several workstations connected to a central hub.

Strategic: A way of thinking in which a plan of action is made and is intended to accomplish a specific goal.

Strategic planning: The process of forming a vision of where the organization needs to head, convert that vision into measurable objectives and performance targets, and craft a plan to achieve the desired results.

Streaming media: Streaming video with sound.

Streaming video: A sequence of compressed moving images that are sent over the Internet.

Structured decisions: Decisions where the procedures to follow for a given situation can be specified in advance.

Structured Query Language (SQL): The most common language used to interface with databases.

Supercomputer: The most expensive and most powerful category of computers. It is primarily used to assist in solving massive research and scientific problems.

Supply chain: The network producers of supplies that a company uses.

Supply Chain Management: Management of the network of suppliers and sub-suppliers that a company interacts with.

Supply network: The flow of materials from multiple suppliers involved in the process of servicing a single organization.

Symmetric Digital Subscriber Line (SDSL): A data transfer format that enables large amounts of data to be sent relatively quickly over existing copper telephone lines; said to be symmetric because it supports the same data rates (up to 3 Mbps) for upstream and downstream traffic; works by sending digital pulses in the high-frequency area of telephone wires.

Symmetric secret key system: An encryption system where both the sender and recipient use the same key for encoding (scrambling) and decoding the message.

System analysis: The second phase of the systems development life cycle, in which the current ways of doing business are studied and alternative replacement systems are proposed.

Systems analysis and design: The process of designing, building, and maintaining information systems.

Systems analyst: The primary person responsible for performing systems analysis and design activities.

Systems benchmarking: A standardized set of performance tests designed to facilitate comparison between systems.

System clock: An electronic circuit inside a computer that generates pulses at a rapid rate for setting the pace of processing events.

System conversion: The process of decommissioning the current system and installing a new system into the organization.

System design: The third phase of the systems development life cycle, in which all features of the proposed system are described.

Systems development life cycle (SDLC): The process of identifying the need for, as well as designing, developing, and maintaining contemporary types of information systems.

System effectiveness: The extent to which a system enables people and/or the firm to accomplish goals or tasks well.

System efficiency: The extent to which a system enables people and/or the firm to do things faster, at lower cost, or with relatively little time and effort.

System identification, selection, and planning: The first phase of the systems development life cycle, in which potential projects are identified, selected, and planned.

System implementation: The fourth phase of the systems development life cycle, in which the information system is programmed, tested, installed, and supported.

systems integration: Making it so that two information system can work together better and/or can exchange data more seamlessly with each other.

System maintenance: The fifth (and final) phase of the systems development life cycle, in which an information system is systematically repaired and/or improved.

System software: The collection of programs that controls the basic operations of computer hardware.

System unit: The physical box that houses all of the electronic components that do the work of the computer.

T1 line: Developed by AT&T as a dedicated digital transmission line that can carry 1.544 Mbps of information.

T3 line: A digital transmission line that provides about 45 Mbps of service at about 10 times the cost of leasing a T1 line.

Table: A collection of related records where each row is a record and each column is an attribute.

Tangible benefit: A benefit of using a particular system or technology that can be quantified.

Tangible cost: A cost of using a particular system of technology that is quantifiable.

Technology: Any mechanical and/or electrical means to supplement, extend, or replace human, manual operations or devices.

Telecommunications: Refers to the transmission of all forms of information, including digital data, voice, fax, sound, and video, from one location to another over some type of network.

Telecommunications network: A group of two or more *computer systems* linked together with communications equipment.

Telecommuting: The process of working at home or at another remote location and "commuting" to the office via computing and networking technologies.

Telemedicine: The exchange of medical information from one location to another via a computer network.

Telnet: Enables users to connect, or log in, to any computer on the Internet.

Terminals: Local input devices used to enter data onto mainframes in centralized computing systems.

terrestrial microwave: The process of using earth-based antennas that require an unobstructed path or line-of-sight between nodes; often used to cross inaccessible terrain or to connect buildings where cable installation would be expensive.

Text recognition software: Software designed to convert handwritten text into the computer-based characters.

token passing: An access method that uses a constantly circulating electronic token, a small packet of data, to prevent collisions and give all workstations equal access to the network.

Top-level domain: Categories of Internet domain names as indicated by their suffix (i.e., .com, .edu, or .org).

Total quality management: A management system in which people within the organization are constantly monitoring what they do to find ways to improve quality of operations, products, services, and everything else about the firm.

Trading exchange: A Web site where multiple buyers and sellers come together to conduct business; also called an electronic marketplace.

Transaction processing system (TPS): An information system designed to process day-to-day business event data at the operational level of the organization.

Transactions: Repetitive events in organizations that occur as a regular part of conducting day-to-day operations.

Transmission Control Protocol/Internet Protocol (TCP/IP): The protocol of the Internet, which allows different interconnected networks to communicate using the same language.

Transmission media: The physical pathway to send data and information between two or more entities on a network.

Transnational information system: A type of international information system that is not specific to any country or any particular organization.

Trojan horse: A destructive computer code whose instructions remain hidden to the user because the computer appears to function normally, but in fact it is performing underlying functions dictated by the intrusive code.

tunneling: A technology used by VPNs to encapsulate, encrypt, and transmit data over the Internet infrastructure, enabling business partners to exchange information in a secured, private manner between organizational firewalls.

Twisted pair cable: Cable made of two or more pairs of insulated copper wires twisted together.

Unauthorized access: Occurs when a person gains access to a computer system who does not have authoritiy to do so.

UN/EDIFACT: One of the formatting standards followed by EDI to specify how information is transmitted electronically.

Unicode: A 16-bit code used code for representing numbers, letters, and other characters in binary form.

Uniform Resource Locator: The unique Internet address for a Web site and specific Web pages within sites.

Unstructured decisions: Decisions where few or no procedures to follow for a given situation can be specified in advance.

Upstream: An information flow consisting of information received from another organization, such as from a supplier.

Usenet: Enables groups of people with common interests to send messages or other binary information to each other. Unlike listserv, Usenet has no master list of subscribers. Rather, anyone with access to Usenet may use a newsreader program to post and read articles from the group.

Utilities or utility programs: Software designed to manage computer resources and files.

value-added network (VAN): Medium-speed WANs that are private, third-party managed networks and are economical because they are shared by multiple organizations.

Value chain: The process of adding value throughout each of the functions within the organization.

Value chain analysis: The process of analyzing an organization's activities to determine where value is added to products and/or services and the costs that are incurred for doing so.

Value system: A collection of interlocking company value chains.

Vanilla: The features and modules that the ERP comes with out of the box.

Vertical market: A market comprised of firms within a specific industry sector.

Very high-speed Backbone Network Service (vBNS+): A cooperative agreement between WorldCom and the National Science Foundation aimed at developing high-performance, high-bandwidth Internet-related technologies and applications.

Video: Sill and moving images that can be recorded, manipulated, and displayed on a computer.

Videoconferencing: The use of integrated telephone, video recording, and playback technologies by two or more people to interact with each other from remote sites.

virtual company: A firm that exists either on paper or on the Internet but has little/no physical components or attributes.

Virtual private network: A secure network that utilizes telecommunications lines from a telephone service provider and enables there to be a connection created when a transmission needs to take place and terminated

once the transmission has been completed and enables the user to scale bandwidth up and down as needed.

Virtual product: A product without tangible features created through the process of digitization.

Virtual teams: Work teams that are composed of members that may be from different organizations and different locations that form and disband as needed.

Viruses: Destructive programs that disrupt the normal functioning of computer systems.

Visual programming languages: Programming languages that have a graphical user interface (GUI) for the programmer and are designed for programming applications that will have a GUI.

Voice mail: Telecommunication technology that allows callers to leave voice messages in a voice mailbox, much like leaving a message on an answering machine.

Voice over IP: A collection of hardware and software that enables the use of the Internet as the transmission medium for telephone calls.

Volatile: Memory that loses its contents when the power is turned off.

WAIS (Wide Area Information Server): Internet tool that enables users to locate information by indexing electronic data using standard keywords.

Watermarked: The process of marking products so that they can be traced to the original purchaser.

Web browser: A software application that can be used to locate and display Web pages including text, graphics, and multimedia content.

Web page: A hypertext document that contains not only information, but also references or links to other documents that contain related information.

Web page builders or HTML editors: Programs for assisting in the creation and maintenance of Web pages.

Web server: A computer used to host Web sites.

Web site: A collection of interlinked Web pages created by the same author.

What-if analysis: A capability of some information systems (e.g., a decision support system) that allows a user to make hypothetical changes to the data associated with a problem and observe how these changes influence the results.

Wide area network (WAN): A computer network that spans a relatively large geographical area; typically used to connect two or more LANs.

Wireless local area network (WLAN): Local area network using a wireless transmission protocol.

Wireless media: The tools used to transmit and receive electromagnetic signals using methods such as infrared line of sight, high-frequency radio, and microwave systems.

Wisdom: Accumulated knowledge, gained through a combination of academic study and personal experience, that goes beyond knowledge by representing broader, more generalized rules and schemas for understanding a specific domain or domains; wisdom allows you to understand how to apply concepts from one domain to new situations or problems.

Work profile matrix: A chart which consists of job categories and work categories and shows how much time is spent on each of the job categories and each of the different types of work.

Workstation: A special class of microcomputer designed for individuals that has the power of some midrange computers but fits on a desktop.

World Wide Web (Web):   A system of Internet servers that support documents formatted in HTML, which supports links to other documents, as well as graphics, audio, and video files.

Worm: Destructive computer code that is designed to copy and send itself throughout networked computers.

Zip drive: A high-capacity, removable diskette drive that typically uses 100MB Zip disks or cartridges.

CHAPTER 1

Applegate, McFarlan, and McKenney. 1996. *Corporate Information Systems Management: Text and Cases*, 4th ed. Burr Ridge, IL: Richard D. Irwin, Inc.

Bakos, J. Y., and M. E. Treacy. 1986. "Information Technology and Corporate Strategy: A Research Perspective," *MIS Quarterly* 10(2): 107–120.

Belcher. L. W., and H. J. Watson. 1993. "Assessing the Value of Conoco's EIS," *MIS Quarterly* 17(3): 239–254.

Blodgett, M. 1998. "NC or Not NC." Information from: **www.cio.com**. Information verified: April 21, 1998.

Brynjolfsson, E. 1993. "The Productivity Paradox of Information Technology," *Communications of the ACM* 36(12): 66–76.

Dragoon, A. 1998. "Come and Get IS." Information from: **www.cio.com**. Information verified: April 21, 1998.

Field, T. 1997. "When Bad Things Happen to Good Projects." Information from: **www.cio.com**. Information verified: April 21, 1998.

Goldratt, Eliyahu M. and Jeff Cox. 1992. *The Goal: A Process of Ongoing Improvement*. Great Barrington, MA: North River Press.

Hagendorf, J. 1998. "Trying to Keep Pace—IS Spending Climbs, Along with Needs, Costs," *Computer Reseller News*. Information from: **www.techweb.com**. Information verified: April 29, 1998.

Harris, S. E., and J. L. Katz. 1991. "Organizational Performance and Information Technology Investment Intensity in the Insurance Industry." *Organization Science* 2(3): 263–295.

Leibs, S., and K. M. Carrillo. 1997. "Research Productivity—Replacing Workers with IS Doesn't Guarantee Maximum Gains, Finds a New Study from Harvard: What Does?: You May Be Surprised," *InformationWeek*. Information from: **www.techweb.com**. Information verified: April 29, 1998.

Pearson, D. 1998. "Clear Steering." Information from: **www.cio.com**. Information verified: April 21, 1998.

Porter, M. E. 1979. "How Competitive Forces Shape Strategy." *Harvard Business Review* 57 (March–April 1979): 137–145.

Porter, M. E. 1985. *Competitive Advantage: Creating and Sustaining Superior Performance*. New York: The Free Press.

Porter, M. E. 2001. "Strategy and the Internet," *Harvard Business Review* 79(3): 62–78.

Sassone, P. G., and A. P. Schwartz. 1986. "Cost-Justifying OA," *Datamation*, (Feb. 15): 83–88.

Shank, J., and V. Govindarajan. 1993. *Strategic Cost Management: Three Key Themes for Managing Costs Effectively*. New York: The Free Press.

Slater, D. 1998. "Business Line Backers." Information from: **www.cio.com**. Information verified: April 21, 1998.

Violino, B. 1998. "Here's what Comes First," *InformationWeek* (April 20): 48–70.

Wheeler, B. C. 2002a. "Making the Business Case for IT Investments Through Facts, Faith, and Fear," ISWorld.net Online Teaching Case and Teaching Note. **www.coba.usf.edu/departments/isds/faculty/abhatt/cases/TN-ITInvestments.doc**

Wheeler, B. C. 2002b. "NeBIC: A Dynamic Capabilities Theory for Assessing Net-Enablement. *Information Systems Research* 13(2).(in press)

Zuboff, S. 1988. *In the Age of the Smart Machine: The Future of Work and Power*. New York: Basic Books.

CHAPTER 2

Castells, M. 2000. *The Rise of the Network Society*, 2nd ed. Cambridge, MA: Blackwell Publishers.

Drucker, P. 1959. *Landmarks of Tomorrow*, 1st ed. New York: Harper.

Farrell, Christopher, Ann Therese Palmer, and Seanna Browder. "A Rising Tide for Workers," *BusinessWeek* (August 31, 1998).**www.businessweek.com/1998/35/b3593010.htm**

Field, T. 1997. "Great Expectations." Information from: **www.cio.com**. Information verified: April 20, 1998.

Koch, C. 1998. "Can Federalism Fly?" *CIO* 11(12): 46–50.

Porter, M. 1985. "Technology and Competitive Advantage," *The Journal of Business Strategy* 5(3): 60–78.

Porter, M., and V. Millar. 1985. "How Information Gives You Competitive Advantage," *Harvard Business Review* 63(4): 149–161.

Reich, R. 1991. *The Work of Nations: Preparing Ourselves for 21st Century Capitalism*. New York: Knopf.

Rifkin, J. 1987. *Time Wars: The Primary Conflict in Human History*. New York: Henry Holt and Company.

Rothfeder, J. and L. Driscoll. 1990. "CIO Is Starting to Stand for "Career Is Over": Once Deemed Indispensable, the Chief Information Officer Has Become an Endangered Species," *BusinessWeek* (February 26, 1990): 78.

Sims-Taylor, K. "The Brief Reign of the Knowledge Worker: Information Technology and Technological Unemployment." Paper presented at the International Conference on the Social Impact of Information Technologies, St. Louis, Missouri, October 12–14, 1998.

Stevens, D. 1994. "Reinvent IS or Jane Will. *Datamation* (December 15, 1994): 84.

Todd, P., J. McKeen, and R. Gallupe. 1995. "The Evolution of IS Job Skills: A Content Analysis of IS Jobs," *MIS Quarterly* 19(1): 1–27.

CHAPTER 3

Boar, B. 1998. "Understanding Data Warehousing Strategically." White paper, NCR. **www.ncr.com**.

Date, C. J. 1995. *An Introduction to Database Systems*. New York: Addison-Wesley Publishing Company, Inc.

Hoffer, J. A., Prescott, M. B., and McFadden, F. R. 2002. *Modern Database Management*, 6th ed. Upper Saddle River, NJ: Pearson Education, Inc.

CHAPTER 4

Berghel,H. 1996. "U.S. Technology Policy in the Information Age," *Communications of the ACM* 39(6): 15–18.

Comer, D. E. 1995. *The Internet Book*. Englewood Cliffs, NJ: Prentice Hall.

Looney, C. A. and D. Chatterjee. 2002. "Web Enabled Transformation of the Brokerage Industry: An Analysis of Emerging Business Models," *Communications of the ACM*, forthcoming.

Sands, D. Z. and K. Bauer. 2001. "Build an Ethical Bridge over the Digital Divide/Reply," *American Medical News* 44(25): 14.

Sarker, Suprateek and Saonee Sarker. 2000. "Implementation Failure of an Integrated Software Package: A Case Study from the Far East," *Annals of Cases on Information Technology Applications and Management in Organizations* 2: 169–186.

CHAPTER 5

Alexander, M. 2001. "IBM Web Site to Drive ASIC Design Collaboration," Information from: **www. internetweek. com/story/INW20010308S0004**. Information verified: July 27, 2001.

Berghel, H. 1996. "U.S. Technology Policy in the Information Age," *Communications of the ACM* 39(6): 15–18

Boeing Company, The. 2001. "MyBoeingFleet.com—Boeing Commercial Aviation Services," **Web.boeing.com/commercial/aviationservices-/guesttour/index.htm** (June 2001).

Carr, N. G. 2000. "Hypermediation: Commerce as Clickstream," *Harvard Business Review* (January–February 2000): 10–11.

Chatterjee, D. and V. Sambamurthy. 1999. "Business Implications of Web Technology: An Insight into Usage of the World Wide Web by U.S. Companies," *Electronic Markets—International Journal of Electronic Commerce & Business Media* 9(2) (Spring 1999).

Christensen, C. M. and R. S. Tedlow. 2000. "Patterns of Disruption in Retailing," *Harvard Business Review* (January–February 2000): 6–9.

Cohen, W. M. and D. A. Levinthal. 1990. "Absorptive Capacity: A New Perspective on Learning and Innovation," *Administrative Science Quarterly* (March 1990): 128–152.

Comer, D. E. 1995. *The Internet Book*. Englewood Cliffs, NJ: Prentice Hall.

Couzin, J. 2000. "Analysis: EBay Fraud Lawsuit Raises Questions," Information from: **www.cnn.com/2000/TECH/computing/11/07/suing.ebay.idg/**. Information verified: July 30, 2001.

DataChannel, Incorporated. 2001. "DataChannel, Incorporated," **Web.datachannel.com**, (June 2001).

Dell 2001. "Welcome to Business Center," Information from: **www.dell.com/us/en/biz/default.htm**. Information verified: August 1, 2001.

Hennessey, T. 2000. "Wiring the Produce Patch," *Progressive Grocer* 79(9): 79–86.

Hill, S. 2000. "From EDI to XML: Making Advanced SCM a Reality," *Apparel Industry* 61(10): 16–20.

Kalakota, R., R. A. Oliva, and E. Donath. 1999. "Move Over, E-Commerce," *Marketing Management* 8(3) (Fall 1999): 23–32.

Looney, C. A. and D. Chatterjee. 2002. "Web Enabled Transformation of the Brokerage Industry: An Analysis of Emerging Business Models," *Communications of the ACM*, forthcoming.

McDougall, P. 2000. "Dell: Beyond the Box?" *Informationweek* 787 (May 22, 2000): 48–57.

Microsoft Corporation. 2001. "Microsoft Business Case Studies," **Web.microsoft.com/business/casestudies/default.asp**, (June 2001).

Pang, A. 1998. "Commerce Bonanza: Is It Real or Imagined?" *Internet Computing* (March 1998): 70–74.

Priceline.com. 2001. "How It Works," Information from: **www.priceline.com**. Information verified: July 30, 2001.

Quelch, J. A. and L. R. Klein. 1996. "The Internet and Internal Marketing," *Sloan Management Review* 63 (Spring): 60-75.

Rebello, K. 1996. "Italian Sausage that Sizzles in Cyberspace," *BusinessWeek* (September 23, 1996): 118.

Rockwell, B. 1999. "Understanding the Evolution to EC on the Internet," *The Journal of Electronic Commerce*: 80–89.

SciQuest. 2001. "SciQuest Corporate Page," Information from: **www.sciquest.com**. Information verified: August 1, 2001.

Sullivan, K. B. 1999. "Boeing Achieves Internet Liftoff," ZDNet eWeek, **Web.zdnet.com/eweek**, (May 10, 1999).

Szuprowicz, B. 1998. Extranet and Intranet: E-commerce Business Strategies for the Future. Charleston, SC: *Computer Technology Research Corporation*.

Tempest, N. 1999. "Charles Schwab Corporation (B)," *Harvard Business School Press* (September 13, 1999).

Turban, E., J. Lee, D. King, and H. M. Chung. 2000. *Electronic Commerce: A Managerial Perspective*. Upper Saddle River, NJ: Prentice-Hall.

Zwass, V. 1996. "Electronic Commerce: Structures and Issues," *International Journal of Electronic Commerce* 1(1): 3–23.

CHAPTER 6

Checkland, P. B. 1981. *Systems Thinking, Systems Practice*. Chichester, U.K.: John Wiley.

EXSYS. 2002. "Class Selection Student Advisor," **www.exsys.com**.

Roche, E. M. 1992. *Managing Information Technology in Multinational Corporations*. New York: Macmillan Publishing Company.

Sprague, R. H., Jr. 1980. "A Framework for the Development of Decision Support Systems," *MIS Quarterly* 4(4): 1–26.

Turban, E. and J. E. Aronson. 2001. *Decision Support Systems and Intelligent Systems*, 6th ed. Englewood Cliffs, NJ: Prentice Hall.

CHAPTER 7

Butler, S. 2001. "From B2B to SCM," *Entrepreneur.com*. Information from: **www.entrepreneur.com**. Information verified: August 16, 2001.

Chandrashekar, A. and P. B. Schary. 1999. "Toward the Virtual Supply Chain: The Convergence of Information Systems and Organization," *International Journal of Logistics Management* 10(2): 27–39.

FirePond. 2001. "FirePond Products," Information from: **www.firepond.com**. Information verified: August 15, 2001.

Frishia, T. 1997. "ERP—The Goldrush Continues," *Manufacturing Systems* 15(1): 22. **www.infotechtrends. com/prenterpriseresourceplanning.htm**

Grosvenor, F. and T. A. Austin. 2001. "Cisco's Ehub Initiative," *Supply Chain Management Review* (July/August) **www.manufacturing.net/?layout= articlePortal_V2&articleid=CA154379&search= webexclusive&text=cisco%27s+ehub**

Hewlett-Packard. 2001. "Customer Support Center," Information from: **www.hp.com**. Information verified: June 22, 2001.

i2 Technologies. 2001. "Southwest Airlines Chooses i2 to Provide Supply Chain Management Solutions," Information from: **www.i2.com**. Information verified: August 16, 2001.

Kelly, S. T. and J. A. Barry. 2001. "Failing to Construct the Seller," *Computerworld* 1(1): 30–33.

Koch, C., D. Slater, and E. Baatz. 2000. "The ABCs of ERP," *CIO Magazine*. Information from: **www.cio.com**. Information verified: August 6, 2001.

Kumar, K. and J. Van Hillegersberg. 2000. "ERP Experiences and Evolution," *Communications of the ACM* 43(4): 23–26.

Kumar, R. L. and C. W. Crook. 1999. "A Multi-Disciplinary Framework for the Management of Interorganizational Systems," *The DATA BASE for Advances in Information Systems* 30(1): 22–36.

Langenwalter, G. A. 2000. *Enterprise Resources Planning and Beyond*. Boca Raton, FL: St. Lucie Press.

Larson, P. D. and D. S. Rogers. 1998. "Supply Chain Management: Definition, Growth, and Approaches," *Journal of Marketing Theory and Practice* 6(4): 1–5.

Manugistics. 2001. "Enterprise Profit Optimization," Information from: **www.manugistics.com**. Information verified: August 16, 2001.

Markus, M. L. and D. Tanis. 2000. "The Enterprise Systems Experience—From Adoption to Success." In *Framing the Domains of IT Reserach: Glimpsing the Future Through the Past*, edited by R. W. Zmud. Cincinnati, OH: Pinnaflex Educational Resources.

Porter, M. E. and V. E. Millar. 1985. "How Information Gives You Competitive Advantage," *Harvard Business Review* (July–August): 149–160.

Ptak, C. A. 2000. *ERP Tools, Techniques, and Applications for Integrating the Supply Chain*. Boca Raton, FL: St. Lucie Press.

Sarker, S. and A. S. Lee. 2000. "Using a Case Study to Test the Role of Three Key Social Enablers in ERP Implementation," *Proceedings of the International Conference on Information Systems*, Brisbane, Australia: 414–425.

Shah, J. B. 2001. "ERP Losing Favor as Businesses Reevaluate What to Target—SCM, CRM Software Now More in Demand," *Ebn* 1265 (June 4): 4–5.

Soh, C., S. K. Sia, and J. Tay-Yap. 2000. "Cultural Fits and Misfits: Is ERP a Universal Solution?" *Communications of the ACM* 43(4): 47–51.

Willcocks, L. and R. Sykes. 2000. "The Role of the CIO and IT Function in ERP," *Communications of the ACM* 43(4): 32–38.

CHAPTER 8

Applegate, L. M., and F. W. McFarlan. 1999. *Corporate Information Systems Management: Text and Cases*, 5th ed. Chicago, IL: Irwin.

Booch, G. 1990. *Object Oriented Design with Applications*. Redwood City, CA: Benjamin/Cummings.

Boynton, A. C., and R. W. Zmud. 1994. "An Assessment of Critical Success Factors." In *Management Information Systems*, 2nd ed., edited by Gray, King, McLean, and Watson. Fort Worth, TX: The Dryden Press.

Caldwell, B. 1996. "The New Outsourcing Partnership: Vendors Want to Provide More than Just Services," *InformationWeek* (June 24, 1996): 50–64.

CIO. 2001. "Global IT-Services Spending to Reach $700 Billion," **www.cio.com** (July 24, 2001).

Coad, P., and E. Yourdon. 1991. *Object-Oriented Design*. Englewood Cliffs, NJ: Prentice Hall.

Court, R. 1998. "Disney Buys Out Starwave," **www.wired.com**, *Wired Magazine* (April 30, 1991).

Fryer, B. 1994. "Outsourcing Support: Kudos and Caveats," **www.computerworld.com**, *Computerworld* (April 11, 1994).

Halladay, S., and M. Wiebel. 1993. *Object Oriented Software Engineering*. Englewood Cliffs, NJ: Prentice Hall.

Hoffer, J. A., J. F. George, and J. S. Valacich. 2002. *Modern Systems Analysis and Design*, 3rd ed. Englewood Cliffs, NJ: Prentice Hall.

Martin, J. 1991. *Rapid Application Development*. New York: Macmillan Publishing.

McConnell, S. 1996. *Rapid Development*. Redmond, WA: Microsoft Press.

McFarlan, F. W., and R. L. Nolan. 1995. "How to Manage an IT Outsourcing Alliance," *Sloan Management Review* 36(2): 9-24.

Mosquera, M. 2001. "Spending on IT Outsourcing is Growing," **www.techweb.com**, *TechWeb* (May 14, 2001).

Nunamaker, J. F., Jr. 1992. "Build and Learn, Evaluate and Learn," *Informatica* 1(1): 1–6.

CHAPTER 9

BSA. 2001. "Sixth Annual BSA Global Software Piracy Study," *Business Software Alliance* (May). **www.bsa.org**.

Elias, S., and P. Gima. 2000. *Domain Names: How to Choose and Protect a Great Name for Your Website*. Soquel, CA: Nolo Press.

Mason, R. O. 1986. "Four Ethical Issues for the Information Age," *MIS Quarterly* (16): 423–433.

Mosquera, M. 2000. "FBI E-Mail Surveillance Raises Privacy Concerns." www.techweb.com/wire/story/TWB20000713S0013

Sipior, J. C., and B. T. Ward. 1995. "The Ethical and Legal Quandary of E-Mail Privacy," *Communications of the ACM* 38(12): 48–54.

TechWeb. **www.techweb.com** (July 13). 2000.

Weisband, Suzanne P., and Bruce A. Reinig. 1995. "Managing User Perceptions of E-Mail Privacy," *Communications of the ACM* (December): 40–47.

APPENDIX A

Freed, L. 1995. *The History of Computing*. Emeryville, CA: Ziff-Davis Press.

Keogh, J. 2002. *The Essential Guide to Computer Hardware*. Ridgefield Park, NJ: Prentice Hall.

APPENDIX B

Chen, M., and R. J. Norman. 1992. "Integrated Computer-Aided Software Engineering (CASE): Adoption, Implementation, and Impacts." In *Proceedings of the Hawaii International Conference on System Sciences* 3, edited by J. F. Nunamaker, Jr. Los Alamitos, CA: IEEE Computer Society Press: 362–373.

Hoffer, J. A., J. F. George, and J. S. Valacich. 2002. *Modern Systems Analysis and Design*, 3rd ed. Upper Saddle River, NJ: Prentice Hall.

Orlikowski, W. J. 1989. "Division Among the Ranks: The Social Implications of CASE Tools for Systems Developers." In *Proceedings of the Tenth International Conference on Information Systems*: 199–210.

Name Index

Organization Index

DISCARDED

Management Information Systems

MIS:

Alter, *Information Systems: The Foundations of E-Business 4/e*

Dickson & DeSanctis, *Information Technology and the Future Enterprise*

Gupta, *Information Systems: Success in the 21st Century*

Jessup & Valacich, *Information Systems Today*

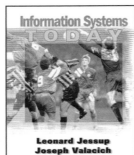

Laudon & Laudon, *Management Information Systems 8/e*

Laudon & Laudon, *Essentials of Management Information Systems 5/e*

Luftman/et al., *Managing the IT Resource*

Martin/et al., *Managing IT: What Managers Need to Know 4/e*

McLeod & Schell, *Management Information Systems 8/e*

McNurlin & Sprague, *Information Systems Management In Practice 5/e*

Miller, *MIS: Decision Making with Applications Software (Cases)*

Nickerson, *Business Information Systems 2/e*

Electronic Commerce:

Awad, *Electronic Commerce*

Farhoomand, *Global E-Commerce: Text and Cases*

Oz, *Foundations of Electronic Commerce*

Turban, *Electronic Commerce 2002, A Managerial Perspective*

Turban, *Introduction to E-Commerce*

Database Management:

Hoffer, Prescott, McFadden, *Modern Database Management 6/e*

Kroenke, *Database Concepts*

Kroenke, *Database Processing: Fundamentals, Design, & Implementation 8/e*